BEYOND
PETROPOLIS

DESIGNING
A PRACTICAL UTOPIA
IN NUEVA LOJA

GRADUATE PROGRAM IN URBAN DESIGN - CITY COLLEGE OF NEW YORK
GRADUATE PROGRAM IN LANDSCAPE ARCHITECTURE
UNDERGRADUATE PROGRAM IN ARCHITECTURE

FACULTAD DE ARQUITECTURA, DISEÑO Y ARTES -
PONTIFICIA UNIVERSIDAD CATÓLICA DEL ECUADOR

BEYOND PETROPOLIS

DESIGNING A PRACTICAL UTOPIA **IN NUEVA LOJA**

PREFACE by Michael Sorkin
EDITED by Michael Sorkin, Ana María Durán Calisto, Matthias Altwicker
ESSAYS by Matthias Altwicker, Ana Maria Duran Calisto, Patrick Radden Keefe, David Leven, Michael Sorkin, Achva Benzinberg Stein, Osvaldo Paladines Zurita
ART DIRECTION by Oscar Riera Ojeda

OSCAR RIERA OJEDA
PUBLISHERS

TABLE OF CONTENTS

PREFACE

Michael Sorkin **8**

INTRODUCTION

Welcome to Petropolis, Michael Sorkin **12** Infrastructure, Future and Memory: The Bicentennial of Territorial Integration in South America, Ana María Durán Calisto **16**
Designing a New Landscape for Lago Agrio, Achva Benzinberg Stein **34** The End of the Petrol Age, Osvaldo Paladines Zurita **38** Timeline **40** Geography **41** Trip **44** Town **45** Jungle **46**
Predator Urbanism: On the Birth and Growth of Nueva Loja, Ana María Durán Calisto **48**

BACKGROUND

SOCIAL Demographics **56** Economy **58** Politics **62**
ENVIRONMENT Climate **66** Vegetation **68** Hydrology **69** The Aguarico River **71** Ecosystem **74**

URBAN INFRASTRUCTURE

Petroleum **78** Energy **80** Water **84** Food and Agriculture **86** Waste **88** Public Facilities **91** Urban Infrastructure **93** Education **95**

PROPOSALS

URBAN DESIGN Regional Organization **102** City Boundary **108** City Organization **112** Barrio Vía Quito **114** Napo - Julio Marín **117** Barrio San Francisco **121** The Orienco University **125**
El Barrio Chacra **130** Barrio La Florida **134** De-Central Park **140** Barrio La Esquina **142** Barrio Isegorida **148** Barrio Puerto Aguarico **152** The Kindling Charcoal **158**
ARCHITECTURE Architectural Infrastructure for the Post Petroleum City, David Leven **174** The Roof Machine **178** Covering, Joining, Hanging **180** Hybrid System **182** Dwelling Prototype **184**
Housing Prototype for a Hot Humid Climate **186** 750 Prototype **188** Single-family Dwelling with Louvers **192** Housing with Nature **198** Stackable Housing **204** Multi-Family Housing: The Departure of the City **208**
Multi-Family Housing: Living in the Amazon **210** Lago Agrio Housing **212** Mobile Classroom: Pop-up School House **216** Mobile Classroom: 0 Waste Prototype **218** Mobile Classroom: Deployable School **220**
Puerto Aguarico Secondary School **222** Green and Blue Primary School **226** The Urban School **228** School as a Tool for Learning: Escuela De Construcción De Nueva Loja, Camille Dunn **232**
SustainableHuman Settlements for the Post-Oil Era in the Ecuadorian Amazon: An Introduction to the Nueva Loja Workshop (FADA-PUCE), Osvaldo Paladines Zurita **238** Productive Landscape – Productive Household **240**
Sustainable Systems **242** Multi-layered Connector **246** Self-sufficient Metabolisms **248** Strips for Growth **252** Material Fusion **256** Sustainable Free-standing Household **260** Protective Canopy **264**

ARTICLE

Reversal of Fortune, Patrick Radden Keefe **266**

CONCLUSIONS

Postscript: A Post Petroleum Nueva Loja, Matthias Altwicker **278** Bibliography **280** Biographies **284** Credits **286** Acknowledgements **287**

MÁS ALLÁ DE PETRÓPOLIS

Spanish Version **289**

PREFACE

MICHAEL SORKIN

Each year, the Graduate Program in Urban Design at The City College of New York takes a trip to a city that is experiencing a revelatory form of stress. In collaboration with students and faculty from a local institution, the class observes and analyzes an urban situation, familiarizes itself with physical, social, economic and environmental contexts, conceives a program, and formulates a series of physical responses. Over the past decade, we have done projects in Nicosia, Havana, Johannesburg, Wuhan, Biloxi, New Orleans, Tijuana, Hanoi, and Bogotá.

In January of 2007, joined by students and faculty from the Catholic University of Ecuador and from the architecture and landscape architecture programs at CCNY, we traveled to the little city of Nueva Loja in the heart of the Ecuadorian Amazon basin. We chose this site, in consultation with our colleagues Ana María Durán and Osvaldo Paladines, because this small city is emblematic of so many of the difficult processes of development in the global south and especially a concern with the interaction of social and environmental ecologies. At the time of our visit, Nueva Loja, which then had a population of around 100,000, had the highest municipal growth rate in Ecuador.

There was one reason for this explosive growth: oil. Since the first major finds in 1967, the Oriente region of Ecuador has seen a wild pattern of exploitation. Located in an extremely sensitive landscape, and home to native peoples whose way of life had been largely uninterrupted for centuries, the town and its hinterland were uniquely susceptible to the ravages of oil exploration and extraction, the pressures of development and the violent spill-over from the nearby Colombian border.

The influx of population that has accompanied the infusion of oil money has mixed with existing social and natural systems to produce a metastasis of violence and destruction. Patterns of life have undergone severe disruptions of "modernization." Thousands of square miles of rainforest – including some of the most complex and little understood eco-systems on the planet – have been scraped away and divided into lots able to support only grazing and speculation. A collusion of money, drugs, human-trafficking, guerilla warfare, and contested political power has created a culture of violence, corruption, dependency, and poverty. It has also goaded organization and resistance and created a critical mass of people and needs that must be better served.

Should current demographic trends continue, the population of Nueva Loja will reach 150,000 in 2021. The year is significant: it's when the oil runs out. This was the problem we sought to investigate: imagining a post-petroleum Nueva Loja. Of course, this is not an entirely architectural project. While we worked through the medium of physical design, I hope that this book shows evidence of a wider range of concerns. We have tried to imagine the kinds of production that might sustain the town over a long future and have shaped our intervention to reflect this. We have included the use of indigenous renewables as alternative energy. We have focused on the range of economic activities that a restored rainforest could sustainably support. We've included tertiary educational facilities because there are none in the region and to plug the widely remarked upon "brain drain" to Quito. We've thought about the restoration of crafts-based production and sustainable forms of agriculture, including the cultivation of medicinal plants. We've included facilities for eco-tourism. We've looked to the region's rivers for transport. Furthermore, we've speculated about a construction industry attuned to the local bio-climate and resources.

We have also looked carefully at the existing town. Sprawling, poorly furnished and maintained, a wasteland for architecture, bereft of much basic infrastructure, Lago nevertheless has qualities of community and urbanity that can be nurtured as the basis for its development. Most important is the town's human capital, its activists and strivers, its energetic immigrants and entrepreneurs, its professional cadres. Although crippled by a fiscal regime in which municipal funds flow from the central government, the local administration, for all the debilitating exigencies of Ecuadorean politics, seems committed to the authentic amelioration of the town. We saw evidence of improvement in services, public space, education and other vital elements of the good city.

The real life of Lago also showed evidence of a vigorous urbanity and suggested many potential areas for future elaboration. Curiously, the town has grown away from its greatest natural asset, the Aguarico River. As one might expect, the pre-petroleum communities lay along its banks but the new need for road access, large sites, and unencumbered territory led to the emergence of a town away from the river. To the extent that its lovely and delicate corridor has been protected from helter-skelter and environmentally indifferent development by this move, this is a positive sign, leaving the river's future to more sensitive and careful actors. The new center of town is bustling and urbane, with vendors lining the sidewalks of the main drag. There is the beginning of a system of arcading that offers pedestrians protection from the intense sun and frequent showers, and a threshold of commerce that identifies this as "downtown." There's a marvelous public market. A big new plaza has been designed with ambition. The crazy quilt of informal construction in both interstices and peripheries, while often slapdash and unsanitary, also presents a kind of vigor and self-reliance that must, with appropriate assistance and constraints, become a crucial component of any new vision for this place.

This book contains proposals at a number of scales. The first is territorial, an effort to promote the larger restoration of a ravaged landscape and to fit Lago Agrio symbiotically within it. Next we've looked at a general pattern of organization for the city itself and have based this on a pattern of neighborhoods; "barrios." These are intended to be semi-autonomous districts that offer both living places as well as a range of commercial, educational, recreational, and productive facilities and as a medium of local politics. We've also investigated the town's natural systems, the reclamation of its waterways, the biological treatment of its waste, and the restoration of its displaced plant and animal life. Finally, many students have worked on particular architectural proposals for housing and shared facilities. These have all been done in a spirit of investigation that privileges local skills, materials, and traditions over the inscription of alien forms and unsustainable practices.

The work of a semester can only scratch the surface of a city's character and design and can only brush lightly against the crucial collaborations that are indigenous to a democratic planning process, one that must remain continuously dynamic. We offer these proposals as a contribution to a conversation that is already happening among community organizations, commercial interests, government, and individuals. On our visit we were especially moved by the optimism and activism of our brother and sister architects in Lago Agrio. Their commitment to their town and to the cause of environmental justice inspired us all and we look forward to continuing our relationship with them and with this fascinating city.

INTRODUCTION

WELCOME TO PETROPOLIS

INFRASTRUCTURE, FUTURE AND MEMORY:
THE BICENTENNIAL OF TERRITORIAL INTEGRATION IN SOUTH AMERICA

DESIGNING A NEW LANDSCAPE FOR LAGO AGRIO
THE END OF THE PETROL AGE
TIMELINE
GEOGRAPHY
TRIP
TOWN
JUNGLE
PREDATOR URBANISM: ON THE BIRTH AND GROWTH OF NUEVA LOJA

WELCOME TO PETROPOLIS

MICHAEL SORKIN

Pink Floyd was playing on the loudspeaker of the ferry that transported our bus over the Rio Napo into the 2,700 square-mile Yasuni National Park in the Amazon basin in Ecuador's Oriente. After hours of slow progress over rutted roads through a largely denuded countryside, we'd missed an earlier ferry and had milled an hour in a shore-side scene of extreme informality – hot sun, muddy, littered, paths along the river, lazing dogs, scattered houses, a small shop and a dirt parking lot for waiting vehicles. The scene on the opposite bank, however, was more like Guantanamo. From the dock, we walked along narrow passages between chain-link fences topped with razor wire, passed though a magnetometer, had hand luggage x-rayed, passports balefully compared to a list we'd sent in advance, and watched our bus taken into a camouflage-painted metal shed for the once-over. No Coke stands or pleasantries here. Instead, there were gun-towers, searchlights, signs forbidding alcohol and drugs, and M-16-toting men in uniform from the Ecuadorian army and private security firms with Orwellian names like Servisafe and Servipro. It was an unexpected gateway to paradise.

Yasuni, a UNESCO "world biosphere reserve," is one of the most biodiverse areas on the planet – a river-laced rainforest teeming with life and home to the indigenous Huaorani and other aboriginal peoples. And to oil. Crossing the river, we were entering "Block 16," one of the giant concessions that have platted Oriente since 1967 when a consortium of Texaco and Gulf discovered huge oil reserves there. By mid-1972, exploitation was in full swing and a 312 mile long pipeline had been constructed to carry crude from the now booming village of Nueva Loja (universally known as Lago Agrio – Sour Lake after Texaco's headquarters in Texas) to the coast, where it is shipped abroad, primarily to the U.S. The high security was intended to protect this resource, to secure the jungle against incursions by terrorists, smugglers, narcotics traffickers, poachers, loggers, the press and settlers. Of course, it did nothing to protect the area from the traumatic impact of petroleum itself. The effects of oil on the Ecuadorian landscape have been profound. On the one hand, it has fueled a boom economy which – especially in the go-go seventies and eighties – generated much middle and upper class prosperity and government investment in public infrastructure. On the other, oil has been an environmental disaster. Thousands of square miles of rainforest have disappeared. The lives of numerous indigenous peoples have been permanently disrupted. And vast areas have become toxic. According to a class action lawsuit filed in 2003 on behalf of 30,000 local inhabitants (endlessly making its way through the Ecuadorian courts), Texaco have not just spilled 30 times more oil in the jungle than leaked from the Exxon Valdez, but also dumped close to twenty billion gallons of toxic wastewater. Much of the oil is extracted via the injection of water under high pressure and, rather than following standard practice of deep re-injection of waste, the company simply dumped it in ground-level pits, saving itself $3 a barrel. Often referred to as the "Rainforest Chernobyl" the devastation has, according to Judith Kimerling in her book *Amazon Crude* (1990), polluted huge areas of land and aquifer, spiked cancer, spontaneous abortions and other diseases, and spread these poisonous effects as far as Peru. The lawsuit is attempting to recover the cost of the estimated $6 billion clean-up, as is an Ecuadorean government suit claiming fraud on Chevron's part.

The oil concessions – covering thousands of square miles – have a very specific spatiality, a format that is, by stages, turning the forest not simply into a degraded, toxic environment but into an urbanism, a city of a new "disarticulated" character that combines webs and nodes, formality and informality, density and dispersion. The components of this jungle city include grids of seismic trails (three meter wide pathways in which a 2 - 5 meter deep hole is dug at 100 meter intervals to hold 10 - 20 kilos of dynamite for acoustic exploration), networks of wells and toxic dumps, pumping stations, refineries, tank farms, pipelines, helicopter landing zones, airports, roadways, security check-points, military installations and a proliferation of camps, depots, towns, strips and villages. In an environmental lawsuit filed against the US oil company Atlantic Richfield in 1993, the plaintiffs inventoried – in this one concession – 339 wells, 18,000 miles of seismic trails, 300 miles of roads, 600 toxic waste pits, and 1,368 helicopter landing sites. Welcome to Petropolis.

The roadways slashing through the rainforest instigate both extraction and attraction, becoming the medium for still larger territorial reorganization. As roads are built, forest is cleared to make way for three rows of agricultural plots, each 250 x 2000 meters, creating a space twelve kilometers wide and, in all, hundreds of miles long, a vast linear settlement occupied by "colonos" – migrants from elsewhere in the country. Well over a quarter of a million have poured into Oriente since the discovery of oil. Much of this is pasture land: rainforest soils are a poor basis for conventional agriculture and clearing the jungle dooms the richly symbiotic biodiversity it supports. The pattern brings a new economic organization as well as new styles of agricultural activity, new homesteads, new villages, and new towns. Much like the Jeffersonian gridding of the American west, the remorseless geometry of subdivision accomplishes a dramatic literal and conceptual shift: what was once "wilderness" becomes urban, part of a global system. The long miles of farms and villages in the cleared jungle and the check-point at Block 16 are part of the same Petropolitan urbanism that produces the freeway morphology of LA and Houston and the glittering skylines of Dubai or Kuwait City.

Of course, an urban environment requires urban citizens and the boom has attracted hundreds of thousands. But what of those already there and their sedulously un-urban lifestyles? Two years after Texaco discovered the huge reserves of oil in Oriente, the Ecuadorian government created a protected "reserve" for the Huaorani. Desperate to cash in on the oil but anxious about the potential cauldron of conflict between native peoples, oil workers, and the accelerating influx of settlers and tourists, Jose Maria Velasco Ibarra, the president at the time, handed the protectorate's administration to the Sumner Institute of Linguistics, a Protestant evangelical group active in Ecuador since the early 50's that specialized in the translation of scripture into native languages.

Like their missionary predecessors from centuries past, the Sumner Institute's tragic endeavor entailed forcing the "natives" into villages, establishing schools with the Bible at the center of the curriculum and introducing capitalism. The results also included the clearing of forest to create larger fields, agricultural specialization and a money economy, as well as the rapid introduction of alien cultural forms, from trousers and radios to beer and zinc roofs. The natives were being urbanized, made into model citizens for a new order. Resistance was not long in developing and there were numerous instances of speared priests and oil-workers. More importantly, there has been remarkable grass-roots political organization and raised consciousness by native peoples, a crucial result of which was the formation in 1986 of the Confederation of Indigenous Nationalities of Ecuador, CONAIE, which has now become a major political power working on behalf of both human and environmental rights.

In 1989 the Ecuadorian government, faced with declining oil prices and eager to keep its revenue stream flowing, prepared (with financing from Conoco Oil) a new "management" plan for the as yet untapped Yasuni Park. Half the park was zoned for oil company use, the other half for the Huaorani. In 1993, a modified plan was put into place in which the Huaorani were nominally incorporated into the administration of the combined entity. For them, this meant jobs as oil workers and security guards in their own formerly peaceable homeland. It also meant new – and desperately inappropriate – houses for some, generally clustered in what can only be described as concentration camps. This for a people that for millennia lived nomadically. It also brought the ravages of imported diseases and a rapid education in modernity. This is not the place to settle the question of the rights of indigenous people nor to debate the respective arguments for literacy, technology, and participation in national life versus the logic of protecting the ability of "primitive" peoples to defend and continue historic patterns of life and settlement. The point is simply that the lives of these people have undergone tremendous rupture and their culture was sent down the road to extinction on the basis of somebody's idea of the greater good – that of the Ecuadorian economy, which continues to float on oil (as it had earlier done on monocultures of cacao and bananas). Oil sales provide between 40% and 60% of government revenue (about half of which goes to the military) and the eventual nationalization of oil reserves in 1989 has put the government in the admirable position of actually owning the source of its own revenue.

The machinations in Yasuní, with the repeated redrafting of the borders of the park, the concessions and the ethnic reserves (for a people whose imagination did not house the concept of such borders) are part of a broader system of overlapping territories, defined by relations of property, that prescribes modern patterns of space and exchange to the jungle. Northern Oriente shows all of this raised to a flashpoint of toxic weirdness. The troops we saw in Yasuni were not simply protecting the oil but keeping out the cocaine industry (increasingly forced toward and over the Ecuadorian border by the U.S.-sponsored "Plan Colombia") which has its own networked system of extraction and a parallel labyrinth of roads, airstrips, laboratories, villages and flows of capital.

Like any city, Nueva Loja overlays infrastructures, territories, interests, technologies, densities, communities, histories and morphologies. Its differences from the "post-urban" edge cities that have become the characteristic mode of urban growth in so many parts of the world are not of kind, simply of degree. Both patterns are environmentally corrosive, both conceptually predicated on the domination of distributed rather than concentrated systems. Both are also based on a model of urban development that privileges extraction – of oil, cocaine, or land values – over sociability, permanence, or culture. Although only half the planetary population, by traditional means of measure, lives in cities, the whole planet is immeasurably more urbanized.

Yasuni – and the Amazon basin – throws this accelerated urbanism into such sharp relief because the rainforest remains our paradigmatic "state of nature" – the antithesis of urban civilization. As our green sensibility grows (and the jungle disappears) we have come to understand the extent to which our own survival depends on the fate of the forest.

In much the same way, respect for indigenous peoples and traditions is an emblem of our understanding of the risks of globalization, which threatens to obliterate difference and freedom of economic action. The Huoarani appear doomed, but in their demise it is urgent that we see ourselves.

INFRASTRUCTURE, FUTURE AND MEMORY:

The Bicentennial of Territorial Integration in South America.

ANA MARÍA DURÁN CALISTO
Translation: Henry Hsu

"...In that Empire, the craft of Cartography attained such Perfection that the Map of a Single province covered the space of an entire City, and the Map of the Empire itself an entire Province. In the course of Time, these Extensive maps were found somehow wanting, and so the College of Cartographers evolved a Map of the Empire that was of the same Scale as the Empire and that coincided with it point for point. Less attentive to the Study of Cartography, succeeding Generations came to judge a map of such Magnitude cumbersome, and, not without Irreverence, they abandoned it to the Rigors of Sun and Rain. In the western Deserts, tattered Fragments of the Map are still to be found, sheltering an occasional Beast or beggar; in the whole Nation, no other relic is left of the Discipline of Geography."

A Universal History of Infamy, **Penguin Books, London, 1975**
Jorge Luis Borges

Territory is a document in continuous transformation: malleable, elastic, bountiful and indomitable. It is no surprise that the science which studies it, geo-graphy, etymologically refers to the act of writing; the actions and impressions made by diverse natural and social forces over the course of time are registered in its varied strata. In 1983, André Corboz compared it with a palimpsest in which memory and oblivion are renewed and reconstructed. South America carves out a new territory and to observe it through the lens of a satellite, is to decipher the economic and political structures that govern the new principles of continental and bicentenary integration. If the independence of Latin America laid the groundwork for ideological unification, and the Centenary celebration brought many of the great works of industrial infrastructure (e.g. railways), the Bicentennial is providing the framework for unprecedented integration, in terms of infrastructure, politics, finance, culture and defense. The institutions which make up this framework (UNASUR, Banco del Sur, IIRSA, CAF, MERCOSUR, OTCA, etc.) are as varied as the discourse on integration. Nevertheless, it is the land itself that embodies these principles and that will provide the setting for this activity, which is why I propose to consider the political and mercantile roles that influence the infrastructure of unification.

IIRSA: INTEGRATIONIST PRAGMATISM, GEO-ECONOMICS AND THE GLOBAL MARKET

Partially due to the rise of uncontainable processes of expansion in the global, capitalist, free market of the 90s, and thanks to the surge of digital technologies that have aided this rise, the cities of Latin America, Asia and Africa have exploded. The anarchic behavior and relative autonomy of the transnational market have unleashed an endless number of global patterns. Chief amongst these are the emergence of local (versus national) governments as the principal nodes of political and economic management; the rise of multinational corporations as some of the main GDPs in the global economy; the direct and indirect opening of political borders as the new modality for access to and exchange of resources, capital and labor; and the rise of China, India, Brazil, Russia and the Middle East as the principal emerging markets on the global scale.

In the southern hemisphere, it is unprecedented in recent history for a South American country to have consolidated itself as one of the main vortices of the international market. It is no surprise that Brazil has taken the lead in the pragmatic process of commercial and infrastructural regional integration. In the year 2000, the then president of Brazil, Fernando Henrique Cardoso, along with a technical team from the IDB (Inter-American Development Bank), presented an Initiative for the Integration of Regional Infrastructure in South America (IIRSA), an ambitious territorial planning proposal, to his South American counterparts. In its early stages, the Initiative´s portfolio encompassed 351 projects for transport, energy and telecommunications, to be implemented between 2003 and 2006, involving a total investment of approximately 37 billion US dollars. In 2010, the IIRSA comprised 524 projects for an estimated investment of 96 billion, 119 million US dollars. The project's plan divides the South American continent into ten axes of development, five transversal and five longitudinal[1]. Even though the proposal demarcates the development of infrastructures for multi-modal transport, energy and telecommunications, 80% of the current proposal is comprised of hydroelectric plants and roads.

There are two principal forces that have awoken the interest of Brazil, the South American giant, in its Hispanic neighbors: on the one hand, the need to open routes to ports on the Pacific side of the continent to trade with Asia, particularly China; and on the other, a need to manage the Amazon River Basin and the hydroelectricity grid it is expected to support. Even though circa 70% of this waterway is found within Brazilian territories, most of its sources are in the Andean glaciers, outside of Brazil[2]. Furthermore, the steep slopes in the eastern foothills of the Andes are ideal for the generation of hydroelectric power. The Amazon basin within Brazilian territory is, instead, relatively flat. Brazil has been forming partnerships with its Andean neighbors in order to develop hydroelectric dams in the eastern slopes of the Andes. The former President of Brazil, Luiz Inácio Lula da Silva, and the former Peruvian President, Alan García, signed an agreement to build six hydroelectric dams in Peru´s rainforest. "Most of the power generated by these plants will] be exported to Brazil to start with, but the proportions [will] slowly reverse and after 30 years Peru [will] own the $4 billion project."[3] The first of these dams is being planned at Inambari, at the intersection of the Madre de Dios, Cusco and Puno departments. Given the increasing need of the expanding Brazilian economy to harness more energy, it is no wonder that still another instrument for integration has been created: the Amazon Cooperation Treaty Organization (ACTO, 2003). The treaty acknowledges that large ecosystems such as the Amazon cannot be dealt with in an isolated manner, within the confines imposed by national borders and that the situation becomes even more critical when what is at stake is one fifth of the fresh water on the planet – a resource that will in very few decades become the most sought-after commodity in the world. The organization, therefore, brings together the eight countries that share the Amazon basin in an attempt to coordinate its conservation and development.

IIRSA AXES OR NODES OF DEVELOPMENT

[1] see www.iirsa.org

[2] It is worth noting that Andean glaciers are receding under the effects of global warming and the impact this recession will have on the Amazon basin is immeasurable.

[3] See "Messing around with dams: First build a road, then flood it," ***The Economist***, Nov. 19th, 2009.

THE MAIN SOUTH AMERICAN ECOLOGICAL REGIONS AND IIRSA; IMAGE DEVELOPED FOR SAP (SOUTH AMERICA PROJECT) BY VÍCTOR MUÑOZ SAEZ

THE CARTOGRAPHIES OF POWER: TERRITORIES AND VISUALIZATION

Territorial planning documents are not innocuous; quite the contrary, maps have a far greater effect than merely illustrating a determined area. They have the capacity to aid its transformation. For this reason, one cannot underestimate the role of Geographic Information Systems, Google Earth, satellite images, remote sensing and other macro, tele, subterranean and supervisory technologies in the reformulation of the South American continent. Paradoxically, the concept of what is 'local' has been transformed by widespread access to devices which are extremely far away, and global in outlook; satellites and related systems are bringing places once regarded as being distant closer. A two-decade planning scheme on the continental scale, such as the IIRSA, would not have been possible without these tools. Every single piece of infrastructure, beginning with the first sketches on paper, constitutes a gesture that will forever alter the terrain on which it is inscribed. The IIRSA´s infrastructural projects will traverse various fragile ecosystems on the South American continent, and for this reason, it is necessary to pay close attention to the Amazonian Region, home to four of the Initiative's ten axes.

Now that the bicentenary is upon us, it is of utmost importance to reinforce the principles of the continental integration made necessary by the challenges imposed by the global economy. Nevertheless, one must wonder what will be the outcome of infrastructural integration within traditionally remote areas that have remained relatively invisible for centuries and have now been mapped, quantified, appraised and reconfigured as mega-geographic stocks and deposits of raw materials (including water), soon to be extracted and commercialized. The movement of humans, commodities, capital and information depends on the construction and consolidation of generic infrastructural networks of transport, energy and telecommunications. Due to their standardized, industrial nature, roads and oil pipelines remain immutable whether they cross marshland, desert or forest. Infrastructural engineering has not been examined closely enough in terms of its response to the varying geographic and social conditions in which it is implemented. What happens when these generic infrastructures and the particular cultural and ecological characteristics of a human settlement or community and an ecosystem meet? One is forced to ask, is South America putting its geography 'up for sale' once more, this time on a monumental scale?

A territory cannot be mapped without taking economic considerations into account, nor can an economy be designed independently of its territory. Furthermore, it is desirable that the design of the infrastructure – its redevelopment, construction, articulation and/or expansion – respond to an organizing logic in a manner that facilitates exchange within the twelve economies of the South American block, so as to permit the sharing of complementary strengths and weaknesses in supply and demand. Although the Brasilia Communiqué from September 1, 2000 alludes to this vision and advocates a complementary integration of South American countries based on the notion of "open regionalism"; a concept that includes the expansion and interconnection of education, information and telecommunications systems, the images published by the IIRSA do not coincide with the text of the Communiqué. It is vital to question whether or not the Initiative is a visionary project that answers the undeniable need to consolidate South America as one economic block with its own market, economy and territory, or whether its program will lead to the repetition of patterns typical of extractive economies. A crucial factor in the IIRSA achieving its purported goals, is to supply the region with an infrastructural system capable of articulating the land, fluvial, air, maritime and digital routes of South America, one that does more than just provide good connections to its Pacific ports. It must also attune energy, agricultural and industrial production systems to a new arena of regional free-trade; "open regionalism," rather than simply opening the gateway for raw material extraction and export.

Since the arrival of the Europeans, South America has experienced a long history that clearly illustrates the underlying logic of the extractive mentality which still to a great extent governs its economy to this day. Neither enlightened Independence nor the Centenary with its industrial aspirations were able to reverse the vicious cycles of the vertiginous boom and depression economies created by the simple extraction of resources and exportation of raw materials or mono-culture products. At the risk of slipping into a reductionism that will surely scandalize economists and historians alike, I would go as far as to say that a disturbing pattern of scars is accumulating on the land. The landscapes of extraction and the infrastructures that facilitate the flow of materials and energy on a regional and global scale pockmark, striate and reduce the South American geography. During the modern period, National State Systems, often ruled by dictatorships, promoted the construction of large scale infrastructural works which defined the exploitation of resources, primarily minerals, in many different countries.[4] These monumental projects for industrializing extraction were financed using geography as collateral to obtain onerous loans that increased South America's international debt to suffocating levels. The problem that arises when infrastructure is constructed with simple extraction as its ultimate goal is that the benefits are not distributed throughout society. On the contrary, they tend to become concentrated in pockets of power which rarely distribute them; they turn into a drain on capital, which is then re-injected into the international financial market, in a perverse cycle that returns only a trickle to the enormous flow of water from which it originated. It is enough to see the conditions in which the communities and settlements that exist in areas of extraction live, to be convinced of the asymmetries generated by this system of production. Furthermore, technological investments fall into disrepair due to lack of use or obsoleteness after the resource is depleted. What is left? What remains is desolation and the informal colonization of the infrastructure; ghost towns (some of which are revived as tourist destinations); external debt; deforestation and the expansion of the agricultural footprint; and last but far from least; an immense social and environmental deficit.

The patterns are just as vicious when governed by the private sector, or public-private alliances. In the 90s, South America experienced the rapid privatization of its infrastructure. In fact, conduits are a key business in this era of branching globalization; infrastructure is not only a medium, it is also a commodity. Transnational corporations have accumulated unprecedented power and strength, and have become the main benefactors of new waves of infrastructural deployment and extraction of the raw materials that feed the incredible global growth of cities, especially in emerging economies such as those in Asia. They have also supported the expansion of digital industries, which, as Saskia Sassen has demonstrated, are

[4] Monoculture is another form of extraction that has played an important role in export-led economies based on the production of primary goods. Their impact on the geography amounts, in some cases, to a near complete substitution of a pre-existing ecology with plantations. The Ecuadorian coast is a case in point: 80 per cent of its mangroves have been replaced with banana plantations and shrimp farms.

not "virtual" and immaterial as their apparently evanescent world depends upon tangible, at times even massive systems of infrastructure[5]. At the end of the 90s, several Latin American economies began to crumble (many names were used to describe the crisis: corralito, the tequila effect, freezing of funds, etc.) under the pressure of neo-liberal policies that reinforced the private sector, increased the porosity of national borders and installed transnational corporations at the pinnacle of the global economy. This took place to the detriment of public spheres and agencies on all scales. A pendulum reaction in South America led to the rise of governments of a neo-socialist liberal ilk across the continent. Their economic policies partially reverted to previous ideologies: mechanisms of alliance emerged; some resources were nationalized, and some processes of privatization were halted. Nevertheless, many of these States lack the financial capacity to develop and undertake extraction, and have renewed their power by playing a strategic role in the economy as they award concessions (or not) to multinational companies and guarantee (or not) a minimum level of security to foreign investment. Even though nation states seem to have lost jurisdiction and autonomy within the new global order; reduced to mere institutional substrata – an anachronism eroded by transnational flows that pass them by – their executive powers have acquired unprecedented control, having affiliated themselves with corporate interests, which have surged ahead in the race for natural resources.[6] Socialist governments extract as much as, or even more than, neo-liberal ones. The creative industries that can add value to the production and export goods of Latin America are dependent on long term health and education policies which could produce the educated majority that lies at the core of a true democracy and a healthy, structural development.mocracy and a healthy, structural development.

At this juncture, it is appropriate to return to the topic of mapping. Take the case of the Petroperú Map [7] which shows the blocks that have been conceded to more than twenty companies with the goal of prospecting and potentially extracting petroleum in the Peruvian Amazon. Just a glance is enough to understand that the territory has been ground down to a relatively autonomous, relatively privatized system of tracts conceded over a period of time. How can one talk of integration during a stage of territorial pulverization? Paradoxically, the only thread that seems to weave together the fragments of a new manner of extraction, is the infrastructure itself. For this reason, the IIRSA, is a hugely important program destined to have a great impact on South America, even though, as the former President of the Republic of Ecuador and first Executive Secretary of UNASUR, Dr. Rodrigo Borja, has noted, it still languishes in relative obscurity[8]. What one must not forget is that whilst infrastructures bind and integrate they can also create rifts and divisions. The IIRSA is a double edged sword from the geographic standpoint; it could stitch the continent together or be one of the final steps in its ultimate fracture.

5 Sassen Saskia. *Cities in a World Economy*. Thousand Oaks, London, New Delhi: Pine Forge Press, 2006.

6 Sassen, Saskia. *Una sociología de la globalización*. Buenos Aires: Katz Editores, 2007

7 www.petroperu.com.pe

8 Personal Interview

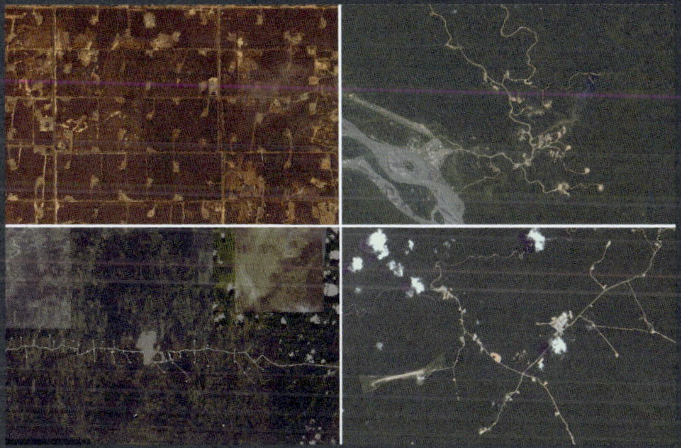

STRIATIONS CAUSED BY THE OIL EXTRACTION INDUSTRY ON THE VENEZUELAN COAST (UPPER LEFT CORNER), THE ECUADOREAN AMAZON (LOWER LEFT CORNER), THE PERUVIAN AMAZON (UPPER RIGHT CORNER) AND THE BRAZILIAN AMAZON (LOWER RIGHT CORNER). COMPILED BY ÁNGEL RODRÍGUEZ FOR THE SEMINAR RESOURCE EXTRACTION URBANISM; FELIPE CORREA & ANA MARÍA DURÁN CALISTO; GSD, HARVARD; SPRING 2011.

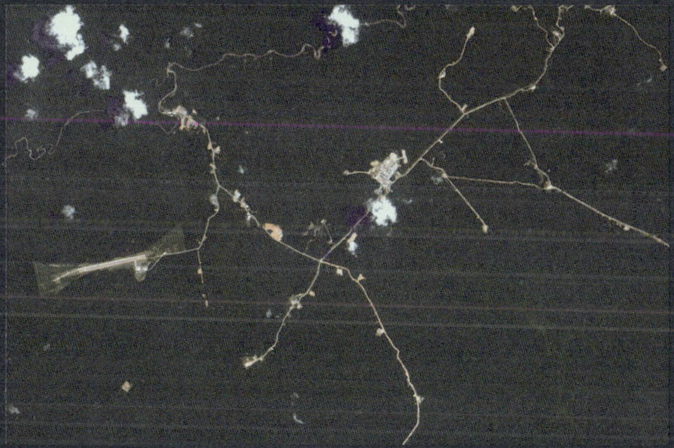

LEFT: PATCHES OF PERUVIAN AMAZON THAT HAVE BEEN CONCEDED TO OIL COMPANIES OF DIVERSE ORIGIN (PRIVATE AND/OR PUBLIC; NATIONAL AND/OR MULTI-NATIONAL). WILL THIS KIND OF TERRITORIAL FRAGMENTATION CONTRIBUTE TO THE INTEGRATION OF THE SOUTH AMERICAN CONTINENT? IMAGE: OIL REPUBLICS, BY SANTIAGO DEL HIERRO AND GARY LEGGETT, 2009

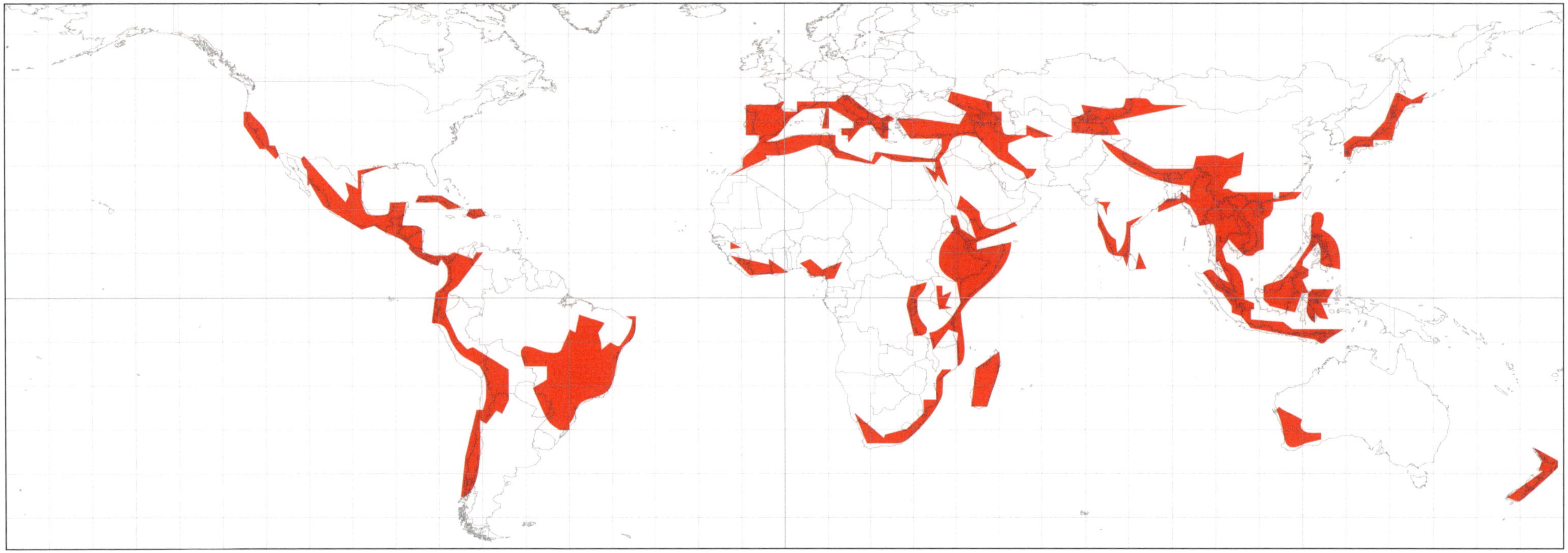

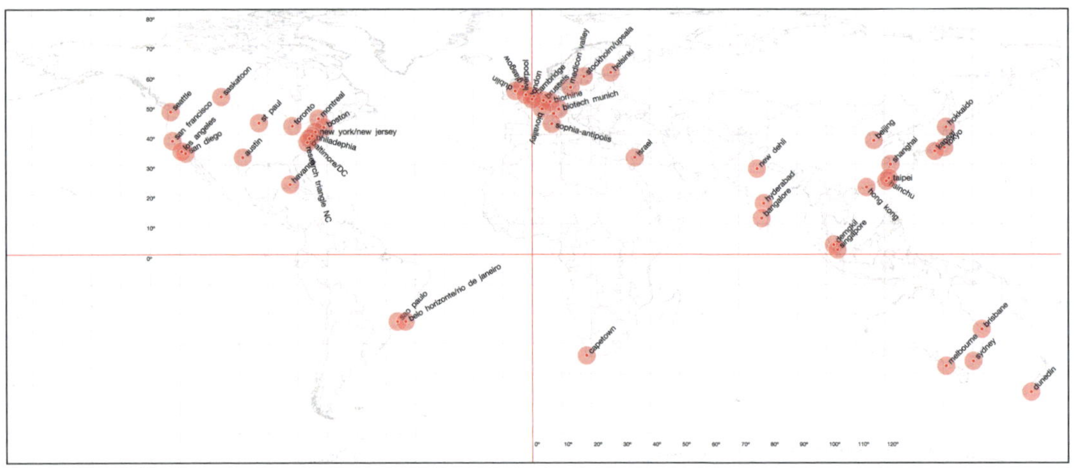

TOP: BIODIVERSITY HOTSPOTS. NOTICE THAT OIL CONCESSIONS IN THE AMAZON OVERLAP SOME OF THE MOST BIODIVERSE ECOSYSTEMS IN THE WORLD, PARTICULARLY ALONG THE STRING WHERE THE AMAZON BASIN MEETS THE ANDEAN CORDILLERA, PROVOKING A SECTION OF INCOMPARABLE ENDEMISM. SOURCE: CONSERVATION INTERNATIONAL. MAP DRAWN BY VÍCTOR MUÑOZ SANZ FOR THE SEMINAR RESOURCE EXTRACTION URBANISM; FELIPE CORREA & ANA MARÍA DURÁN CALISTO; GSD, HARVARD; SPRING 2011

LEFT: BIO-TECH CLUSTERS: AS THIS MAP ILLUSTRATES, SOUTH AMERICA LAGS BEHIND IN THE DEVELOPMENT OF BIOTECHNOLOGIES EVEN THOUGH THESE ARE BECOMING CRUCIAL TO ITS FUTURE SURVIVAL. MAP DRAWN BY VÍCTOR MUÑOZ SANZ FOR THE SEMINAR RESOURCE EXTRACTION URBANISM; FELIPE CORREA & ANA MARÍA DURÁN CALISTO; GSD, HARVARD; SPRING 2011

FROM FREE TRADE AGREEMENTS (FTA) TO SPECIAL ECONOMIC ZONES (SEZ)

It would be valuable, for example, to pause and observe the patterns of proliferation of the Special Economic Zones (SEZ) that are springing up around the South American continent with increasing frequency, linked to airports that are being built or renovated on its coasts, jungles, mountains and grasslands. The SEZs, by opening gateways of exchange in countries whose neo-socialist policies have often impeded the application of Free Trade Agreements (and the concomitant opening of their borders), achieve a goal via infrastructure which had previously been pursued by political means. And they do so in a more efficient manner, by avoiding troublesome political negotiations. The alternate strategy brought about by the apparently anarchic and organic system of the global market (punching holes in the barriers rather than relaxing border controls entirely) generates areas of economic impunity where the uninterrupted flow of imports and exports is permitted. These zones may have industrial, technological or service components – outsourcing is a case in point. That is to say, they are true cities, an industrialized version of gated communities, which are constructed to accommodate the manufacturing (maquilas) and production output of transnational companies. They benefit from the difference in labor costs, inadequately referred to as "comparative advantage," or they seek to establish themselves in a strategic manner in order to facilitate the trade of raw materials or the provision of services. It is an undeniably brilliant tactic; achieving economic goals while simultaneously avoiding the relative corruption and inefficiency of local bureaucracies. SEZs create their own legal bubbles in which tariffs and import/export limits do not apply; within them anything is possible: borders within borders, the borders of a global market system that embed themselves within the jurisdiction of a nation state in order to inject components and finished and semi-processed products from abroad and/or to absorb manual, intellectual or natural resources from the interior. Inevitably, the affiliation between the threshold and the floodgates triggers a distinctive kind of infrastructural urbanism.

Many FTAs are built in remote areas, such as the Peruvian coast to the west of Arequipa, where an FTA is being proposed and financed by a group of Chinese investors, or the island of Santa Rosa in the Peruvian Amazon, where it would form a strategic triangulation with Leticia in Colombia and Tabatinga in Brazil. It is no surprise that the most developed and extensive FTA in Brazil is located in Manaus: an industrial, commercial and agricultural center in the heart of the Amazon rainforest. Even though the insertion of FTZs into remote areas does benefit the economy by contributing to decentralize resources, it nevertheless irreversibly alters the environment and the cultures of extremely fragile ecosystems. Although all of this is happening as this essay is being written and the port areas are being articulated within a system of global intercommunications, we still have time to design the future of geographic infrastructures that are in danger of succumbing to entropy – the waste material of "development" – in an intelligent fashion, taking advantage of the synergies between culture and nature.

This juncture is crucial. Instead of repeating the models of industrialization of North America, Europe and Asia, South America could become an ideal setting for the development of sustainable, post-industrial models. If minerals were the blood of the industrial era, organic matter may be the future in the post-industrial era. If biotechnology is the future, the Amazon is its center and South America would thus play a pivotal role in the formulation of more sustainable modes of production, lifestyle and metropolises. From the technological and ideological points of view, one may question whether the IIRSA is a leap forward. Does it promote green infrastructural construction, healthy populations and an industry with added value? Does it stimulate the development of new technologies that might help us to improve our products and services above the baseline of extraction? In order to survive in a complex ecosystem, a successful organism must discover and appropriate an unexplored niche within a territory. It is through diversification,

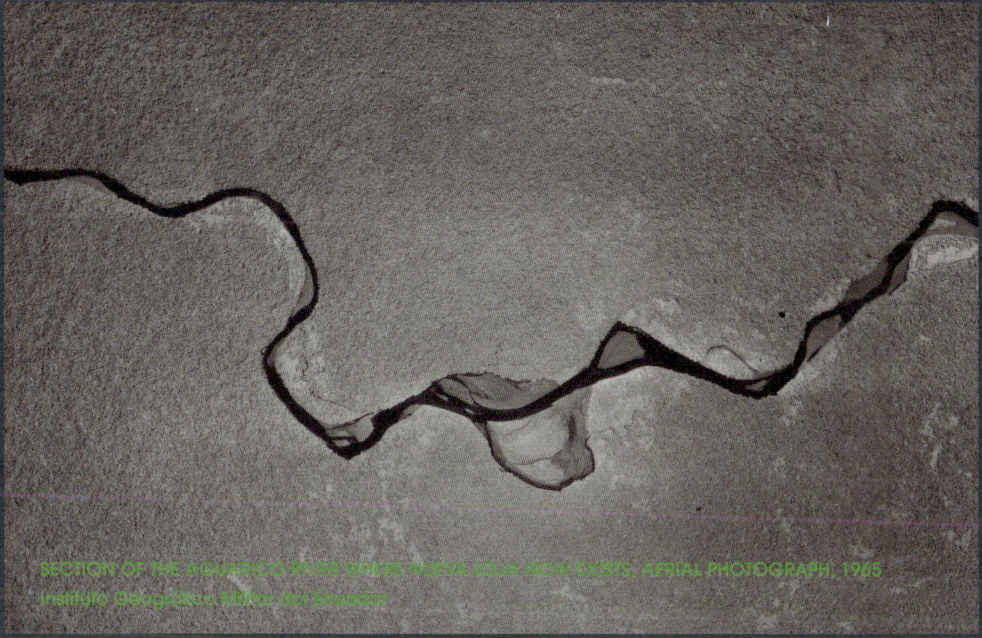

SECTION OF THE AGUARICO RIVER WHERE NUEVA LOJA NOW EXISTS, AERIAL PHOTOGRAPH, 1965
Instituto Geográfico Militar del Ecuador

NUEVA LOJA AERIAL PHOTOGRAPH, 1985
Instituto Geográfico Militar del Ecuador

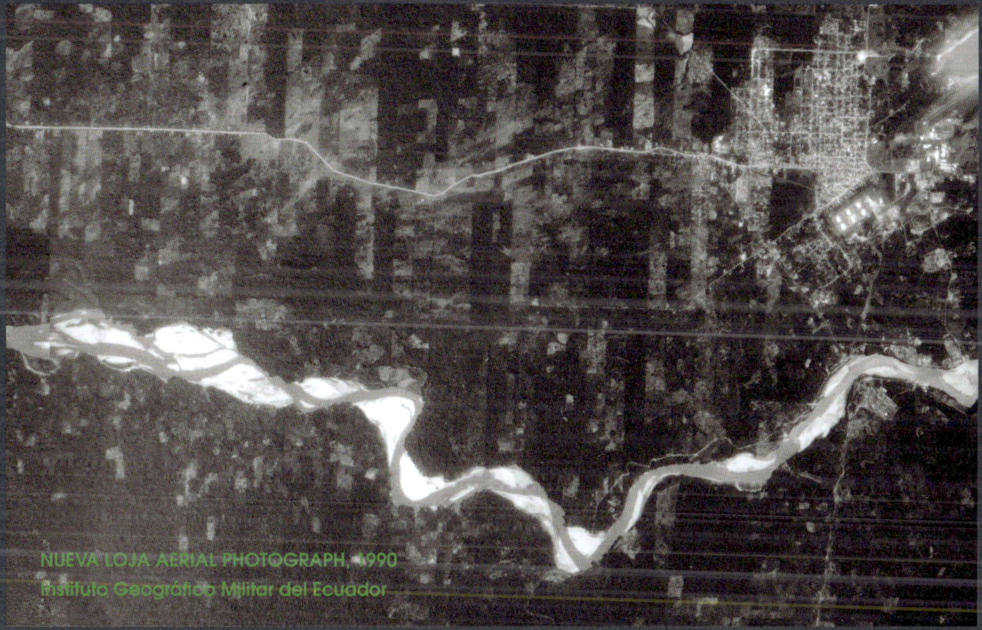

NUEVA LOJA AERIAL PHOTOGRAPH, 1990
Instituto Geográfico Militar del Ecuador

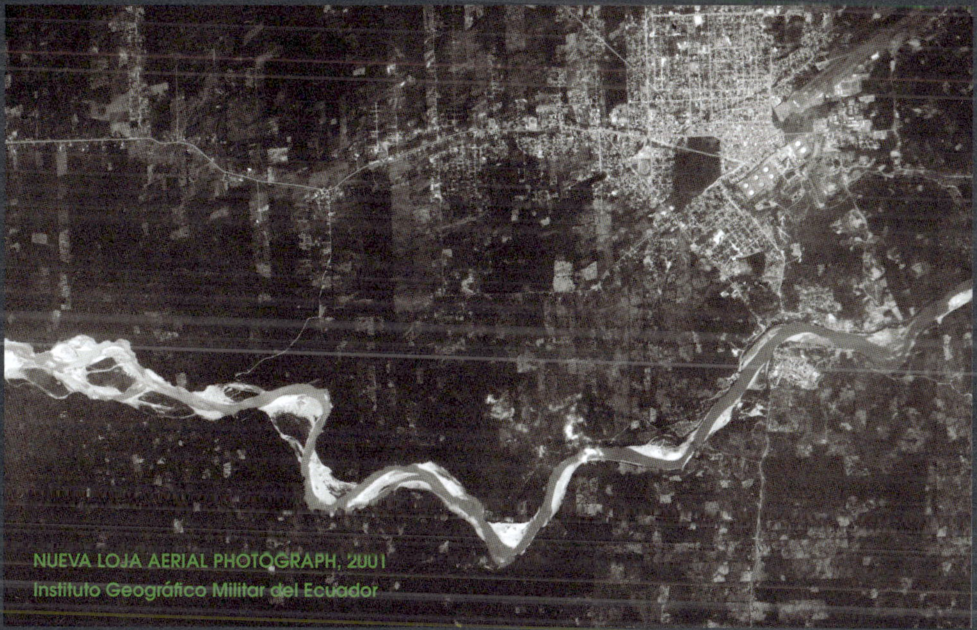

NUEVA LOJA AERIAL PHOTOGRAPH, 2001
Instituto Geográfico Militar del Ecuador

INFRASTRUCTURAL URBANISMS

The IIRSA clearly stipulates that one of its fundamental objectives is to "facilitate access to areas with major productive potential that have remained isolated or underutilized."[9] We know very well what it takes to open pathways to sources of raw materials or areas with great energy potential. Railway systems are laid out, as are air, maritime and fluvial routes, but most often, roads are built. What differentiates the latter method from the other modes of transport is that the pattern of development that is generated does not respond to a sequence or spine, with well-defined points of intervention. Water and air can be contaminated, but not striated, whereas the land is inevitably scarred by the deployment of roads and highways in a system that behaves like a fractal: the lines of main roads bifurcate into secondary roads, which in turn generate tertiary roads, causing a transversal and continuous form of entropy. To open the pathway to sources of raw materials is to open the floodgates of colonization and to trigger processes of hyperactive and multi-directional migration. The phenomenon that occurs at the intersection of global necessity and the physical reality on the local level could be described as "infrastructural urbanism" or "entropic infrastructural urbanism."

If South America, in order to "develop itself," needs to deploy an infrastructural network, it is fundamental to analyze what are and will be the spatial and geographic consequences – and eventually, social, cultural and environmental ones – of its construction and renovation. Traditionally, the focal points of occupation and eventual urbanization of the ground have been access to sources of water, soils rich in nutrients, or commercial routes. Infrastructural urbanisms in remote areas derive from a different logic; they occur along "routes to nowhere" (extraction areas) in often hostile geographies and generally depend on the provision of external products to survive. Furthermore, urban growth inevitably triggers a concurrent expansion of agricultural zones. The counterparts of the urban explosion are the immense pasturelands and monoculture agriculture that sustain it, as well as the ulcers of diverse forms of mining.

GREEN INFRASTRUCTURES

According to *The Financial Times*[10], to add four points to the annual growth of a country's Gross National Product, it is necessary to invest between five and nine percent of its budget in infrastructure. An economy is bound to grow as a result of an infrastructural stimulus. Nevertheless, one would have to wonder if the return varies for elements that serve mainly for extraction purposes, adjusting the curve for long-term investment to account for environmental and social costs. Otherwise, an economy that remains territorially blind builds oil pipelines, canals, dykes, highways, bridges, ports, cable networks and endless modes of mobilization without questioning the very nature of the infrastructure, which might be designed differently, or the specific interests that it serves. If detrimental impacts were included in the cost-benefit analysis, governments and companies would probably invest more money in the development of green infrastructures. For example, if one were to take into account the environmental costs of the construction of a hydroelectric plant or any other project whose sheer scale is enough to detonate an impact with extremely high social and environmental costs, one might develop alternate systems of micro-infrastructures, which, due to their smaller scale, would have less impact. A system of micro-hydroelectric dams might cost more initially, if constructed to produce the same amount of energy as one mega-dam, but in the long run its impact would be far less marked and the savings generated would end up benefitting society much more than a centralized mega-system. The same could be said, for example, for water collection and energy production micro-systems; an off-the-grid strategy that, rather than connecting to a central network, could act in a wireless or un-plugged fashion, granting the user autonomy and the capacity to save, and triggering, by a chain reaction, a reduction of environmental degradation. We know from mathematics and the

9 www.iirsa.org

10 www.ft.com/home/us

analysis of dynamic systems that an infinitesimal change in the initial stages produces a substantial transformation on a major scale in the final reckoning. Future infrastructural developments can benefit from the amplified effect of tiny changes and are able to mediate the encounter between the continental and local scales. Even from a security standpoint, micro-infrastructures constitute a better option than larger engineering works, insofar as the latter serve as targets for vandalism; when they collapse, the entire system collapses. Ironically, in an era of intense interconnection, an ability to disconnect is becoming key to survival. Instead of being aimed at centralizing resources, infrastructures could become a medium for democratization. They could also serve as points of distribution for public services and contribute to enhancing access to education and health for large sectors of the population. Latin America, if it took advantage of its marginal status to work towards a plan for integration and innovative economic development, could trigger a process of global renewal. The relative isolation in which we have remained gives us an advantage: the advantage being that we have not developed under the guidelines of an unsustainable industrial paradigm.

NEW CENTRALITIES: THE PERIPHERIES OF THE PERIPHERIES - THE CASE OF THE AMAZON

The Amazon is an ideal laboratory in which to study, in the dendrites of capitalist intelligence, the relationship between global and local forces – their effects on the very fringes of geography, the periphery of peripheries, where the very restrictions of the system are latent like nowhere else. At these critical locations, the hope is that one can find the ideal terrain on which to formulate new paradigms for development. Here, one could test all that is "green": green infrastructures, green industry, urban ecologies, clean energy, mixed agricultural and forestry systems, urban agriculture, potentialities of biotechnology, or possibilities for anthropogenic landscapes and soils. Archeologists have already demonstrated that human activity can have a positive effect in the Amazon. Its pre-hispanic cultures not only knew how to take care of, but also how to enrich poor soil to increase its agricultural productivity. Mentioning this, I do not mean to say that I favor an agricultural conquest of the jungle, nor that I view a return to former ways of living as desirable. I simply view the relationship between humans and nature with optimism, as inextricable, and believe that the land can be managed even within extremely fragile ecosystems. On the other hand, I remain optimistic about technology, understood anthropologically, as a culture, as the human ability to interact with, modify, and be modified by the environment. In addition to giving us solutions through environmental design, technology could provide us with the tools necessary to improve social welfare. To cite a specific case in the Amazon, as we traversed it in the summer of 2008, we discovered a solar-powered communication system that has been implemented in various indigenous communities in the Brazilian forest, in order to give their members the benefit of immediate inter-connection in a context where patterns of population dispersion predominate. This system has contributed to strengthen the power of indigenous groups and to consolidate their participation in the political arena, particularly with regard to policies that directly affect the livelihood of their communities.

TRAVEL AS A RESPONSE TO THE TERRITORIAL BLINDNESS OF GEO-ECONOMIES

Often, the logic of economics has suffered from a territorial blindness. Economics affiliates itself with Engineering and Politics and decides how to extract what from where. Its strategies have often unfolded without the appropriate planning of physical space. Its fundamental tools are cartographies and enormous databases that correlate diverse parameters of econometric planning. Maps which work with the territory at great distances pulverize it, with the advantage of unveiling patterns, structures, substructures and even causes of phenomena, thanks to the elimination of detail. These, though, need to be complemented with other maps that have been drawn by walking, navigating, and traversing the minutiae of space, taking into account the fact that observers – near or far – are an inextricable component of a system.

If we look, on the one hand, from afar at the Amazon Basin, we see that infrastructures like the trans-Amazonian highway or the BR 163 that connects Santarem with the Bolivian border, inevitably generate patterns of land clearing. Paradoxically, the same mapping systems that facilitate the design of infrastructures and their insertion in the land have also become the mechanisms that are used to protect it from diverse forms of invasion. The geo-referential systems of information such as GEOSUR, decentralized networks of map servers, geo-integrating mechanisms (open source), geo-spatial data, the regional visualization of national data and the CONDOR 2 program (the first attempt to offer an interactive mapping tool for South America hosted by the International Andean Development and Conservation Corporation)[11] provide another form of integration, building a preliminary framework within which to estimate the environmental and social impact of large scale infrastructural road system projects, as well as establishing diverse control mechanisms.

Why has control become such a preponderant concern in the Amazon? Because the Amazon is plagued with illegalities: it has become one of the main global centers of coca leaf and poppy seed plantations; the river is a vital artery for the trafficking of cocaine and opium; sexual exploitation of children occurs along the entire length of the river; selective deforestation is creating an ever shrinking forest canopy; full deforestation is occurring even in the most remote regions; disregard for the intellectual property of indigenous communities is a common occurrence; illegal animal trafficking is endless; and human slavery continues to exist as a form of labor exploitation (in the literal sense of the word)[12]. Even illegal infrastructures exist; not only those constructed by the drug trafficking industry but others open for logging and/or settling. According to Imazon (Institute of Men and the Environment in the Amazon)[13] "the Brazilian jungle has at least 95,355 km of illegal roads; ten times the number of official roads." Many new "ghost" towns or settlements are also illegal – might not this be the reason that the GPS does not identify several Amazon sites, regardless of their size? It is interesting to observe that illegal activities seem to find the perfect hiding place in the canopy of the rainforest, and that their response to aerial and satellite monitoring has been to pulverize the traces of their existence. Large agricultural fields are replaced by archipelago agriculture, deforestation by selective deforestation, and shifting streams become the preferred means of transportation rather than the main navigation arteries. The performance of satellite monitoring systems is improving as quickly as new strategies for the fracture of territory are being developed.

THE BUILT WORLD AS A NATURAL RESOURCE AND THE IMPORTANCE OF DESIGN

Architecture, the city and infrastructure need to be re-conceptualized as natural resources, and new development plans cannot continue to be formulated without the participation of designers (architects, urban planners, urban designers, landscape architects, etc.) who can develop proposals in conjunction with politicians, engineers, economists, ecologists, mathematicians and experts in diverse fields. The collaboration of different fields of knowledge is another vital form of integration that we must strive to achieve in the midst of the enormous social and environmental challenges currently facing us. After all, the construction industry absorbs 50% of the acquisition and extraction of materials producing 217 different types of ecological impact; it consumes 26.15% of overall energy generated and produces 50% of the pollution from which we all suffer.[14] Designers working alongside the extraction agencies, as well as those working in the areas of material accretion, are being called upon to provide effective answers to the

11 www.caf.com

12 www.csmonitor.com/2004/0907/P01504-woam.html

13 www.imazon.org.br

14 http://vlex.com/vid/materiales-construccion-medio-ambiente-41651434

15 It is important to mention that the system of parks and nature preserves encumbers urbanization: population densities dilute around protected zones. In addition to the public reserves, private ones are playing an increasingly important role in terms of environmental conservation, generally in association with the tourism industry.

environmental problem. The participation of the design community has nevertheless been minimal, if not completely nil, within territorial planning programs. The catastrophic consequences that derive from this absence are apparent in developed nations, where many cities are shrinking and myriad recovery projects in large industrial areas retroactively seek out the design discipline to find new forms of spatial rehabilitation in areas whose infrastructure was originally designed exclusively following now obsolete economic and engineering logic. Large infrastructures from the industrial era are being retrofitted as parks and public spaces. If we learn the lessons from the North, we can design the infrastructures of the future, taking their life cycles into account, in the South.

We should even question whether designers are equipped to respond to the unique conditions of an ecosystem using tools based on the application of standards and regulations, however environmental they may seem. Mechanisms that are purportedly green, such as LEED certification, collapse when they are applied to an ecosystem like that of the Amazon. Is it even possible to respond to ecologies with unique characteristics using standardized, generic certificates, however "combinatory" or purportedly "local" they may be? Aren't these systems a mere variation on the generalizations of the industrial mentality? Are not urban parametrics and dynamic urban ecological models better alternatives for the design of future interventions? In the specific case of the Amazon, and taking into consideration all the answers that can be found in the territory itself (be it in formal or informal versions), the basin could be rethought as a productive landscape, where the main components of infrastructure and urbanism are buoyant. There is much to be learnt from floating cities such as Iquitos; even from the fluvial hospitals and schools that already populate the river in an attempt to provide educational and health alternatives that are in harmony with the surroundings they are meant to serve. In an era in which designers and researchers are investigating potential responses to water level changes, as we face the challenges posed by global warming, the nature of cities like Iquitos becomes worthy of deeper analysis and should not be effaced in the name of development.[15]

THE BICENTENNIAL AS A SYMBOLIC DIMENSION OF INFRASTRUCTURE

Infrastructures are not silent systems; simple a-semantic, functional objects devoid of content and ideology. Quite the contrary: infrastructures signify progress and development; they symbolize strength and unification. Several of the infrastructural projects that had already been planned by the Ministries of Public Works of several governments in South America have been included in the IIRSA's project portfolio, and several others are being or will be inaugurated in commemoration of the numerous Independence Bicentennials that are being celebrated in the majority of South American countries.

The alliance is perfect: as we celebrate two centuries of independence, and in order to survive inclement global market competition, we will unify our infrastructures. In addition to its triple meaning: autonomy, integration and progress; the "infrastructural Bicentennial" provides a platform for remembrance, self-evaluation and the evaluation of the ideological discourses and economic aims embedded in the infrastructures of the IIRSA.

And if I could end this essay with an atypical contemporary optimism, an optimism instilled in me after traversing the South American continent along the Amazon River, I would even dare say that if the Nile was the forefather of the Egyptian civilization, the Volga of the Russian, and the Yangtze of China; the civilization that has been bred and shall spring from the Amazon River is destined to be grandiose, in accordance with the power of the jungle and the life, generosity and magnificence of the river-ocean. South America cannot afford to ignore the fundamental role it is being called upon to play as the paradigm of the future post-industrial world is written, and Brazil will have to continue leading this process, as is expected from the only country that shares its borders with every other country in the continent, with the exception of two; Chile and Ecuador. Every landscape is a way of thinking. The Amazon is the supreme symbol of ancestral youth, of a system that renews itself – perennial – as it makes itself from continuous small deaths... from this river we shall learn how to contrive new strategies for development.

Updated from October, 2008

BIENVENIDOS
A la Jugueria

C.C. La Bahía

COMERCIAL
COMERCIAL
LOAIZA
Camisetas
BRASIELES
TOALLAS
COLCHAS
VIKINES
Etc.
CHEVROLET
LAGO AGRIO
TELF. 830 780

DESIGNING A NEW LANDSCAPE FOR LAGO AGRIO

ACHVA BENZINBERG STEIN

The Amazon River system is a complex interconnected network of thousands of rivers merging into one another. In the vicinity of Lago Agrio, the Cuyabeno River flows into the Aguarico River, which empties into the Napo River, which in turn discharges into the Amazon (also known as the Solimões). This ecosystem still supports the largest number of species on earth – over 2,000 trees and shrubs, close to 600 birds, 100 amphibians, more than 80 reptiles and nearly 80 bats. There are 60 species of social bees and more than 100,000 species of insects per hectare. Altogether this yields more than six trillion individual living beings.

But human habitation has had a profound impact on this region. Traditionally, the indigenous peoples of the Sucumbíos province, where Lago Agrio is located, had a delicately balanced relationship with the environment – it nourished and protected them. Since the middle of the last century, however, with the laying of roads and extraction of oil, new colonizers have inflicted major devastation on the area and its inhabitants. The resulting contamination of the upper river system has created havoc downstream – the global, political, social and economic implications are yet to be fully understood.

In their book *The Sixth Extinction: Patterns of Life and the Future of Humankind*, Richard E. Leakey and Roger Lewin suggest that human beings are triggering a "sixth extinction" similar to the five others which took place before our species arrived. Looking at contemporary Lago Agrio, and the human activity that has caused such vast destruction, their thesis seems not just plausible but convincing.

Today the urban landscape of Lago Agrio – environmental, physical, infrastructural – is in large part the result of haphazard settlement, facilitated by oil drilling and the subsequent internal migration of labor. Some of the structures in and around the town have been built well enough, but just as many are rundown, make-shift or both. Cultivated land has been fragmented into small farmsteads, while housing colonies for the migrants tend to be near roads and oil extraction sites rather than arable land, reflecting the state of rural poverty the newcomers are forced into.

Oil pollution in this area is ubiquitous: it permeates the ground, seeps into rivers and streams and collects in large depressions and puddles both in the town and on the periphery. As a result, Lago Agrio's hydrological cycle has been damaged and its carbon and nitrogen cycles disrupted. Where human settlements have grown up, natural vegetation has been disturbed at best, destroyed at worst. Native populations – human and non-human – and the resources needed for their survival have been marginalized, at times entirely overlooked.

The extraordinary biological wealth around Lago Agrio – and the continuing damage being inflicted upon the land – has challenged scientists to think of ways to protect the forest from human encroachment. Ideas about how to restore a balance to the web of physical, economic, social, and institutional forces, however, remain elusive. The conservation, repair and creation of new landscapes is the core work of the environmental designer. We set our students the task of preparing designs that would help, halt, or perhaps even reverse the situation they found at Lago Agrio. The results compiled here are meant not as a prescription but rather a critical exercise. All are examples of practical solutions for a sustainable human future, not just the future of Lago Agrio.

The urban design and landscape architecture students who prepared the urban master plan for Lago Agrio took to heart the challenge of repairing and healing the land. They sought to address the inevitable increase in waste and effluents that will occur as the city's population grows. They called for chemical and biological recycling systems to be incorporated into the development plan, in particular water storage and recovery systems. They studied cycling and water filtration in depth. Their critical green solutions included floating wetland structures to increase river vegetation and eliminate toxic nitrogen oxides and a system of constructed wetlands to filter volatile and non-volatile hydrocarbons and organic and inorganic material at petroleum refinery sites and landfills. They proposed, too, planting native riparian plants (those naturally acclimatized to the ground adjacent to streams, lakes and other water sources) to recycle and filter polluted water before it reaches the aquifer and other bodies of waters.

Since these are passive treatment systems, they require only sporadic maintenance and a small financial investment compared to other technologies – a prerequisite in such an economically-driven climate. At all times, effort was made to ensure these proposals were feasible as well as sound. The solutions offered here are not merely temporary. These measures could provide treatment well into the long term; perhaps in perpetuity. They are land intensive, which is an advantage in this region since large tracts of land here have been rendered uninhabitable to humans. The proposed combination of ponds, wetlands and infiltration basins would be attractive additions to these damaged sites. In time, a new ecosystem would be created, filled with fauna and flora adapted to the new conditions.

Unplanned and irregularly developed, Lago Agrio is blighted by depressions and erosion gullies. The students propose the creation of swales and rain gardens that would direct water away from impervious surfaces, walkways, roads and downspouts, and allow the rain to saturate the soil. The rain gardens would be planted with low maintenance, native plants with appropriate root systems to filter the water before it reaches the aquifer. These gardens could reduce the amount of pollution reaching creeks and streams by up to a third.

Solar energy farms and solar roofs were seen as crucial elements in the production of alternative energy, as was the use of turbines submerged in the river. Focusing on the river would direct the town's attention to this important natural resource not only as a source of energy, but as a surface transportation system in need of major upgrading and as a recreation area for residents.

The urban master plan creates an extensive system of urban agriculture. It restores indigenous agricultural techniques and animal husbandry to the farms at the edge of town and uses native trees and shrubs to replace exotic plants in the streets, plazas and other public open spaces. The plan also proposes commercial bamboo farming. Bamboo is a useful, quickly regenerated and sustainable material both for construction and manufactured flooring.

The students called for better educational resources at all levels. They considered programs for elementary and secondary education and the expansion of higher education. Their plan sites this faculty on a major water course, to act as a linear park providing both recreation and water filtration and as a base for the study of natural resources. In fact, intrinsic to the plan for this institution is a multidisciplinary training center, focused on management of commercial and natural resources – an informational as well as training hub for local, community, and larger scale regional projects.

While these design solutions were developed specifically to curb the exploitation of resources and to repair destroyed sites, they will also have a profound visual, ecological and socio-economic effect on the landscape of Lago Agrio. The repair of damaged ecological systems is an easy concept to understand. Conservation, however, is a more challenging idea for both students and professionals, since it involves not just the repair of harm inflicted in the past, but the imposition of restrictions in the present and the future. Where the primary conservation needs are organizational and educational, the meaning and value of these measures are particularly hard to grasp.

One standard conservation strategy is to designate forest land as "reservation" for recreational use. But this approach cannot prevent the air, water and soil contamination or the dust and noise pollution that bring about habitat destruction and the loss of plant and animal life. Recreational open space is designed for human use and for visual impact – not for resource conservation. Even eco-tourism takes a high toll on the forest, from the poaching of timber and wildlife to erosion by motor boats which also threaten low-level nesting birds. The cutting of new trails, to keep up with ecotourists' hunger for novelty, leads to severe habitat loss. Areas near the reserve must be developed to house the large numbers of visitors during the peak season, effectively turning the forest into an island ecosystem, eroding the integrity of the reserve and gradually destroying the area altogether.

Eco-tourism, even when managed carefully, disturbs native cultures by raising false expectations for leisure and escape. For conservation to be effective there has to be a comprehensive management program that embraces all categories of open space – from urban infrastructure and agriculture, to gardens, parks and nature reserves – rather than simply patches of portioned-off green space.

We do not design landscapes. A landscape is born out of a myriad of large and small actions by individuals and the collective. It mirrors the large-scale processes at work upon it. All landscapes are constantly in flux from a dynamic interplay of ecological, social and economic forces. When human and non-human species come together in relative harmony, a landscape feels "natural." When it combines the varied conditions necessary for all life, it can function without force, coercion, high levels of mortality or disarray.

To achieve such a state of coexistence in Nuevo Loja will require a shift in paradigms from one of exploitation and extraction to one of reconciliation. Only when professionals working with the land stop trying to separate culture from nature and strive for integration will design on the land assume a different form. When that happens, the landscape will reflect those changes. It is not enough, however, for the architect, urban designer or landscape architect to produce a coherent program. There are enormous issues to resolve. For any physical plan to be implemented, the multitude of often conflicting claims on the land will have to be heard and reconciled. A tall order.

SCENES FROM THE CITY

THE END OF THE PETROL AGE

OSVALDO PALADINES ZURITA

In 2007 Rafael Correa, the President Elect of Ecuador, came to the historic decision to ban all drilling for oil in the Ecuadorean subsoil in protected zones, natural reserves, or national parks in the Amazonian basin. As if this weren't enough, the government has also implemented a series of new regulations for the extraction of precious minerals, which for decades has caused massive pollution of the rivers and land with mercury and other heavy metals. With these first regulatory measures, mining has come under scrutiny for the first time in this country.

This new direction, apart from demonstrating a much more severe and strict environmental conscience (not a very popular stance amongst supporters of the free market policies that dominate almost the entirety of the South American continent), poses fresh challenges for both architects and city planners. Apparently, the much-feared end of the Oil Era has already arrived in Ecuador. Or at least the indiscriminate exploitation so characteristic of it over the past three decades has ended.

When we began to plan the Design and Research Studio with our friends at the City College of New York, we optimistically estimated that Ecuador's oil resources would be exhausted in 25 years. It seems that we were off by a wide margin. We said that the oil cities of Amazonia would have enough time to plan ahead and adjust their planning policies before the wealth earned from the black gold ran out. The dilemma about what to do with the encampments that grew into cities was far into the future. But events have precipitated this change and our task has taken on critical importance.

From the beginning, the academic challenge was fascinating. Experiencing the city of Lago Agrio at first hand, we observed the ways in which its frontier nature has created a unique set of circumstances; it is a distribution center, has undeniable links with Colombian guerillas, and is also an urban center experiencing rapid, almost entirely unplanned, growth. The analysis of the policies of urban development, the con stant destruction of the jungle soil and the potential of Nueva Loja to become a typological example of a post-oil city were worthy of not one but many collaborative studios.

It seemed to us that the objective contributions of an external group of interested and curious colleagues of diverse origin – together with those of several civil authorities and a group of determined architects in Nueva Loja – would allow us to study, analyze, and finally put forward some preliminary ideas about how the growth of cities of this kind, historically haphazard in their "planning," improvisational in their human development policy, and marginalized by violence and the neglect of a succession of governments, should evolve. Now the problem is at our doorstep: there is little time to transform traditional habits, ideologies, and prejudices in urban planning.

Ecuador is beset by a Modernism that won't go away; and this is true in every area of design. The Modernism of the 20th century is so deeply-rooted here that only a few saw Postmodernism, with its critical aspects pass them by. This country is chained to the socializing urban practices of the 60s, and we all suffer their consequences without the least hope that this state of affairs in our cities will change any time soon.

The presentation of new planning visions to the authorities was a challenge that we set ourselves from the beginning, and after a couple of days in Lago Agrio we were able to provide a comparison for local stakeholders and reinvigorate the studio with the wishes and proposals of a wonderful group of architects in charge of the renovation of the urban center of the city.

But perhaps the most gratifying experience was the visit to the research station run by the Universidad Católica, deep in the Ecuadorian rainforest at the edge of Yasuní National Park. And even there, where the rainforest remains in a state of apparently untouched virginity, we found oil drilling encampments which definitely shouldn't have existed.

The contrast between this scene of human exploitation and the dignity of the natural landscape was so chilling that most of us, professors and students alike, awoke to a reality impossible to ignore. The idea became rooted in our brains with such force that we committed to entering into the constant practice of environmental conservation in every aspect of design and daily life.

Amongst the most vivid and powerful experiences of those days was the visit we made to a Huaoroni community. Moved and quite overwhelmed by the clash of cultures, we observed ancient ancestral rites that have now been blurred by Western customs or adapted to tourists´ expectations.

We were honored with some ancestral songs and, trying to give them something in return, we sang Silent Night (the only song we could come up with that everyone in our diverse group knew), which, despite weird resonances with missionary "education," sounded sincere in the large straw hut built for tourists.

The academic experience was continued with animated group evaluation days in which we put forward our proposals and listened to those offered so kindly and determinedly by the students of City College. The exchange was enriching and helped us to establish many of the essential guidelines that might aid the future planning of post-oil cities. We became aware of and expressed a number of certainties, which is more than a workshop can hope for, discovered the true meaning of *sinchi sacha* (the power of the jungle), and the capacity of the Amazonian wilderness to enter into the city and be a constant presence in everyday activity. We got rid of our prejudices and realized how right Van der Laan was in his famous comparison of a house with a sandal:

"In the house, it is not only a question of it coming between our feet and the ground, but the coming together of our being and the natural surroundings. The terms under which this harmony between the two is established are not simply that of a piece of soft sole under our feet, but a piece of habitable space separating us from the natural environment through walls... Whilst the sandal is tied to our feet it completes the body and allows us to walk over hard ground, the house should be seen as an addition to nature, through which natural space is completed and made habitable for us..."[1]

And so the students in the studio designed their proposals for sustainable households in Amazonia. The projects presented here are the result of these and other considerations about the role human beings should play in extremely endangered natural environments.

The conclusions and results may not produce concrete results in the short term. We will have to hope that the next generation of Ecuadorian architects decides to decisively take the next step towards genuinely sustainable planning and make a huge effort to bring to an end the abusive and uncontrolled extermination of the great Amazonian resource which will eventually save the rest of the earth.

[1] Dom Van Der Laan, 'Nature and Architecture', taken from 'The Place of Architecture'.

NUEVA LOJA TIMELINE

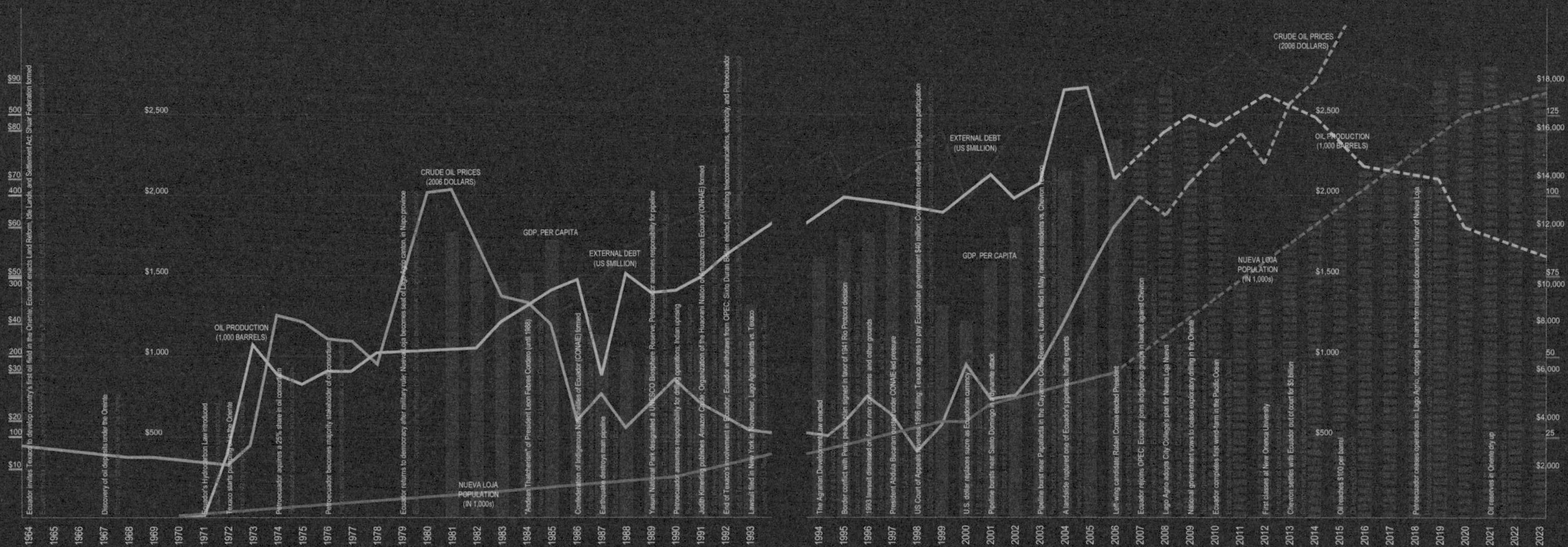

PETROLEUM TIMELINE

SOURCES: **GDP.** http://www.ocontasts.com/woo/CV049V015.html
CRUDE OIL PRICES: http://www.wtrg.com/prices.htm
OIL PRODUCTION: http://www.cedatos.com.ec/contenido.asp?id=774
EXTERNAL DEBT: http://www.latin-focus.com/latinfocus/countries/ecuador/ecudebt.htmLAGO AGRIO POPULATION:
http://www.inec.gov.ec/, http:www.citypopulation.de/ecuador.html

GEOGRAPHY

MAP OF ECUADOR

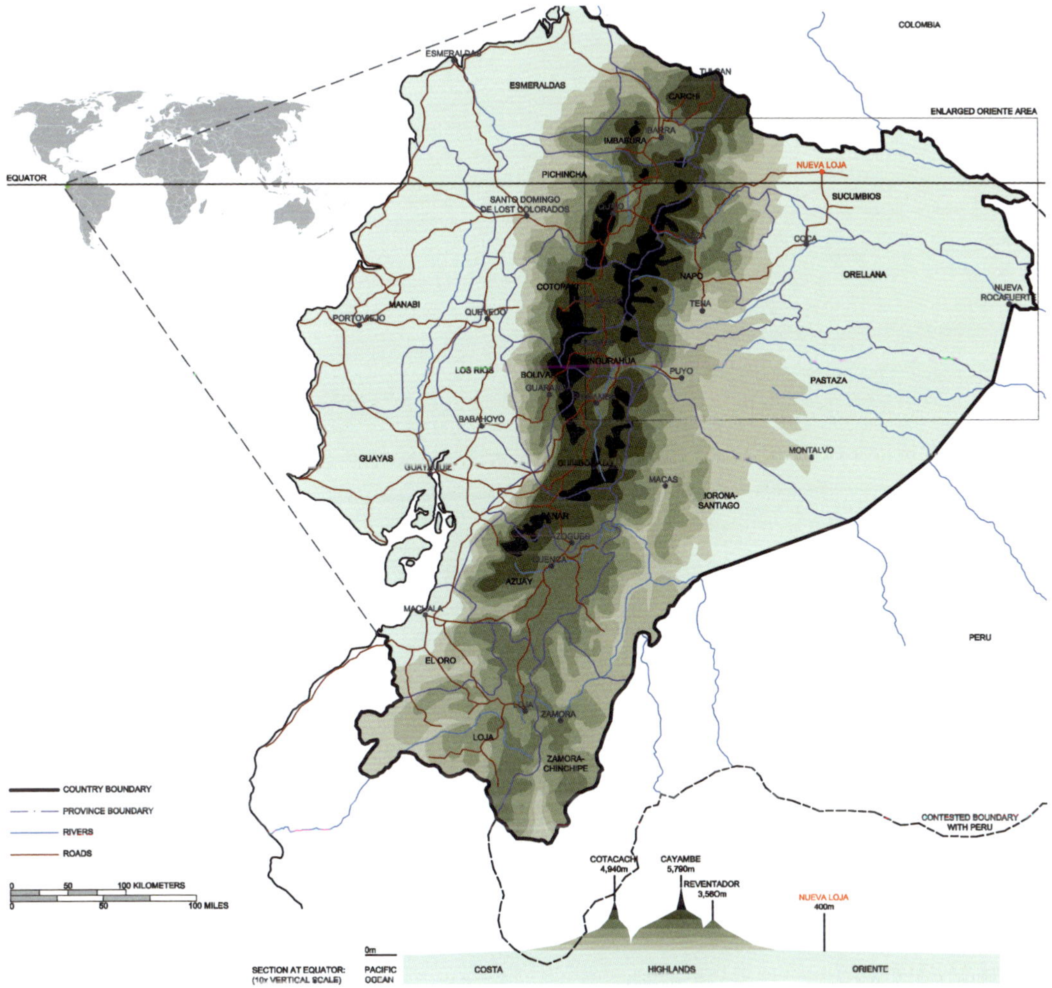

TOP: ORIENTE

BOTTOM: HIGHLANDS, COAST

INDIGENOUS POPULATIONS

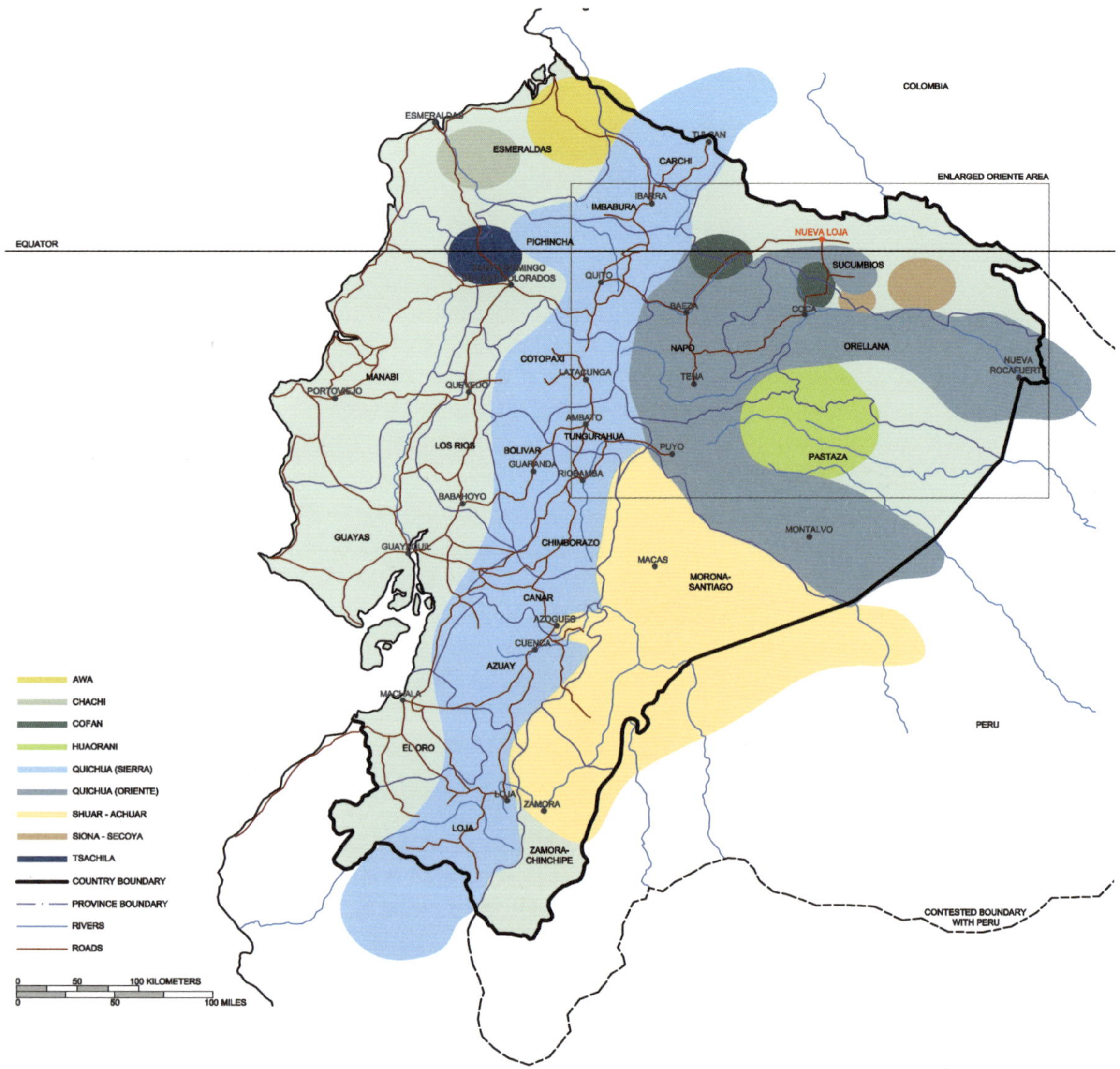

PETROLEUM CONCESSIONS

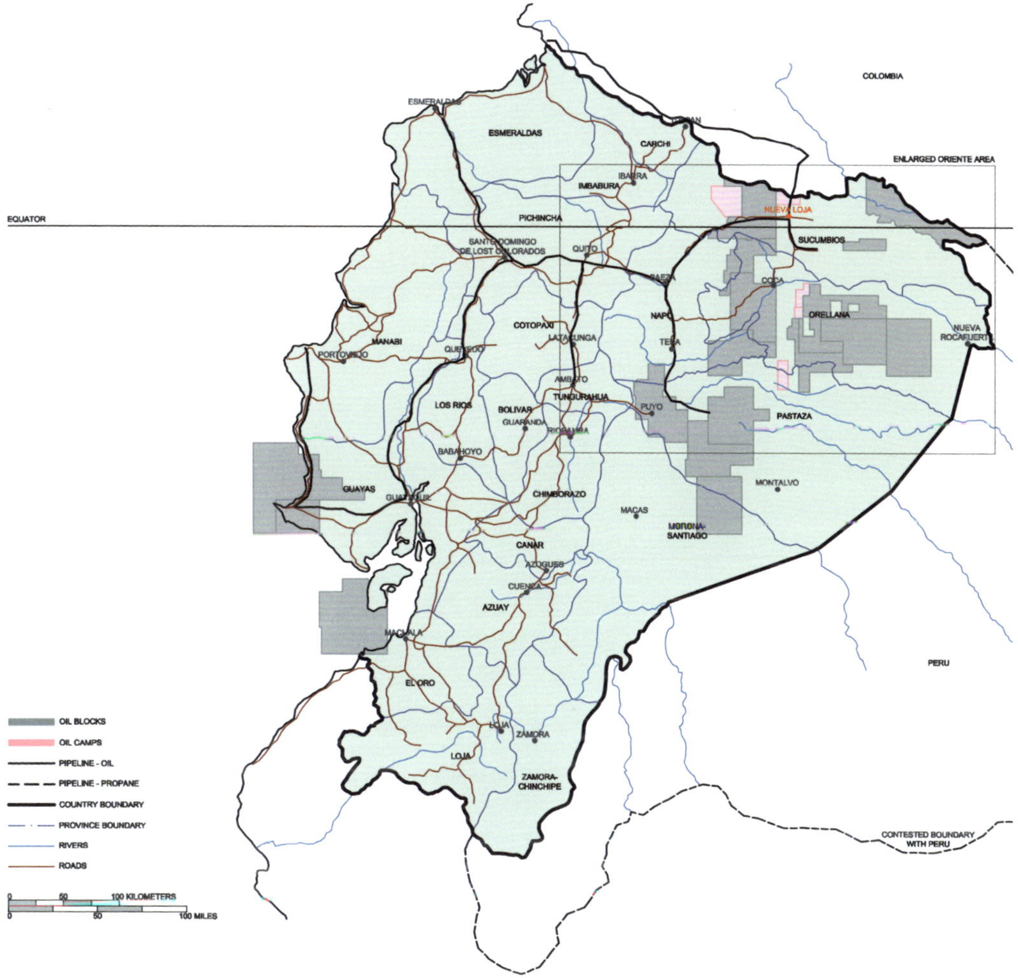

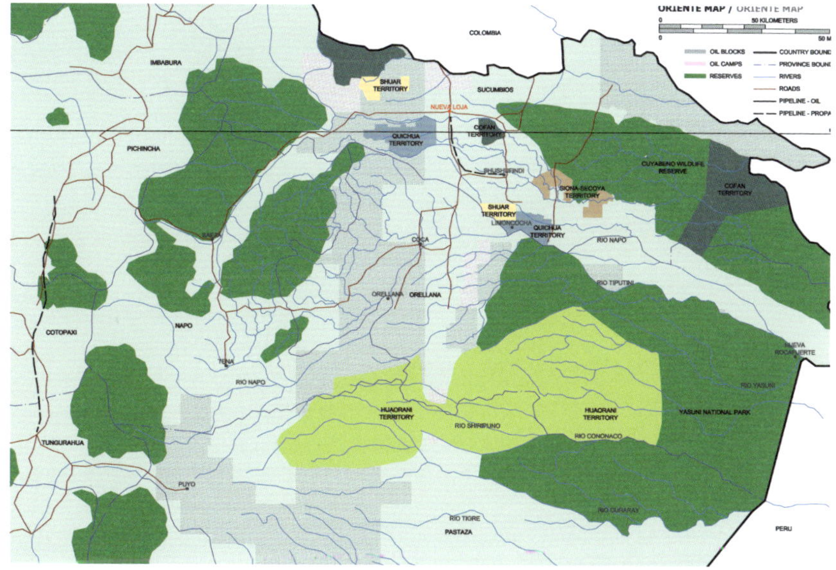

OIL IN ORIENTE

TRIP

HOLLY KALLMAN

We begin our trip in the crystal cool air of Quito and the Andes. Urbane and colonial, Quito has a gorgeous history, clashing Catholic factions, Rapid Bus transit and stunning vistas and monuments. We find it hard to believe it is "unsafe." We're from New York City and we're tough. Ha!

An astonishing landscape rolls below us. This road is so precarious – it's no urban armature. Our view is a sectional slice through the landscape. Volcanic altitudes fall away to meet the red clay of swift-flowing rivers. The oncoming traffic passes an inch from our hurtling bus. We hear the bus wheels land on steel as we cross a bridge high over coursing waters. Always running along at our side is the crude steel of the pipeline, snaking silently through brilliant tones of lush vegetation. The pipe is the reason this road is here. Texaco laid them together in 1972, opening the Amazon up to us, to everyone.

We come to the River Napo and cross it by boat, finally able to feel the furious current. The bus takes a separate barge. We are stewarded by able and capable hands; this is an able and capable land.

Nueva Loja is all city. Commerce driven and competitive, the markets are stocked and bustling. But the urbanity I am accustomed to, settled layer by layer over time, is not here. There is only a single layer, as thin and fragile as the rainforest topsoil, and just as difficult to cultivate.

Awash in vivid color, the Amazon feels rich with raw beauty and wildness.

TOWN

ROBERTA KORCZ

With the discovery of oil in 1967, the original agricultural community at Nueva Loja became a municipal entity. Oil infrastructure determined the grid of the new city. It set the street pattern and the distribution of people. It also drove the destruction of the rainforest. Today, with the human population set to grow exponentially over the next quarter of a century, this oil-based pattern of organization will become ever more ingrained in the framework of the city.

Over the same 25 year period, the oil here will run dry and its infrastructure will become obsolete. Although it's possible to imagine a long-term, post petroleum future for Nuevo Loja – in which the oil industry's footprint is expunged from the landscape, the soil and water are toxin-free, animal and plant life have returned and the economy is diversified – the city's past will shape that future.

Nueva Loja, a frontier town composed predominantly of migrants and informal settlements, is quite unlike a traditional Latin American city. Its linear urban form is concentrated along the town's principal street, Avenida Quito. A dynamic urban street, Avenida Quito abruptly splits into nothing at the city's eastern edge in an area dubbed "the petro-wall" for its concentration of oil infrastructure.

Nuevo Loja is organized around a fragmented network of oil infrastructure, arterial buildings, parks, farmland, and roads. Ironically, this layout has echoes of the Amazon's indigenous patchwork of forest, savannah, scrubland, and floodplain. Nuevo Loja is the locus of two apparently contradictory landscapes the city framework spreading outwards and the rainforest forced out beyond the periphery. There are some exceptions to this general pattern; it folds and overlaps where the boundaries between the two systems are more fluid.

JUNGLE

GARETH MAHON

Eco-Tourists venturing east from Quito, the Ecuadorian capital, bound for the Oriente and the Amazon Basin will no doubt read of Nueva Loja as being a gateway to the jungle and a jumping-off point for their Amazonian adventure. It is true that Nueva Loja, by virtue of its location and infrastructure, is a natural point of departure for a trip to the Cuyabeuno Reserve or the Yasuni National Park, but as we begin to think about a design proposition for the future of this jungle city we need to look deeper at our understanding of the jungle and how we relate it to a contemporary urban environment.

"Jungle" accounts for almost six percent of the earth's land mass. In climatic and geographical terms it is typically defined as a tropical rainforest biome and found in the equatorial regions of Africa, Asia and South and Central America. Jungles are zones of extreme bio-diversity and home to over half the species of plants and animals on the planet. Yasuni National Park in Ecuador has been described as the most biodiverse place on earth and the Amazon rainforest alone produces twenty percent of the world's oxygen. These facts, together with the knowledge that the rainforest is being depleted at a rate of one and a half acres each second, begin to shape our contemporary understanding of the jungle.

But the idea of the jungle has been taking shape for much longer than modern statistics have been available and more often than not it has been shaped by juxtaposing two opposing beliefs, or experiences, that together create an idea of place that we recognize today. For the 200,000 indigenous people of the Amazon rainforest the jungle has always been a place to be revered as much for its rich supplies of food and shelter as for the dangers it presents in the form of illness and relative position on the food chain. For the visitor – conquistador, scientist, industrialist, missionary or tourist – the jungle has presented itself in many guises – a wealth of gold and natural resources to be exploited, an ungodly place in need of salvation, or an Eden-like wonderland to be explored and recorded before it disappears.

In the first years of the 19th century the German naturalist and explorer, Alexander von Humboldt, travelled throughout much of Central and South America, including visits to Ecuador and Peru. His rich depictions of the landscapes, plants and animals were warmly received in Europe and North America by proponents of the newly developing Romantic Movement. Over subsequent decades Americans especially would begin to be obsessed with landscape as a means of connecting with a higher being. As America looked to the picturesque wilderness of the west, many of the artists of the day, including the Hudson River School painter Frederic Edwin Church, travelled to South America to record the jungle scenes described in such detail by von Humboldt. These depictions, embodied with references to the sublime, began to shape one of the formative ideas of the jungle that is still powerful today. This romantic view, enhanced by transcendentalist ideas, placed man and god firmly within the landscape. With so many of those early American wilderness areas depleted, the torch would now seem to have been passed to the jungle as the home of the spiritual landscape.

In contrast, the events that began unfolding over three hundred years before von Humboldt's expedition, with the arrival of the Spanish conquistadors in South America, set into play a different dynamic. The conquistadors came in search of gold and treasures and the goal of ensuring Spain's position as a 16th Century Superpower. They also came to bring Christianity to a godless place. Their methods were brutal and the genocide and destruction of Aztec, Inca, and other societies ensued. The jungle and its inhabitants were often portrayed as savages aligned with the devil. As these stories filtered back to Europe they created a dark picture of the jungle as a place to be feared. European explorers to Africa and Asia also helped to perpetuate pejorative perceptions of native peoples who were portrayed as cannibals all too keen to have them for dinner. This myth has been explored and embellished in popular culture, literature and film over the last century, with the jungle providing the stage for battles between good and evil and a sanctuary for the dark side of the human psyche.

Reconciling the opposing depictions of the jungle as a place akin to heaven or hell has been an ongoing struggle throughout much of the last two centuries. It should be clear that they are not mutually exclusive and that the savage wilderness and the pristine rainforest are one and the same. The most popular movie of all time, Avatar, deals directly with this issue. Through wonderful scenery the stage is set for the battle between the indigenous and the exogenous. The viewer ultimately must take sides, but how could anyone not love the Na'vi? The contemporary artist Walton Ford explores the dialogue with more success in his large format paintings. Ford depicts wild animals in natural settings that, upon further inspection, show a barbaric sub-theme of suffering and death that is as much a part of life for these beasts as the stunning environment they inhabit.

The reality is that the jungle is a complex landscape of overlapping systems. And for better or worse many of these systems are controlled or influenced by both modern and indigenous man to suit

our ever changing needs. William Cronon, the environmental historian, notes in *Uncommon Ground* that when thinking about nature and wilderness "we gaze into the mirror that [wilderness] holds up for us [and] too easily imagine that what we behold is Nature when in fact we see the reflection of our own unexamined longings and desires." The jungle must bear this burden. For some it remains a rich supply of natural resources to be harvested. For others it will always be a mascot of the environmental movement and a metaphor for all things green. Or perhaps it is the last remaining wilderness and our closest point of contact with the sublime. For many it is their home and their livelihood. A modern city in the jungle must meet all of these needs and share the jungle's burden.

TOP LEFT: VOLLEYBALL AFTER WORK
TOP RIGHT: "NILA" BY WALTON FORD

PREDATOR URBANISM: THE BIRTH AND GROWTH OF NUEVA LOJA

ANA MARÍA DURÁN CALISTO

"Quirin, the god of production, or Hermes, who presides over exchanges, can sometimes wield violence in a more efficient manner than Jupiter or Mars and, to reach their goals, they may use the same procedures as the latter."

Michel Serres, *The Natural Contract*
Translation from Spanish by the author

Anyone who has watched the movie "The Gods Must be Crazy" (Jamie Uys, 1980) probably remembers the scene in which a glass Coke bottle lands in the middle of the Kalahari desert. The history of Nueva Loja has a similar plot, but it wasn't a Coke bottle that landed, it was a Texaco light aircraft; and the land was not the Kalahari desert in southern Africa, it was the northwestern edge of the Amazon Rainforest in South America. And who were the characters? Not the Ju/ hoansi of the desert, but the Kichwas and Cofanes of the jungle. What remains common to both stories – however fictional and speculative the former may be – is that the presence of this foreign element which landed on indigenous territory changed the life of their communities forever. As I write, the Huaorani, the famous headshrinkers who first came into contact with the outside world in the 50s and used to be known as Aucas, face a similar plight while the subsoil of their territory and the Yasuní National Park, one of Ecuador´s largest oil reserves, is being negotiated for carbon credit or other so-called "environmental services" in the international market, in order to "keep the oil in the soil" – as the motto of the ITT (Ishpingo-Tiputini-Tambococha) Initiative succinctly has it. The ultimate goal is to spare this land and these peoples from experiencing the same fate as that of Nueva Loja and its surroundings.

Nueva Loja is an unnatural town, and I mean "unnatural" in the urban, not the environmental, sense. It was not born from an indigenous settlement which grows and prospers (the original inhabitants of the Amazon are, for the most part, nomadic or seminomadic – or were). It was never a colonial implant with a gridded bone structure whose adiposity increases as the blocks surrounding the central plaza with its Catholic Church and the headquarters of the city government become occupied, all in accordance with the Laws of Indies that dictated the first and most impressive process of systematic urbanization in the Americas. It didn´t stem from an orderly Mission and develop from a rural, agricultural or hacienda pattern. Nor was it the spontaneous outgrowth of commercial forces driven by the bustling vehicle of urbanism; it is not a "road town", built to service major traffic arteries. It was not a tertiary fluvial port from the rubber boom, reactivated in Modern times, nor was it ever a company town. The heart of Nueva Loja is an oil well; this town is the bastard child of car-based cities in the middle of one of the many ecosystems that sustain them. It simply sprang up. A point and a line were its cradle; the mechanism of its inception. First came the plane (in the 60s), then the oil prospecting strips, then the dots of the oil wells that were interconnected in a branching structure as they multiplied. These were linked by road to the settlement which started as an oil camp and turned into a boom town; this is in turn linked to the more "natural" settlement along the Aguarico River. One could argue that the secondary town revolved around the water source, and the main town around the oil source. As the pioneering arrival of the plane implies, the oil wells brought with them an airport strip, highways, and, eventually, pipelines: the SOTE (Sistema Oleoducto TransEcuatoriano) in 1972 and the increased capacity of the OCP (Oleoducto de Crudos Pesados) in 2003. Both link Nueva Loja to the outskirts of Esmeraldas, a port in the Pacific Ocean, after crossing the Andean Cordillera.

If we try to wedge Nueva Loja into some sort of urban typology, it does not fit. It provokes a taxonomic impulse; it lacks a last name, a genealogy, as its offspring proliferates throughout the Ecuadorian Amazon and beyond: is it an extraction slum? An entropic settlement? Hernán Orbea Travez, former Dean of the School of Architecture, Design and Art at the Universidad Católica del Ecuador, refers to it as "predator urbanism." I picked his insightful name as the title of this short essay because it captures the essence of both settlers and settlement. Most citizens of Nueva Loja are there temporarily; the town is, or was, a passage to a better, more prosperous life elsewhere. Mines and petroleum engineers (generally male) move to Nueva Loja for finite periods from Quito and abroad; oil workers flock from many different provinces, attracted by the higher wages of the oil companies; prostitutes migrate to the town to profit from the newfound wealth; refugees displaced by violence from Colombia build a temporary shelter in its peripheries, hoping one day to return home; businessmen arrive into the area in order to open up liquor stores, supermarkets, restaurants and all sorts of entertainment venues; narcotraffickers and paramilitary and guerrilla members cross the border for rest, entertainment and to build local partnerships; loggers come and go with their trucks and their chainsaws; and the very few who moved to the area in order to settle, cultivate cash crops and raise cattle (many of them motivated by the 1964 Land Reform and Colonization Law), become displaced as the land is rendered useless. The informal sector of Nueva Loja is also a vibrant commercial force that has attracted settlers who see a better future for their children in its promise of wealth and fortune. And those who are claiming their stakes may be at the right place, for, in spite of its problems, or for this very reason, Nueva Loja lies at the center of a struggle that will transform environmental laws and transnational commercial relationships forever. A group of 30,000 inhabitants of the Ecuadorian Amazon were fearless enough to stand up to a mighty corporate giant – Texaco/Chevron – and demand that it clean up the mess it left behind. It is this very town – the lost and invisible Nueva Loja – that "will set a precedent, forcing companies operating in developing countries to comply with the same anti-pollution standards as in the industrialized world." Both the ITT Initiative to "leave the oil in the soil" and the Texaco/Chevron lawsuit constitute an attempt to develop what Michael Serres has termed a "natural contract." National and transnational negligence, which he terms "objective violence" (the violence caused by raw economic thinking) can have devastating social and environmental consequences comparable to an undeclared war. There is currently no law regulating these encounters. Thanks to Lago Agrio, this may not be the case in the future.

GROWTH PATTERNS

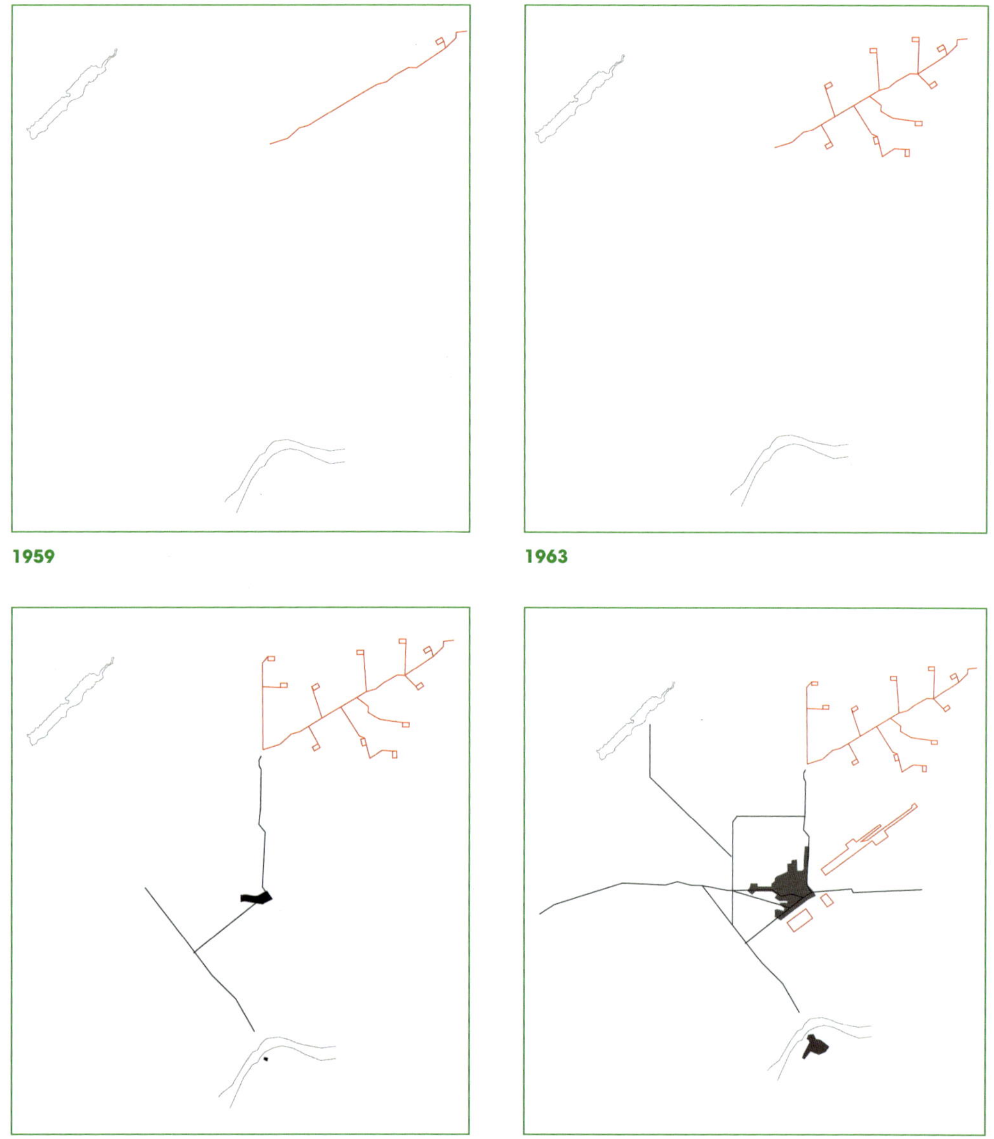

1959 1963 1968 1976

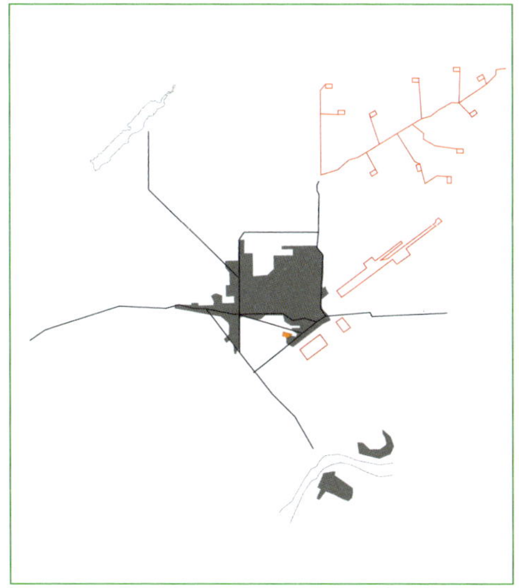

1985

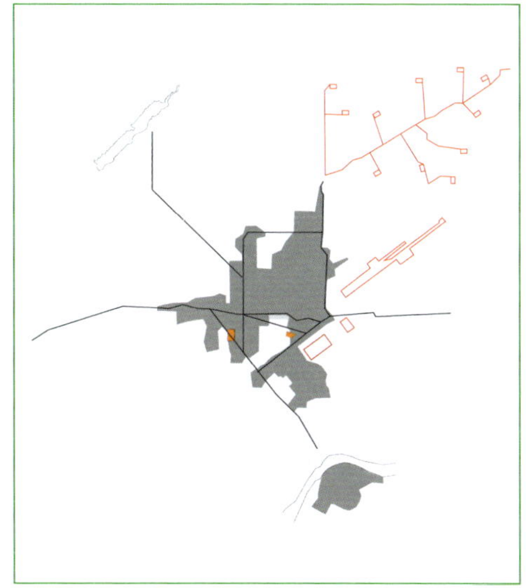

1991

1998

2020

BACKGROUND

SOCIAL

DEMOGRAPHICS
ECONOMY
POLITICS

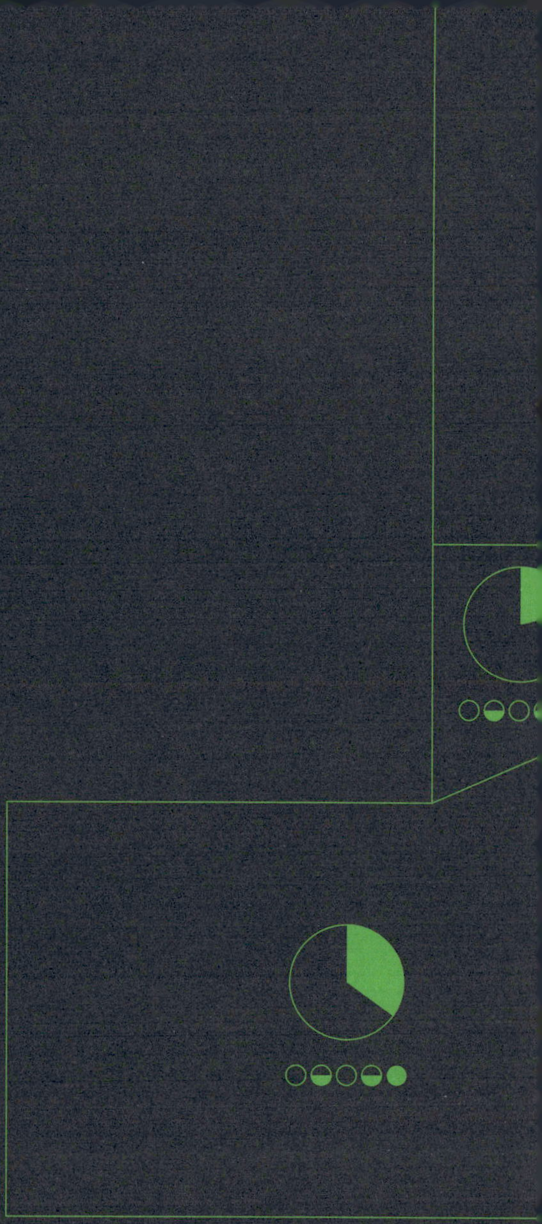

DEMOGRAPHICS

DEMOGRAPHIC MAP

YEAR 2002

ZONE — SAN FRANCISCO

POPULATION — 9,943

HOUSEHOLDS W/ELECTRICITY — 94%

MUNICIPAL SERVICES — WATER, SANITARY SEWER, STORM SEWER, ELECTRICITY, GARBAGE PICK-UP

= NO

= YES

= YES, BUT INADEQUATE

NET DENSITY (PERSONS/HA):

- 200+
- 100-200
- 50-100
- 5-50
- 0-5

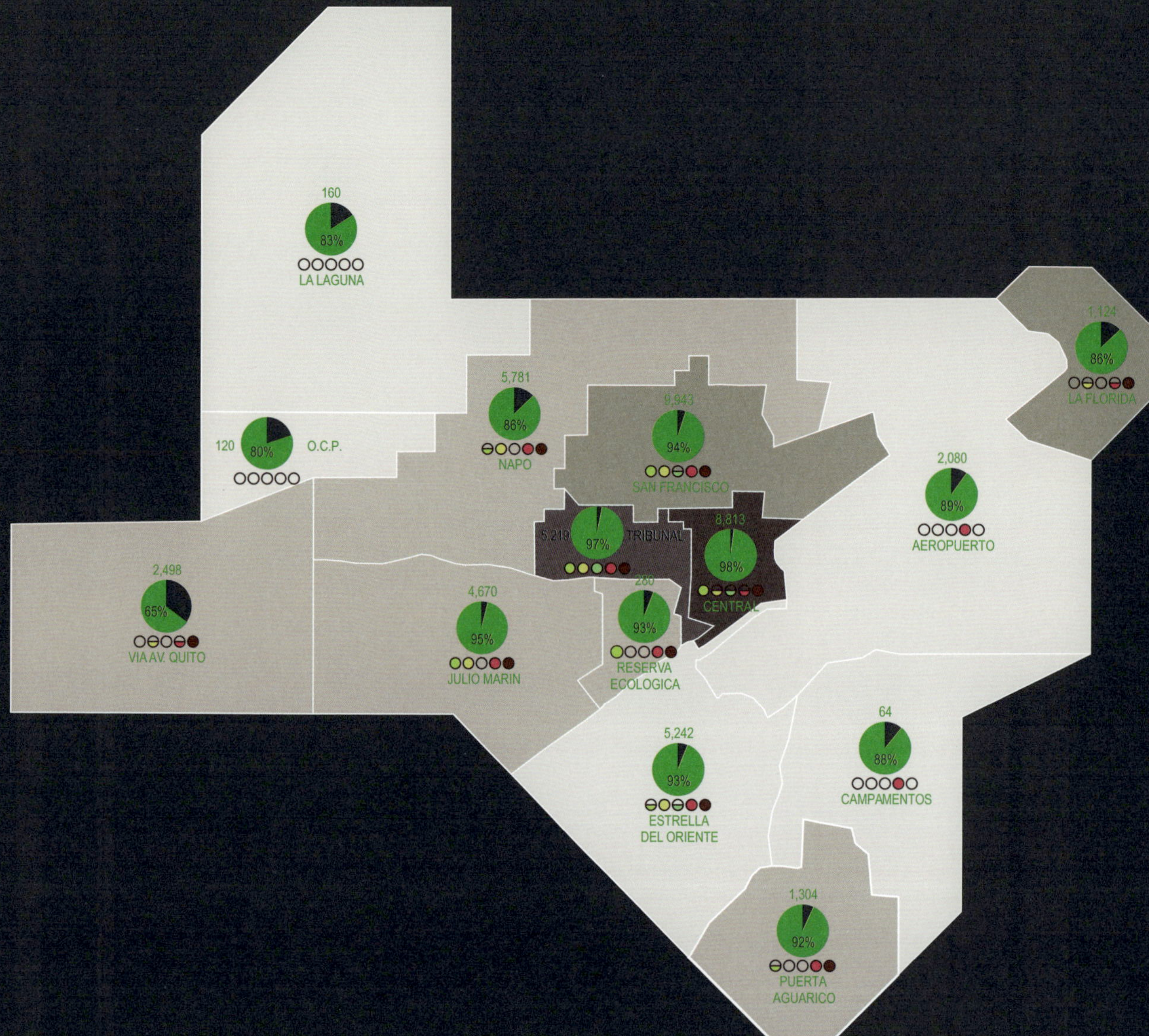

NATIONAL - REGIONAL DEMOGRAPHICS

POPULATION SHIFT:

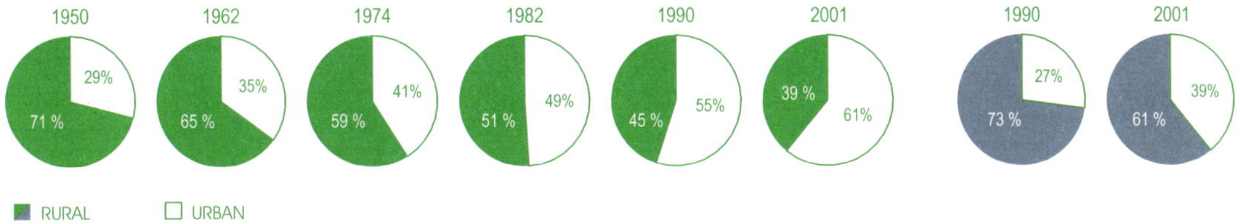

POPULATION BY REGION

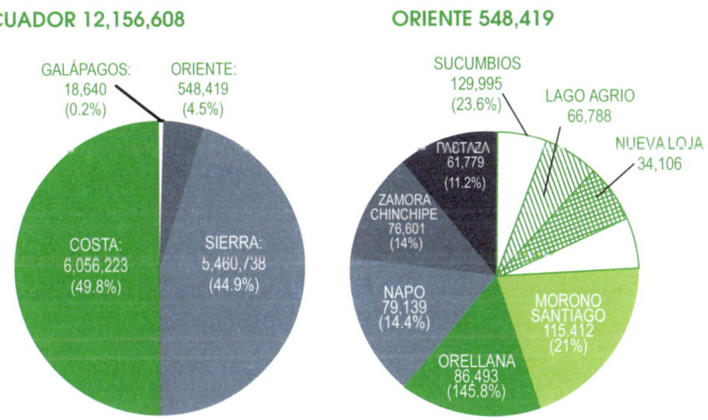

POPULATION PYRAMID

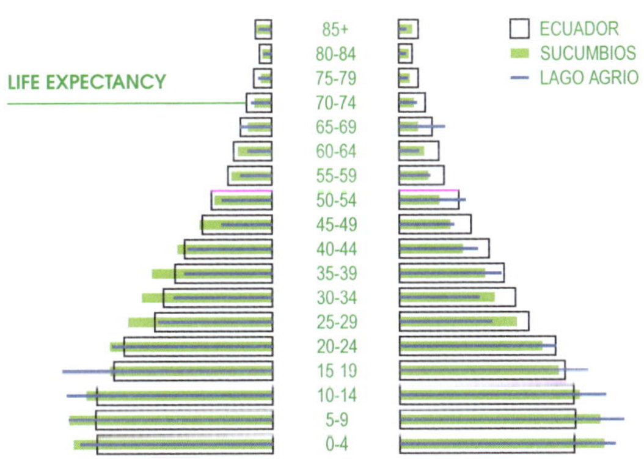

ANNUAL GROWTH RATE

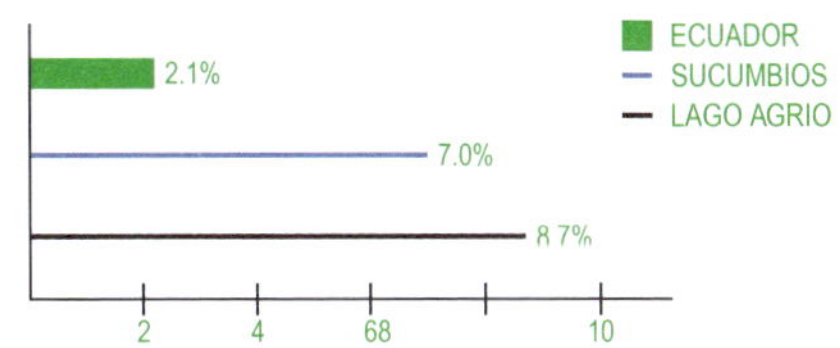

BIRTH/DEATH STATISTICS

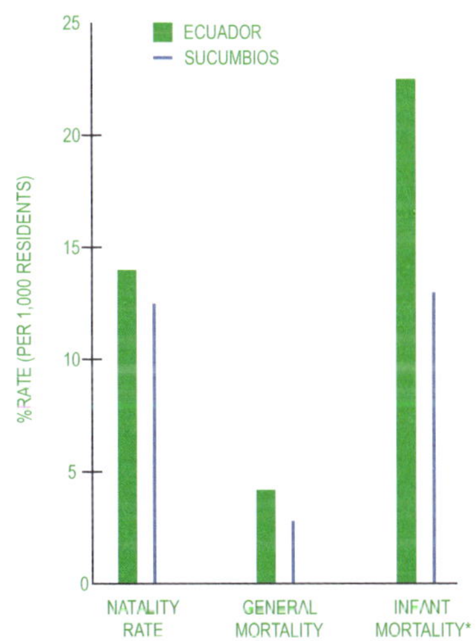

* VERT. SCALE = PER 1,000 BIRTHS

LOCAL DEMOGRAPHICS

POPULATIONS

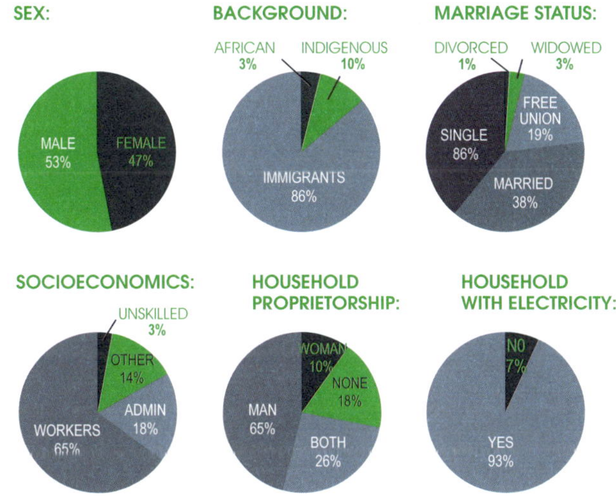

MISCELLANEOUS STATISTICS

LIVING:	AVERAGE FAMILY SIZE	2.95 PERSONS
	HOMELESS RATE	3.5%
HEALTH:	DIRECT ACCESS TO HEALTHCARE	58%
EDUCATION:	PRIMARY SCHOOL ENROLMENT	85%
	SECONDARY SCHOOL ENROLMENT	40%
	LITERACY RATE	95%
HOUSING TYPES:	HOUSES	56%
	QUARTERS	24%
	PREFAB HOUSE	13%
	APARTMENT	4%
	INN	1.2%
	FARM	1%
	OTHER	0.1%

ECONOMY

GARETH MAHON

A CHANGING ECONOMY

By 2025, Nueva Loja will no longer be a center of oil production in Ecuador. The regional wells will have run dry, industry will have moved elsewhere and Nueva Loja will be left to fend for itself in a new post-petroleum era.

A city that has never known life without oil will face a fresh set of challenges. The wealthy oil class will be gone. Local businesses created to serve the petroleum companies and their employees will need to find new markets. Some will follow the oil money. And while the old economy favored imported staples over local produce, these goods will become prohibitively expensive.

The Way Forward

The city of the future must take as much interest in the design of its economy as the design of its streets, parks and homes. We need to think about how current economic sectors will impact the economy of tomorrow. The new economy will need a framework that allows it to develop sustainably with growth from within. It must respect the environment and nurture the well-being of all Nueva Loja's citizens. New economic sectors will have to meet the requirements of a changing community and their own – whether home grown micro-businesses or modified existing industries; they will need to grow symbiotically across the region, city and neighborhood as well as over time.

With its jungle location, climate, soil, hydrology, renewable resources and ever-expanding population, Nueva Loja is an extraordinary place. Given a set of guiding principles and a strong supporting framework, the city could flourish and become an example for other communities facing similar challenges.

Principles – For A Sustainable Economy

Self Sustaining: Economic growth should be driven from within the region. Both industry and consumers should source and sell goods from within the region without the need for protectionist methods or a decline in the quality of those goods.

Environmentally Sustaining: All new economic activity must respect the environment. All existing activity should be assessed and altered to meet new standards and minimize ecological impact.

Quality of Life Sustaining: All economic activity must respect fair trade, workers' rights and a fair family wage.

Support Framework

In order to nurture emerging economic sectors, a framework of support systems and practices should be put in place. A range of services should be available to new and existing businesses offering advice on financial and environmental "best practice." Support should take a variety of forms including training and education, credit and micro-loan programs, improved infrastructure and regional marketing programs. These in turn need to be facilitated through government initiatives, international aid programs and a network of Non-Governmental Organizations (NGOs).

Measuring Success

The new economy must include a system for measuring success and failure. New forms of inclusive economic reporting are needed that will consider the wellbeing of citizens and the environment alongside strict financial reporting. A genuine progress indicator will be needed to provide feedback for existing industry and help identify and encourage new sustainable development. Any future reading of the economy will balance not only financial capital but also natural and human capital.

THE ECONOMY: OIL

Ecuador's economy was transformed in 1964 when the country opened up its oil reserves to exploration by multinational companies. A chain of events was set in motion that turned Ecuador into South America's fifth largest producer of oil. Production currently stands at over 500,000 barrels per day. With foreign investment, however, came external debt which also made it, per capita, South America's most indebted country. In 2000, a combination of low oil prices and rapid inflation prompted the government to replace the national currency with the US dollar.

Over 40% of the country's export earnings are attributed to oil, with over one third of the central government budget funded by these exports. Nueva Loja, however, despite being the heart of the country's oil drilling industry, remains one of the poorest areas in Ecuador. Although local employment statistics are unclear, evidence suggests that oil workers are not recruited from the local population but are rather brought into the region on a rotating shift basis. Much of the crude coming from this region is now under the control of state owned Petroecuador.

THE ECONOMY: AGRICULTURE

Ecuador is predominantly an agricultural country; the coastal and mountain regions are the most productive. The sector makes up approximately 15% of the country's GDP with total exports exceeding imports by almost 700%. Ecuador is the world's largest exporter of bananas, which make up half of these exports. Shrimp, coffee, cocoa and cut flowers make up the rest.

An estimated 30% of the population is employed in agriculture with that figure rising to almost 50% in Oriente. Urban expansion and the rise of large corporate farming practices put a particular stress on small farmers, while issues of land ownership and rights are as pressing in Ecuador as they are in the rest of South America.

AGRICULTURE IN ECUADOR

15% GDP
30% National Population Employed in Agriculture
50% Lago Agrio Population Employed in Agriculture

THE ECONOMY: INFORMAL

In Ecuador generally, and particularly in Nueva Loja, informal employment accounts for a sizable sector of the economy. National statistics show unemployment at 10% and underemployment at almost 50% with official unemployment in Nueva Loja measured at 50%. These figures may account for the large and diverse informal sector that spans commerce, domestic service, day laborers and micro-businesses.

Despite the size of the informal sector it remains unorganized and as such is open to exploitation, unregulated labor is carried out for meager payment, often by children. In 2010, the minimum wage was set at $240 per month (average family food costs are around $440 per month) with most workers in the formal sectors earning more than that. Reports exist, however, of informal farm laborers being paid just $50 a month.

Informal practices are also evident in land ownership and residential construction methods. Money sent home by migrant workers from Spain and the United States is another often overlooked factor in the informal economy.

THE ECONOMY: ILLEGAL

Lago Agrio feels and functions like a frontier town. Less than eighteen kilometers from the Colombian border, removed from the watchful eye of the central government, it has a thriving illegal economy. Traditionally known as a rest and relaxation spot for Colombian rebels it has also become a gateway for almost 20% of Colombian cocaine exports and the chemicals needed to dxevelop the drug. The conversion of the currency to the American dollar has facilitated the business of money laundering. The ebb and flow of criminal activities such as stealing oil and kidnapping has had the knock-on effect of increasing employment in private security firms. (Prostitution in Ecuador is legal and therefore not a factor in the illegal economy.)

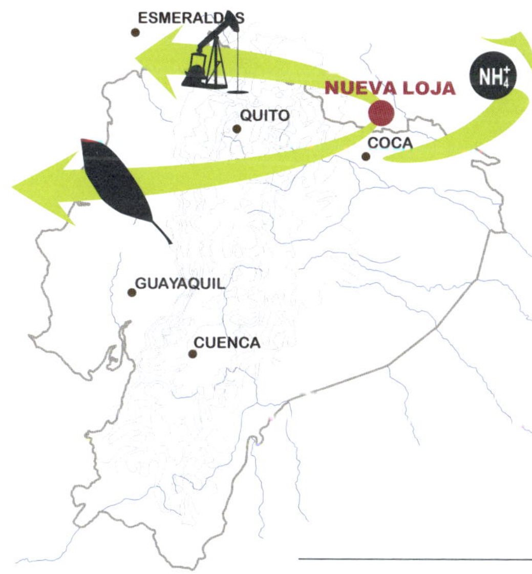

Time for a change
Nueva Loja has always been a center of globalization – it's just the product that needs to change.

CHANGING ECONOMY

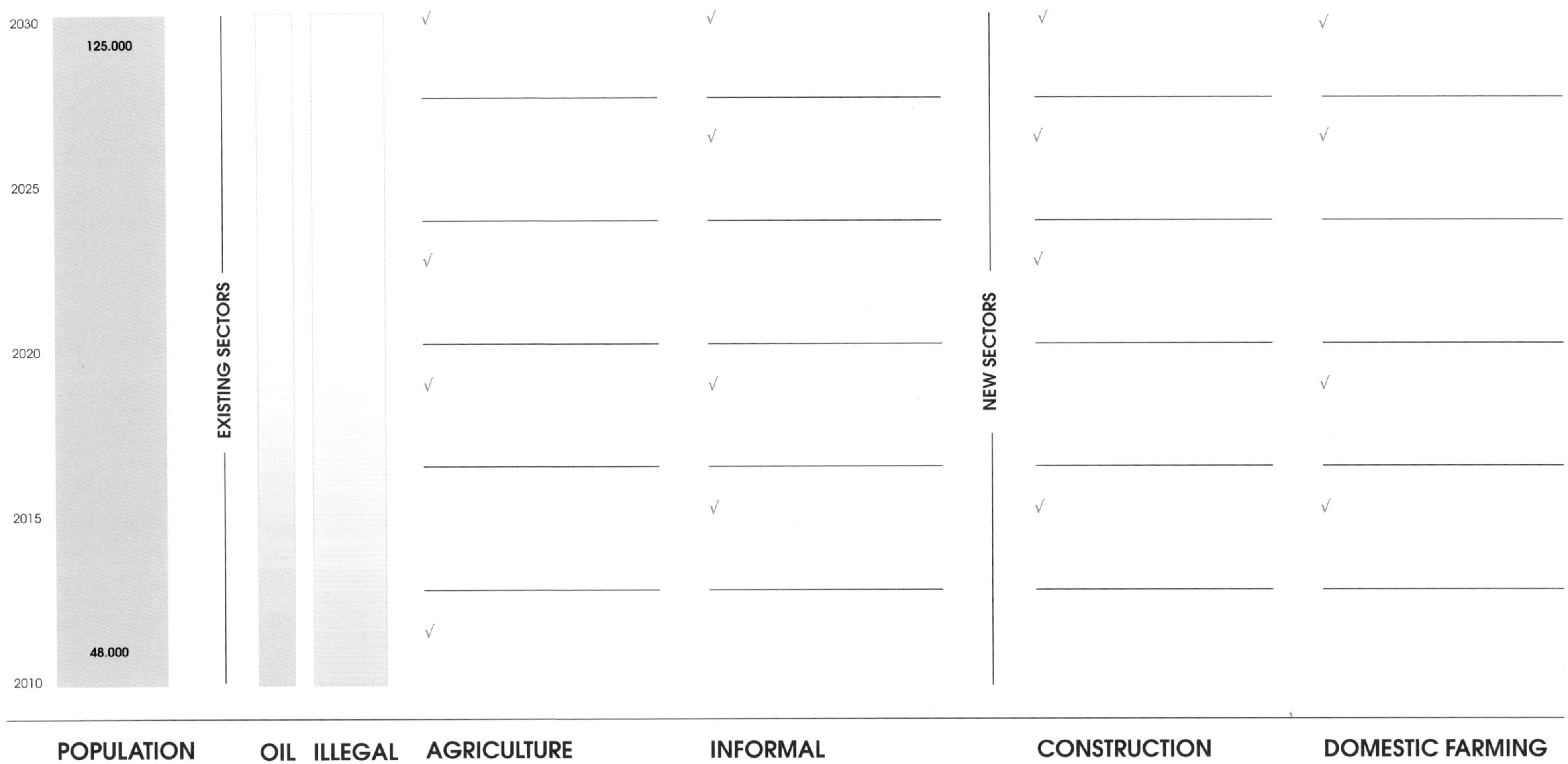

AGRICULTURE: Large scale farming for export will continue and new practices will be introduced.

INFORMAL: The informal economy will get stronger and be recognized.

CONSTRUCTION: New locally sourced materials will be used for residential and municipal infrastructure.

DOMESTIC FARMING: New methods, crops and markets will drive this sector.

SUPPORT SYSTEM	ALTERNATIVE FUELS	BAMBOO	EDUCATION	ECO-TOURISM
TRAINING AND EDUCATION	√	√	√	√
NGO MENTORSHIP	√	√		
INFRASTRUCTURE				
PROMOTION				√
CREDIT PROGRAMS			√	√
DEVELOPMENTAL AID	√		√	
	Locally grown and manufactured technologies will replace oil.	Climate and soils are ideal to develop bamboo production and manufacturing into a new industry.	Nueva Loja will become a center of sustainable learning. An eco-university will forge the way.	Already an emerging sector in Lago Agrio, this will continue to grow along sustainable principles.

POLITICS

JOHN HILL

The politics of Ecuador's Oriente region revolves around three key issues: oil, agriculture and the indigenous population. Since 1964 – when Texaco arrived to search for oil deposits at the invitation of the Ecuadorian government, land reforms were enacted and the first indigenous federations were formed – these three issues have shaped the area, intersecting in difficult and sometimes violent ways.

TOP: AGRICULTURAL PATTERNS IN THE NUEVA LOJA AREA

POLITICS: OIL

Oil has been pumped in Ecuador since 1917. But it was only after 1964, when Texaco began exploration in Oriente, that oil became a primary factor in the country's economy and politics. Before then, the Amazon basin was an inaccessible area, navigable only by river and on foot. But in the five years following the discovery of oil in 1967, a network of roads and pipelines was laid. This infrastructure was paid for by the Ecuadorian government and built by Texaco using local workers on low wages.

In 1992, the national oil company Petroecuador assumed responsibility for all operations. Although Texaco (now Chevron) has left Oriente, a class action lawsuit filed by Lago Agrio residents against the company for damage to the landscape is still pending. For its part, Chevron contends the Ecuadorian government is at fault for permitting the use of substandard practices in its drilling operations. Whichever way the case goes, the Ecuadorian government, determined to build an economy on oil revenue, has undoubtedly played a role in the environmental damage.

POLITICS: AGRICULTURE

When Ecuador enacted land reforms in 1964, it redefined land as a productive resource. Crops and cattle are now officially considered the two primary agricultural land uses in Oriente (monoculture crops typically preceding cattle grazing). Indigenous practices that nurture the rain forest are not defined as agriculture since they do not fall within the "productive" category. After oil was discovered, farmers migrated to the area and began the severe deforestation that continues to this day. Deforestation remains a means of laying claim to land, in line with the government's land tenure laws.

POLITICS: INDIGENOUS PEOPLE

The government's position on land, oil and agriculture conflicts with that of indigenous people. While the government prioritizes the exploitation of the land, the indigenous population believes in nurturing the land – both for its continuing survival and for its own.

Since the first indigenous federation sprung up in 1964, these organizations have multiplied. In 1997, with the ousting of President Abdalá Bucaram under pressure from CONAIE (the Confederation of Indigenous Nationalities of Ecuador), the indigenous population became a key player in Ecuador's political decision-making. Indigenous groups now commonly stage protests to voice their anger at government policies on oil, agricultural deforestation and land rights. Occasionally action has escalated, with protestors blocking roads, dynamiting pipelines and even committing murder.

The Ecuadorian government now finds itself in the uncomfortable position of having to balance oil interests (internal and external) with those of farmers and indigenous people – an unenviable task, but one necessary for the survival of the rainforest and all those who depend upon it.

POLITICS: THE BORDER

Nueva Loja's location – only 18km (11 miles) from the border with Colombia to the north – creates a complicated and sometimes violent context for the town and its inhabitants. The natural characteristics of the area: – dense jungle, numerous rivers (including the San Miguel and Putumayo Rivers which flow between the two countries) and a remoteness from urban areas like Quito and Bogota – have aided the flow of goods, people and even airborne contaminants from one side of the border to the other. Since 2003, Colombia, attempting to reduce illegal, drug-related activities in its capital, has succeeding in pushing them out towards its shared borders with Venezuela to the northeast and Ecuador to the south.

Colombian insurgency

The major players in Colombia´s narcotics activities (primarily coca and poppy cultivation) are the drug cartels; the formerly left-wing insurgency groups and paramilitary groups which exercise muscular power. These organizations require land, goods, people and weapons to operate – the latter three accounting for much of the illegal traffic across the Colombian-Ecuadorian border. Colombian migrants enter Ecuador searching for a safe haven free from insurgency, while members of the paramilitary groups cross the border to hide from the military crackdown on narco-terrorism. (In early spring 2008, Colombia raided a camp in Ecuador, killing not only a top FARC commander and 20 others, but also an Ecuadorian.) Ecuador has become the resting ground of the narco-traffic industry. Since its economy was dollarized in 1999, it has provided ideal financial support for money launderers. Weapons illegally trickle over its border into Colombia. It is undeniable that its policy of neutrality with regards to the Colombian armed conflict has indirectly contributed to perpetuate the region's instability.

The US presence

The U.S. channels aid to the region through its two anti-narcotics, anti-insurgency strategies, Plan Patriota and Plan Colombia. Both try to curb illegal activities in the country and its border regions, and both have been ineffectual; neither the flow of drugs nor the violence have diminished. With both plans focused on military and police training and the supply of arms, their social and economic impact has also been negligible. The US has failed to address the flow of people, goods and poverty across the border. It even ignores border distinctions entirely during the aerial spraying of illegal crops, when damaging airborne contaminants drift into northern Ecuador.

Ecuador's response

The impact of the insurgency in Colombia, drug cultivation and other illicit activities on Ecuador extends well beyond the immediate border areas. Foreign and domestic oil companies in the eastern provinces have had personnel kidnapped and infrastructure targeted. They now spend millions of dollars on security. And while Ecuador deploys over 10,000 troops to monitor the 600km border with Colombia, it remains permeable. Ecuadorians go to work in the coca fields to the north, the raw material is transported west within Ecuador, back into Colombia for processing and then south for distribution from the Ecuadorian ports of Esmeraldas or Guayaquil.

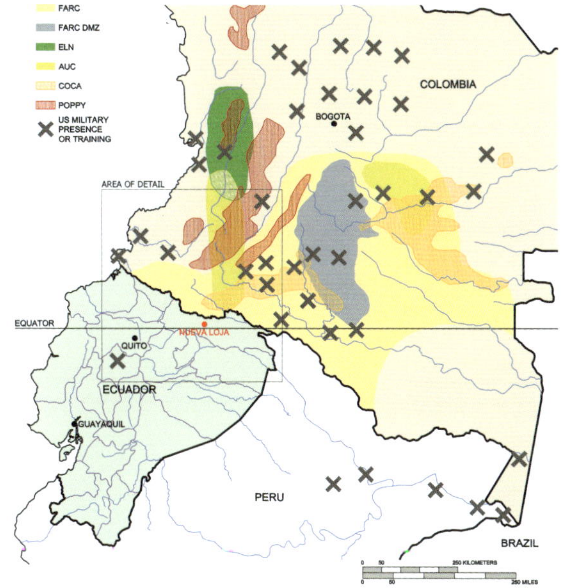

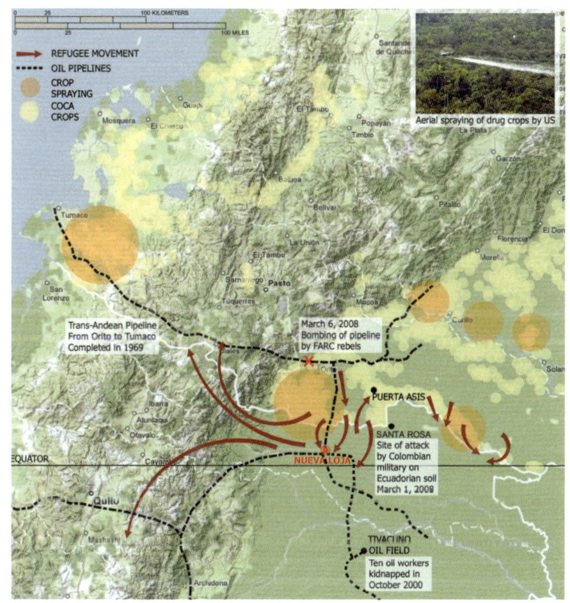

TOP: DRUGS AND INSURGENCY
BOTTOM: DRUGS AND REFUGEES

ENVIRONMENT

CLIMATE
VEGETATION
HYDROLOGY
THE AGUARICO RIVER
ECOSYSTEM

CLIMATE

MATTHIAS ALTWICKER

The Ecuadorian Amazon lies at the eastern foot of the Andes and at the western edge of the Amazon basin which stretches east to the Atlantic coast. Its geographic position creates a hot and humid climate. Temperatures typically range from 77-97 degrees Fahrenheit and heat is exacerbated by humidity and the lack of wind. Cloud cover averages 25% annually and rainfall is high; winter and spring are twice as wet as summer and fall. When properly harnessed, the rain can be an advantage – it can significantly reduce the perceived temperature and reduce discomfort.

RECOMMENDATION:
ARCHITECTURAL RESPONSE TO CLIMATE

Surprisingly, the architecture of Nueva Loja does not respond responsibly to its climate. This failure is not due to a shortage of materials or space but a lack of basic knowledge of the area and the most appropriate way to build there on the part of migrants who are used to other climates in Ecuador. The use of shading in homes and outdoor public space is rare.

This proposed series of morphological transformations responds to climate in both a protective and positive way. Lifting the building off the ground (or separating the roof from the floor below it) promotes cross ventilation, protection from flooding and creates a shaded area that can also be used to collect and remediate rainwater runoff. These principles can also be applied to public spaces.

CLIMATE FACTORS

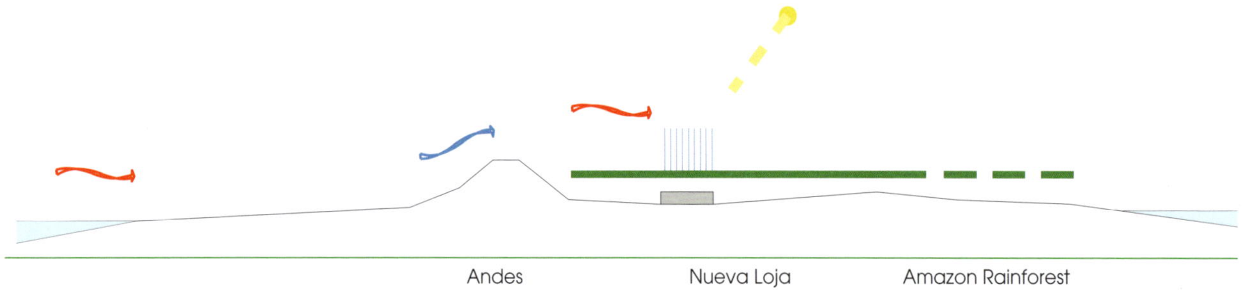

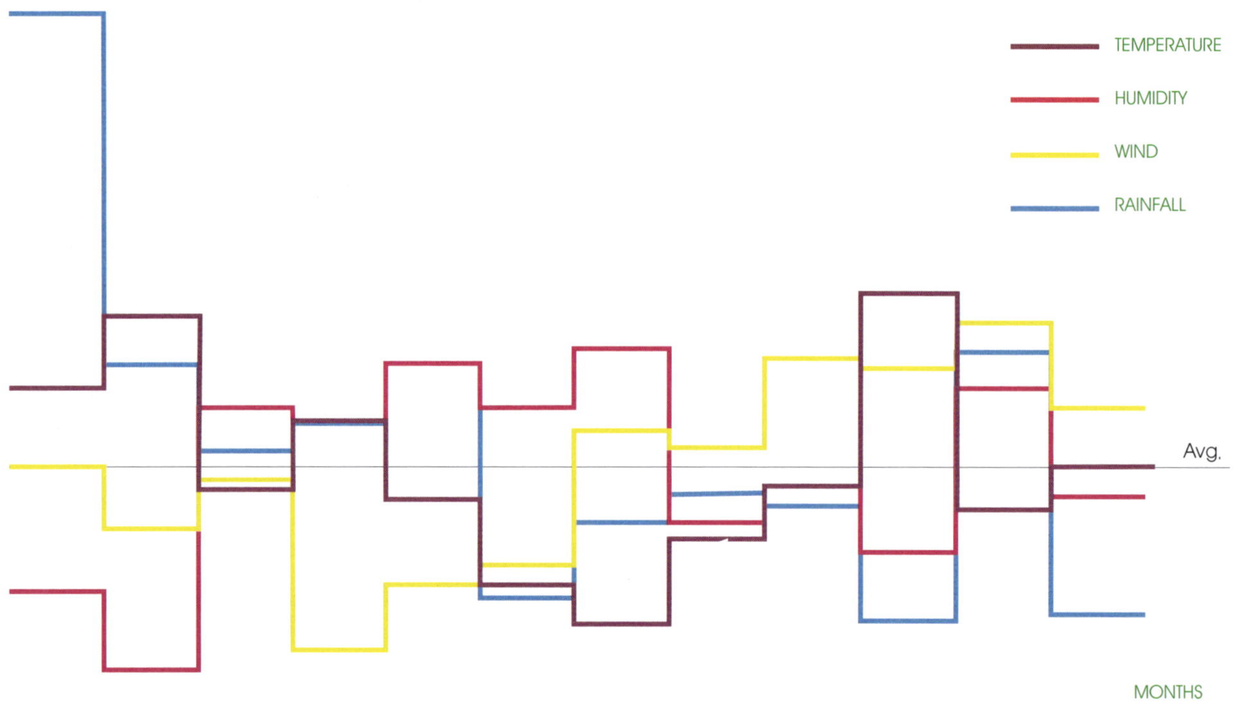

Nueva Loja, Ecuador Elevation: 299 meters / Latitude: 0°5' north / Longitude: 76°54' west

TOP: UNRESPONSIVE ARCHITECTURE

CONFIGURATION PRINCIPLES:

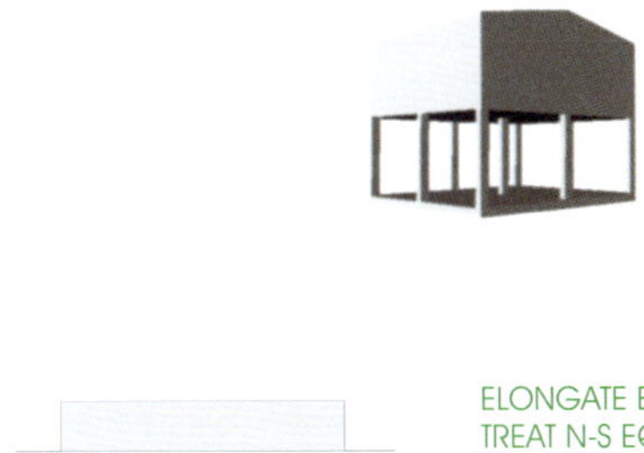

ELONGATE E-W;
TREAT N-S EQUALLY

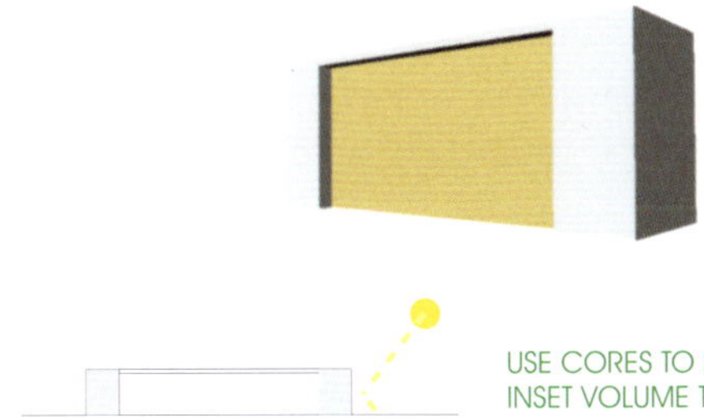

USE CORES TO BLOCK E-W SUN;
INSET VOLUME TO N-S

USE DEEPER OVERHANGS TO E-W;
SHORT OVERHANGS TO N-S

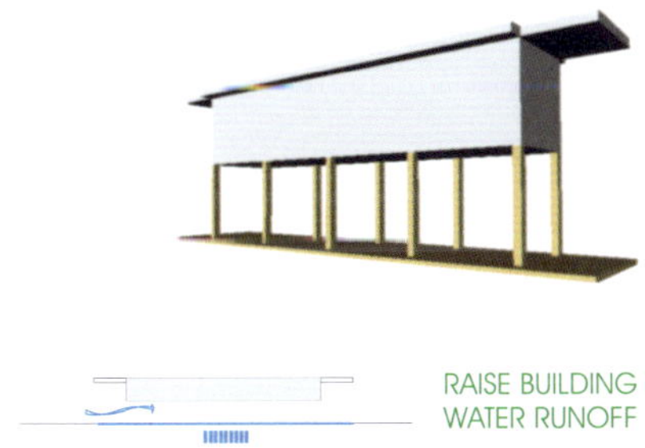

RAISE BUILDING TO ALLOW
WATER RUNOFF

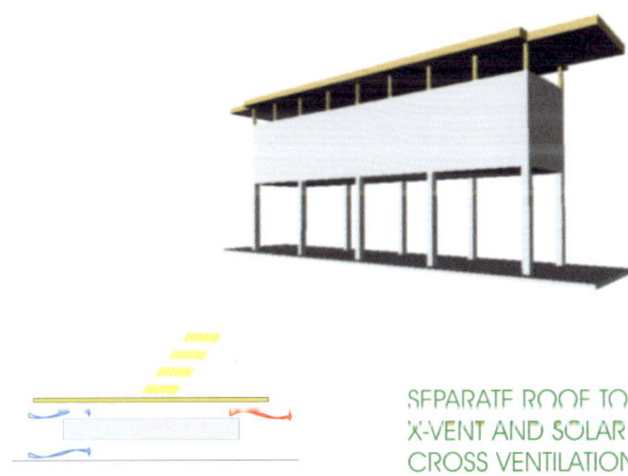

SEPARATE ROOF TO ALLOW
X-VENT AND SOLAR SEPARATION
CROSS VENTILATION

DIFFERENTIATE E-W ACCORDING
TO SUN INTENSITY

VEGETATION

CHRIS SYRETT

The Ecuadorian Amazon is the world's most bio-diverse region. It contains between 9,000 and 12,000 species of vascular plants, many of which are only found in the forests around Lago Agrio. A recent report by the Global Environment Fund found 1,200 plant species within a single two square kilometer tract of land in the Cuyabena Reserve. The exact number of species here, however, remains unknown. An estimated 30% of the total biota of the region has yet to be identified.

The rainforest canopy rises to over 40 meters, with rich and varied strata of sub-canopy trees below – lianas, bromeliads, understory trees and shrubs. There are three main types of rainforest within the Ecuadorian Amazon, *terra firme, várzea* and *igapó*. Terra firme forest is found on higher ground not subject to flooding, várzea on land subject to seasonal flooding by whitewater rivers and Igapó on poor soils that are seasonally or permanently flooded by blackwater or low sediment filled rivers. Distinct and varied vegetation is found in each type of forest.

Amazonian plants are also a rich source of food, medicine and materials. If they survive Ecuador's deforestation, they could be the key to a sustainable source of wealth for the region.

HYDROLOGY

PATRICK WEISEL

SURFACE HYDROLOGY

Like much of the Amazon Basin, the Nueva Loja area is hydrologically complex. The basin once drained into the Pacific Ocean before continental drift formed the Andes, forcing rivers on land to the east of the rising mountain ridge to reverse course and drain into the Atlantic. The flooded forest, or *igapó*, found just east of Nueva Loja in the Cuyabeno Reserve, is an excellent example of the continent's still shifting and unresolved drainage patterns.

REGIONAL HYDROLOGY

Within the Amazon Basin's unique hydrology, Nueva Loja is even more remarkable. Sitting atop an extremely low and ambiguous ridge dividing the Putumayo and Napo watersheds, Nueva Loja contains the active tributaries of both rivers, sometimes separated by less than a kilometer of dry land. Consequently, rain falling in the city's northern neighborhoods will not converge with rainfall in the rest of the city until each joins the Amazon River nearly 1,000 kilometers downstream in Brazil. The city sits at a hydrologic crossroads, and has a major influence on two important watersheds.

LOCAL HYDROLOGY

Central Nueva Loja sits on another ridge dividing the Teteyé and Aguarico Rivers. Watersheds flow generally northward from Avenida Quito (which sits atop the ridge) into the Teteyé and its main tributary, the Orienco. Water falling to the south of Avenida Quito flows generally southward into several smaller tributaries feeding the Aguarico. Within the city's three major watersheds – Putumayo, Teteyé and Aguarico – there are eight smaller watersheds. The city's Putumayo watershed collects largely into Nueva Loja while three others, including the Orienco and Teteyé, meander slowly through the saturated bottomlands north and east of the city, eventually joining the Aguarico some 15 kilometers downstream. These four northern watersheds can hold vast quantities of slow moving water so the potential for contamination is considerable. The remaining four watersheds, two north of Rio Aguarico, and two in Puerto Aguarico south of the river, join the Aguarico after shorter flows over steeper gradients.

PREVIOUS PAGE: NUEVA LOJA WATERSHEDS
THIS PAGE TOP: OIL
THIS PAGE LEFT: RIDGELINE AND MAJOR WATERSHEDS

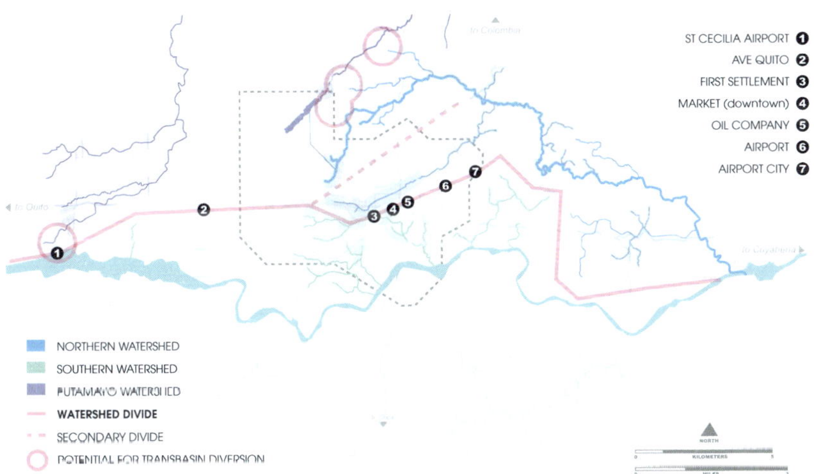

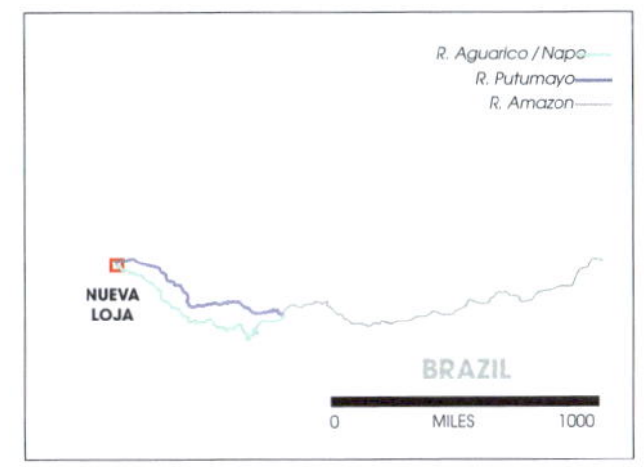

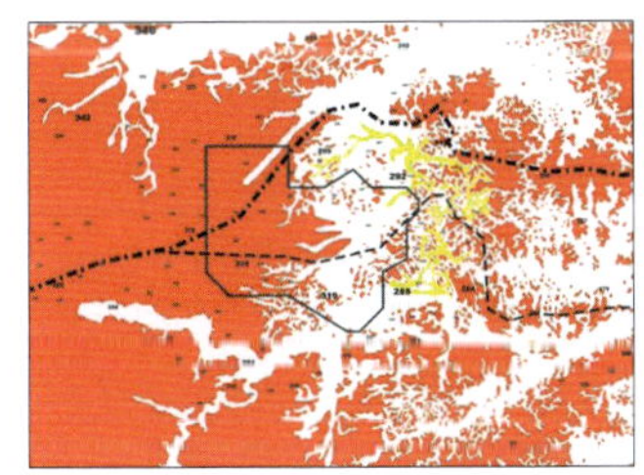

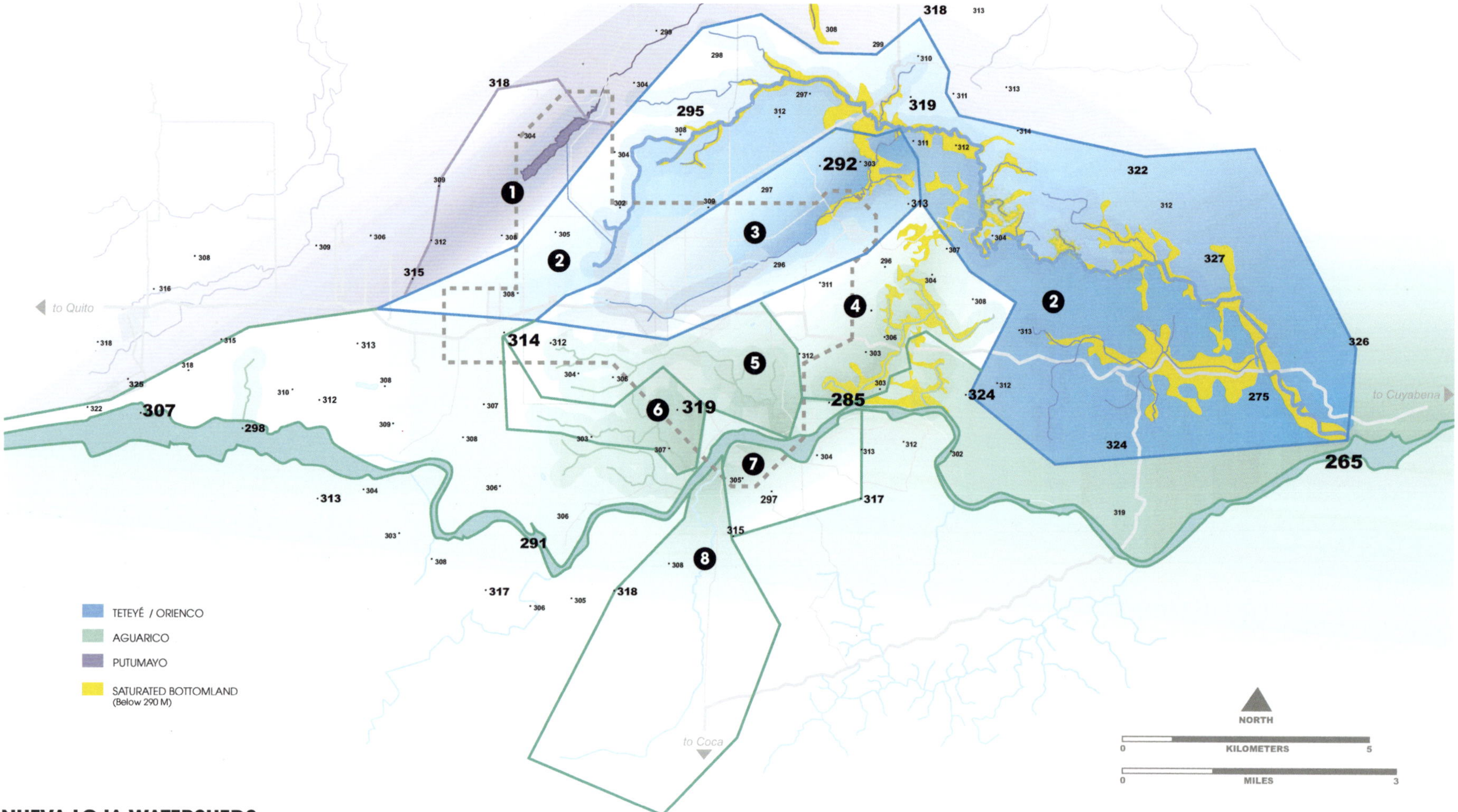

NUEVA LOJA WATERSHEDS

WATERSHED AREA	1 2	3	4	5	6	7	8
Lago Agrio 8 Km^2	**Teteyé** 22 Km^2 (pre-Orienco) 45 Km^2 (post-Orienco)	**Orienco** 14 Km^2	**Petróleo** 10 Km^2	**Esmeraldas** 8 Km^2	**Coop. Sionas** 4 Km^2	**Puerto** 4 Km^2	**Gasoducto** 19 Km^2

THE AGUARICO RIVER

MARIANNA CASTILLO

The Aguarico River occupies the central and northwestern part of Sucumbios province. One of the major tributaries of the Napo River, for generations it provided the indigenous communities of Sucumbios and Nueva Loja with much of their sustenance. Its banks were where women washed clothing, families took baths, children played games and the community harvested food.

Since the start of oil exploitation in Sucumbios, toxins from oil spills have contaminated Rio Aguarico. Although the damage is not immediately visible, it has profoundly affected the lives of those who depend on the river. Their traditional water source is toxic, the fish are gone and new diseases have appeared. Indigenous people must now rely on rainwater, even when the rain turns black from the clouds of toxic smoke from burning oil wells. They must find ways to make money to buy food once provided by the river, to pay for wells for clean water and medical care to treat new diseases.

The Aguarico River remains a vital resource for the people of Nueva Loja, as a transport artery for the indigenous communities and for tourists traveling through the Ecuadorian Amazon. During the week, women still wash clothes and children bathe and play on its banks. At weekends, the waterfront is an important place of recreation.

RECOMMENDATION: A NEW RIO AGUARICO

The Aguarico River is one of Nueva Loja's greatest assets: a spectacular natural landscape and a convenient transport route. With the repair of the river ecology, it could become the site of new recreational and economic activities.

The river and its waterfront must be treated as an integral part of Nueva Loja. It must enhance the city's vitality, offer a diversity of cultural, commercial and recreational uses and be physically and visually accessible for both locals and tourists. The plan for a new Aguarico River must reinstate those parts of the natural environment lost over time and its indigenous heritage and role as a regional artery used to give character and meaning to future waterfront development. The preservation of its past is integral to its sustainable redevelopment.

MAP: RIO AGUARICO BASIN

IMAGE: RIVER FRONTS

Data

Source: Cordillera de Pimampiro, 77°35'W; 0°25'N
Total length: 390 km
Major tributaries: Cofanes, Tetetes, Eno, Shushufindi, Zabalo, Pacayucu
Outlet: Napo River
Area: 10,290 km2

	April - June	November - February
DEPTH m	4,58	2,37
WIDTH m	216	194
SPEED m/s	1,34	0,99
FLOW m3/s	1258	440

WATER LEVEL

APRIL - JUNE

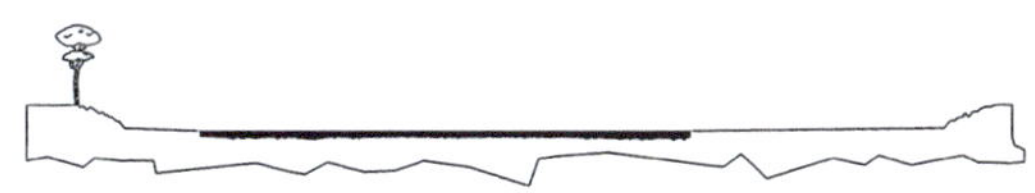

NOV - FEB

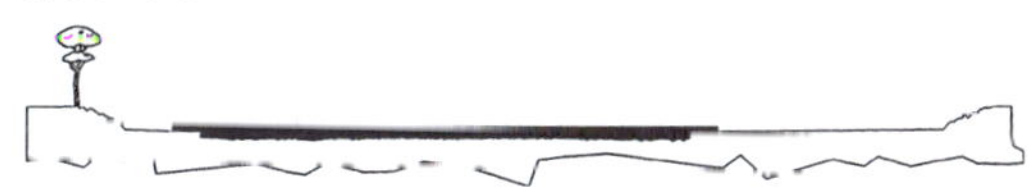

ECOSYSTEM

CHRIS SYRETT

The Amazon rainforest is a highly complex ecosystem. A single tree in the forest hosts more species of ants than can be found in all of England. There are more species of trees within a few hectares here than in the whole of North America. But while the biodiversity of the forest is truly impressive, the real complexity of this ecosystem derives not from the astounding quantity of species but from the many relationships and interdependencies between them.

The Brazil nut, for example, depends on a number of specific creatures to complete its life cycle. Its flowers, found near the forest canopy, are pollinated by a single species of bee, the engoline orchard bee. Once the nuts ripen, they fall to the forest floor and are scattered throughout the area by a single species of rodent, the agouti.

The deforestation of Ecuador's Oriente has profoundly disturbed this complex web of life. Any loss of canopy cover means habitat destruction for many forest species and the disruption of complex ecological systems evolved over millennia.

A comprehensive land use plan must be developed to preserve the rainforest and protect these ecosystems. Historically, forest land designated as "reserves" eventually succumbs to deforestation amidst pressure for more agricultural and pasture land. Any new plan should therefore incorporate multifaceted, flexible programs that highlight the value of the forest. This could be achieved through the sustainable extraction of woodland resources, woodland agriculture or chacra farms.

The Ecuadorian Oriente is part of the vast Amazon River Basin.

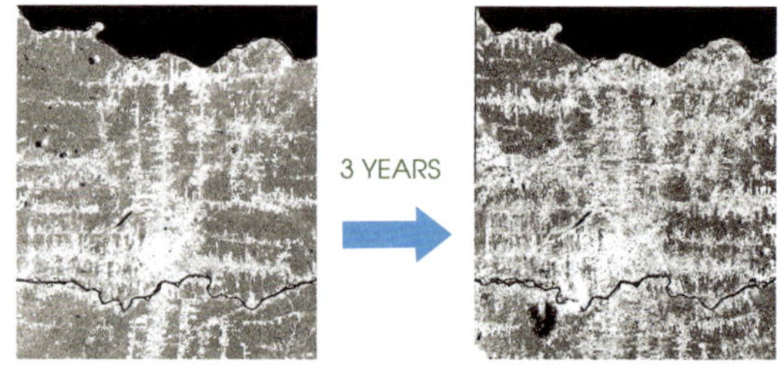

The deforestation of the Ecuadorian Amazon is happening at an accelerated rate.

While disturbance is an important aspect of forest succesion and diversity, anthropogenic disturbance produces profound, often detrimental, changes to the environment.

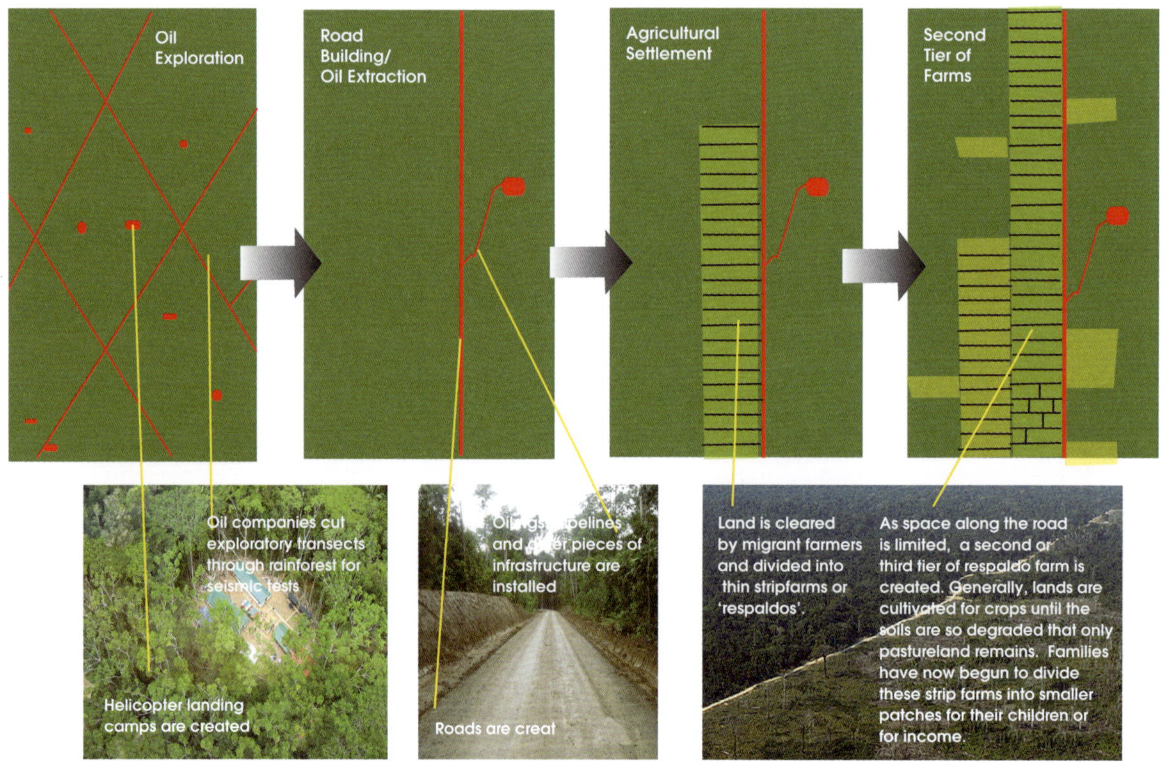

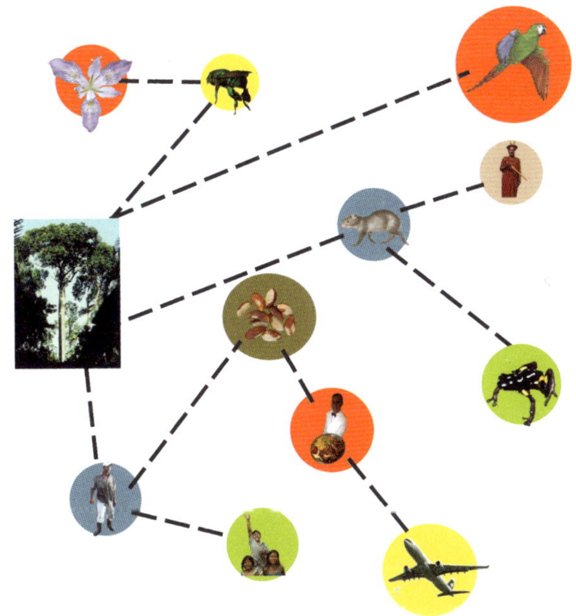

The life cycle of the Brazil Nut makes a distinct ecosytem. The sustainable harvesting of such forest products as the Brazil nut can keep the complex system intact and provide Nueva Lojans with income.

Value of one hectare of Amazonian Rainforest if used for pasture: **$148**

Value of one hectare of Amazonian Rainforest if clear cut for timber: **$1000**

Annual value of one hectare of Amazonian Rainforest if sustainably harvested for its timber and non-timber products: **$6,820**

Recent studies have shown that the sustainable use of both timber and non-timber forest products can be more profitable than current agricultural practices.

Rainforest species inhabit specific levels of the rainforest canopy. By using different strategies to keep canopy cover in place, specific habitats and ecosystems can be maintained

URBAN INFRASTRUCTURE

PETROLEUM
ENERGY
WATER
FOOD AND AGRICULTURE
WASTE
PUBLIC FACILITIES
URBAN INFRASTRUCTURE
EDUCATION

PETROLEUM

ALAN FOX

Since the first oil wells were established in 1967, Nueva Loja has served as the hub of the region's expanding petroleum production. Pipelines and roads built to reach the oil reserves cover much of the region.

By the time Texaco left the Ecuadorian jungle in 1993, it had spilled 30 times more oil than the Exxon Valdez and created over 600 open waste pits and other facilities that continue to leak highly toxic waste. This environmental catastrophe has affected more than 30,000 local people. With the results of the billion-dollar lawsuit against Texaco still pending, Petroecuador and private producers continue the degradation of the rainforest. To date, in the Upper Oriente the oil industry has caused the deforestation of approximately two million hectares (20,000 square km, / 7,700 square miles) of rain forest.

Nonetheless, Ecuador remains just as hooked on oil as the countries it sells to. Crude oil accounts for almost 50% of Ecuador's exports. Revenues provide 50% of the government's income which it uses to pay back its significant debt to the International Monetary Fund. Ecuador's oil industry is set to go the way of Lago Agrio's oil well LA-01. In 1967, LA-01's output was 1,500 barrels per day. Today it produces just 10% of that. While Ecuador's total current oil production is 550,000 barrels per day, by 2037 this is expected to fall to 10% of 2006 levels. The country's oil fields are believed to hold 4.5 billion barrels. At the current rate of extraction, Ecuador's oil will run out in 2029.

NUEVA LOJA'S FIRST OIL WELL - LA-01

SEPARATION FACILITY

This separation facility contains an oil pit, one of many scattered around northeastern Ecuador - and a natural gas flare - off structure. Ecuador lacks the infrastructure to collect natural gas, so much of it is burned off.

ECUADOR'S OIL PRODUCTION

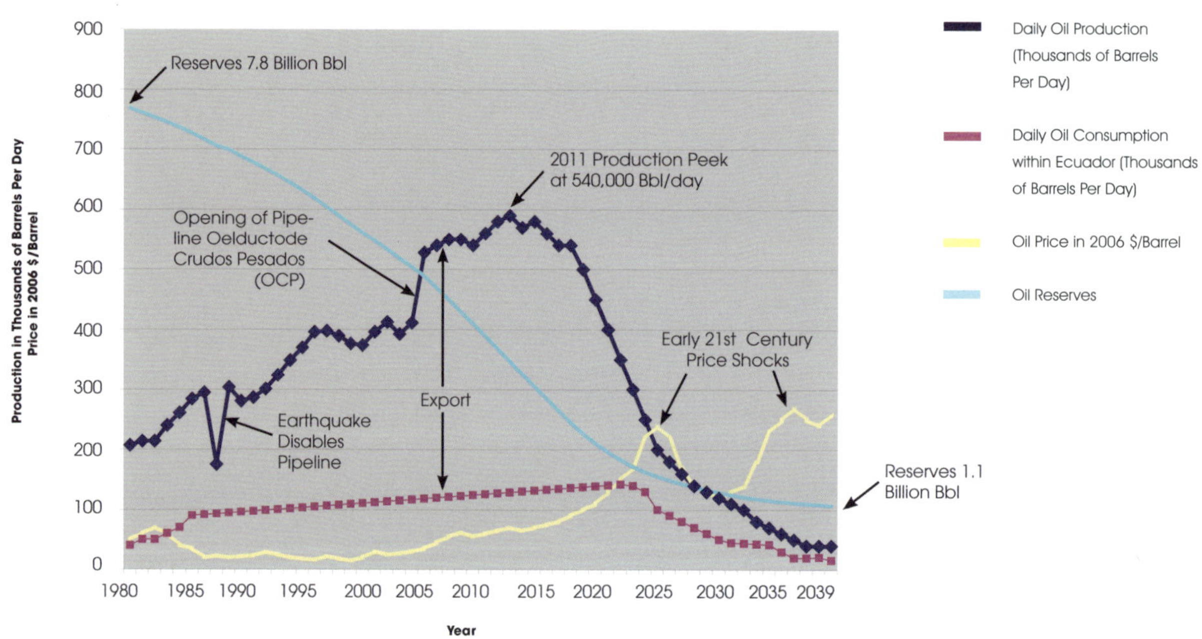

ECUADORIAN OIL PRODUCTION 2007

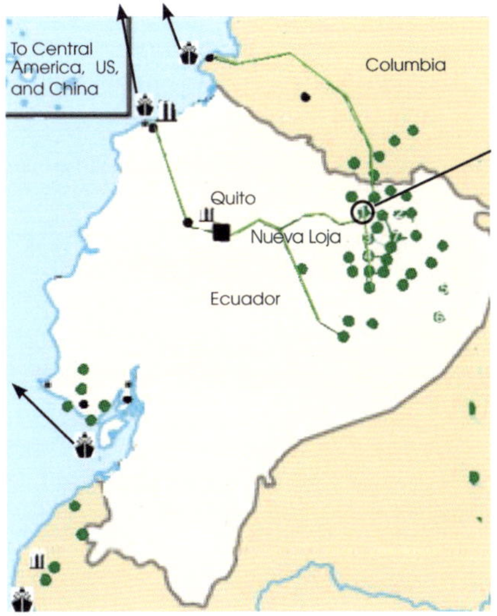

- Oil Field
- Shipping
- Refinery
- Pipeline

GREATER NUEVA LOJA OIL PRODUCTION 2007

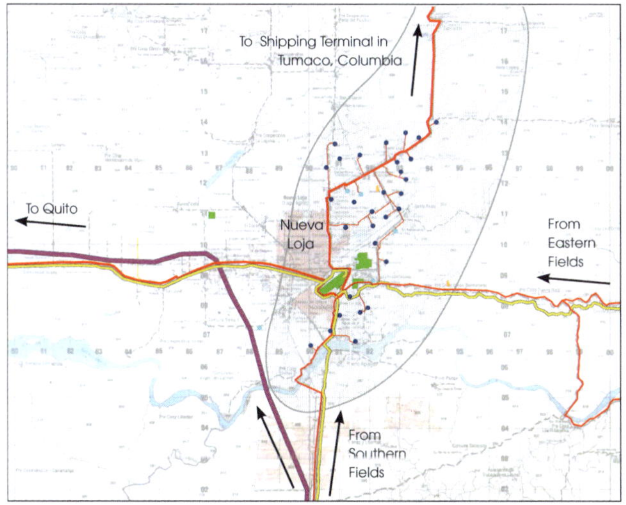

- Oil Pipeline
- OCP Oil Pipeline
- Natural Gas Pipeline
- Oil well
- Inactive Oil Well
- Other Petroleum Industry Facilities
- Oil Contamination Mitigated
- Oil Field

NUEVA LOJA OIL PRODUCTION 2007

- Oil Pipeline
- OCP OIL Pipeline
- Natural Gas Pipeline
- Oil Well
- Inactive Oil Well
- Other Petroleum Industry Facilities
- Oil Contamination Mitigated
- Oil field

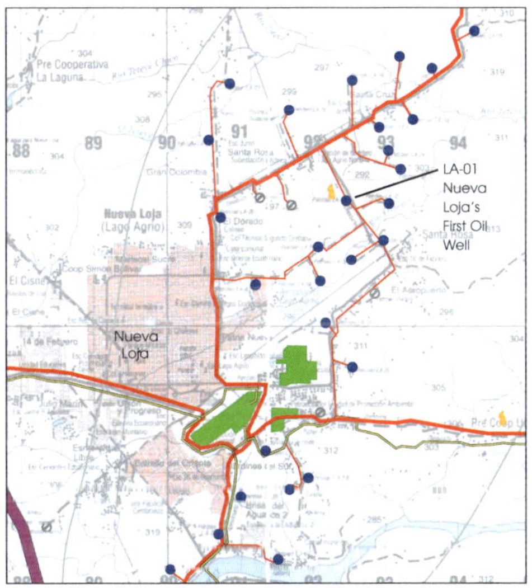

NUEVA LOJA OIL PRODUCTION 2037

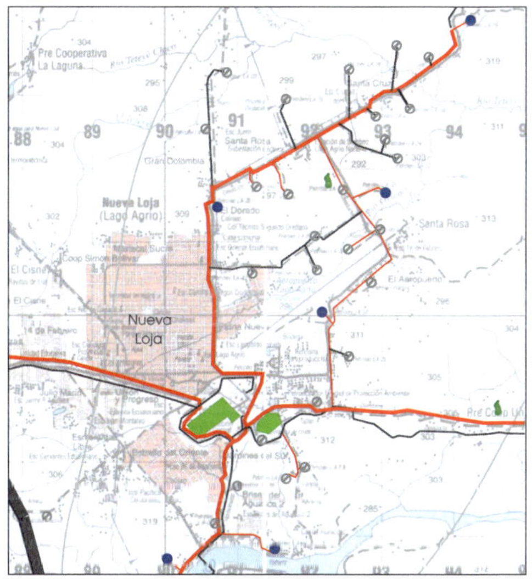

ENERGY

ALAN FOX AND HOLLY KALLMAN

ELECTRICITY CONSUMPTION: 2007

Ecuador meets about 60% of its electricity needs through hydroelectricity with hydroelectric plants on the Paute River in southern Ecuador providing over 50% of the nation's needs. The rest is generated through conventional thermal production using diesel and natural gas fueled plants.

Meeting the country's growing electricity requirements is a continual challenge. Ecuador's economy is expanding, and its appetite for electricity is increasing even faster. In August 2007, Ecuador's president proclaimed "a state of emergency in the nation's power sector." Last year demand increased by 8%. At the same time, supply has fallen due to a reduction in water through the hydroelectric plants and a shortage of investment.

Nueva Loja has an electricity shortfall along with the rest of the country. Diesel power is the least expensive and most accessible form of electricity in the city but its diesel fired generators cannot produce enough, particularly during peak usage periods in the late afternoon and early evening. Neighborhood blackouts are common. Many of the city's wealthier residents have their own diesel generators as back ups when the city supplies fail.

Empresa Electrica Sucumbios S.A. distributes power in Nueva Loja. Its network is the only one not connected to the national power grid. Increasingly, private consumers will be expected to meet their additional electricity needs.

ELECTRICITY PROJECTIONS: 2037

By 2037, the population of Nueva Loja will have increased from 34,000 in 2007 to over 150,000. We estimate that individuals will be spending three times more on electricity than they did in 2007. But they will also have more electrical devices, so their electricity needs will have risen more than their income. The cost of diesel will have risen too and caps on carbon dioxide emissions will further curtail its use, although diesel will still be used to make up for shortfalls during peak periods.

Hydroelectricity will be the primary source of power for Nueva Loja. Half the city's power will be generated by hydroelectric facilities in the Andes Mountains, owned by the city, private businesses and individuals. Electricity will be brought in along the same routes used to send the diminishing supply of oil out of the city. The city, province, and citizens will also have invested in photovoltaic panels and small and large wind turbines. These capital investments will have been substantial at first, but a move to free fuels will begin to pay off over the long term. Energy collectives will have formed to share the cost burden.

Any excess electricity will be sold on the open market. The city owns and maintains the distribution system and charges a fee to users. Some individuals will have built small and micro hydro facilities on their properties using the power for their own use or selling it to the city.

NUEVA LOJA'S 2007 COMPARATIVE ELECTRIC POWER CONSUMPTION

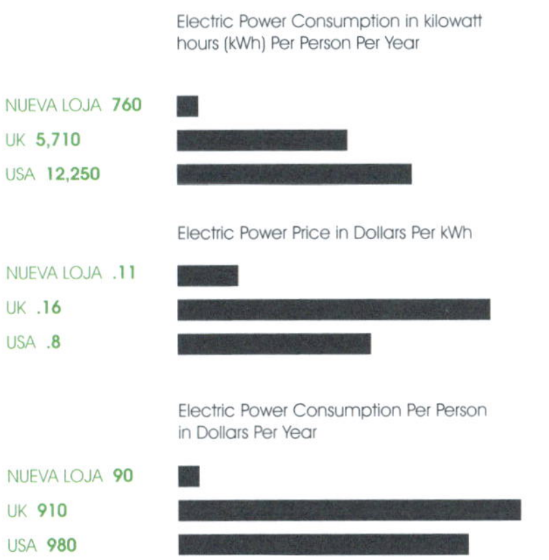

NUEVA LOJA'S 2007 ELECTRIC POWER GENERATION

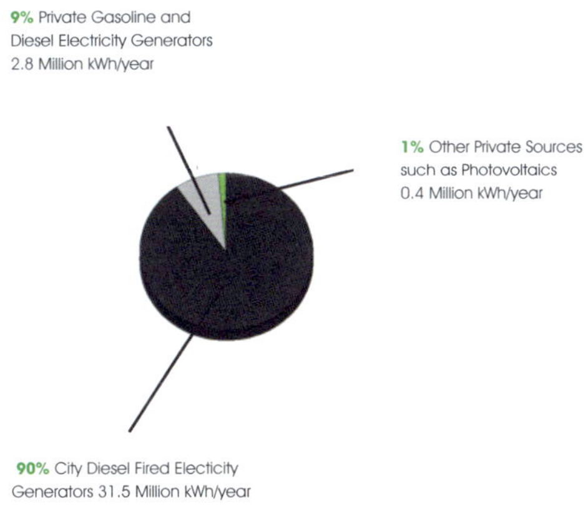

ECUADOR'S 2037 COMPARATIVE ELECTRIC POWER CONSUMPTION

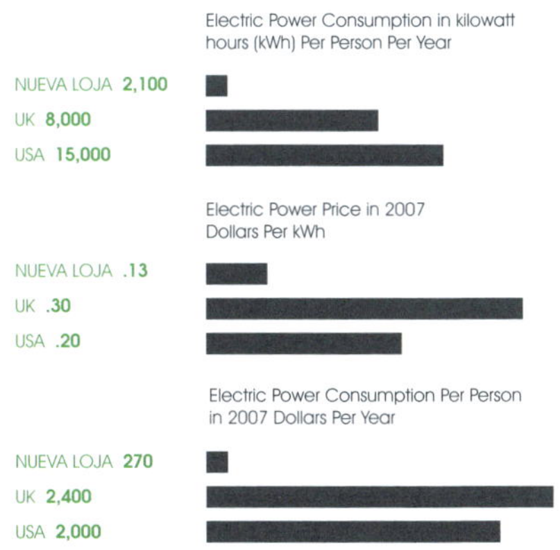

NUEVA LOJA'S 2037 ELECTRIC POWER GENERATION

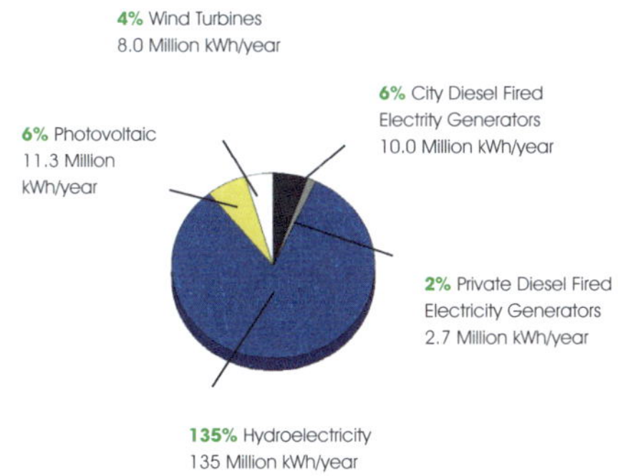

NUEVA LOJA'S 2007 DAILY ELECTRIC POWER CONSUMPTION

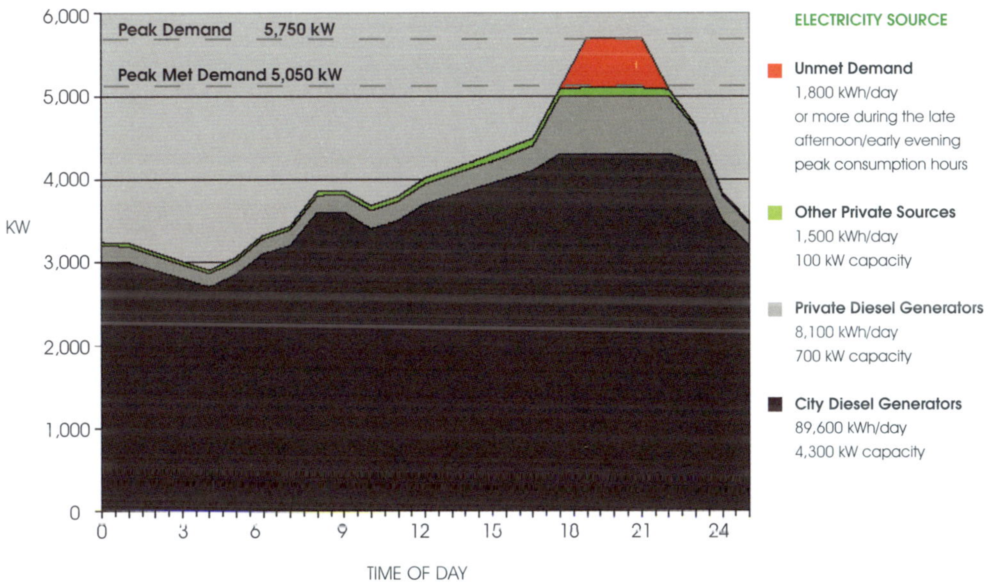

NUEVA LOJA'S 2037 DAILY ELECTRIC POWER CONSUMPTION

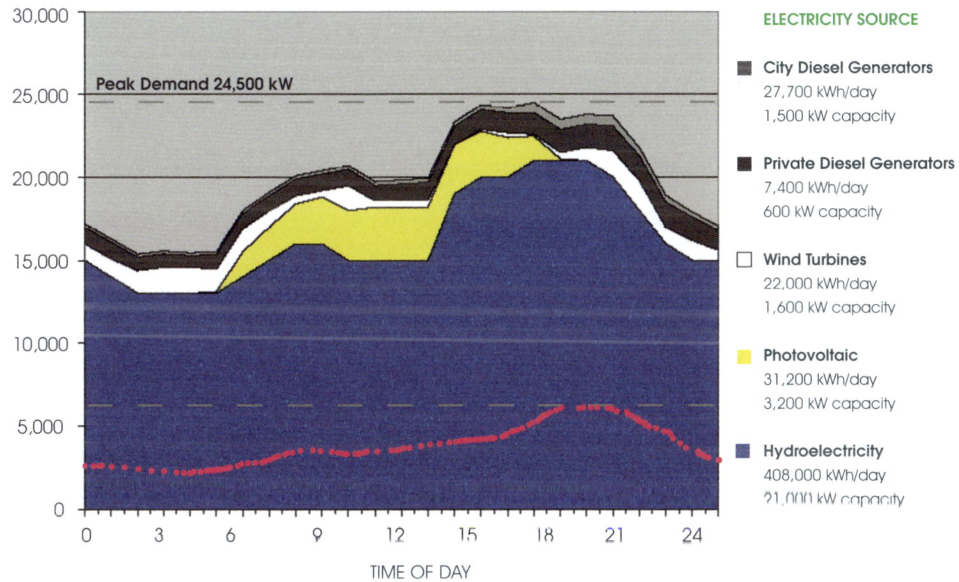

NUEVA LOJA ELECTRICITY GENERATION COMPARISON PER kWh

	DIESEL	HYDROELECTRIC	PHOTOVOLTAIC	WIND
CO_2 OUTPUT	X X X X	X X	X	
SURFACE IMPACT		X X X X	X X	X
INSTALLATION COST	X X	X	X X X X	X X X X
OPERATIONAL COST	X X X	X	X	X
FUEL COSTS	X X X X			
TRANSMISSION DISTANCE	X	X X X X	X	X X
2007 PRICE IN 2007 $	.11	.05 - .15	.24 - .48	.10 - .20
2037 PRICE IN 2007 $	.30	.03 - .08	.12 - .25	.07 - .15
FUTURE	Quick to install, proven method of generating power. Requires inputs of bought diesel fuel. As the fuel supply becomes increasingly expensive and CO_2 emissions are limited, its share of electricity generation will be yielded to hydroelectricity.	Low construction and maintenance costs. Fuel is free. However there are substantial local impacts, especially submersion of rainforest and settlements. Global impacts include the possiblity of significant CO_2 and other greenhouse gas releases from decaying vegetation in a hydroelectric dam's reservoir. These impacts can be minimized with foresight and consideration of local sentiment. Also, dams are not a requirement of hydroelectricity. Topography and rainfall make eastern Ecuador, especially near the Andes, an ideal region for hydroelectricity.	High panel costs. Fuel is free and maintenance is minimal. The region's high intensity sunlight is optimal for producing electiricty. However, sunlight is variable due to the high frequency of clouds. Costs will continue to decline.	High machinery costs. Fuel is free and maintenance is minimal. Intermittent and slow winds do not make the region optimal for generating wind-based electricity. However, there may be enough daily wind to make it competitive in tandem with photovoltaics. Large sized wind turbines can start generating power with winds as low as 14 km/hour, small turbines 5 km/hour. Cost will continue to decline.

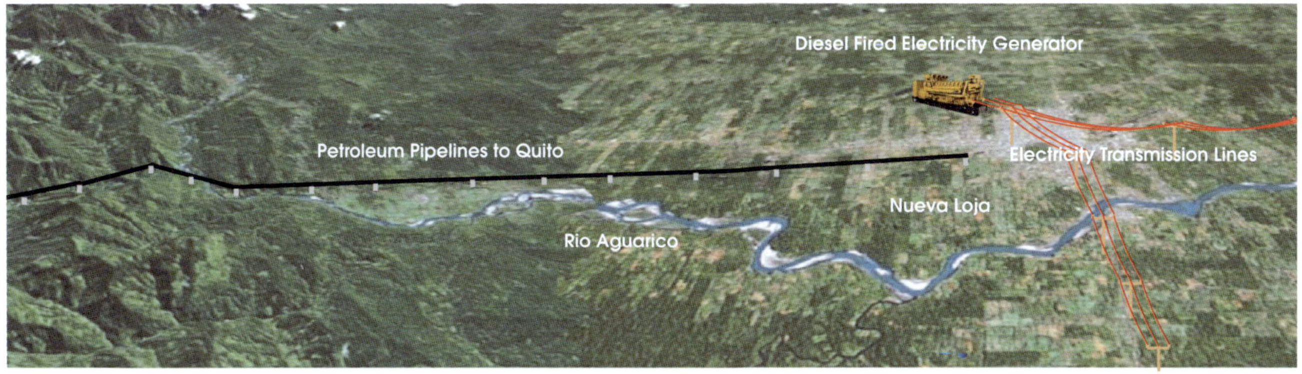

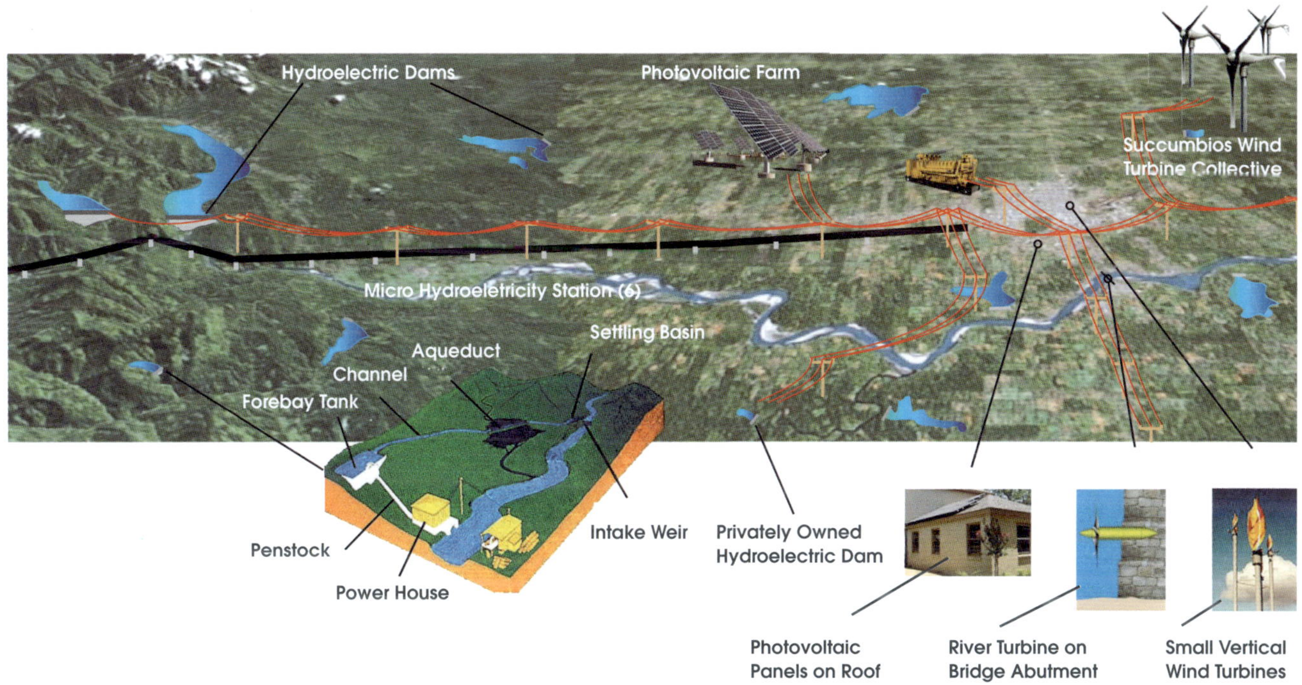

TOP. 2007 NUEVA LOJA ELECTRICITY GENERATION MAP
BELOW: 2037 NUEVA LOJA ELECTRICITY GENERATION MAP

WATER

PATRICK WEISEL

Nueva Loja receives an average of 340mm of rainfall per day in the wet season and 190mm in the dry season for an average total of 3500mm per year. Management of such a great quantity of water is essential to the quality of life in an urbanized area, but the effective infiltration and absorption capacities of the area's original forest have been lost.

THE MISSING THIRD

Rainforest canopy, which previously covered the entire area, absorbs roughly a third of all rainfall before it reaches the ground. Even without paved impermeable surfaces, natural absorption cannot compensate for the loss of the forest canopy. Flooding, increased stream velocities, and erosion destroy habitat, destabilize the soil base, and alter the water table – all of which has potentially serious consequences. The solution to an excess of surface water seems obvious: collect as much rainwater as possible and store it for household and commercial consumption.

WASTEWATER TREATMENT

In addition to stormwater and drinking water deficiencies, Nueva Loja lacks an effective sewage treatment system. Creation of decentralized wastewater treatment tied to the collection, storage and management of rainwater could replace the function of the missing rainforest canopy.

STRUCTURAL HYDROLOGY

Rainwater collection, storage, and treatment are interdependent and cannot be considered separately. Balancing allocations at the neighborhood and lot level will inform building placement and living densities, leading to a hydrologically healthy and sustainable Nueva Loja.

RAINFOREST | **URBAN STRUCTURE**

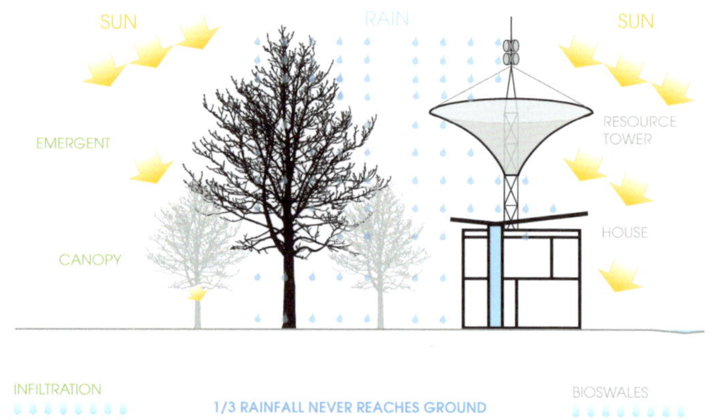

PUMP & TREAT
GROUNDWATER FLUSHING

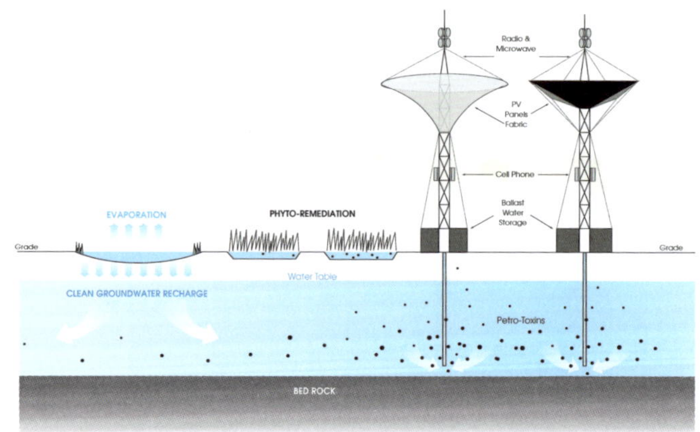

ROOF

150 m2 outdoor living space
66 m2 garden space
12 m3 water storage pool

STORAGE & FOOD PRODUCTION

WATER COLUMN

7 m3 vertical rainwater storage

RESOURCE TRANSPORT VOID

2nd FLOOR

250 m2 indoor living space

GROUND FLOOR

250 m2 commercial space

WATER TREATMENT

septic tank primary treatment
36 m2 secondary wetland
36 m2 tertiary treatment

RECYCLING

TYPICAL HOUSE

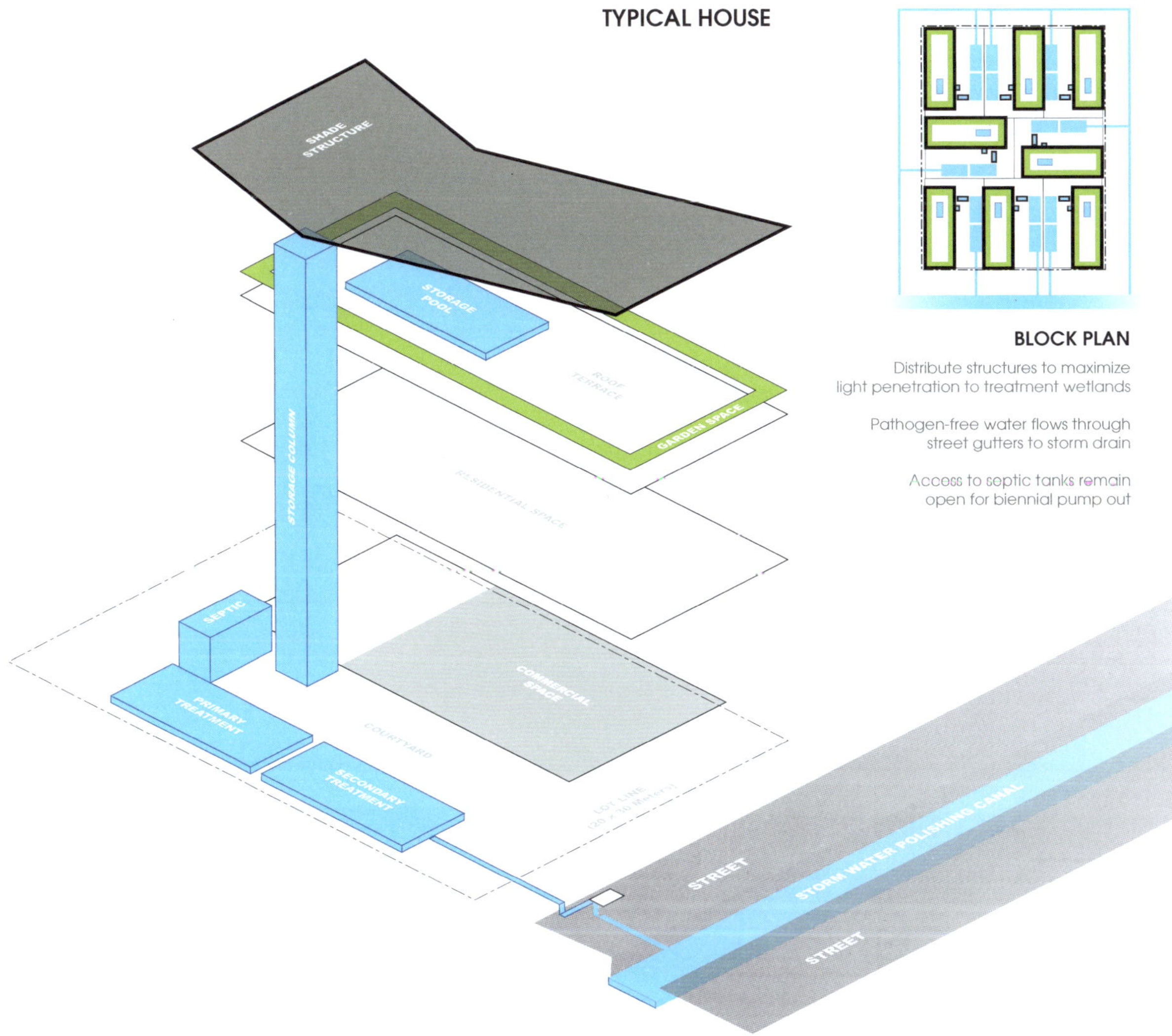

BLOCK PLAN

Distribute structures to maximize light penetration to treatment wetlands

Pathogen-free water flows through street gutters to storm drain

Access to septic tanks remain open for biennial pump out

WATER USE AND POPULATION DENSITY

(PER PERSON)

CATCHMENT AREA (m2)	STORAGE (3 days in m2)	TREATMENT AREA (m2 per stage)	USAGE (gal/day)
15	.34	1.78	23
20	.46	2.40	31
25	.58	3.02	39
30	.69	3.56	46
39	.89	4.65	60

A HARVESTING SYSTEM

FOOD & AGRICULTURE

CHRIS SYRETT

Secumbios Province currently ranks well in most global hunger indexes, but over the next few decades feeding the population of Nueva Loja will become more of a challenge. Population growth, soil degradation, shifting and unclear land ownership, poor farming practices and the effects of global warming could all undermine food production and food security in the region.

Using the right strategies, however, many of these problems could be addressed and a sustainable, dynamic agriculture developed at Nueva Loja. The indigenous chacra system of shifting cultivation could be used to preserve and restore the fragile rainforest soils, for example, while effectively feeding the city. Harvesting of native non-timber products could provide a lucrative alternative to the current dependency on unsuccessful cash crops. These non-timber products, such as avocado, could also supplement Nueva Loja's access to fresh fruits, vegetables and nuts.

Urban agriculture could be another source of food for residents, who might use garden plots to produce all their food, or at least, to supplement their diets or bring in some extra income. City farming has other benefits – it eliminates the financial and environmental cost of transporting food from other areas and reduces packaging waste.

FARMERS AROUND NUEVA LOJA ARE HEAVILY DEPENDENT UPON A FEW CASH CROPS.....

OVERALL LAND USE

PASTURE		14,8%
COFFEE		5.8%
CACAO		3%
SUBSISTENCE FOOD		1.2%

....WITH LITTLE WEALTH BENEFIT FOR LOCAL FARMERS...

WORLD BANK POVERTY LINE WAGE - PER MONTH	$ 62 USD
MONTHLY FAMILY EARNINGS FOR LOCAL FARMERS	$ 38 USD

....HEAVY INPUTS FOR LITTLE OUTPUT....

1 Ton of Rainforest

=

1 Double Cheeseburger

.... AND WITH SIGNIFICANT DESTRUCTION TO THE ENVIRONMENT.

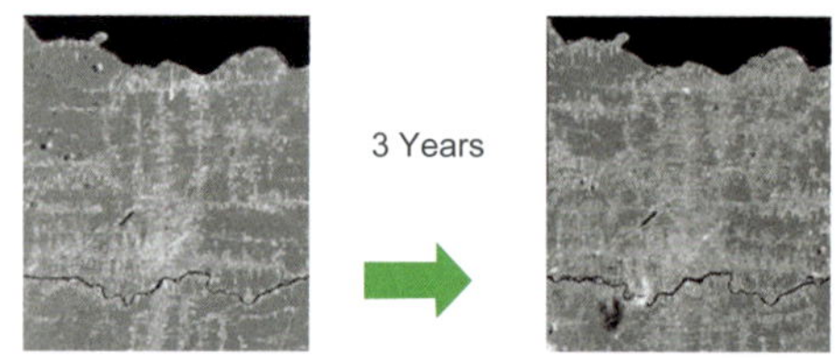

Population growth, cattle grazing and continued soil degradation will limit the ability to sustainably feed Nueva Loja and Sucumbios Province.

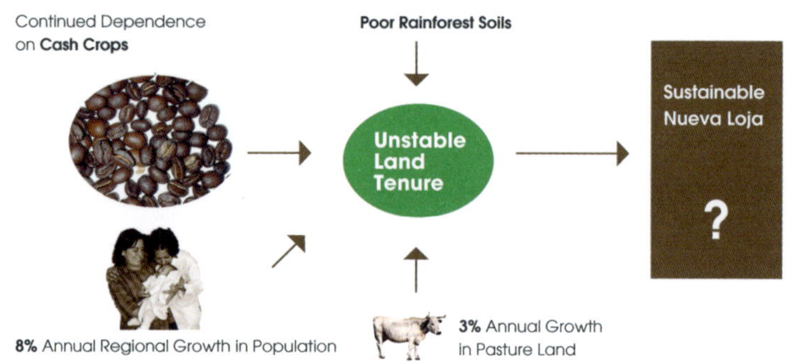

THE CHACRA SYSTEM

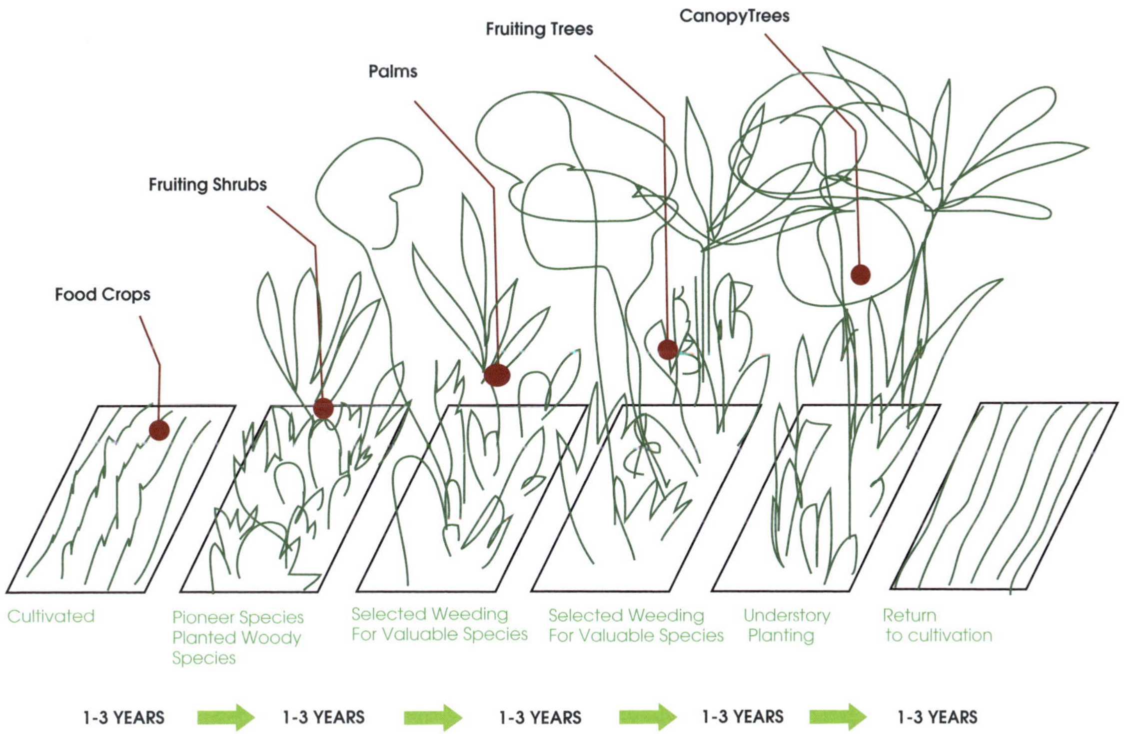

"THE CHALLENGE OF SUPPLYING NUTRITIONALLY ADEQUATE AND SAFE FOOD TO CITY DWELLERS IS SUBSTANTIAL."

FAO Report on Urban & Peri-Urban Agriculture

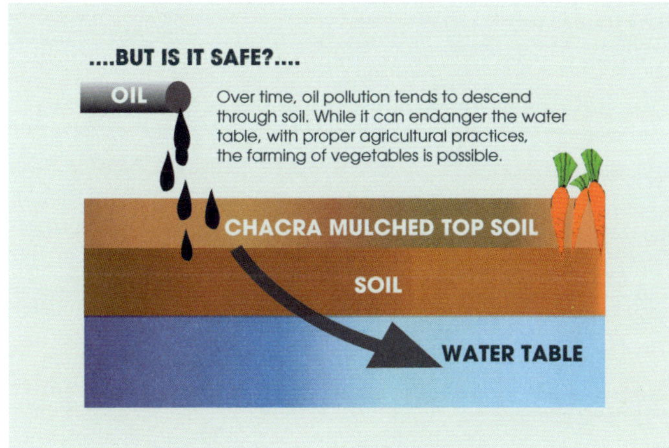

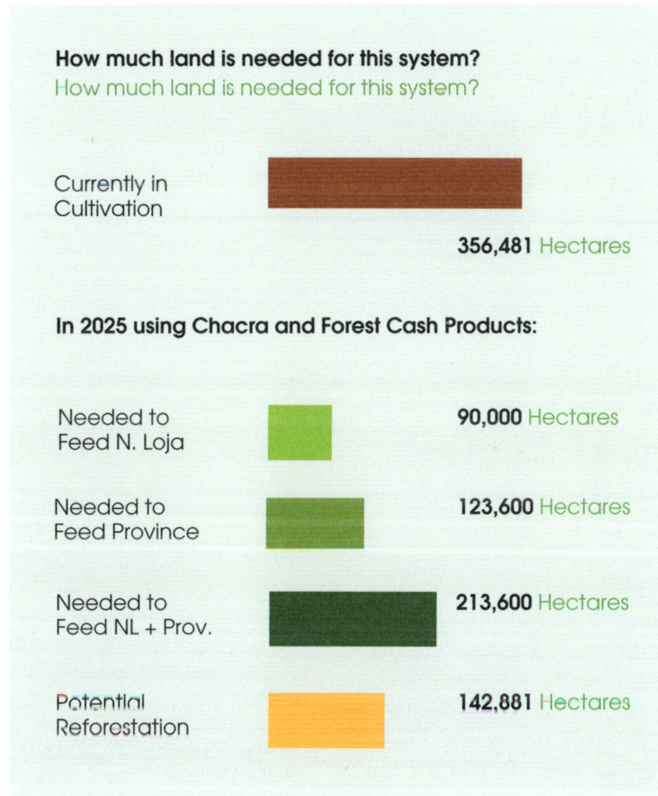

WASTE

GARETH MAHON

PROBLEMS

COST

In developing countries, 30 - 50% of municipal operational budgets are spent on solid waste management. Systems are typically centralized, top-down and privatized, making them capital intensive. Funding for waste projects often comes in the form of international loans from bodies such as the World Bank.

EFFICIENCY

In most cities, only 50 - 80% of household waste is collected.

EXCLUSIVE

The informal waste collection community, particularly active throughout Ecuador, is marginalized when centralized systems of waste management are implemented.

HEALTH

Poorly managed landfills are often sited near informal settlements creating health and pollution problems.

STAKEHOLDERS' OBJECTIVES

THE CITIZENS OF NUEVA LOJA

To live in safer, more sanitary neighborhoods

THE MUNICIPALITY

To create jobs
To reduce health problems
To lower raw material costs
To find economical and socially viable solutions

INFORMAL WASTE COLLECTORS/PICKERS

To find secure jobs
To escape poverty
To enjoy better health
To have security

THE ENVIRONMENT

To eliminate toxic pollution
To reduce landfill sites
To conserve resources

OBJECTIVES

MINIMIZE

The production of waste

MAXIMIZE

Reuse and recycling of waste

COMPOST

All organics

SOLID WASTE **ORGANIC WASTE**

GRAPHIC: SOLID AND ORGANIC WASTE

WASTE: A QUITO MODEL FOR NUEVA LOJA?

Lago Agrio does not recycle its waste. Trash is collected from most parts of the city and taken to a landfill site five miles east of town. (Trash collection at Lago Agrio appears to be fairly efficient, though according to the World Bank, local governments in South America spend 20 to 50 percent of their revenue on solid waste services but only 50 to 80 percent of waste is actually collected.)

Early efforts at recycling in the capital Quito offer some lessons for Nueva Loja. Quito began its first pilot recycling programs in 1993 in lower and lower-middle class neighborhoods. Studies released in 2002 show how they have evolved over the intervening years and some of the problems encountered along the way.

The Quito programs built on the informal systems of waste management already in existence. Families performed the initial sorting of the products; neighborhood teams or "micro-enterprises" organized curbside pick-ups of sorted recyclables (paid a fixed salary by the city); and the city collected the waste from drop off depots and took it for recycling. Local neighborhood groups worked with the micro-enterprises to secure the best prices and to re-distribute some of the profits back into the community.

The overriding goal was to reduce municipal overheads while providing jobs locally. Among the unexpected side-effects was a general improvement in sanitation and an increase in neighborhood pride.

But as time progressed, problems began to arise. Waste was not being sorted correctly and the overall volume of recycling began to fall – the result of local dissatisfaction with the program. A follow up study funded by USAID and carried out in part by local NGO Corporación OIKOS 17, identified the main factors that caused the demise of the program.

It blamed poor follow-up education and training; dissatisfaction in the work performed by the micro-enterprises; cultural beliefs and self-image (many residents felt that the separation of waste was demeaning and should be left to scavengers); and a general resistance to giving away valuable wast e to the micro-enterprises.

The study also found that the Quito program gave insufficient consideration to the informal system it replaced. In an attempt to reduce the informal practice of 'Minadore' who comb the landfill for scrap, it also put a stop to the tradition of 'Cacharreros' who went door to door buying up scrap directly. Gender played a role too. Women were responsible for starting many of the micro-enterprises and performing the task of waste separation, but often the men, who did not understand the system or the effort involved, were opposed to it for self-image or financial reasons.

The results of this study suggest that for a recycling system to work in Lago Agrio, it must start with buy-in from the community and follow through with clear initiatives linked to a public education program. Some financial gain from the resale of recycling material should reach the household and any informal system of recycling already in place must be incorporated.

WASTE: RECOMMENDATIONS

REDUCE WASTE GENERATION

- Establish education programs in schools and community centers.
- Encourage efficiency in local industries.
- Encourage local industry to reduce packaging.
- Introduce Municipal Codes promoting long life reusable products.

DECENTRALIZE WASTE MANAGEMENT TO LARGE BARRIOS

SET TARGETS FOR THE INFORMAL SYSTEM

- Aim to recycle 90% of all waste.

SUPPORT A DECENTRALIZED SYSTEM

- Recognize waste as a resource.
- Involve all stakeholders on the ground in the management of this resource.
- Enable waste pickers to form cooperatives with help from CBOs (community-based organizations) and NGOs (non-governmental organizations).
- Identify markets – local, regional and national – for reusable and recyclable waste.
- Provide space in each community for waste separation and storage.
- Provide space for composting.
- Provide space for bio-gas generators.

Develop a system of compensation

- Give waste pickers rights to all waste collected.
- And/or create a fee based service.

Generate secondary services

- Introduce street cleaning.
- Introduce tree pruning.

Identify and work to resolve problems

- Overcome "Nimbyism."
- Involve residents not participating in the system.
- Engage residents not performing initial separation.

IN THE BARRIO

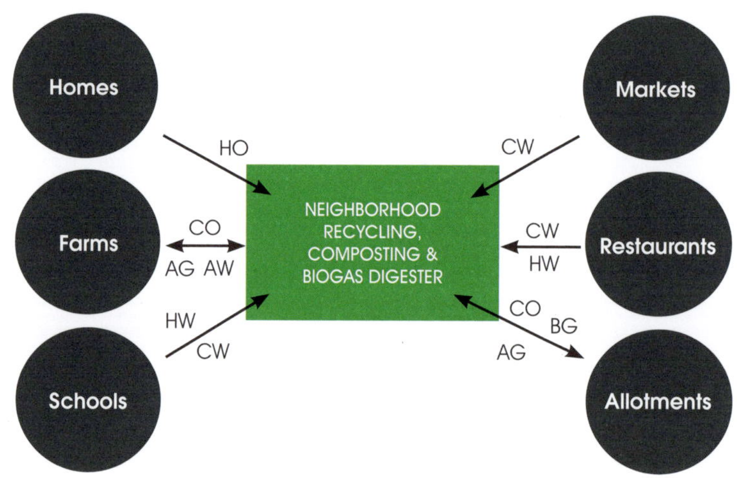

HO - Household Waste
HW - Human Waste
CW - Commercial Waste
AW - Animal Waste
AG - Agriculture Residue
CO - Compost
BG - BioGas

PUBLIC FACILITIES

MATTHIAS ALTWICKER

Nueva Loja's poorly distributed infrastructure falls woefully short even for its current population, which, if predictions are correct, is set to explode.

A new public infrastructure for the city should focus on quantity, distribution and sequencing. Exterior public spaces and educational facilities are critical to the development of any neighborhood. These should connect with city-wide public transport and anchor the community.

During a second phase of development, a variety of markets must tie in with the economic strategy of the region.

In both phases, links between the local, urban and regional levels will be critical – they will determine sites for new infrastructure.

Each neighborhood of 3,000-5,000 inhabitants will have two centers – economic and educational – and the neighborhood will develop between the two.

Some primary infrastructure not located within these neighborhoods – the large market, the bus station and the stadium – will be evenly distributed across the city to encourage movement and interaction between the different neighborhoods.

EXISTING INFRASTRUCTURE

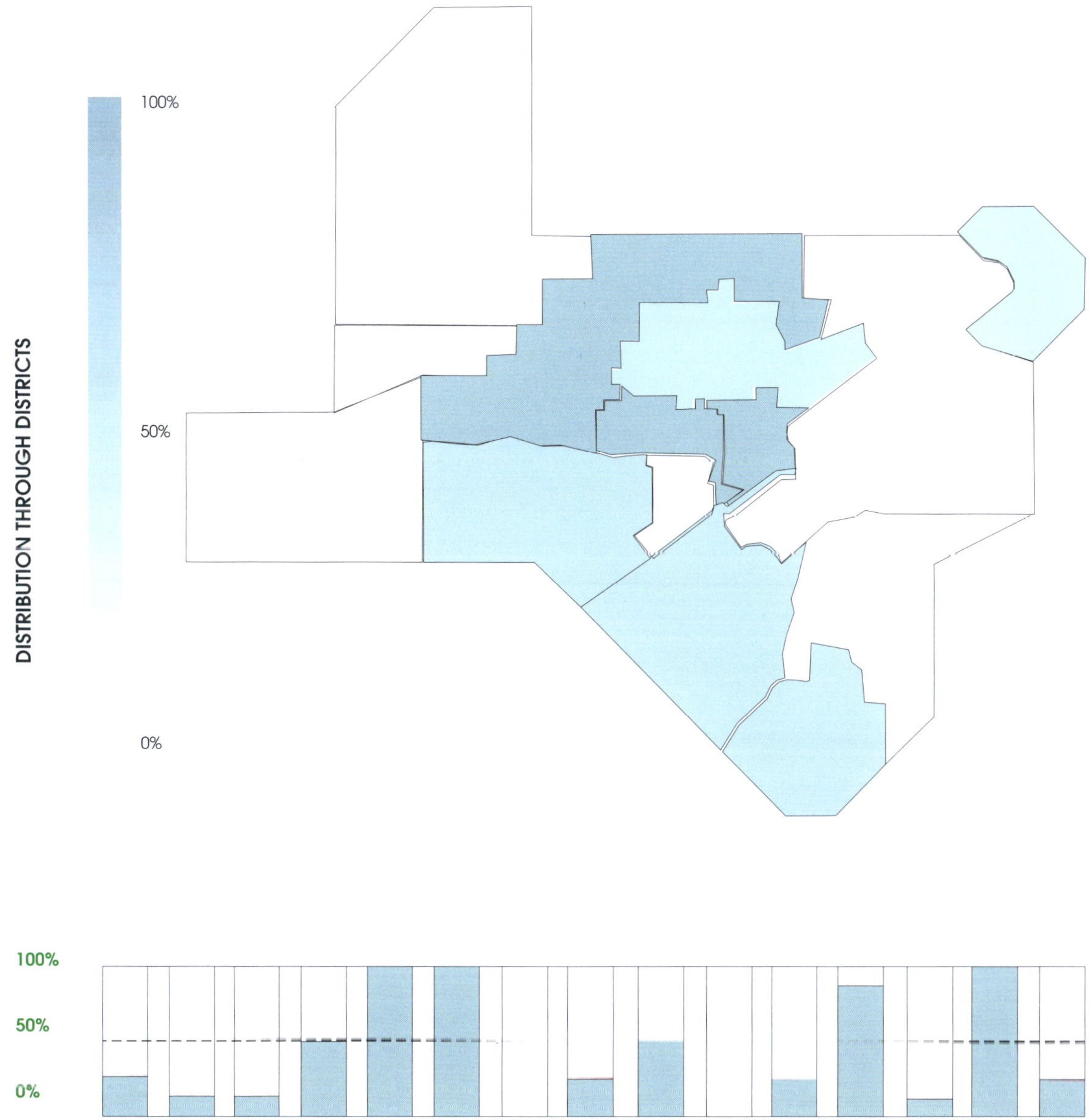

REQUIRED INFRASTRUCTURE

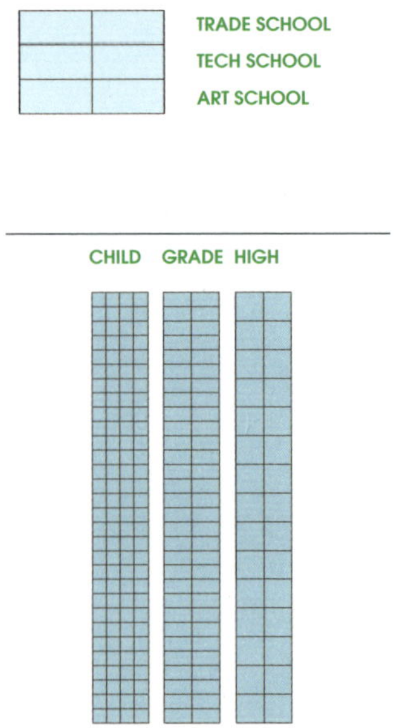

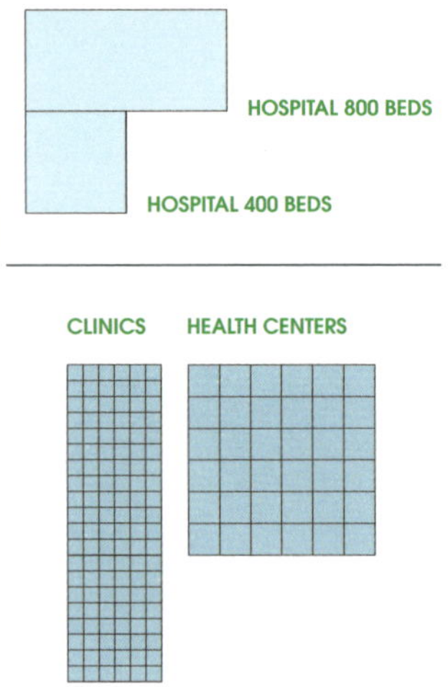

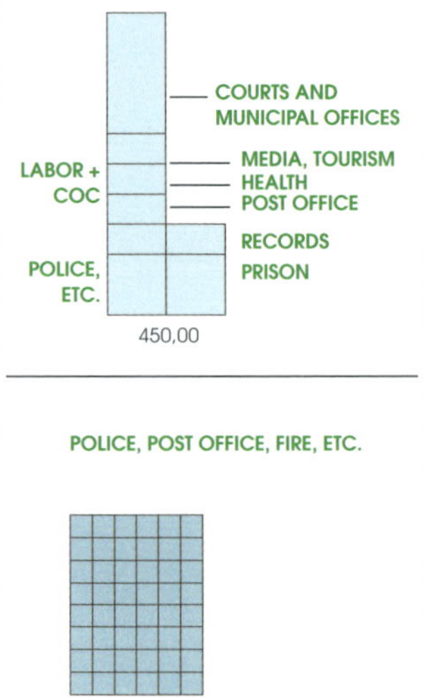

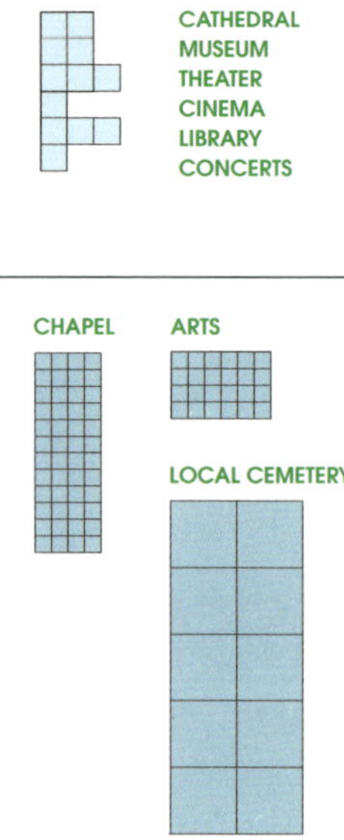

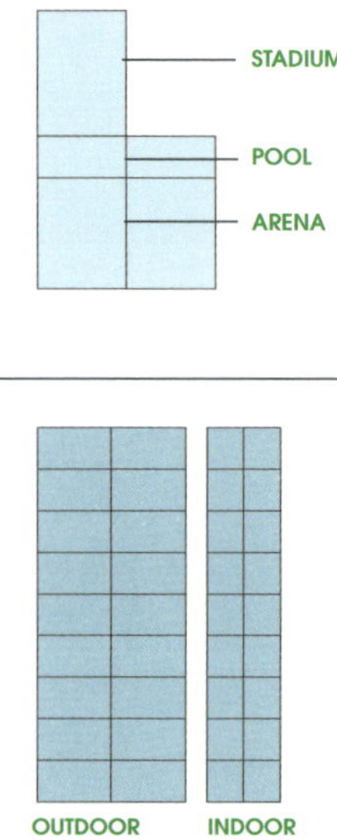

EDUCATION	HEALTH	MARKET	MUNICIPAL	CULTURAL	SPORTS
DAYCARE / KINDERGARTEN 1/1500p = **84**	CLINIC 1/1500p = **84**	CORNER STORE 1/1000p = **125** OPEN 7 DAYS/WK	MEETING HALL 1/500p OR NEIGHBORHOOD CTR 1/5000p	SHOULD BE COMBINED WHENEVER POSSIBLE	RECREATION SHARED BETWEEN EDUCATIONAL AND PRIVATE ENTITIES
PRIMARY SCHOOL 1/3000p = **42**	HEALTH CENTER 1/5000p = **25**	STREET MARKET 1/4000p = **31** STORE + STREET VENDORS	3 policemen/1000p = **450**		
SECONDARY SCHOOL 1/6000p = **41**	HOSPITAL 400 b/30000p = **2000 beds**	OPEN MARKET 1/1000p =**13** OUTDOORS, 3X/WK	FIREMEN 1/3000p = **50**		
UNIVERSITY/TRADE SCHOOL 1/50000p = **3**		DISTRICT MARKET 1/5000p = **3** COVERED 2 DAYS/WK MAX.	PRISON CELL 1/1000p = **125** CAN BE CENTRALIZED		

URBAN INFRASTRUCTURE

MATTHIAS ALTWICKER

COMPONENTS

I. The first element will be a primary school or a high school.

II. It will be sited next to a green space and public transport routes.

III. A shaded public space will be designed adjacent to the school.

MARKETS

I. Corner stores: Small informal shops sited 150m apart and within residential areas.

II. Street markets: Sited 500m apart; a separate structure with imported goods and fixed hours.

III. Neighborhood markets: Sited 1500m apart; close to circulation routes and the production of goods; they contain both open and closed spaces.

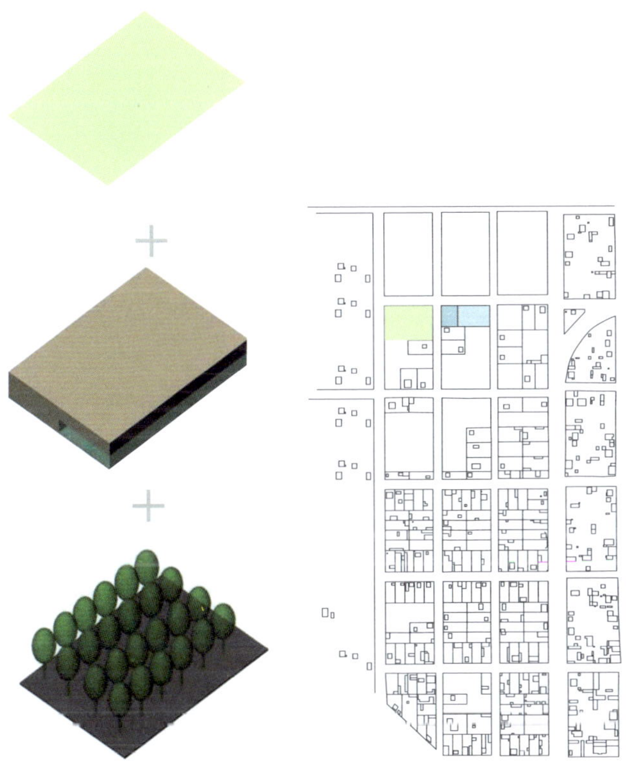

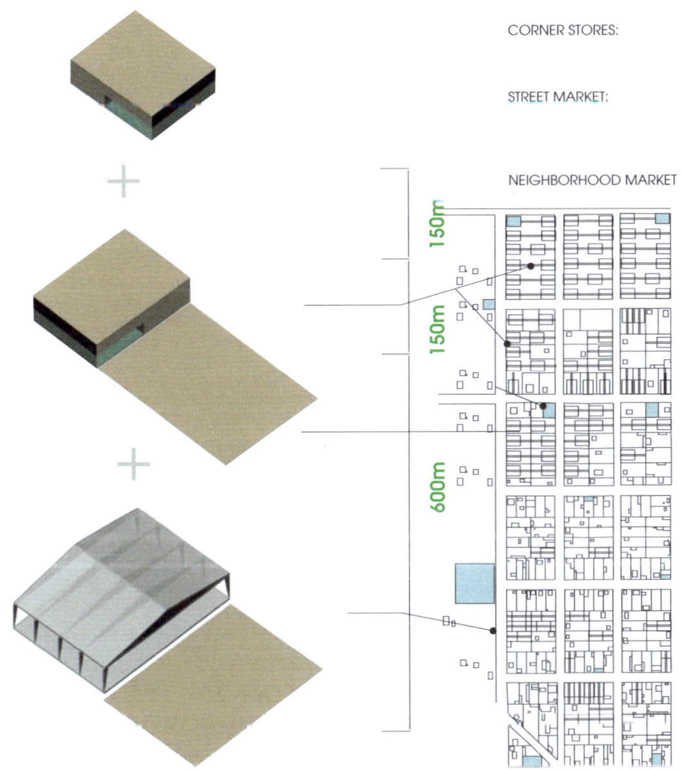

ADJACENCIES

I. Additional public programs may occupy the school building or be located elsewhere.

II. As the school takes on a variety of uses as a result of these programs, an adjacent exterior space will be added to accommodate a gathering of 1,500 people.

III. The siting of municipal services and markets will not be permitted adjacent to the school.

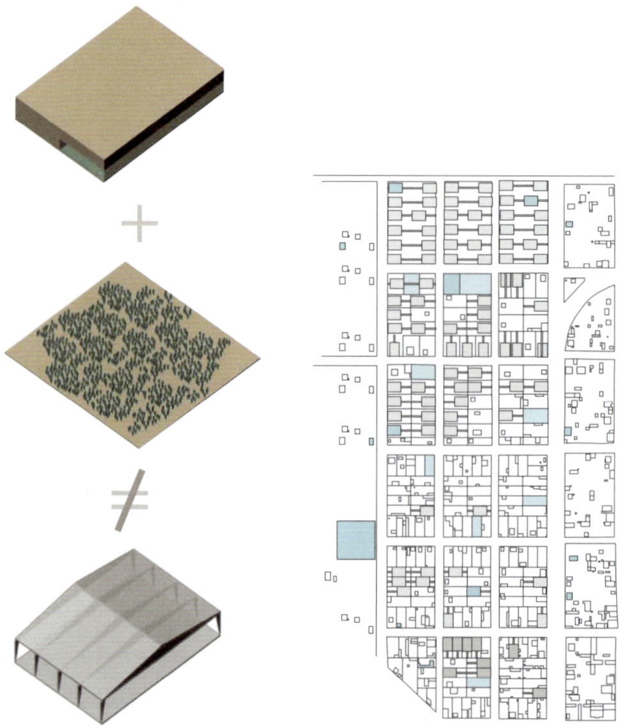

PARAMETERS

I. The municipality will maintain the open public space.

II. The community will be responsible for siting the commercial and public infrastructure.

III. Each building and space must be accessible to all.

IV. Construction should use passive systems of shading, lighting, and ventilation.

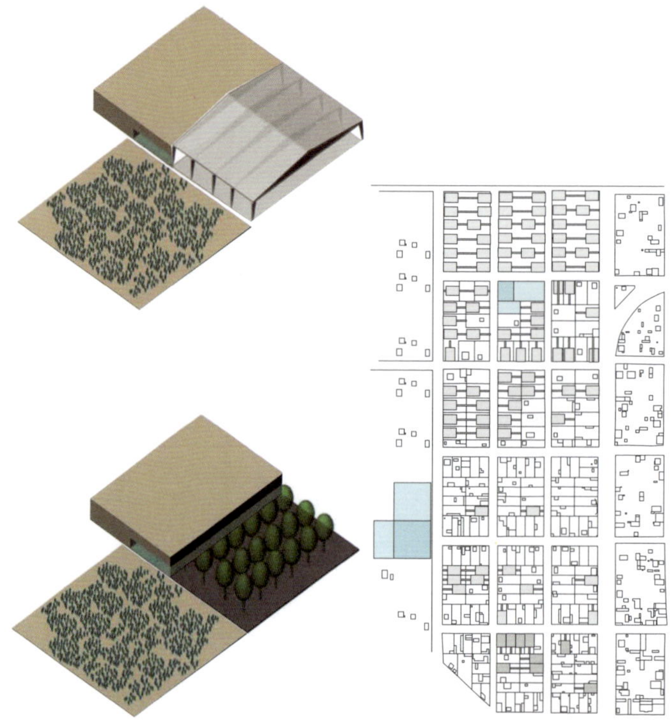

EDUCATION

HOLLY KALLMAN

RECOMMENDATIONS

THE ECONOMICS OF AN AMAZONIAN UNIVERSITY

"The plain fact is that the planet does not need more 'successful' people. But it does desperately need more peacemakers, healers, restorers, storytellers, and lovers of every shape and form. It needs people who live well in their places. It needs people of moral courage willing to join the fight to make the world habitable and humane."

Environmentalist David Orr

UNESCO keeps a close eye on global education statistics. Through its UNI TWIN program, it manages, mentors and monitors education in developing countries. The amount of schooling a child can expect is one of the most significant divisions between the world's richest and poorest countries. And the most significant cause of these differences is the provision of tertiary education.

Support for an Amazonian University could come from a number of public and private universities that have expressed an interest in funding and staffing satellite research sites. These could include MIT, CityTech, CUNY, Penn State and Duke University. The Organization of the Petroleum Exporting Countries (OPEC) is interested in funding research to mitigate the impact of oil extraction.

The European Union (EU), the World Bank and private companies such as Intel are also potential supporters.

The creation of a university at Nueva Loja will reinforce a sense of identity for the Amazon, helping the new Nueva Loja become a powerful emblem for the region and bringing sustainable prosperity to the city. Students will learn directly from the land around them and a new educational model will be established, closely related to "studio culture."

ABOVE: THE AMAZON

INPUTS	2013	2018	2023	2028
FULL TIME FACULTY	20	45	75	100
INSTRUCTORS	25	50	125	200
STUDENT BODY	500	1,000	2,000	3,000
IN-HOUSE MAINTENANCE				
MAINTENANCE CONTRACTORS CONSTRUCTION INDUSTRY	150 people employed 20 new businesses			(1,500) people employed 150 new businesses
SERVICES				
SUPPLIES				
ANNUAL BUDGET				

PROCESSES	2013	2018	2023	2028
CURRICULUM				
UNESCO MENTORING AMBASSADOR	Discovery and Development in Phyto Remediation	Cancer treatments found	New Technology in fresh water recovery	Solar and Hydroelectric energies made reliable

OUTPUTS	2013	2018	2023	2028
DEGREE PROGRAMS:				
BIOLOGY & LIFE SCIENCE		Oil drilling halts except for domestic use, which is strictly managed.		
EDUCATION	Teachers up to 10%	Up to 20%		Ecotourism model
AGRICULTURE	Sustainable	Pesticide free	Market trading	
NURSING	A collaboration between health care initiatives and traditional herbal lore is established.	Health care system run by nursing experts	Model for alopathic medicine as costs are 1/20 of standard medical costs in developed world.	World model for wealth building
HUMANITIES & THE ARTS	Secondary education in the Amazon	Graduate level degree offered	Prime research published by alumni and professors	Training of nurses and doctors
TECHNOLOGIES	Solar/Energy	Building-Recycling	Reforestation	Destination Education
DENTISTRY				
BUSINESS	Small Business Bureau Initiates	Markets are implemented	Mortgage and home ownership underwritten	Management=stewardship

OUTCOMES
HIGHER EDUCATION AVAILABLE IN AMAZONIA
REMEDIATION TECHNOLOGY REVOLUTIONIZED
ECONOMIC ANCHOR FOR CITY & REGION
UNIVERSITY: DESTINATION EDUCATION
DISTINGUISHED ALUMNI
WORLD LEADERS IN SUSTAINABILITY PRODUCED

PROPOSALS

URBAN DESIGN

REGIONAL ORGANIZATION
CITY BOUNDARY
CITY ORGANIZATION
BARRIO VIA QUITO
NAPO - JULIO MARIN
BARRIO SAN FRANCISCO
THE ORIENCO UNIVERSITY
EL BARRIO CHACRA
BARRIO LA FLORIDA
DE-CENTRAL PARK
BARRIO LA ESQUINA
BARRIO ISEGORIDA
BARRIO PUERTO AGUARICO
THE KINDLING CHARCOAL

REGIONAL ORGANIZATION

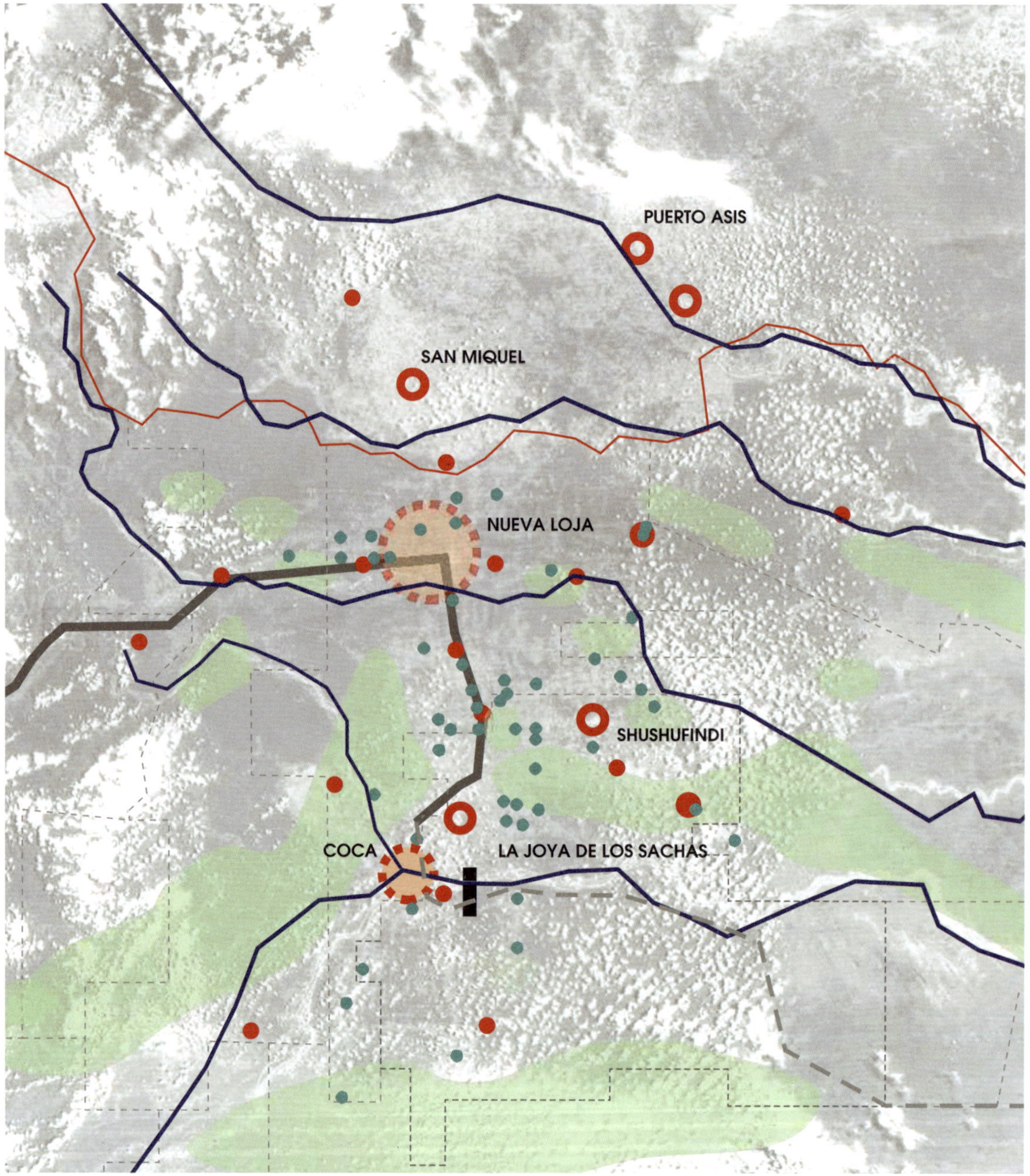

ECUADOR - COLOMBIA BORDER

URBANIZED AREAS (30,000p)

TOWNS (5000p)

VILLAGES

COMMUNITY CENTERS

INDIGENOUS REGIONS

OIL CONCESSIONS

HYDROELECTRIC PLANT (planned)

BI-OCEANIC HIGHWAY (planned)

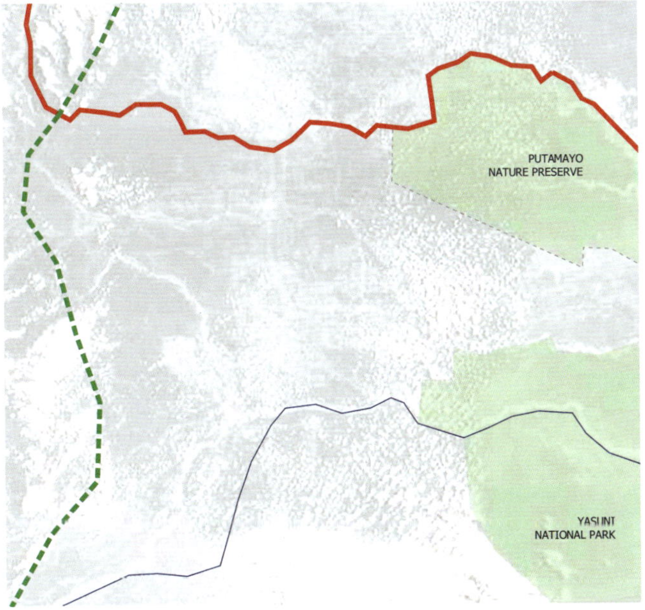

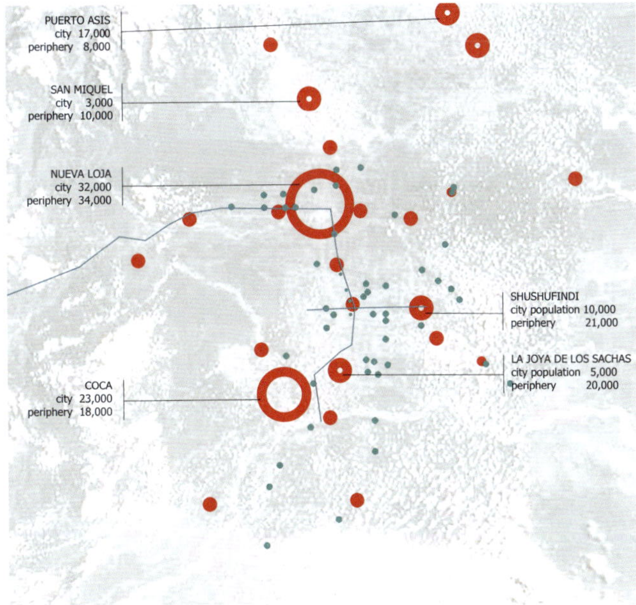

NATURE PRESERVE

RIO NAPO

ANDEAN HIGHLANDS

COLOMBIA - ECUADOR BORDER

CLEAR CUT AGRICULTURE

PETROLEUM CONTAMINATION

URBAN AREAS >20,000p

URBAN AREAS <10,000p

TOWN CENTERS

PAVED MAJOR ROADS

RIVER SYSTEMS

SECONDARY ROAD NETWORK
(PARTIALLY PAVED)

TOP LEFT: REGIONAL LIMITS
TOP RIGHT: DEVELOPED MARKETS+CENTERS
BOTTOM LEFT: ECOLOGICAL RISK ZONES
BOTTOM RIGHT: MOVEMENT SYSTEMS

ECONOMIC ORGANIZATION

MATTHIAS ALTWICKER

EXISTING

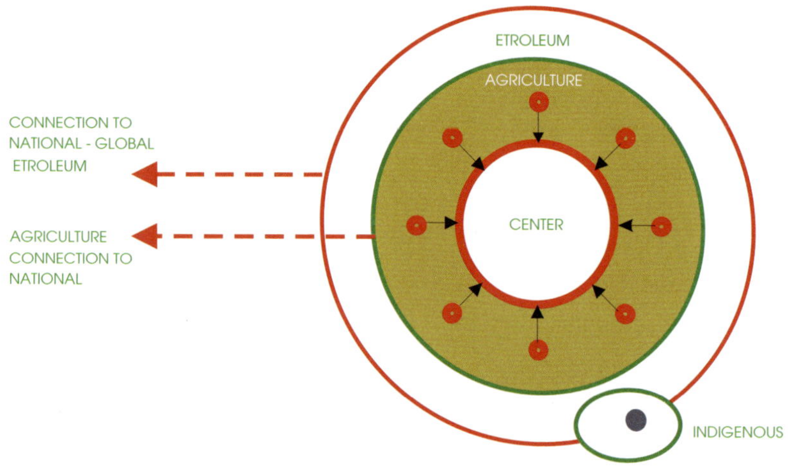

PROPOSED

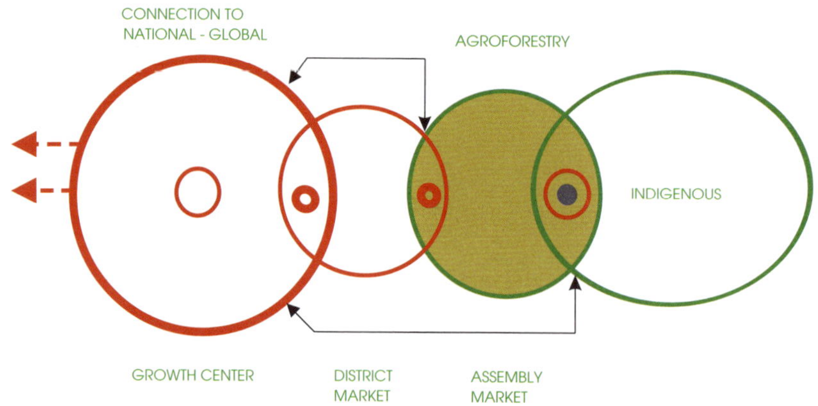

FOOD + SPACE: AREA REQUIREMENT

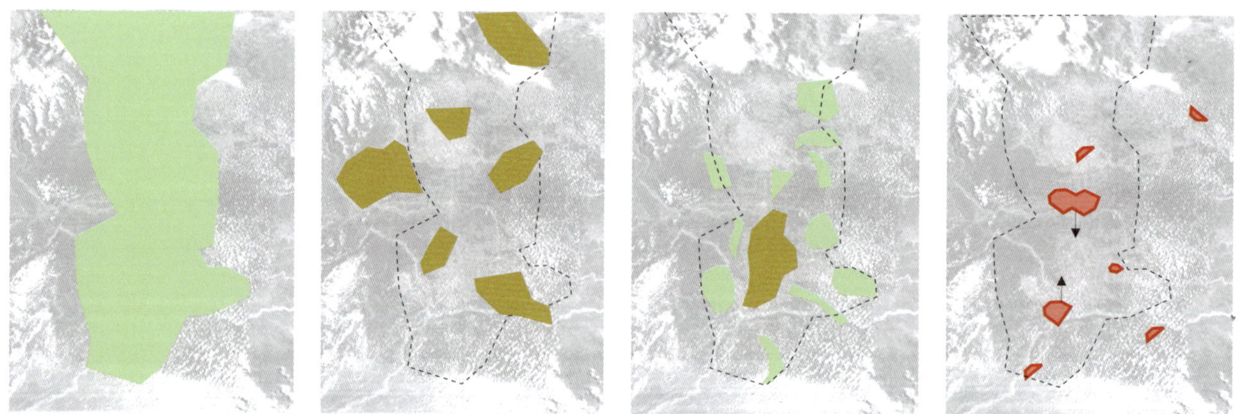

FROM LEFT:

EXISTING AGRICULTURE 360,000 ha; 60% efficiency
REQUIRED AGRICULTURE for Region: 240,000 ha
REFORESTATION & REMEDIATION necessary for rehabilitation: 90,000 ha
"HARD" DEVELOPMENT urbanization and density: 30,000 ha

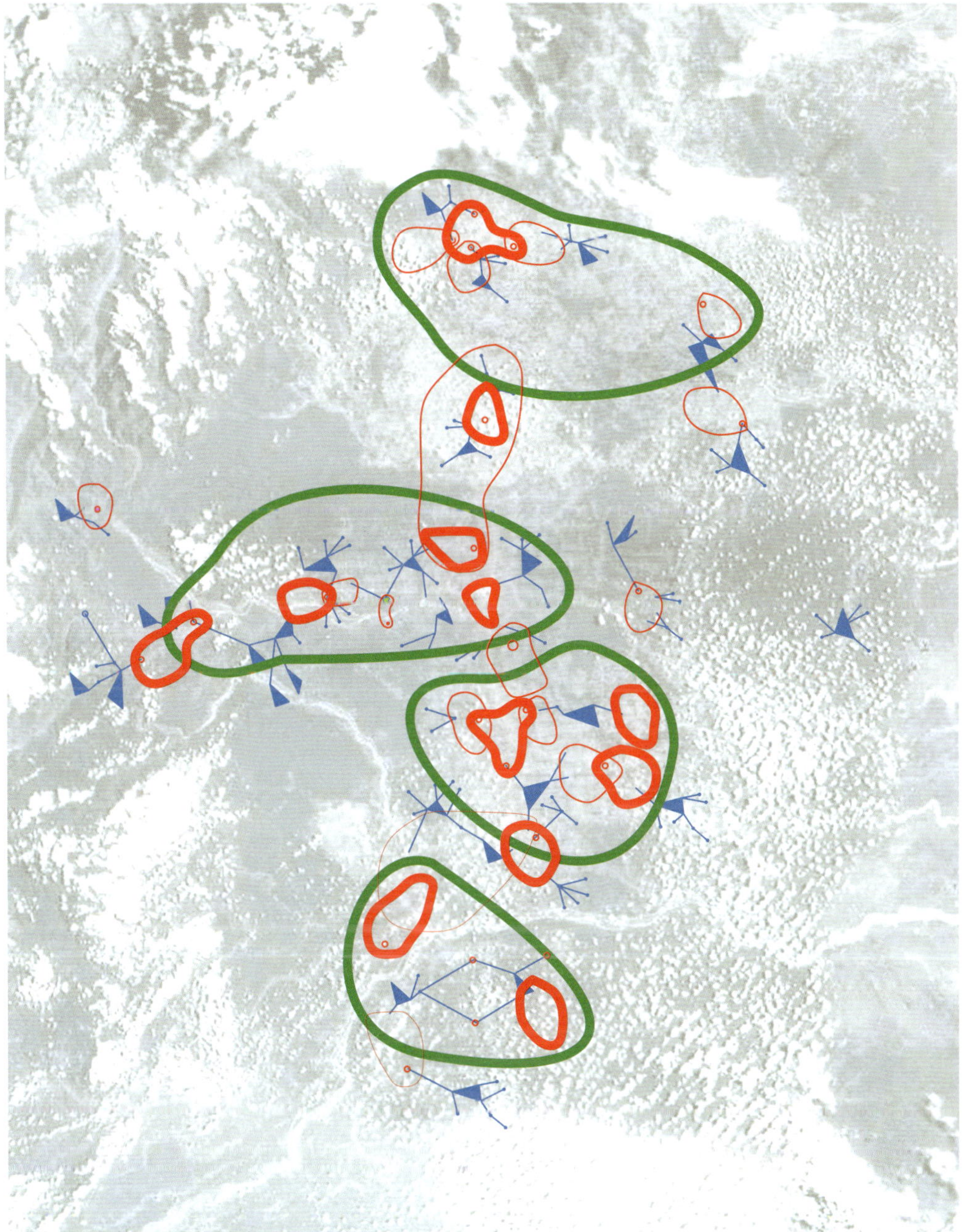

WEEKLY MARKET SCHEDULE

MARKET - PRODUCE REORGANIZATION

ECONOMIC REGION

- 4 regions within the Northeastern Ecuadorian Amazon are developed around proposed density of services and existing natural conditions.
- All necessities, including imported produce, are provided.
- Connection to the global market.
- Municipality monitors balance.

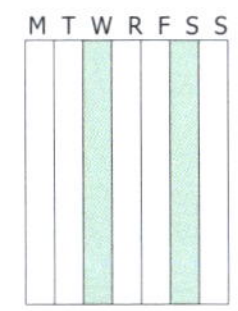

LARGE MARKET

- Scheduled bi-weekly with consistent vendors and rented spaces.
- Provides collection of products from the entire economic region.
- Occurs in concert with district markets for continuous provision of products.

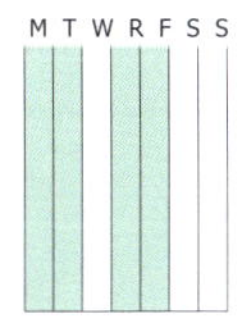

DISTRICT MARKET - AREA CATCHMENT

- Scheduled small markets of specific product, evenly distributed.
- Provides interface between local/commune and urbanized large markets.
- Occurs in concert with large markets.

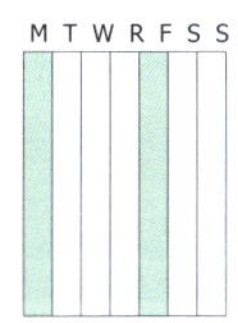

ASSEMBLY MARKET - TOWN CATCHMENT

- Occurs weekly or sporadically.
- Mobile markets collecting available goods via truck.
- Provides products for local consumption from inaccessible large markets; trading goods for others.

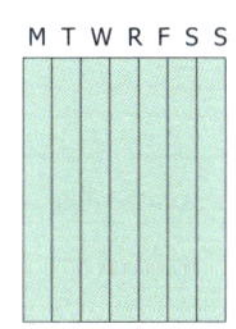

LOCAL NETWORK

- Small markets located at source.
- Provides food and services.
  Surplus traded via assembly market or commune membership.
- Individually maintained, seasonal.
- Promotes indigenous interaction.

TWIN CITIES: NUEVA LOJA-COCA

GOAL

Nueva Loja is the regional anchor of Sucumbios, and Coca is its administrative center. Considering Nueva Loja and Coca as twin gateway cities would strengthen both urban centers and balance their expansive and shared periphery. Each city would maintain its own local identity, while also becoming symbiotically linked through shared functions and resources.

AVAILABLE RESOURCES: GENERAL

The twin cities can draw on indigenous culture, ecological reserves and a strong primary education framework.

POPULATION	Nueva Loja	Coca
Urban - projected	150,000	60,000
Periphery - projected	40,000	20,000
Total	165,000	80,000

AVAILABLE CONNECTIONS

Connections-international	Colombia	Brazil
Connections-national	Andes	S. Oriente
Transport	airport	Rio Napo

KEY INVESTMENTS REQUIRED

Energy sources: Private technical sponsors, research grants.

Education initiatives: UN development grants, private university collaborators.

BORDER ZONES

GOAL

To promote productive relationships across existing borders. To change how the Colombia-Ecuadorian border area is perceived, from a dangerous and contested place to a safe one. This will create a "controlled" area with incentives for settlement and opportunities for cross-border collaboration.

LOCATION/AVAILABLE RESOURCES

International: The Colombia - Ecuador border. Existing, dispersed river towns will be organized into collectives. Building products will form a new manufacturing base that takes advantage of reforestation and new development along the border.

REGIONAL: SUCUMBIOS - NAPO BORDER

A conservation strategy is to be developed with the oil companies operating to the south, which limits development to the Sucumbios-Napo border zone and the urban centers.

KEY INVESTMENTS REQUIRED

Settlements: Local municipalities deed property rights and assist with basic infrastructure.

Development: Money from the US's Plan Colombia and Ecuador's military funds will be redirected towards private investment in manufacturing.

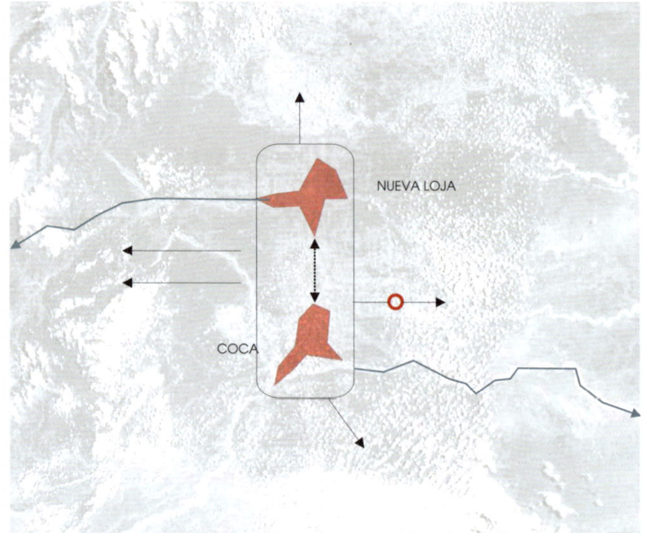

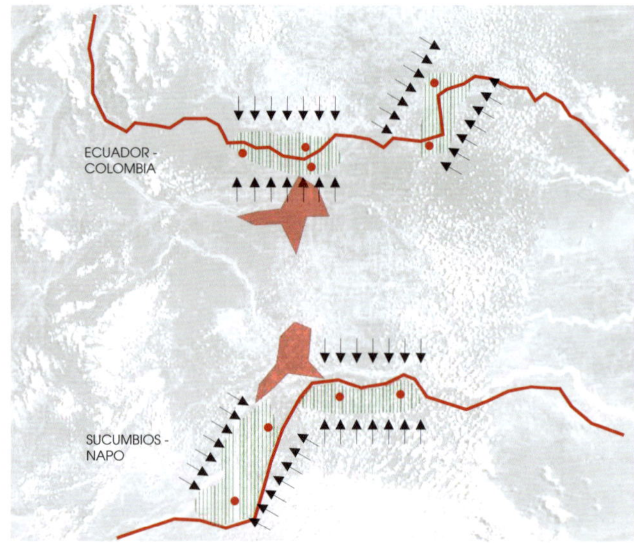

TOP: TWIN CITIES: NUEVA LOJA-COCA
BOTTOM: BORDER ZONES

AGRICULTURAL ZONES

GOAL

Agriculture, though the primary source of commerce in the region, is inefficiently managed. Through education, training and revision of land use practices, over time it could become both more productive and more sustainable.

COMMUNES

Co-operatives have a reputation for mismanagement and taking advantage of new settlers. These will slowly be restructured into communes linked by proximity. Crops will be balanced to ensure collaboration within the commune rather than competition.

AGRO-FORESTRY

New settlers will be taught productive reforestation and orchard management in order to improve efficiency of land use. 80% of land will be used to serve local and national needs.

CHACRA: EFFICIENT FARMING METHOD

Moving to this indigenous farming method will be an improvement on current subsistence farming methods and will support the regeneration of the environment and the reintegration of the indigenous culture.

KEY INVESTMENTS REQUIRED

The World Bank and UN Development Funds for re-education; private investment in agro-industry.

RESTORATIVE ZONES

GOAL

To restore and manage the area's ecology through land stewardship practices and by minimizing settlement and access. This regional hinterland, removed from the global market place, will become a place of local opportunity instead.

REFORESTATION: EDGES AND CORRIDORS

A continuous edge of forest reserve will be created by "filling in the gaps." Settlers, hired as forest wardens, will support themselves through selective cutting and subsistence farming along with subsidies from the local and national government. This is a long-term schedule of restoration: it will be ten years before it yields returns.

DETOXIFICATION

Fungal-phyto remediation will be used to clean up petroleum zones. The initial process takes several months, but within a year these areas will produce mushrooms and potatoes. This project will be managed closely by the Ecuadorian government, the educational system and watchdogs to ensure trust and cooperation.

KEY INVESTMENT REQUIRED

Reforestation: Local governments, ecotourism, the UN and the World Bank.

Detoxification: Ecuadorian government, petroleum corporations.

TOP: AGRICULTURAL ZONES
BOTTOM: RESTORATIVE ZONES

CITY BOUNDARY

ROBERTA KORCZ

GROWTH DISCREPANCIES

Both municipal and informal data show Nueva Loja expanding at a rapid rate. The two sources, however, show different patterns for this growth. City maps record a fairly even radial growth pattern, while satellite imagery reveals urban and agricultural expansion to be more sporadic and fragmented, extending out along oil infrastructure lines and major roadways.

This pattern is largely due to the informal nature of settlements in the Oriente. As a result, forested and urbanized land is becoming increasingly disconnected as agricultural land sprawls into rural corridors. At the same time, distances are increasing between settled areas and urban centers, building a dependency on cars.

URBAN GROWTH BOUNDARY GOALS:

- To limit urban and agricultural sprawl.
- To prevent ecological habitat fragmentation.
- To delineate a networked pattern of urban, agricultural, and natural land use.
- To inhibit the city's negative interactions with surrounding ecosystems.

MUNICIPAL GROWTH PATTERNS

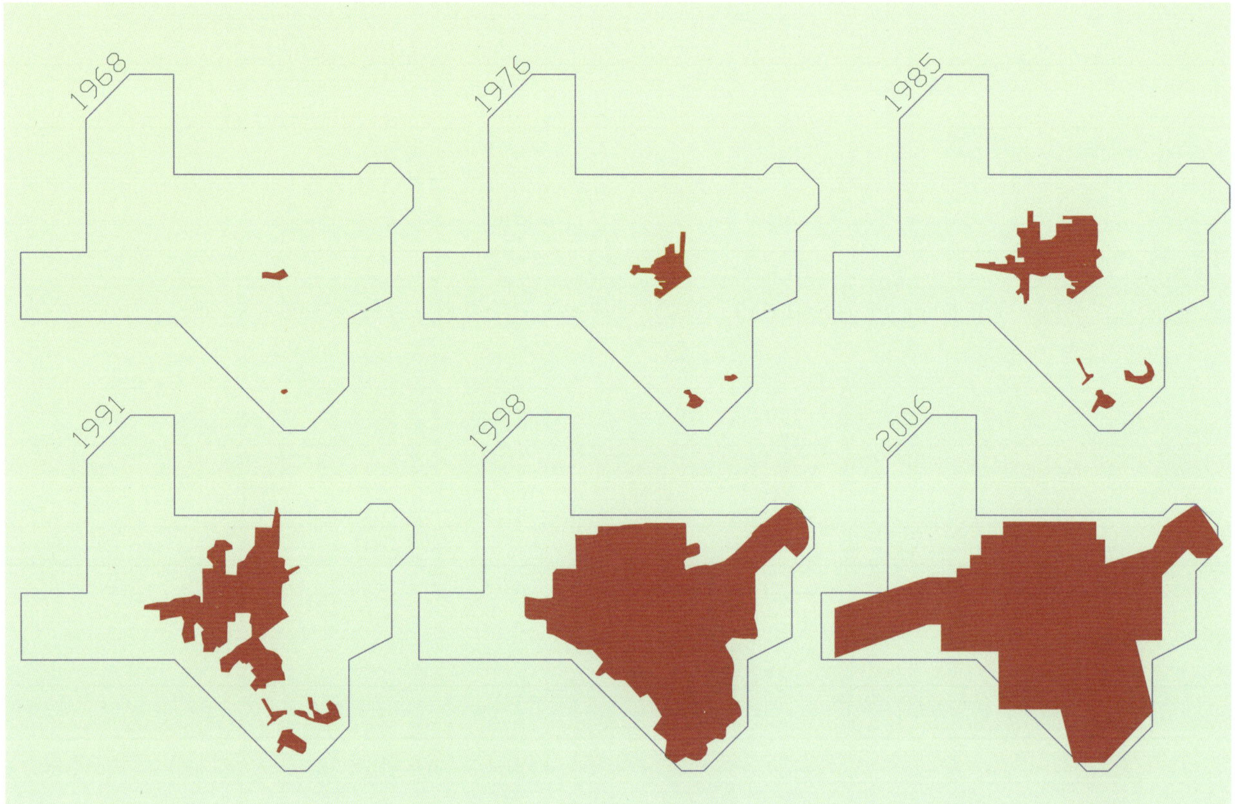

Growth Factors: sporadic housing, oil, roads, agriculture

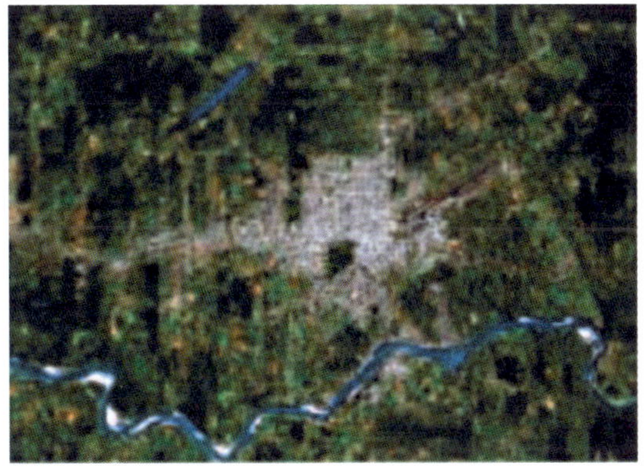

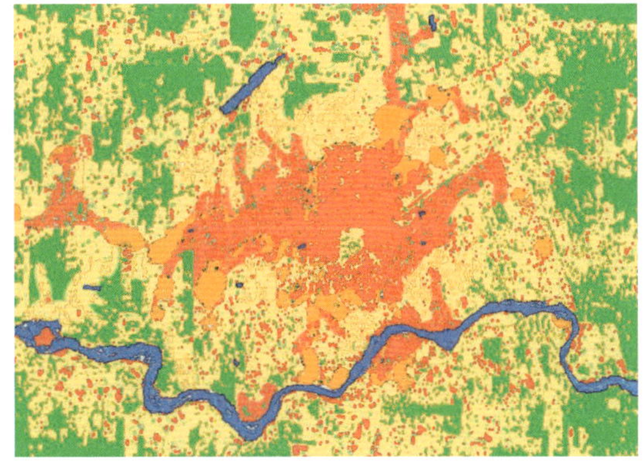

ACTUAL GROWTH

Above left: Satellite imagery shows a linear pattern of urban and agricultural growth, which extends out along oil infrastructure lines and major roadways.

Above right: Projected growth is based on 1999-2005 growth patterns. Urban and agricultural lands merge creating areas of fragmented ecological habitats.

Below left: Key developmental nodes are connected to establish a boundary of urban (red), agricultural (orange), and environmental (yellow) zones of growth.

Below right: Existing and projected growth patterns show agricultural expansion to the north and south, and westward sprawl along Avenida Quito.

Below: Changes in land use, ownership, size and accessibility between 1990-1999.

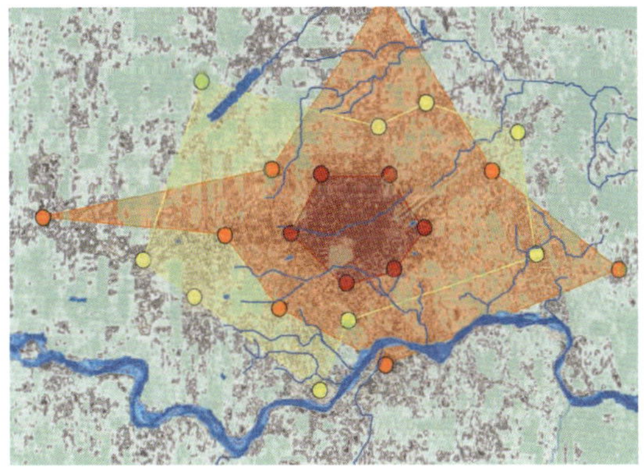

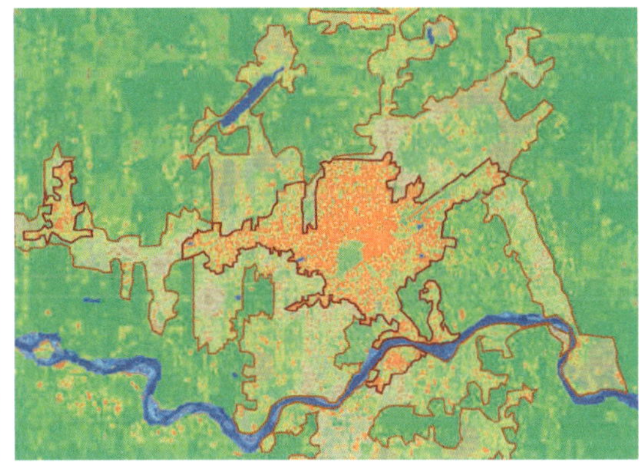

PLOT SIZE (HA)

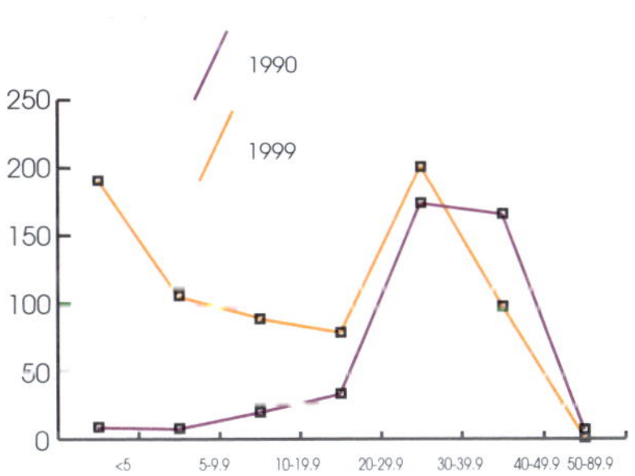

ACCESSIBILITY BY DISTANCE (KM)

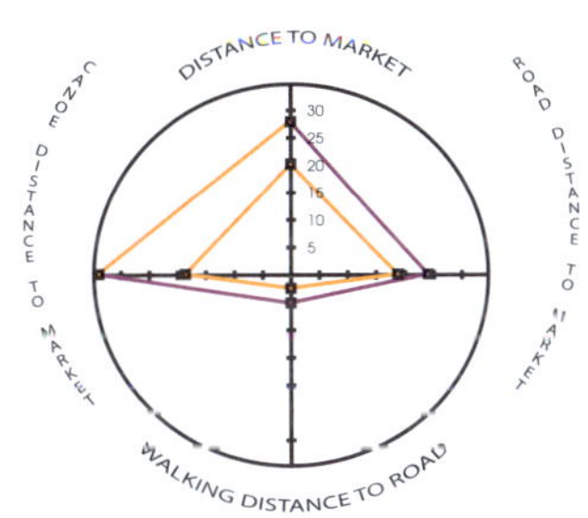

LAND TENURE

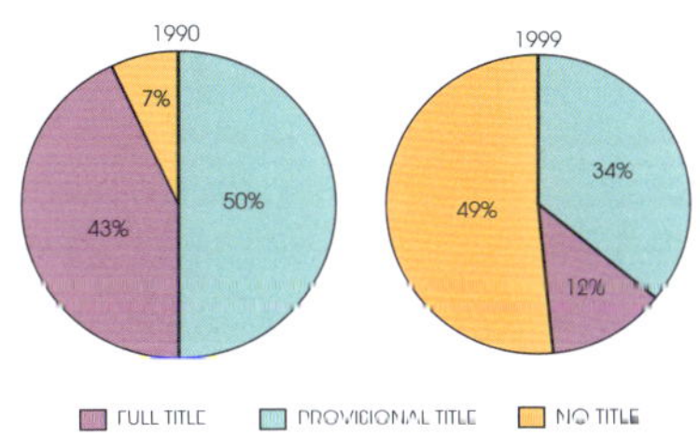

LAND USE FOR 1990 AND 1999 (HEA)

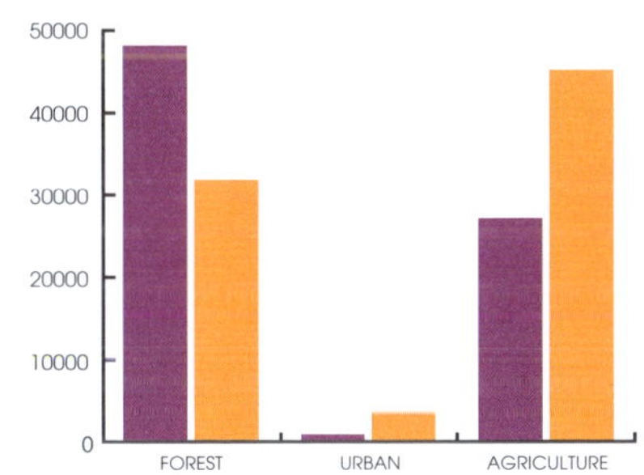

SAMPLE URBAN EDGE CONDITIONS

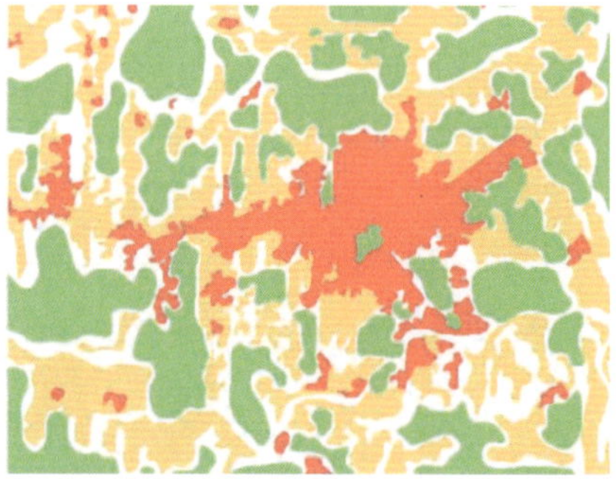

CURRENT URBAN FORM

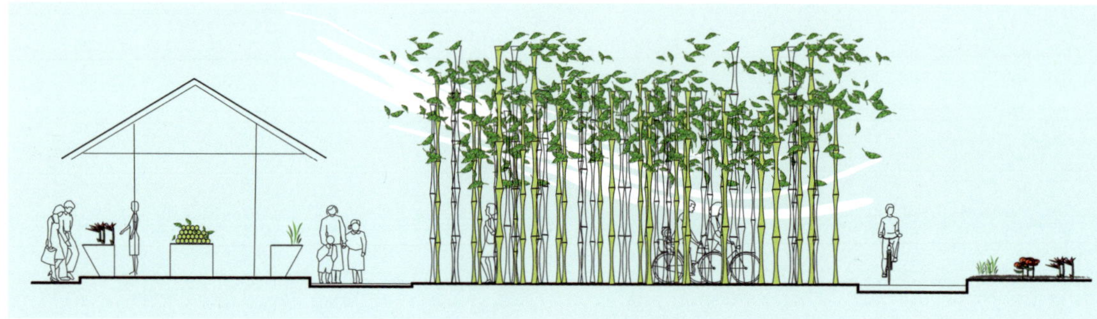

Agricultural edge condition - Bamboo wall between urban and rural land uses

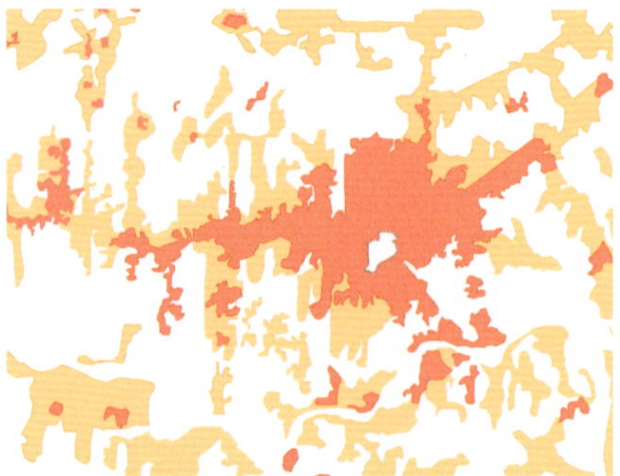

SPORADIC GROWTH, RURAL SPRAWL

Bridge overpass connecting urban areas with minimal disturbance to environmental areas

FRAGMENTED GREENERY

Ecological corridor running between urban areas to minimize habitat fragmentation

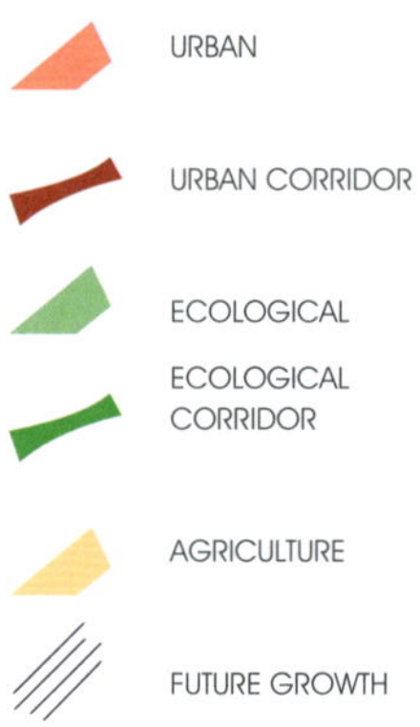

FINAL CONDITION

PROPOSED NETWORK FORM

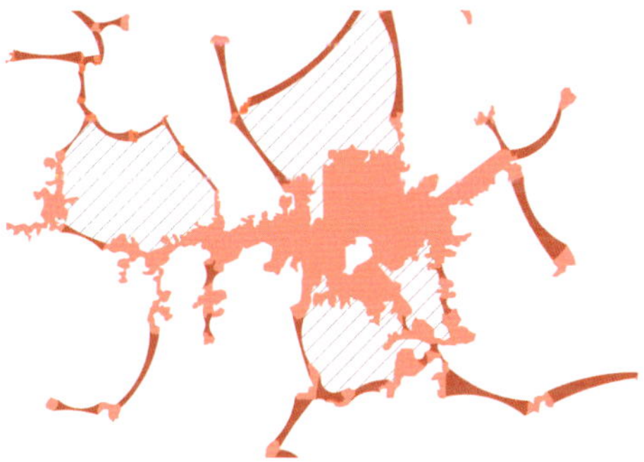

URBAN AND GREEN CONNECTION CORRIDORS

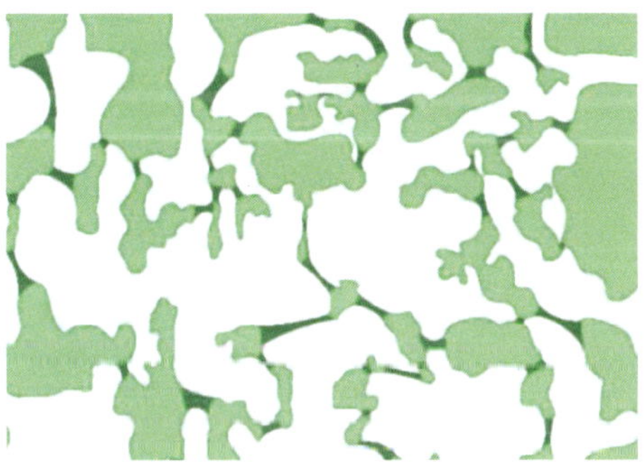

Urban networks connect outer populated areas directly to the city center creating areas for possible future growth. Green connections create ecological corridors to prevent habitat fragmentation. In between are agricultural areas, creating a protective barrier to potentially invasive species.

IMPLEMENTATION STRATEGIES

Implementation strategies will combine design, policy, and community based initiatives. They will:

- Create direct connections between peripheral urban areas and the city center.
- Create ecological corridors - all designated green space will be connected to other designated green space.
- Incorporate environmental elements such as constructed wetlands, reforestation and ecological preserves into the city system as semi-porous urban edge conditions.
- Emphasize independently-owned and maintained farming practices to limit the spread of the rural frontier area and to help contain potentially invasive species such as bamboo.
- Form urban empowerment zones which contain all the municipal facilities, services, and economies needed by the local community to exist relatively autonomously.
- Establish infrastructure networks, including (but not limited to) schools, clinics, parks and transportation, easily accessed within community centers.
- Implement land cost and entitlement incentives so that appropriate buildable land is available at more affordable costs and land tenure is linked to self-development.

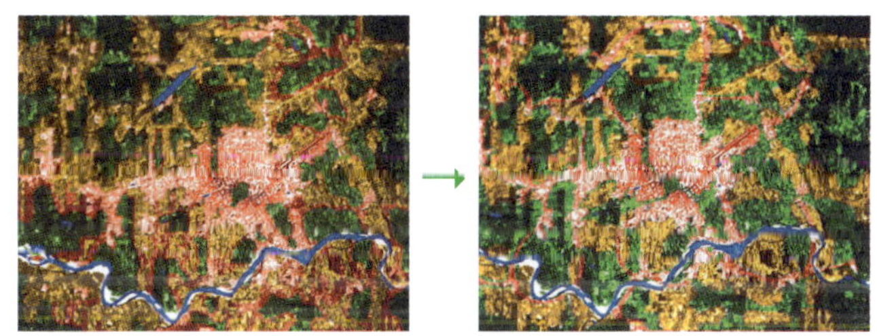

CITY ORGANIZATION

EXISTING MICRO-BARRIOS

The critical parameter in the current form of the city is the micro-barrio, a political entity created in an ad-hoc manner by citizens to provide themselves with a vote and a voice; micro-barrios may be as small as 500 people. Giving a voice to local concerns is undermined by the small scale of the local voice, which cannot develop larger scale resistance to the municipality and consequently influence urban form.

PROPOSED GRAN-BARRIOS

Our intentions are for the Gran-Barrios are to tie together micro-barrios in larger organizations. The organizations are intentionally determined by crossing physical boundaries typically used to divide constituents (roads, lot lines), instead tying together barrios based on shared infrastructural concerns.

ECOLOGICAL CORRIDORS

The dearth of open space gives an opportunity to leave sites unbuilt/protected to provide ecological corridors through the city that in turn allow the ecosystems of the periphery to reestablish themselves throughout the development.

TRANSPORTATION SYSTEMS

Primary transportation for industry is diverted to the south of the city. Within the city limits an extensive series of looping bus routes links together public infrastructure.

PUBLIC SPACE

The specific public space of the city not programmatically defined here is distributed with an even pattern throughout the city limits. It exists as much at the periphery as it does at the existing core. It is always connected to municipal functions.

EDUCATION-ECONOMY

The connection of these two is critical for both a productive and successful coexistence of the two systems. Agro-economy and agro-education are the primary way the city and the region will continue to exist. These spaces are intentionally distinct and separate from the municipal public space.

EXISTING MICRO-BARRIOS

PROPOSED GRAN BARRIOS

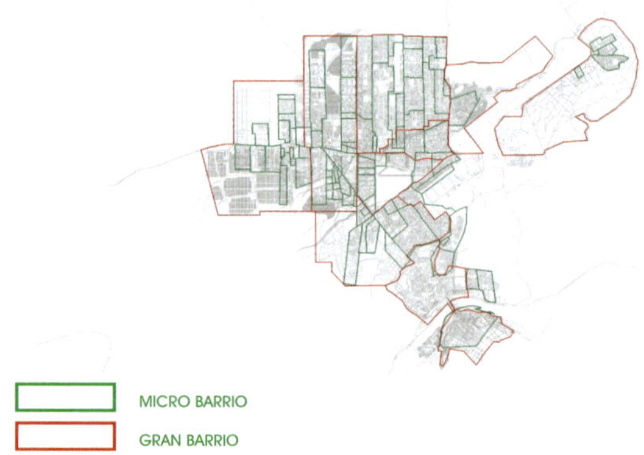

ECOLOGICAL CORRIDORS

PUBLIC SPACE

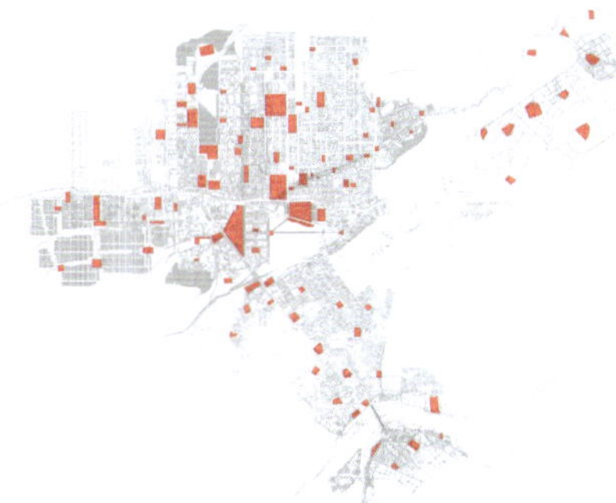

TRANSPORTATION SYSTEMS

REGIONAL VEHICULAR ROUTES

CITY BUS SYSTEM

LOCAL BUS LOOPS

EDUCATION - ECONOMY

EDUCATION

AGRO-ECONOMY

REFORESTATION/PERIPHERAL AGRICULTURE

BARRIO VIA QUITO

PAUL KING

Barrio Vía Quito, located on the south-western edge of Nueva Loja, will serve as the entrance to the city for visitors arriving from Quito.

ECONOMY

Barrio Via Quito will be a mixed-use residential, commercial and manufacturing neighborhood which will develop and support a bamboo products-based economy. Bamboo will be grown to the south where soil conditions are adequate. Several non-invasive clumping species will be grown in a sustainable forest certified by the Forest Stewardship Council (FSC).[1] Bamboo will be harvested and brought to the *barrio* for processing.

The correct growth cycle and harvest time for bamboo varies by product. Bamboo for textiles and weaving can be harvested in two to three years: furniture and composite materials require three to four years; and structural products require five to six years. Bamboo products can be divided into three broad categories: Crafts and textile products; furniture and composite products; construction products and modular housing components. Craft and textile products include baskets, mats and other woven products as well as bamboo yarn and textiles. Bamboo produces a naturally anti-bacterial yarn that can be used to make clothes. The production of furniture and composite products will require training in carpentry skills. Furniture and fencing products include bamboo flooring and "plyboo," a bamboo plywood panel. Construction products include those used for structural scaffolding and in modular housing units.

SOCIAL PROGRAMS

Barrio Vía Quito will be modeled on the housing projets of the Hogar de Cristo Foundation[2], a similar charitable project in Guayaquil. It will produce modular housing products for the upgrade and improvement of informal construction in Nueva Loja. Units will be pre-manufactured, assembled and then broken down for delivery and re-assembly on site. Those accepted onto the program will be sold a house on the condition they contribute to an education program for women starting up in business.

BAMBOO MARKET SQUARE

In addition, bamboo market stalls will sell finished products. The buildings at the center of the market square will house charitable groups and provide classrooms for adult education, retraining in the production of bamboo products, counseling and support.

EDUCATION

Trade high schools in Barrio Via Quito will specialize in teaching students the skills they need to become productive members of the bamboo economy. One high school will focus on "soft products"– craft and woven products including mats and textiles as well as clothing.

A second will specialize in "hard products," teaching the carpentry skills required for the production of furniture, composite products and modular housing components.

Both high schools will be located within a short walking distance of the central Market Square.

An apprenticeship program will be set up to provide job opportunities and work place training for students. At weekends, students will demonstrate the assembly of modular housing components in the Market Square.

The market will showcase the use of bamboo and provide a focus for activities in the barrio. At the market entrance, a "totem" sculpture will welcome visitors to the town. Beyond this, visible from the road, a large open-air bamboo pavilion will provide a showcase for the material's structural capabilities. Large groups will be able to gather in the pavilion, protected from the sun and rain. At weekends, there will be bamboo product making demonstrations and modular housing units will be on sale.

[1] This certification ensures that sustainable methods of growth and production are used. Adherence to the program increases the marketability of products, which can carry the FSC logo.

[2] www.hogardecristo.org

BAMBOO

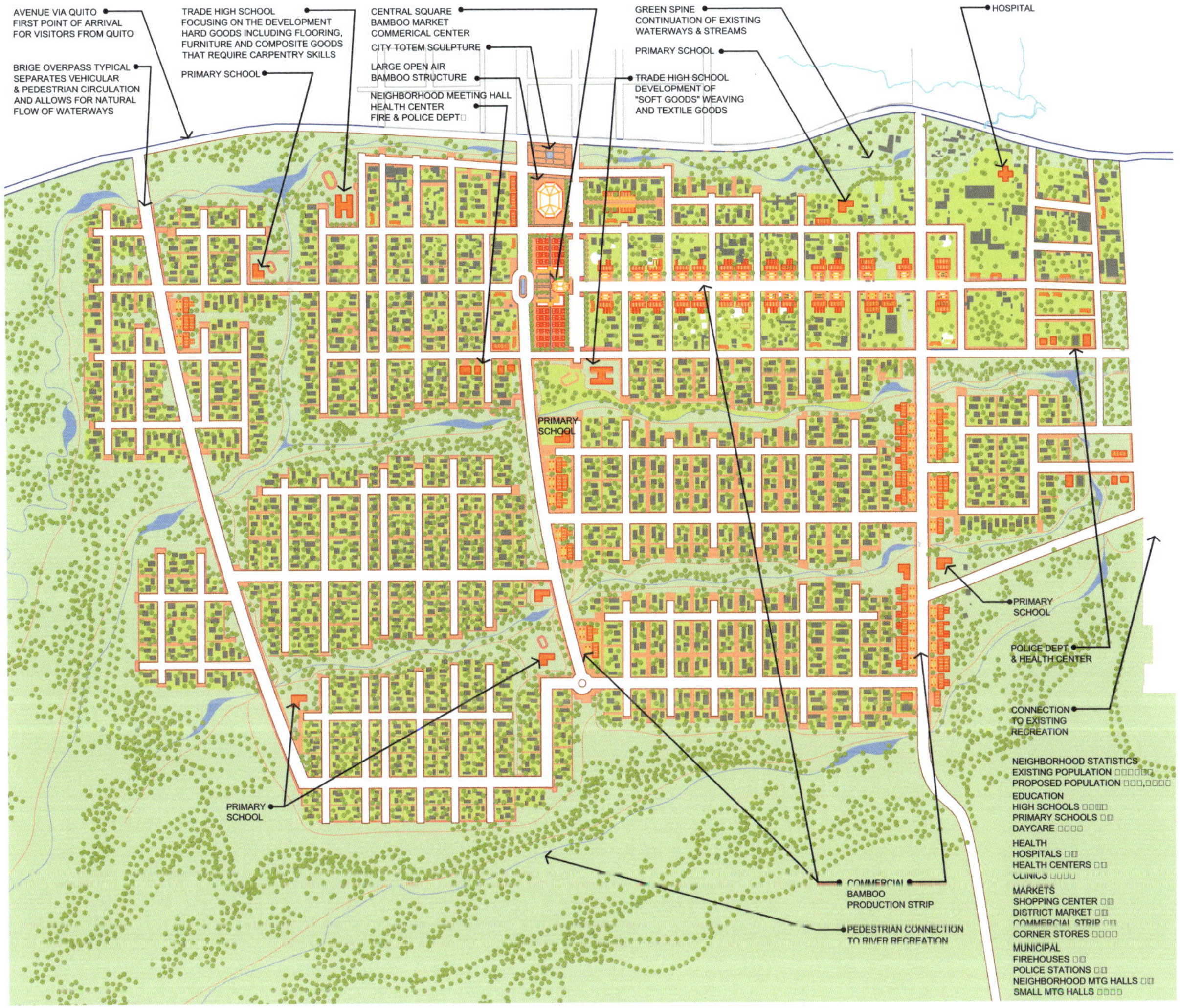

FROM THE TOP:
VIEW OVER MARKET BOOTH
MARKET BUILDINGS
CENTRAL MARKET SQUARE
LARGE CENTRAL BAMBOO PAVILION

MARKET

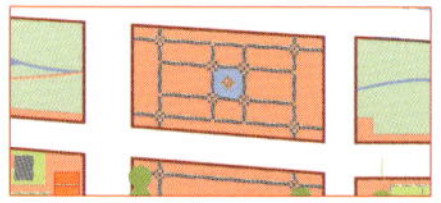

TOTEM SQUARE

Sited along Via Quito, the square contains the Neuva Loja Totem which marks the entrance to the city.

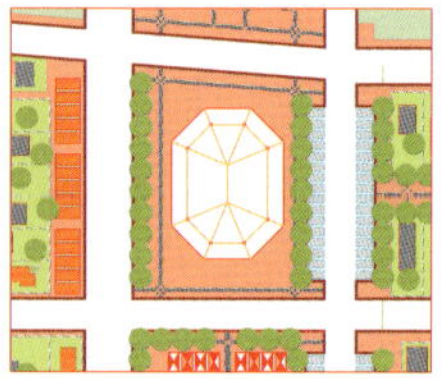

LARGE CENTRAL BAMBOO PAVILION

A large, flexible open-air space used for community meetings and the display of bamboo modular housing systems and other large products.

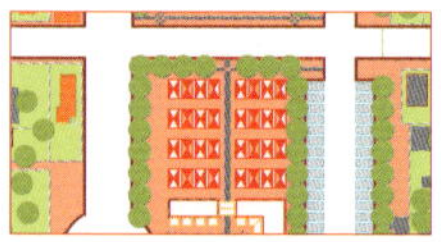

OPEN AIR MARKET BOOTHS

Smaller market booths selling bamboo products including baskets, mats, furniture, textiles and clothing.

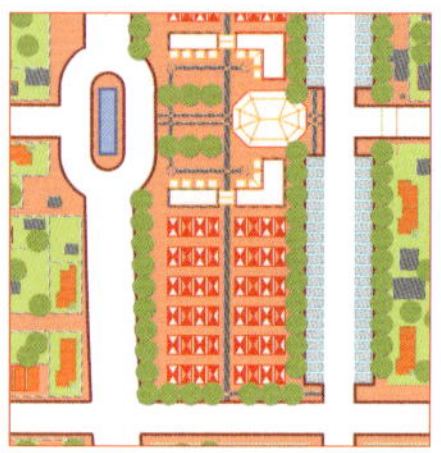

CENTRAL MARKET BUILDINGS

Contains classrooms for continuing adult education and training in bamboo skills and facilities for the bamboo housing.

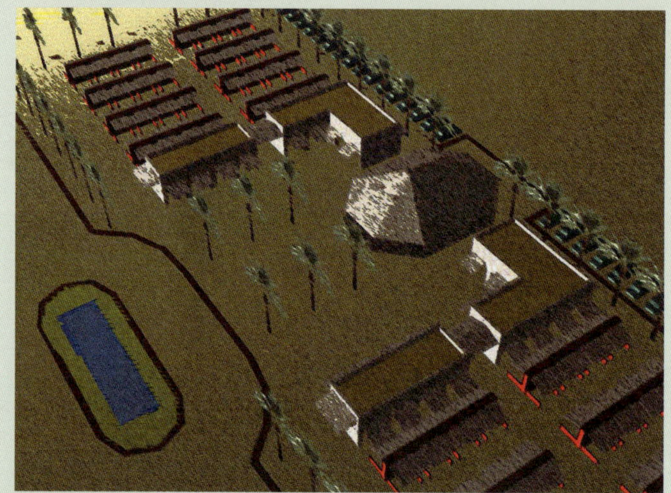

FROM THE TOP:

CENTRAL MARKET EDUCATION BUILDING

CENTRAL MARKET EDUCATION BUILDING WITH SMALLER BAMBOO PAVILION

CENTRAL MARKET EDUCATION BUILDING

NAPO – JULIO MARIN

MATTHIAS ALTWICKER

Informal development, which accounts for 40% of all construction in Nueva Loja, is taking place at Napo-Julio Marin. Informal development leads to a wide range of problems. Settlers tend to squat on land of questionable ownership and development potential which can bring them into conflict with the municipality, which controls land use, and with the land owners. Settlers typically form quasi-legal "communities" to gain legal ownership and/or services from the city. In most cases the official land owner allows the city to resolve the problem by providing necessary services. Municipal regulations on construction, the environment, health, and safety are not evenly enforced. The sense of community established by the original settlers breaks down after the city starts providing services and settlers soon return to a competitive, subsistence existence. The city, unprepared for the new cost of these unplanned developments, is unable to cope with the increased demand for services.

COUNTER PROPOSAL

To solve these problems, the municipality must adopt a more proactive approach to informal developments, following trends and identifying new developments at the earliest stage. It should erect micro-infrastructure for new settlements which puts in place three essential controls for informal building, neither making it illegal nor turning a blind eye. First, the city should define the limits of the informal development and establish property rights on the land adjacent to the settlement. Second, it should introduce a system for ad-hoc additions and development. The municipality will see a return on its investment in the short term from energy collection and control of the water supply. The city will also see a return on its investment in the long term by having infrastructure already in place for future development. The city starts providing services before development begins. These services are provided through environmentally sound methods to ensure maintenance over time.

FROM THE TOP:
SINGLE FAMILY HOMES CREATED WITH MAKESHIFT ACCESS AND SECURITY.
DEVELOPMENT ALONG ROAD NETWORK TO ACCESS ELECTRICITY
GROUPINGS OF HOMES FORCE CITY TO PROVIDE INFRASTRUCTURE.
HOMES IMPROVED IN AN AD HOC FASHION.

PERIPHERAL INFORMAL SETTLEMENTS 1965-2005

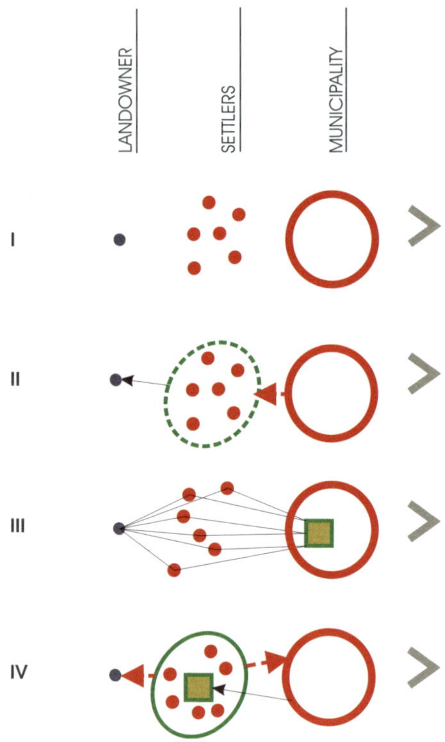

AERIAL VIEW OF LOCATION

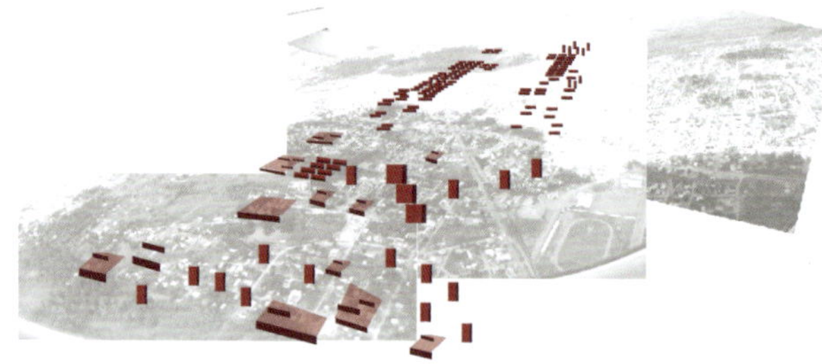

NEW SETTLEMENTS

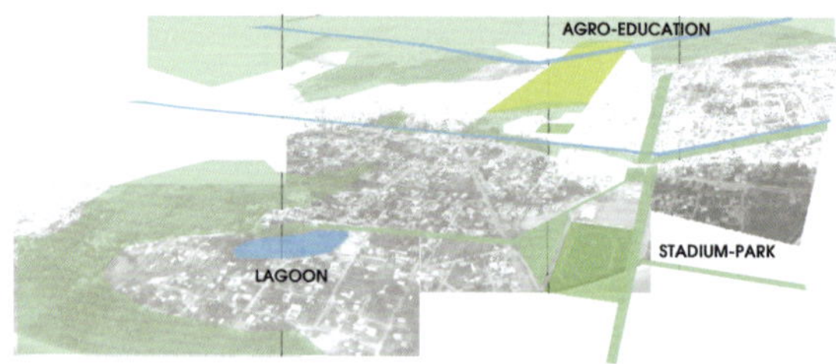

NATURAL NETWORKS

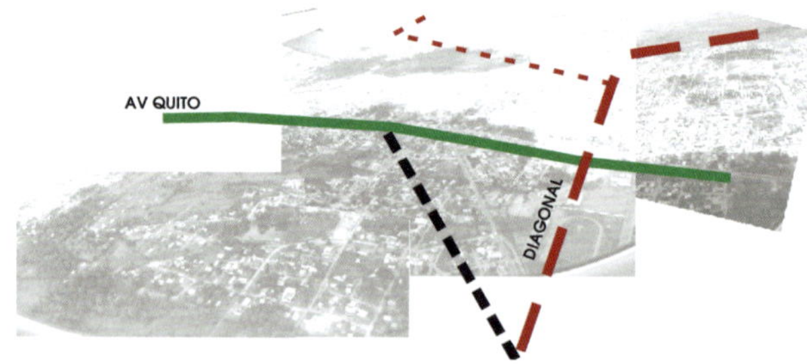

PRIMARY CIRCULATION

PUBLIC FACILITIES

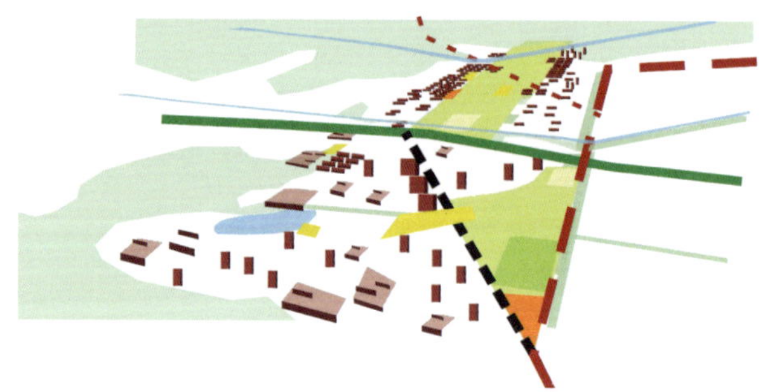

COMPOSITE

WALL INFRASTRUCTURE

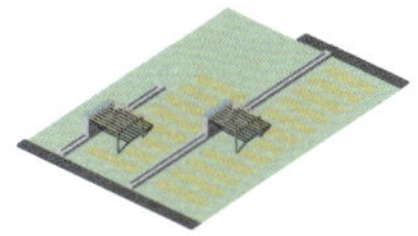

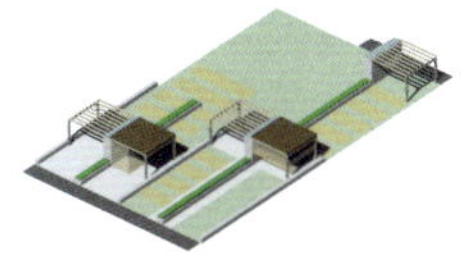

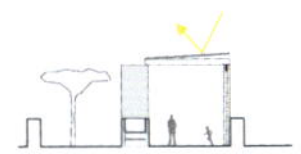

Infrastructure walls placed at current lot width; wall contains water collection on the roof and filter / bathroom in the core with hookups for kitchen+electric. Wooden roof shading structure to provide for those working outdoors in the area.

LOT-DIVIDING WALLS AND PROVISIONAL INFRASTRUCTURE

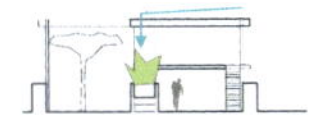

Secondary walls are placed adjacent to columns to halve the site; the yard is defined by user farming or low-impact industry or commerce. Plant bed is irrigated by rainwater collection from the roof. Additional unit is added adjacent to the existing core.

FURTHER LOT-SUBDIVISIONS, ESTABLISHMENT OF PLANT BEDS

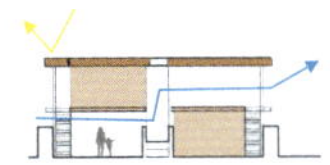

Lots are either closed to the back and adjacent lots or open to allow the owner to cultivate the adjacent site. Build out is done with whatever means are available; no more than half of the volume may be built out so as to maintain space for cross ventilation and a shaded exterior space.

APARTMENT BUILD-OUT

TOWER INFRASTRUCTURE

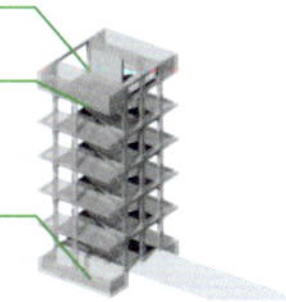

CONCRETE CORE STRUCTURE

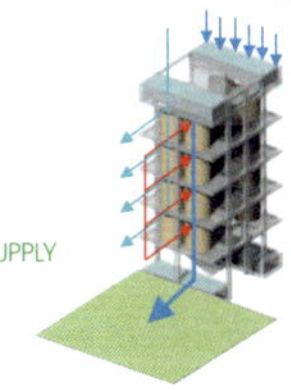

WATER COLLECTION AND DISTRIBUTION

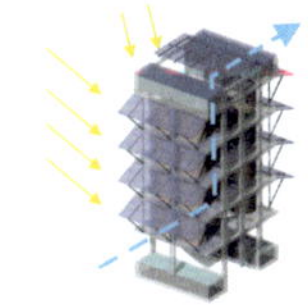

SOLAR ENERGY COLLECTION AND VENTILATION

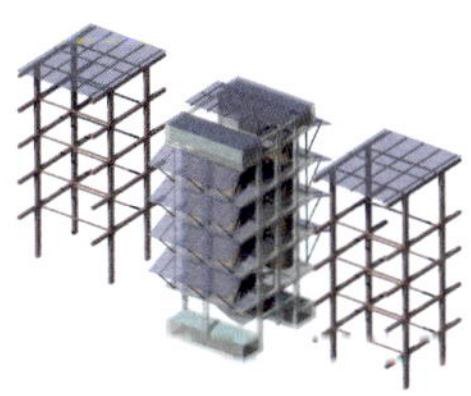

SECONDARY SCAFFOLDS + SOLAR TOWERS

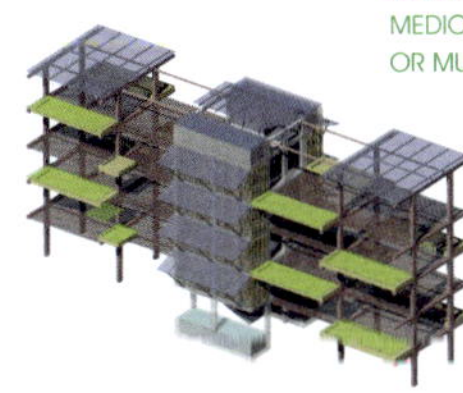

VERTICAL FARMING

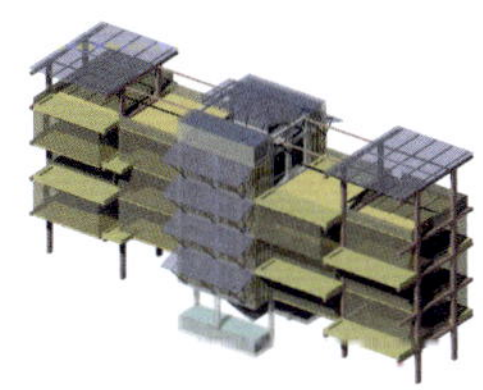

APARTMENT BUILD-OUT

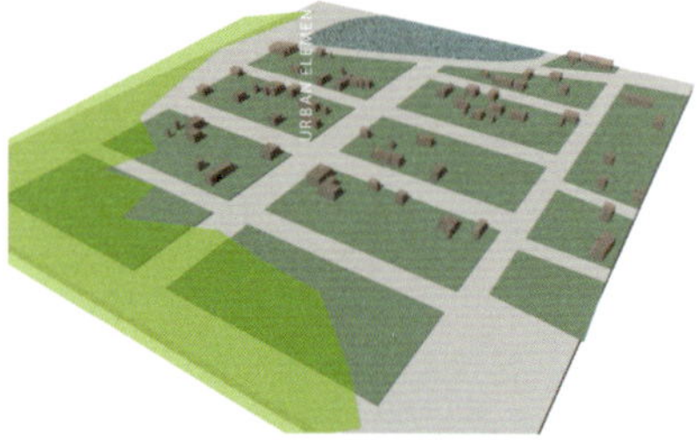

EXISTING STREET AND BLOCK GRID

TYPICAL BLOCK SIZE 50 x 75m

TYPICAL LOT SIZE 25 x 1m

FIRST PHASE - BASE INFRASTRUCTURE

TOWERS DEFINE CONTINUOUS GARDENS/WATER SYSTEM.

PRIMARY SCHOOL IS PLACED TO THE SOUTHWEST ADJACENT TO THE GARDENS.

WALLS DEFINE CITY BOUNDARY AS FARM STATIONS BEGIN LAND OWNERSHIP.

ROADS ARE DEAD ENDED TO LIMIT VEHICULAR THRU-TRAFFIC.

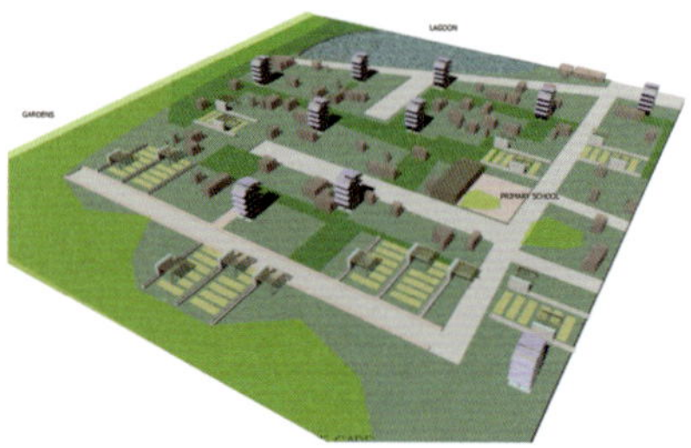

SECOND PHASE - DEVELOPMENT

INITIAL FRAMEWORK IS FILLED OUT AS NECESSARY.

WALL-BASED UNITS MAKE EXPLICIT CONNECTIONS TO STREET OR TO THE LANDSCAPE.

TOWER UNITS EXIST IN VARIOUS PHASES OF DEVELOPMENT.

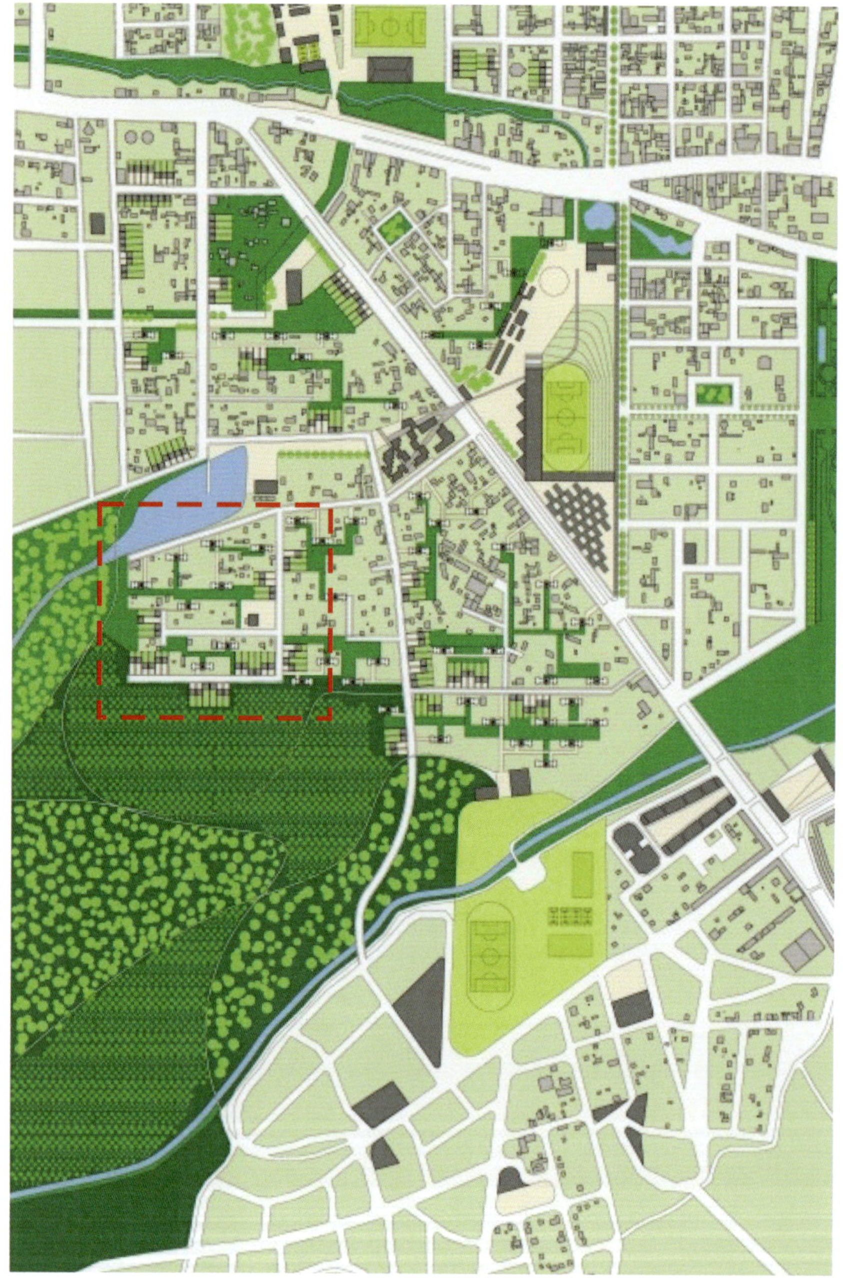

BARRIO SAN FRANCISCO

JOHN HILL

The development strategy for this built-up area north of downtown Lago Agrio is infill housing and evenly-distributed public infrastructure. Proposals include the ecological rehabilitation of flagging lots that coincide with the existing water network; the creation of mixed-use frontage zones with commercial strips; a green network of boulevards, parks, waterways and renewed forest; and a public transport network giving priority to pedestrians and cyclists.

SITE PLAN

GROUND PLAN

EXISTING BUILDINGS
NEW MIXED-USE OFF-SITE
NEW UNIVERSITY BUILDINGS
NEW GOVERNMENT BUILDINGS
NEW MIXED-USE (PUBLIC)
NEW MIXED-USE (PRIVATE)

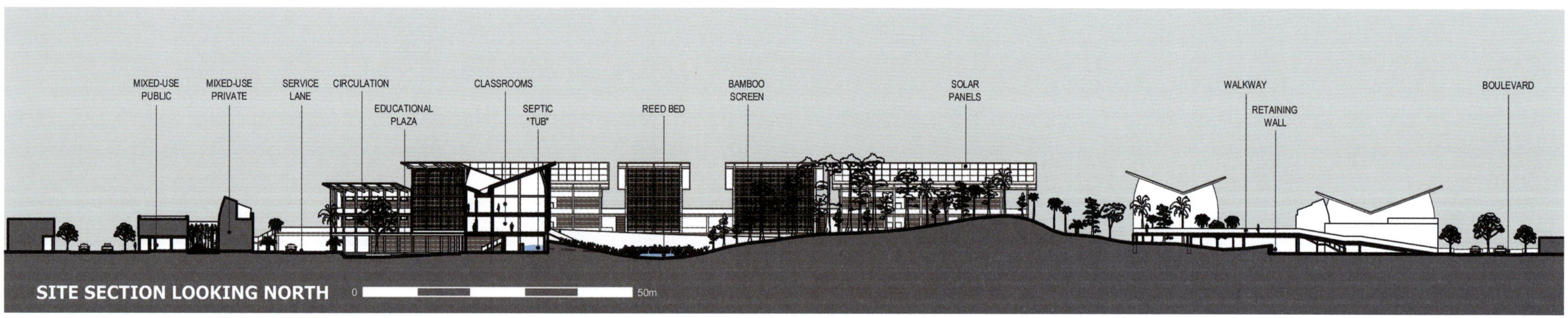

SITE SECTION LOOKING NORTH

TRIPLE GRADIENT DEVELOPMENT

This six-block development will be a major economic, environmental and social addition to the San Francisco barrio. The project consists of three layers from inside to outside (hence the name Triple Gradient): a central park linked to the northern boundary via an unobstructed linear park; new buildings for the Orienco University for the study of agro-foresty, medicinal research and forest conservation; and a mix of uses at the perimeter with ground-floor retail and housing. Additionally, a public plaza anchors the southeast corner, local and national governmental offices are aligned on the east edge, and a look-out tower sits near them. Each piece of the development is dependent upon the center – a hybrid public park and educational area of forest regrowth which contributes to forest conservation and brings the forest into the city. They all, therefore, have a vested interest in conserving it: the educational facilities working the forest; the retail outlets serving the university; and the public enjoying the park, plaza and look-out tower.

UPPER FLOOR PLAN

NEW UNIVERSITY BUILDINGS
NEW GOVERNMENT BUILDINGS
NEW MIXED-USE (PUBLIC)
NEW MIXED-USE (PRIVATE)

ROOF PLAN

NEW UNIVERSITY BUILDINGS
NEW GOVERNMENT BUILDINGS
NEW MIXED-USE (PUBLIC)
NEW MIXED-USE (PRIVATE)

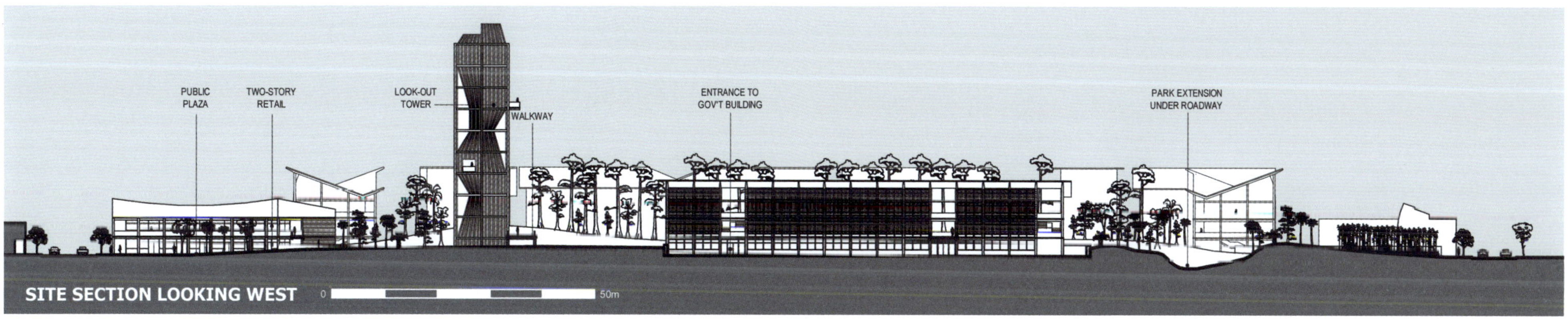

SITE SECTION LOOKING WEST

COMPONENTS

Around the perimeter of the development are small, deep, narrow lots that are built up over time. As well as this street frontage, there are entries to the service lanes between the mixed-use and education buildings; walkways from the street to the main, second level of the school; and "jungle creep," where the forest reaches out to the street, inviting passers-by into the park. The school buildings feature natural ventilation, rainwater recycling, sewage treatment, and exterior circulation that alternates from one side to the other, interacting with the walkways.

VIEW SOUTHEAST FROM EDUCATIONAL BUILDING

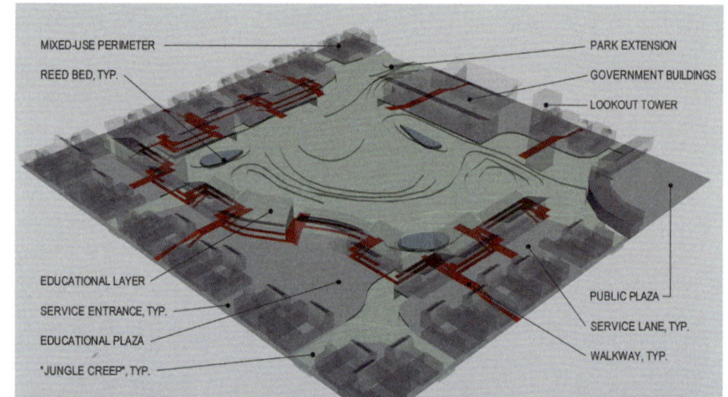

SITE DIAGRAM

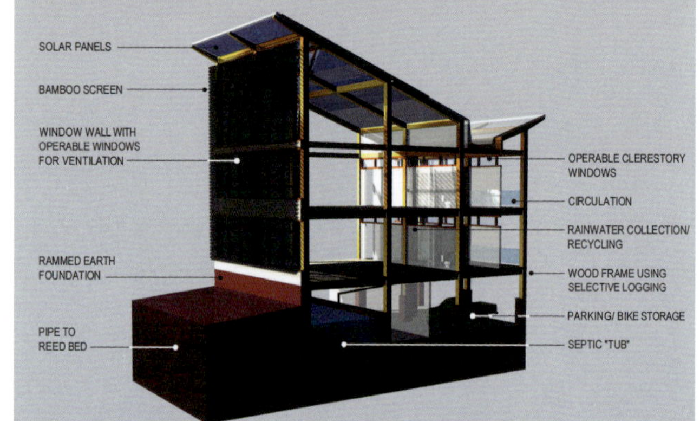

EDUCATIONAL BUILDING SECTION

SITE SECTION LOOKING SOUTH

THE ORIENCO UNIVERSITY

HOLLY KALLMAN

The Orienco River flows through the most important neighborhood in Lago Agrio. From the western entrance to the town, the stream runs northeast along Avenida Quito past City Hall and the Mayor's office.
In most growing cities, a stream like the Orienco would be considered a nuisance. Residents dump their garbage in it and bridges must be built to cross it. In time the town will usually decide to cover it over, running its waters through a drain pipe, until periodic flooding, with loss of property and lives perhaps, reminds the city of its forgotten watershed.

The Orienco could have a different future. It could become a "place," enhanced and built upon, even heavily, for a mixture of uses. It could become the site of a university for the Amazon.

A university sited here would also host primary and secondary schooling and provide housing and classroom space for community and adult education classes. It would train adults to become teachers, initially through a system whereby parents and guardians are paid to accompany groups of students to their local schools.

The Orienco University will work with the city to lay the foundations for a prosperous and humane society, by creating new centers of expertise and attracting residents concerned with the health and welfare of the community and the development of the region's resources.
Courses at the university will cover: health care; sustainable agriculture; arts and culture; soil and water remediation; forest and wildlife regeneration; renewable energy; renewable, locally managed, intelligent transport and building technologies.

The Orienco's position at the center of Nueva Loja, and its significance as a watershed crossroads, make it the ideal site for the new university. The current water level will be maintained, with the stream acting as an overflow system, a water recycling system and an amenity to enjoy. For the university to succeed, the Orienco must be developed as a sustainable place.

One idea is to implement a covered living system for processing black water. This must be carefully planned, since the University here will increase the density of the area. The campus must become a model for, and innovator of, such systems.

The construction of the university spans 20 years, divided into phases. UNESCO-UNITWIN's mentoring program will set up a plan for the university with set targets.

The university could be funded by OPEC and by multi-national oil companies since they have an interest in researching remediation technologies. The sort of long-term research needed to achieve real results would be prohibitively expensive if conducted at a university in the United States. This type of research would attract other research teams to the area to lead and teach.

Funding for the schools of education, biology and life science, and agriculture and forestry would come from large research universities, multinational energy companies, the World Bank and NGOs. The university will attract world-class educators to the region to fill the local skills shortage.

TOP: CENTRAL ADMINISTRATION WITH PRESIDENTIAL OFFICE, FACULTY AND ADMINISTRATION HOUSING, AND ARENA VENUE

UNIVERSITY OF NUEVA LOJA STRUCTURAL OUTLINE

UNIVERSITY DEPARTMENTS	
ARTS & THE HUMANITIES	CREATIVE WRITING ART HISTORY WORLD CIVILIZATIONS TRIBAL LORE PAINTING, SCULPTURE CLASSICAL LITERATURE CONTEMPORARY LITERATURE
SCHOOL OF BUSINESS	HOTEL MANAGEMENT SMALL BUSINESS ACCOUNTING LEGAL AID
EMERGING TECHNOLOGY	COMPUTER SCIENCE VIDEO GAME DESIGN COMPUTER GRAPHICS
BUILDING TECHNOLOGY	STRUCTURAL TECHNIQUES STATICS & STRENGTHS PHYSICS
AGRICULTURE SCHOOL	HORTICULTURE BIOLOGY ECOLOGY AGRICULTURE FORESTRY
BIOLOGY & LIFE SCIENCE	RESEARCH & DEVELOPMENT GLOBAL CIRCLES HERBAL LORE PHYTO-REMEDIATION BROWNFIELFD DEVELOPMENT
SOCIAL WORK	NEIGHBORHOOD NETWORKS SOCIOLOGY PSYCHOLOGY ONTOLOGY
NURSING	GENERAL HEALTH PEDIATRICS OB & GYN MIDWIFERY PREVENTION EMERGENCY CARE
DENTISTRY	PROFESSIONAL PRACTICE DENTAL HYGIENE
THEATER & FILM	

NEIGHBORHOOD TIE-INS

DANCE, THEATER, OPERA — NEIGHBORHOOD NETWORKS & NGOS — PARKS DEPARTMENT — HEALTH CARE CLINICS & NETWORK — PUBLIC ART, EVENTS

THE CENTRAL SCHOOL DISTRICT OF THE ECUADORIAN AMAZON IN NUEVA LOJA
TO PROVIDE AN EDUCATION FREE FROM LIMITATIONS, TO PLANT AND NURTURE THE SEEDS TO BRING FORTH A NEW GENERATION

- SCHOOL OF BUILDING TECHNOLOGIES
- SCHOOL OF SOCIAL WORK
- SCHOOL OF BUSINESS
- SCHOOL OF EMERGING TECHNOLOGIES
- SCHOOL OF THEATER AND FILM
- SCHOOL OF ARTS AND HUMANITIES
- CENTRAL ADMINISTRATION
- SCHOOL OF EDUCATION
- SCHOOL OF BIOLOGY AND LIFE SCIENCE
- SCHOOL OF AGRICULTURE AND FORESTRY
- SCHOOL OF NURSING AND MEDICINE
- SCHOOL OF DENTISTRY

KEY TO COLLEGES ALONG THE ORIENCO

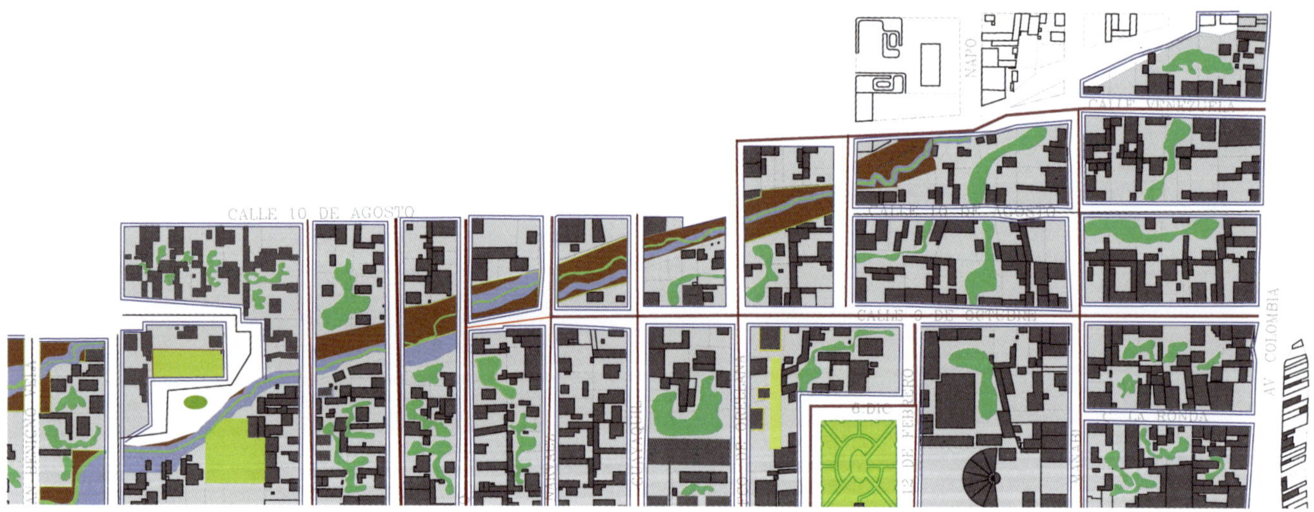

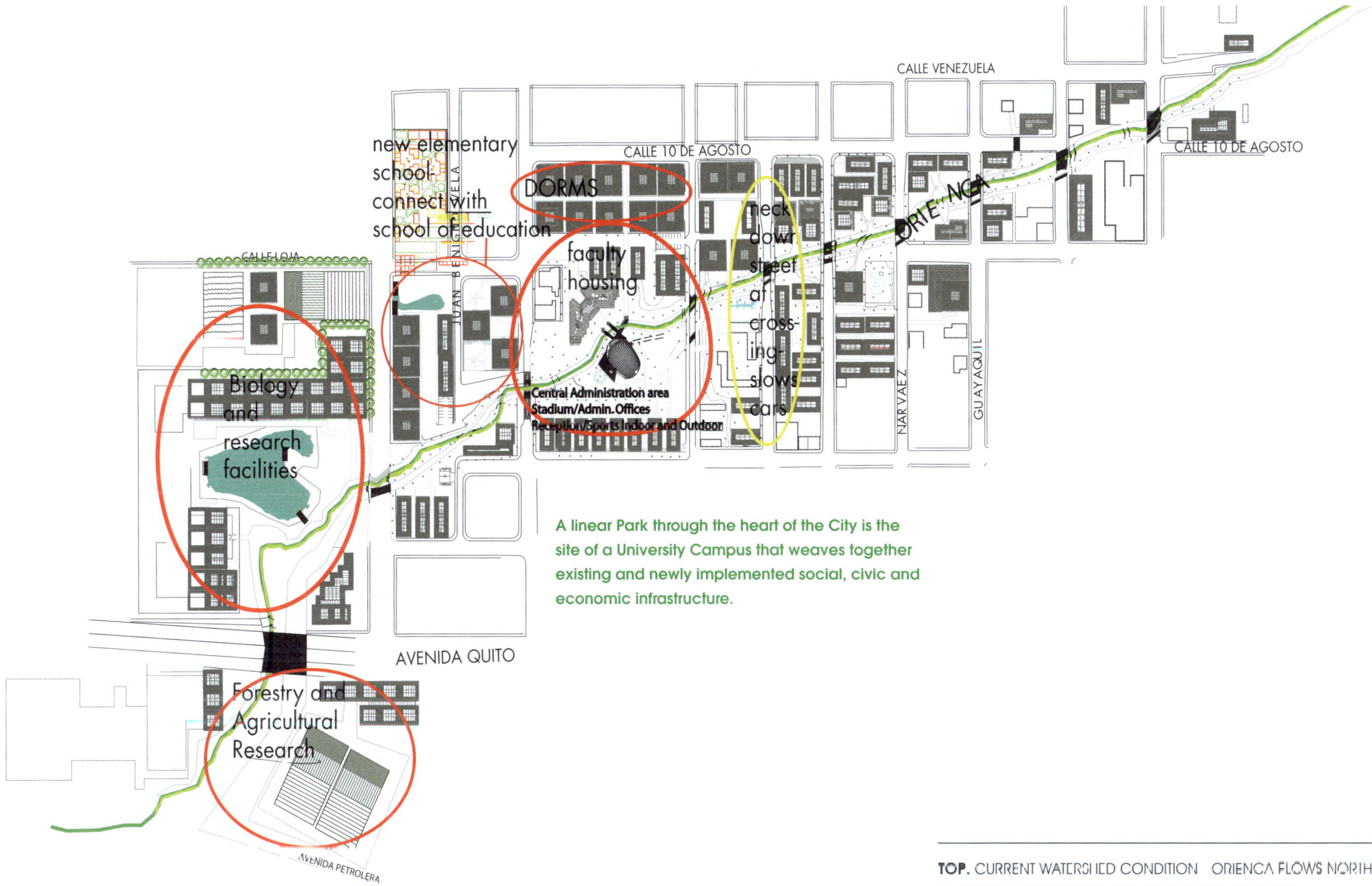

A linear Park through the heart of the City is the site of a University Campus that weaves together existing and newly implemented social, civic and economic infrastructure.

TOP. CURRENT WATERSHED CONDITION - ORIENCA FLOWS NORTHEAST & CURRENT CONDITIONS - POLLUTED AND A NUISANCE

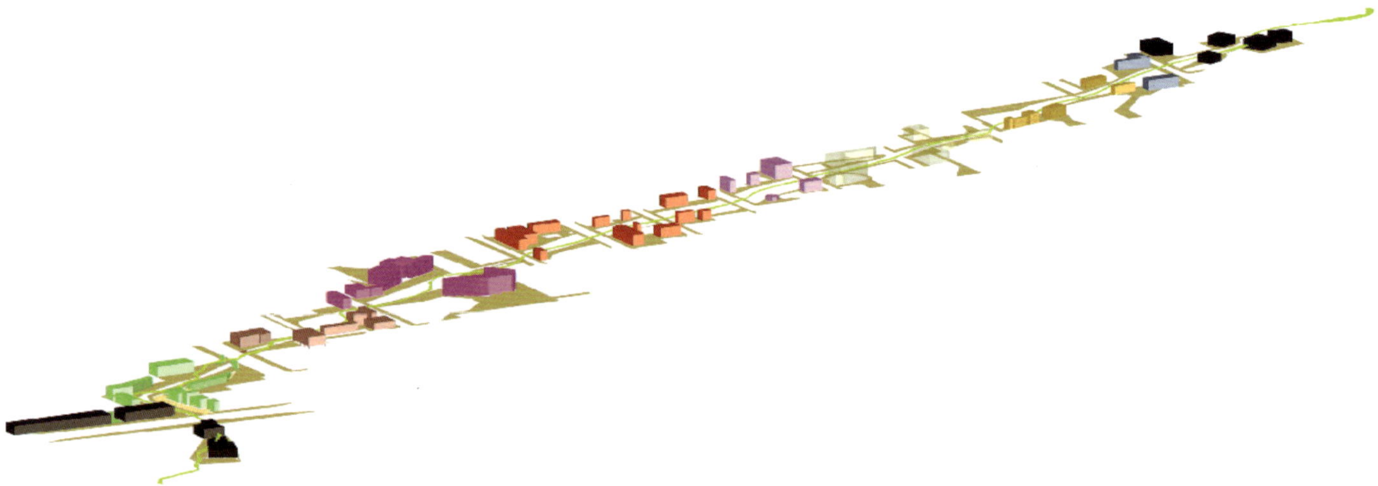

TOP: CONCEPT MODEL FOR THE UNIVERSITY
BOTTOM: ORIENCA UNIVERSITY: A LINEAR CAMPUS FOR A SUSTAINABLE CITY IN THE AMAZON

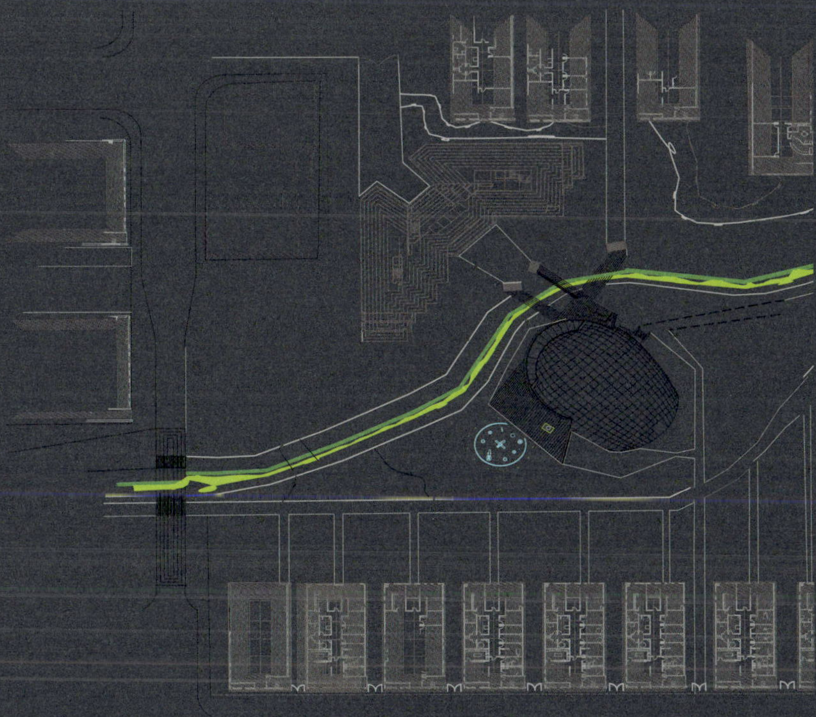

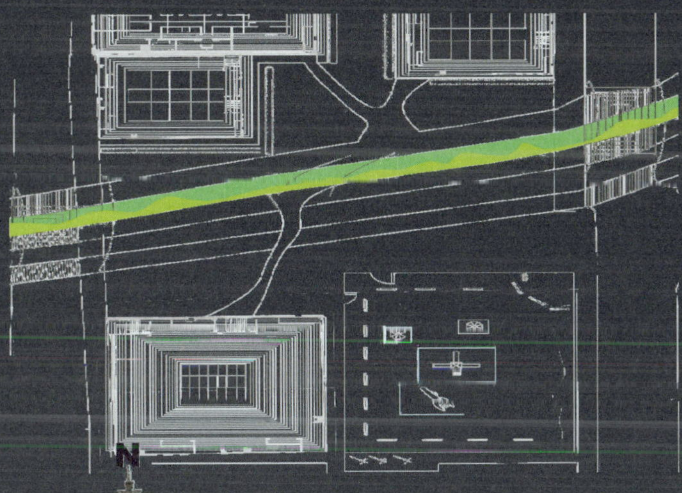

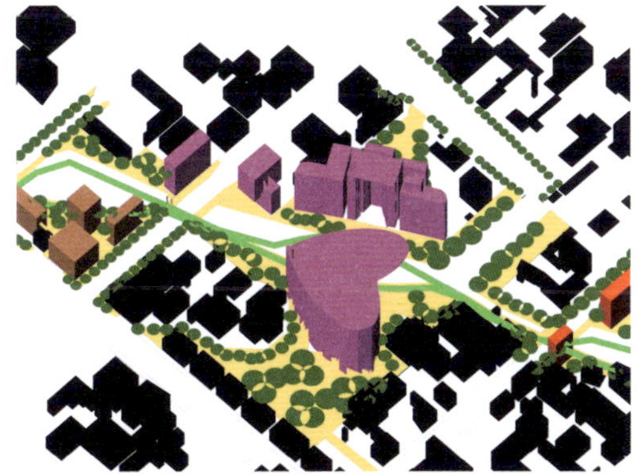

TOP: EARLY CONCEPT MODEL FOR CENTRAL ADMINISTRATION
& CURRENT CONDITIONS AT PROPOSED CENTRAL ADMINISTRATION

EL BARRIO CHACRA

CHRIS SYRETT

The redesign of El Barrio Chacra is built upon a dynamic, sustainable agricultural and forestry-based economy.

The barrio will be separated into 11 smaller neighborhoods. Each of these 'micro-barrios' will include a tract of forest located outside Nueva Loja. Non-timber forest products, jobs and other benefits derived from these individual forests will increase the collective and individual wealth of each micro-neighborhood.

The barrio's current population is 1,500. With the introduction of this chacra design scheme the population will increase to 3,000. Each household within the community will be given two agricultural plots to supplement their food stores and their income. Using the indigenous chacra system of crop rotation, households must keep a significant section of their holdings fallow. This will allow for the replenishment of the soil and canopy cover. The plots will be accessed along moveable wooden walkways placed on fallow fields. Each micro-barrier will have a central meeting and recreation space and additional infill housing. There will also be at least one shared store per community. The center will be a place to play sports, hold community meetings, stage political actions or simply hang out and relax.

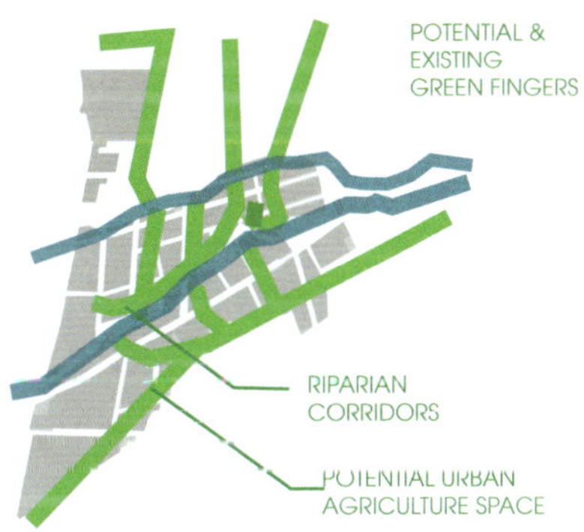

TOP MAP: PLAN OF INDIVIDUAL MICRO-BARRIO

IMAGES: EXISTING CONDITIONS

FOREST>CITY **CITY**>FOREST
COLLECTIVE FORESTRY AS ECONOMIC AGENCY & EDGE CONDITION

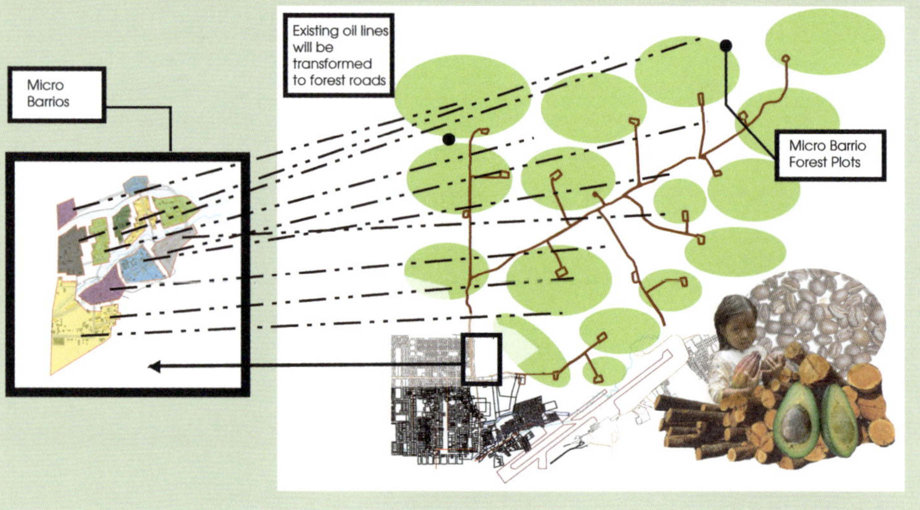

LIFE CYCLE OF A CHACRA FIELD

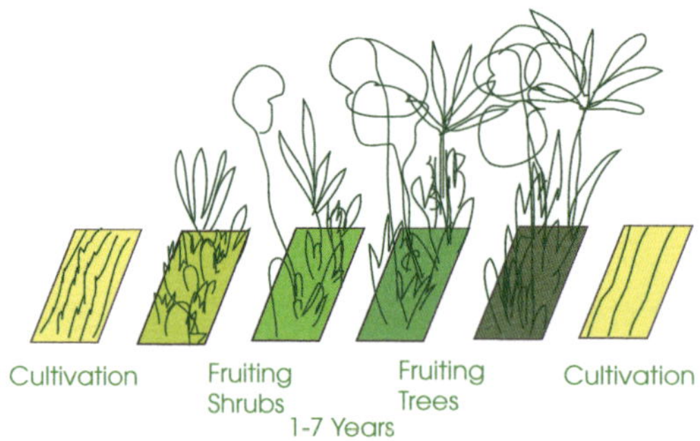

EACH HOUSEHOLD WILL HAVE 2 OR MORE CHACRA FIELDS

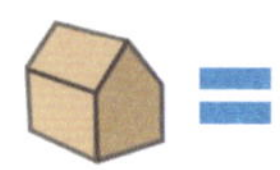

ONE HOUSEHOLD

TWO 180 SQ. METER CHACRA FIELDS

Chacra in Cultivation

Chacra in Succesion

Economic Agency - Each micro-neighborhood will have collectively owned forest holdings outside the urban limit. Neighborhoods will benefit in jobs, income, and in harvested food from the sustainable wealth of these tracts. Use and investment of the forest will ensure protection of these valuable resources and in the complex ecosystems of the rainforest. These holdings will also ensure that Nueva Loja does not continue to sprawl into adjacent forested land.

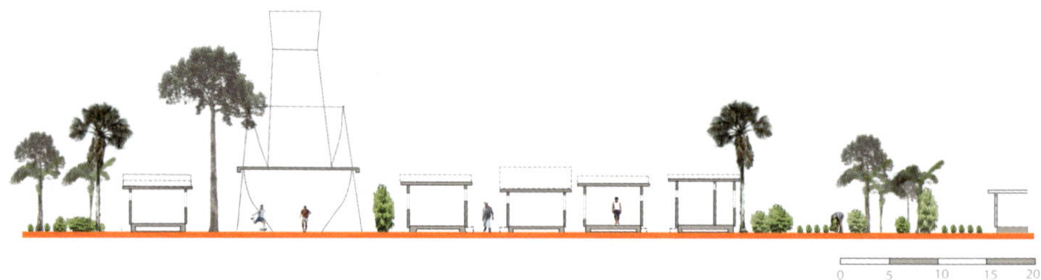

ROTATING CHACRA FIELDS WITH MOVEABLE WOODEN PATHWAY

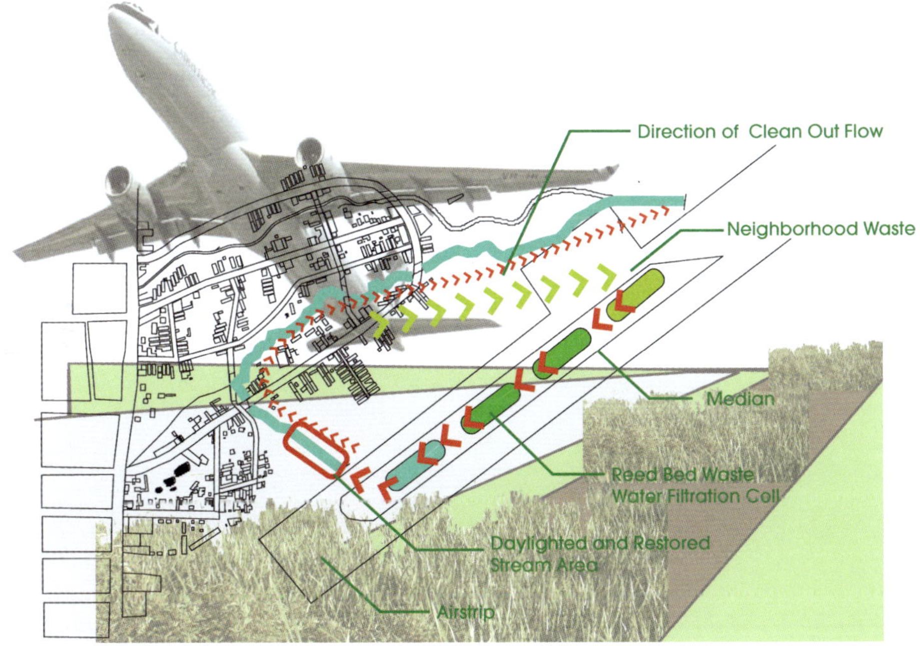

TOP: AIRPORT UTILIZED TO TREAT GREY WATER WASTE

BARRIO LA FLORIDA

ROBERTA KORCZ

La Florida lies in the northeastern section of Nueva Loja. It borders the airport to the north, a major oil camp to the west, lowlands to the south, and a small residential community to the east, it is located on what has been termed the petrowall – a stretch of the city dense with oil infrastructure.

Also influencing the character of La Florida, are intermittent fingers of rainforest that creep back into the city, creating a surreal juxtaposition of metal and vegetation.

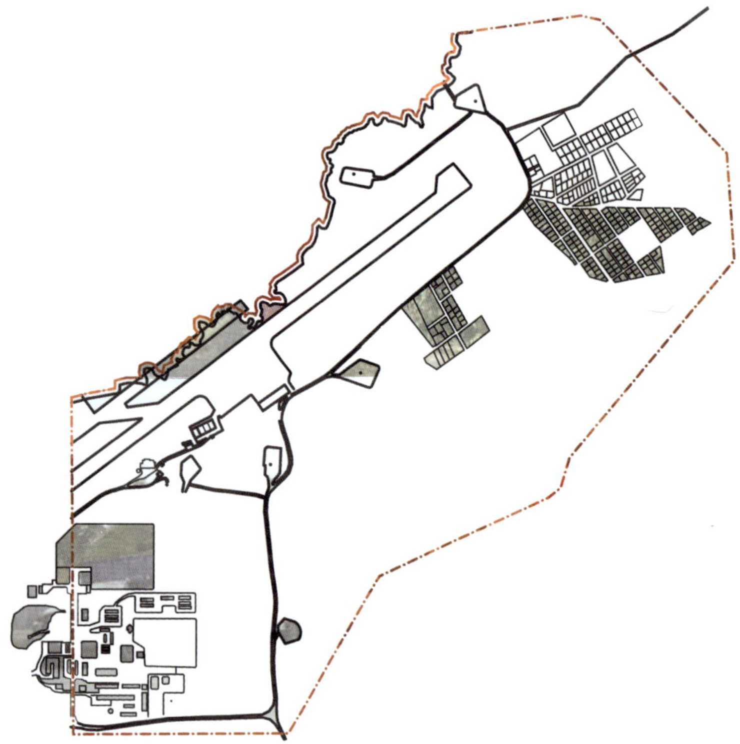

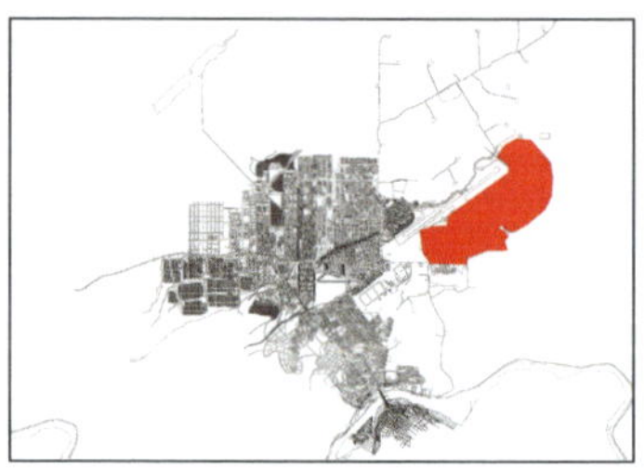

Zoned Uses

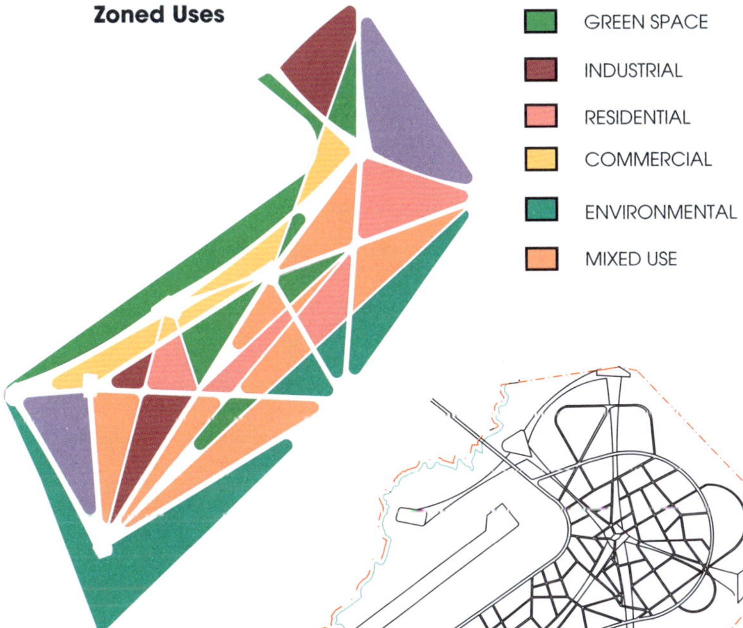

Site Analysis

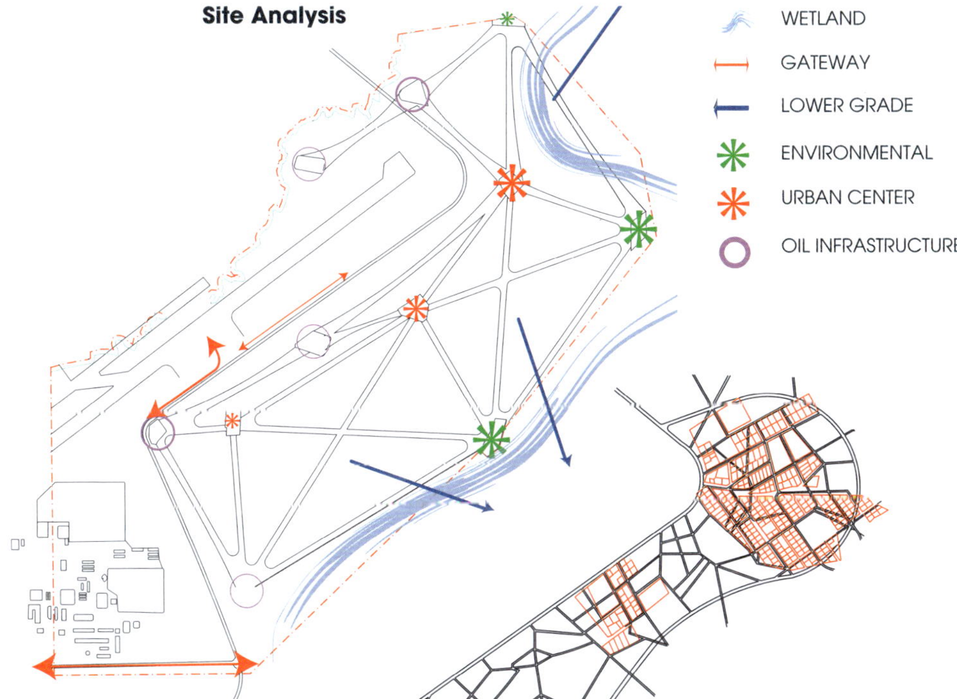

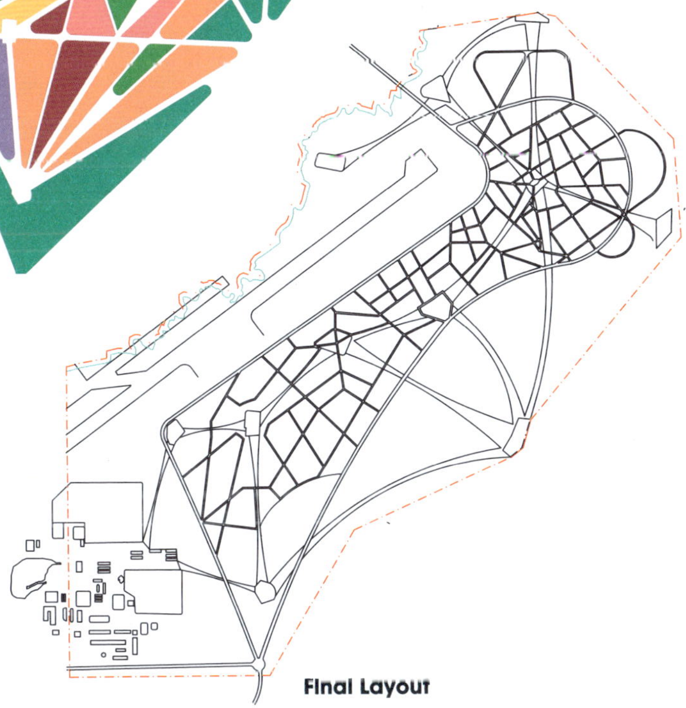

Final Layout

Street Networks

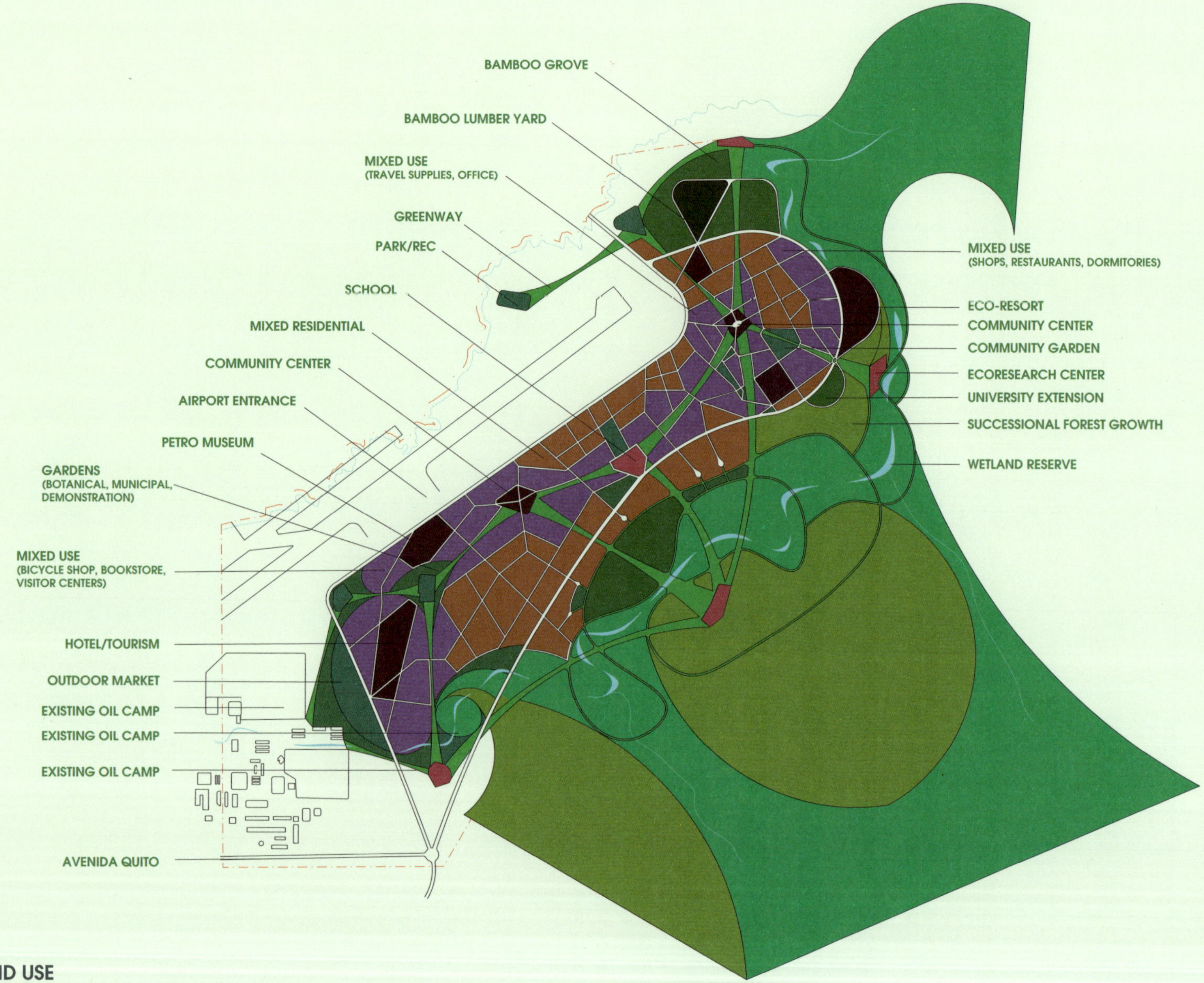
BAMBOO GROVE
BAMBOO LUMBER YARD
MIXED USE
(TRAVEL SUPPLIES, OFFICE)
GREENWAY
PARK/REC
SCHOOL
MIXED RESIDENTIAL
COMMUNITY CENTER
AIRPORT ENTRANCE
PETRO MUSEUM
GARDENS
(BOTANICAL, MUNICIPAL,
DEMONSTRATION)
MIXED USE
(BICYCLE SHOP, BOOKSTORE,
VISITOR CENTERS)
HOTEL/TOURISM
OUTDOOR MARKET
EXISTING OIL CAMP
EXISTING OIL CAMP
EXISTING OIL CAMP
AVENIDA QUITO
MIXED USE
(SHOPS, RESTAURANTS, DORMITORIES)
ECO-RESORT
COMMUNITY CENTER
COMMUNITY GARDEN
ECORESEARCH CENTER
UNIVERSITY EXTENSION
SUCCESSIONAL FOREST GROWTH
WETLAND RESERVE

LAND USE

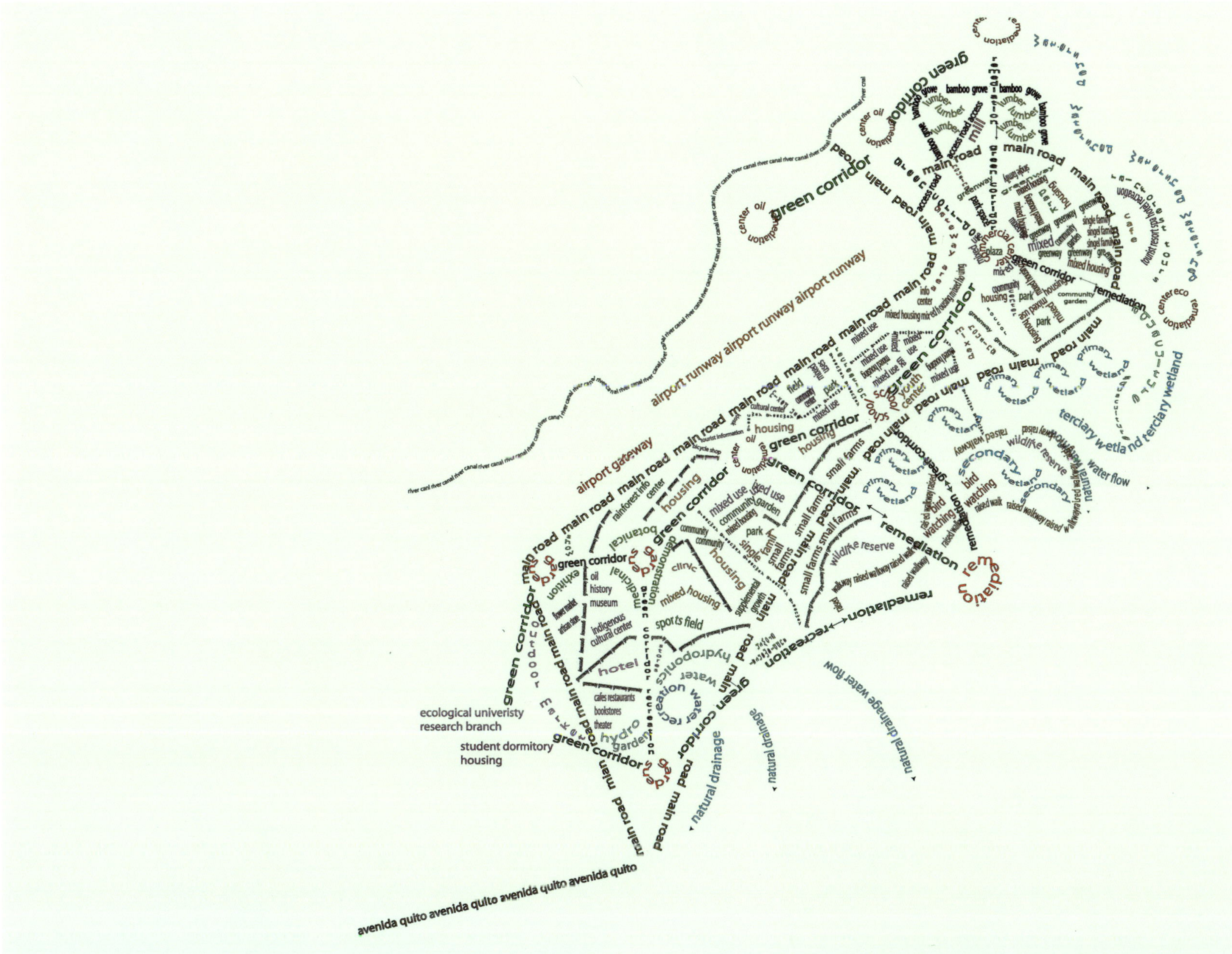

WORD DIAGRAM

ACTIVE GREENWAY

THE GREENWAY, WHICH RUNS THROUGHOUT LA FLORIDA, SERVES THE PURPOSES OF TRANSPORTATION, RECREATION, PHYTO-REMEDIATION, AND COMMUNITY COHESION.

ECO-LODGE

A ECONOMIC FEATURE OF LA FLORIDA'S POST-PETROLEUM FUTURE IS TOURISM. LOCATED NEAR THE AIRPORT AND ECOLOGICAL RESERVES, THIS NEIGHBORHOOD BENEFITS FROM ITS ABUNDANCE OF VISITORS. ESTABLISHING A TOURISM INDUSTRY IN NUEVA LOJA ALSO SERVES THE PURPOSE OF LESSENING THE STRAIN ON THE SURROUNDING AMAZON RAINFOREST.

COMMERCIAL CENTER

COMMERCIAL CENTER IN THE NORTHWESTERN SECTION OF THE GREENWAY EMBRACES PREEXISTING OIL INFRASTRUCTURE AS AN IDENTITY MARKER. IT'S AN EASY-ACCESS POINT IN THE NEIGHBORHOOD (ACCESSIBLE BY CAR, BUS, BIKE, AND FOOT) AND A NATURAL MEETING GROUND.

OUTDOOR DINING

AN ATTRACTIVE ASPECT OF LA FLORIDA IS ITS PROXIMITY TO THE RAINFOREST. THIS IS EMBRACED IN INFRASTRUCTURAL COMPONENTS, SUCH AS RESTAURANTS; ANOTHER KEY POINT OF IDENTITY.

The design for La Florida is based on a system of greenways connecting major nodes of the neighborhood.

Nodes are established based on the preexisting oil infrastructure. It is assumed that as oil runs out over the next 25 years, these nodes will morph to encompass the new area economies such as bamboo production, tourism, gardening, and ecological endeavors. As these centers develop, they will incorporate the frames of oil infrastructures as a component of place identity. The greenways connecting places will serve to create a walkable neighborhood.

Development with an eye on greenery rather than streets is aimed at limiting the need and desire for automobiles. A public transit system will run around the periphery of the neighborhood, providing easy access to the rest of the city. Second, these greenways will provide phyto-remediation to help clean the soil of toxins left by the oil. These networks of densely planted greenways will anger their way throughout the neighborhood. Towards the southernmost edge of La Florida is a semi-constructed wetland. This is an area at lower grade and serves as a natural place for drainage runoff. This wetland is to be developed as a reserve for recreational and ecological purposes. It is hoped that residents, tourists, and researchers will use this area to limit the stress on surrounding rainforest reserves.

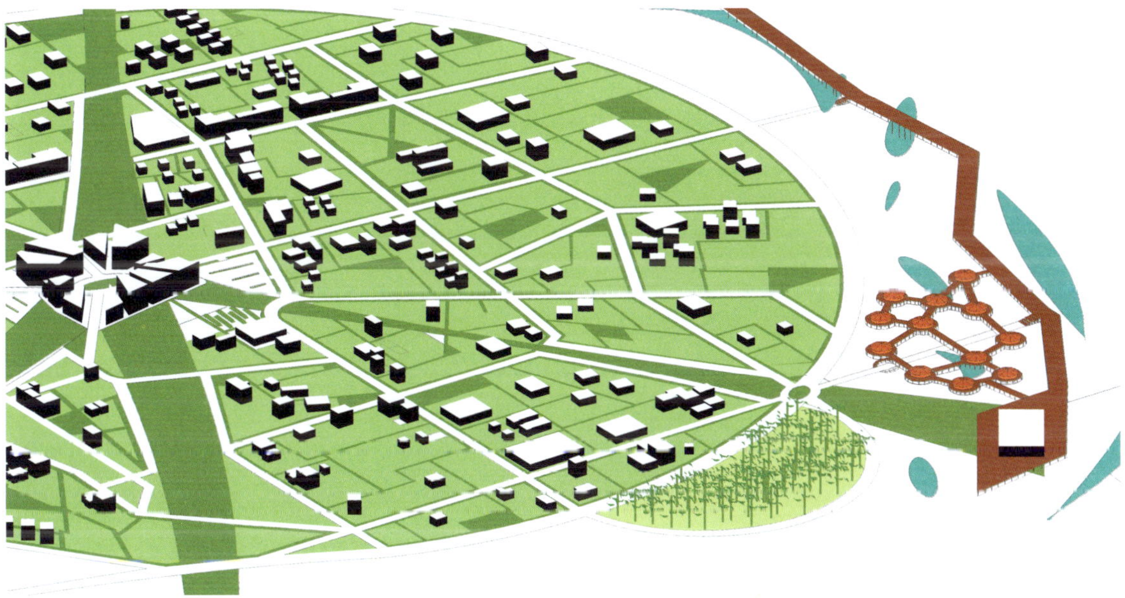

DE-CENTRAL PARK

PATRICK WEISEL

INITIAL DESIGN CONSIDERATIONS

The pattern of development here has been determined by oil infrastructure networks – its lines of connection then filled in by businesses and housing. It lies along an important edge of the city, with major national parks and ecological reserves to the east and south. The boundary condition is the merging of the built environment and the forest. Because of the airport to the north, building ordinances limit height allowances at certain locations.

This neighborhood to the northeast of the city will serve four major functions. It will provide a gateway to Nueva Loja from the airport and nearby national parks. It will establish the northeast edge of the city. It will create a precedent for the conversion of oil infrastructure into functional, attractive places as oil runs out over the next 25 years. It will be a catalyst for the region's tourist industry.
Geographically, this neighborhood will be divided up into three main areas of development:

1. To the northeast, the redundant oil wells will be preserved and set within new landscaping. These areas will be transformed into parks, greenways, and tourist areas while still recognizing the city's oil history.

2. The airport, which is central to this neighborhood with the petro-wall running horizontally through it, will continue to serve as a major gateway to Lago Agrio. The area will become a symbol of both the city's oil history and its sustainable future.

3. The easternmost section of Avenida Quito contains major oil camps still in use. This is the first stretch of the city visitors will see as they enter from the airport and the last as they exit to surrounding national parks. The juxtaposition of oil infrastructure and natural scenery has the potential to create a dynamic edge condition that is both attractive and ecologically responsible.

SECTIONS

PASILLO CENTRAL

MARKET ARCADE

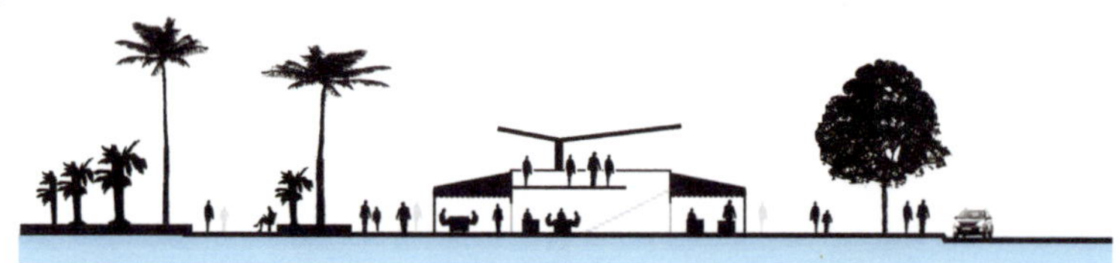

CENTRAL MARKET

Phase 1 • Edges Phase 2 • Northern Phase 3 • Forest 1 Phase 4 • Forest 2 Phase 5 • Axis Phase 6 • Oil Infra

FORCES + AGENTS = NUEVA AMAZONAS

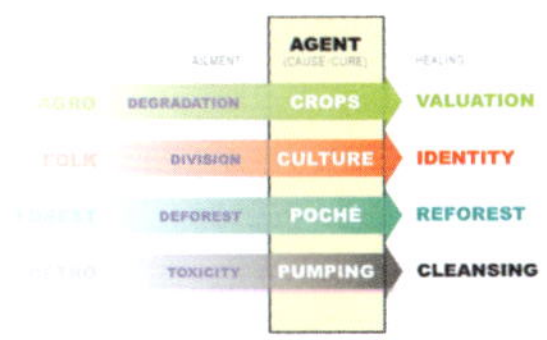

PROGRAM

1. STADIUM
2. BOTANIC GARDEN
3. CULTURAL CENTER
4. LIBRARY
5. ZOO
6. ARBORACULTURE
7. AGRICULTURAL TEST FIELD
8. MARKET SQUARE
9. MARKET
10. FLORACULTURE
11. FOREST PRESERVE
12. GROUND WATER REMEDIATION
13. COMMUNITY GARDENS
14. OPERA / PETRO MUSEUM

BARRIO LA ESQUINA

GARETH MAHON

All roads lead to the corner: La Esquina lies at the convergence of several of the city's most important arteries including the 'Diagonal,' the boulevard between the Rio Aguarico and Avenida Quito. Situated at the southern entrance to the central park, it will be both a destination and a residential neighborhood.

A multifunctional central plaza will serve as a gathering place, a park entrance and a cultural center, identifiable throughout the city. The neighborhood will have a strong education network that includes several vocational schools. The neighborhood's green network will include a visible, decentralized system of waste management.

LOCATION

EXISTING CONDITIONS: THE NEIGHBORHOOD BOUNDARY LOOKING SOUTH TOWARDS RIO AGUARICO

EXISTING CONDITIONS

Area	80 ha
Dwellings	440
Population	1600
Density	20 people/ha
Municipal Districts	9

PROPOSED CONDITIONS

Population	8000
Density	100 people/ha

REQUIRED INFRASTRUCTURE

Medical Center	1
Medical Clinic	6
Daycare Centers	6
Primary School	3
Seconday School	1
Police Station	1

SYSTEMS AND NETWORKS

PARKS, PLAYING FIELDS, ALLOTMENTS AND RECYCLING CENTERS.

- decentralized recycling centers
- pedestrian network
- protected open green space

CIRCULATION

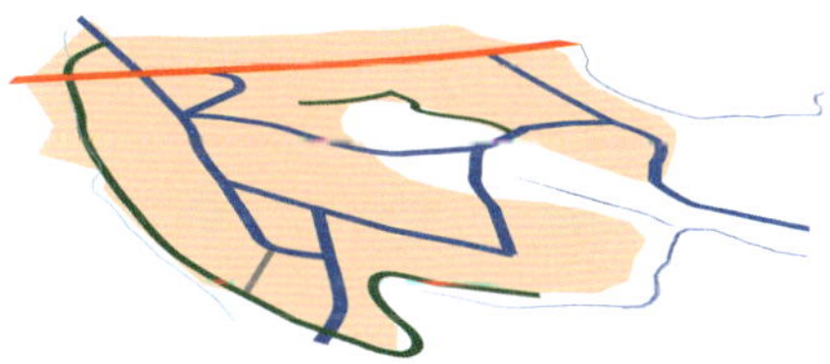

'The Diagonal' boulevard
30-35m wide property line to property line
Four car lanes and bike lanes
Commercial buildings and outdoor eating on the sidewalk

Secondary streets
15m wide property line to property line
Two car lanes plus one bike lane
Commercial activity at street level

Greenways
3-4m wide
Two way bike lanes and pedestrian walkway

EDUCATION

- Shared sports fields
- Schools: vocational, high and grade schools

RESOURCES
Clinic within 250 meters
Neighborhood center within 500 meters
Shared sports fields
Park or allotments within 250 meters

LINKS
Greenway to school | Bus route to school

COMMUNITY CENTERS

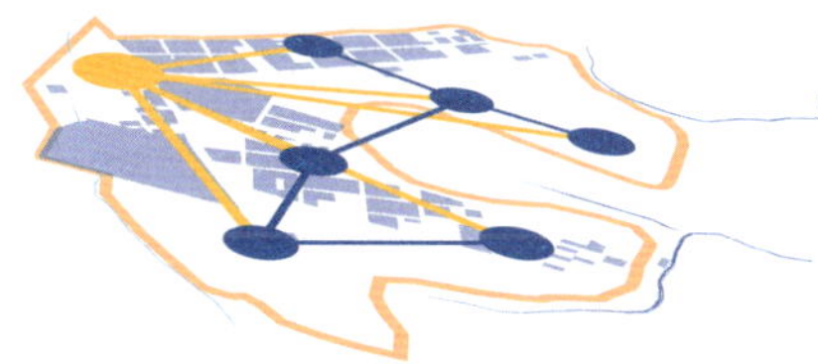

Commercial use and social services
Neighborhood identity
Link to the greater city
City to barrio link
Direct bus, greenway and main road/boulevard

BARRIO CENTER
Emergency services – fire, police and medical center | Main local attractor | Barrio identity |
Park or plaza

BARRIO TO NEIGHBORHOOD LINK
Indirect bus, greenway and mixed-use streets linked via other neighborhoods

NEIGHBORHOOD CENTER
Basic services, community center and health clinics | local identity | open space
Serves 1,500 people

NEIGHBORHOOD TO NEIGHBORHOOD LINK
Greenway link and mixed-use streets
Shared resources

Minimum distance between each is 500 meters

BOUNDARY AND PRESERVED LOTS

The boundary expands the limits of the existing built perimeter to within 15 meters of all waterways. The edge is maintained with agricultural land including agro-forestry.
Empty lots, indicated in the city plans, are removed.

EXISTING CONDITIONS AND TOPOGRAPHY

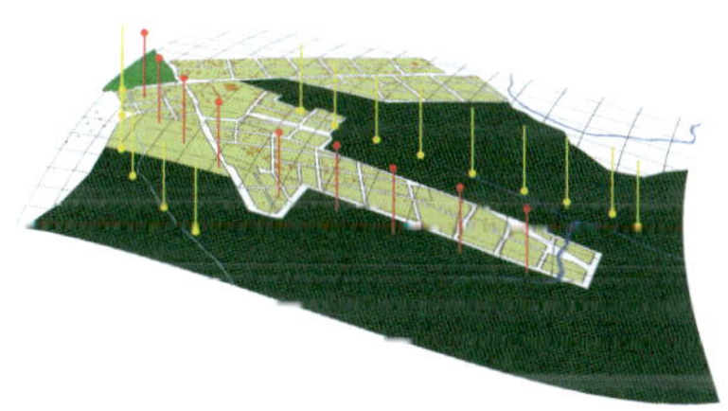

Existing formal and informal expansion along higher elevations.
The total elevation change across the site is 10-15 meters.
The ridge line along the northern edge of the barrio provides an elevation change for the plaza.
Streams and lower drainage areas.

1. Central park
2. Plaza, park, cultural center and entrance to the central park
3. Commercial and administrative center
4. Solid waste management: recycling and reuse
5. Solid waste management: composting
6. Central allotments
7. Community sports fields

NEW DEVELOPMENT BLOCKS

EXISTING BLOCKS, LOTS AND BUILDINGS

COMMUNITY CENTERS

EDUCATIONAL

ALLOTMENTS AND COMMUNITY GARDENS

NEIGHBORHOOD PARKS AND PROTECTED OPEN SPACE

EDGE AGRICULTURE AND AGRO-FORESTRY

0m 100m 500m

1. Entrance to the central park
2. Park with sloped terracing
3. Volleyball courts and childrens' playground
4. Outdoor theater/volleyball court
5. Plaza overlook
6. Upper plaza
7. Terraced water management swales
8. Residential with commercial on plaza level
9. Residential – municipal – cultural
10. Lower street plaza
11. Residential with commercial on lower level
12. Mixed use one way street
13. Narrow arcade
14. Boulevard – the 'Diagonal'

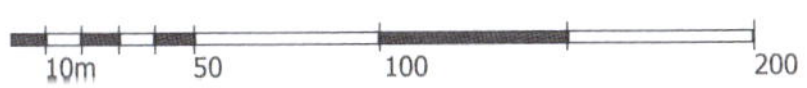

Street level public space

Plaza, sidewalks, streets, ground floor buildings

PLAZA
CENTER
MEETING PLACE
RELAXATION
BUSINESS
MARKET
ICONIC
DESTINATION
HOME
CONSIDERATIONS
SUSTAINABILITY
CIRCULATION
SHADE
SEATING
SURFACE
WATER

HAPPENINGS
MUSIC
PEOPLE WATCHING
SPORTS
BAND STAND - RETRETA
KIOSK
DAILY MARKET
LOTTERY
SHOESHINE
EDUCATION
VENDORS
MOVEMENT
GO AROUND IT
GO THROUGH IT
PARKS ON IT
PUBLIC TRANSPORTATION

BICYCLES
CARS
ECUADOR
POWER
TOURISM
SPANISH - COLONIAL
RELIGIOUS - CIVIC
GOVERNMENT - MILITARY
ATTRACTOR
BOULEVARD + PLAZA
PLAYGROUND - PARQUES - PLAZA
CLASS ISSUES
MAYBE
PROSTITUTION
DRUGS
ROBBERY

BARRIO ISEGORIDA

ALAN FOX

Isegorida will be a new artisan neighborhood for 10,000 residents, its form echoing the welcoming proportion and scale of a medieval European city. The squares, alleys, passageways, parks and streets will feel like the extension of residents' living rooms. This will encourage a sense of community and inclusion. Amenities will all be within a 20 minute walk of each other, reducing transport needs.

EXISTING CONDITIONS
PUBLIC INFRASTRUCTURE

EDUCATION	
DAYCARE CENTER	7
PRIMARY SCHOOL	4
HIGH SCHOOL	1
TRADE SCHOOL	1
HEALTH	
CLINIC	7
HEALTH CENTER	2
HOSPITAL	1

MARKET	
CORNER STORE	10
STREET MARKET	3
SHOPPING CENTER	1
MUNICIPAL	
MEETING HALL	3
POLICEMEN	30
FIREMEN	4
PRISON CELLS	10

1. Neighboring New Neighborhood: La Esquinia
2. Neighboring New Neighborhood: Puerto Aguarico
3. Waterwheel Bridge
4. Avenida Quito
5. Agora
6. Sucumbios Square
7. Industrial Enclave
8. High School
9. Technical School
10. Fuggeri Retirement Enclave
11. Stormwater Treatment and Retention Streams
12. Wastewater Treatment Wetlands
13. Sports Stadium
14. Mountain Biking Tracks and Trails
15. Open Field and Woods
16. Wet Park
17. Beach
18. Beer Garden
19. Artisan Enclave

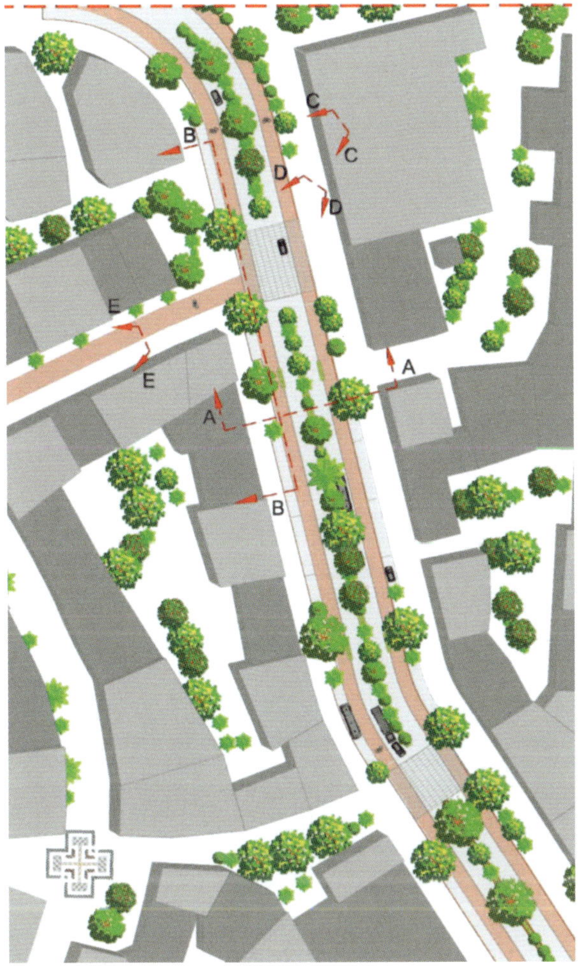

Avenida Quito is located as item 4 on the previous page.
Sections D-D and E-E are shown on the following two pages.

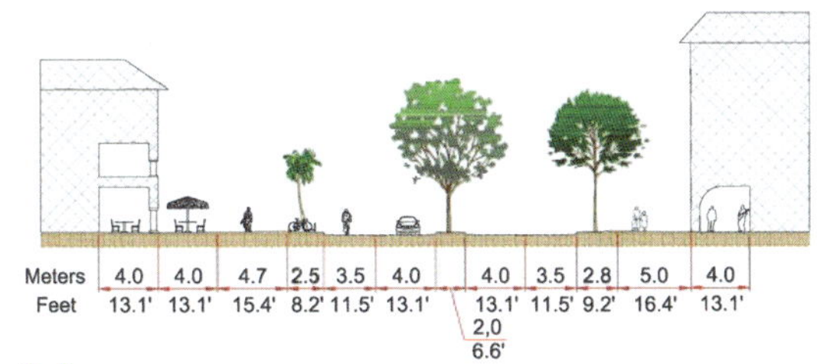

A-A

B-B

C-C

D-D AVENIDA QUITO

E-E SIDE STREET

WATERWHEEL BRIDGE

The Waterwheel Bridge, like the improved Avenida Quito, will serve as a destination as well as a transport path. The sidewalk along half the length of the bridge will be widened to allow people to leisurely make their way across. This sidewalk will also have benches, trees and small kiosks. The waterwheel will encircle the bridge at its center, the large machine serving as a point of interest and a gateway between neighborhoods. It will be powered by the river below, connecting the people to their environment.

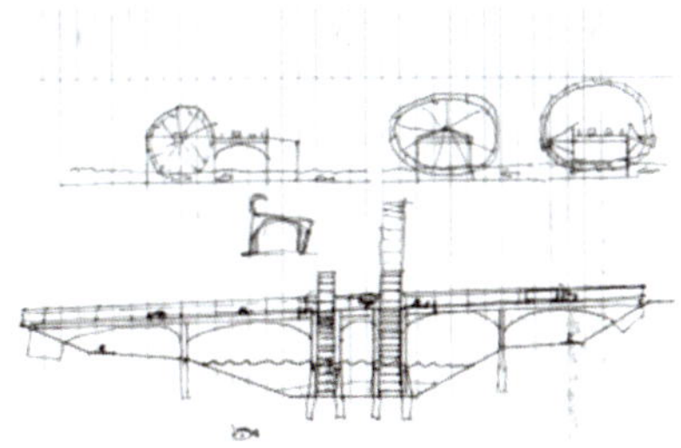

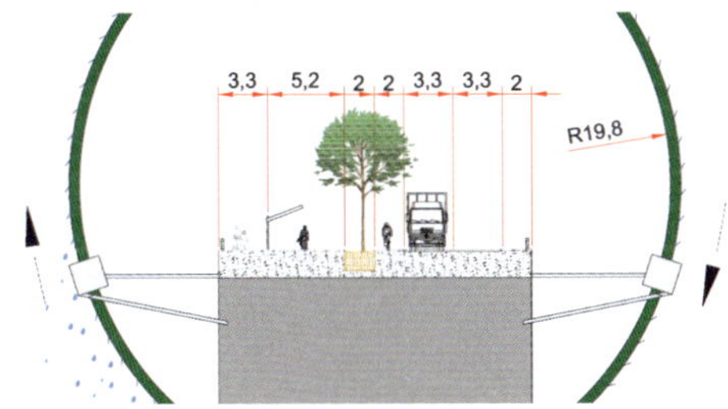

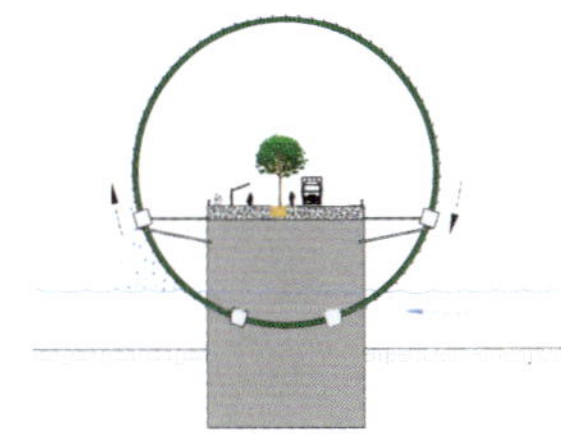

B-B

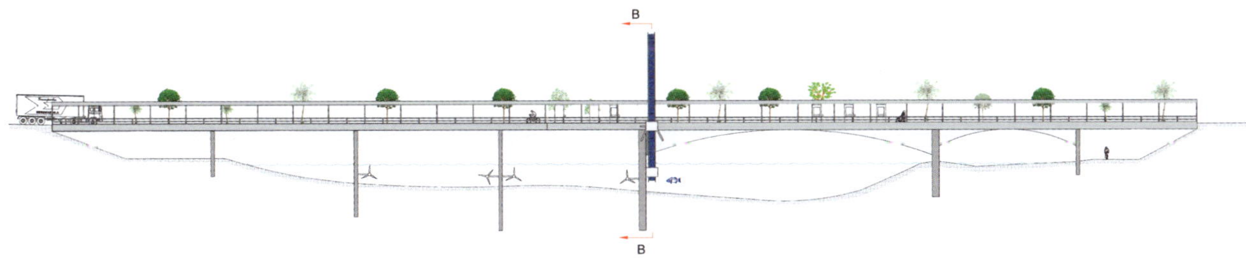

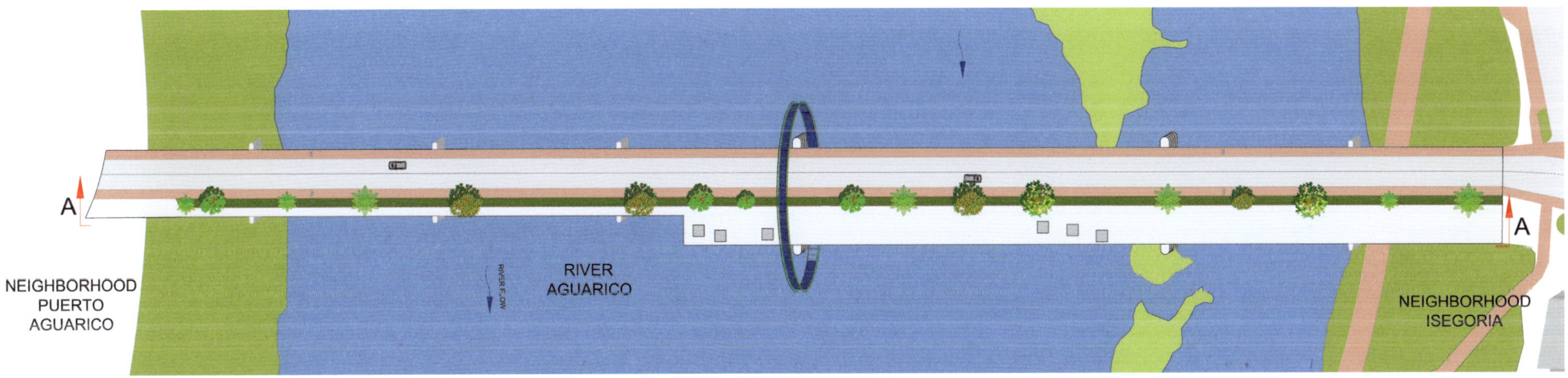

BARRIO PUERTO AGUARICO

MARIANA CASTILLO

PUERTO AGUARICO

AREA 34 Ha
POPULATION 900 p

DENSITY 13 p/hs

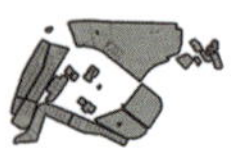

LOW DENSITY AREA
HIGH DENSITY AREA

HOUSING

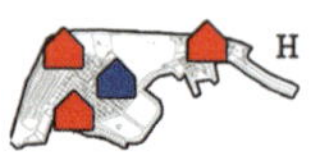

TOTAL 727
ONE-STORY 265
TWO-STORY 7
HOUSING DENSITY 8 Ha

GREEN GRID

- Nature preservation
- Communal gardens
- Recreation
- Sports

INTEGRAL FARMING

- Edge definition
- Food source
- Social, economic and ecological development

AQUARICO RIVER
BEACH
AQUAPONICS
FOREST
PUBLIC GREENSPACE
INTEGRAL FARMING
PUBLIC INFRASTRUCTURE
COMMERCIAL STRIP
MIXED-USE
HOUSING 1-2 STORY
HOUSING 3-5 STORY
COMUNAL SPACE
EXISTING FABRIC

INFRASTRUCTURE

MAIN CIRCULATION
- Regional network

COMMUNAL SPACE
- Urban fabric link

COMMERCIAL STRIP
- Economy
- Tourism

PUBLIC INFRASTRUCTURE
- Education
- Health
- Market
- Institutions
- Sports
- Recreation

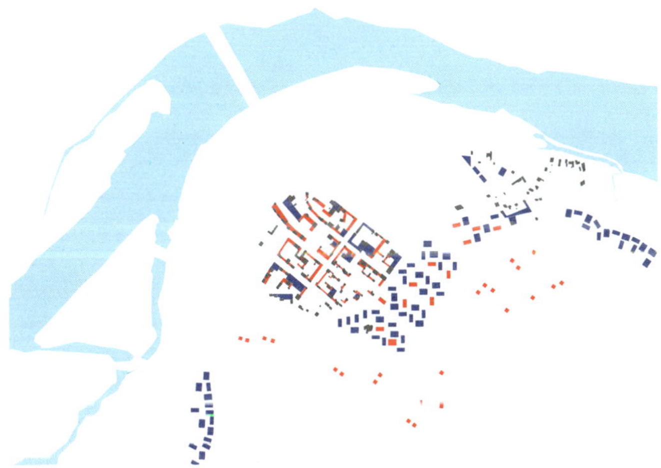

DENSITY

AREA	46 Ha
POPULATION	3000 p
DENSITY	65 p/hs

HOUSING NETWORK F M

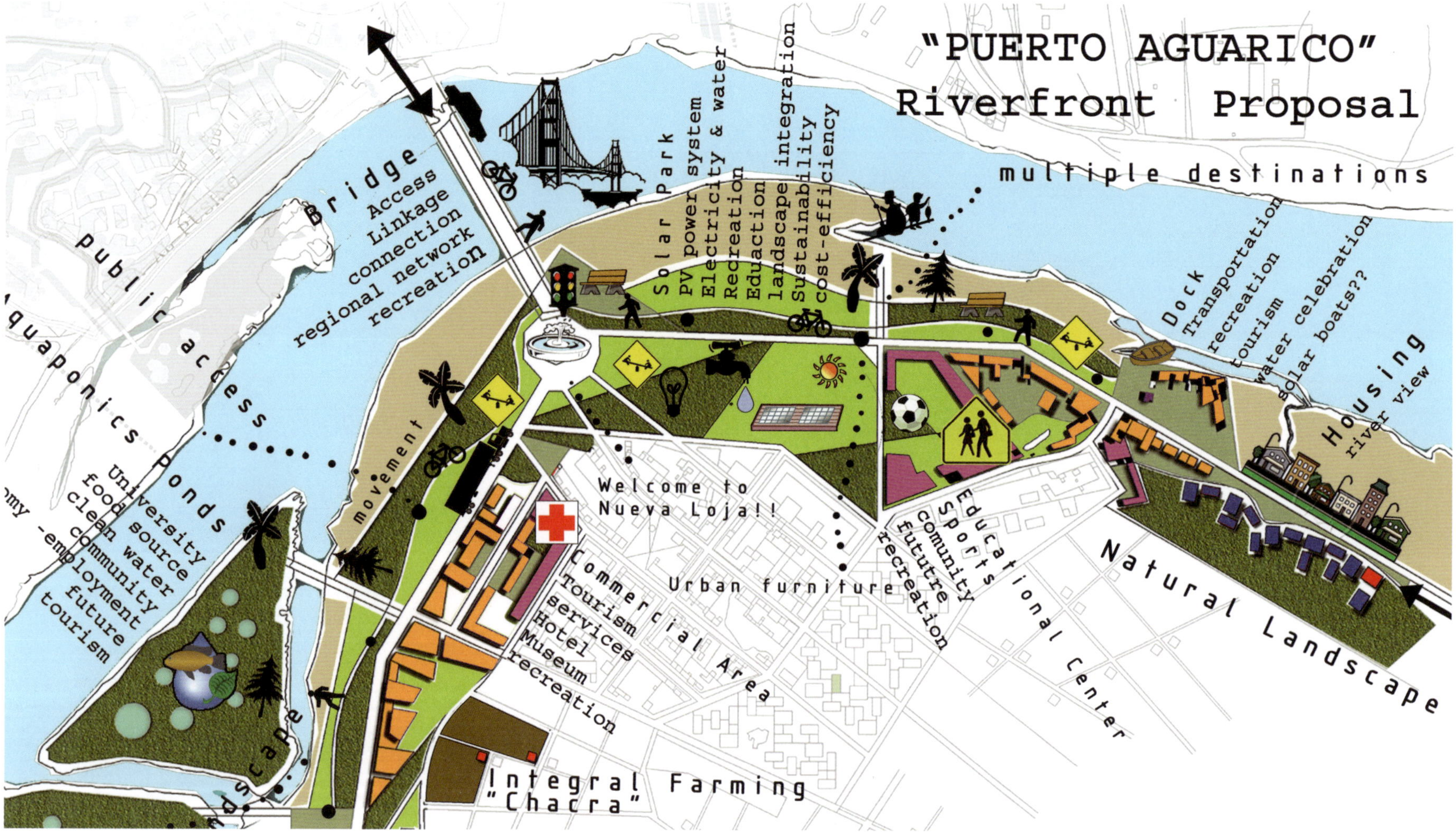
"PUERTO AGUARICO"
Riverfront Proposal
multiple destinations
Bridge
Access
Linkage
connection
regional network
recreation
public access
aquaponics ponds
University
food source
clean water
community
-employment
future
tourism
movement
Solar Park
PV power system
Electricity & water
Recreation
Eduaction
landscape integration
Sustainability
cost-efficiency
Dock
Transportation
recreation
tourism
water celebration
solar boats??
Housing
river view
Welcome to
Nueva Loja!!
Urban furniture
Educational Center
Sports
comunity
fututre
recreation
Commercial Area
Tourism
services
Hotel
Museum
recreation
Natural Landscape
Integral Farming
"Chacra"

A'
Beach
B
A
Dock
Solar Park
Commercial strip
Housing
Educational Center
Farming
Aquaponics
Farming
Housing
B'
N
W
E
S

SECTION A

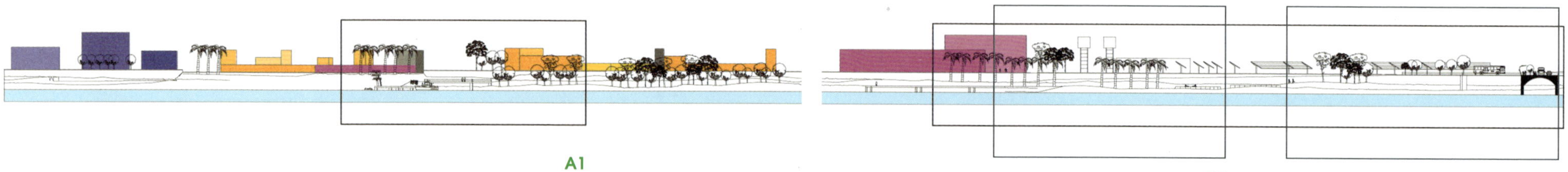

A1 A2 A3

SECTION B

B1

A1

A2

A3

B1

THE KINDLING CHARCOAL

PILYUN AHN

This project distributes new paving throughout the city to exchange local identity, manage rainwater and re-use waste oil. A network of swales, gardens and cascades will be created along the street edge allowing stormwater to be absorbed directly into the ground or via drainage channels.

The drainage system is inspired by Seattle's Street Edge Alternative project, which began as an experiment in a low-density, residential neighbourhood of single family homes. Following the success of the program, Seattle's public works agency extended the experiment to increasingly large and dense urban areas, showing that these innovative techniques could be applied not just to relatively undeveloped "greenfield" sites, but also to high-density city environments.

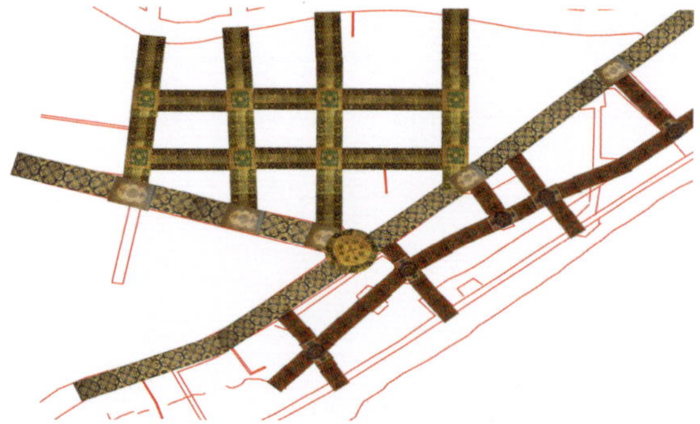

Paving patterns are inspired by local carpets.

Natural drainage systems, such as this grassy swale, absorb run-off from the street.

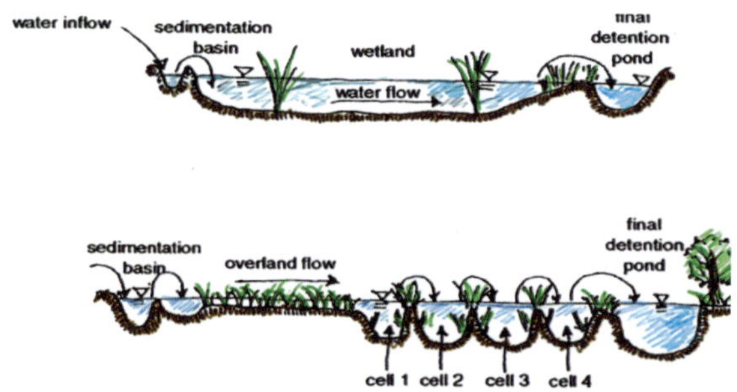

WASTEWATER TREATMENT

NARROW STREETS, BORDERED BY BEDS OF DENSE PLANTING, ALLOW FOR MINIMIZED RUN-OFF AND NATURAL INFILTRATION.

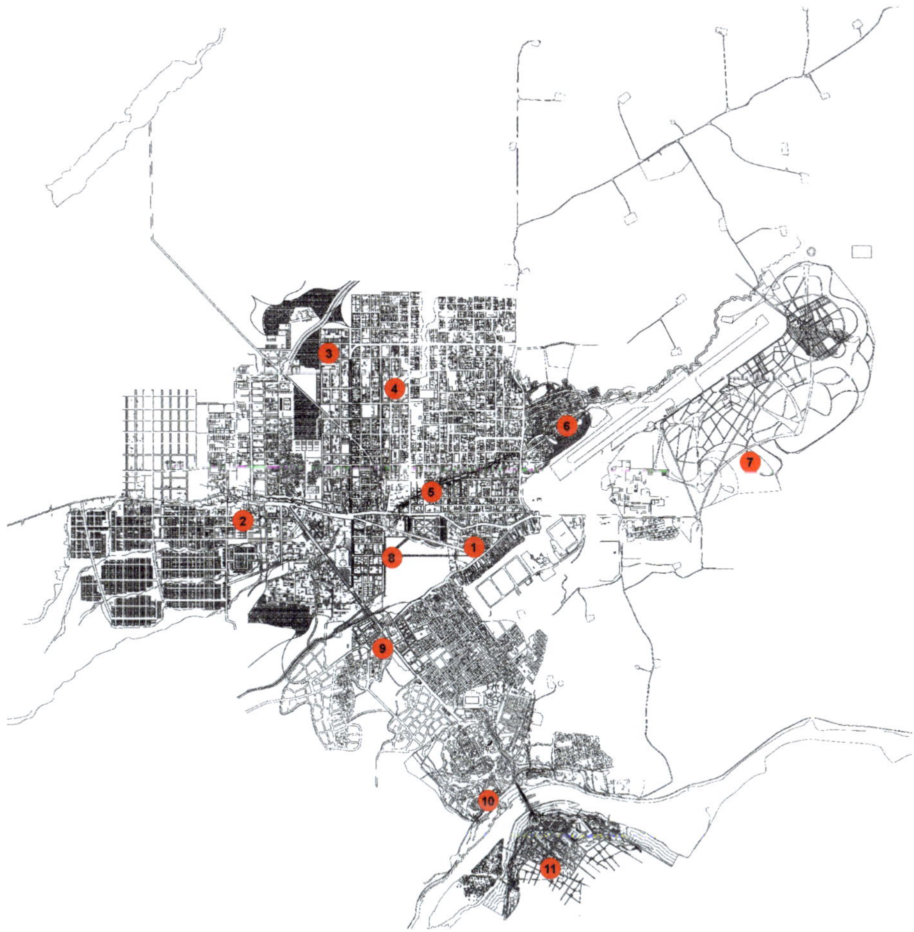

ONE SPECIAL PAVING INSTALLATION HAS BEEN DESIGNED FOR EACH GRAN BARRIO.

4. PILYUN

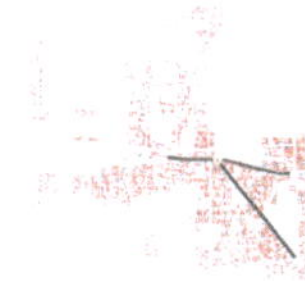

2. PAUL

3. MATT

4. JOHN

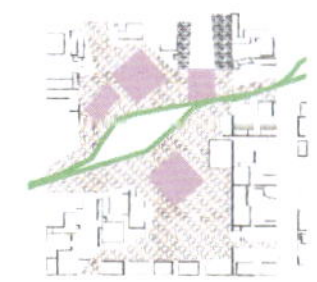

5. HOLLY

6. CHRIS

7. ROBERTA

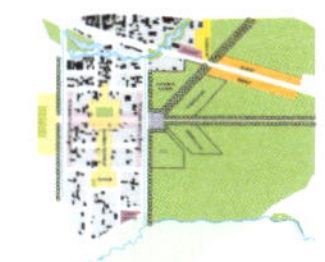

8. PATRICK

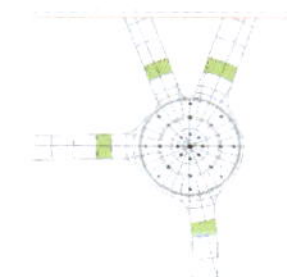

5. GARETH

10. ALAN

11. MARIANA

AMAZONAS

CALLE ROCAFUERTE

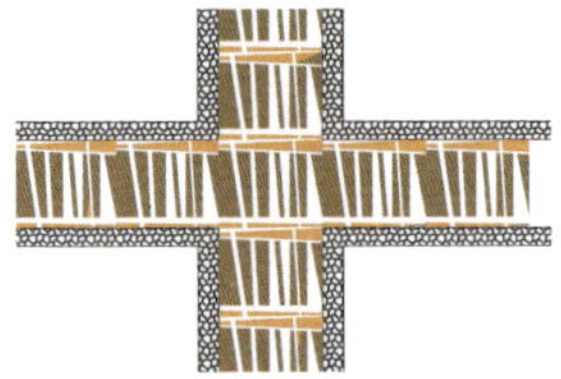

PETROLERA

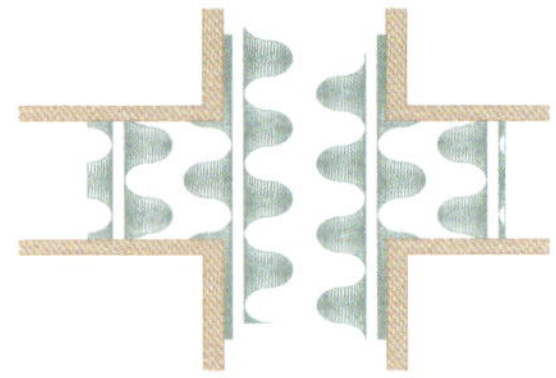

QUITO

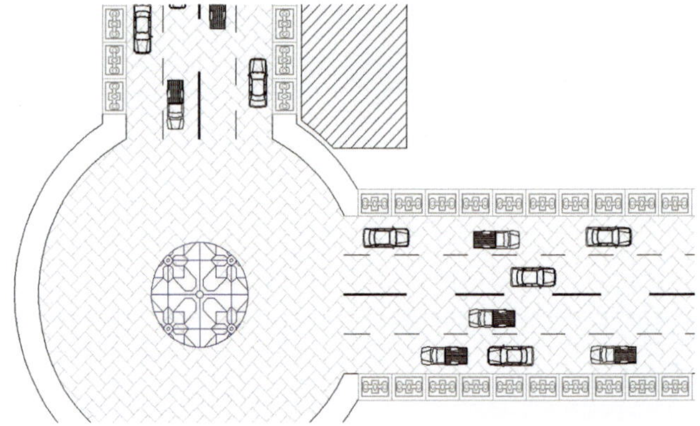

ROUNDABOUT (A)

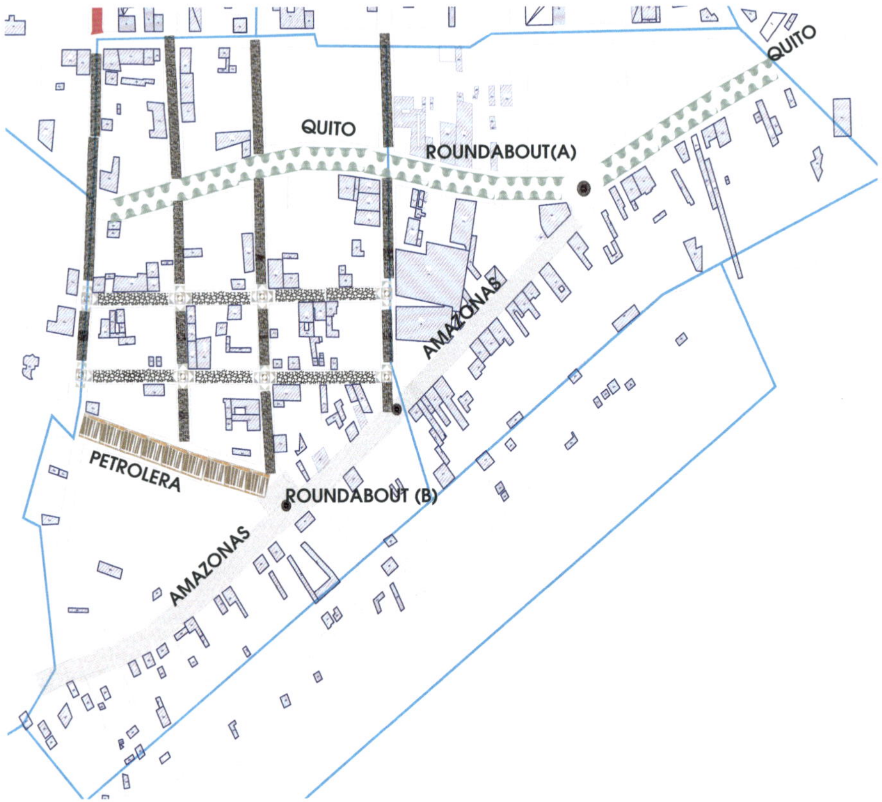

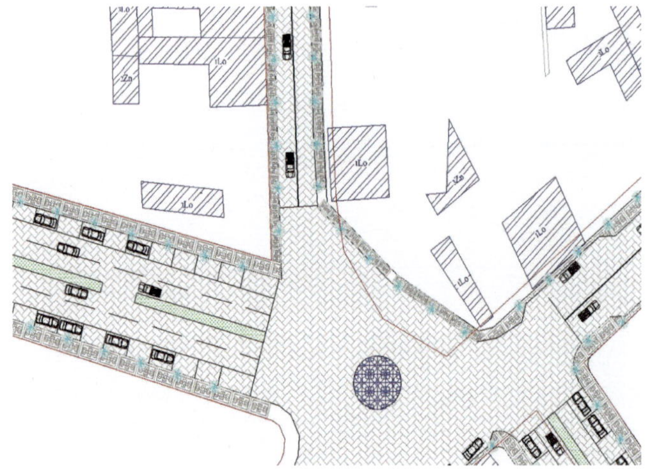

ROUNDABOUT (B)

THE KINDLING CHARCOAL

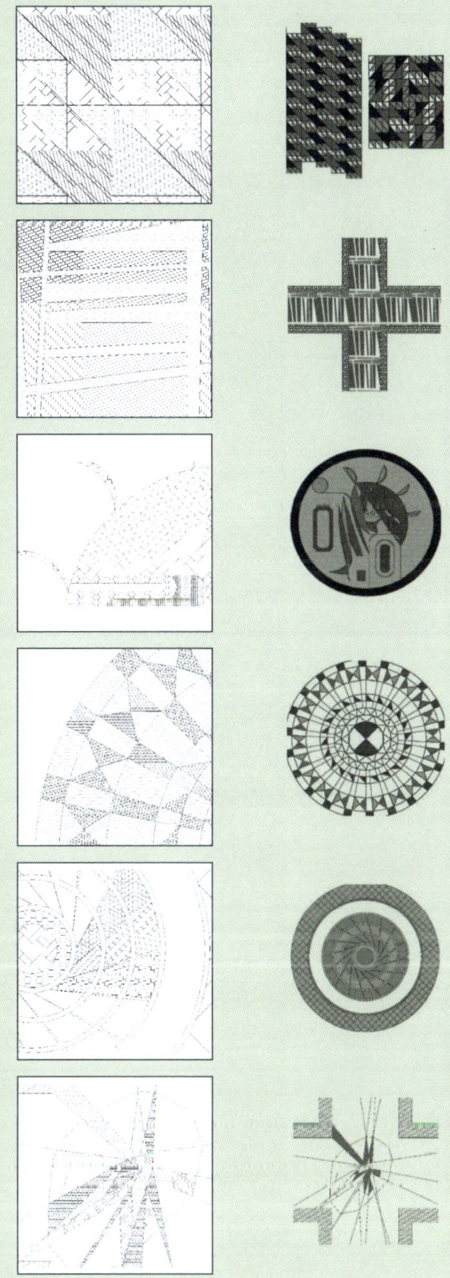

LA ESQUINA

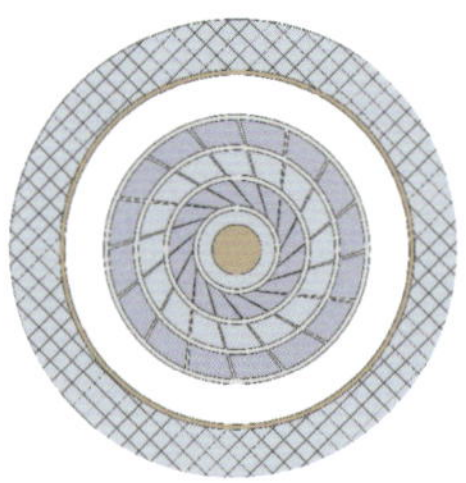

ENGINE OF CREATION

THE PATTERN IS A SPIRAL TO REPRESENT INFINITY.
IT IS 18 METERS IN DIAMETER.
IT CREATES A PLACE FOR MEETING AND RELAXING.
IT WILL HELP TO INCREASE PROPERTY VALUES.
THE THREE COLUMNS REPRESENT NATURAL RESOURCES, PEOPLE, AND SCIENCE.
IT IS SET WITHIN A CAR ROUNDABOUT.

CAN

A TOOTHED WHEEL

TRADITIONAL GRINDER

PUERTO AGUARICO

INFINITY

A ROUNDABOUT.

A PLAZA, 30 METERS IN DIAMETER.

ITS FUNCTION: BIKING, ROLLER SKATING, JOGGING.

THE TREE PROVIDES SHADE.

THE PATTERN IS A SPIRAL TO REPRESENT INFINITY.

UMBRELLA

A BRANCH

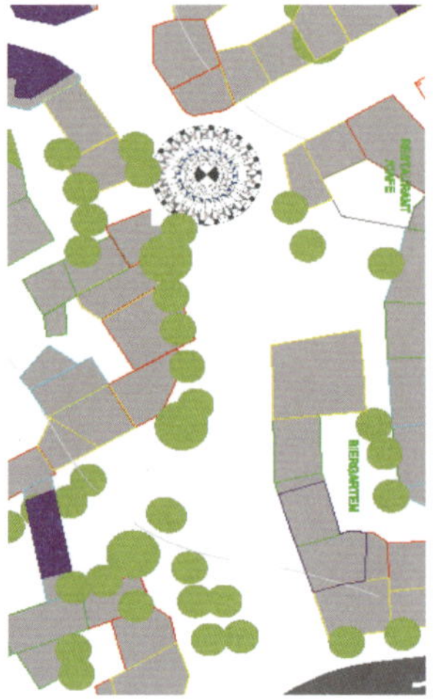

ISEGORIDA

LANDSCAPE

TRANSPARENT CLOCK

SUNDIAL

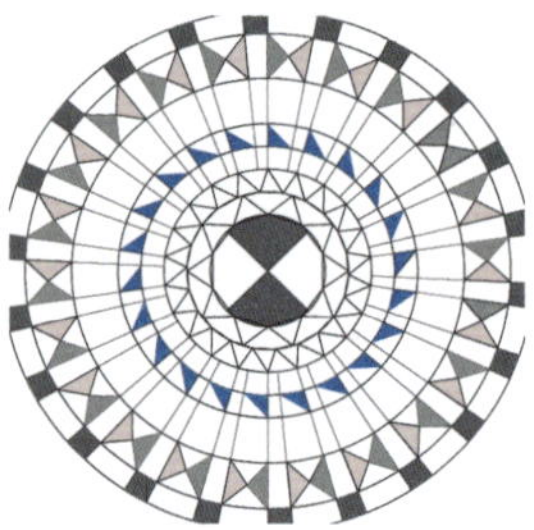

KARMA

A PLAZA WITH SUN – A SUNDIAL AND SEE-THROUGH CLOCK

A SUNSHINE PLAZA – FOUR WITHIN THE NEIGHBORHOOD

EL BARRIO CHACRA

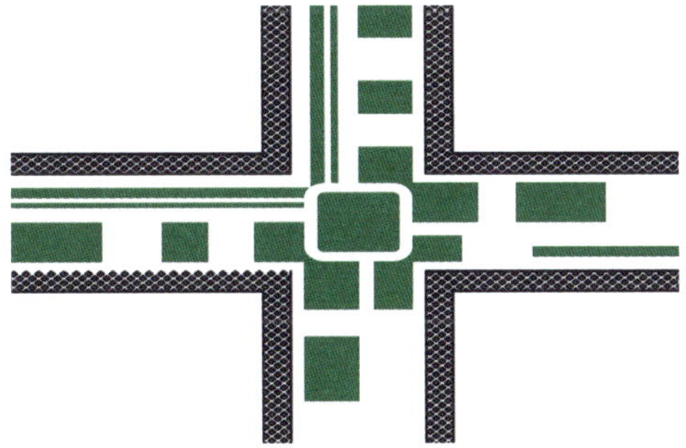

JUXTAPOSITION

JUXTAPOSITION

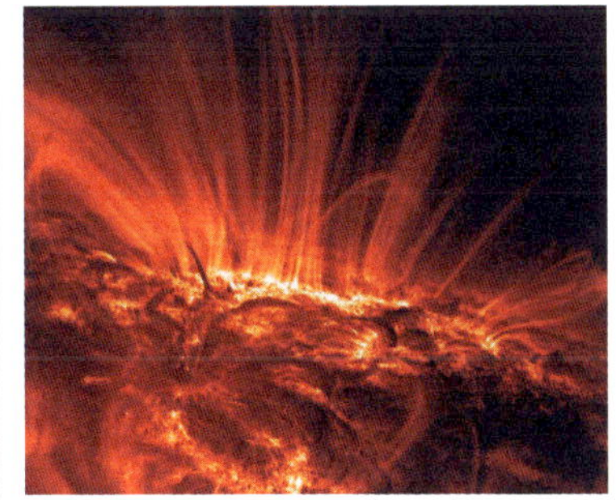

FIRE

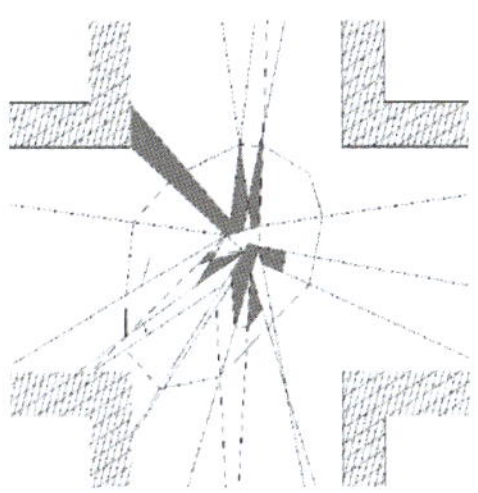

PLAZA WITH MOONLIGHT

THE JUXTAPOSITION OF HOT PASSION AND COLD GEOMETRY.
AN AGRICULTURAL SPACE: THE FARMERS NEED
A PLACE TO REST.

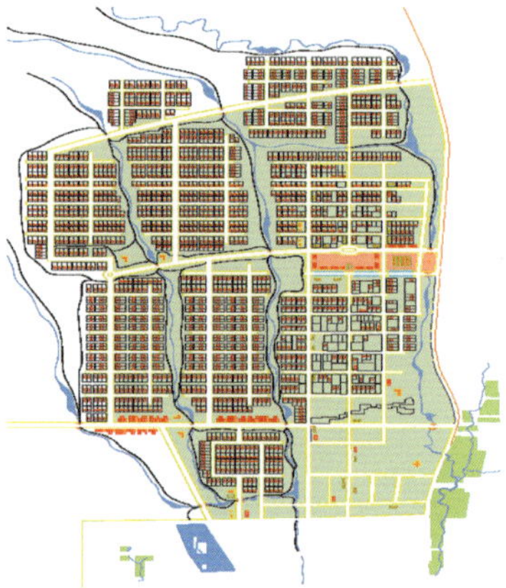

VERTICAL LIGHT

DEEP RECTANGLE

HORIZONTAL LIGHT

BARRIO VIA QUITO

THROUGH THE LOOKING GLASS

THE CONCEPT IS REFLECTION.
THE MODULES: HORIZONTAL LIGHT,
VERTICAL LIGHT AND A DEEP RECTANGLE.
THE PATTERN IS LOGICAL AND ORGANIC.
A WALL OF TREES CREATES SHADE.

THE ORIENCA UNIVERSITY

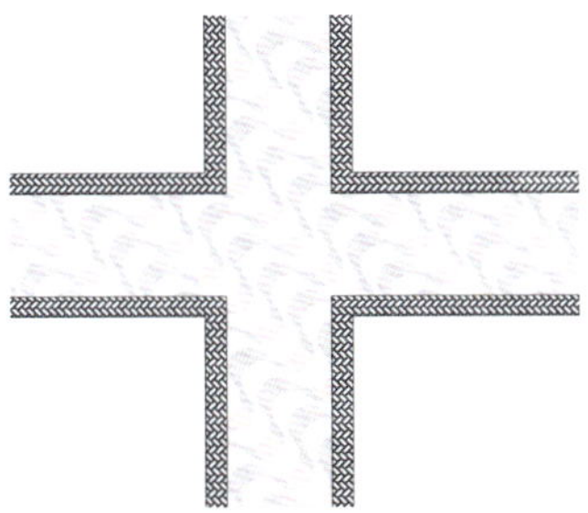

A FULL MOON

AN ATHENIAN SCHOOL: LOGICAL, CLASSICAL PATTERN AT THE ENTRANCE.

A WAVE PATTERN INSIDE. EDUCATION BRINGS NEW WAVES OF THINKING.

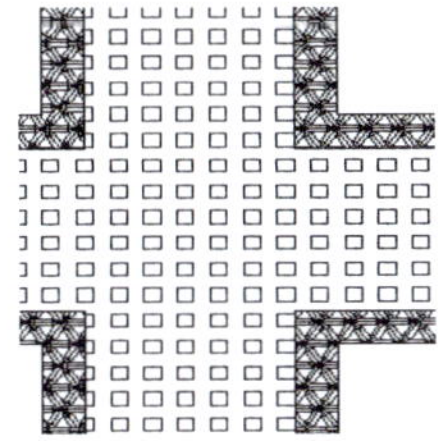

PAVING

PARTHENON

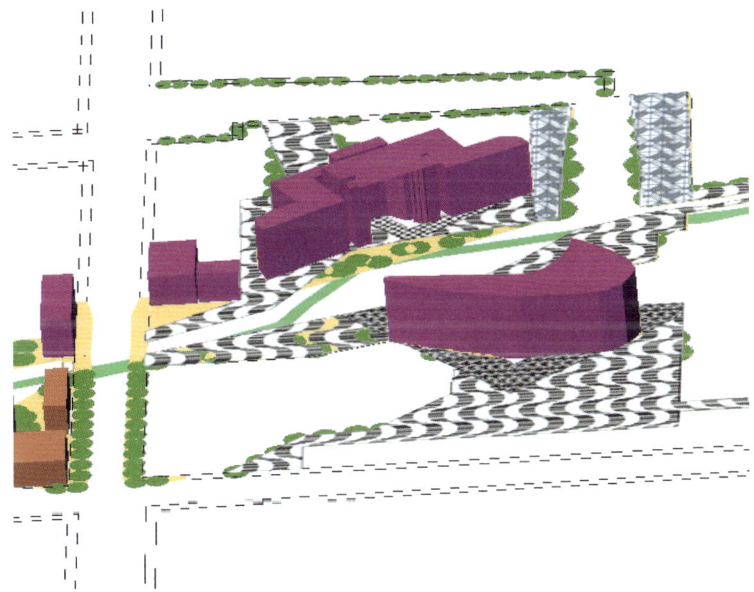

SAN FRANCISCO

Neighborhood concept: An infill of new housing and social infrastructure; reclaiming green and blue spaces for a sustainable future. A large development that includes an educational component focused on sustainable forest management.

TRIUMPH PLAZA

A BLOSSOMING FLOWER, INFINITY RECTANGLES, MOON PHASES, AN EAGLE FLYING

THE INCOMING TIDE: AN ACTIVE PLAZA

WILD FLOWER

SEQUENCE OF MOONS

EAGLE FLYING

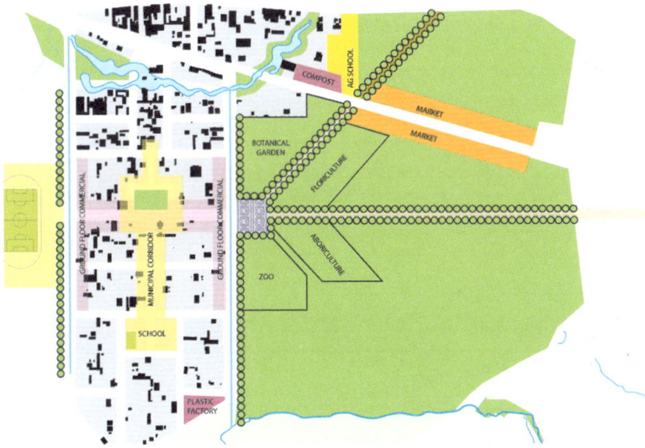

DE-CENTRAL PARK

PAVING

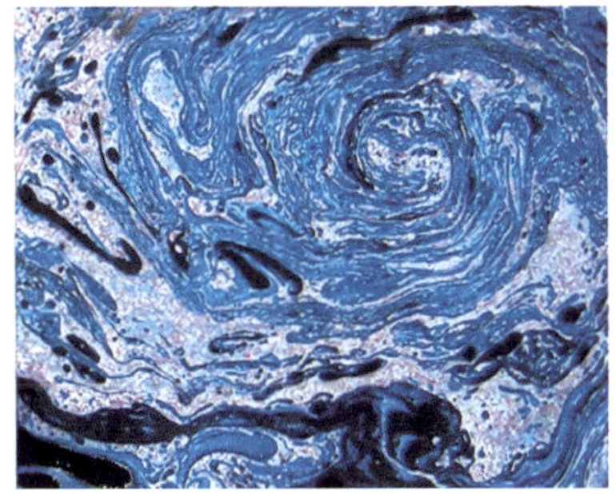

UMBRELLA

A BRANCH

WAVE

SPINNING, WHIRLPOOL, OPTICAL ILLUSION

THE THIRD WAVE (SCIENTIFIC): AN ACTIVE FEELING

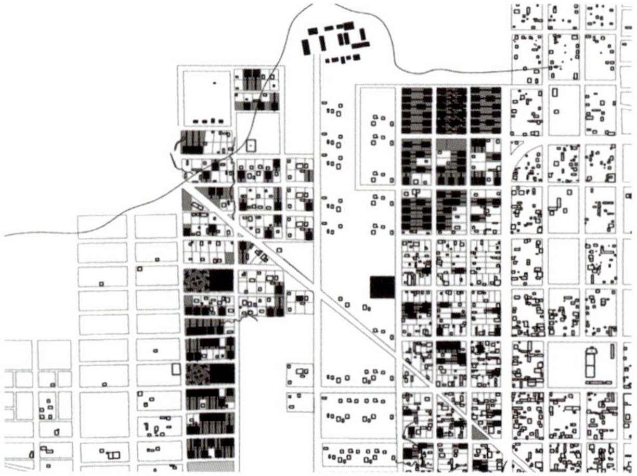

NAPO - JULIO MARIN

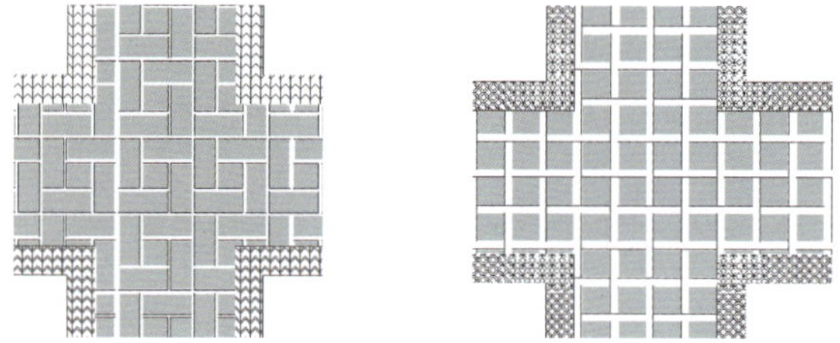

PAVING

GEOMETRIC

ORIGIN

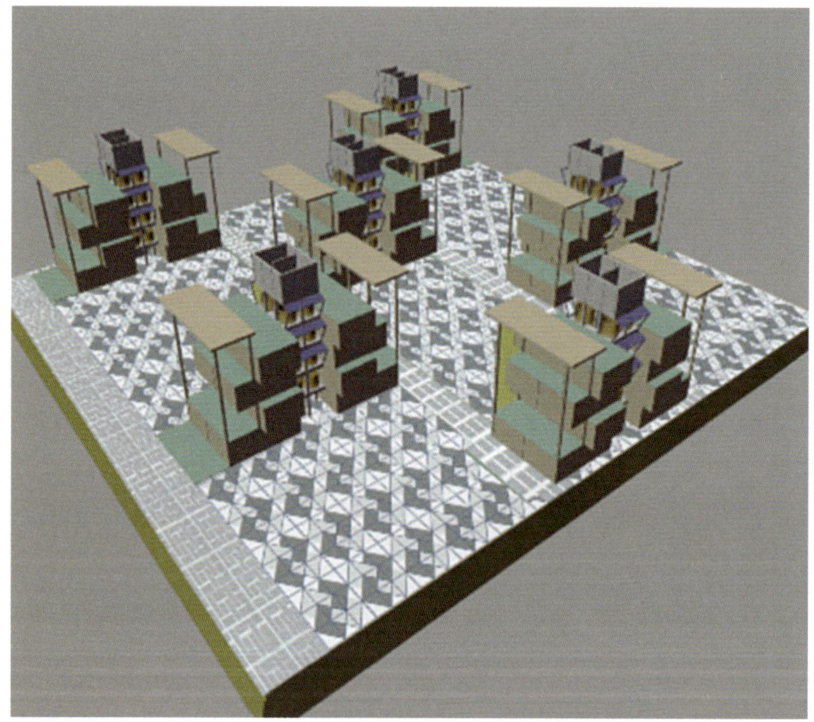

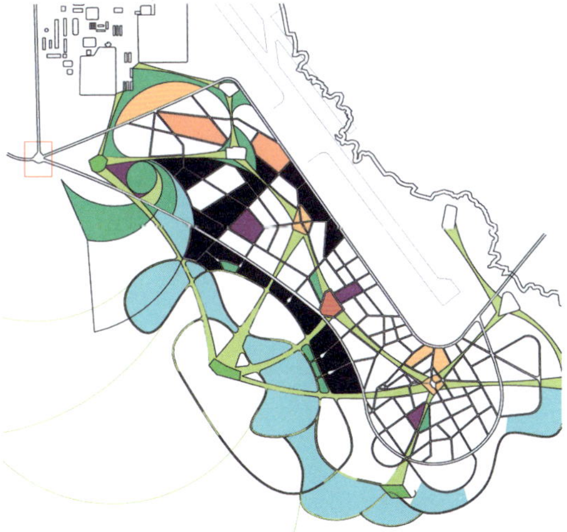

LA FLORIDA

KALEIDOSCOPE

ROSE

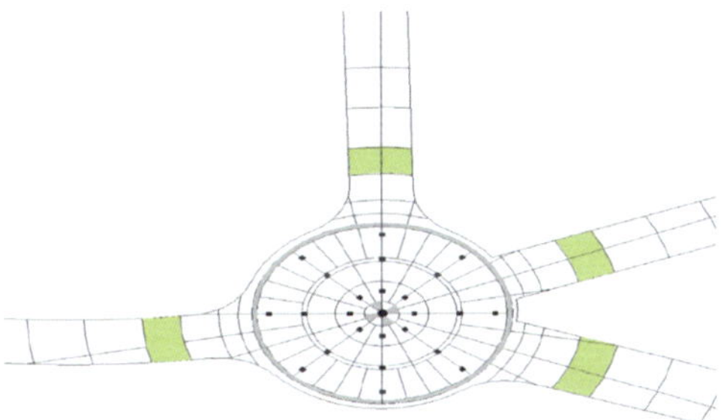

BLOSSOM

FUNCTION: CAR AND PEDESTRIAN CIRCULATION, SHADE

ARCHITECTURE

ARCHITECTURAL INFRASTRUCTURE FOR THE POST PETROLEUM CITY

THE ROOF MACHINE
COVERING, JOINING, HANGING
HYBRID SYSTEM
DWELLING PROTOTYPE
HOUSING PROTOTYPE FOR A HOT, HUMID CLIMATE
750 PROTOTYPE
SINGLE-FAMILY DWELLING WITH LOUVERS
HOUSING WITH NATURE
STACKABLE HOUSING
MULTI-FAMILY HOUSING: THE DEPARTURE OF THE CITY
MULTI-FAMILY HOUSING: LIVING IN THE AMAZON
LAGO AGRIO HOUSING
MOBILE CLASSROOM: POP-UP SCHOOLHOUSE
MOBILE CLASSROOM: 0 WASTE PROTOTYPE
MOBILE CLASSROOM: DEPLOYABLE SCHOOL
PUERTO AGUARICO SECONDARY SCHOOL
GREEN AND BLUE PRIMARY SCHOOL
THE URBAN SCHOOL

SCHOOL AS A TOOL FOR LEARNING:
ESCUELA DE CONSTRUCCIÓN DE NUEVA LOJA

SUSTAINABLE HUMAN SETTLEMENTS FOR THE POST-OIL ERA IN THE ECUADORIAN AMAZON: AN INTRODUCTION TO THE NUEVA LOJA WORKSHOP (FADA-PUCE)

PRODUCTIVE LANDSCAPE – PRODUCTIVE HOUSEHOLD
SUSTAINABLE SYSTEMS
MULTI-LAYERED CONNECTOR
SELF-SUFFICIENT METABOLISMS
STRIPS FOR GROWTH
MATERIAL FUSION
SUSTAINABLE FREE-STANDING HOUSEHOLD
PROTECTIVE CANOPY

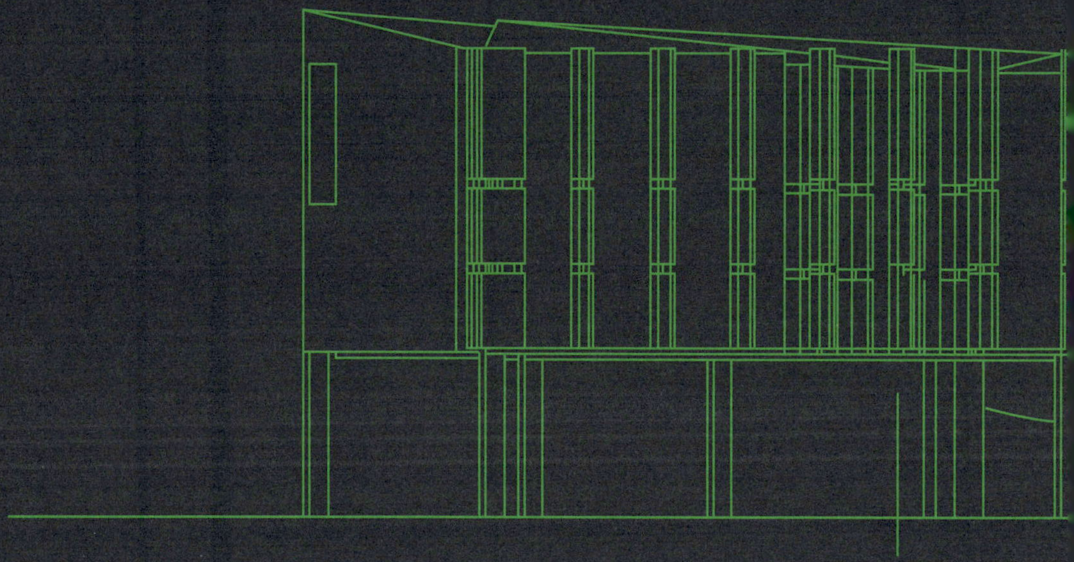

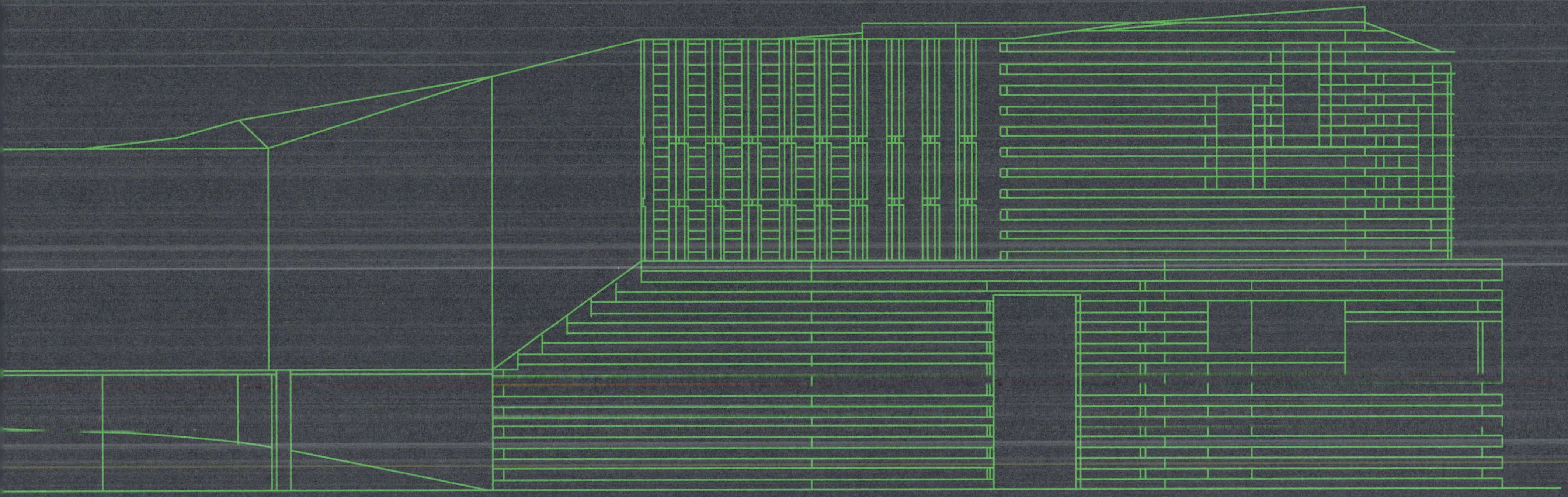

ARCHITECTURAL INFRASTRUCTURE FOR THE POST PETROLEUM CITY

DAVID LEVEN

Lago Agrio, or Nueva Loja, in local parlance, is a small dusty Amazonian oil town in eastern Ecuador. Considering the pressures acting upon it, the town could either explode or dissolve back into the jungle after its 40 years in existence. An explosion could come in various forms and at various scales: economic growth due to internal migration; social upheavals due to neo-liberal first world pressures and inequities in the oil economy; pressures from the cross border narcotics trade; environmental degradation by oil and lumber companies; or the actual explosion of an oil well. On the other hand, dissolution could take place as oil in the region runs out and no new economic base replaces it.

A visit to the town, however, reveals a vibrant, often contradictory, largely informal settlement full of human activity. Life goes on and patterns of habitation, social interaction, community and co-existence with the climate abound. By studying these patterns, it's possible to find integrated ameliorative architectural solutions to make a healthy, sustainable, equitable and beautiful city that supports myriad activities, economies and populations. The architecture students, whose work is shown here, grappled with the architectural implications of the interplay of traditional and modern societies. Their proposals, responsive to both tradition and climate, are infused with appropriate modern and traditional materials, methods and processes of construction.

PROPOSITION: ARCHITECTURAL INFRASTRUCTURE

Since the purview of the architect is the built and social geography of a place, we have focused on two building types (and sub-typologies within them): housing and schools. We considered housing in terms of its locality, history, typology and infrastructure. We considered schools as part of a 20th century tradition (particularly early 20th century when the fever for social ideals ran high) and a community-centered design methodology.

The students tackled housing at various scales from the single-family shelter to the larger housing agglomeration where services and utilities are shared and the organization of the buildings facilitates community groupings. When they moved from the study of the individual, detached house to the systematic, urban arrangement of multiple units, housing was considered as "infrastructure" – connected to the urban pattern, designed to create efficiency and urban continuity. They also conceived access to humane, sustainable housing as a right.

This idea, of infrastructure as configuring place, can be seen in the oil infrastructure of the Oriente. Ecuador's oil pipeline, a neo-liberal global infrastructure, ever-present from the Andes down into the Amazon basin, runs along the one main road from Quito to Lago Agrio, Shushufindi and other Amazonian oil towns. The impassive pipe, often black and smooth, sometimes painted with political slogans, physically and economically bypasses the people who live along its length – even though many are forced into its service. By contrast, the "infrastructures" proposed here by the students challenge the neo-liberal policies that colonize place around a narrow set of economic rules. Rather, their solutions open up discussion about the integration of various economies (including big oil while it lasts), social formations and sustainable practices that can reconfigure the post petroleum city around positive urban and architectural ideals.

The seemingly heretical idea in Western Capitalism that housing can be thought of as an infrastructure that gives shape to a city, presupposes that (like clean water) housing is a right. This infrastructure, however, was not conceived by the students as monotonous, impersonal and top down – like much state housing – but rather as tactile, tectonic, reflective of community and in harmony with nature.

The main models of school architecture as community-derived and community-configuring are the mid 20th century architects Aldo Van Eyck and Herman Hertzberger. Their work formed the basis for our thinking about a community centered urban jungle school. It also encouraged comparisons between school building following the world wars and school building in this post-petroleum region which is also ravaged by the Colombian drug trade and the military response, recruiting by insurgents and prostitution (there is in fact a brothel next to one of the high schools in Lago Agrio).

POST PETROLEUM HOUSING THROUGH THE LENS OF POST WAR HOUSING

In cities experiencing the aftermath of a cataclysm, building booms are common.

Less typical, but occasionally possible, is a reassessment of the social project of architecture. In 1928, in post World War I Europe, the Congress International d'Architecture Moderne (CIAM) was founded by a group of modern architects led by Le Corbusier and Sigfried Gideon. CIAM aimed to shape the principles of Modern architecture and to declare architecture a social art. CIAM's second conference in 1933 focused on the minimum dwelling where the ideas of "Existenzminimum" were presented as a new model theory for the provision of social, humane housing. The sixth conference in 1947 – two years after World War II had left many European cities in ruins – focused on the reconstruction of cities. The CIAM conferences also formalized certain material and technological methods that would shape the built environment of the modern world. These three themes – social dwelling, the reconstruction of cities and the far reaching effects of the global materials industry – all have serious implications in this remote jungle town.

Although by no means on the scale of a world war, the impact of Texaco and other oil companies on the Ecuadorian jungle can be seen as cataclysmic – in the depth of degradation of the environment and its inhabitants and the lengthy after effects of oil extraction in the Amazon basin. When Texaco first set up camp, the methods of inhabitation were solely indigenous, primitive and environmentally and climatically attuned and sophisticated. A case in point is the typical, inherently temporary, Huaorani dwelling made of long thin long thin trunks of wood woven with overlapping leaves to form a self-ventilating skin. The simple technological innovation of rows of leaves in a tight overlap also make this skin highly resistant to water infiltration from the persistent rain forest deluge.

The dwelling sits on the ground, but hammocks and storage nets are suspended from the structure, whose skin provides ventilation.The roof has a covered aperture at the top so that cooking smoke can escape and the entire dwelling can be fumigated to remove jungle insects. When indigenous people were sequestered in reservations, their housing was also transformed into the far inferior, permanent, modern and ubiquitous cement block or wood shack, with a non ventilating galvanized metal roof that blazes in the sun and is deafening in a rain storm. These cement blocks and the larger concrete buildings found all over Latin America are hangovers of the international modern movement's adoption of concrete as the material with which to build the entire modern world, regardless of climate, social structure, or material culture.

Forty years later in Lago Agrio, an informal town has grown up with a largely random block and lot structure formed by individual acquisition and contingency. The town takes the form of a haphazard grid surrounding an airstrip, an oil storage encampment, a series of creeks turned sewage ditches and a large green space protected from oil company and military acquisition by a private owner, before petering out to the South where it reaches the Aguarico River. The dimensions of the city blocks range from 60 meters square to 60 meters by 90 meters and up to 140 meters with random lot structures and building arrangements. Residential building on these lots often takes the form of a grouping of houses, workshops and sheds nestled closely to one another, sharing informal lot lines with neighboring structures. As always, the jungle tries to grow back wherever it's not cut down or paved over. The material of the town is concrete and concrete block, galvanized metal, and wood. Informally settled, dense areas of the town contain lots and structures with overlapping residential, commercial and industrial uses in long thin sliver forms butted up to the oil encampment. These slivers are approximately 5 meters wide by 30-40 meters deep from the street. Other housing forms are informal rural shacks without utilities or multi-story, unfinished concrete buildings, inhabited at the lower levels and often used for laundry drying and storage at the upper levels.

The first challenge for the students was to understand the existing housing patterns described above. The second was to determine what local intelligence, methods, technologies and materials were useful. The third was to propose integrated architectural schemes at the single lot and single family dwelling scale, and the larger agglomerative multi-unit housing scale. And finally, they needed to consider appropriate external technologies, morphologies and sustainable practices.

Students looking at housing and school buildings needed to work within an urban master plan from the outset, to ensure their proposals were integrated with the surrounding communities. These projects also had to understand which infrastructures were already in place, which had to be reinforced and which needed to be built before their ideas would work.

CONTEMPORARY TRADITIONS

Various contemporary architects and architectural projects exemplify the approach pursued by the students. Alvaro Siza's Evora Housing in Portugal (1977-1997), configures the entire urban plan around a series of infrastructural aqueducts that carry water and utilities to the housing units. The aqueducts were constructed first, plans and model buildings were configured around Modernist minimum existence principles, and the community continues to fill in the master plan. In Siza's plan the genius of the architecture resides in the reliance on a visible, physical infrastructure that provides for growth but also creates conditions of community in a very modest economic condition. Similarly, Alejandro Aravena's Iquique Housing (2004) in Iquique, Chile, presents a pared down building module in a repetitive plan with gaps between units that can be filled in by the residents as finances become available.

The owner of a unit purchases the minimum affordable space and the block structure of the complex is completed over time. As a result, conditions of community are evolving and dynamic.

The work of Estudio Teddy Cruz on the border of San Diego and Tijuana is another exemplar of the informal and communal. In the Casa Familiar, the informal configurations of housing and social buildings are bundled together and slipped amongst one another to create a community that does not conform to accepted local codes but addresses the needs and patterns of the inhabitants.

HOUSING SCHEMES

The housing schemes here explore a range of issues particular to this jungle environment. Initially, the students pared down the design parameters for jungle habitations to three operations: hanging, covering and joining. As a result, issues of climate, tectonics and ergonomics could be isolated as discrete design problems, and conditions that would later be integrated into full architectural schemes.

One project, a leaf-like roof covering system, employs traditional bamboo as a structural system and combines it with aluminum or steel fastening methods. Another, the Roof Machine, goes a step further, proposing a flexible configuration that allows for the modulation of air-flow in the structure. System, a structural component method, looks at natural processes of spider webs and water bugs to derive form and structural efficiency. The genius of System lies in its joining system and its separation from the ground – an acknowledgement of the soil pollution caused by oil exploration. The Dwelling Prototype Module takes similar issues – joining, lifting from the ground and bamboo technology – and applies them through dispersed, non-linear, non hierarchical patterning systems attuned to the ordered chaos of the jungle. This project bridged the initial exercise of "hanging, joining and covering" and the prototypical single unit housing study.

In the design of the single unit dwelling, the appropriate size, materials, building methods, energy requirements and waste remediation for dwellings in Nueva Loja were determined by the students from the start. Issues of proximity to other dwellings, community circulation and repeatability were injected into the study. In the prototypical dwelling project, the appropriate transformation from indigenous to modernized forms was investigated in depth. The three prototypes presented here respond to the climate by lifting the buildings off the ground and by making louvered and permeable wall systems to address air flow. Structural systems were also of paramount importance in this exercise,exemplified by Prototype 750 which uses ubiquitous steel pipe – detritus from the oil industry – to structure a flexible demountable housing unit that could be moved easily on a truck bed and erected in any area of the city or region. Other schemes employed demountable systems fabricated from various diameters of bamboo trunks harvested from indigenous and or proposed harvested trees. The multi-unit dwelling presented a diverse set of requirements and conditions, larger, more complex and decidedly more urban than the single unit dwelling. In these schemes the master plan of the neighborhood was required to understand the urban grain of each locale at both large and small scales. The master plans included issues relating to access, urban character, bulk and zoning proposal, edges and context responses, proposals for existing transportation systems and grid systems, and community making and amenities. Once established, the master plan was developed into programmatic configurations, cognizant of site, that included various dwelling units, communal areas, access to public and private transportation, parking for bikes and larger vehicles for commercial use, commercial facilities, shading strategies at the level of the unit and the community and green programs and formations.

SCHOOL SCHEMES

The school system in Nueva Loja is seriously inadequate for the existing population: in its number of schools per population, its buildings and facilities for students, teachers and the wider community and in its methods for achieving sustainability. The school system, including day care facilities, primary schools and secondary schools (Ecuador only divides its schools into these two main groups) is at risk of a facilities lag and subsequent population overload of the current system when the city population grows to the projected 125,000-150,000 in the next decade. In addition, it is common in Ecuador for students to attend schools in shifts – morning and afternoon or evening – in order to service double the number of students with one building. Here, the permanent school buildings were primary. But we also recognized a need for temporary solutions since current schools are inadequate and school building in the future may be outpaced by the population expansion.

To that end, the students' first exercise was to design temporary, potentially mobile buildings of flexible dimensions to meet the changing needs for classroom, clinic and assembly space. The model of Architecture for Humanity's 2002 Mobile Health Clinic to Combat HIV/AIDS in Sub-Saharan Africa was studied as a precedent. The idea behind this competition – for flexibility, affordability, sustainability, social justice and smart efficient design in spaces for learning and assembling – was their starting point.

The next exercise (the student's main project) was the design of model schools at each level: primary and secondary. As in the multi-unit housing schemes, program and site were extensively analyzed, the concepts of the educational approach, which came out of precedent studies by the likes of van Eyck and Hertzberger, were determined, the connection to the community, as always, was stressed and construction methods appropriate to the region and the sustainability of the building, were employed in an overall effort to create viable designs for those school buildings.

THE ROOF MACHINE

IMAN ANSARI, ONUR EKMEKCI

The tropical conditions at Nueva Loja – heavy rain and sunlight – create specific challenges for the design of a new building system. The most crucial elements needed are roofs and coverings. Because of concerns about sustainability and global warming we need to think about ventilating and shading in different ways and about the building's consumption and production of energy.

The building contains two or more spaces, each covered with a roof system. These spaces are connected to each other at the side, and are open for ventilation and light at the front and back. The spaces could be built to different dimensions, allowing for a variety of uses. Each roof system within a space functions independently of the others, again allowing for different uses.

The sliding roof systems allow for shading and covering, as well as ventilation and water collection. The roofs would also be flexible – allowing for maximum cover in the event of heavy rain or sunlight or minimum cover at other times.

A crucial aspect of this project is its reduced energy consumption. Aside from the control of sunlight through the use of sliding roofs, air is compressed and directed into the building. The system then acts as a cooling system, particularly when the roof structure is filled with rainwater. The water collected will then be directed and stored for other uses.

The design of the Roof Machine also grew out of an analysis of bamboo as a potential structural material. The Roof Machine consists of a series of bamboo poles cut in half which are then connected by a simple joint, which allows for the circular movement of the pieces. A long piece of metal connects the joints to the barring wall. Railings placed inside the wall allow the roof to move in either direction. This area also consists of a channel for collecting and removing water from the roof.

BAMBOO SYSTEMS

Bamboo is a sustainable material that can used both formally and structurally. The Roof Machine draws on its internal structure as a water barrier or container, and on its strength and length – bamboo pieces are connected through a system of joints, which will allow infinite variation and flexibility. The joint can connect up to six different bamboo pieces. The system can carry a structural skin and expand in various directions. It can also be used as a space frame.

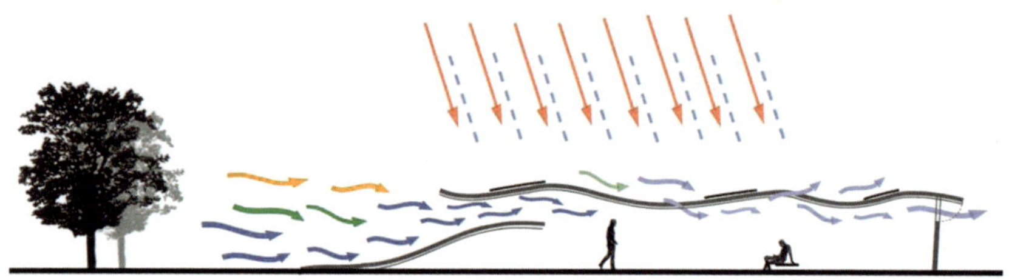

ENERGY DIAGRAM

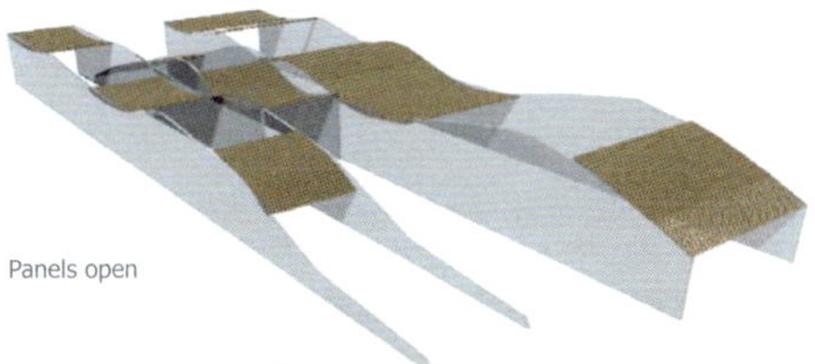

Panels open

Semi-closed

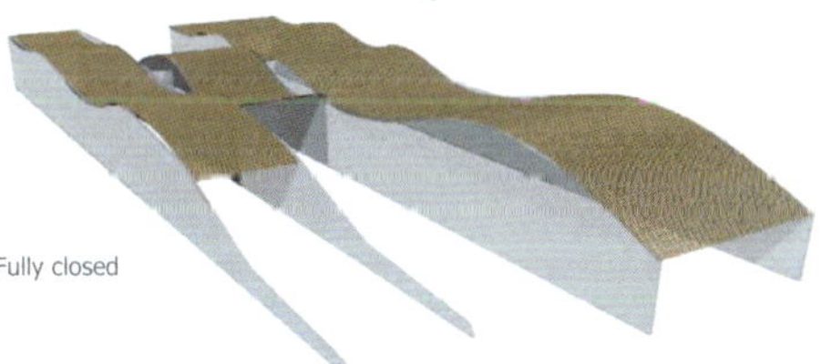

Fully closed

TOP + TOP LEFT: CONNECTION DETAILS

COVERING, JOINING, HANGING

ROMMEL GORDILLO, JAVIER CARACAMO

THE CHALLENGE

To create a covering / joining/ hanging system.
How can it be developed as a prototype? How can it grow?

THE CONCEPT

Nature is the most complex system of growth. We analyzed the growth of leaves and trees to learn about complex growth.

THE STRUCTURE

It begins looking like a simple geometric form. It is composed of two systems on the same axis. The adherent system follows the same pattern. This creates a vertical growth.

THE PROTOTYPE

This system can be arranged in multiple configurations simply by rotating the entire structural joint. Some configurations create spaces that can be inhabited. Various configurations make a joining, covering, hanging system.

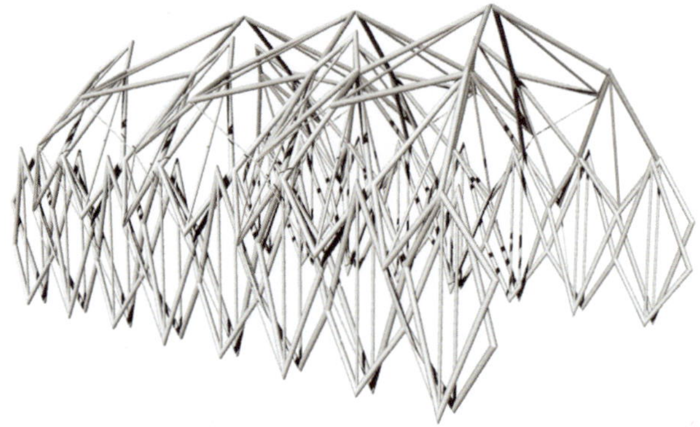

TOP: VIEWS OF STRUCTURE
BOTTOM: VIEWS OF STRUCTURE

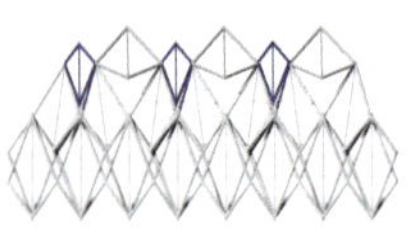

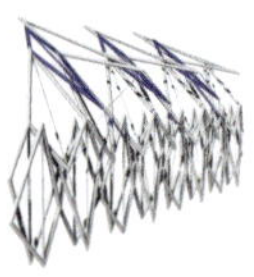

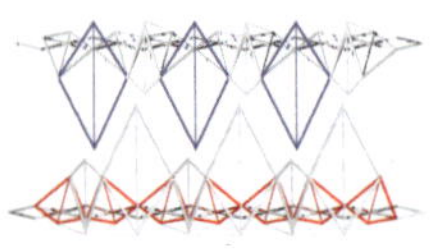

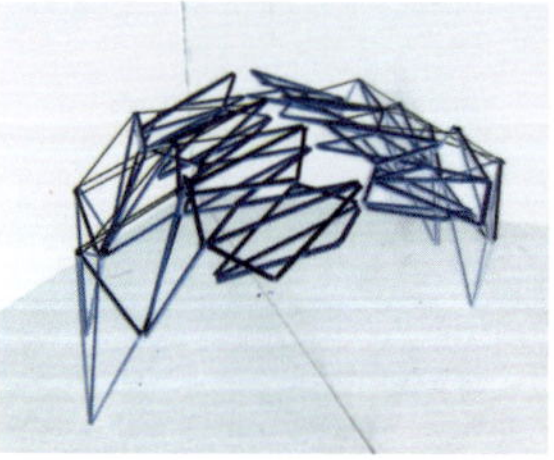

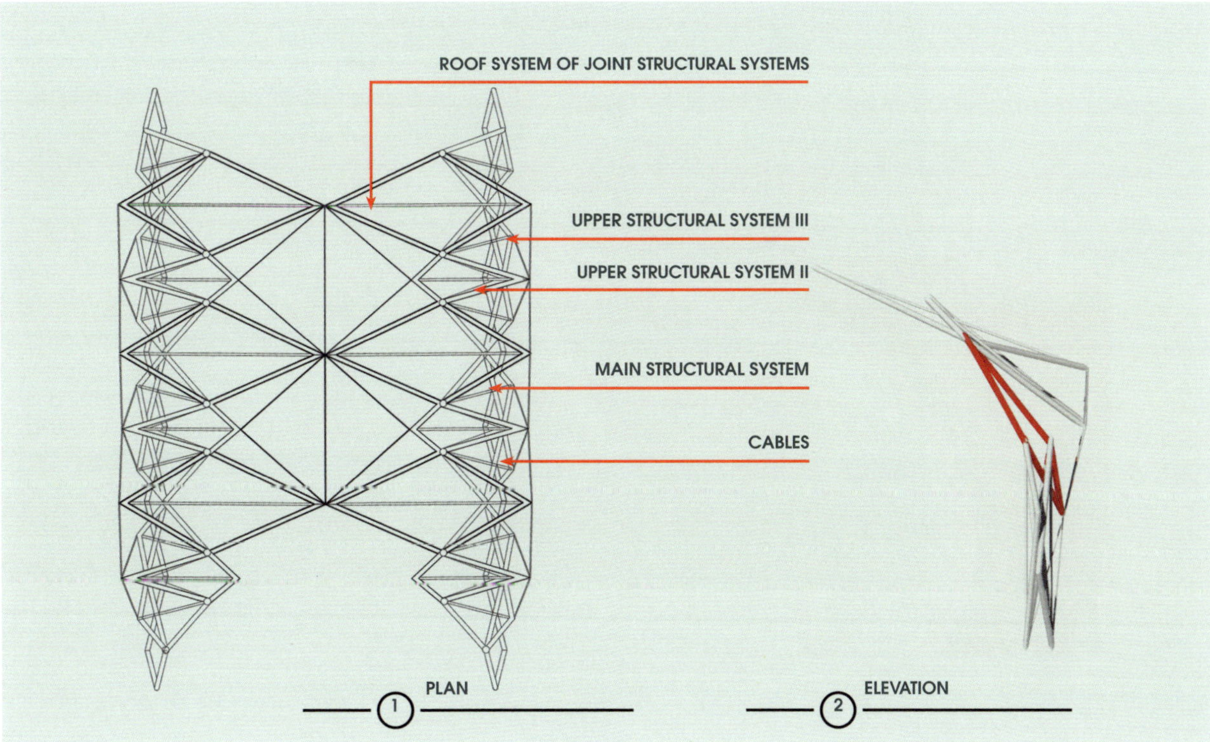

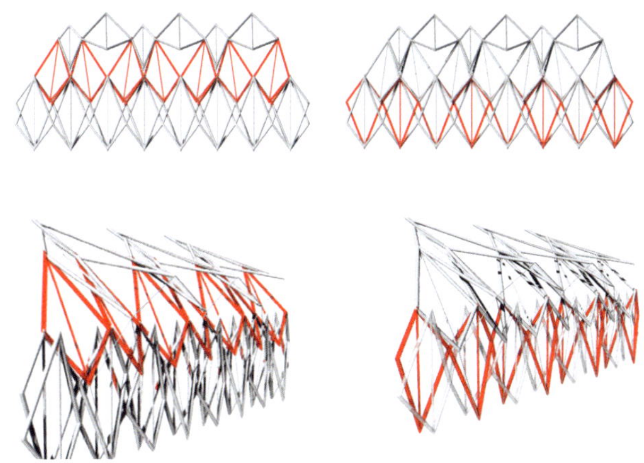

TOP: COMPONENT
BOTTOM: FOLDING STRUCTURE
LEFT: JOINT DETAIL

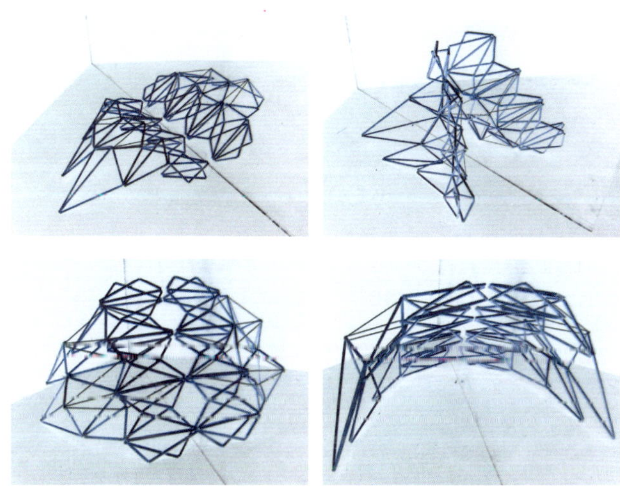

The system involves three ideas (join, cover and hang).
It began from an examination of leaf structures. The concept was to bring the leaf arrangement and jointing to a structure that functions spatially.

The result is a structural form: a prototype that incorporates these three ideas: joining, hanging, and covering.
It is constructed from bamboo, an efficient, sustainable material, easily found in hot climates.

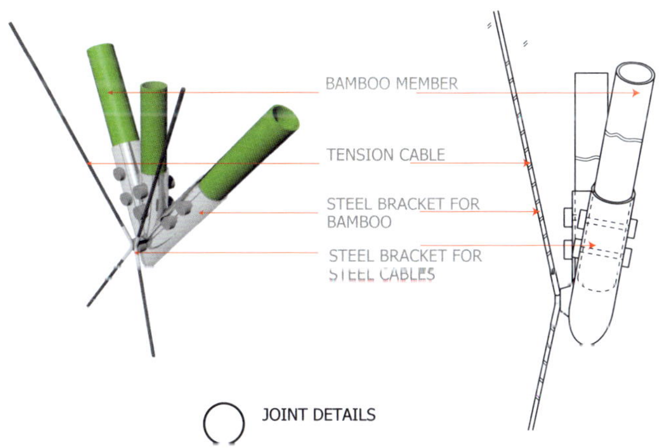

HYBRID SYSTEM

PATRICK ISAAC AND SUJIN JEONG

This system is a hybrid between the structure of a spider web and the suspension technique of a water bug. The idea was to create a human shelter with a structure raised up off the ground to minimize its impact on the site.

The project will provide new housing for the expanding city. At the same time it will encourage a more direct relationship between human settlers and the soil as it undergoes decontamination. It will aid the establishment of a new ecosystem at Lago Agrio.

The vertical joint has three members: two parallel horizontal members and one diagonal member placed at various angles.

This joint works by allowing a rotating adjustable inner joint to secure an incoming member set at an incline.

The horizontal members that make up the web will be attached with metal plates that bolt them together. The arrangement will still allow a level of play between the two connecting members, though never allowing them to form a 90 degree angle.

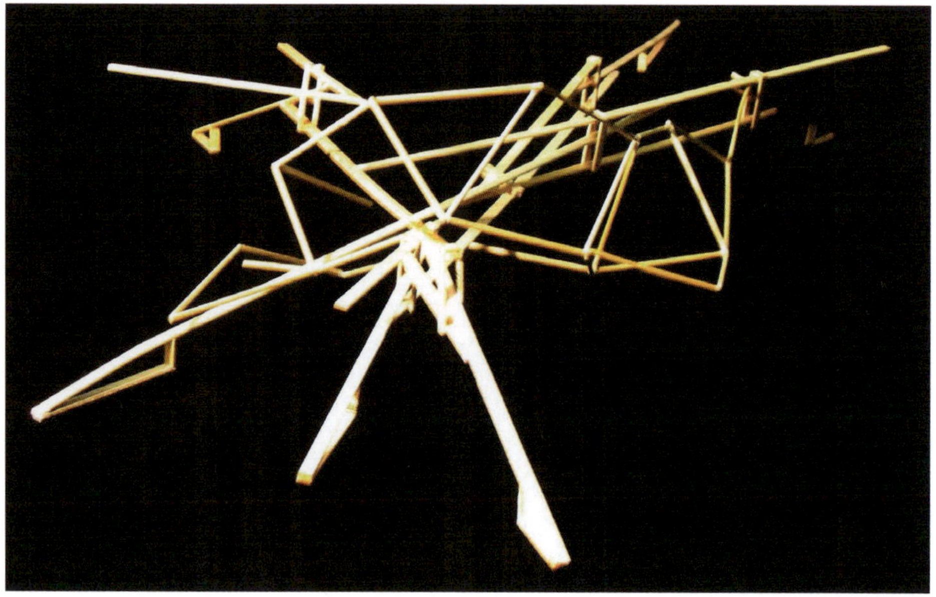

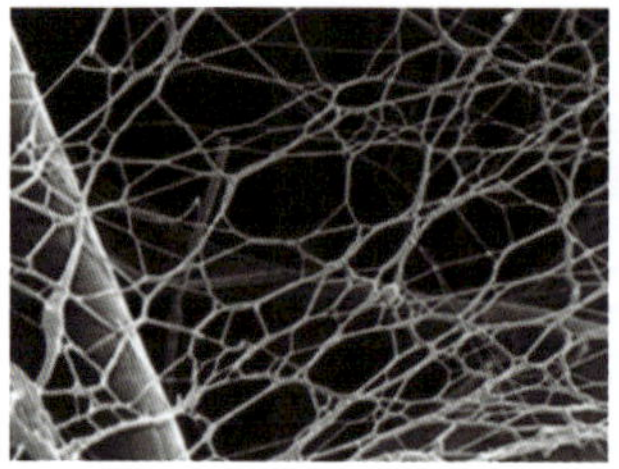

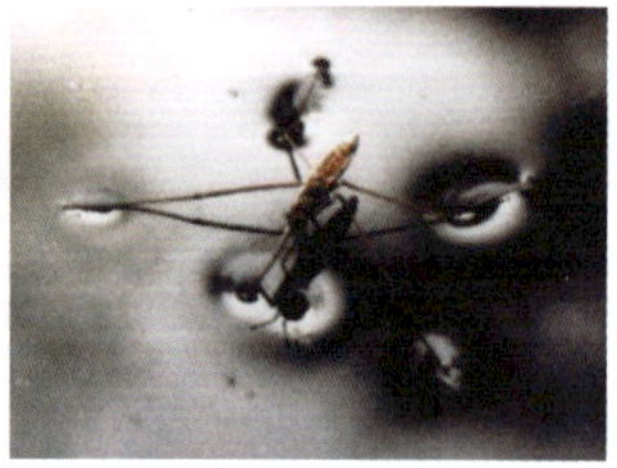

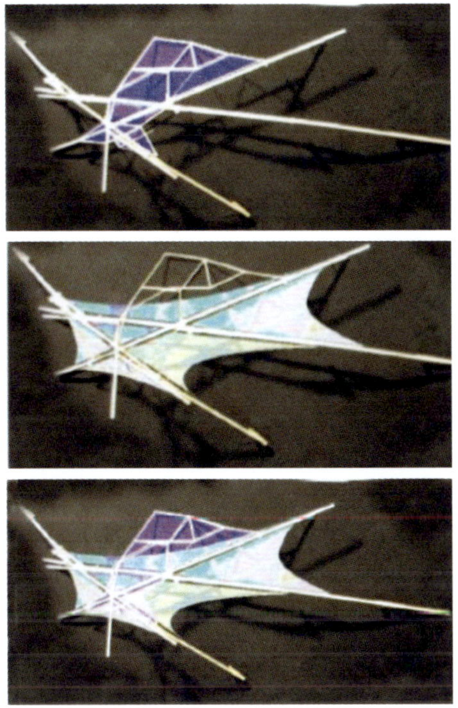

COVERING

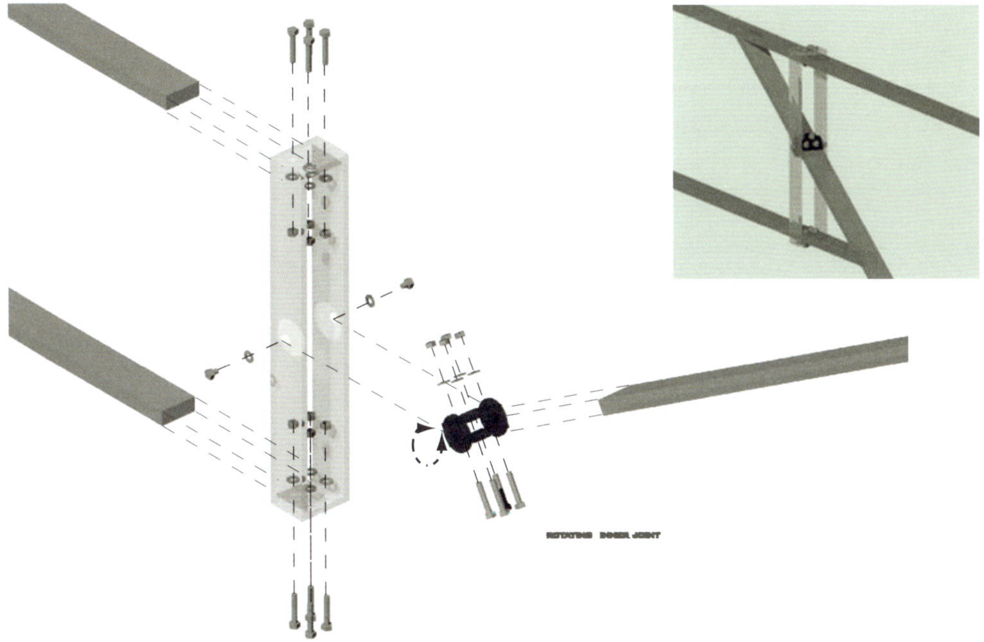

The vertical joint

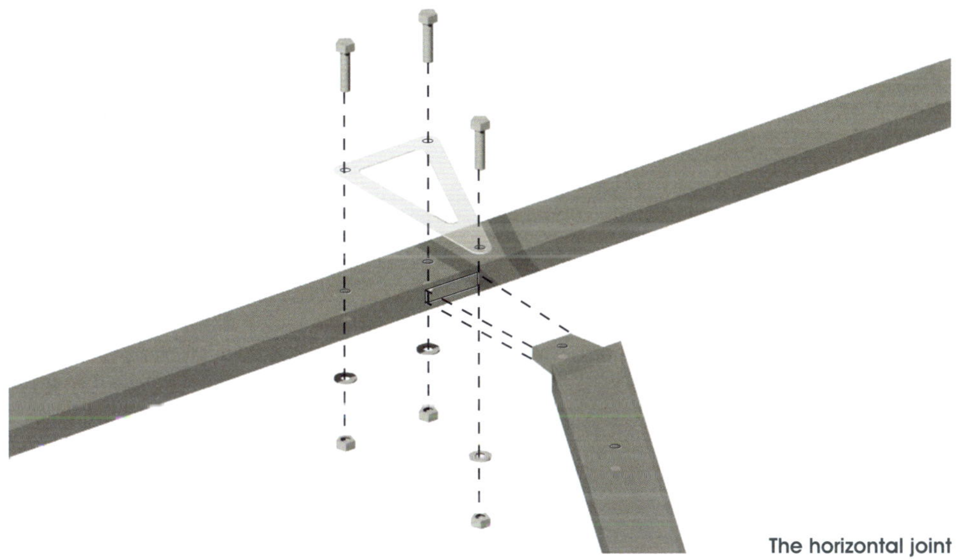

The horizontal joint

DWELLING PROTOTYPE

ERIK SCANLON AND YULYA LLIZAROV

This prototype for an Amazonian dwelling is inspired by natural growth systems. The modules are designed to sit harmoniously within the environment. They will be placed within an area of dense trees, which supply the structure. The modules are variations on a triangular form since this requires the least number of connection points with the structural trees to create an enclosed space. The modules are attached to the trees at various heights depending on whether they are above land or water.

The structure of the modules is based on the construction of scaffolding. Movable clamps at each joint allow a variety of connection options. The walls of the module consist of a double skin of rope penetrated by foliage.

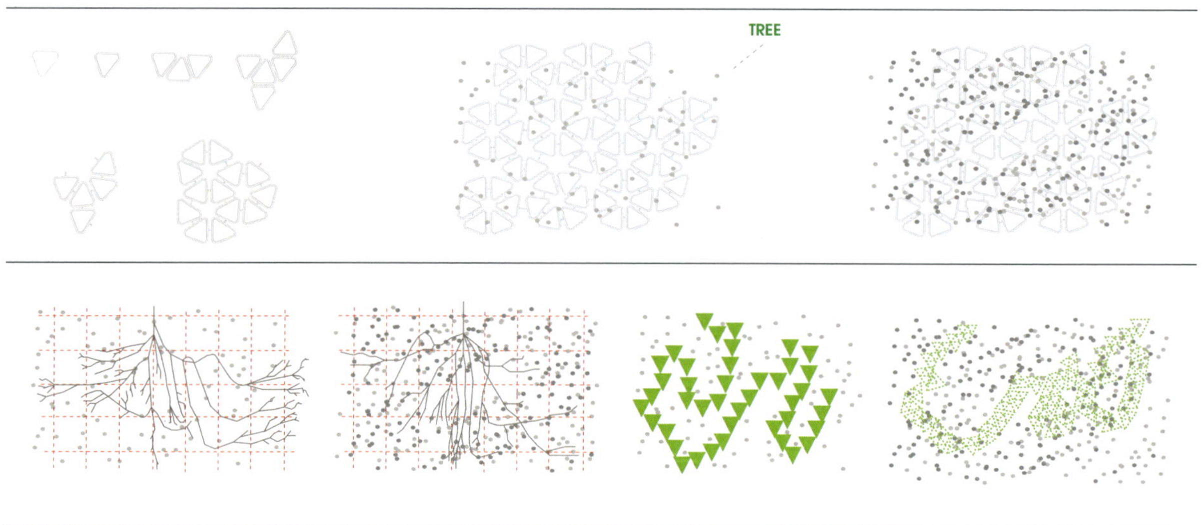

STRUCTURAL FRAMES

WITH VERTICAL SUPPORTS

WITH ROPE SKIN

TOP: DWELLING PROTOTYPE

SYSTEM

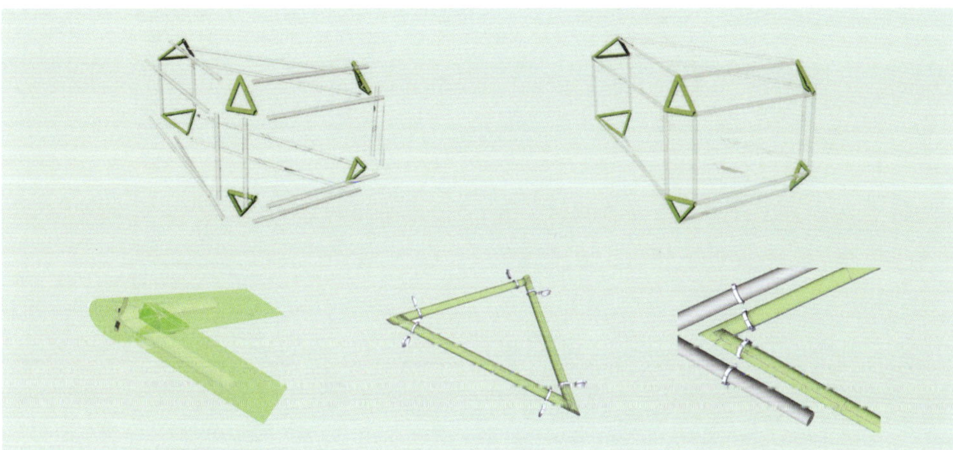

CONNECTIONS

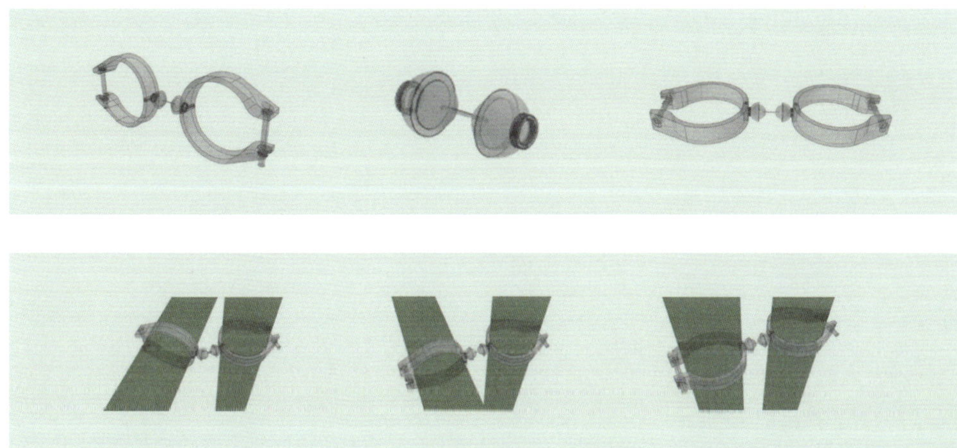

HOUSING PROTOTYPE FOR A HOT HUMID CLIMATE

YULIYA ILIZAROV

This housing prototype for the Amazon's hot and humid climate contains both public and private zones. The public zone is the large central space, with different areas separated by slight changes in elevation. The private nodes are arranged around the main public space. There are variations for both the public and private zones which allows for a variety of arrangements.

The public zone is broken up into a kitchen area, living area and two outdoor areas. Their arrangement can be varied to alter the relationship between indoor and outdoor spaces. The private nodes allow for a number of different family groups to share the dwelling. They can be added on as needed as the extended family grows. The nodes feed into the central public zone – the central area for the family to gather together.

The prototype has a bamboo frame with tension cables that are used to hang the private nodes from the main public zone. Each outer wall is skinned in a double layer of thin bamboo strips, with foliage between the two layers for air purification. The bamboo strips are woven into the structure of the prototype. They can be either densely or loosely woven to create varied levels of privacy. The roof is skinned in a photovoltaic fabric to produce energy. Beneath the bathroom is a composting bin for collection and use by the community.

COMBINATIONS

PUBLIC MODULES

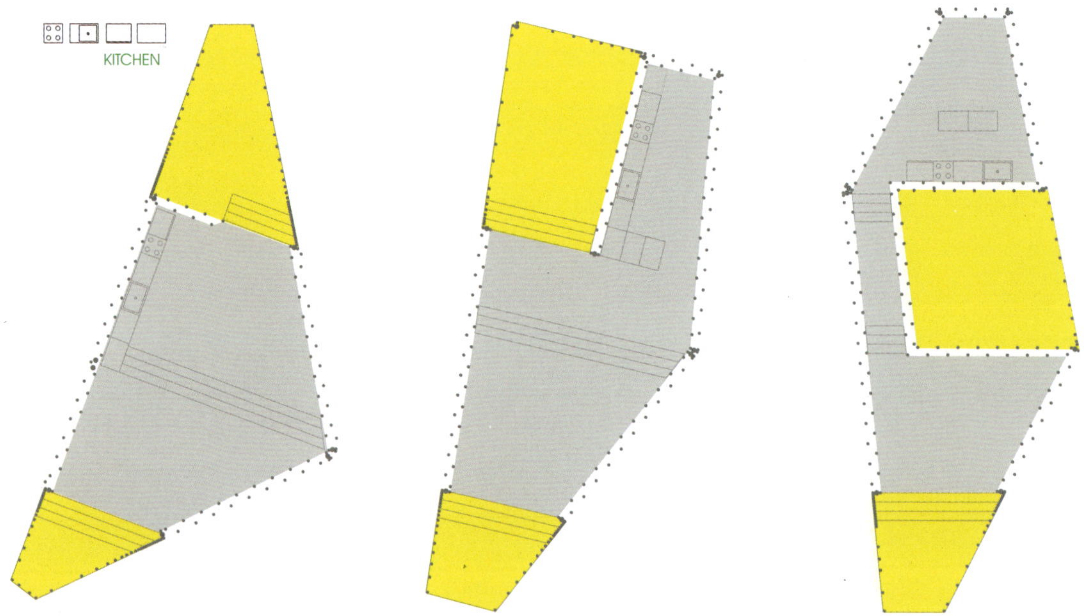

PRIVATE MODULES

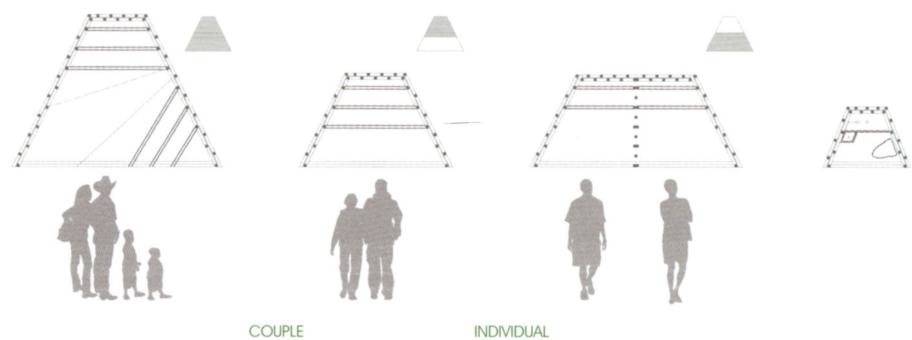

SECTION A-A

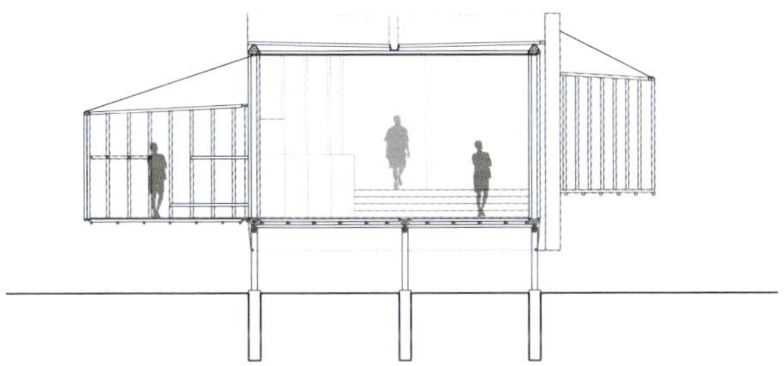

SECTION B-B

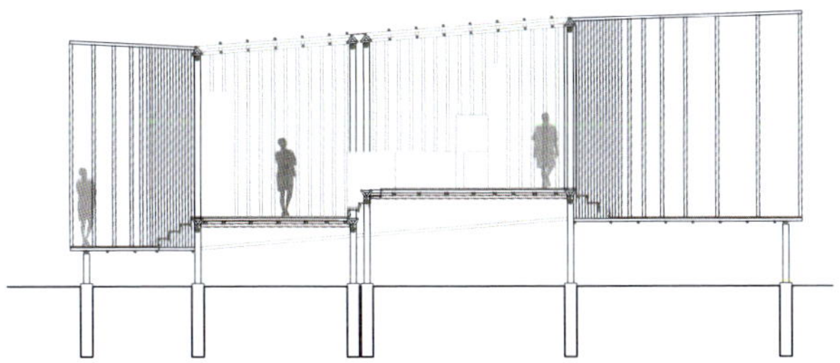

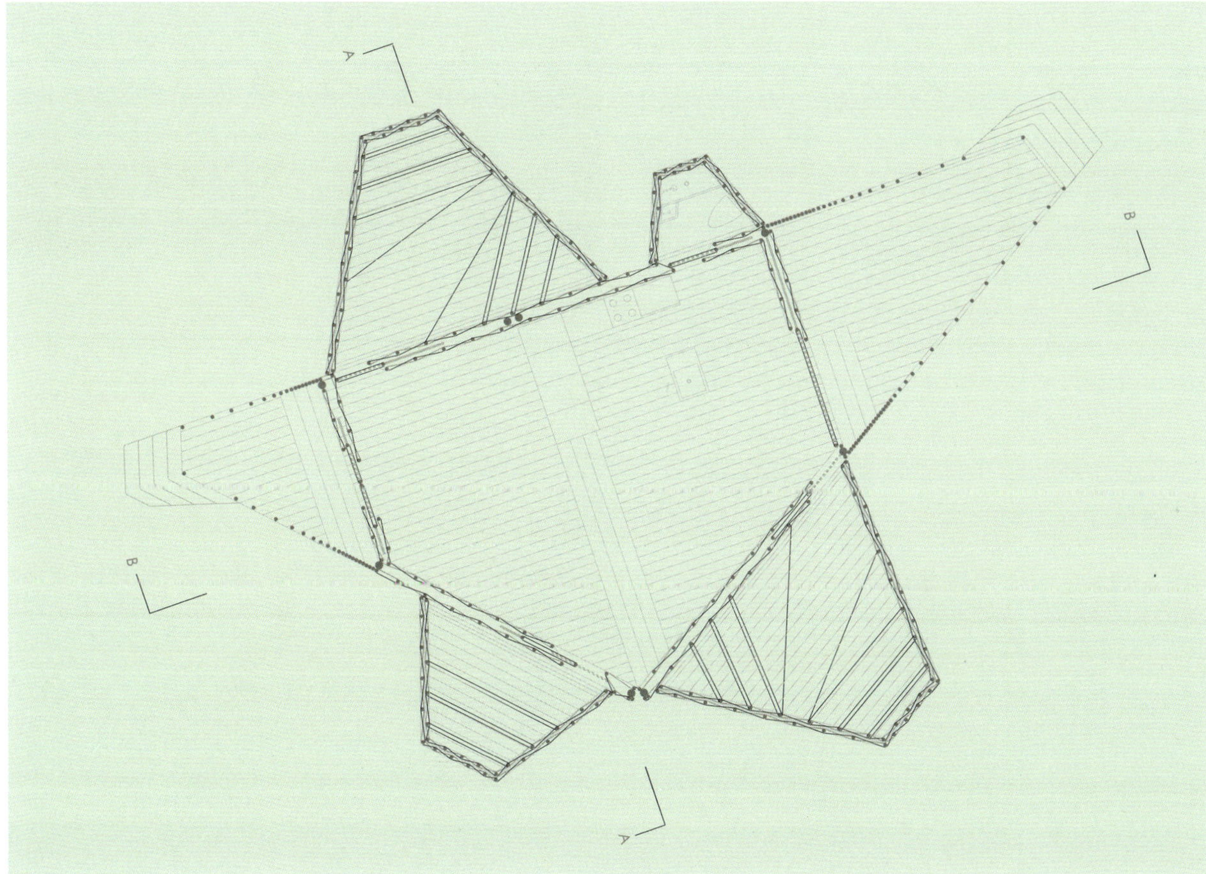

TOP: PLAN OF DWELLING

750 PROTOTYPE

ERIK SCANLON

The 750 PROTOTYPE is a model for urban housing in Lago Agrio. With the population projected to increase from 25,000 to 150,000 by 2021, the project had to achieve optimal efficiency in terms of affordability, function and construction, while also responding to Lago Agrio's very particular urban, climatic, cultural and development conditions.

SYSTEM COMPONENTS

The 750 PROTOTYPE is a pre-fabricated, easily assembled housing system built from local materials. The structural frame is made up of bamboo segments connected with steel inserts and bolted together. The floor surface is made from rope wrapped around a concealed three-point adjustable mechanical frame that can be positioned as bed, lounge chair, seating and preparation surface. This flooring system is used in the bedrooms and in the family room.

The exterior wall system is a series of triangulated panels wrapped in a bamboo and mesh weave that can be opened along the roof line to create air circulation. Additionally, the bottom panels could be deployed to act as an extension of the living space, increasing the square footage. The operational mechanisms in the 750 PROTOTYPE allow for these possibilities.

The materials could be replaced by other more accessible or affordable materials, giving each family the chance to express its individual identity through their own design. The ultimate goal behind the 750 PROTOTYPE is to be an answer rather than "The Answer."

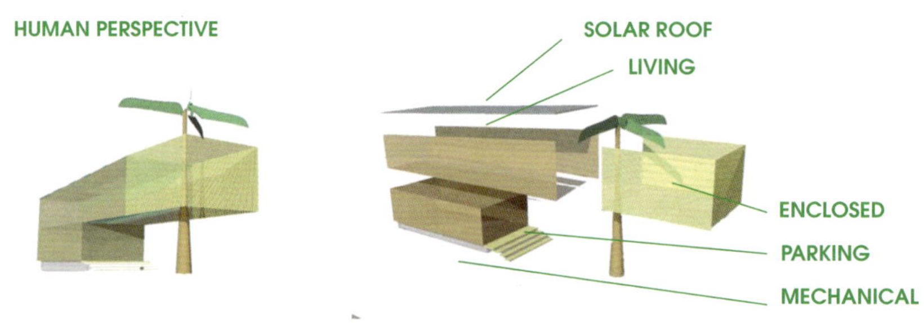

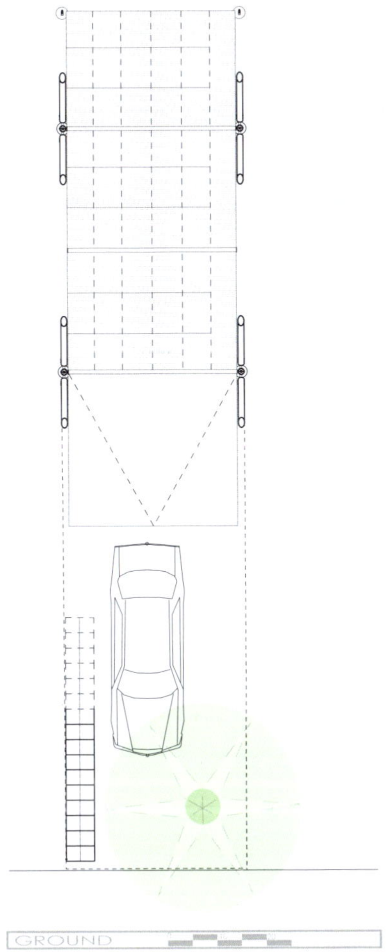

GROUND FLOOR PLAN

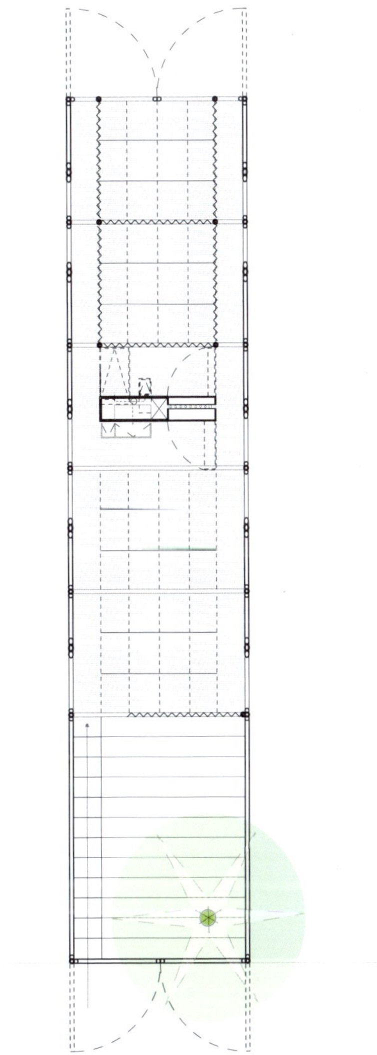

FIRST FLOOR PLAN

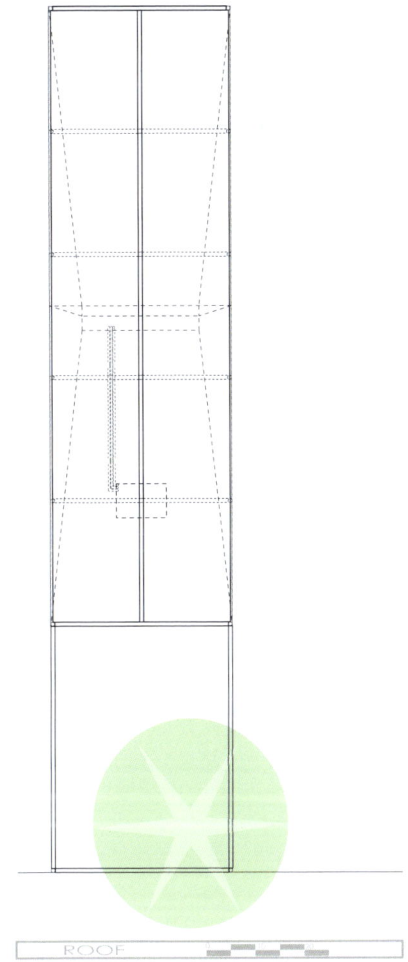

ROOF

750 + 850

UNFOLDING SCHEME

WEST ELEVATION

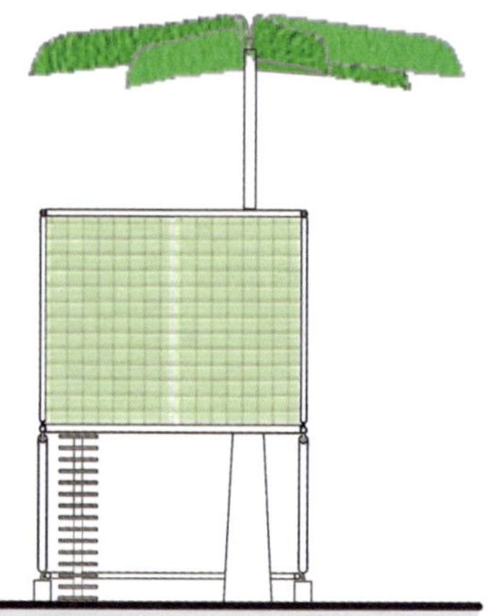

SOUTH

750 + 850

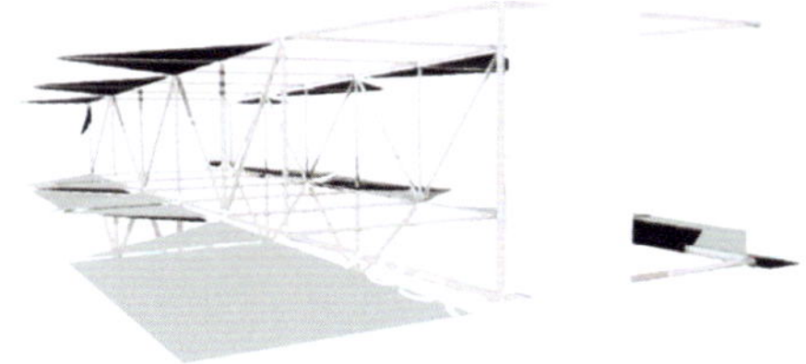

UNFOLDING SCHEME

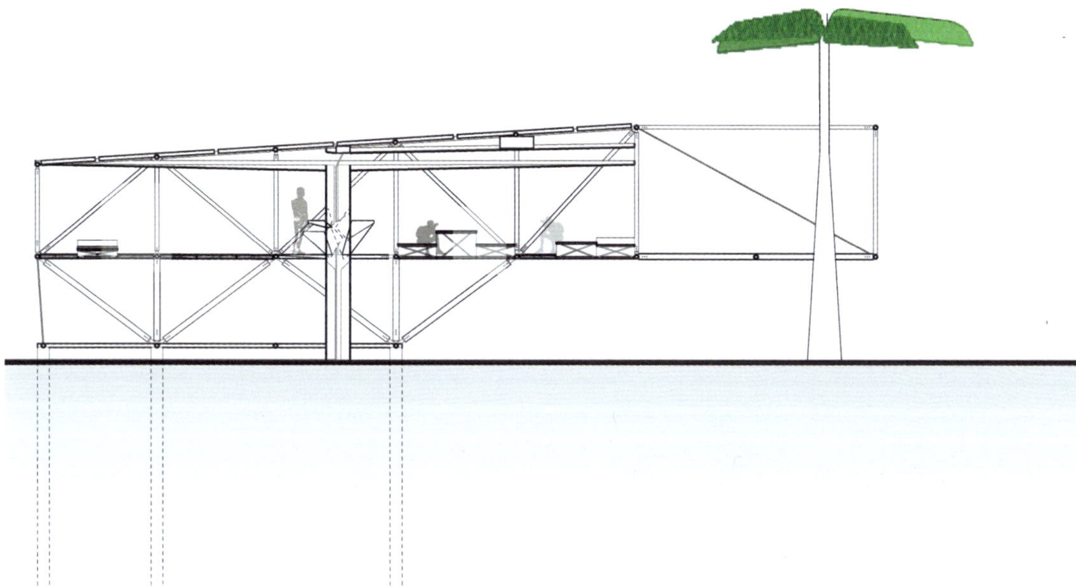

LONGITUDINAL SECTION

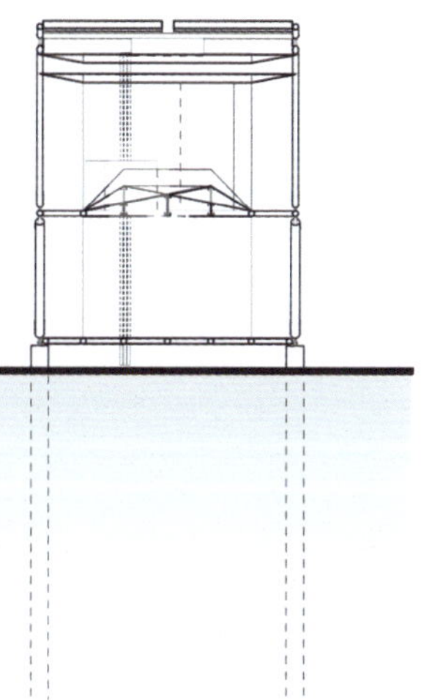

CROSS SECTION

SINGLE FAMILY DWELLING WITH LOUVERS

ROMMEL GORDILLO

THE CHALLENGE

To design a single family prototype dwelling for a hot climate. How can this system become a prototype? How can it grow?

THE CONCEPT

Nature is the most complex system of growth. We analyzed the growth of leaves and trees to gain an understanding of complex growth.

The back of the house is elevated. It serves as a recycling water system. The open space in the middle of the house serves as a water filter.

PRIVATE AREAS

These are at the back and upper levels to enhance privacy.

PUBLIC SPACES

These begin at the entrance and circulate upwards to make a "u" shape. The public areas have louvers and views to open them up to the outside.

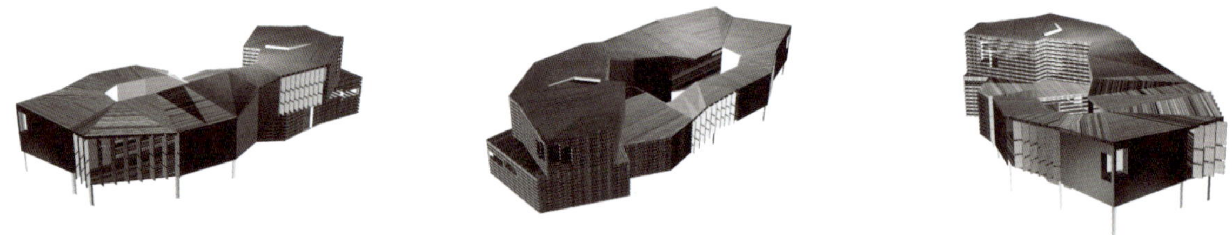

VIEWS

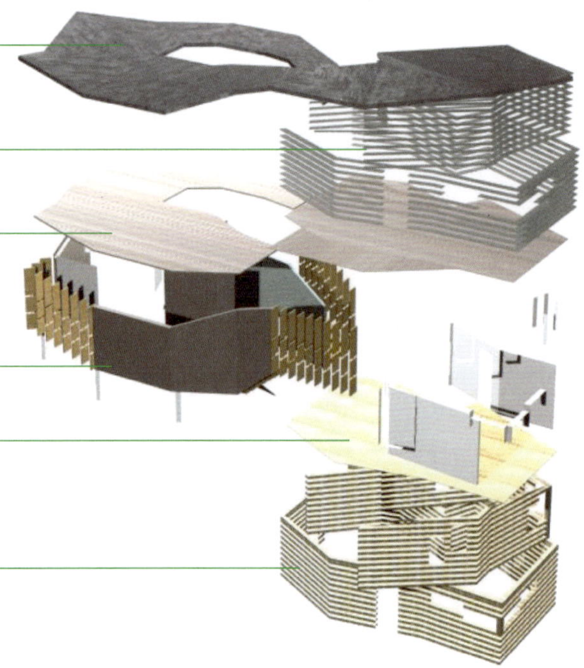

LOUVER DIAGRAM

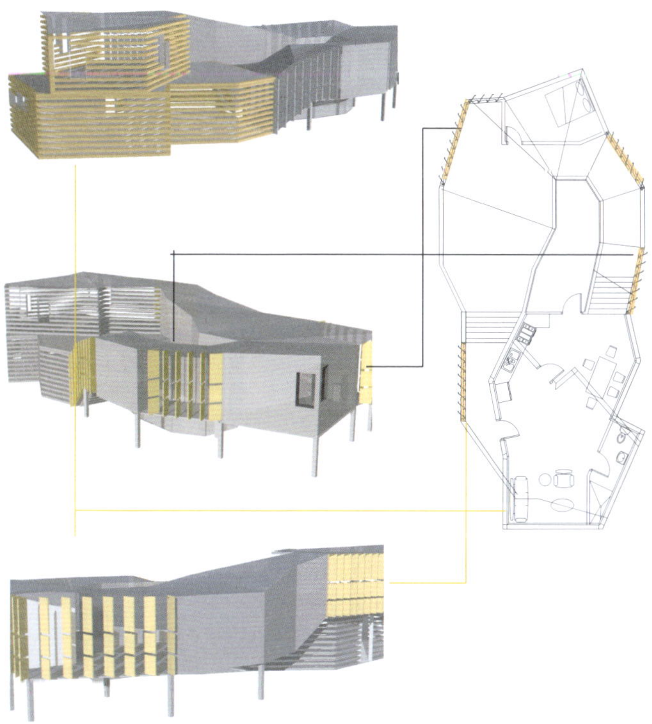

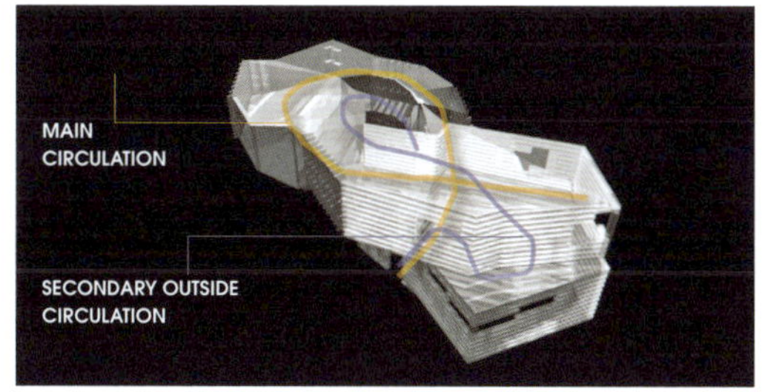

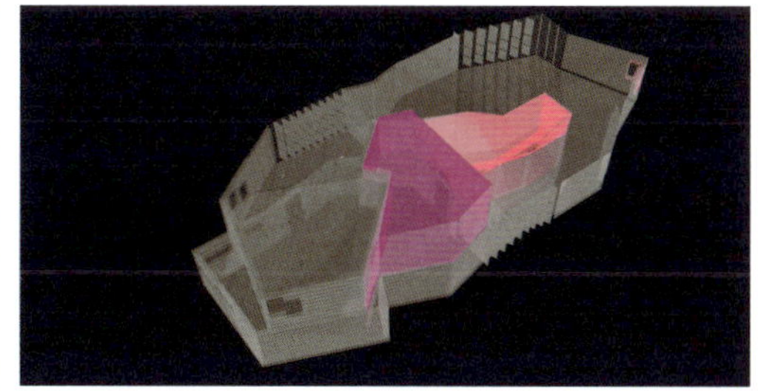

PRIVATE

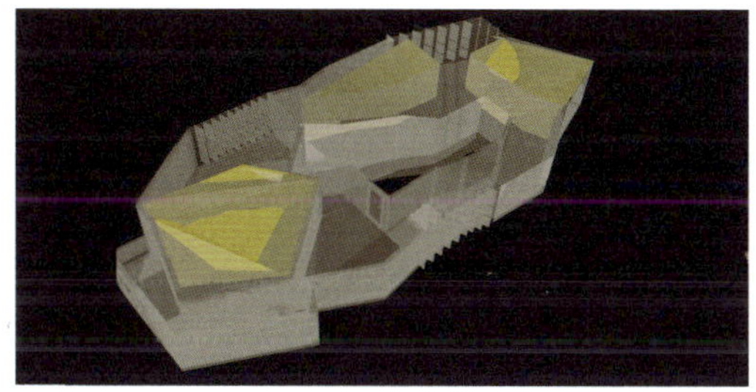

GREEN PUBLIC

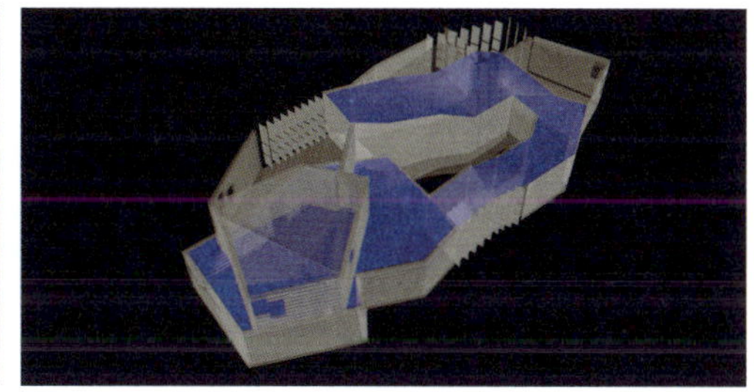

PUBLIC

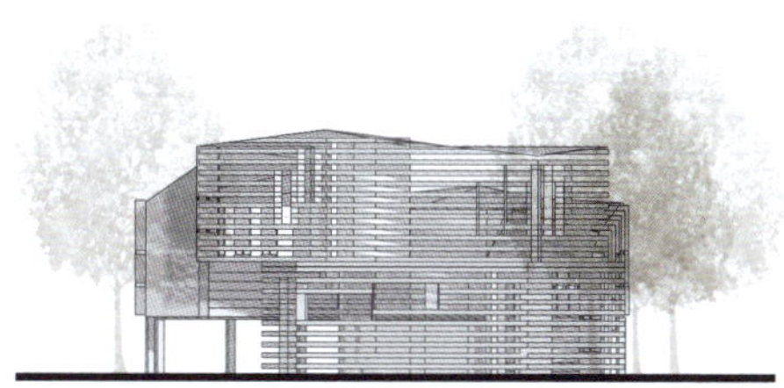

SOUTH ELEVATION

NORTH ELEVATION

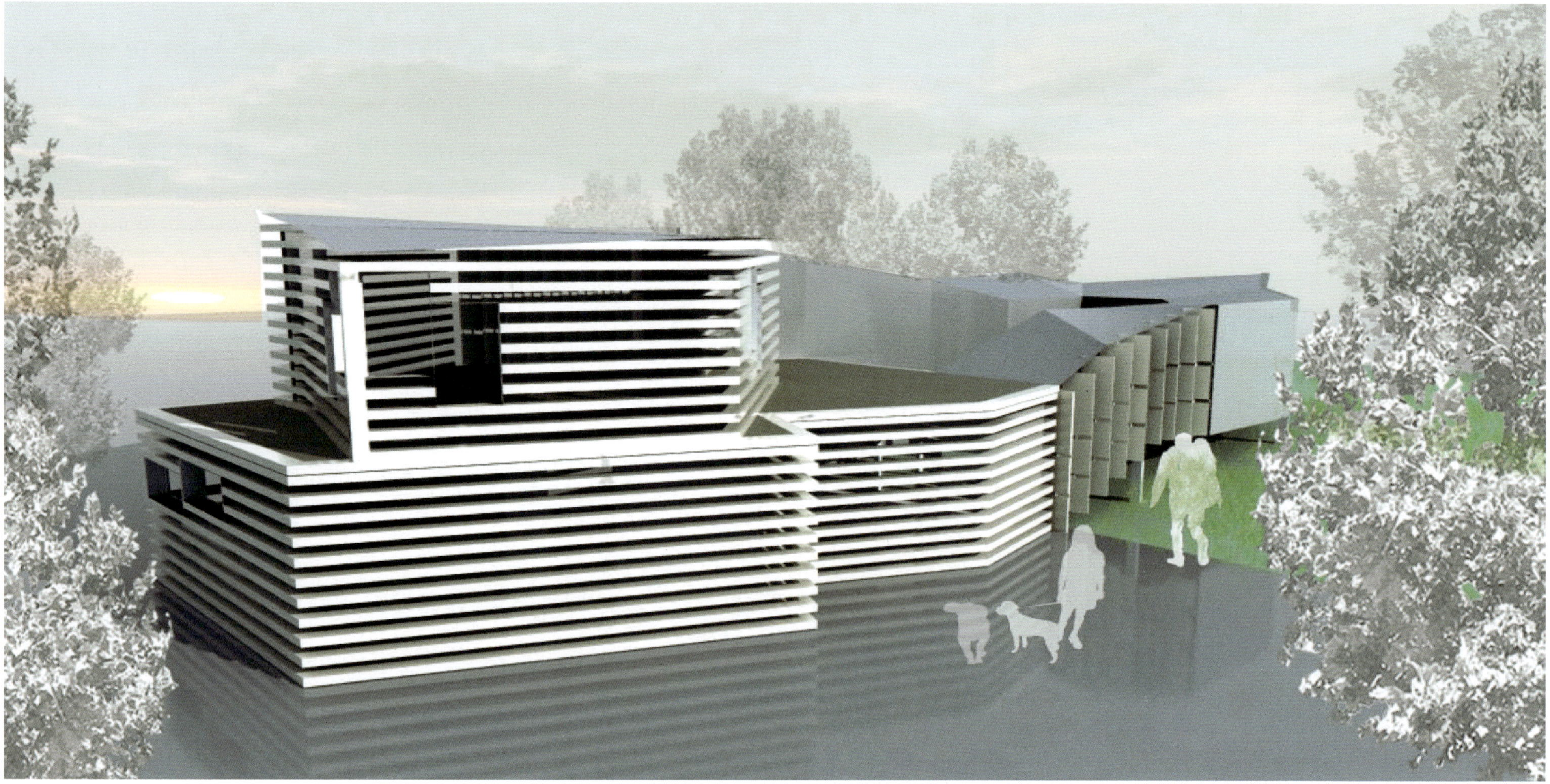

ROOF

The roof was designed at a pitch, sending rain water to a well at the center of the house where it is collected and used. The structure is mainly composed of wood with aluminum louvers which let in air while preventing water penetration when closed. The structure is placed onto the main walls that hold the house together.

PARTY WALL - Connects the units
WET WALL - Collects water for recycling and re-use
LOUVER WALL/OUTSIDE WALL - Lets in air and light
OUTSIDE/INTERIOR WALL - Provides privacy and cooling

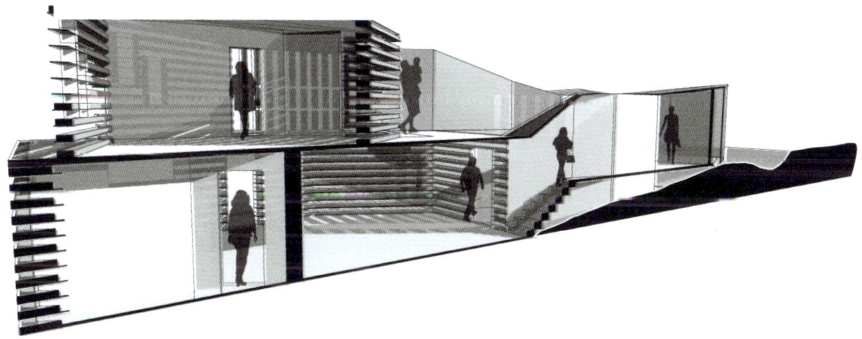

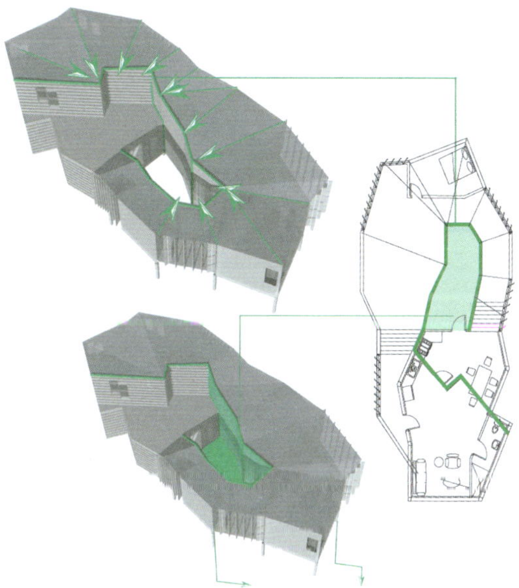

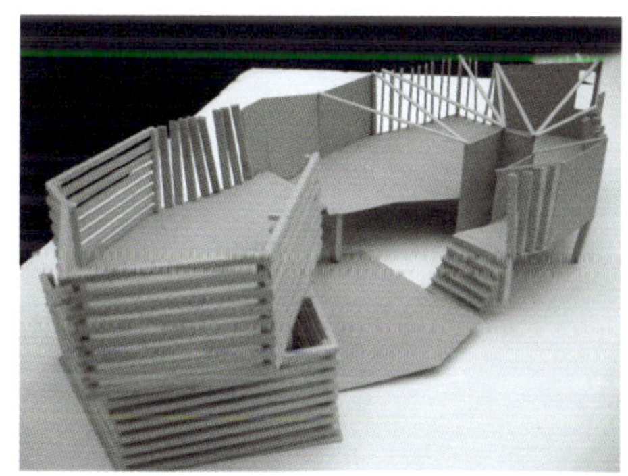

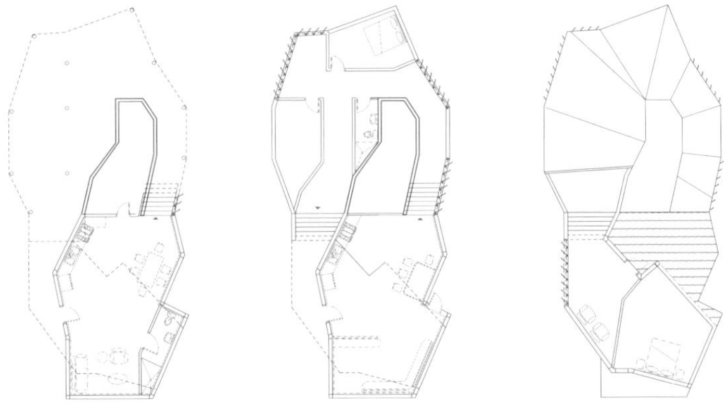

FIRST FLOOR PLAN

SECOND FLOOR PLAN

THIRD FLOOR PLAN

VIEW: EAST ELEVATION

HOUSING WITH NATURE

PATRICK ISAAC

Our point of departure is the creation of an infrastructure that will allow newcomers to plug themselves into the city. Architecturally this translates into an "auto-constructed peripheral in which [people build] their own homes." This creates individual, private housing while the residents' social needs become the basis upon which the city functions. One solution is a "parking garage" like building – pure infrastructure that attempts to pick up on the dynamic of the city street and render it in the vertical. Citizens can appropriate a parcel of built space, similar to a plot of land, and build at their own leisure. The vertical prolongation of the street into the buildings will connect the individual to common social spaces and activities.

CIRCULATION PATTERN

Development site
City grid

HOUSING COMPLEX AND SITE RESTRICTIONS

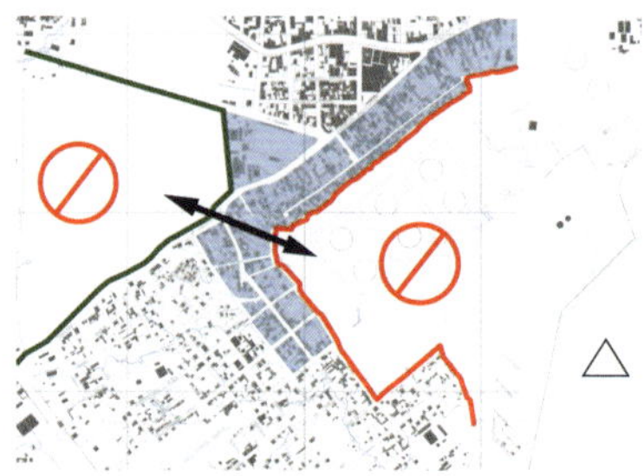

Construction site
Green barrier
Petroleum barrier
Interchange boundary

IMAGES: SITE CONTEXT

TOP: EXISTING SITE CONDITIONS
RIGHT: SITE INTERVENTION

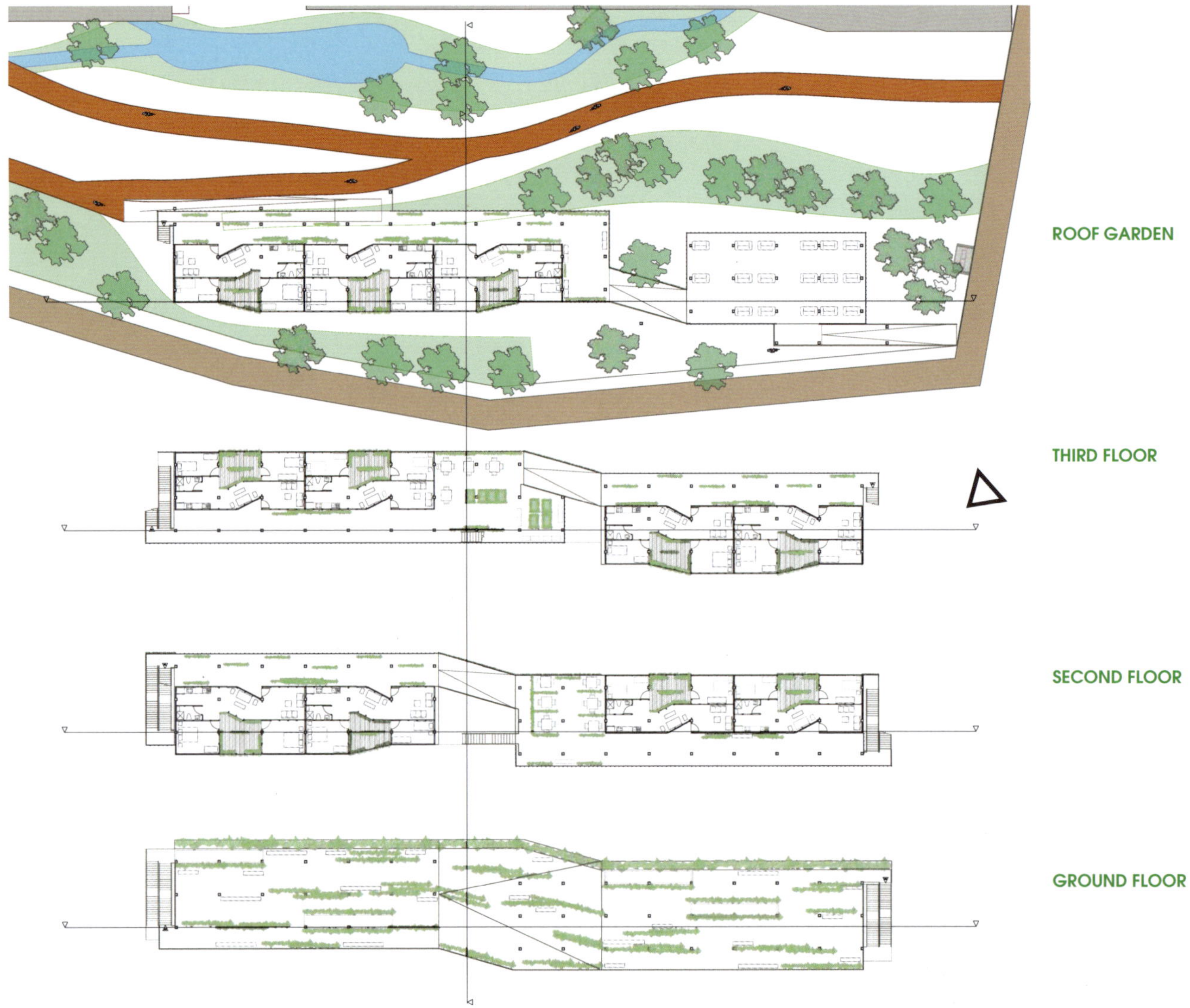
ROOF GARDEN
THIRD FLOOR
SECOND FLOOR
GROUND FLOOR

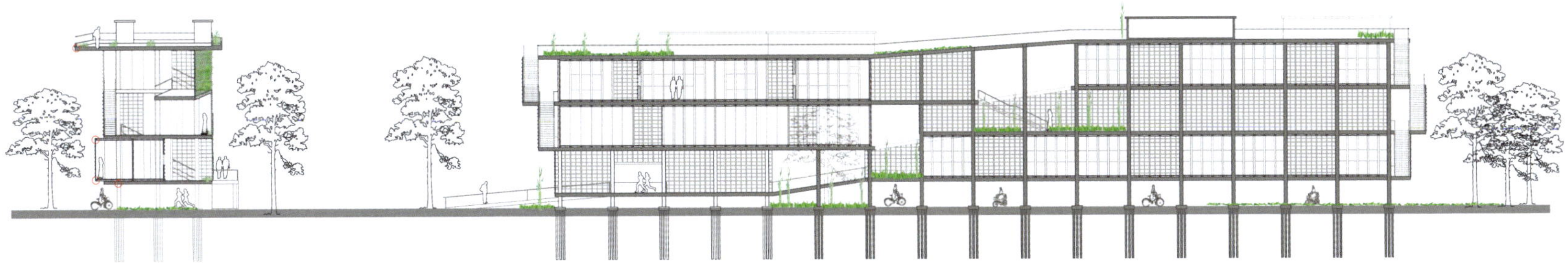

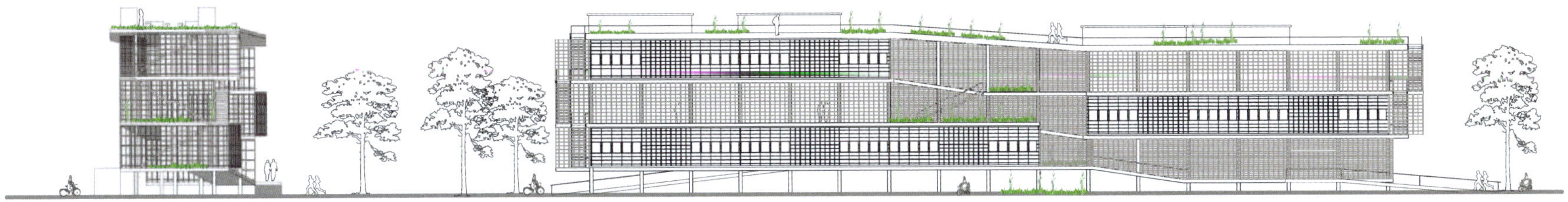

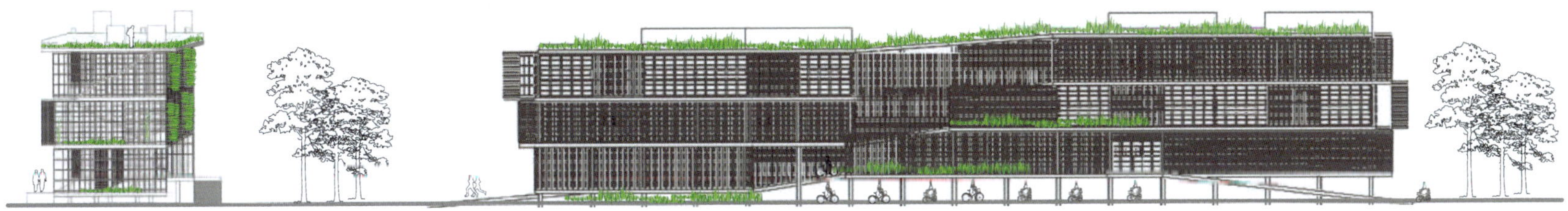

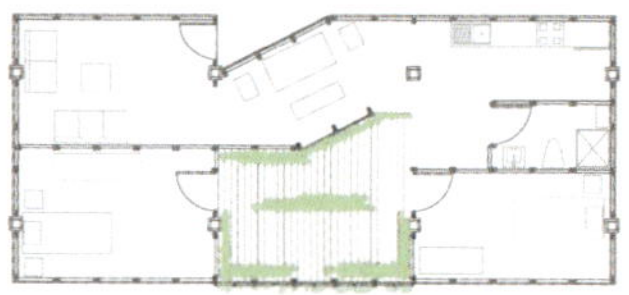

UNIT WITH TWO SINGLE BEDROOMS
FACING EAST, OIL REFINERY VIEW

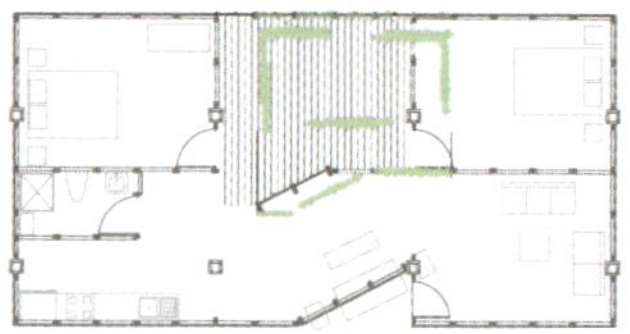

UNIT WITH TWO DOUBLE BEDROOMS
FACING WEST, CITY VIEW

UNIT WITH ONE SINGLE AND ONE DOUBLE BEDROOM
FACING WEST, CITY VIEW, SOUTH ORIENTATION

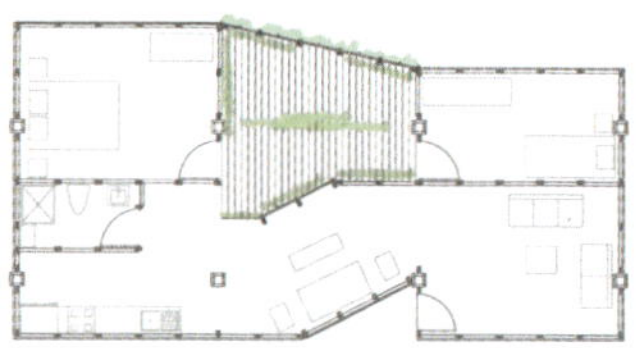

UNIT WITH ONE SINGLE AND ONE DOUBLE BEDROOM
FACING WEST, CITY VIEW, NORTH ORIENTATION

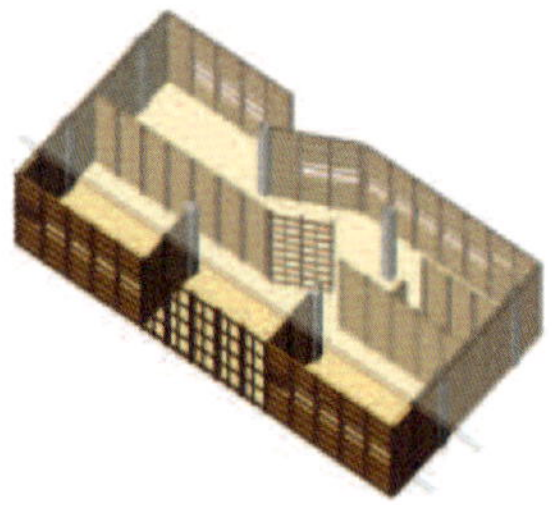

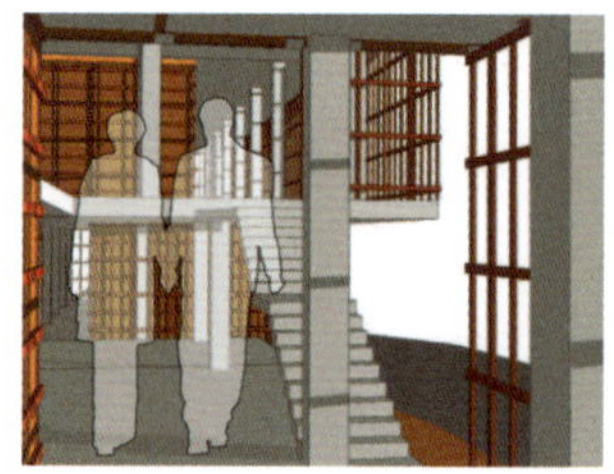

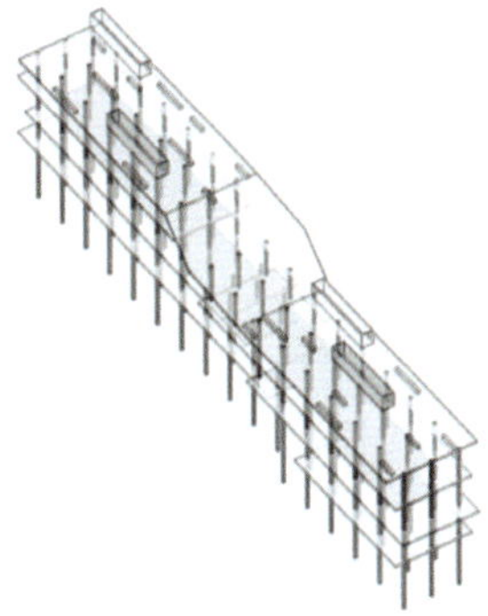

CONCRETE FRAME

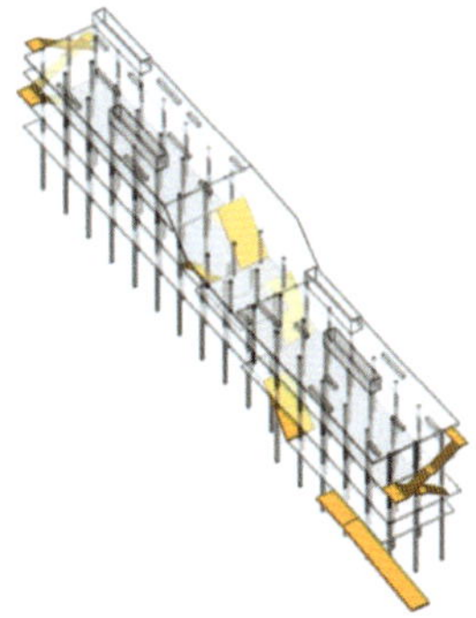

CIRCULATION

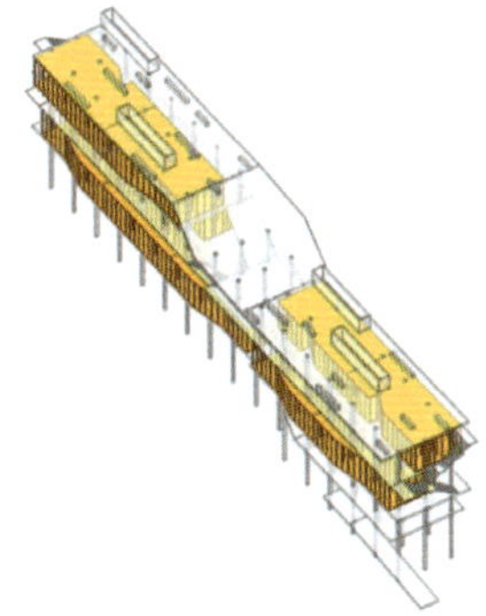

SECONDARY WOOD STRUCTURE

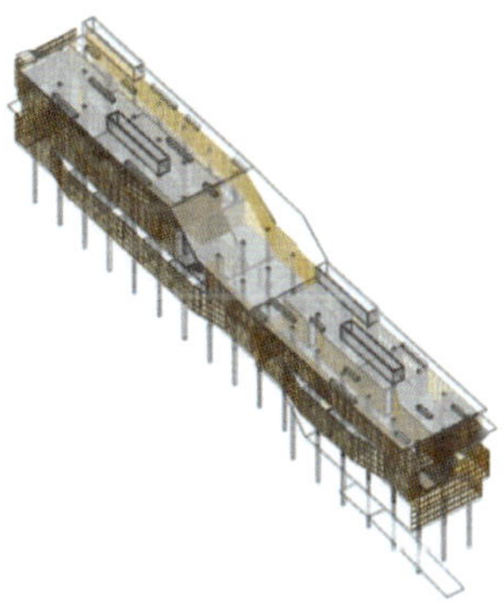

SKIN

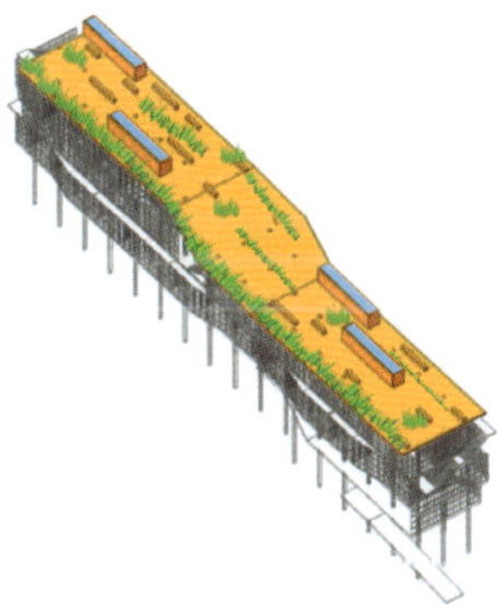

SUSTAINABLE ROOF GARDEN

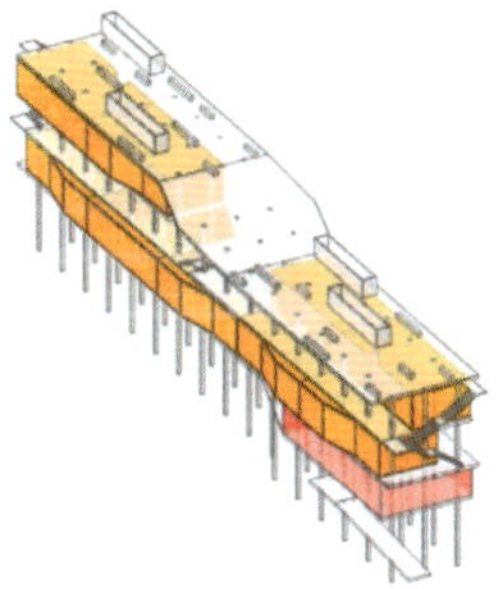

PROGRAM

STACKABLE HOUSING

YULIYA ILIZAROV

This linear housing model is for a sparsely populated area south of the Aguarico River. The linear settlement begins at the artificial southwestern limit of the city. At the boundary, public farmland supports the developing community with an agricultural market to serve the whole city. A relatively dense urban grid of housing, communal urban gardens, markets, pedestrian, bike and vehicular circulation paths and open public spaces follow the strip of linear farms.

The living units are composed linearly with a series of terraces, overhangs and courtyards to create outdoor spaces that range from private to semi-private and public. The most public open space houses the communal urban gardens, which produce food for both local consumption and for sale by the different living clusters. An exterior lattice of circulation, structure and infrastructure supports the living unit cluster.

GROUND FLOOR | FIRST FLOOR | SECOND FLOOR | THIRD FLOOR | ROOF

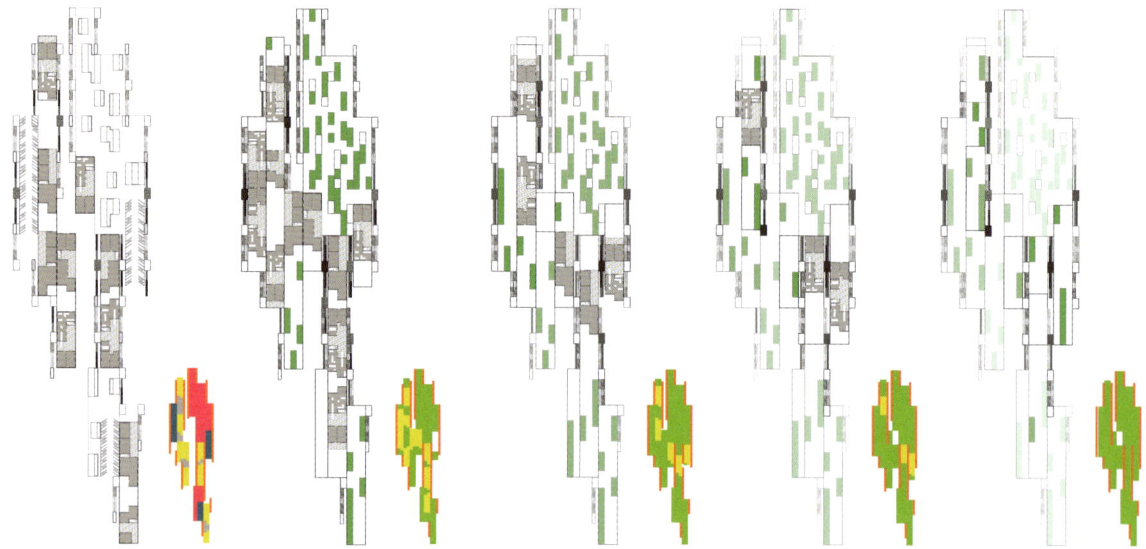

MARKET

STORAGE + BICYCLE RACKS

LIVING UNITS

CIRCULATION + STRUCTURE + INFRASTRUCTURE LATTICE

OPEN SPACE + URBAN GARDEN

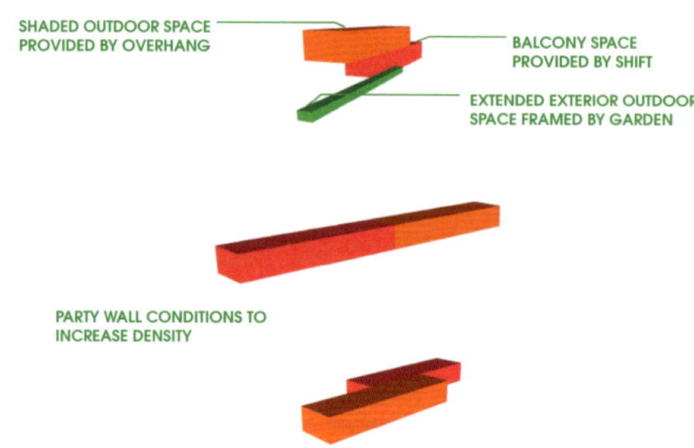

THREE GRADIENTS COMPOSE HOUSING

PUBLIC TO PRIVATE

LOWER TO HIGHER

LESS GREEN TO MORE GREEN

MORE PUBLIC SPACES

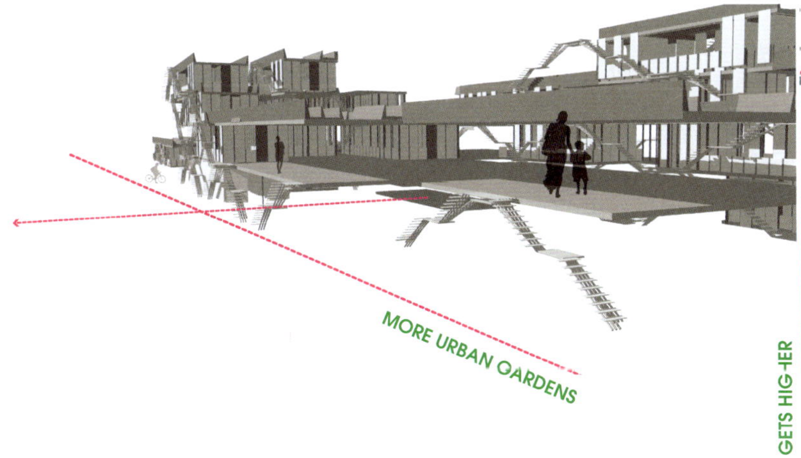

NORTH-SOUTH ELEVATION

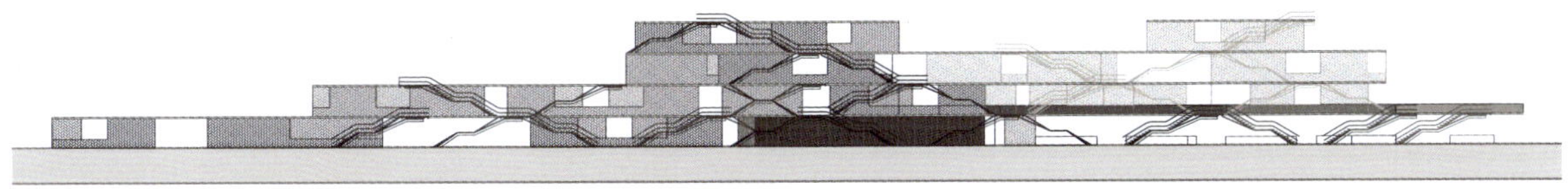

EAST-WEST ELEVATION

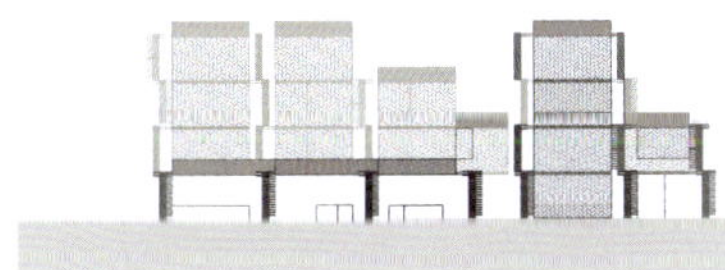

CROSS SECTION

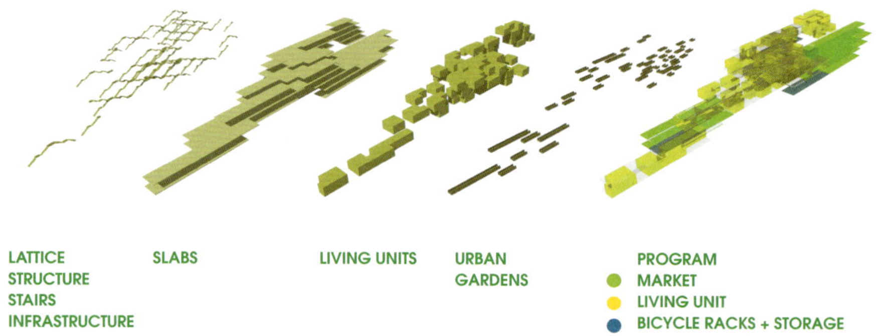
LATTICE
STRUCTURE
STAIRS
INFRASTRUCTURE
SLABS
LIVING UNITS
URBAN
GARDENS
PROGRAM
MARKET
LIVING UNIT
BICYCLE RACKS + STORAGE

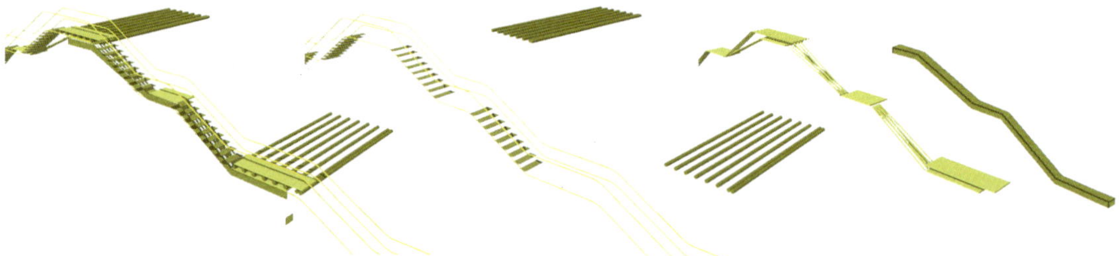

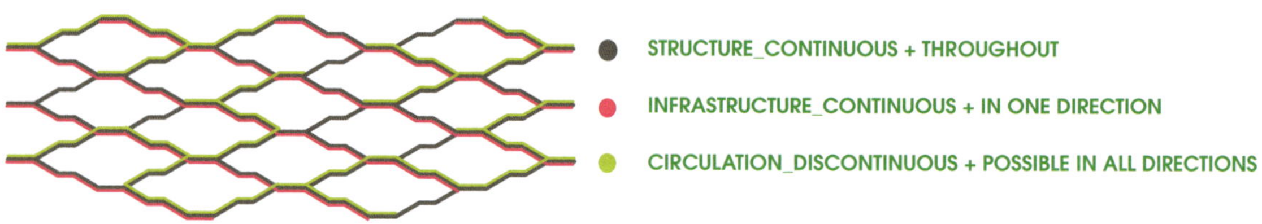
STRUCTURE_CONTINUOUS + THROUGHOUT
INFRASTRUCTURE_CONTINUOUS + IN ONE DIRECTION
CIRCULATION_DISCONTINUOUS + POSSIBLE IN ALL DIRECTIONS

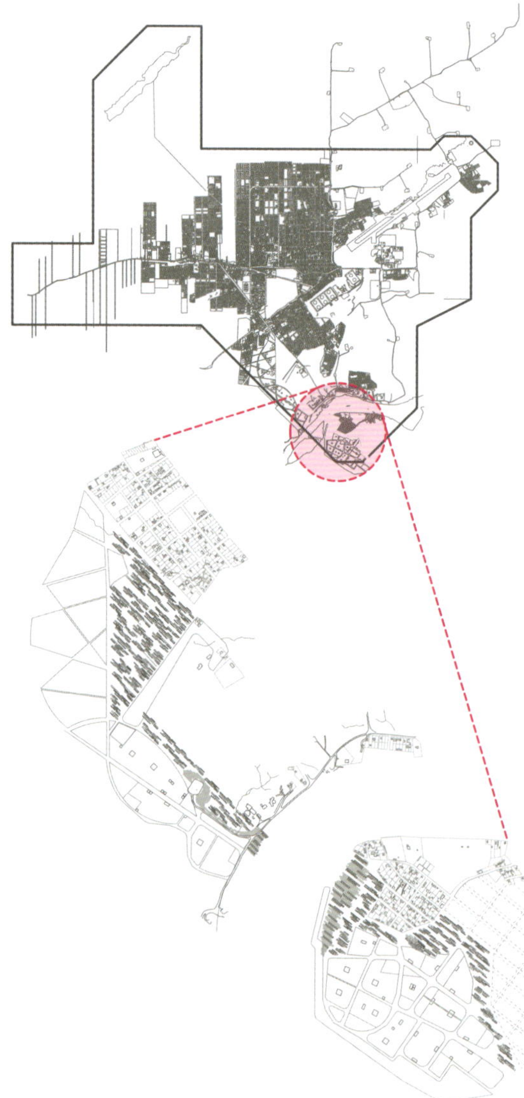

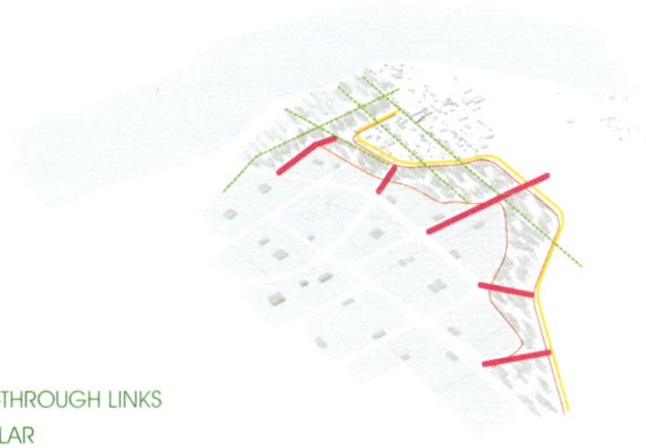

CIRCULATION

- CROSS-THROUGH LINKS
- VEHICULAR
- PEDESTRIAN + BIKE
- IMPLIED EXTENSION OF CITY GRID

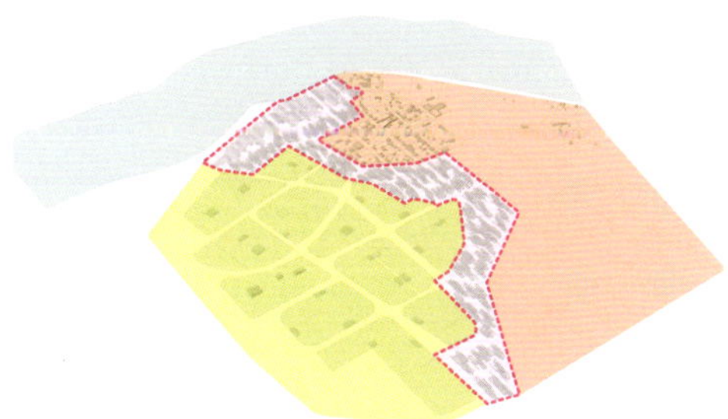

CONCEPT

BUFFER ZONE BETWEEN
LOW DENSE FARMS + HIGH DENSE CITY

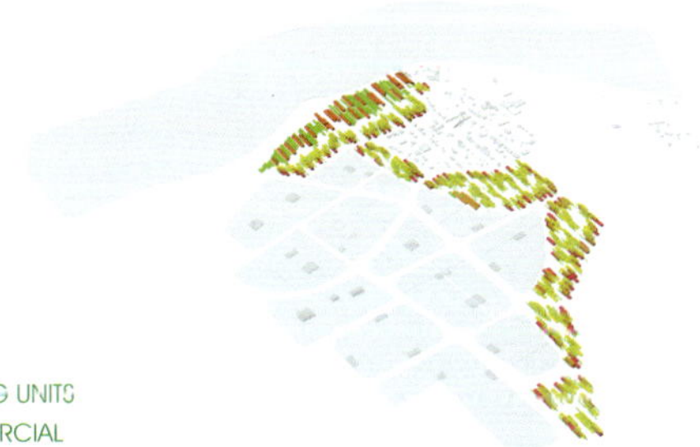

PROGRAM

- HOUSING UNITS
- COMMERCIAL
- MARKETS
- MUNICIPAL

UNIT DISPERSAL

GRID

BUFFER

EVOLUTIONARY DEVELOPMENT

GREEN + BLUE

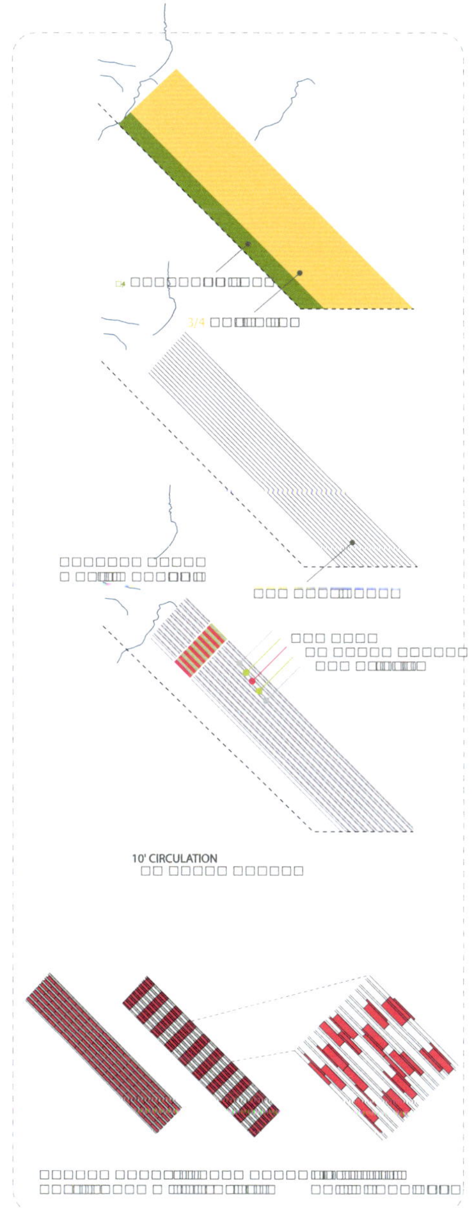

MULTI-FAMILY HOUSING: THE DEPARTURE OF THE CITY

IMAN ANSARI

The neighborhood is located at the northeastern edge of the city and is aligned with the existing airport runway. The structure of the site is a metaphor for the city as it departs and disappears. The current density of the neighborhood is fairly low. The new design therefore seeks to address this.

A new grid structure creates spatial opportunities within the neighborhood. Density is increased by the center and the main circulation and axis of the existing plan fitted within the new system.

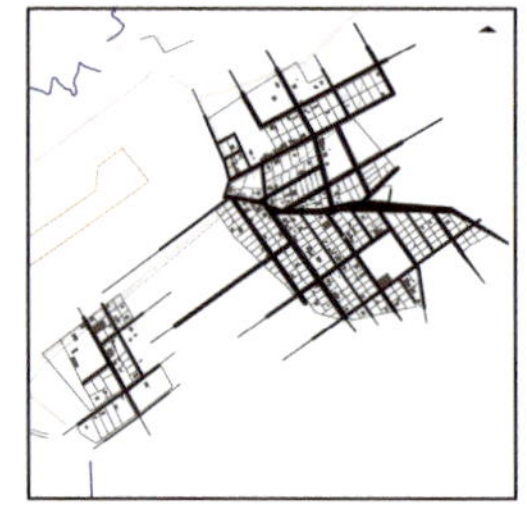

EXISTING STREET SYSTEM

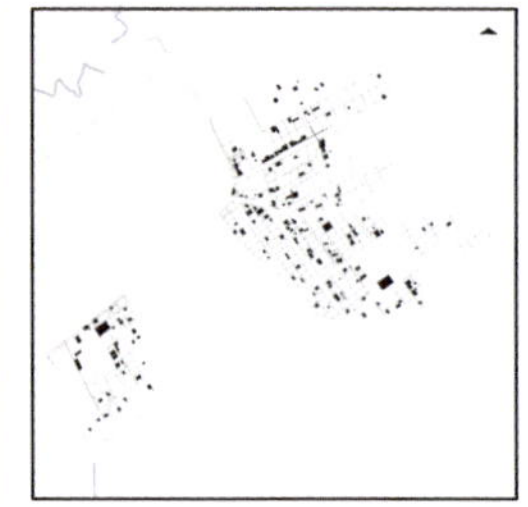

EXISTING BUILT STRUCTURE

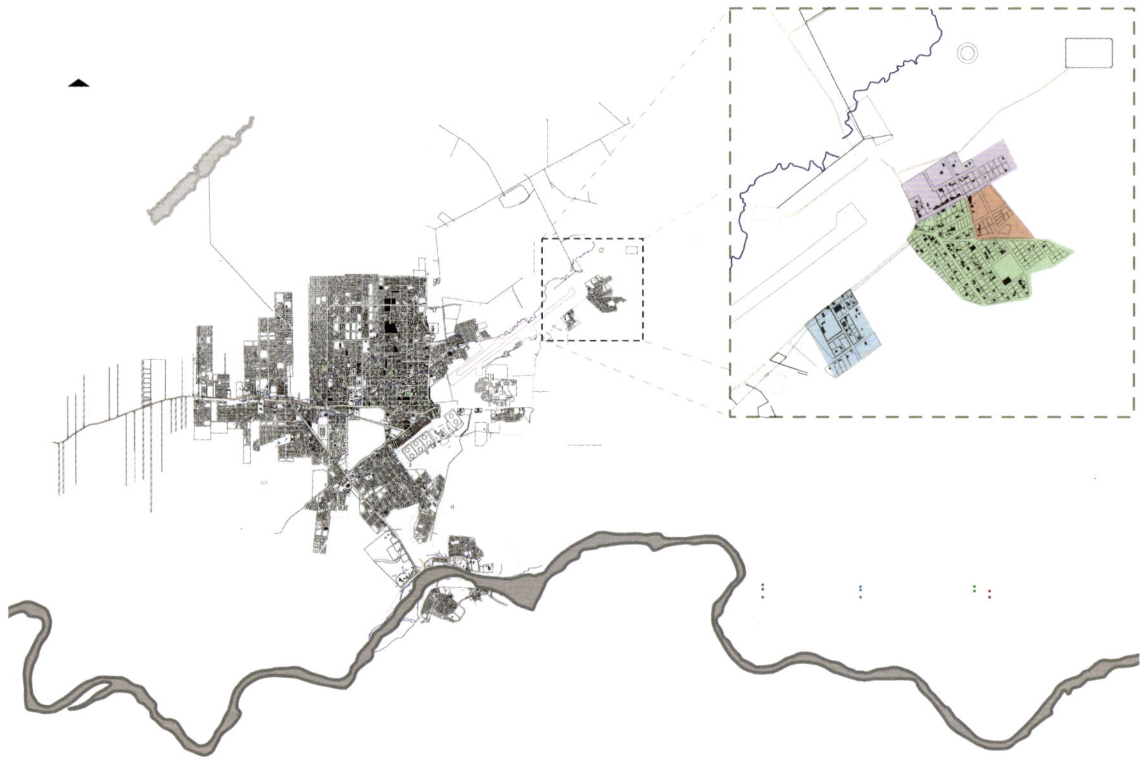

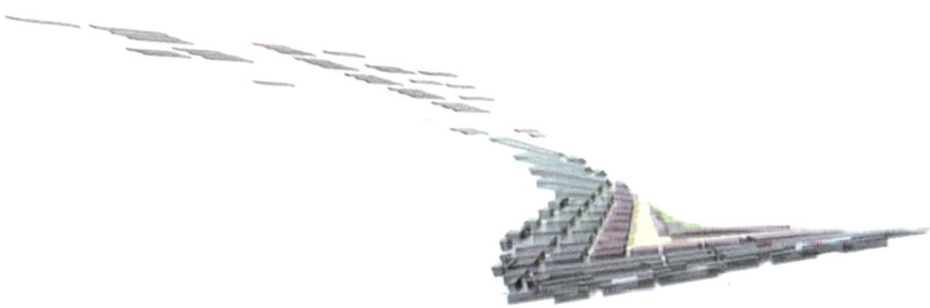

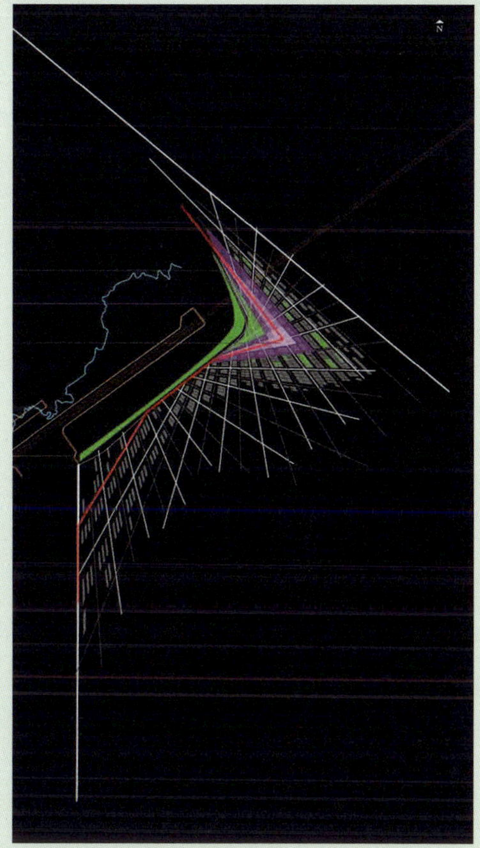

MULTI-FAMILY HOUSING: LIVING IN THE AMAZON

IMAN ANSARI

This project is a new system for large-scale housing: The repetition of a single folded structure which contains two living units, and two gardens. The second structure sits next to the first one, yet faces the opposite direction. This pattern is then repeated.

One living unit is always surrounded by gardens on four sides. Each unit will also have its own private garden in front to improve energy efficiency and cooling. The ground level will be given over to commercial and public use. This will create an active public space beneath the building. There is a communal space within the building for public activities.

ENVIRONMENTAL STRATEGY

DETAIL

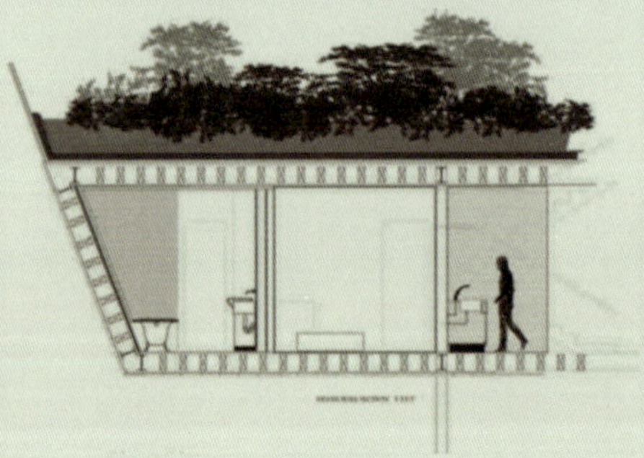

BUILDING SECTION

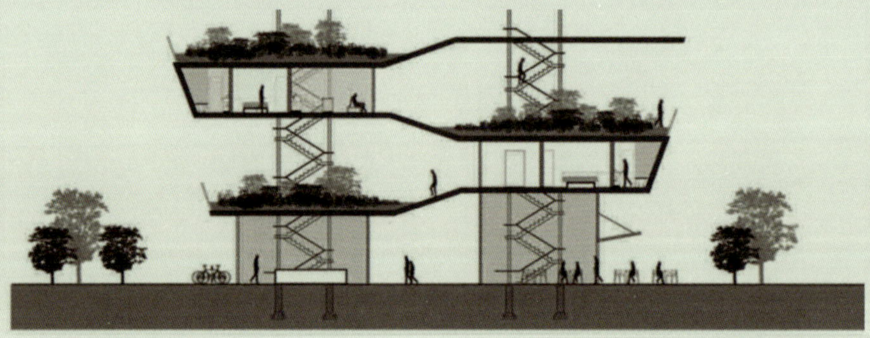

IMAGES: VIEWS OF HOUSING

LAGO AGRIO HOUSING

LAWRENCE JACQUETTE

This project relies on the completion of the as yet unfinished bridge over the Aguarico River and on the construction of a second pedestrian/cycle bridge to the east.

A multi-stranded linear housing development will sit on the river's south bank, between these two bridges, providing a link between them.

The project includes various sustainable waste management solutions including on-site grey water treatment. The buildings are self-ventilating, sustainable and have day care facilities for parents working in other parts of the city.

The combination of housing and commercial use at ground level, and the creation of a public square at the head of the proposed pedestrian and cycle bridge, will create a major new piece of infrastructure on the river's south bank.

STRUCTURAL FRAME

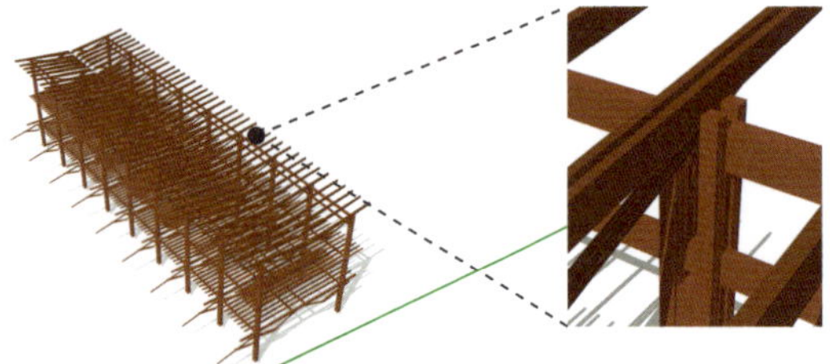

DOUBLE SPLIT COLUMN UTILIZES SMALLER STRUCTURAL MEMBERS TO MAKE COLUMNS AS WELL AS HAVING GIRDERS

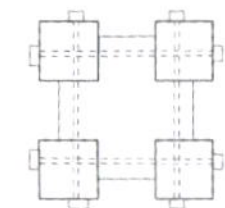

COLUMN CROSS SECTION @ CONNECTION

SECTION A

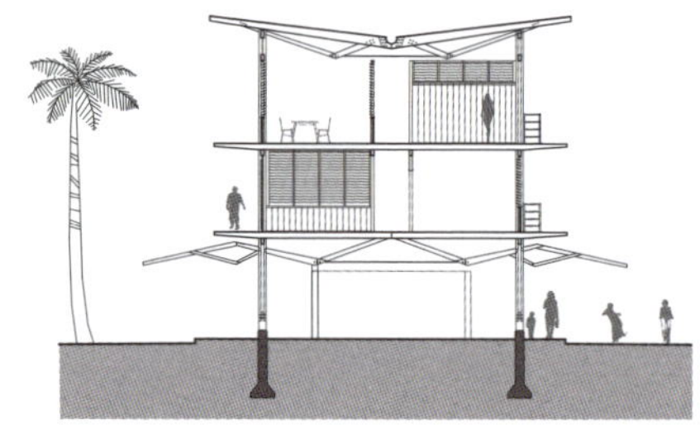

INFILL PANELS OF LOUVERS AND EARTHEN PLASTER ALLOW FOR AIR FLOW

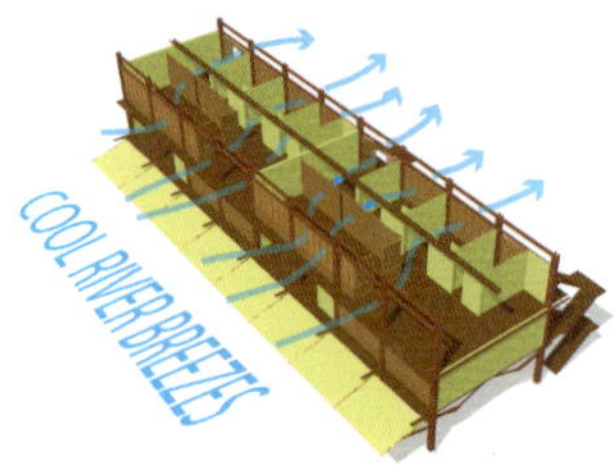

SOUTH ELEVATION

INVERSE PITCHED ROOF CATCHES RAINWATER FOR COLLECTION IN CISTERNS

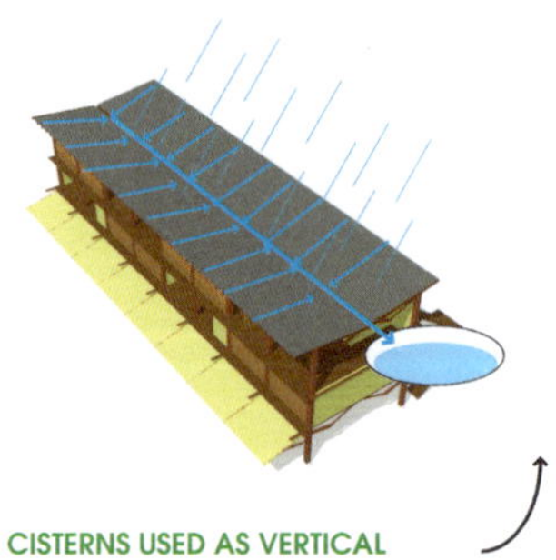

CISTERNS USED AS VERTICAL CIRCULATION UP TO UNITS

NORTH ELEVATION

SCALE 1:100

ROOF PLAN

1St FLOOR PLAN

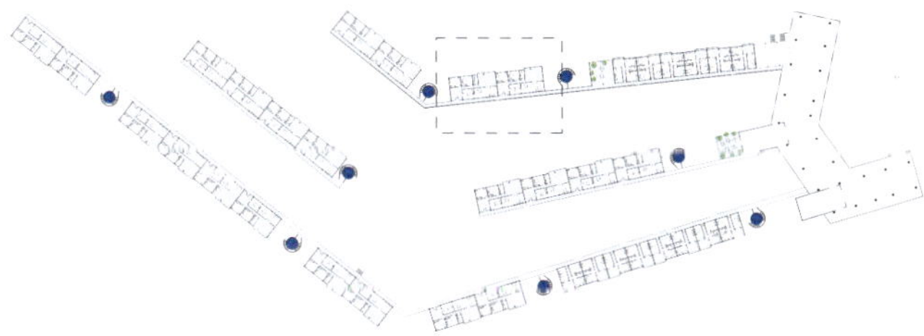

OPEN MARKET

BAR/RESTAURANT

GROUND FLOOR PLAN

SCALE 1:1000

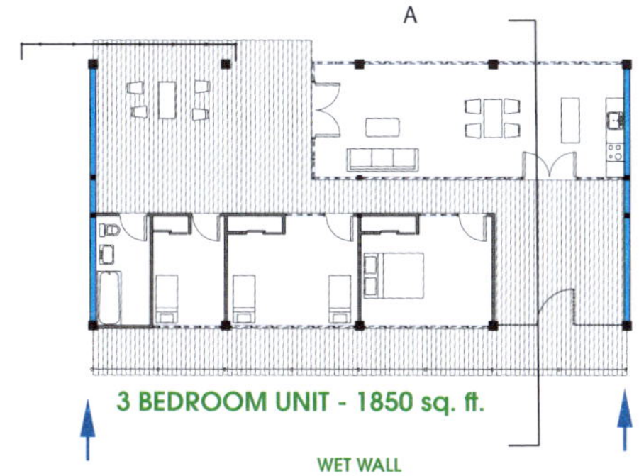

3 BEDROOM UNIT - 1850 sq. ft.

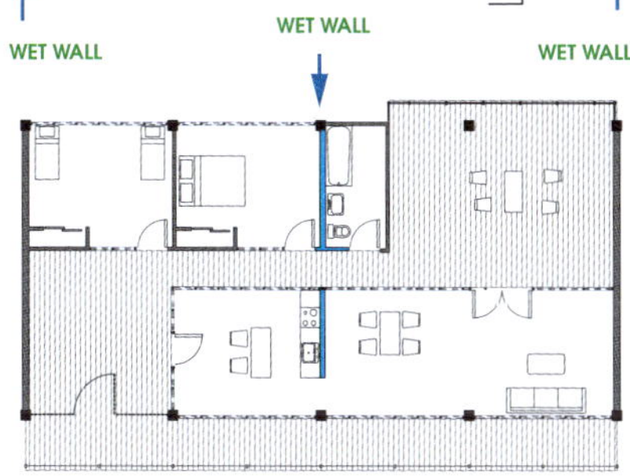

2 BEDROOM UNIT - 1850 sq. ft.

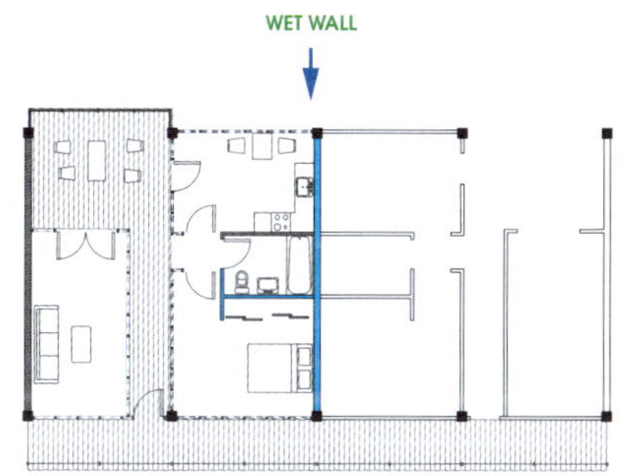

3 BEDROOM UNIT - 925 sq. ft.

SCALE 1:100

MASTER PLAN

LAGO AGRIO HOUSING

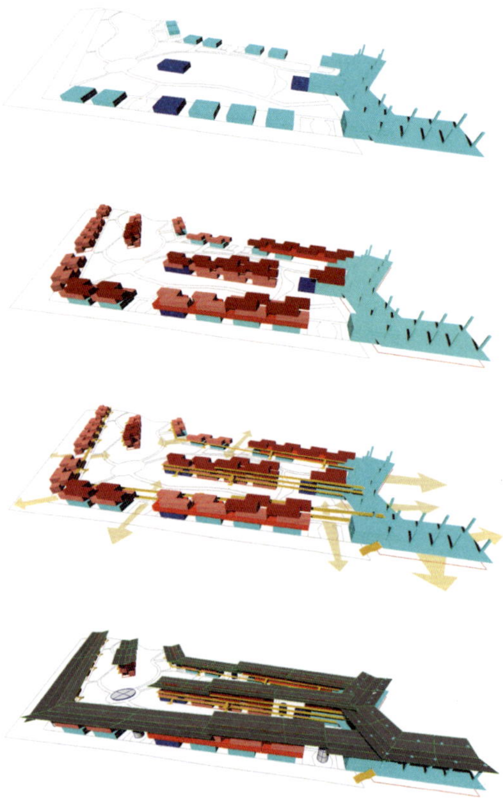

LEGEND

- COMMERCIAL
- COMMUNITY
- 3 BEDROOM
- 2 BEDROOM
- 1 BEDROOM
- CIRCULATION

WALL SECTION DETAIL

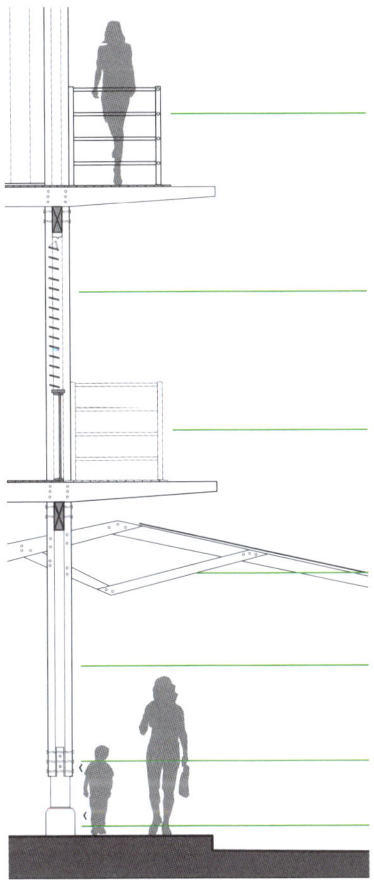

TOP: 3 BEDROOM OUTDOOR LIVING SPACE RENDERING

BOTTOM: MARKET STALL ARCADE RENDERING

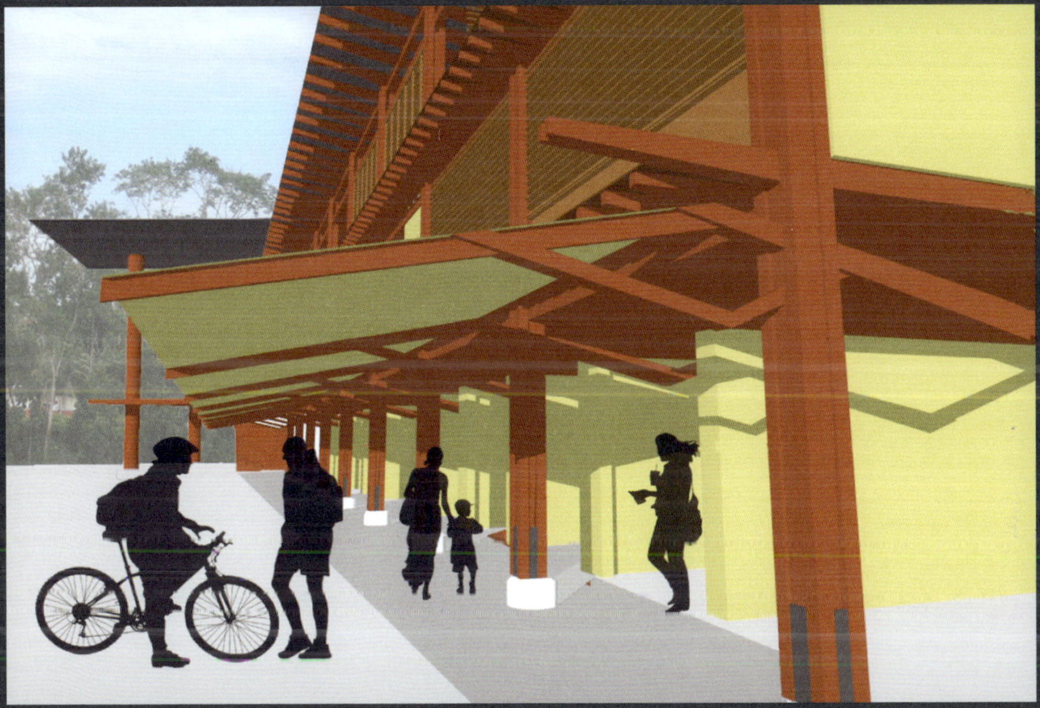

MOBILE CLASSROOM: POP-UP SCHOOLHOUSE

LAWRENCE JACQUETTE AND CAMILLE DUNN

This portable, two-room, off-the-grid schoolhouse is designed for use by the indigenous peoples of the rainforest near Nueva Loja. The flexible interior houses the school by day and functions after hours as a community space with room for meetings and small assemblies. The structure, skin and furnishings of the pop-up schoolhouse fit entirely within a wooden shipping container, which unfolds to become the school's flooring. Bamboo columns placed in steel brackets support the roofing system and create a grid for panel modules to be plugged into. These modules can be arranged according to climatic or programmatic needs.

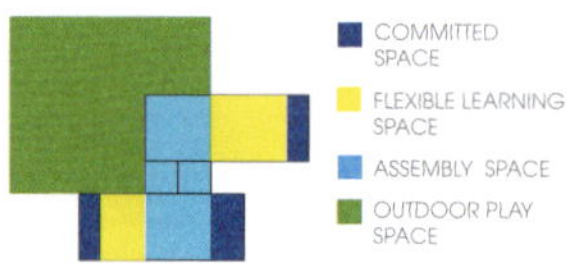

PROGRAMMATIC DISTRIBUTION OF CONFIGURATION "B"

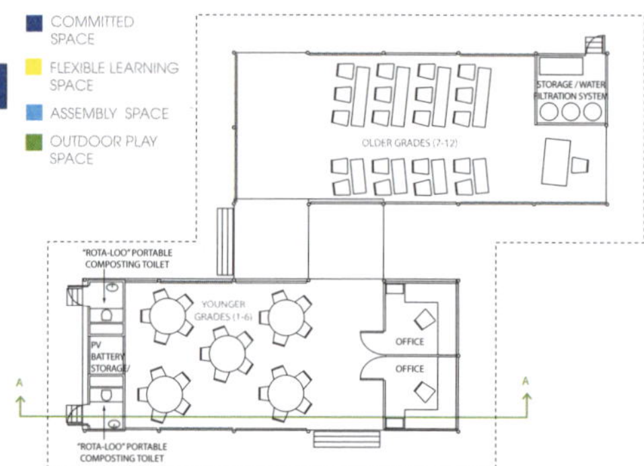

PLAN

UNITS CAN BE CONFIGURED IN A VARIETY OF WAYS TO RESPOND TO SITE AND PROGRAMMATIC RELATIONSHIPS

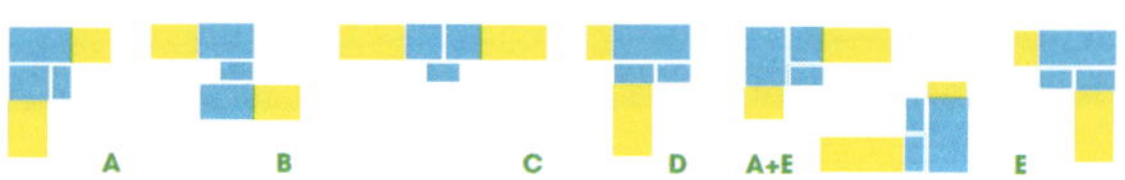

STACKABLE/UNPACKABLE

THE POP UP SCHOOL PARTS COME PACKAGED IN A WOODEN SHIPPING CONTAINER THAT FOLDS OUT TO BECOME THE SCHOOL'S FLOOR SLABS

THE ROOF TRUSSES FOLD TOGETHER AND NESTLE WITHIN ONE ANOTHER, WITH THE ROOF AND WALL FABRIC ROLLED UP. SMALLER SPACES ARE FILLED UP BY FURNITURE, OFFICE SUPPLIES, BOOKS AND INSTALLATION MATERIALS.

SECTION AA

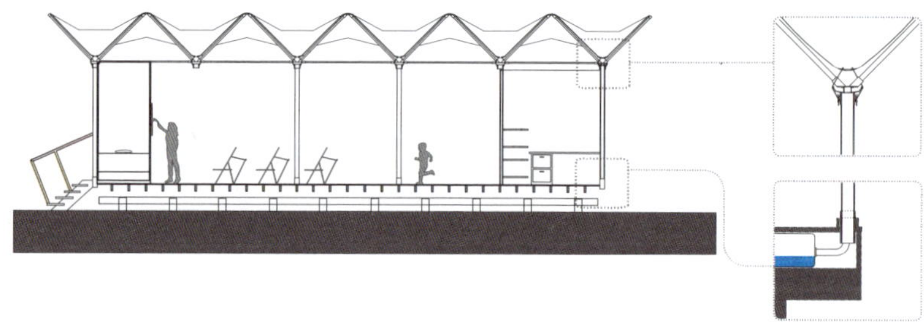

SCALE 1˝=1´

EXPAND-O-TRUSS

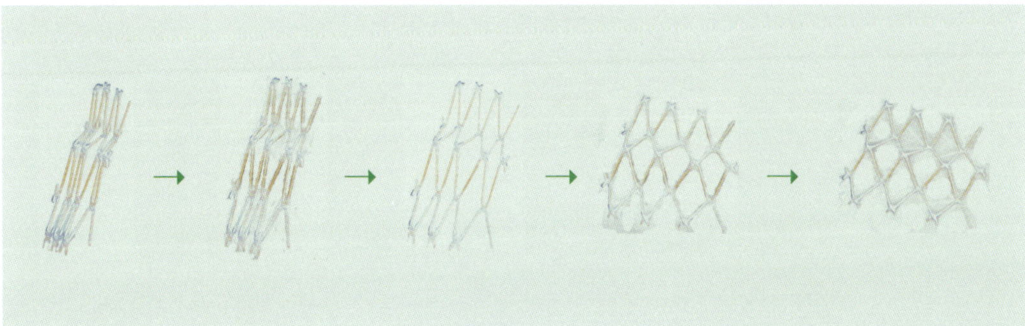

MOD-U-PANEL SYSTEM

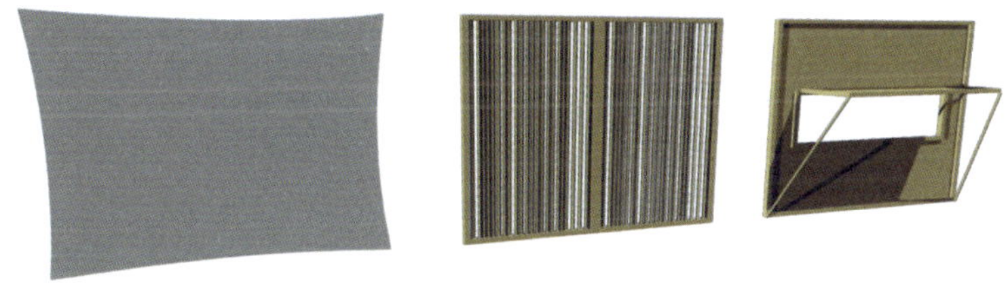

LIGHTWEIGHT ROLL-UP TENSILE PANELS: CONTROLS VIEWS AND PROVIDES A SENSE OF ENCLOSURE

HINGED "BAMBOUVERS": CREATE A SECURE ENCLOSURE AND ENCOURAGE VENTILATION

SOLID SHEAR PANEL: PROVIDES STRUCTURAL SUPPORT AGAINST RACKING AND CREATES A SECURE ENCLOSURE

SOUTH ELEVATION

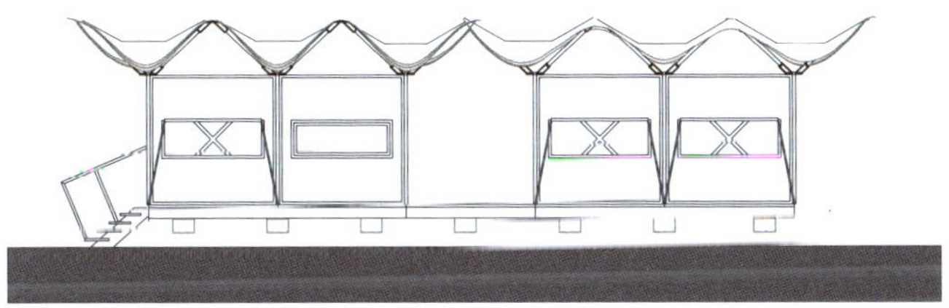

EAST ELEVATION

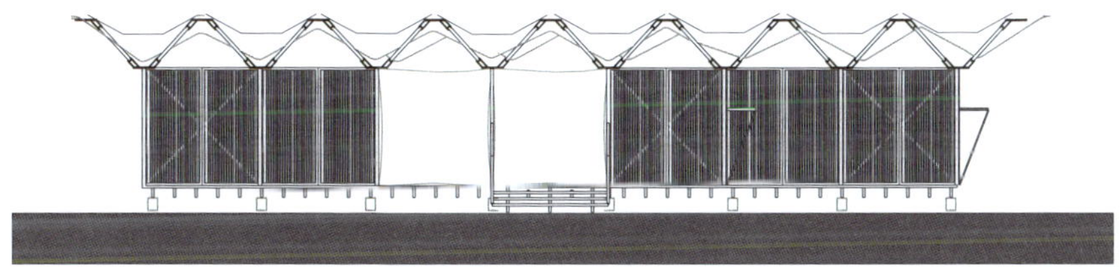

MOBILE CLASSROOM: 0 WASTE PROTOTYPE

ERIK SCANLON AND YULIYA ILIZAROV

The 0 Waste Prototype for a portable classroom is made from a metal shipping container that is cut and reconfigured into a two level foldable and portable container housing office, bathroom and utility spaces on the ground level and a classroom/meeting area above.

The interior is faced with plywood, while the exterior is the bright colored shell of the metal container. The walls are made of a metal frame with mesh to create a sense of enclosure while letting in light and air. On the walls of the classroom/meeting area there are folded chairs and desks in an array of colors which can be taken down and used as needed.

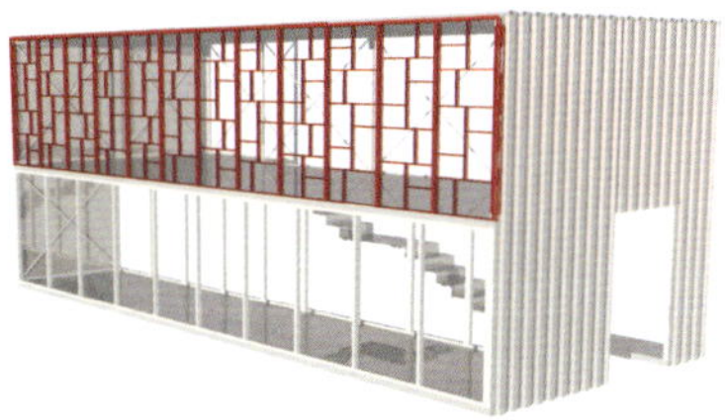

PROGRAMMED PANELS

FOLDED

UNFOLDED

FOLDED

UNFOLDED

GROUND FLOOR

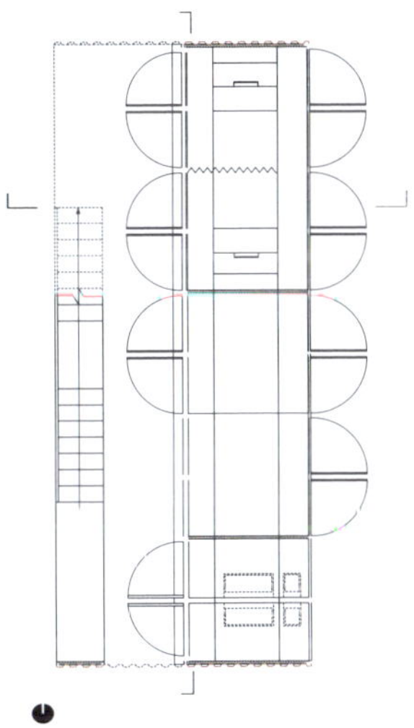

UPPER FLOOR

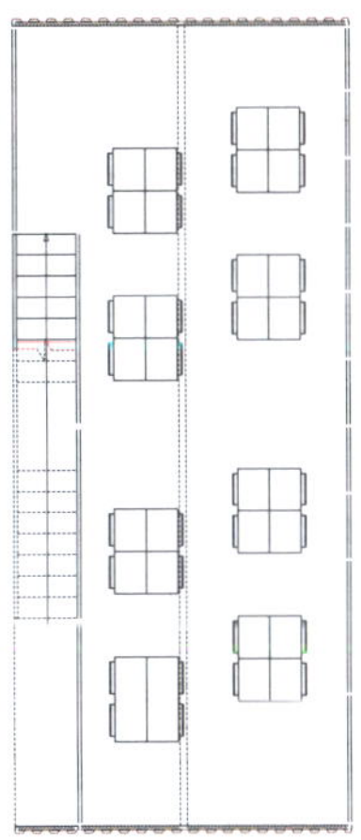

ROOF

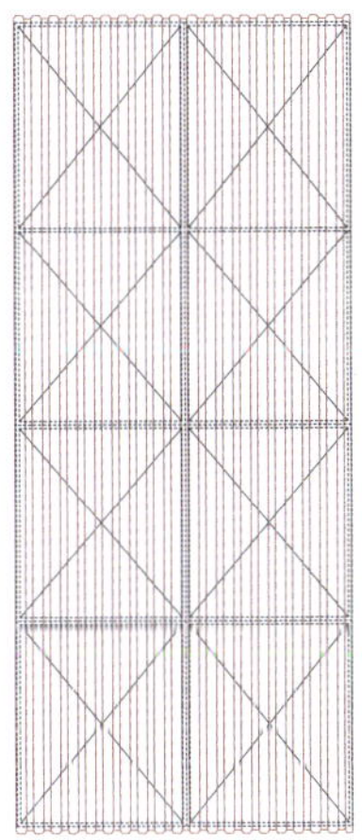

NORTH

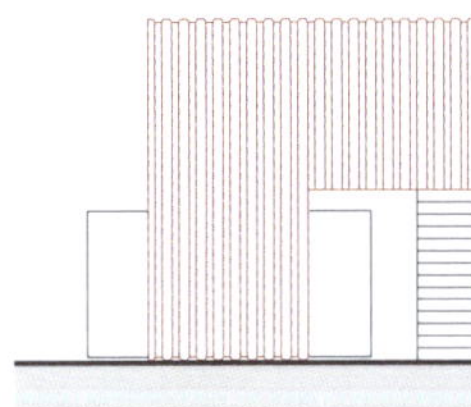

WEST

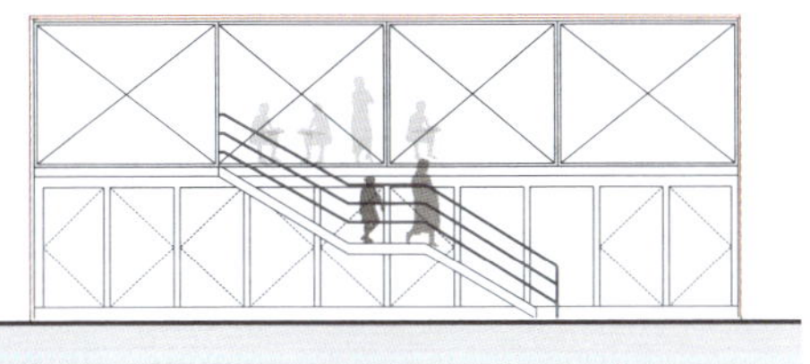

SOUTH

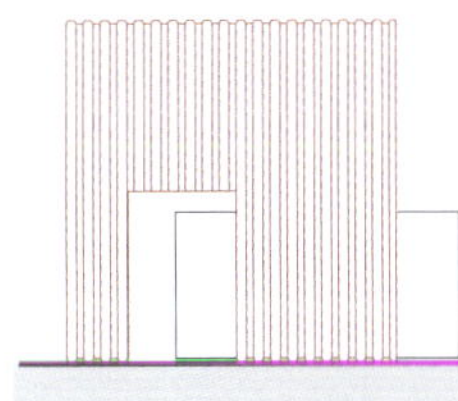

EAST

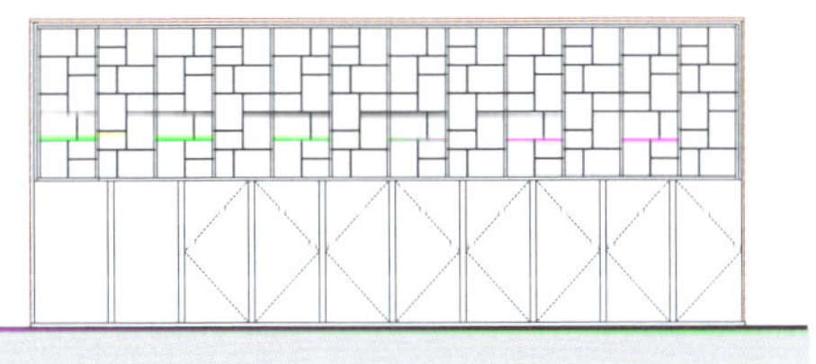

MOBILE CLASSROOM: DEPLOYABLE SCHOOL

EDITH ALTAMIRANDA AND YURIY TKACHENKOV

The success of a mobile school relies on how easily it can be transformed and adjusted to the needs of different users and activities. So the design of the prototype had to be flexible and adjustable.

This project uses a combination of removable and deployable partitions so that spaces can be easily arranged and re-arranged, and a combination of local (bamboo and wood) and mass-produced materials. It uses easy installation systems based on simple but reliable technology. Movable and removable partitions minimize the use of electricity. Exterior and interior partitions are designed using similar technology for easy storage. Bamboo weaved partitions provide shading and allow for the ventilation of classrooms.

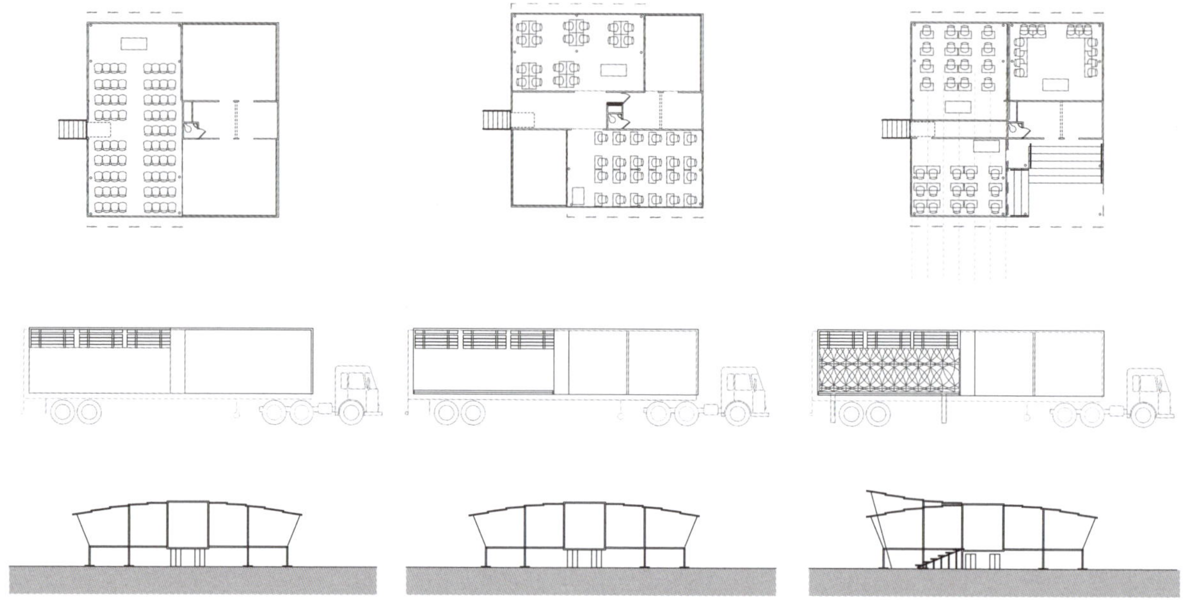

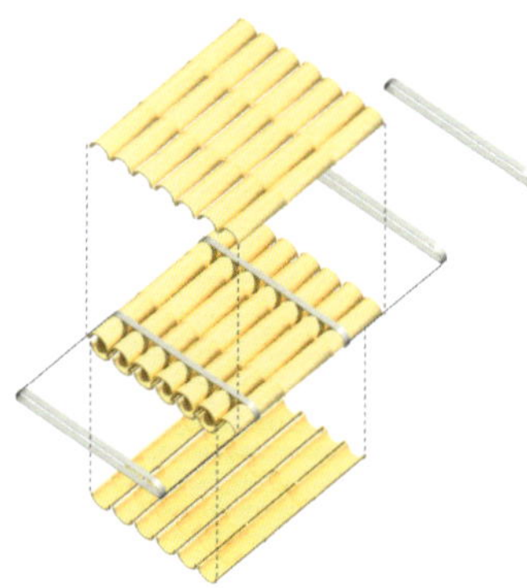

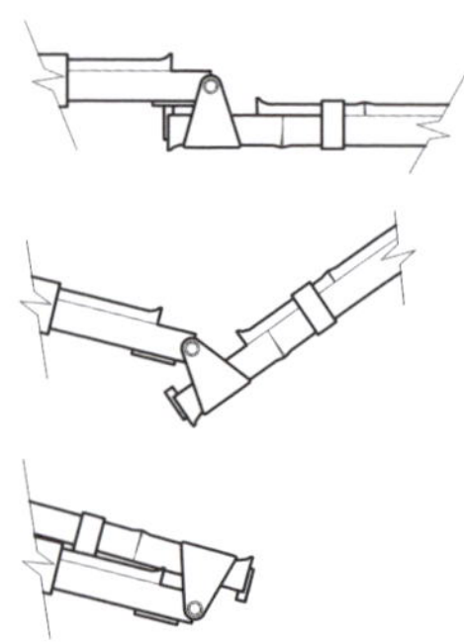

MOBILE

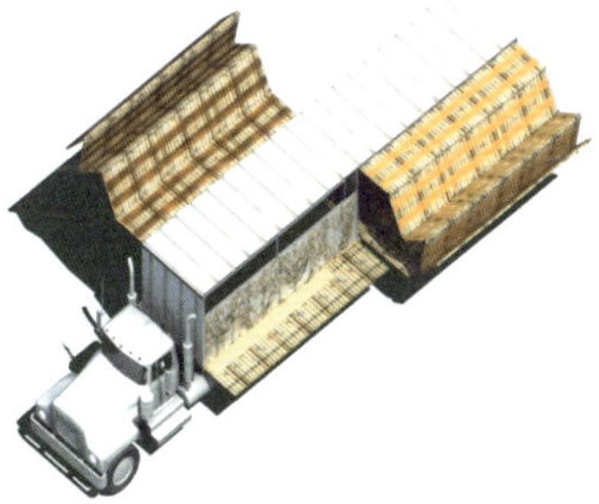

DEPLOYABLE

SCHOOL

ELEVATION A

ELEVATION B

PUERTO AGUARICO SECONDARY SCHOOL

EDITH ALTAMIRANDA

Puerto Aguarico, a municipality at the south of Nueva Loja across the Rio Aguarico, is one of the oldest, most attractive areas of the city. Its lack of bridges means it has limited communication with the rest of the city. Boats and canoes are used instead.

MAP:

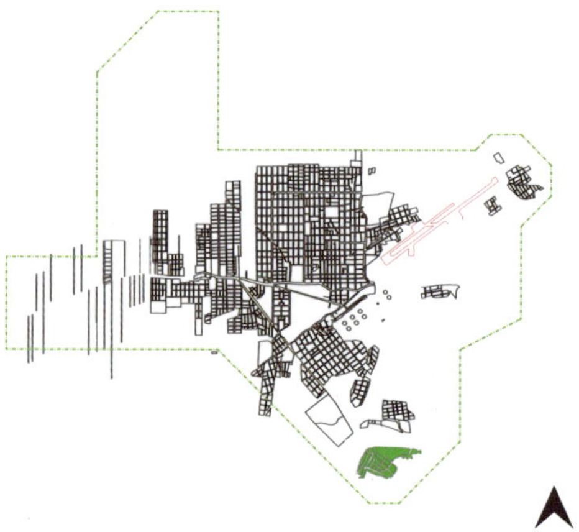

GREEN DIAGRAM

LOW DENSITY AREAS

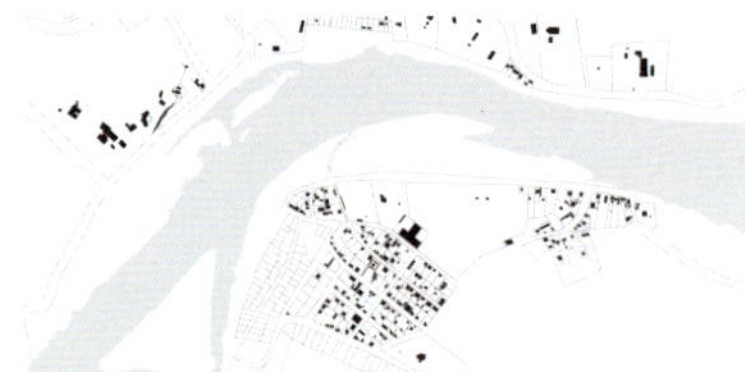

FIGURE GROUND

EXISTING ROAD SYSTEM

TOPOGRAPHY

PROPOSED TRAFFIC CONNECTION

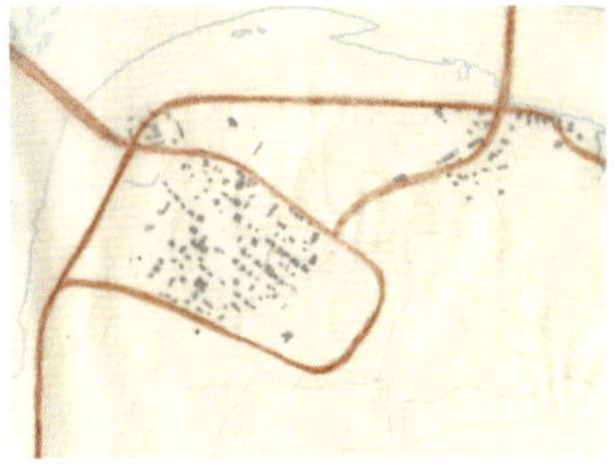

EXISTING ROAD SYSTEM

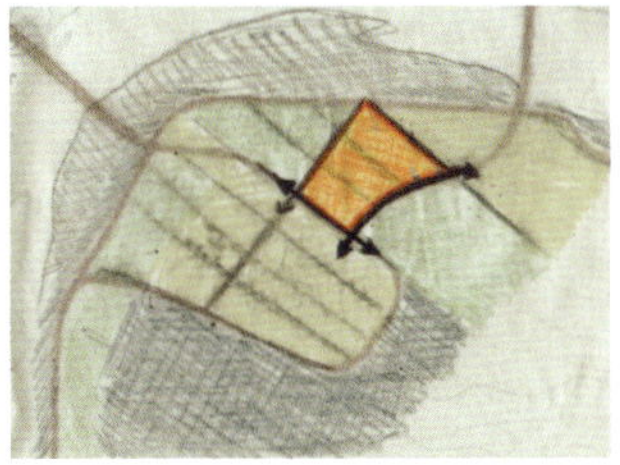

PRIMARY POINT OF INTERSECTION

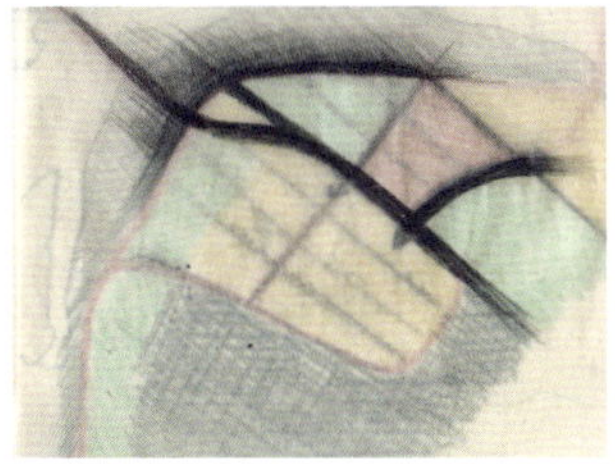

ACCESSIBILITY STUDY

CITY GRID COMPOSITE

POTENTIAL POINTS OF CONNECTION

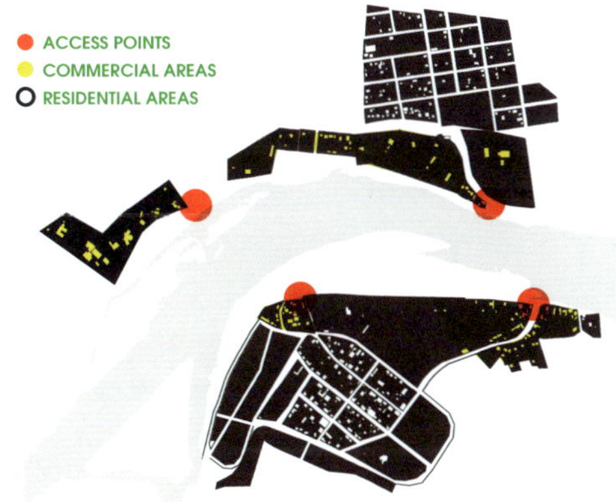

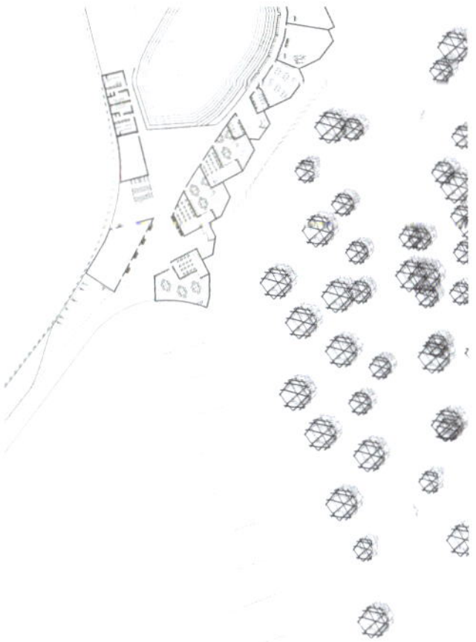

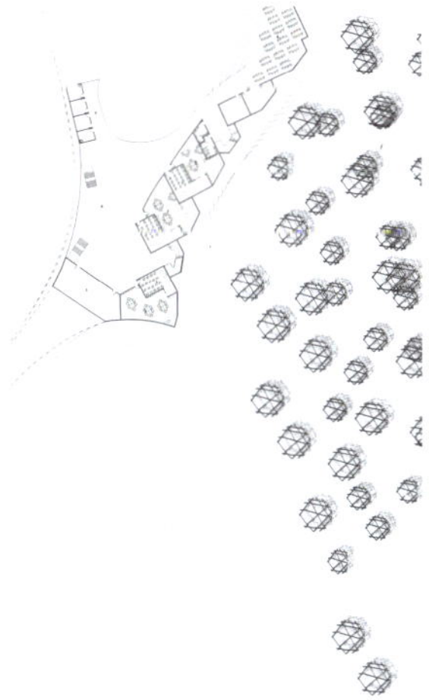

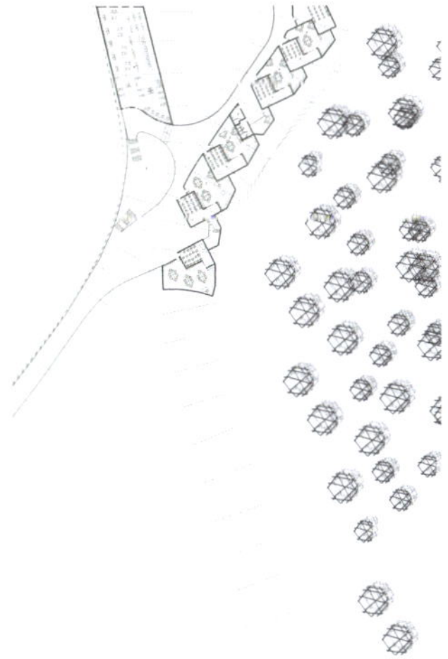

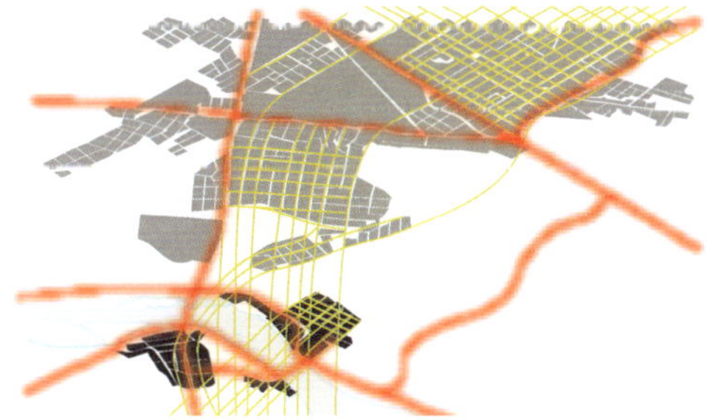

EXTENSION OF THE CITY GRID

MAIN ROADS
LOCAL ROADS

EXISTING ROAD SYSTEM

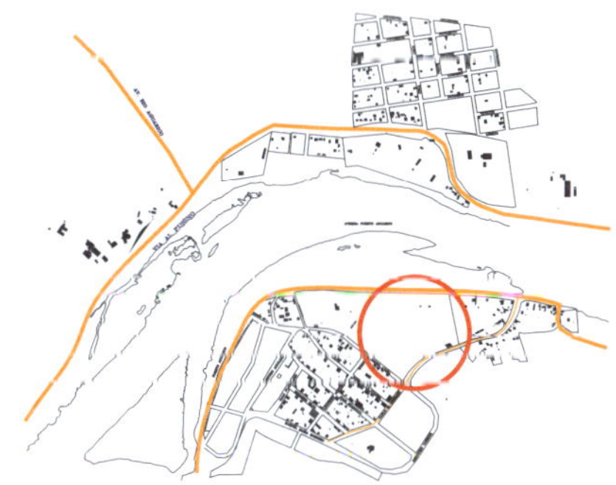

3RD LEVEL

1. CLASSROOM
2. WORKSHOP
3. LIBRARY
4. COMPUTER ROOM
5. BATHROOM

2ND LEVEL

1. CLASSROOM
2. WORKSHOP
3. TEACHER'S LOUNGE
4. ADMINISTRATION
5. NURSERY
6. CAFETERIA

1ST LEVEL

1. CLASSROOM
2. WORKSHOP
3. GYM
4. ADMINISTRATION
5. BIKE STATIONS
6. LOCKER ROOM

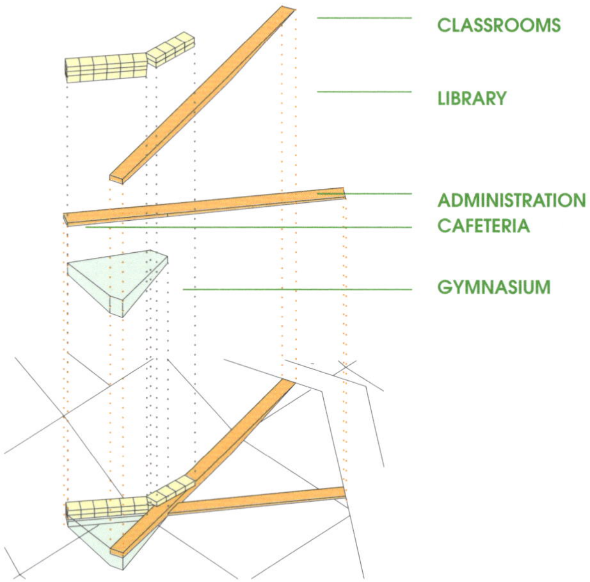

Spaces on the east side of the school have views towards the forest, away from the urbanized areas of the town. Working spaces and social spaces are located on the west side of the school.

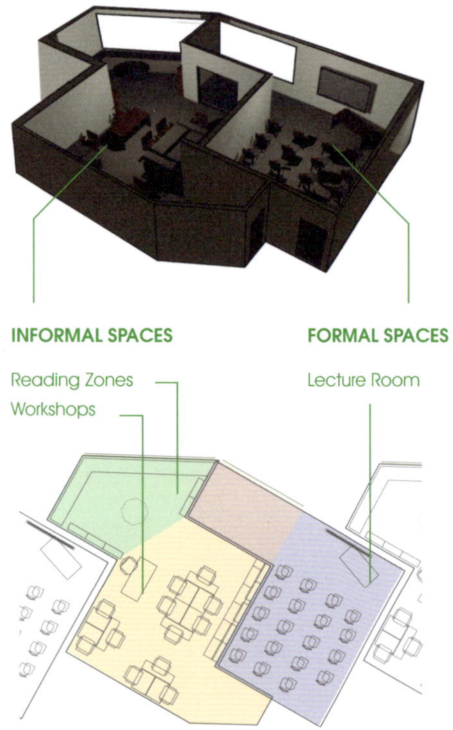

MULTIPURPOSE CLASSROOM

Elements for a diverse learning environment.

Environmental

Properly lit spaces, pleasant views and functional areas.

Psychological

Different learning methods adjusted to the diverse subject areas.

Sociological

Formal and informal individual learning groups: workshops, lectures, and individual activities.

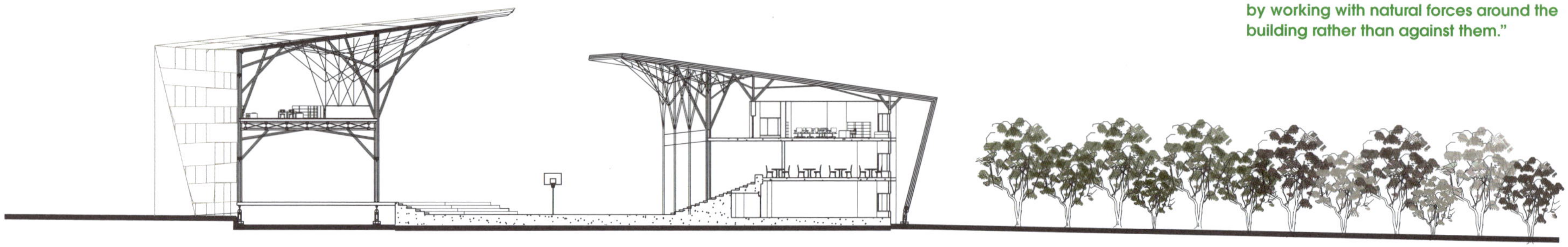

"Manipulating the environment within buildings by working with natural forces around the building rather than against them."

IMAGE VIEW: VIEW OF COMMON SPACES

GREEN AND BLUE PRIMARY SCHOOL

YULIYA ILIZAROV

The Green and Blue Primary School is organized along two opposing systems; the imposed city grid and the naturally occurring streams that run through the area. Situated on an un-built site of a roughly gridded neighborhood bisected by a river, the school wraps around the river with a cluster of classrooms, labs and offices. The various elements of the school sit as discrete yet connected particles beneath a container roof/skin structure that maintains the grid structure present in the neighborhood. The interior courtyard is the center of school activities – an open, yet private and secure space for learning. The container structure extends beyond the edge of particles that make up the school to enclose a sheltered outdoor space accessible to the community at large. This space mediates between the private interior of the school and the public exterior of the pedestrian street.

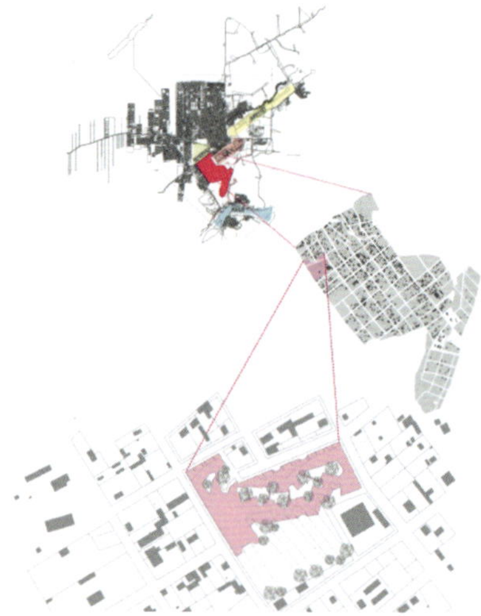

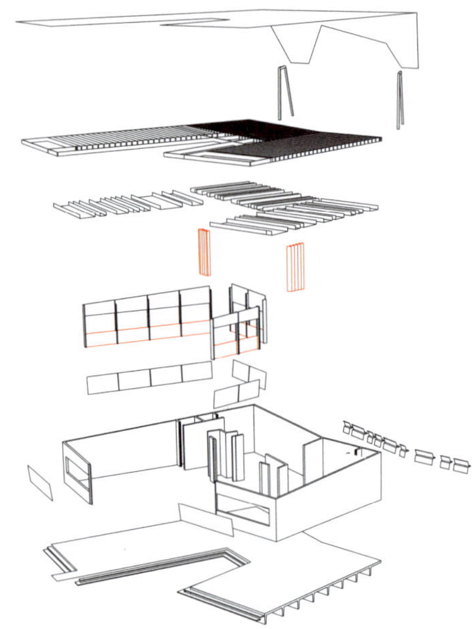

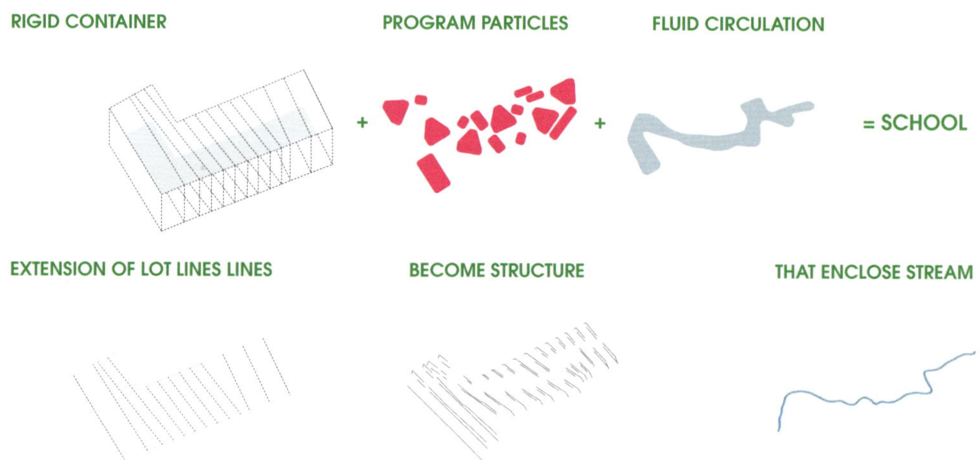

GREEN (COURTYARDS)

CIRCULATION

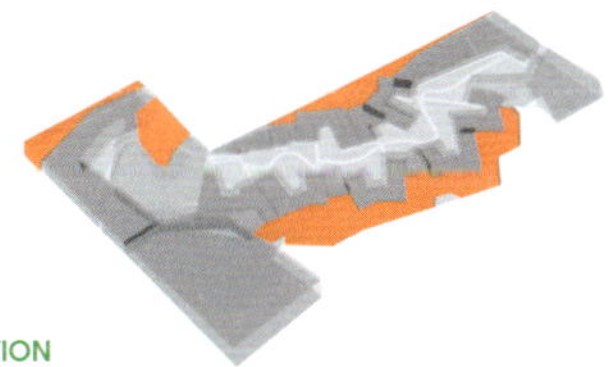

COMMUNITY CONNECTION

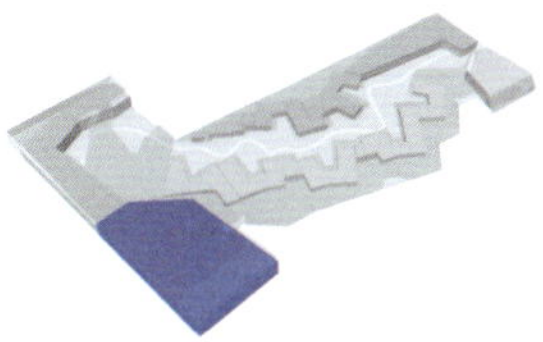

GYMNASIUM

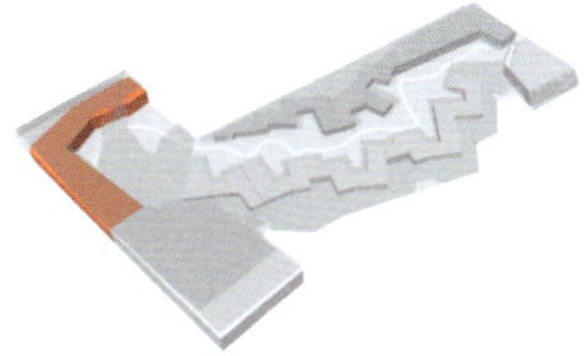

ADMINISTRATION

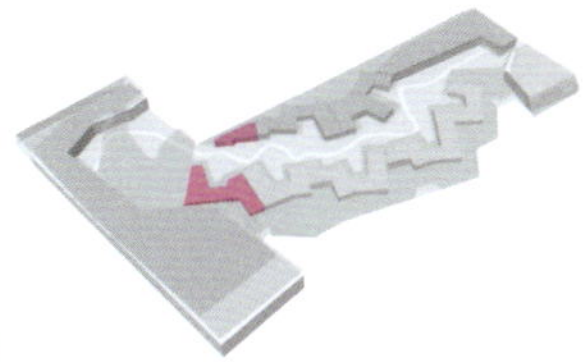

TEACHER OFFICES AND FACILITIES

CLASSROOMS

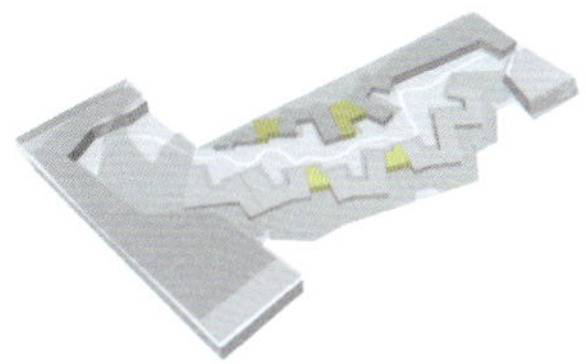

SCIENCE + ART LABS

VIEW FROM WALKWAY

LIBRARY

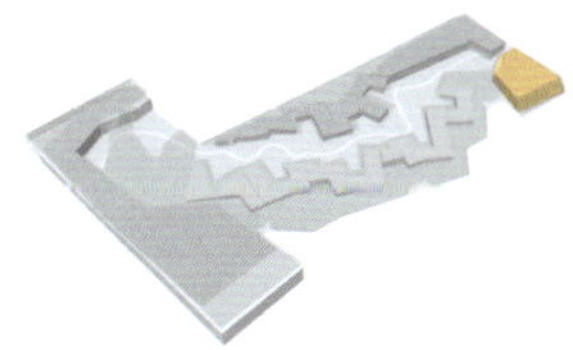

AUDITORIUM

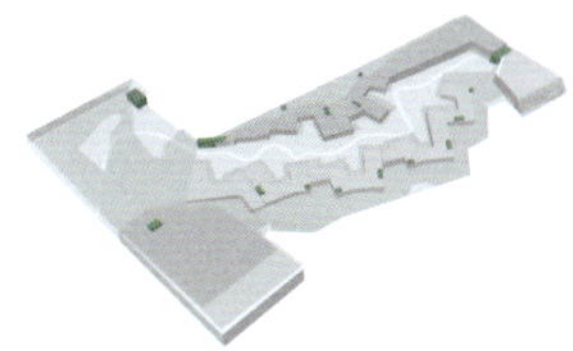

BATHROOMS

THE URBAN SCHOOL

IMAN ANSARI

The neighborhood where the school is to be located is perhaps the densest area of Lago Agrio and contains the city's main social, secular and sacred centers. The super *barrio* is also surrounded by major avenues such as Avenida Colombia in the east and Avenida Quito in the south and is divided in two by the river running through it. This breaks up the city grid, creating varied city blocks. The school will become part of the new university revitalizing the abandoned areas around the river. It will therefore need to maintain its own identity within the university campus. Due to the density of the site, the school will be comprised of city infill along the river, connected through a series of bridges.

The school recreates the city grid at a smaller scale. By elevating the school, the ground level will be opened up to the public allowing circulation, traffic and trade to take place underneath. This system, of in-fill spaces bridged across the river, could be repeated anywhere along the river in order to expand the school or the university in the future.

1

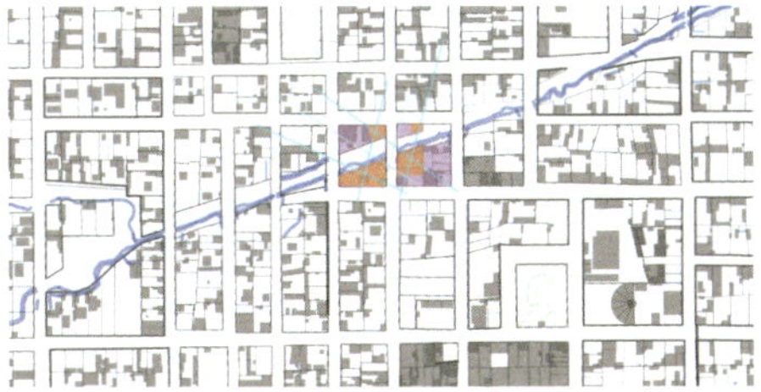

2

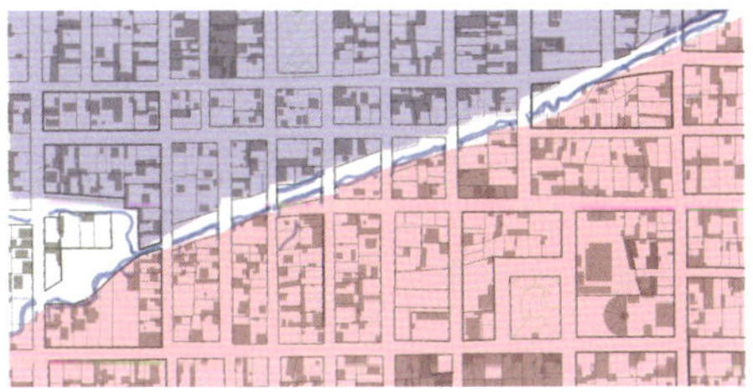

3

4

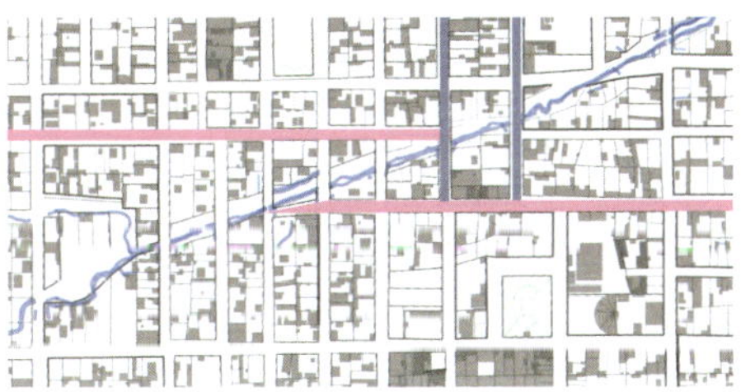

5

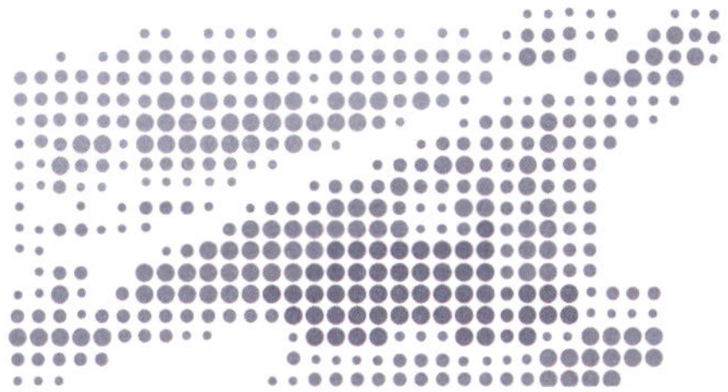

6

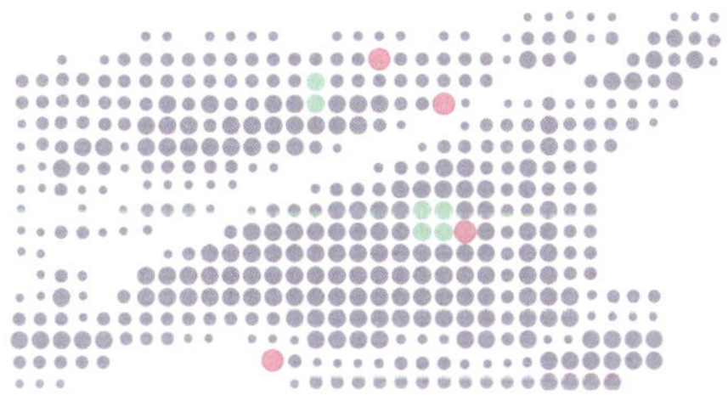

7

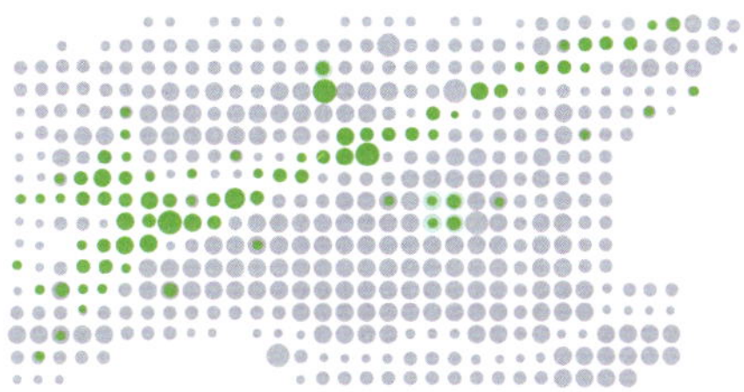

8

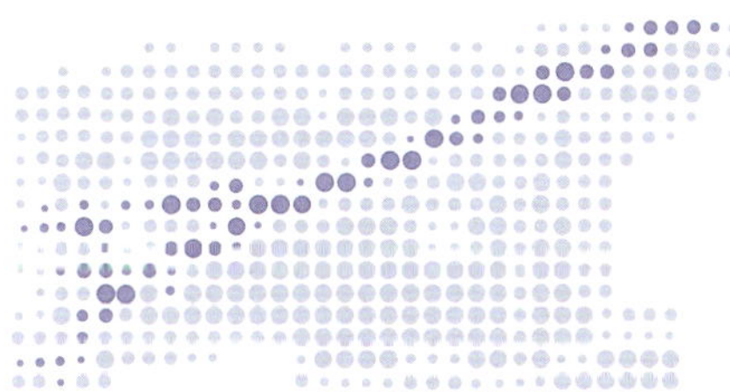

9

10

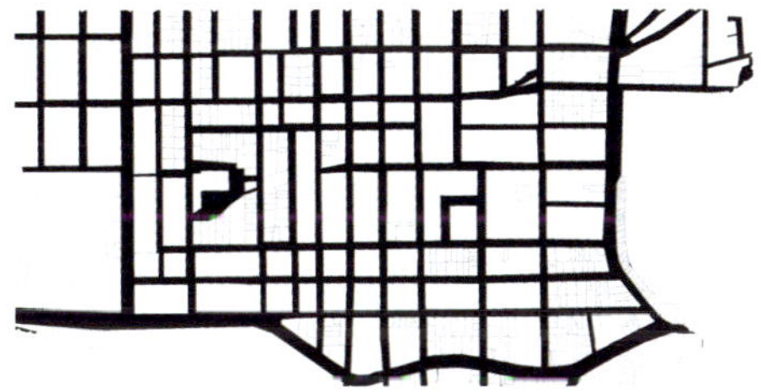

1. PROGRAM DIAGRAM
2. SEPARATION OF CITY BY THE CANAL
3. VARIATIONS OF CITY BLOCKS
4. ACCESS TO AND AROUND THE SITE
5. DENSITY DIAGRAM
6. CIVIC CENTERS AROUND THE SITE
7. GREEN DIAGRAM
8. WATER DIAGRAM
9. FIGURE GROUND DIAGRAM OF THE SITE
10. CIRCULATION DIAGRAM

CONCEPTUAL SPACE DIAGRAM

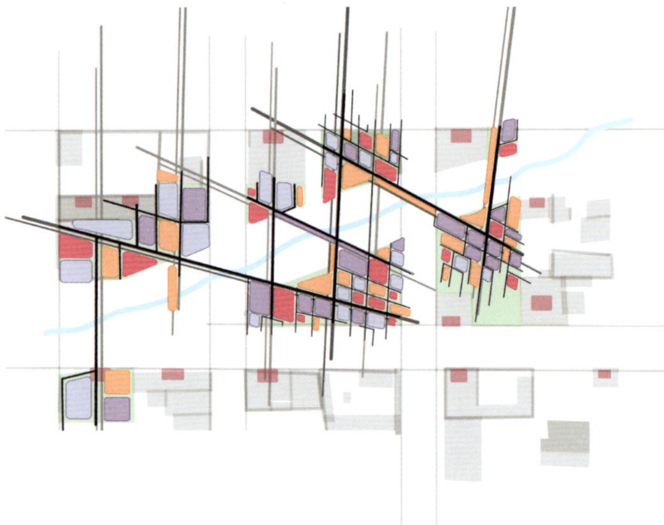

PROGRAM DIAGRAM

GROUND FLOOR PLAN

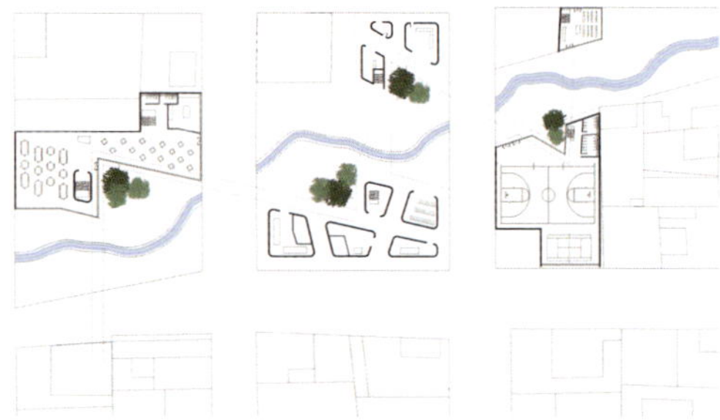

FIRST FLOOR PLAN

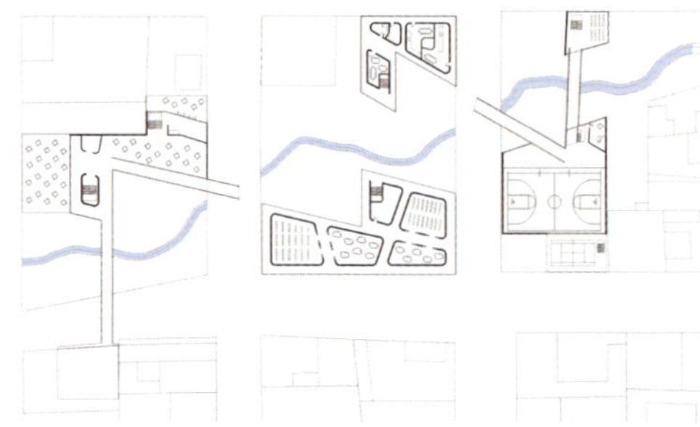

SECOND FLOOR PLAN

ROOF PLAN

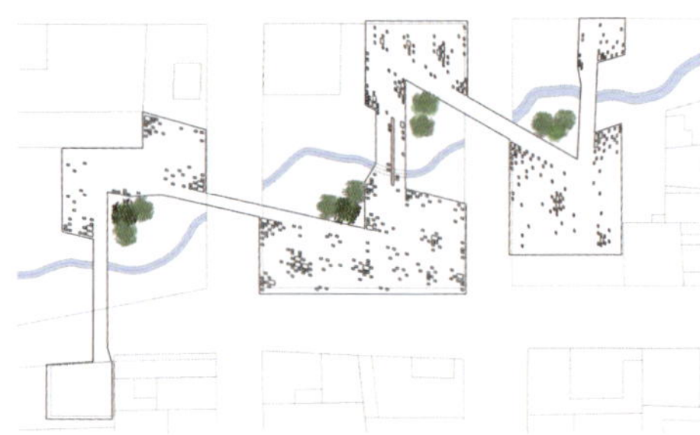

CONCEPTUAL SPACE DIAGRAM AND PROGRAM DIAGRAM LEGEND

- BOOKSTORE
- CORE
- SOCIAL
- GYM
- OFFICE
- LAB
- CLASSROOM
- STORAGE
- CAFETERIA
- KITCHEN
- TERRACE
- DAYCARE

VIEWS OF CIRCULATION

VIEWS OF ROOFTOP SCAPE

SCHOOL AS A TOOL FOR LEARNING: ESCUELA DE CONSTRUCCIÓN DE NUEVA LOJA

CAMILLE DUNN

The Escuela de Construcción de Nueva Loja, or ECNL, is a vocational school for the instruction and development of sustainable construction techniques. By teaching responsible building practices the school will disseminate ideas and strategies to promote sustainable growth and foster local industry in Sucumbíos province.

La Esquina is situated at the corner of Avenida Amazonas, the road that continues into the Amazon, and Avenida Aguarico, the main northwest-southeast artery that runs from the river into the heart of the town. It is a neighborhood poised to see an increase in traffic and important social, infrastructural and green development (in the form of a proposed park).

As the town grows, thought must be given to the building methods used here. Currently, a large percentage of development is informal – constructed without building permits. Building materials are low quality; building methods are ad hoc and poorly executed; and waste, utility supply, and road infrastructures are often nonexistent. As a result, these informal residential neighborhoods are at risk of breaking down and disappearing back into the jungle within a short period of time.

This project for a technical school devoted to construction means, methods and materials occupies a site just off the Avenida Aguarico/Avenida Amazonas intersection. Siting the school here – near this intersection, at the end of an open utility zone, near residential neighborhoods, toward the river (and hopefully reconstructed bridge), and out toward the jungle –will reinforce a sense of place within the neighborhood and make the school (and the technology and know-how it will produce) accessible to the rest of the city.

The design of the school reflects the beauty of the place, the vibrancy of the town and the possibilities for intelligent, sustainable jungle building methods. The Nueva Loja School of Construction is a living laboratory for sustainable tropical construction. The structure of the school forms a framework onto which classroom units can be added or subtracted. Students will take classes to investigate the materials, form, ventilation and shading systems of the building – a reminder for students and instructors of the mission of the town and the building culture of the region.

LIVING LABORATORY

ENCL is conceived of as both a place in which to learn and a place on which to learn. Students will be trained in sustainable building techniques for use in their professional practice.

The classrooms, study centers and offices are all temporary structures developed and assembled by teams of students providing them with an opportunity to test new sustainable construction methods and materials at full scale. The framework of the school is designed to hold and engage these experimental units with a pulley/wench system that lifts new units into place.

FORMAL STRATEGY:

Tropicalizing the University of Virginia Academical Village

Thomas Jefferson's iconic plan for the "Academical Village" at the University of Virginia provides a precedent for campus planning at ENCL. Both ENCL and the University of Virginia have an open horseshoe plan with the library at the apex. This form creates a cohesive campus which frames a central campus green. However there are a number of ways in which ENCL departs formally from the University of Virginia in its response to both climatic conditions and the surrounding community.

- The plan is rotated to minimize exposure to the sun and to give full morning sun.
- Whereas the University of Virginia has private gardens, the ENCL has a public streetscape and plantings on the facade for the benefit of all.
- Instead of an insulating layer of faculty housing, ENCL is surrounded by community housing.
- The volume of ENCL is more porous both for the free circulation of air and to make the interior accessible to the community rather than insular like the University of Virginia.

FORMAL STRATEGY:
Passive Cooling in the Tropics

ENCL uses passive cooling strategies for its interior spaces. To take advantage of cooling breezes, ENCL promotes the movement of air and cross breezes through the school by keeping the building porous and shallow.

To minimize the building surfaces' exposure to the sun, ENCL is long and narrow, oriented to minimize surfaces on the east and west facades that are exposed to the light of the morning and evening sun. At midday, when the sun is at its hottest, the parasol-like tensile panels which make up the roof system form a canopy to shade the classroom and circulation spaces below.

PASSIVE TECHNOLOGIES:
Integrated Living Machine Biological Wastewater Treatment System

ENFL will have a program to educate students and the community about the construction and maintenance of decentralized, low-tech, sustainable water treatment solutions. In addition, the school will harvest and treat rainwater for use on campus, giving students first hand experience of these systems.

Rainwater is first collected by the tensile roof panels, which funnel the water into inlet columns diverting it to underground collection pipes which feed the Living Machine water treatment system. The Living Machine system is a series of tanks and constructed wetlands in which an ecosystem of plants, algae, bacteria, molluscs and fish act as a biofilter, processing wastewater and making it safe for non-potable uses such as irrigation and toilet flushing. Some of the treated water is then diverted to additional filtration systems to make it safe for drinking. The potable and non-potable water is kept separate and stored in tanks for on-campus use.

TORRE BIBLIOTECA

The library tower serves as a focal point for the campus and a symbol of the school's commitment to innovative and comprehensive sustainable construction practices.

Firstly, it is an integral part of the library's passive cooling system. The face of the tower is a black, folded-plate concrete slab angled to catch the morning sun. By applying a thin transparent layer of ETFE film to the slab, the recesses in the concrete become pockets of air warmed by the thermal mass of the concrete. As the heated air rises to the top of the tower it rushes past vents from the library interior creating suction (the effects of the Bernouli Principle). This suction powers the passive cooling system by pulling air from outside through the geothermal loop heat exchange to cool the interior of the library and computer lab. Secondly, the tower holds tanks filled with both treated grey water and treated potable water from the school's living machine system. The height of the tower generates pressure that allows water to be distributed around campus for use in kitchens, restrooms and irrigation.

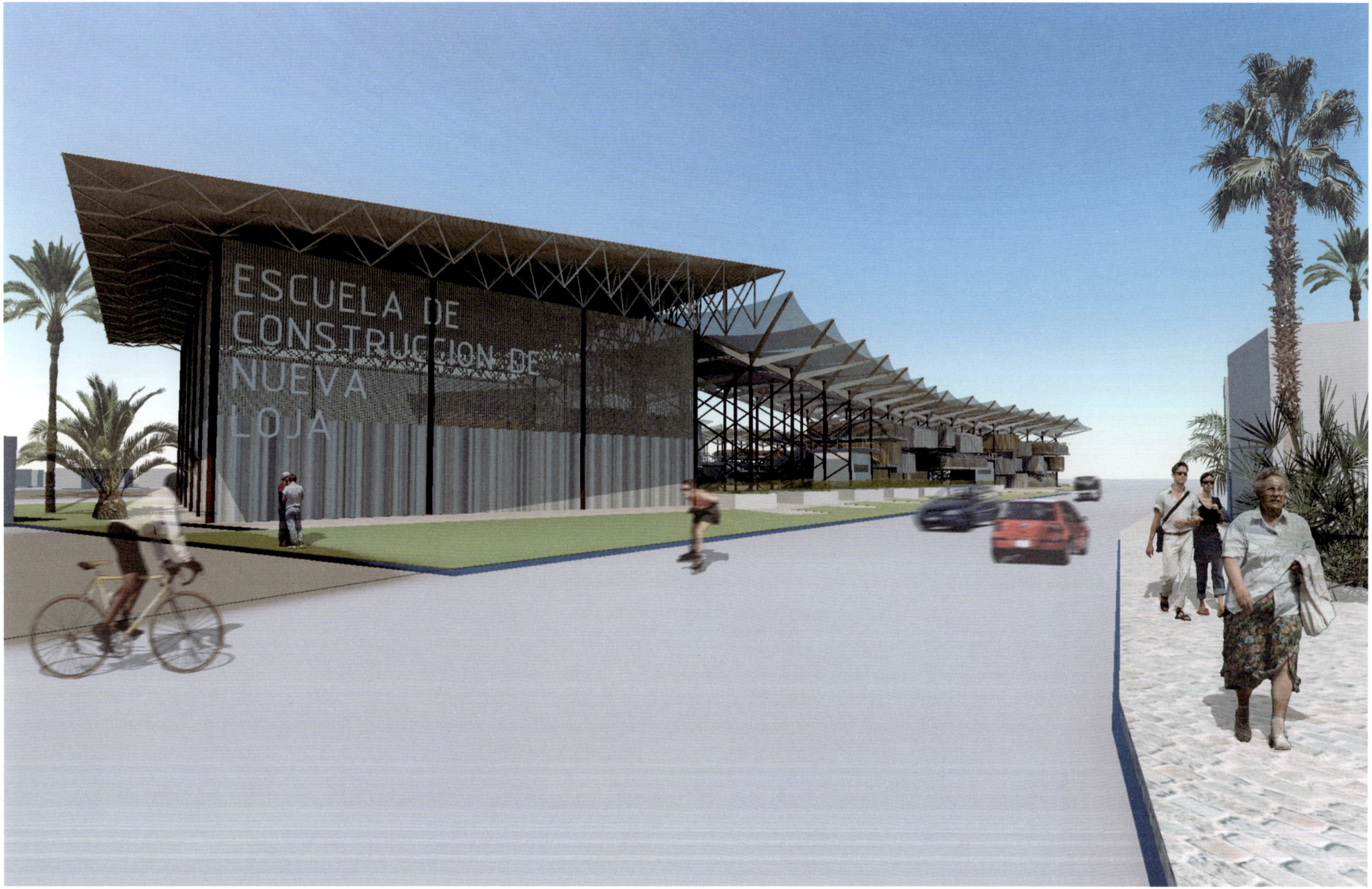
ESCUELA DE
CONSTRUCCION DE
NUEVA
LOJA

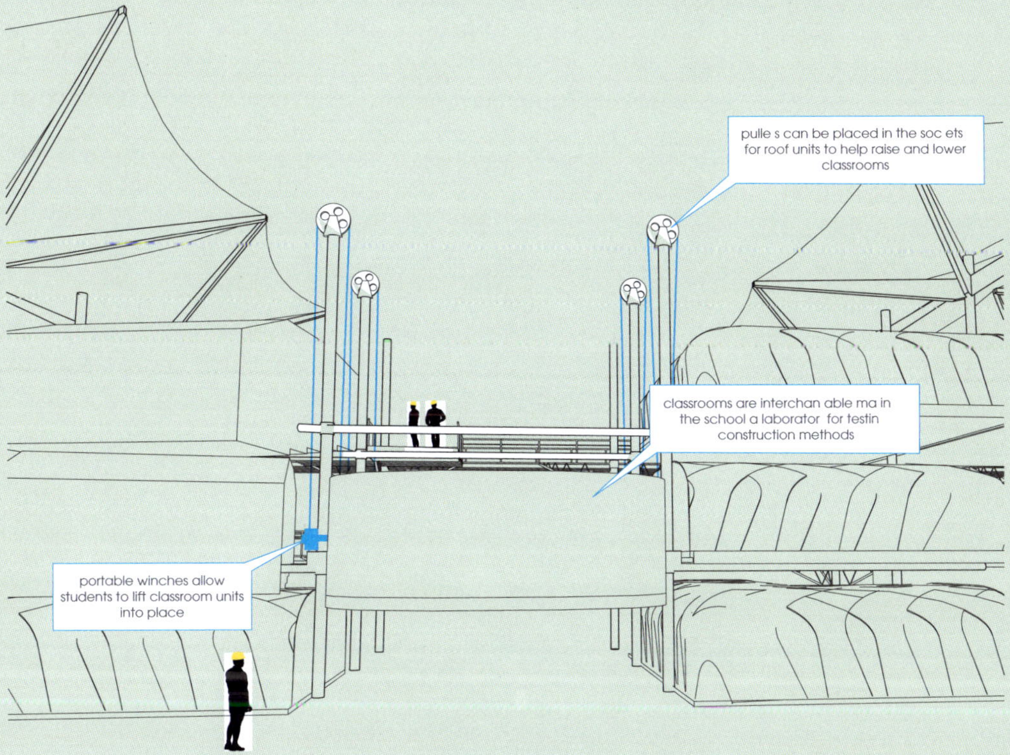

IMAGES: SYSTEM OF CONTAINER DEPLOYMENT

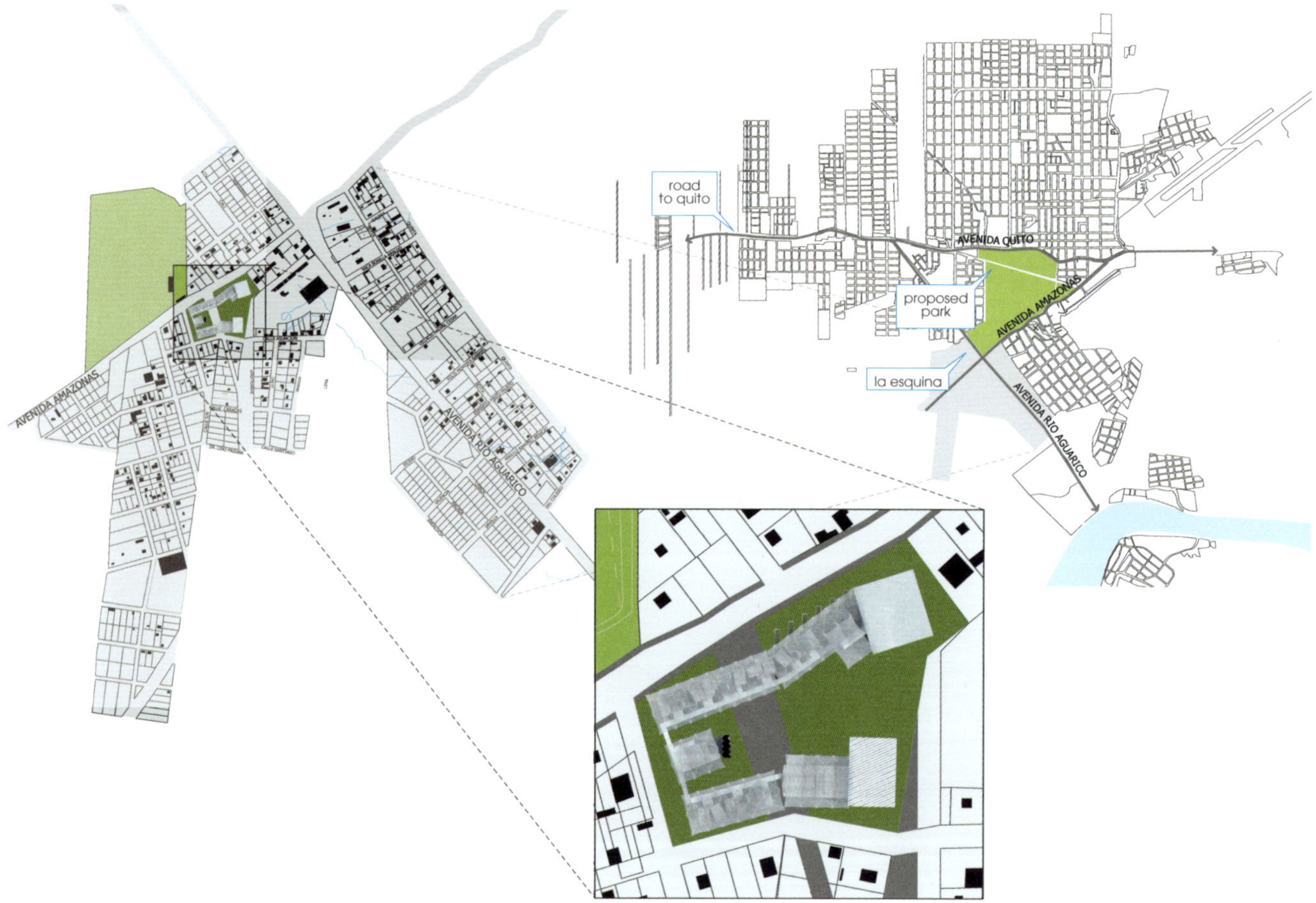
AVENIDA AMAZONAS
AVENIDA RIO AGUARICO
road to quito
AVENIDA QUITO
proposed park
AVENIDA AMAZONAS
la esquina
AVENIDA RIO AGUARICO

PLUG IN UNITS

WHISTLE-SHAPED CLASSROOM ENCOURAGES FOCUSED GATHERINGS

L-SHAPED CLASSROOM ALLOWS FOR MULTIPLE STYLES OF LEARNING SPACES

STEPPED CLASSROOMS FUNCTION AS LECTURE HALL

THE WET UNIT HOUSES RESTROOMS AND SHOWERS

TOWER FUNCTIONS AS SOLAR CHIMNEY, WATER TOWER AND BILLBOARD

TENSILE ROOF SYSTEM SHADES FROM SUN AND RAIN FUNNELING RAINWATER INTO PIPE COLUMNS FOR COLLECTION AND TREATMENT

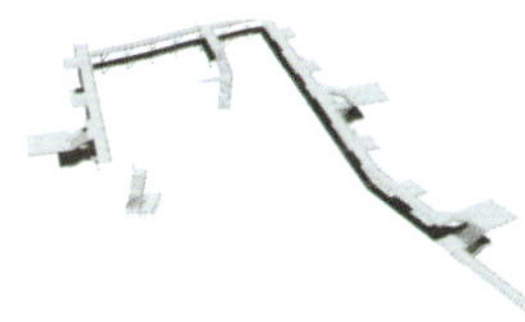

CIRCULATION SYSTEM HOLDS SOCKETS WHICH CONNECT TO PLUG IN UNITS

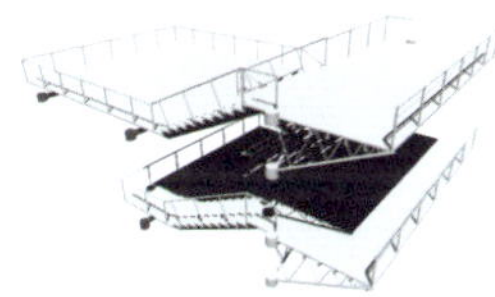

STAIRS OFFER VERTICAL CIRCULATION, SOCIAL SPACE AND WAY FINDING FOR THE WET UNITS BELOW

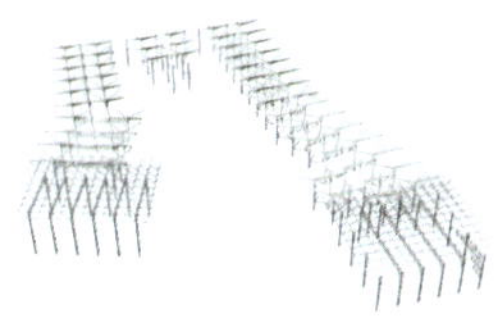

STRUCTURAL SYSTEM ACCEPTS UNITS AND DEFINES THE SHAPE OF THE SCHOOL

STRUCTURAL SYSTEM ACCEPTS UNITS AND DEFINES THE SHAPE OF THE SCHOOL

SUSTAINABLE HUMAN SETTLEMENTS FOR THE POST-OIL ERA IN THE ECUADORIAN AMAZON:

AN INTRODUCTION TO THE NUEVA LOJA WORKSHOP (FADA-PUCE)

OSVALDO PALADINES ZURITA

The city of Nueva Loja, also known as Lago Agrio, is an urban settlement that was founded to meet the housing, recreation and communication needs of workers for foreign oil companies established in the Western Ecuadorian Amazon. Because of its strategic location, close to the Colombian border, Nueva Loja has also become a center for the stockpiling and distribution of illegal goods that are smuggled into the country. Furthermore, it is the entry point to the Yasuní Biosphere Reserve, one of the most bio-diverse areas on the planet.

The Nueva Loja Workshop was undertaken in the Faculty of Architecture, Design and Art of the Pontificia Universidad Católica of Ecuador during the Spring semester of 2007, as a collaboration with the Spitzer School of Architecture of the City College of New York. The curriculum of the studio was divided into three stages:

A VISION AT THE URBAN SCALE OF HUMAN SETTLEMENTS IN AMAZONIA

The objective of the Workshop was to oscillate between utopia and reality, with the aim of exploring new creative visions of urban problems and their causes and to find possible paths towards solutions. The ultimate goal was to unravel the urban matrix and propose alternatives for a contemporary sustainable city, within a general vision of urban growth.

The different causes for the founding and growth of the city of Lago Agrio and its impact on the jungle were studied, taking into account the river, vegetation and native nomadic movements as well as possible models for accommodating a projected 150,000 inhabitants. To this end, emphasis was placed on direct contact and familiarization with the area through an organized visit.

The end product of this first stage was a general proposal for the growth of the city of Nueva Loja, which was expressed in an educational document intended for the children and youth of the area. In this document, students had to describe clearly and informatively the main characteristics of their proposal for the future city of Nueva Loja, as well as outlining the individual commitments that each member of society would have to make in order to implement it. The printed publication was complemented with audio-visual material in digital format geared towards facilitating dissemination and understanding, as well as making the information accessible to the members of the community.

THE SELF-SUFFICIENT HOUSEHOLD UNIT FOR THE FUTURE CITY OF NUEVA LOJA

The post-oil period will arrive in less than 25 years, making the study of new architectural solutions for oil cities a theme of vital importance. Historically, settlements that have flourished spectacularly owing to the exploitation of a single natural resource have eventually been abandoned as ghost towns when this resource runs out (as was the case with the saltpeter towns in Chile, gold-rush cities, etc.)

Rainforest oil cities, because of their strategic location and potential to attract tourism, should not meet the same fate, given that they can be restructured so that in every aspect of their operation they become examples of the sensible use of resources and conservation of energy. The second section of study thus concentrated on the household unit, understood not as a box/machine to be simply plugged into the energy supply infrastructure, but as a base unit that would guarantee the survival of these cities as part of a system integrated with other urban scales, with the countryside, and with the jungle.

**During this stage of the workshop,
the following subjects were studied:**

Energy – Alternative means of energy production: solar, wind, water, ethanol and their impact on the design of housing and the city.

Food – The capacity of the territory to produce food, based on the conditions of the rainforest's natural cycle.

Water – Analysis of the complete water cycle, guaranteeing its efficient use, re-use, etc.

Waste – Analysis of every level of the production of waste and how it can be recycled so that the settlement generates no contaminating footprint at all.

Construction Technologies – Recuperation and implementation of construction techniques well suited to the place, the economy and the climate.

Materials – Use of materials found in the region; tensile structures made with fibers, wood, and giant bamboo.

PRODUCTIVE LANDSCAPE – PRODUCTIVE HOUSEHOLD

TATIANA ARMIJOS

This project proposes the generation of circulation axes that run along existing environmental corridors (rivers and streams) to create a permanent connection with nature and to generate a series of dynamic borders between Nueva Loja and the water with a series of recreational, agricultural and touristic spaces. Commercial and agricultural functions are also proposed for the household, where they become linked to its domestic uses. Its perimeter is conceived as a skin that facilitates an exchange with the environment: it breathes, feeds itself and produces. The household takes advantage of the characteristics of its location: it draws from the surrounding commercial activity; is built over several levels using the elevation changes of the site; optimizes the use of water (capturing, recycling and re-using it for agricultural irrigation) and waste (generating useful fertilizer for agricultural activity). The household has areas for the exhibition and sale of its products, as well as a place for its storage. Concrete and brick were selected to fulfill cultural expectations of solidity, improvement and capacity for growth. The structural composition uses a system of gaps to provide cross-ventilation without obstructing the view of the exterior.

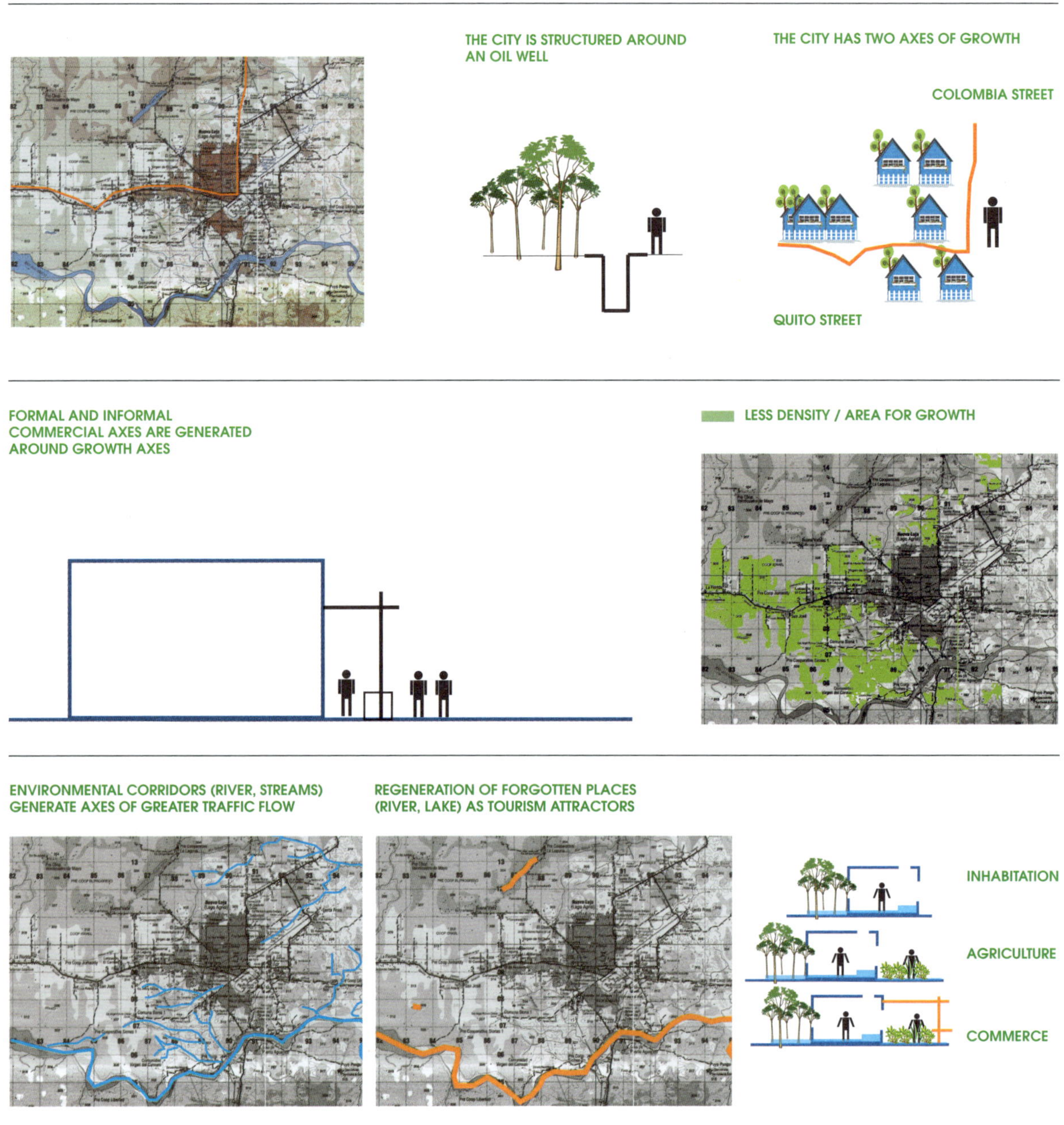

A. DYNAMIC BORDERS / GREEN AREAS FOR RECREATION

B. AGRICULTURE

C. COMMERCE / COMMUNAL AREAS AS ELEMENTS OF CONNECTION

- WATER / IRRIGATION
- PRODUCTION / AGRICULTURE
- HABITATION
- EXHIBITION
- COMMERCIAL

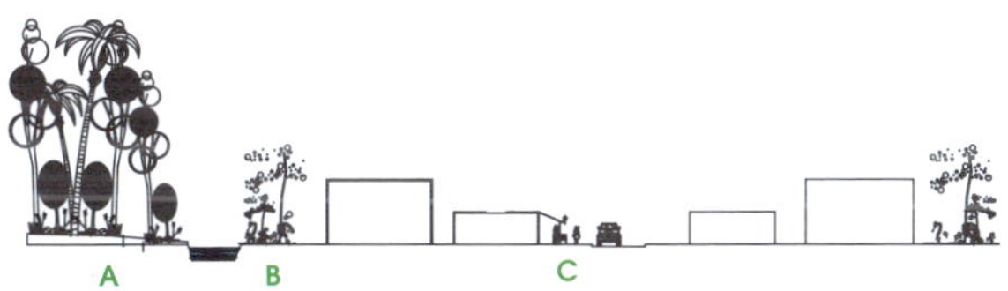

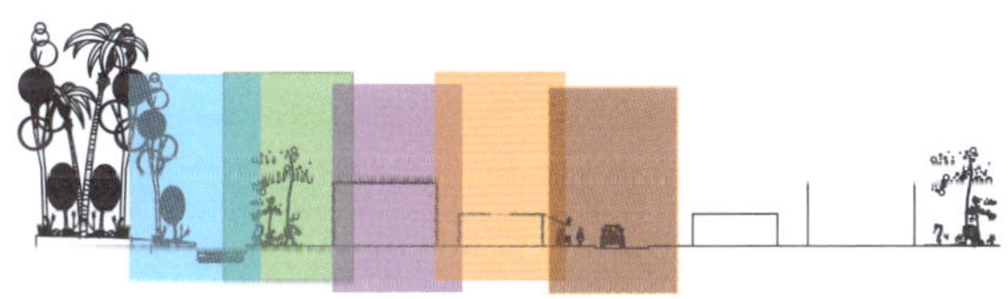

SUSTAINABLE SYSTEMS

JOSÉ LUIS GALLEGOS

We propose that the sustainable, substantive future for the city of Nueva Loja be an overarching system made up of a series of sub-systems or neighborhoods placed at four strategic points where they will fulfill designated functions (tourism, commerce, fish farming and agriculture) and work independently of the current city even as they sustain and feed it, in an era without oil. Each one of these neighborhoods is in charge of its own energy, water, waste and transport systems.

The household constitutes a third sub-system and reflects urban needs on an architectural scale. Its structure is made up of recycled tubing from the oil era; its services are designed so that it will be self-sufficient in water, will re-use and recycle it; its waste will be used as fuel or sorted and entered into the neighborhood and city recycling system. Owing to the high rainfall in Amazonia the facades treat it in the same way as roofs and collect rainwater in a lightwell that traverses the household. Facades are also designed to facilitate cross-ventilation. The shape of the architectural volume is a distorted cube, which seeks to allude to rainforest sensations.

The economy of the neighborhood, located on the shores of the Aguarico River just like its households, is based on fish farming and the cultivation of Amazon fruits to satisfy both internal consumption and to provide goods for export.

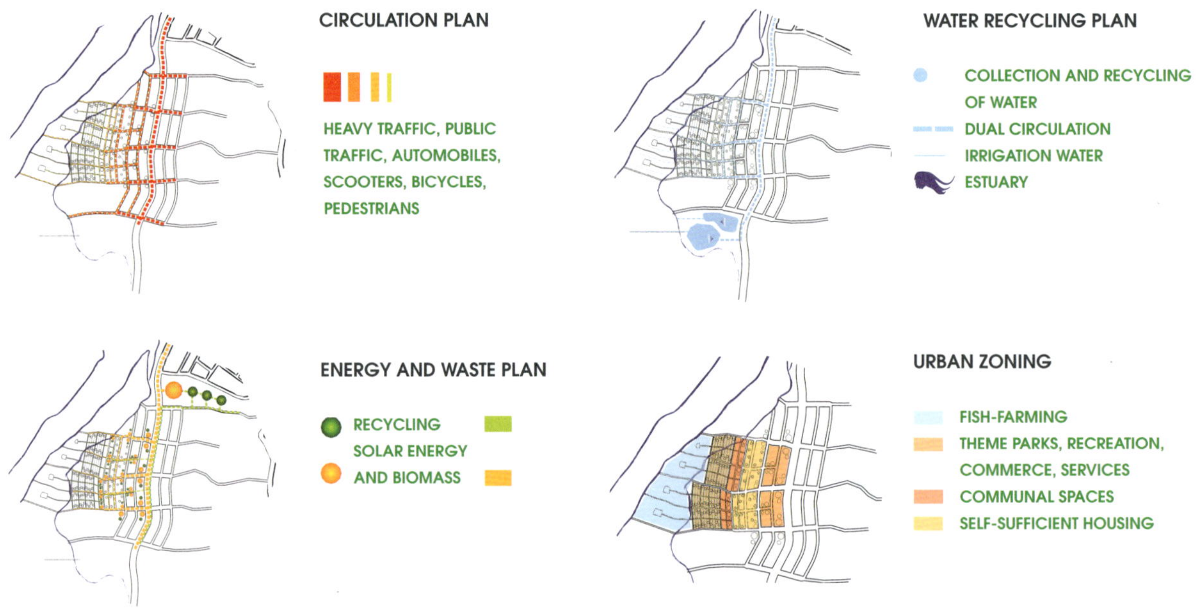

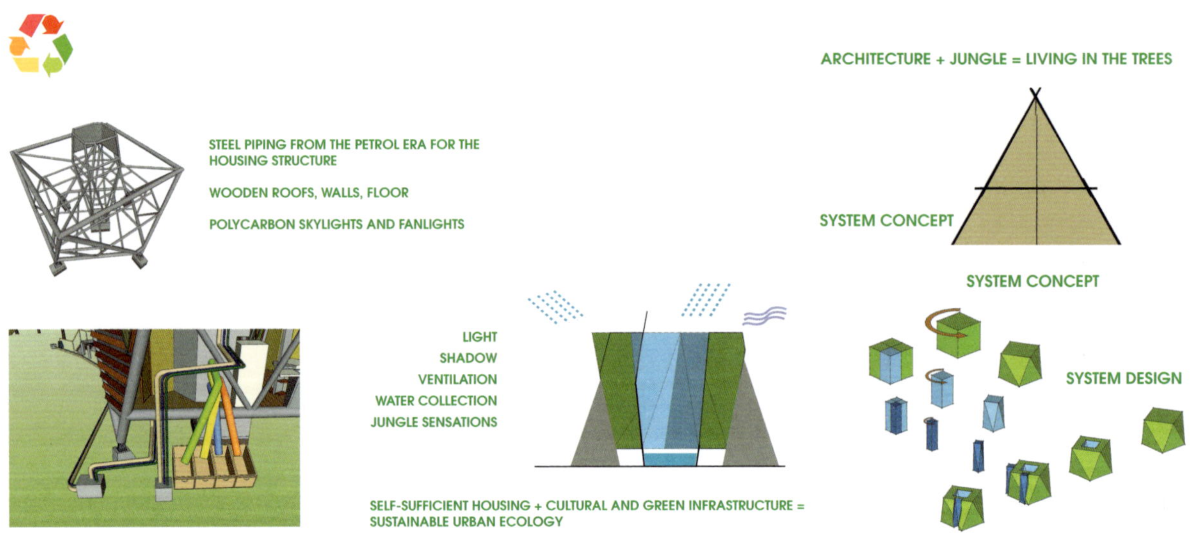

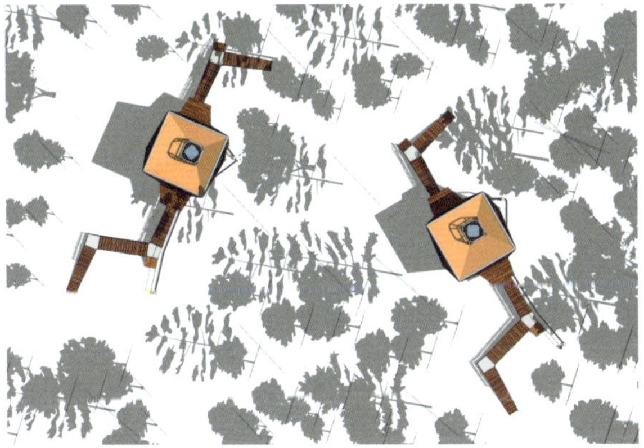

GROUND FLOOR

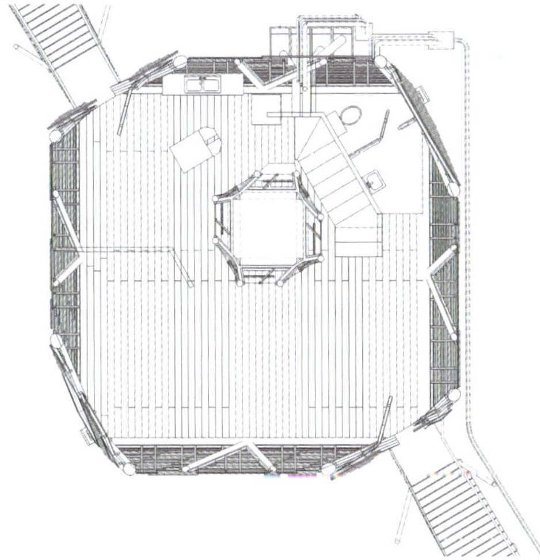

FIRST FLOOR

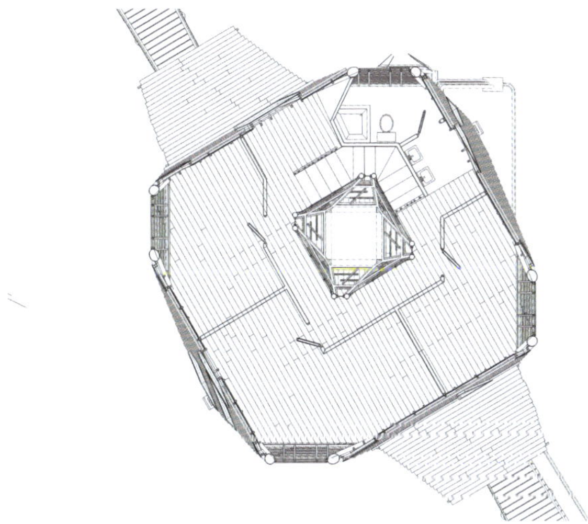

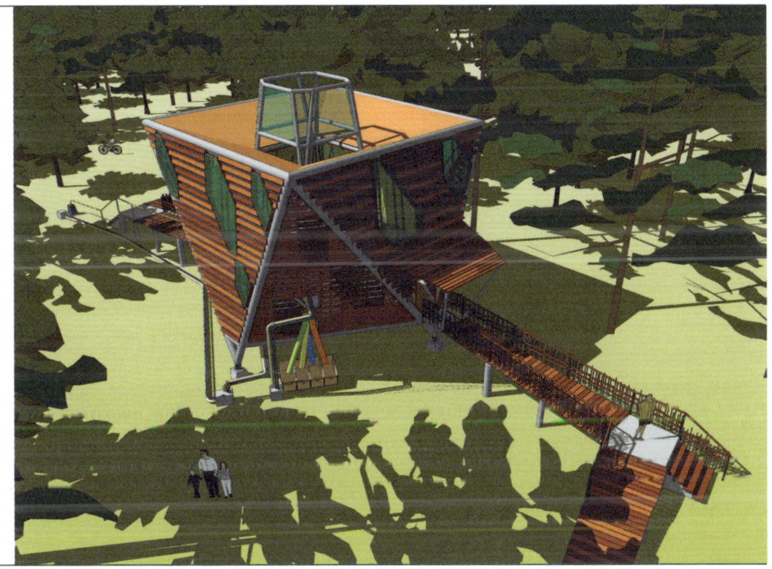

MULTI-LAYERED CONNECTOR

ESTEBAN SÁENZ LAVERDY

Nueva Loja has grown in an arbitrary, chaotic manner. It is necessary to revitalize the city and support its future growth by generating new centers of development, work opportunities and micro-businesses. Using the metaphor of the rain forest and its plant species, which fight amongst themselves to reach the light above them, the idea is to inject new life into the Orienco estuary, which runs across the entire city. It is hoped that new centers of commerce and recreation will compete along its shores, facilitated by a public water-transport system. A second aspect of the plan involves the introduction of exhibition and business spaces and of forms that transition from one shore to another. This network is designed to encourage social, cultural, and commercial exchange in a collective environment in a manner characteristic of a unified community. The third aspect addresses the household, which is designed as a sustainable domestic space. It is hierarchical in its design and implementation. A system of blinds acts as a trellis to aid the growth of vegetation along the facades. This in turn prevents a build-up of heat to create comfortable living spaces. Rainwater is collected and filtered for human consumption.

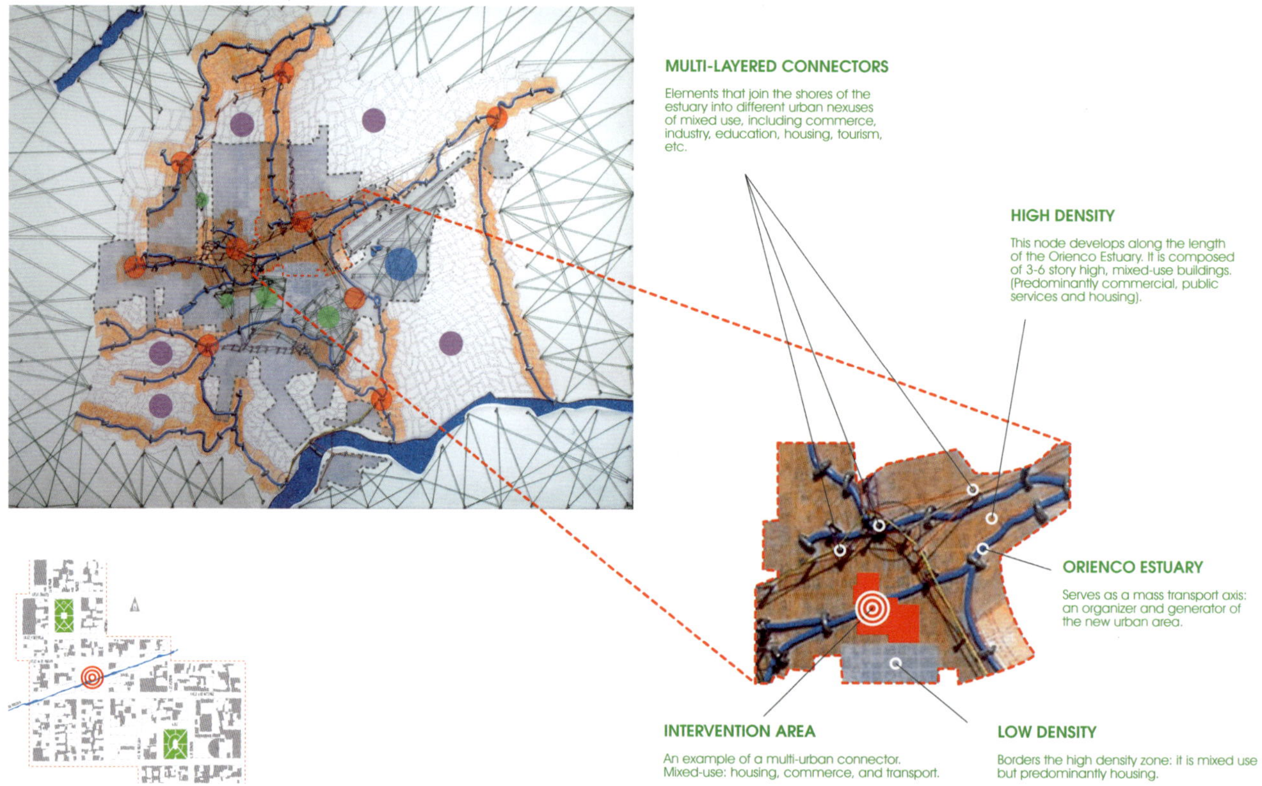

WATER AXIS
Orienco estuary and tributaries
A central axis of growth and urban planning
Circulation axis / Mass transit

URBAN NODE
Concentric generation point of different functions and services. Each one houses institutions; services, housing, commerce, etc. A self-sufficient and fully pedestrian sector where everything is within easy reach of the user.

ENERGY PRODUCING PARK
The re-use of the current oil processing plant as an alternative energy generator, which can also serve as a leisure and recreational park for the education and training of the general public.

NETWORK OF COMMUNAL VEGETABLE GARDENS
Development of gardens for community use in abandoned or under utilized sites, where the population generates economic activity in the region and elsewhere, for the creation, consumption and commercialization of agricultural products.

NEW URBAN AREA
Is created by the parallel waves of expansion along the length of the estuaries; the central organizational axes of the city.

The original, traditional, orthogonal layout and the estuary create a new urban zone.

RAINWATER IS COLLECTED AND TREATED. IT PROVIDES MOST OF THE NECESSARY DRINKING WATER.

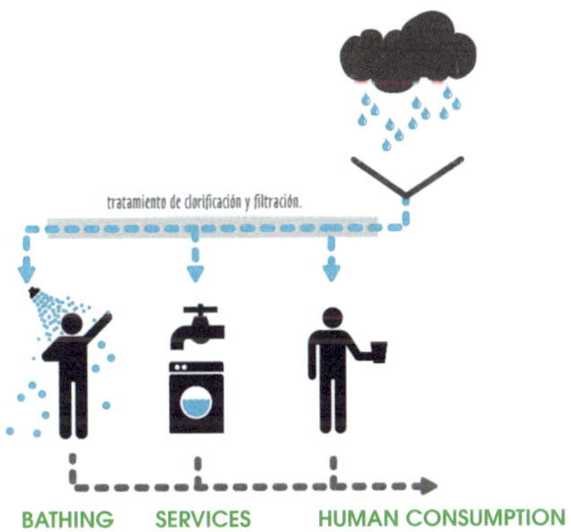

VEGETATION FILTERS ON THE FACADES AND ROOFS SERVE AS LAYERS OF THERMAL INSULATION THAT REDUCE ENERGY CONSUMPTION.

GREEN FILTERS THAT SUPPORT PLANT GROWTH PREVENT HEAT CONCENTRATION, CREATING COMFORTABLE HABITABLE SPACES.

CURRENTS OF COLD AIR ENTER TO COOL THE SPACE, WITH HOT AIR ESCAPING THROUGH THE TOPS OF THE BUILDINGS.

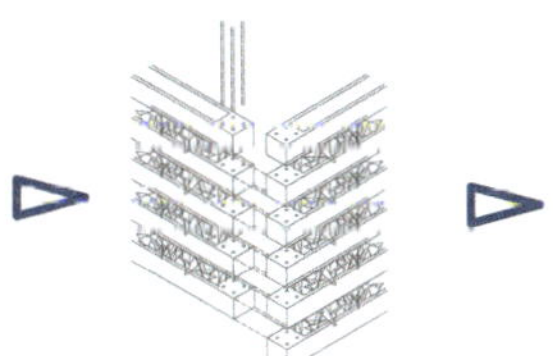

SELF-SUFFICIENT METABOLISMS

MARÍA LUISA BORJA

This project is part of an urban proposal for the growth of the city of Nueva Loja. Its urban model envisions the creation of several nuclei generated around a green center (parks) bordered by large circulation avenues. The households grow less dense as one moves from the center, which has the highest density, to the periphery. This project is located on a corner opposite a park and, in accordance with the urban plan, must have a high density of households, business units and public spaces. In an addition to the integration of these elements, the project takes into account several sustainability parameters with the key objective of creating a collective living unit that functions, like nature, as a self sufficient system: it must produce its own energy; renew its own resources and recycle its waste in a circular metabolism that will minimize the impact on the environment and the jungle. The urban proposal also seeks to reproduce the model of a self sufficient system on a large scale. It is anticipated that in the future human activity will adapt (from an ecological point of view) to the natural world to become a single symbiotic system. The management of energy attempts to diminish energy consumption. In this same spirit, the architecture satisfies light, ventilation and temperature needs through a bio-climatic design that keeps the household cool, lit, and ventilated. The materials used are modified to keep waste to a minimum and, in the case of the wood, certified.

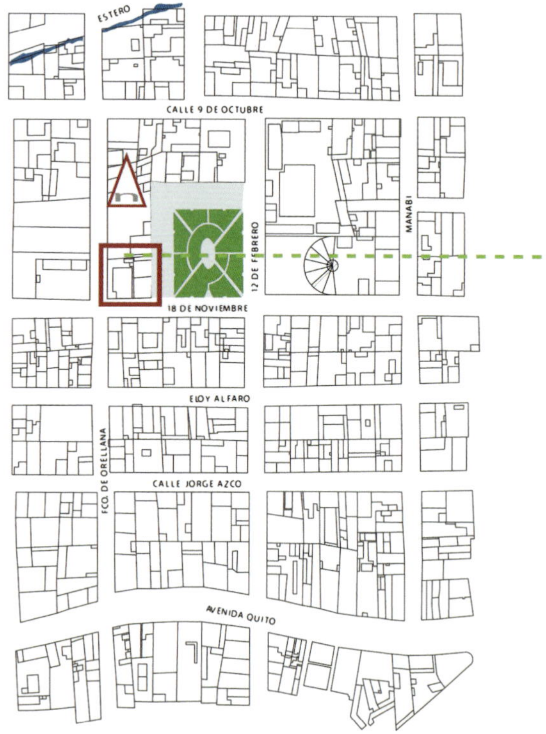

LOCATION

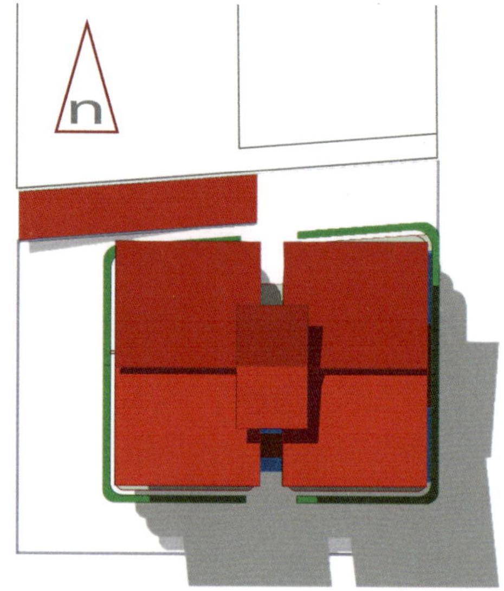

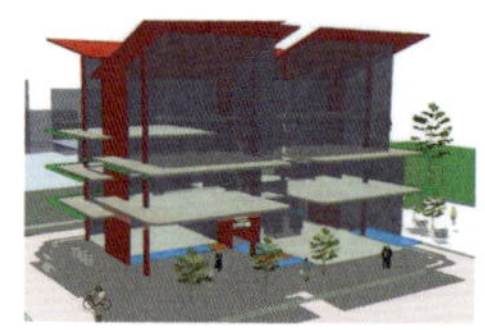

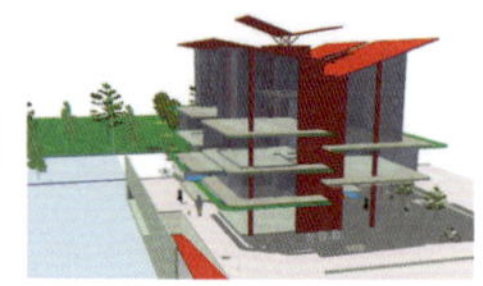

CONCEPTUAL SCHEME

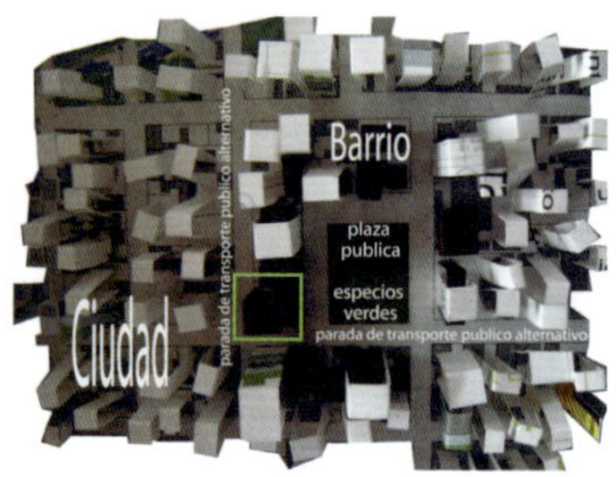

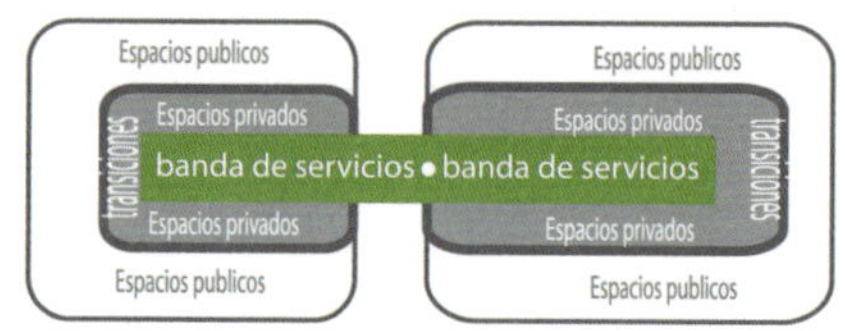

DIAGRAM

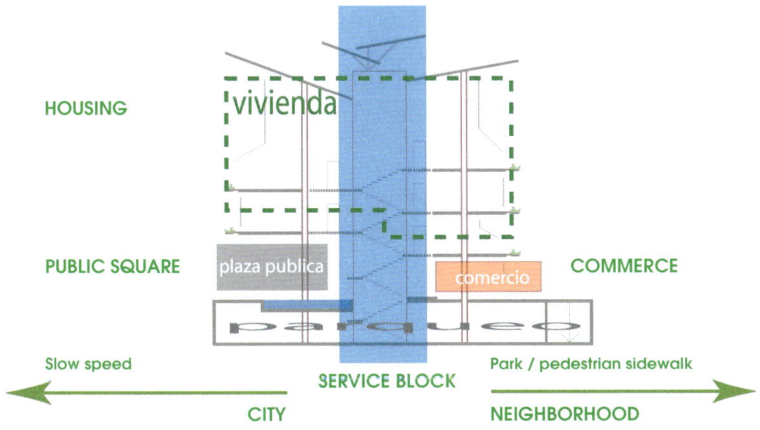

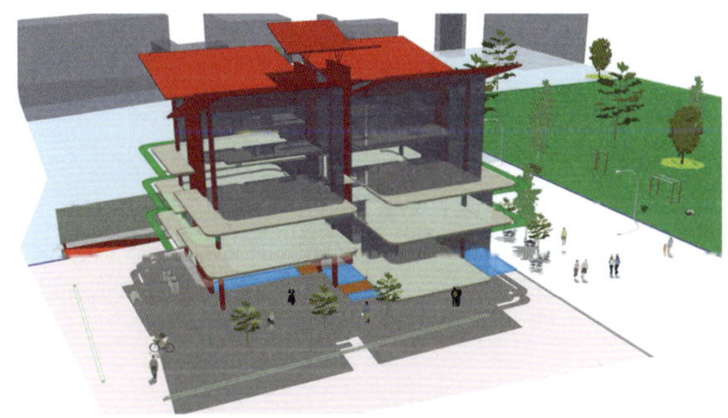

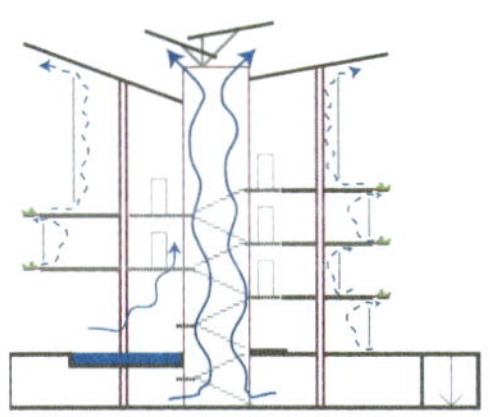

CROSS VENTILATION

Horizontal and vertical circulation of air throughout the building. Piles of volumes prevent the entry of sunlight but allow the flow of air.

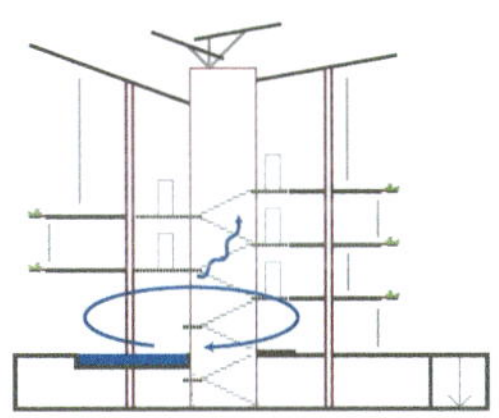

REFLECTIVE PONDS

Provide cooling for the rooms. They are re filled through the collection of rainwater.

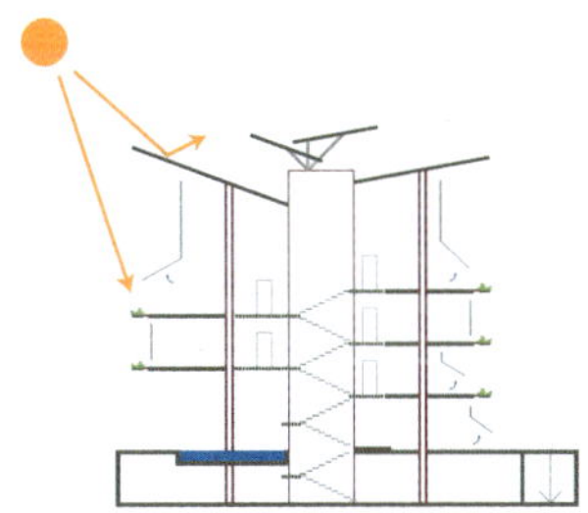

PROTRUDING ROOF GARDENS

Provide shadow to the rooms and allow the entry of light but not heat. They function as passages and extensions of the spaces. Windows follow a north-south orientation.

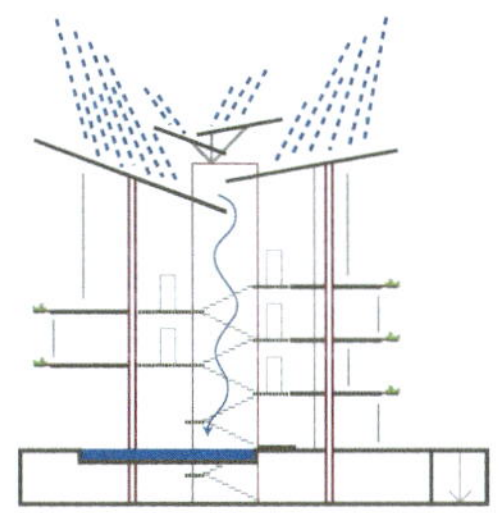

COLLECTION OF RAINWATER

Inclined roofs and water collection systems provide drinking water and fountains.

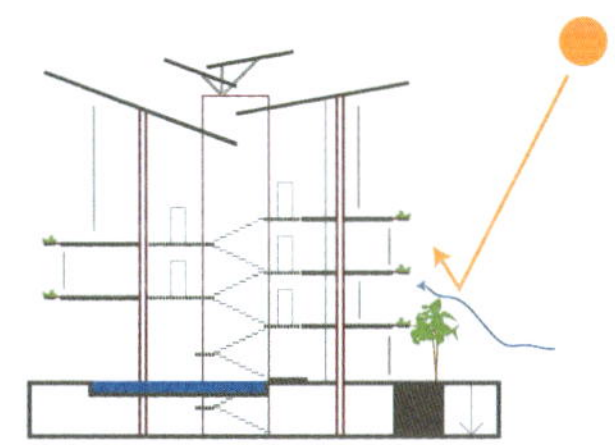

INCORPORATION OF VEGETATION

Helps to regulate temperature and natural ventilation. Simple vegetable gardens are provided in each apartment for family use. Trees offer shade in public spaces.

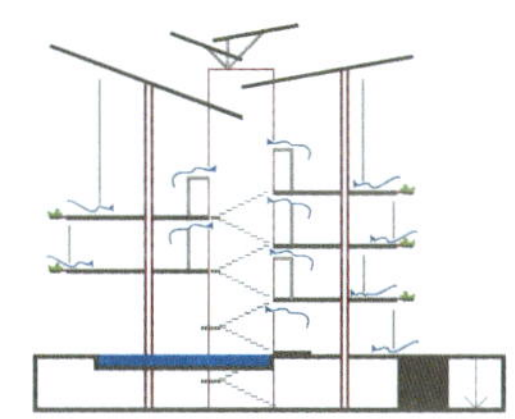

INTERNAL VENTILATION: CONSTANT AIR RENEWAL

Through a central air duct and inner walls that do not reach the ceiling, as well as the provision of high mezzanines.

GROUND FLOOR

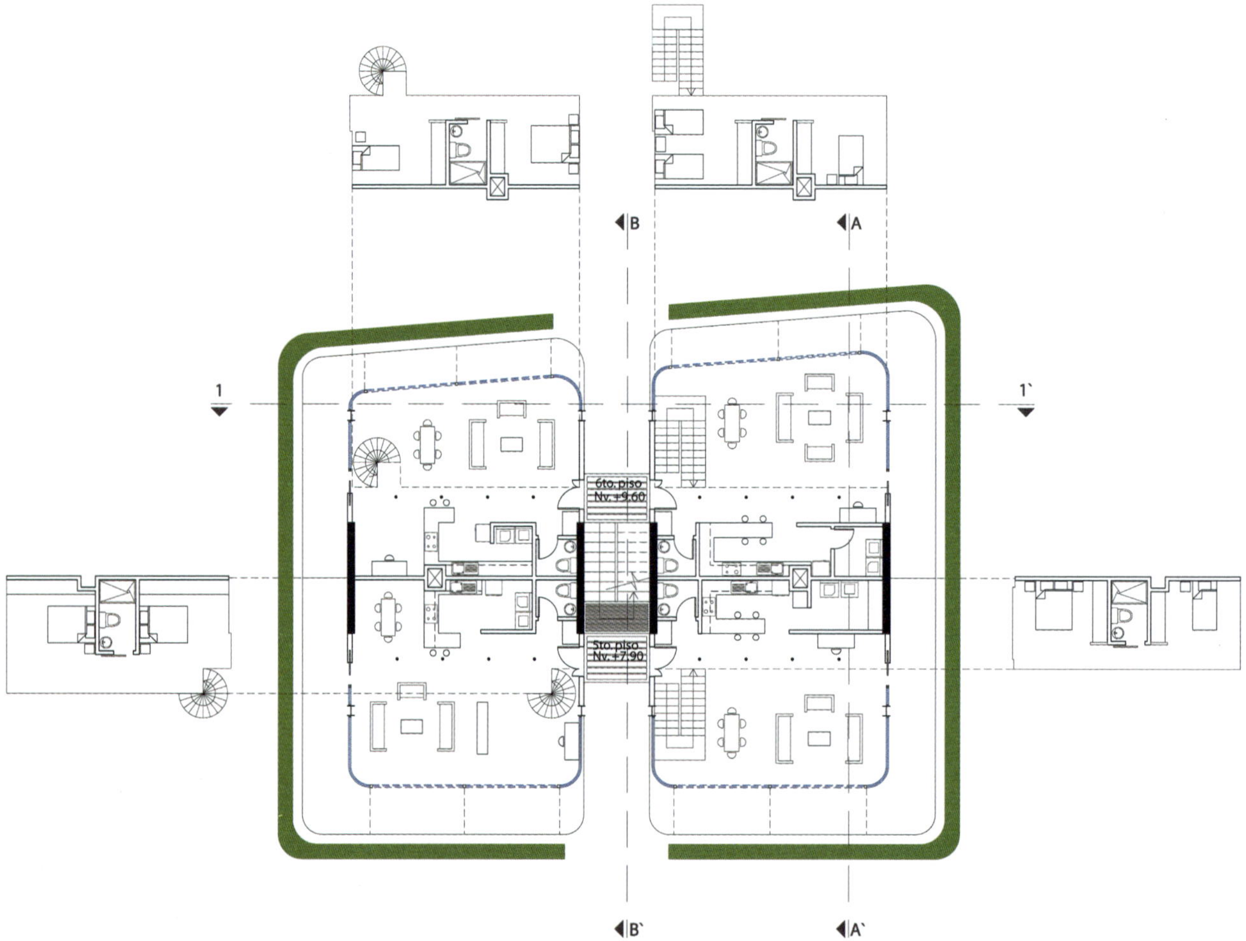

WEST ELEVATION

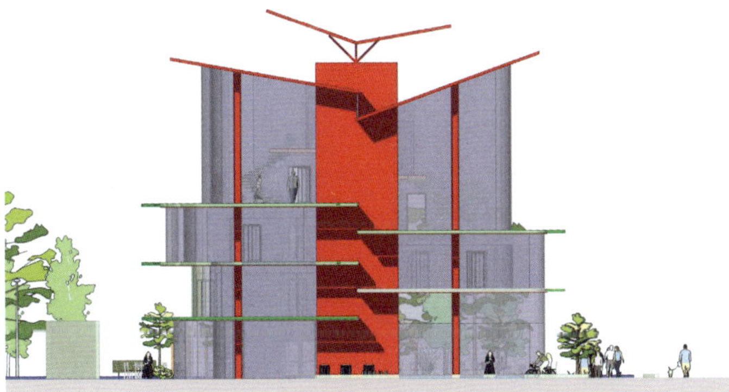

EAST ELEVATION

NORTH ELEVATION

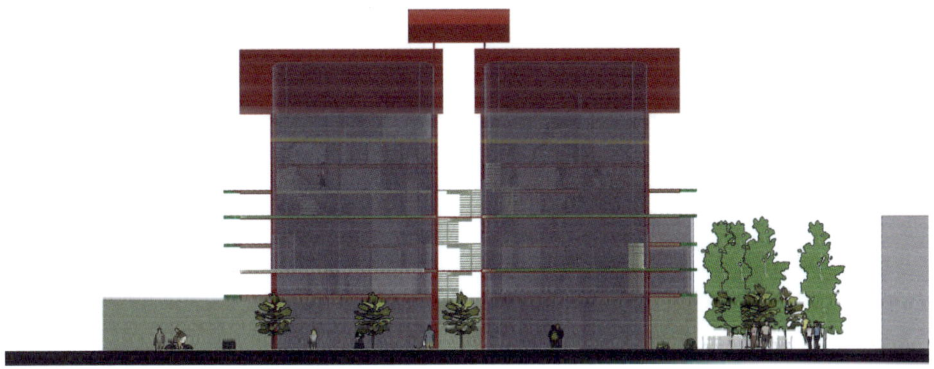

SOUTH ELEVATION

STRIPS FOR GROWTH

ANDRÉS PERALVO

The rainforest is constantly changing; it adapts to its surroundings in order to continue its growth. The city, as a living organism, is no different; it adapts to new necessities and conditions. Each part of the city finds its own space. What's missing is a design that will facilitate ecological growth, in which each organism can interact with the environment and take advantage of the existing resources of the site.

My proposal for Nueva Loja is to concentrate the city and bring various services to its citizens to reduce the need for movement as much as possible. The project inserts a central zone in the city, with its development being based on a series of incremental strips that generate several spaces for different kinds of housing. The growth strips adapt to different environmental needs and functions; they seek to reshape borders between departments, exteriors and interiors, society and nature. In the household itself, emphasis has been put on communal areas that house activities such as urban agriculture, communal washing machines (which run on rainwater) and parking areas for bicycles. To create a better relationship between constructed and natural environments, the benefits of local resources and features have been identified and made use of and the environmental impact on a zone as fragile as the rainforest has been minimized.

CONCEPTUAL DIAGRAMS

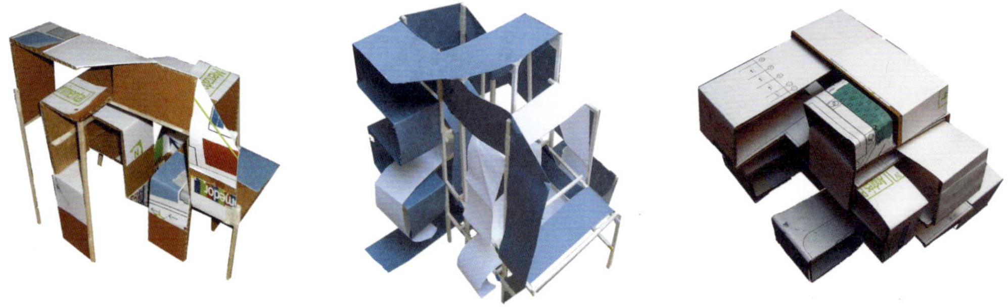

RETHINK LIMITS AND CONTINUITY SPACE, INTEGRATION OF INDOOR AND OUTDOOR SPACES / VERSATILITY

METABOLISM

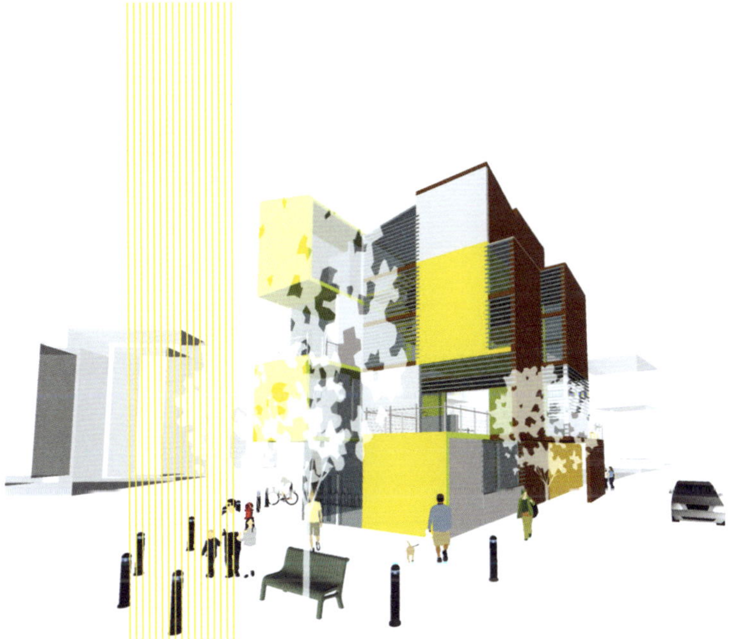

AVENIDA QUITO
AVENIDA AMAZONAS

SECTIONS

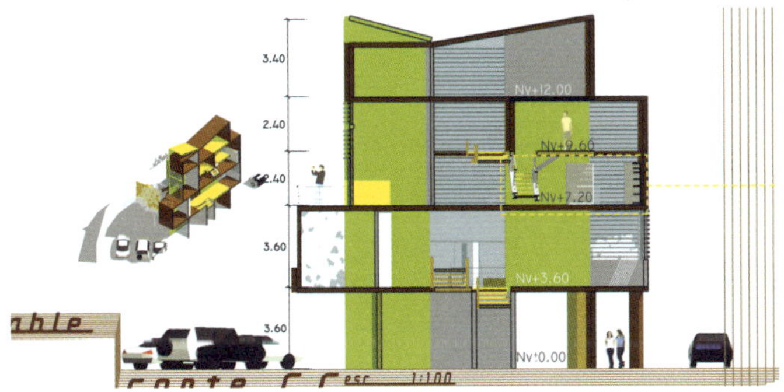
3.40
2.40
2.40
3.60
3.60
Nv+12.00
Nv+9.60
Nv+7.20
Nv+3.60
Nv:0.00
1:100

4.60
3.60
3.60
3.60
Nv+12.00
Nv+10.80
Nv+7.20
Nv+3.60
Nv:0.00

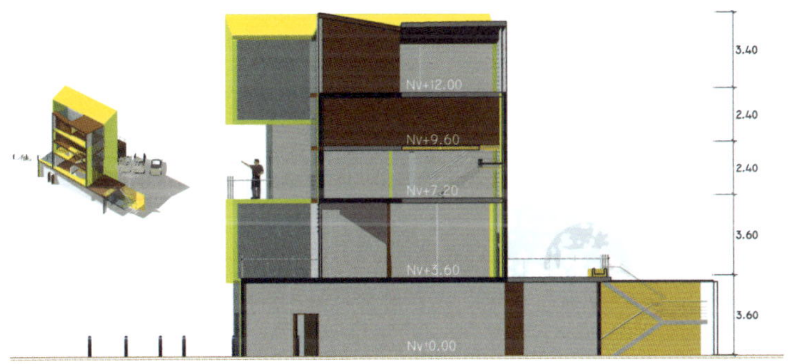
3.40
2.40
2.40
3.60
3.60
Nv+12.00
Nv+9.60
Nv+7.20
Nv+3.60
Nv:0.00

MATERIAL FUSION

NICOLÁS GALLEGOS

From the programmatic point of view this proposal for a household fulfills the basic requirements of any dwelling but also looks to respond to new environmental necessities through bio-climatic design and a reformulation of the service infrastructure. The facades are equipped with a semi-permeable skin, which controls the climate of the household and can be opened completely to improve ventilation. The roof makes use of frequent Amazonian rain showers to collect rainwater which is then recycled and re-used for household services. A series of materials are fused together to fully take advantage of their properties. The steel piping from the oil era is recycled in the structure and wood from aged fallen trees is used for platforms and skins.

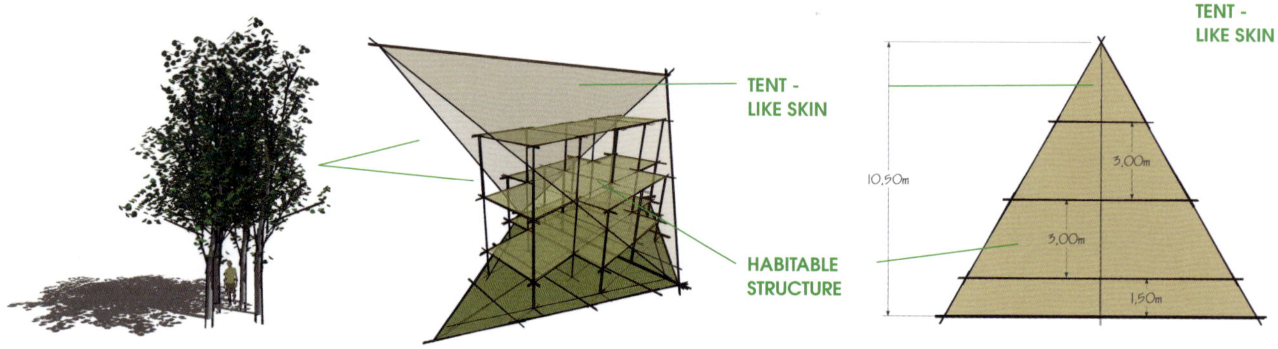

STEEL PIPES OF OIL INFRASTRUCTURE RE-USED AS STRUCTURAL COMPONENTS IN HOUSEHOLD

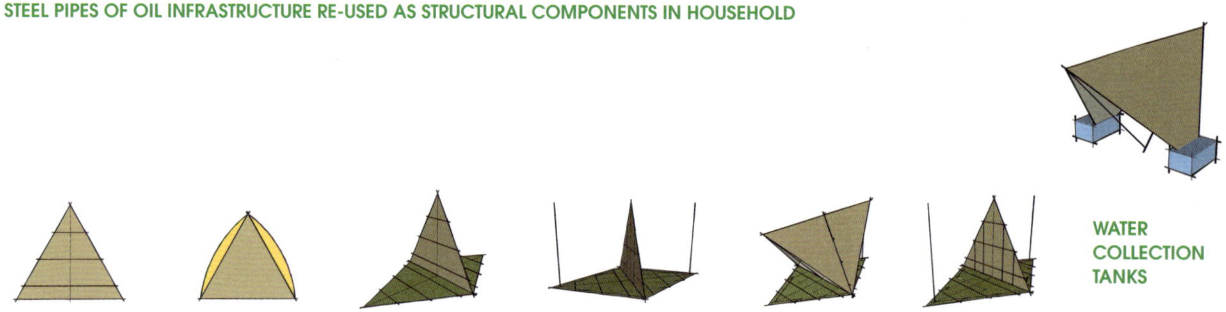

WOODEN BEAMS 20M X 20M

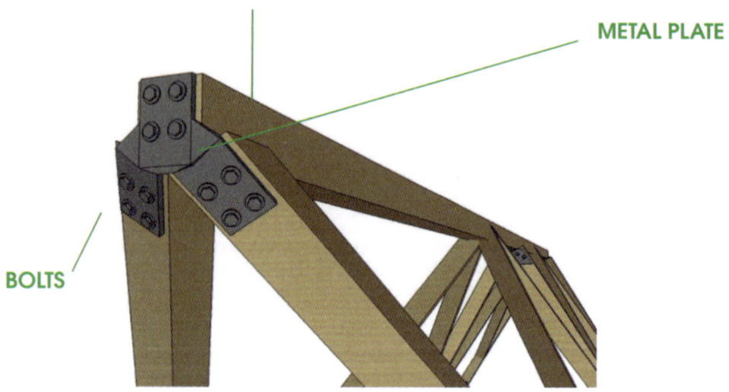

ROOF STRUCTURE

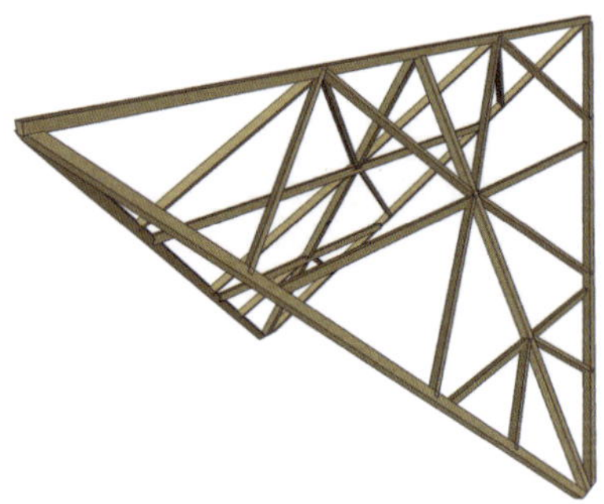

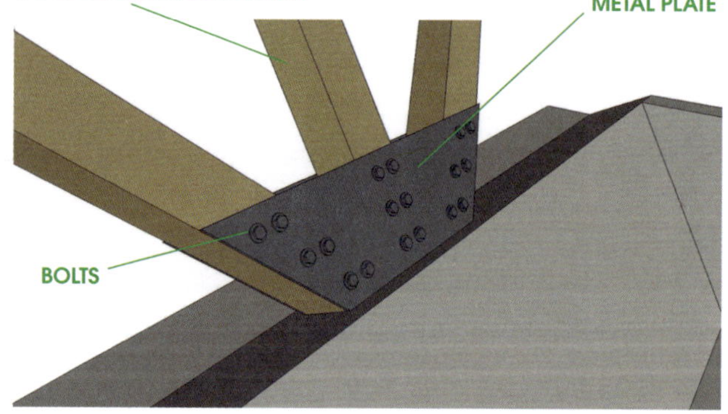

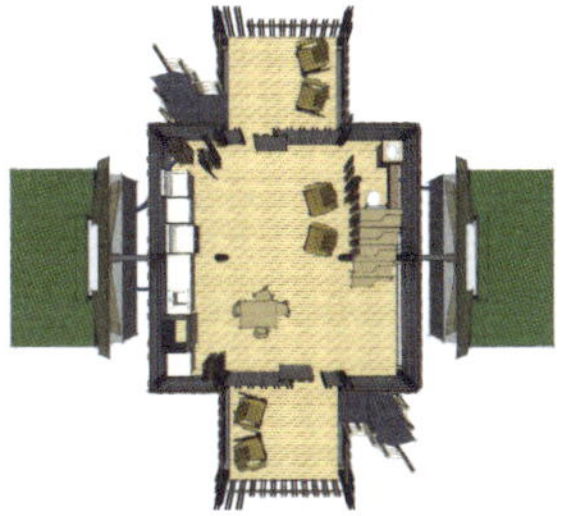

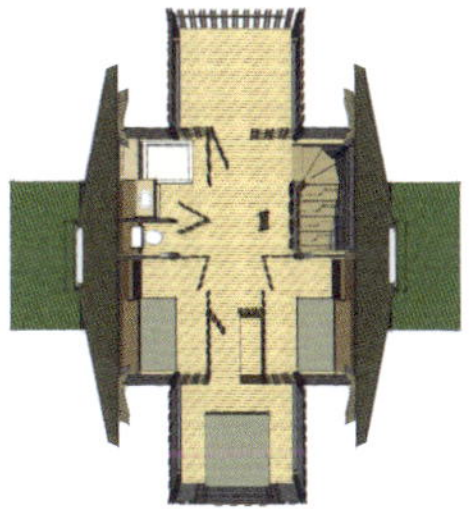

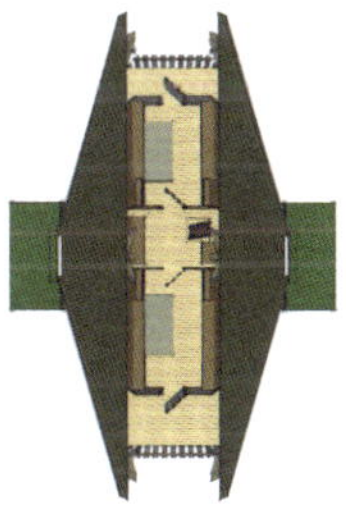

SECOND FLOOR

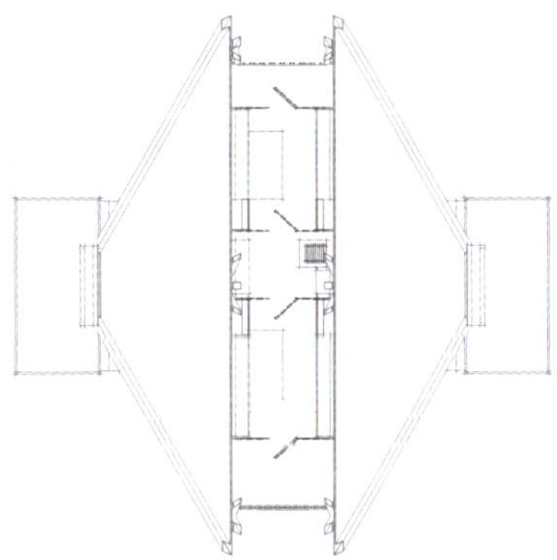

FIRST FLOOR

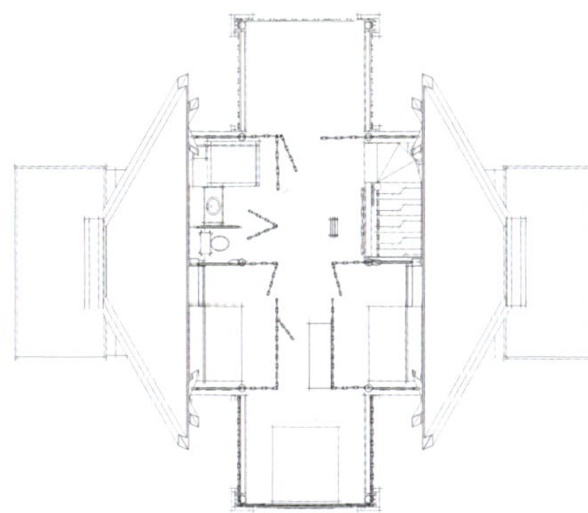

GROUND FLOOR

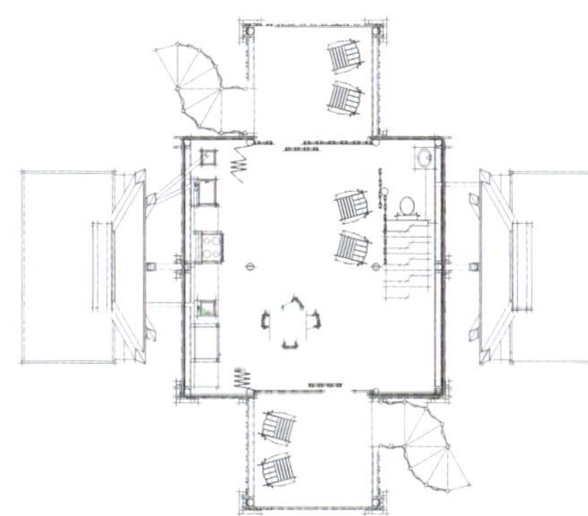

FACADES

A

B

C

D

PERSPECTIVES

1

2

3

4

SUSTAINABLE FREE-STANDING HOUSEHOLD

VERÓNICA GUERRA

Before beginning the design of this project, a proposal for the growth of Nueva Loja was developed. Then the elements that would direct this growth in a certain direction were analyzed: natural limits, such as the Aguarico River and the lake; and artificial ones, such as the airport. It was proposed that growth should be directed towards these places as they have great touristic, commercial and natural potential. A study of urban areas was carried out, based on a pixelization of the geographical elements. Their behavior was observed over time and this knowledge was then applied to the morphology of growth in Nueva Loja, the use of the soil and the design of the households.

Once the analysis and the urban scale proposal had been carried out, a site was established that would also provide for agriculture and commerce (complementary activities for the household). Concepts such as canopies, connections and pixels provided the basis for the design. Building facades are fragmented into a porous mosaic that allows the household to breathe. A rotational agricultural system is proposed for the plantation to avoid exhausting the soil and a place is set aside for photovoltaic panels. The architectural program of the household is thus widened to include productive components.

MODEL

PIXELS
LAYERS
CONNECTIONS
AREAS
TENSIONS
BORDERS

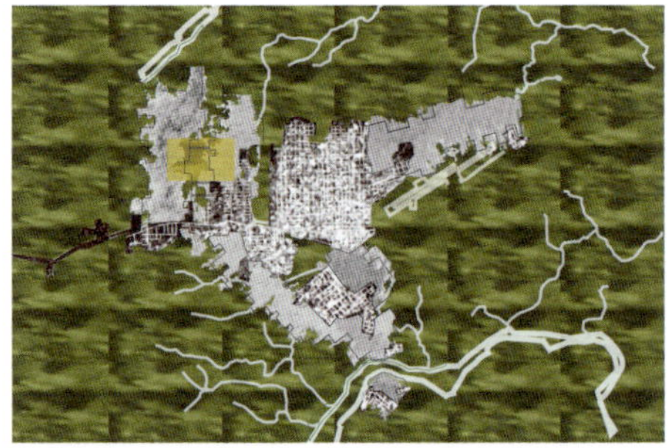

INTERVENTION ZONES

SELF-SUFFICIENT HOUSING

CLOSE TO THE BORDER:

AGRICULTURAL RELATIONSHIP

CONTACT WITH COMMERCE

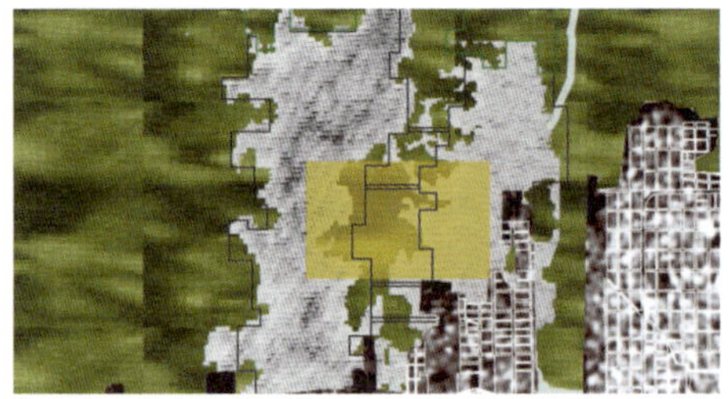

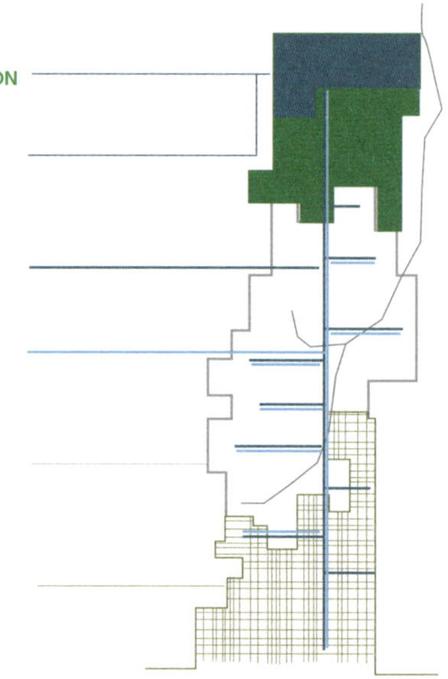

SYSTEMS LAYOUT

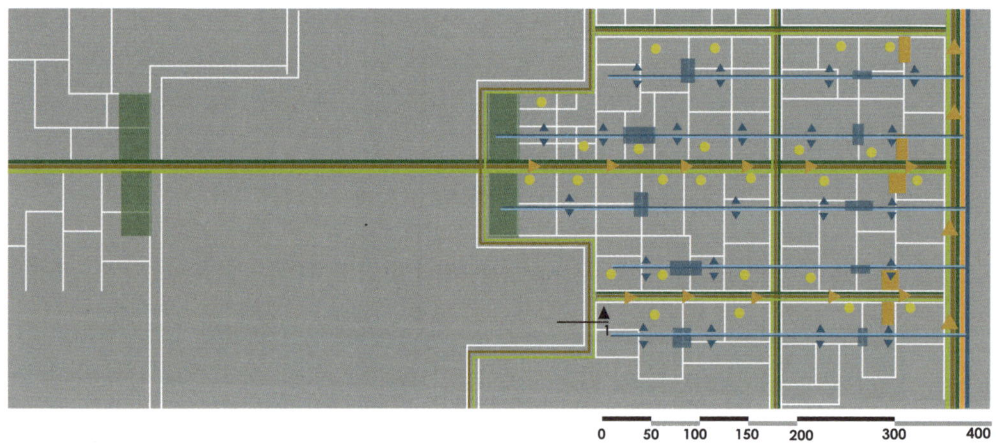

HOUSING IMPLEMENTATION

ORIENTATION

MOSTLY OPEN SURFACES (WINDOWS AND SKINS) WITH A NORTH-SOUTH ORIENTATION – FACILITATE ACCESS TO LIGHT, NOT HEAT, AND ALLOW THE PREDOMINANT WINDS COMING FROM THE SOUTH TO VENTILATE THE INTERIORS.

SKINS

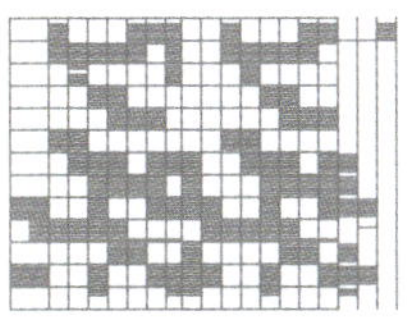

GAPS WILL ALLOW HOUSE TO VENTILATE AND PROVIDE PATTERNS OF LIGHT AND SHADOW

COLOR PATTERN - SKIN - REMOVED

CONNECTION WITH NATURE

DISTRIBUTION

HOUSEHOLD LAID OUT AT DIFFERENT LEVELS

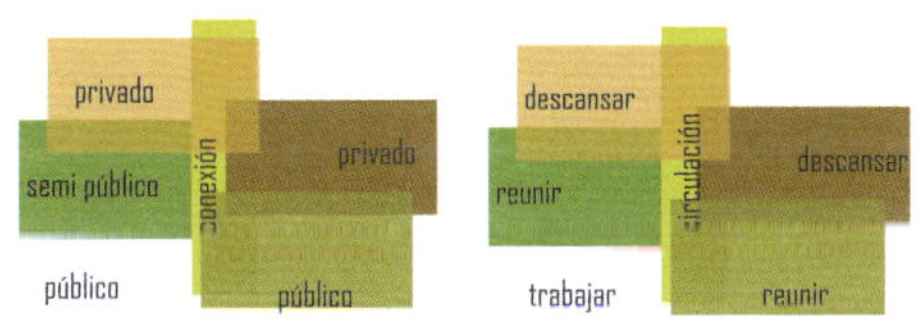

STAIRCASE ARTICULATES ALL SPACES

1 GROUND FLOOR

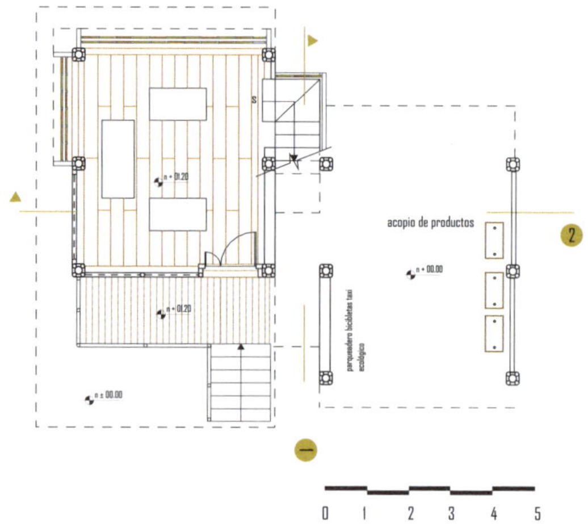

2 FIRST FLOOR

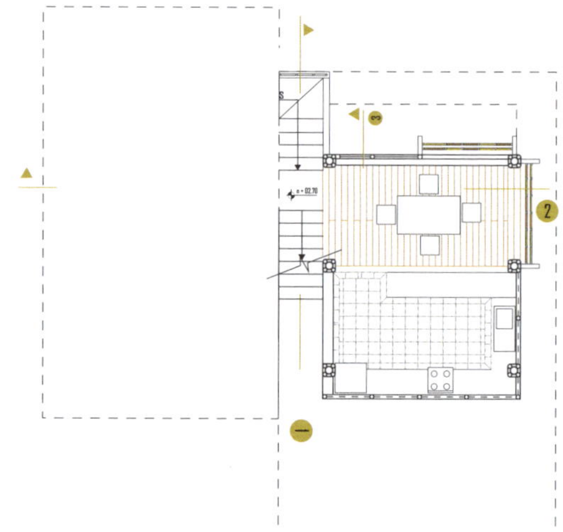

3 SECOND FLOOR

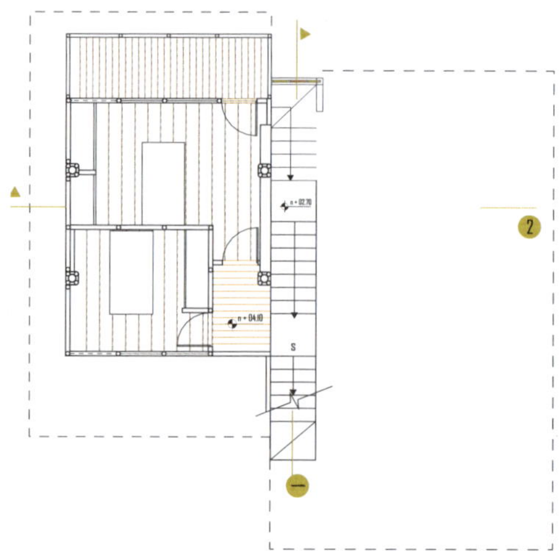

4 THIRD FLOOR

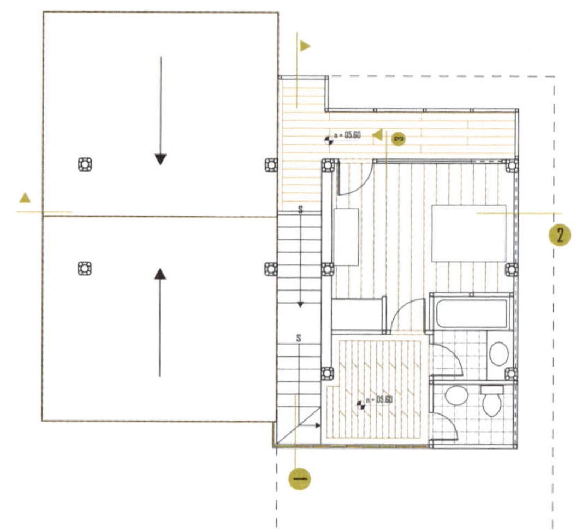

ELEVATIONS

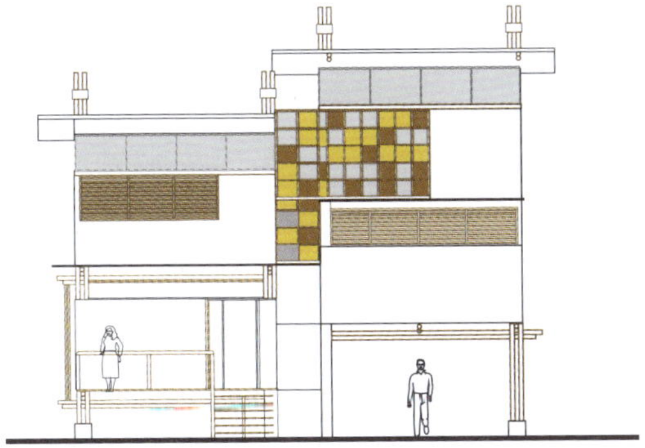

PROTECTIVE CANOPY

MARÍA JOSÉ LEÓN

The objective of this project was to create the kind of household that would adapt to the climate of the Nueva Loja region. On analyzing Amazonia and its forests in particular, I was able to observe that in spite of the fact that the climate is described as tropical – humid and warm – the interior of the forest, thanks to the effect of the trees and vegetation, actually has a cool, shady micro-climate. The forest provides a protective canopy which alleviates the effects of the tropical climate. During the design process, this canopy was developed to create a household that might make use of the protective characteristics of trees. The roof becomes similar to a canopy as it spreads away from the bedrooms. The skins are folded to create closed, open, and semi-open environments. The scale is small and the architectural program minimal. The structure is built with a renewable resource; wood, and is based on the rainforest's mechanisms of renewal.

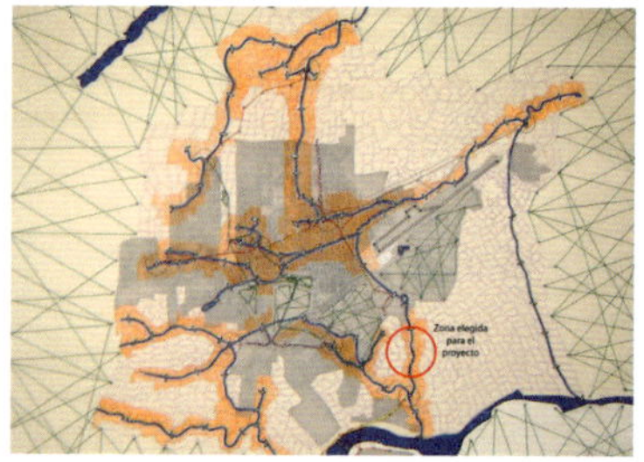

LOCATION

SUN PROTECTION LAYER PLANS

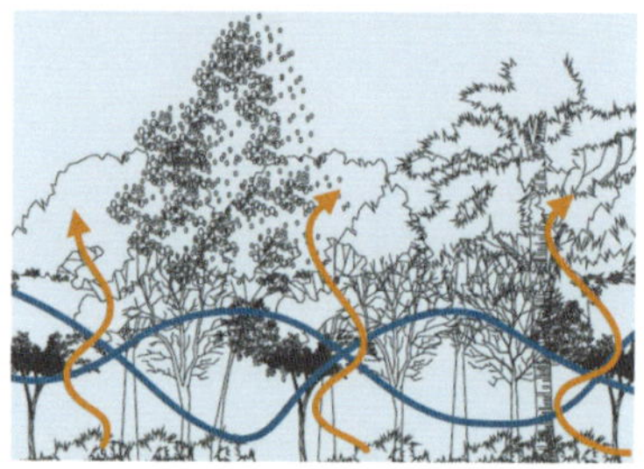

WINDS

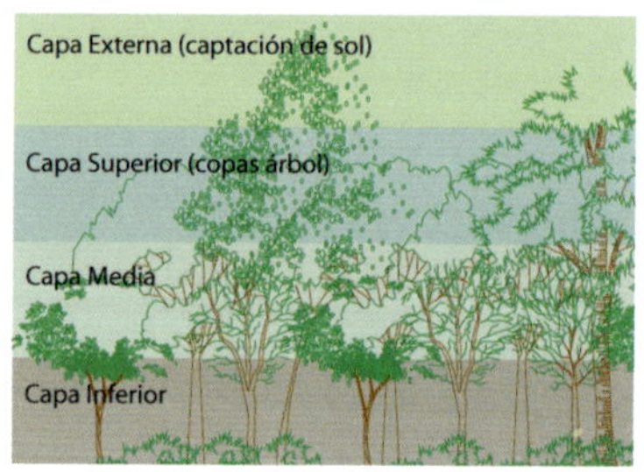

WOODS LAYER

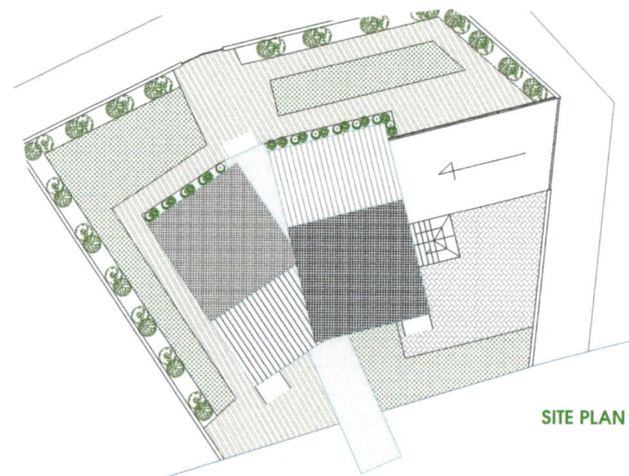

SITE PLAN

GROUND PLAN

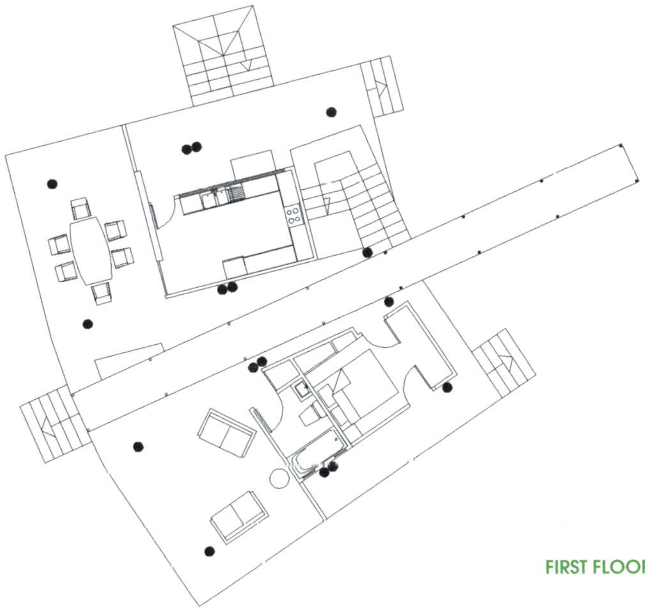

FIRST FLOOR

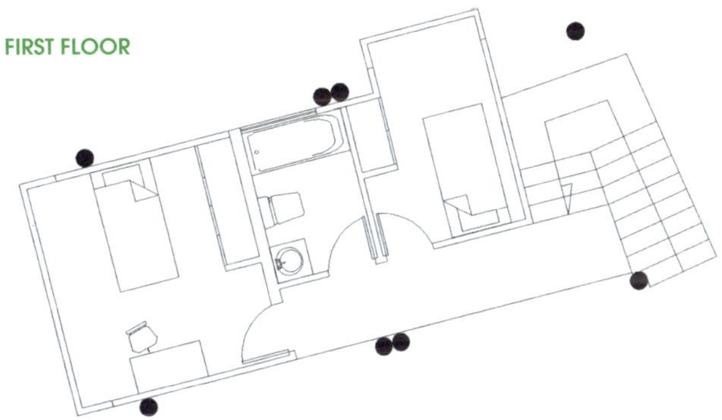

SECOND FLOOR

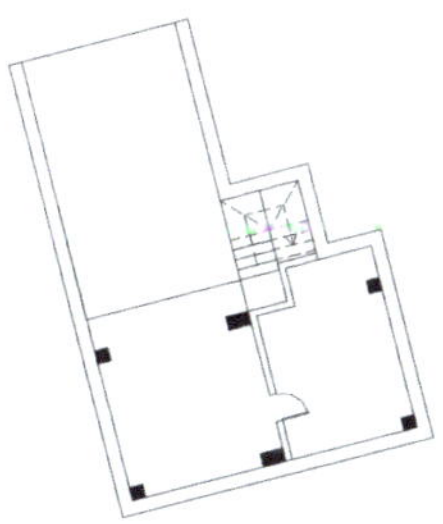

REVERSAL OF FORTUNE

PATRICK RADDEN KEEFE
Published in *The New Yorker*, January 9, 2012

The jungle outpost of Lago Agrio is in northeastern Ecuador, where the elevation plummets from the serrated ridge of the Andes to the swampy lowlands of the Amazon Basin. Ecuadorans call the region the Oriente. For centuries, the rain forest was inhabited only by indigenous tribes. But, in 1967, American drillers working for Texaco discovered that two miles beneath the jungle floor lay abundant reserves of crude oil. For twenty-three years, a consortium of companies, led by Texaco, drilled wells throughout the Ecuadoran Amazon. Initially, the jungle was so impenetrable that the consortium had to fly in equipment by helicopter. But laborers hacked paths with machetes, and, eventually, Texaco paved roads and built an airport.

Today, Lago Agrio feels squalid. The buildings look thrown together, as if no one had believed that the boom might last. Stray dogs prowl the dusty streets, and a slender oil pipeline snakes alongside each major road, elevated on stilts, waist high, like an endless bannister. The Colombian border is ten miles to the north, and drug traffickers and paramilitaries have infested the Oriente, as have sicarios—paid assassins—who post ads online and charge as little as twenty dollars. In 2010, in a single month, the bodies of thirty murder victims were found along a stretch of road near the border.

One day last February, a judge in Lago Agrio, presiding over a spare, concrete courtroom in a shopping mall on the edge of town, issued an opinion that reverberated far beyond the Amazon. Since 1993, a group of Ecuadorans had been pursuing an apparently fruitless legal struggle to hold Texaco responsible for environmental destruction in the Oriente. During the decades when Texaco operated there, the lawsuit maintained, it dumped eighteen billion gallons of toxic waste. When the company ceased operations in Ecuador, in 1992, it allegedly left behind hundreds of open pits full of malignant black sludge. The harm done by Texaco, the plaintiffs contended, could be measured in cancer deaths, miscarriages, birth defects, dead livestock, sick fish, and the near-extinction of several tribes; Texaco's legacy in the region amounted to a "rain-forest Chernobyl."

By the time the judge, Nicolás Zambrano, issued his decision, the case had been going on for eighteen years. It had outlasted jurists on two continents. Zambrano was the sixth judge to preside in Ecuador; one federal judge in New York had died before he could rule on the case. The litigation even outlasted Texaco: in 2001, the company was subsumed by Chevron, which inherited the lawsuit. The dispute is now considered one of the nastiest legal contests in memory, a spectacle almost as ugly as the pollution that prompted it.

Chevron, which operates in more than a hundred countries, is America's third-largest corporation. Its annual revenue, which often tops two hundred billion dollars, is nearly four times as much as Ecuador's economic output. The plaintiffs, who named themselves the afectados—the affected ones—included indigenous people and uneducated settlers in the Oriente; some of them initially signed documents in the case with a fingerprint. They were represented by a fractious coalition of American and Ecuadoran lawyers, most of whom were working for contingency fees. An environmental lawsuit against a major corporation can resemble a war of attrition, and in 1993 few observers would have predicted that the plaintiffs could endure as long as they did. But, on February 14, 2011, their persistence was rewarded. Judge Zambrano ruled that Chevron was responsible for vast contamination, and ordered it to pay eighteen billion dollars in damages—the largest judgment ever awarded in an environmental lawsuit.

It was an extraordinary triumph, particularly for one of the plaintiffs' lead lawyers, a tenacious American named Steven Donziger, who had been a key figure in the case since its inception. Donziger speaks Spanish, and for years has shuttled between Ecuador and New York. "This trial is historic," he has said. "This is the first time that a small developing country has had power over a multinational American company."

Chevron categorically denies the charges made in the lawsuit, insisting that it bears no responsibility for pollution in the Amazon and that Texaco's operations were "completely in line with the standards of the day." A Chevron spokesman told me that "there is no corroborating evidence" of adverse health effects related to oil development in the Oriente, and blamed "trial lawyers" for "perpetuating false information."

In recent years, Chevron has invested millions of dollars in remolding its public image. Elegant television commercials, narrated by the actor Campbell Scott, emphasize that the company aims to "practice and espouse conservation." A print advertisement features a photograph of two smiling African women, and the caption "Oil Companies Should Support the Communities They're a Part Of." This fall, at a breakfast discussion on "Business and Human Rights," in New York, Chevron's manager for global issues, Silvia Garrigo, said that the company makes "social investments" wherever it operates, noting, "We're in countries for the long haul."

In the courtroom, however, Chevron has been far less conciliatory. Not long ago, after the company successfully defeated a lawsuit seeking to hold it responsible for the shooting deaths of protesters on an offshore oil platform in Nigeria, it tried to compel the impoverished Nigerian plaintiffs, some of whom were widows or children, to reimburse its attorneys' fees. (No fees were awarded, and a judge admonished Chevron for trying.) "That's how they litigate," Bert Voorhees, one of the Nigerians' lawyers, told me. "The point is to scare off the next community that might try to assert its human rights."

Chevron has been especially defiant in the face of the Lago Agrio accusations, which its lawyers have labelled "a shakedown." In addition to defending itself in Ecuador, it has fought the case in more than a dozen U.S. federal courts, hiring hundreds of lawyers and producing what its own attorneys have called "an avalanche of paper." Donziger has maintained that Chevron is motivated not merely by fear of an adverse judgment but by a desire "to destroy the very idea that indigenous people can bring an environmental lawsuit against an oil company." In 2008, a Chevron lobbyist in Washington told Newsweek, "We can't let little countries screw around with big companies like this." One Chevron spokesman has said, "We're going to fight this until Hell freezes over—and then we'll fight it out on the ice."

When the verdict was issued in Lago Agrio, Chevron declared the judgment to be "illegitimate and unenforceable," and said that the company, which has no assets in Ecuador, would not pay. Instead, it countered with an audacious move—suing Steven Donziger, the architect of the suit against it. At the very moment that Donziger might have been celebrating a landmark victory in Ecuador, he found himself facing charges of extortion and fraud in New York.

When Donziger is not in Ecuador, he works out of the paper-strewn kitchen of a two-bedroom apartment that he shares with his wife and young son, on the Upper West Side. But Donziger also does a lot of business in restaurants. He will set up shop over lunch at the Ocean Grill, opposite the Museum of Natural History, and work his phone until all the other patrons have left. Wherever he goes, a MacBook Air is tucked under his arm.

If discretion is a signature imperative of the legal profession, Donziger is a rather unorthodox lawyer. He is a compulsive talker, his incessant conversational stream tracking the course of his volatile emotions. Roused by his own orations, he often crescendos, suddenly, into a shout. At six feet four, with big facial features, close-cropped charcoal-gray hair, and enormous hands, Donziger is a formidable physical presence. Friends from Harvard Law School refer to him as "Big Steve." He played basketball at Harvard with Barack Obama, another member of the Class of 1991. Since then, Donziger has devoted his career to a single case.

Shortly after Donziger graduated from law school, a Massachusetts attorney named Cristóbal Bonifaz began considering a lawsuit against Texaco. Bonifaz was a courtly émigré from a prominent Ecuadoran family. (His grandfather had served, briefly, as President.) In April, 1993, after learning about the environmental damage in the Oriente from an Oxfam report, he assembled a team of lawyers, doctors, and specialists from the Harvard School of Public Health for a reconnaissance trip to the Amazon. Bonifaz invited Donziger, a family friend, to join the expedition.

When Texaco struck oil in Ecuador, the country was unstable and impoverished; its chief export was bananas. As Judith Kimerling, the author of the book "Amazon Crude," has written, the "first barrel" of Ecuadoran oil was paraded through the streets of Quito. In 1972, when Texaco completed construction of a pipeline to funnel oil to the Pacific coast, Ecuador instantly became the second-largest oil exporter in Latin America, after Venezuela. Within a decade, per-capita G.D.P. had nearly doubled.

One challenge of drilling oil wells is what to do with "produced water"—a malodorous liquid, fortified with heavy metals, that comes mingled with the oil that is pumped out of the ground. In the United States, it is standard practice, once the oil has been isolated from this mixture, to "reinject" the produced water, pumping it deep underground into dedicated wells, in order to prevent damage to the local habitat. But reinjection is expensive, and in Ecuador Texaco simply dumped the liquid into swimming-pool-size pits. Produced water does not biodegrade, and when Donziger and his colleagues visited the Oriente they discovered that hundreds of oily pools pockmarked the rain forest.

The government of Ecuador had been aware of Texaco's techniques from the start, and for many years Texaco was in a consortium that included the national oil company. Texaco's practices did not directly violate Ecuadoran law; in fact, the country had no meaningful environmental regulations at the time. Most Ecuadorans knew little about the science of petroleum extraction—and most of what they learned came from Texaco. Lago Agrio was named for Sour Lake, the East Texas town where Texaco was established, and, as the oil camp grew into a boom town, pipeline spills became common. Texaco trucks sprayed roads with oil, to keep down dust. In Quito, I met a woman named Margarita Yépez, who spent eighteen years as a social worker for Texaco. In the early days, she said, gringo oilmen told Lago Agrio locals, in jest, that oil was good for one's health; a coffee can full of crude could cure arthritis or male-pattern baldness—just rub some on the affected area. "They were the authority, so we trusted them," she said. "We were dumb."

Initially, the indigenous tribes were the only Ecuadorans affected by the drilling. And though the oil lay under their native land, they weren't entitled to any of the profits, because the government retained all "subsurface" rights. ("The meek shall inherit the earth," the oilman J. Paul Getty once observed. "But not its mineral rights.") The tribes cut down trees to block Texaco's trucks, and launched attacks on oil workers. In 1987, the bishop from a local Capuchin mission volunteered to reach out to one particularly reclusive tribe, the Tagaeri, who lived on land that another oil company wished to explore. A helicopter deposited the bishop, along with a nun, in Tagaeri territory. When the pilot returned, the next day, he discovered their corpses, pinned to the jungle floor by twenty-one heavy wooden spears.

Such gestures of rebellion proved futile. In the decade after Texaco began paving roads, a hundred thousand Ecuadoran settlers moved to the Oriente, lured by free acreage and the promise of work. They razed the forest to accommodate crop farming, and local tribes were reduced to selling trinkets at the oil camps, or to retreating further into the bush. "It was the absolute destruction of their lives," Miguel Angel Cabodevilla, a Spanish monk who has worked with the tribes for decades, told me.

In November, 1993, Cristóbal Bonifaz filed a class-action lawsuit against Texaco in a federal court in Manhattan, on behalf of thirty thousand afectados. Texaco rejected the allegations, maintaining that it had "operated under sound industry practices and complied with all Ecuadoran laws."

Donziger, initially, was involved less in the legal strategy than in a public-relations campaign against Texaco. Before law school, he had worked in Central America as a journalist, and he was unabashed about using a little stagecraft to dramatize his clients' story. At important court hearings in Manhattan, Donziger presented them to the press in their native beads and war paint. Development had exposed most of the plaintiffs to modern customs, and, after appearing in feathers at a press conference, they often changed into jeans at their hotel, then went shopping in Times Square. But journalists were smitten with the transplanted tribesmen. A Times article bore the headline "JUST TOURISTS ON BROADWAY, BUT BAREFOOT AND CRAVING ROAST MONKEY."

For eight years, Texaco fought to have the lawsuit dismissed, on the ground that it should be tried not in the U.S. but in Ecuador. Donziger and his colleagues feared such a turn: Ecuador's judicial system was notoriously corrupt, and its government relied on oil revenues for a third of its annual budget. "Texaco ran that country for twenty years," Chris Jochnick, a law-school friend of Donziger's who lived in Ecuador at the time and now works for Oxfam America, told me. "They had the U.S. Embassy in their pocket. They had the military. Politically, there was no way that Texaco was going to be held accountable in Ecuador." Texaco denied that Ecuador was incapable of offering a fair trial, insisting that the country's legal norms were "similar to those in many European nations."

In 2001, Texaco prevailed. A federal judge in New York dismissed the case, ruling that it had "everything to do with Ecuador and very little to do with the United States." By that time, Texaco's acquisition by Chevron was under way. In a print advertisement, Donziger and his colleagues warned Chevron shareholders that "Texaco comes with a lot of assets, and one huge liability." But it must have seemed that the lawsuit had run its course. Just before the acquisition, a Chevron spokesman said that the company felt no need to "particularly highlight" the Ecuadoran claims to shareholders.

In 2003, Donziger and his colleagues re-filed their case, in Lago Agrio, despite their misgivings about the Ecuadoran legal system. They recruited a team of Ecuadoran lawyers, and Donziger began making regular trips to the region. Because he was not licensed to practice law in Ecuador, his role was ostensibly an advisory one. But he relished the rigors of litigation in the sweltering Oriente, and, by virtue of his galvanic personality and his repeated visits, he gradually supplanted Bonifaz as the driving force in the case.

Not everyone embraced Donziger's leadership. Esperanza Martinez, who runs Oilwatch Sudamérica, an environmental group in Quito, told me, "I confess, the intense personality that Steve has, it's a struggle for me." Sarah Leah Whitson, a longtime friend of his, who is now at Human Rights Watch, acknowledged that some people are put off by Donziger's stubbornness and his theatricality. But it was precisely these qualities, she said, that enabled him to take on an oil giant: "He's a leader, and the fact is that he's the one who has been with this case for over a decade and has kept it going."

As the lawsuit moved forward in Ecuador, Donziger and his team felt daunted by what seemed like grave disadvantages. In his diary, Donziger lamented that trying to hold oil companies accountable in Ecuador "goes against the flow of the entire economy." The country does not have jury trials, so enormous discretionary power is invested in judges, who, for the most part, are poorly paid civil servants; Donziger worried that they might be susceptible to bribery. In the U.S., lawyers are forbidden to meet with a judge "ex parte," or outside the presence of opposing counsel. But in Ecuador at the time no such rules applied, making it difficult to monitor whether a judge had been subjected to improper influence.

Julio Prieto, a young Ecuadoran lawyer working for the plaintiffs, told me that when he was in law school in Quito "it was always on the table that there's a way things should be, but in practice there's a lot of dirt." I asked him if it was dispiriting to work in such a system. "Have you ever bribed a cop?" he asked. I shook my head. "In Ecuador, everybody does," he said. "But that doesn't mean we don't need cops."

Chevron hired a fleet of local lawyers, who were often accompanied in Lago Agrio by bodyguards. Donziger grew obsessed by the vast power of his adversary. "No matter what I do, they can outmaneuver me with money," he complained. Anytime a new judge or technical expert entered the case, Donziger wondered whether the person was contagiado—corrupted. Members of the plaintiffs' legal team came to believe that they were under surveillance by Chevron agents. After the brother of Pablo Fajardo, the lead Ecuadoran lawyer for the plaintiffs, was murdered near the Colombian border, in 2004, some members of Donziger's team insinuated that Chevron was involved. Donziger worried about his own safety, wondering if he might also "become a victim." (Chevron strenuously denies involvement in the murder, and the plaintiffs have offered no support for this theory.)

The plaintiffs' greatest asset, in Donziger's view, was the incontrovertible evidence of environmental contamination—the disfigured forest, the toxic pits. When journalists visited the Amazon, the plaintiffs ferried them from site to site, in a routine that became known as "the toxic tour." At the same time, Donziger feared that, in the end, the legal outcome might hinge not on the truth but on manipulations of the system.

These concerns intensified in 2006, when Donziger heard accusations that a new judge assigned to the case, Germán Yánez, was, as Donziger put it, "a womanizer" and "a drinker." (Around this time, Yánez was accused of sexually harassing an intern, a charge that he dismissed as politically motivated.) Yánez had "the perfect psychological profile for blackmail and corruption," Donziger thought. Some nights, he glanced up from his laptop and, seeing his face in a mirror, was struck by how much older he looked than he had when the case began. He fretted about what he had come to think of as "the fool's-errand problem."

The law firm of Gibson, Dunn & Crutcher is more than a century old and has a thousand attorneys. One day this fall, I visited the firm's New York offices, on the forty-sixth floor of the MetLife Building, to meet Randy Mastro, a fifty-five-year-old partner who, for the past two years, has represented Chevron in the Ecuador case. Mastro, who has peaked eyebrows and unruly white hair, is soft-spoken, but, even by the pugilistic standards of the New York bar, he has a reputation as a merciless litigator. In the courtroom, wearing a conservative suit, with his spectacles perched on the tip of his nose, Mastro springs to life. He bounces on his toes to underscore the obviousness of his logic, and dices the air with his hand, keeping time with his argument, like a rapper. His swagger is transfixing.

As a federal prosecutor, and then as a deputy mayor under Rudolph Giuliani, Mastro fought the New York Mob, cleaning up the Fulton Fish Market and the San Gennaro Festival, despite death threats. At City Hall, he occasionally wielded a baseball bat during meetings, to accentuate a point. The Daily News once observed that Mastro was the only person in the Giuliani administration who made the Mayor seem like a nice guy.

When Mastro entered the plush conference room where I was waiting, he carried a towering stack of binders containing thousands of pages of Chevron briefs and affidavits. I could barely see his face. He set them on the table with a thud. "Clients look to our firm to give them the kind of zealous advocacy that can help turn around a case," Mastro told me, and Gibson, Dunn has been lauded for its success in rescuing major corporations from legal threats. In 2010, Walmart, after a successful defense in a major employment lawsuit, credited the "lifeboat lawyers" of Gibson, Dunn. Others have suggested that the firm can go too far. Several years ago, in an unrelated case, the Montana Supreme Court reprimanded Gibson, Dunn for engaging in "legal thuggery."

The lawsuit in the Amazon is meritless, Mastro assured me—Donziger was merely "out to make a buck." But the fact that Chevron solicited Mastro's aid suggested that the company was anxious about its prospects in the case. Donziger's court-the-press strategy had proved exceptionally effective. In 2005, he approached Joe Berlinger, a well-regarded New York filmmaker, and suggested that he make a documentary about the case. The film, "Crude," was released in 2009. That same year, "60 Minutes" ran a segment that was highly critical of Chevron. In it, Silvia Garrigo came across as a caricature of heartlessness as she downplayed the health hazards of petroleum. "I have makeup on, and there's naturally occurring oil on my face," she said. "Doesn't mean I'm going to get sick from it."

Donziger, in addition to his roles as a lawyer and a P.R. strategist, had become, by necessity, an expert fund-raiser. He was relentless and creative in cultivating celebrities for the cause, including Sting and Daryl Hannah, and in eliciting support from wealthy patrons such as Russ DeLeon, a law-school contemporary who had made a fortune through an online-gambling venture. "You've got to figure out ways that you can sustain efforts like this," Donziger explained in a recent speech, because when you sue a multinational corporation its "main strategy is to exhaust you." For years, the case was underwritten largely by a Philadelphia law firm, Kohn, Swift & Graf, which gave financial and legal support in exchange for contingency fees. But, as the case dragged on, the wire transfers from Philadelphia did not arrive regularly enough to cover expenses.

Looking elsewhere for financial support, Donziger found it in the emerging field of "litigation finance." In recent years, certain hedge funds have started investing in class-action lawsuits, providing up-front capital to cover the expenses of a case in exchange for an equity share in a successful outcome. These arrangements are unregulated and controversial. But for Donziger they presented a crucial opportunity to keep the litigation alive. He offered investors a high-risk, high-reward proposition. The judgment could run to billions of dollars, he said, with attorneys' fees making up roughly a third of that figure. In confidence, he noted that his personal fee alone could amount to two hundred million dollars. Eventually, a fund called Burford Capital, which is based in the Channel Islands, made a multimillion-dollar investment in the case. A powerful law firm in Washington, D.C., Patton Boggs, also joined the plaintiffs' team.

As Randy Mastro sees it, the wealthy, for-profit players who are bankrolling Donziger's efforts betray an underlying cynicism behind the plaintiffs' case. This suit is driven not by poor Ecuadorans, he told me, but by "lawyers and consultants and financiers." Donziger's ambition was certainly grandiose, but it seemed motivated as much by a combative idealism as by a desire for riches. He wanted to recalibrate the power dynamic that had traditionally made it difficult for marginalized foreigners to sue American companies. He felt that he was creating a viable "business model for a human-rights case."

In 2006, Ecuador elected a new President, the left-leaning economist Rafael Correa. Donziger was elated. On the day of Correa's inauguration, he told Berlinger's camera crew, "There is no way under an administration led by this man that Chevron could ever get away with what it usually does here, which is bribes, backdoor meetings, and manipulation of government power." The next year, after lobbying by the plaintiffs, Correa visited the Oriente, and surveyed the waste pits. "Let's not deceive ourselves," he said, at a press conference in Lago Agrio. "There was a crime against humanity here."

The surest sign that the momentum in Ecuador had shifted against Chevron came on November 26, 2008, when a geological engineer named Richard Cabrera, who had been appointed to serve as an independent environmental-damages expert, delivered a report recommending that the court find Chevron responsible for twenty-seven billion dollars in damages. Chevron denounced the report, saying that it contained "fabricated and erroneous evidence" and suggesting that Cabrera was biased toward the plaintiffs. But Donziger's team commissioned a peer review of the findings from Stratus, an environmental consulting firm in Boulder, Colorado, that has done extensive work for the U.S. government. Stratus endorsed Cabrera's report as "sound, reasonable, and consistent with approaches used in other environmental-damage cases."

By this time, the leadership at Chevron may have come to regret Texaco's strenuous efforts, in the nineties, to move the lawsuit out of the U.S. Chevron representatives now expressed alarm at the dire state of the Ecuadoran judiciary, likening due process in the country to what one might find in North Korea. The danger, as Mastro later explained, was that the Correa regime might put a "thumb on the scale" of justice in favor of the plaintiffs.

In August, 2009, Chevron offered startling evidence to support its claim that Ecuador was hopelessly corrupt: it released video footage that allegedly implicated the judge then presiding over the Lago Agrio case, Juan Nuñez, in a bribery scheme. An Ecuadoran businessman named Diego Borja had been hoping to secure a cleanup contract in the event of a judgment against Chevron. But when Borja met with the judge and a Correa administration official, the company explained, he was informed that he first needed to pay a million dollars each to Nuñez, to the administration, and to the Lago Agrio plaintiffs. Borja and an associate secretly recorded the discussions, using cameras embedded in a watch and a pen. Charles James, a Chevron executive, declared, "This information absolutely disqualifies the judge and nullifies anything that he has ever done in this case."

Judge Nuñez stepped aside. But he insisted that he was innocent. The videos, which Chevron posted online, showed Borja and the official elliptically discussing the possibility of a bribe with Nuñez, but offered no proof that the judge had solicited or accepted one. Nuñez told me that the scandal was a setup, and Donziger has called the incident "a Chevron sting." It has subsequently emerged that the purported Correa administration official was in fact a Quito car salesman and part-time caterer, whose name does not appear in a party database of registered members. The businessman, Borja, was a former Chevron contractor.

Chevron insists that it did not prompt Borja to raise discussions about paying bribes, and says that he was not compensated for his efforts. But, according to court documents, Borja and his wife were relocated, at Chevron's expense, to the U.S., and supplied with a house, a car, a generous monthly stipend, and the services of a top criminal-defense attorney. The attorney would not make Borja available to speak with me, but a friend of Borja's, Santiago Escobar, told me that Judge Nuñez was innocent, and that Borja concocted the scheme to entrap him. "He's not a good Samaritan," Escobar said. "He was looking for money."

A few months ago, I took the toxic tour. For half the day, my guide was a spokesperson for Donziger and the plaintiffs; for the other half, I was accompanied by a Chevron representative. Both sides now employ full-time public-relations specialists. In fact, they have spent so many years contesting one another that the controversy can resemble a vituperative political campaign—a constant volley of talking points and rebuttals. No scientific or historical assertion goes undisputed by the other side. (Miguel Angel Cabodevilla, the monk, told me, "In the jungle, there is more literature than history.")

Chevron has hired dozens of ecological consultants, who challenge nearly all the plaintiffs' empirical claims. The company denies that the contamination and the health dangers posed by it are anything close to what Donziger has alleged. When the plaintiffs produced a study showing unusually high rates of cancer in the Oriente, Chevron countered with a study of its own, maintaining that cancer rates in the area are actually lower than elsewhere in Ecuador. Silvia Garrigo, the global-issues executive, has complained that the afectados blame Texaco for their every affliction: "If their cow dies, it's Texaco. If their wife has diabetes, it's Texaco."

During the plaintiffs' portion of the tour, a local man named Donald Moncayo showed me around. Wearing white surgical gloves, he dug up a fistful of black mud and held it so that the sunlight caught the telltale blue-orange tint of petroleum. At one fetid pit in a jungle glade, he stepped gingerly onto the surface of the pool, where the solid matter in the produced water had congealed into a tarlike crust that was sturdy enough to support him. Smiling a little, Moncayo shifted his weight from one foot to the other, until the whole surface began to undulate beneath him. He looked like a kid on a waterbed. According to the plaintiffs, there are nearly a thousand of these pits in the Oriente, scattered across an area the size of Rhode Island.

Watching Moncayo, I had a sense of déjà vu. He is the regular master of ceremonies on the toxic tour; I had read accounts of his routine, and had seen it enacted, in nearly identical fashion, in "Crude," the Berlinger documentary. But, if Moncayo's cadences were rote, there was nothing feigned about his indignation. He led me down a steep ravine to a creek. In the gauzy light filtering through the canopy, the water, which was only a foot deep, looked crystalline. Moncayo drove a stick into the creek bed and churned the mud until the water grew clouded by sediment. At his encouragement, I skimmed my hand across the surface of the creek. My palm was coated in an acrid film.

Moncayo watched me with grim satisfaction. "We tell Chevron, 'If you think this is O.K. for human consumption, then why don't you drink from it?' " he said.

Jim Craig, a Chevron spokesman, took me around Lago Agrio. He told me that the company has taken its own water samples in the Oriente, and has never identified a positive reading for hydrocarbon contamination. He speculated that, in some cases, the plaintiffs may have "spiked" local water sources after Chevron did its tests.

Craig told me that the skin infections and gastrointestinal problems attributed by the plaintiffs to oil pollution were more likely caused by sewer lines that run into local streams and rivers. "You can imagine all kinds of stomach problems arising from the ingestion of that crap," he said.

A few miles outside Lago Agrio, we stood on the lip of a waste pit, and Craig told me that the vile looking residue on its surface was only a few inches thick. To illustrate this point, he picked up a rock and lobbed it into the pit. It landed, with a sickly thud, on the surface. "If we had a bigger rock . . ." he said, and threw a much larger one. It, too, failed to sink.

In Chevron's reckoning, however, these environmental claims and counterclaims are all somewhat beside the point, because the company's defense ultimately rests not on science but on law. In 1995, Texaco acknowledged that it had made a mess in the Amazon, and committed itself to doing some remediation. But the company also emphasized that it had been part of a consortium in Ecuador—one that included the national oil company—and that its stake in the partnership had been thirty-seven per cent. Texaco therefore agreed to clean up only thirty-seven per cent of the pits, even though, as the consortium's sole "operator," it had been responsible for both drilling the wells and digging the pits.

Texaco spent forty million dollars on the cleanup, and in 1998 the Ecuadoran government granted the company a release from any future claims against it. Chevron freely admits that large sludge pits still dot the Amazon, but denies that it has a legal obligation to clean up more of them. Instead, it suggests, that responsibility should fall to the national oil company, Petroecuador, which has managed extraction in Lago Agrio since Texaco's departure and has been accused of polluting extensively in the region. "This is not about dirt in Ecuador," a Chevron lawyer once remarked. "It is about a contract and how to interpret it."

In January, 2009, Donziger travelled to Park City, Utah, to attend the première of "Crude," at the Sundance Film Festival. The film depicts him as a domineering presence; at one point, when he believes that Chevron's lawyers may have manipulated an elderly judge in Quito, he storms into the judge's chambers, towering over the man. "Be very careful with the Texaco lawyers," Donziger warns. "They play dirty." To the camera, he concedes that he would never do such a thing in America, but explains that in Ecuador "this is how the game is played."

In another scene, Donziger coaches one of his indigenous clients, Emergildo Criollo, preparing him to crash Chevron's annual shareholders' meeting, in Houston. He tells Criollo not to be cowed and suggests some rhetoric: " 'You spent twenty-eight years in my territory. I can spend three minutes in your territory.' " Pleased with the line, he says, "That's a good one, right?" In the next scene, Criollo delivers the sound bite to the shareholders.

When Randy Mastro and his colleagues scrutinized the film, they noticed a tiny discrepancy between the version that aired at Sundance and the one that was subsequently released on DVD. A scene in the film captures a consultation between the plaintiffs' lawyers and a tribe that they represent. At Sundance, a Spanish physician named Carlos Beristain was visible in the scene. In the DVD version, he was edited out. This struck Mastro as potentially significant, because after the meeting in question Beristain had gone to work for the independent environmental-damages expert. Had the director edited out the physician at the plaintiffs' request?

"That had our antennae way up," Mastro told me.

He wondered what other "outtakes" might exist from the three years that Berlinger spent filming Donziger, and in April, 2010, he asked a federal judge in New York to compel Berlinger to turn over all his raw footage. Mastro cited a little-used statute that entitles an American litigant facing a lawsuit abroad to pursue extensive "discovery" inside the United States. Chevron needed the outtakes, Mastro argued, "to prove it was denied due process" in Ecuador.

Berlinger's lawyers objected that Chevron was on a "fishing expedition," and invoked the journalist's privilege. Mastro responded that "Crude" was not journalism at all but "an unapologetic work of propaganda." Because Donziger had pitched Berlinger to make the film, Mastro argued, and because Berlinger had cut the shot of the Spanish doctor at the plaintiffs' request, he was not a truly independent filmmaker.

Despite the interventions of news organizations, including the Times, which argued that obliging Berlinger to turn over the footage would set a dangerous precedent, both the judge, Lewis Kaplan, and an appeals court sided with Chevron. Mastro's team was soon in possession of six hundred hours of footage.

It was not long before Mastro requested another hearing before Kaplan, an acerbic but respected senior federal judge, who worked as a corporate lawyer before his appointment to the bench, by Bill Clinton, in 1994. "If we were on a fishing expedition, we caught a whopper," Mastro announced in court. Donziger appeared to have grown so comfortable with Berlinger's crew that he disregarded the fact that they were recording everything he said. As Mastro played a series of outtakes for Judge Kaplan, Donziger's outspokenness was on full display. He riffed, indignantly, about the inadequacies of the Ecuadoran legal system. "They're all corrupt," he says of Ecuadoran judges in one clip. "It's their birthright to be corrupt."

Judging from the outtakes, Donziger's fear that the case would not be decided on its merits had led him to doubt the importance of the evidence itself. In one scene, a scientific expert for the plaintiffs tells him that one measurement of groundwater contamination was not as strong as he had thought. "This is Ecuador, O.K.?" Donziger says. "At the end of the day, if there's a thousand people around the courthouse you're going to get what you want." As for the scientific data, he adds, it's "just a bunch of smoke and mirrors and bullshit."

It was a devastating presentation. Just as Chevron was asserting that Ecuador was too corrupt to ever guarantee a fair trial, here was its adversary, effectively saying the same thing. The documentary was the plaintiffs' "undoing," Mastro told me.

In another scene that Mastro showed to the court, Donziger chats with associates over dinner at a restaurant. Someone at the table, referring to the popular antipathy toward Chevron in Ecuador, suggests that if the judge in Lago Agrio ruled against the plaintiffs he might be killed.

"He might not be," Donziger replies, cradling a glass of red wine. "But he thinks he will. Which is just as good."

In the course of several hearings, Judge Kaplan exhibited a palpable dislike for Donziger. He described him as "the field general of a political and media offensive," and seemed to take umbrage at what he called the "flat-out admissions by Donziger that what's going on in Ecuador is mud wrestling, not bona-fide litigation."

Donziger's lawyers tried to play down his loose talk. But Mastro argued that the outtakes exposed a criminal conspiracy, in which Donziger was exploiting the corruption of the Ecuadoran system to pressure Chevron into a huge settlement. Suddenly, the very qualities that had enabled Donziger to remain steadfast in the face of staggering odds—his runaway rhetoric, his knack for P.R.—had placed him, and the entire case, in peril. "Knives are effective for cutting through things," his friend Sarah Leah Whitson told me. "But sometimes you can slice your own finger."

Mastro, emboldened by his success with the outtakes, decided to go one step further. The video footage revealed such outlandish impropriety, he argued to Judge Kaplan, that Chevron should be entitled to Donziger's own documents. Because much of what Donziger did was fund-raising and publicity, rather than lawyering, Mastro suggested, he should not be afforded attorney-client privilege; and, even if he was entitled to the privilege, he had waived it by inviting Berlinger's cameras to film him. "He has one privilege left," Mastro told Judge Kaplan. "He can assert the Fifth Amendment."

Normally, a lawyer who is subpoenaed creates a log of any confidential documents to be withheld. But Chevron was requesting Donziger's entire case file—documents spanning nearly two decades—and Donziger did not have a staff of associates to help him go through it. When he failed to deliver a privilege log that met Kaplan's approval, the judge agreed with Mastro that "the genie is out of the bottle"—and granted Chevron access to Donziger's confidential documents. Donziger was forced to turn over two hundred thousand pages of material.

Twenty Gibson, Dunn associates set to work reviewing stacks of memos and e-mails marked "Confidential" and "Attorney Work Product." They averaged five thousand pages a day. Gibson, Dunn also requested, and received, Donziger's tax returns, his bank-account information, and his personal computers. Technicians forensically scanned his hard drives, and Gibson, Dunn copied everything they found. An attorney for Donziger protested that this meant that Chevron's lawyers could interrogate his communications with his wife, as well as other unrelated matters.

"He doesn't have any other matters," Kaplan said. "This is his life."

Kaplan's decision was extreme; rarely had such a wealth of sensitive material been handed to a legal adversary. As Gibson, Dunn attorneys fanned across the country, appearing before seventeen federal courts to request further information, one appellate judge noted that the sheer extent of this kind of discovery was "unique in the annals of American judicial history." Kaplan even granted Chevron permission to depose Donziger—a highly unusual move.

"No lawyer wants to be deposed," Stephen Gillers, a legal ethicist at New York University School of Law, told me. "It unnerves us, as a profession. We like to believe that we operate in this zone of privacy that no one can pierce, unless we permit it. Indeed, that enables us to do our jobs."

For fourteen days, in a conference room in a midtown skyscraper, Mastro and other Chevron attorneys questioned Donziger, under oath, about the financing of the case, and about various legal strategies that he had used. Donziger soon grew brittle and exhausted. One task of the inquisitor in a deposition is to confine the person being questioned to simple yes or no answers. But Donziger insisted on defending his conduct loquaciously, to the point where Judge Kaplan reprimanded him, remarking, "The man could have a career as a filibustering senator."

At one point, Donziger was asked whether he kept a diary. Initially, he said no. But his diary, which he had maintained for several years, was saved on one of his laptops, and Gibson, Dunn found it on his hard drive. When Chevron filed the text, unexpurgated, with the court, it became part of the public record—another humiliation for Donziger. In the diary, he details his doubts and aspirations, and returns, obsessively, to the subject of his adversary, who in his shorthand is simply "Tex." He recounts arguments with his wife and makes unsparing observations about his colleagues.

Donziger also describes meetings with Judge Yánez—the judge he had feared would be vulnerable, because of his alleged womanizing and drinking, to blackmail. In one entry, Donziger wrote, "I called the judge and he asked that we bring over some whiskey or some wine. We didn't." On another occasion, he described Yánez asking him for help in obtaining a visa, so that his girlfriend might visit America. Donziger did not help him, but noted in his diary that the plaintiffs had drawn up a complaint about Yánez's conduct, and had informed him that "we might file it if he does not adhere to the law and what we need."

Donziger had worried that Yánez could be manipulated into making a corrupt ruling. But, in urging him to remain upright, the plaintiffs were exploiting Yánez's vulnerabilities as leverage. "So instead of a strong judge who sees the viability of our case," Donziger wrote, "we now might have a weak judge who wants to rule correctly for all the wrong, personal reasons."

Esperanza Martínez, the Quito environmentalist, told me that, in the complex moral landscape of Ecuador, there are different types of "pressure" that can be exerted on a public official. If you pressure an official to abrogate the rights of someone, that is unquestionably corrupt. But if you pressure the official to uphold someone's rights, Martínez maintained, that "is the farthest thing from corruption."

As Mastro and his associates made their way through the trove of material on Donziger, the information that most interested them had to do with the independent environmental-damages expert, Richard Cabrera. Originally, when the decision was made to appoint a single damages expert, Donziger had worried that in Ecuador anyone with that much influence over the outcome of a multibillion-dollar case could be bought. But he was pleased about the appointment of Cabrera—indeed, the Gibson lawyers discovered, Donziger knew in advance that Cabrera would be the court's choice. "We have an expert," he says in one outtake. "The judge is going to appoint a guy in Ecuador to be the expert. But really, you know, we'll be supporting him with our work."

The appointment decision fell to Judge Yánez. The plaintiffs had never filed their complaint against him, and Donziger felt that Yánez owed him a favor. "We saved him," Donziger wrote of the judge, in January, 2007. "And now we are reaping the benefits." (A spokesperson for Donziger told me that "reaping the benefits" simply meant that Judge Yánez was acting independently of Chevron.)

Another outtake captures a plaintiffs' meeting on March 3, 2007, two weeks before Cabrera's official appointment. Donziger attended, along with the lead Ecuadoran lawyer, Pablo Fajardo, and Cabrera himself. On video, Fajardo explains to the team that Cabrera will soon be asked to produce an independent evaluation of Chevron's liability. He will "give his opinion, sign the report, and review it," Fajardo says. "But all of us have to contribute."

"But not Chevron," somebody says—a joke, met with laughter.

Before the meeting concludes, the camera captures Donziger turning to Cabrera. "Richard, of course, you really have to be comfortable with all that," he says. As the meeting wraps up, Donziger exclaims, "We could jack this thing up to thirty billion dollars in one day!"

Mastro and his colleagues were stunned. "It's the kind of shocking revelation that would ordinarily have blown up a plaintiff's case," he told me. "That's the amazing thing about this case—it's smoking gun after smoking gun."

Gibson, Dunn subpoenaed Stratus, the Colorado consulting firm that had endorsed Cabrera's report recommending a twenty-seven-billion-dollar penalty for Chevron. When Julio Prieto, the young lawyer for the plaintiffs, learned that Chevron was seeking information from Stratus, he sent a frantic e-mail to his colleagues. Disclosure of Stratus's documents could be "potentially devastating," he wrote, adding that he and his Ecuadoran associates "might go to jail."

What Mastro's team recovered from Stratus was a document, in English, that the company had sent to Ecuador a few days before the publication of Cabrera's report. The first line of the Stratus document said, "This report was written by Richard Cabrera." It was a draft of the "independent" damages assessment. As Mastro put it to me, "The plaintiffs' team had ghostwritten his report."

The plaintiffs have since insisted that there was nothing improper about Stratus submitting materials to Cabrera for his consideration, and that Chevron could have done the same. But Donziger, in his deposition, acknowledged that Cabrera's final report was drawn "pretty much verbatim" from the Stratus document.

One oddity of Gibson, Dunn's ongoing discovery was that, in something close to real time, Chevron's lawyers were able to obtain internal e-mails in which Donziger and his colleagues discussed how best to deal with these very revelations. "I wonder whether we do better by explaining that we authored the report," one of Donziger's American associates wrote, "rather than letting Chevron tell that story like Nancy Drew." The e-mail was subsequently turned over to Gibson, Dunn.

During the deposition, Donziger was asked, "Was it agreed that Stratus would draft the report in a form that could be submitted to the Ecuadoran court by Mr. Cabrera?"

"That was the general idea," he said.

It may be that the logic of systemic corruption is akin to that of doping in athletics. If you have good reason to believe that everyone else is gaining a competitive advantage through surreptitious transgressions, then you may conclude that to do otherwise, on principle, would fatally undermine your case. "I think it is a miracle how much we have accomplished with so little," Donziger wrote in his diary. "But in the end of the day that means nothing if we don't win."

Donziger's deposition concluded on January 31, 2011. The next day, Chevron sued him in federal court, along with other members of the plaintiffs' team, alleging that they were part of a racketeering conspiracy, and had colluded with corrupt elements in Ecuador to extort billions of dollars.

After questions arose about the independence of the Cabrera report, Nicolás Zambrano, the judge in Lago Agrio, said that he would not rely on it to reach his verdict. But Chevron was not placated. Zambrano's judgment would be fraudulent, Mastro argued, and he asked Judge Kaplan to issue an injunction that would prevent the plaintiffs from attempting to collect damages from Chevron. "We are facing the ultimate sword of Damocles," he said.

Gibson, Dunn, in its discovery, had obtained an internal memo describing the plaintiffs' plan to enforce the Ecuadoran judgment by going after Chevron assets in foreign countries. Mastro called this strategy "vexatious," and asked Judge Kaplan to bar Donziger and his colleagues from trying to collect on the judgment not just in New York but anywhere in the world. Mastro assured Kaplan, "You have the right to enjoin litigation here and overseas."

Kaplan was sympathetic to this position. As he put it, "I don't think there is anybody in this courtroom who wants to pull his car into a gas station to fill up and find that there isn't any gas because these folks have attached it in Singapore or wherever else." He granted the injunction. When, that same month, Judge Zambrano issued his eighteen-billion-dollar decision against Chevron, it was unclear if the plaintiffs would ever receive a penny.

One evening in September, in New York, I met a man named Humberto Piaguaje, who is a member of the Secoya tribe. He was born in the Ecuadoran Amazon in 1964, and he has been involved in the case for nearly half his life. We met in the Mandarin Oriental Hotel, on the thirty-fifth floor of the Time Warner Center. One of the lawyers in the case was staying there, and Donziger and his colleagues had colonized the lobby bar and turned it into a meeting space. Piaguaje wore a polo shirt and jeans. He has been speaking to American journalists for years, and smoothly recited the indignities that his people have suffered. "We're poor," he said. "There are no animals to eat. We don't have our traditional medicines from plants. We don't have clean water. Chevron left us in poverty." In recent years, he said, seven of his relatives had died of cancer. He expressed outrage that his people, after being denied the opportunity to bring their case to America, were now being told that they could not find justice in Ecuador, either. Perhaps, he said, Chevron would like to hold the trial in Heaven. "I'm sure they would decide that wasn't good enough, and ask to move it somewhere else," he added.

Outside the hotel, dusk began to settle over Central Park, and lights flickered on in the buildings across Columbus Circle. If Piaguaje was struck by the incongruity of his surroundings, he did not let on. I asked him if it ever seemed that the case had taken on a life of its own, disconnected from what really happened in the Oriente. He shrugged. "It's a search for justice," he said. "How can we do that without lawyers?"

Piaguaje had flown to New York to attend an oral argument before the Second Circuit Court of Appeals, centering on whether Judge Kaplan had the authority to stop the plaintiffs from collecting on the Ecuadoran judgment anywhere in the world. If Kaplan's injunction was upheld, it would create a major precedent, effectively allowing American courts to pass judgment on the transparency or corruption of their foreign counterparts, and set aside verdicts against American companies when the legal systems issuing them were deemed problematic. The prospect was breathtaking: Chevron looked poised not only to avoid liability but also to acquire greater immunity in its actions abroad. Shell, Dole, and Dow Chemical submitted a brief to the court, urging it to side with Chevron.

On September 16th, three appellate judges took their seats in a courtroom in downtown Manhattan. A contingent of Chevron lawyers was in attendance, as were Donziger, his legal team, and Piaguaje. Randy Mastro argued that the plaintiffs' wrongdoing was so severe that the only solution was to invalidate the Ecuadoran court's judgment. "In thirty years of practice and as a former prosecutor, I've never seen a record so shocking of illegal and improper conduct," he said. "We don't tolerate judgments procured by fraud."

"Anywhere in the world?" one judge asked incredulously. "We will not tolerate a South African judgment being procured by fraud and enforced in Russia?"

The oral arguments took place on a Friday. Normally, appeals courts take several months after hearing arguments to rule on a case, but the judges were ready the following Monday. In a terse, unanimous decision, they reversed Judge Kaplan, and dissolved the injunction. This fall, I had half a dozen long conversations with Steven Donziger about his time in Ecuador and his battle with Gibson, Dunn. Ultimately, he chose, on the advice of his lawyers, not to answer any questions on the record. ("He knows now that anything he says can be used against him," a Chevron representative told me.) In a statement, Donziger argued, "The story of this case is not about the lawyers. It is about the people of Ecuador and how they have suffered at the hands of an American oil company that flouts the law and will stop at nothing to protect its ill-gotten profits."

Chevron's racketeering lawsuit against Donziger has been stayed, for the moment, but if it proceeds Kaplan will likely remain the judge in the case. In an act of desperation, Donziger formally requested that Kaplan be removed, arguing that he had shown a consistent bias toward Chevron. But the request was denied.

Civil racketeering suits seldom go to trial, and some observers suggest that Gibson, Dunn employed the countersuit as a harassment tactic to smear and intimidate the plaintiffs. "Deflect and defame—that's a strategy," one of Donziger's law-school friends told me.

When I aired this theory to Randy Mastro, he gave a thin smile and murmured, "I look forward to the trial."

A person close to the case told me, "What's so unfortunate here is that we're going up against a giant corporation that has acted in such a callous way. They don't get exposed for the way they've acted, because instead the spotlight shifts to this rogue lawyer. Steve should have known. If you want to engage in this kind of David-and-Goliath fight, you've got to focus on your own conduct. Because, if you don't, you give them exactly the ammunition they're looking for."

Chevron has appealed the eighteen-billion-dollar judgment in Ecuador. It has also tried to block the lawsuit by appealing to an arbitration tribunal in The Hague. But the case could still end in a settlement. This might seem hard to imagine, given the rancor on both sides, but it has nearly happened before. Cristóbal Bonifaz told me that in 2001 the plaintiffs indicated, in writing, that they would drop their claims in exchange for a hundred and forty million dollars. But, on the eve of the Chevron merger, Texaco walked away from the offer. Chevron will not comment, but the plaintiffs estimate that the company now spends roughly that amount each year to fight the case.

One day in February, 2007, Donziger sat down with a Chevron lawyer in New York. The meeting was secret. The lawyer indicated that Chevron was ready to find a way to conclude the matter. "We don't want our children or grandchildren to be litigating it," he said.

In his diary, Donziger expressed ambivalence about a settlement, wondering how he could end something that had "so defined" his life. Ultimately, the two sides did not come to terms. "We all have become prisoners of our own creation," Donziger wrote, in another entry. "We all have too much invested to stop.

Ecuador: Chevron Will Not Apologise For Pollution, Even to Save $9.5 Billion

Chevron said Friday that it had no intention of apologizing for the environmental damage to the Amazon rain forest for which an Ecuadorean court ruled it responsible. Attorneys for both sides have said that if Chevron apologized, its legal liability of $18 billion would have been cut to $9.5 billion. Ecuador's judiciary had set Friday as the deadline for an apology. James Craig, a Chevron spokesman, said an apology would be "a false admission of responsibility." Chevron has no assets in Ecuador, so the plaintiffs must try to collect the award abroad.

New York Times
AP, February 4, 2012

CONCLUSIONS

A POST PETROLEUM NUEVA LOJA
BIBLIOGRAPHY
BIOGRAPHIES
CREDITS
ACKNOWLEDGEMENTS

POSTSCRIPT: A POST-PETROLEUM NUEVA LOJA

MATTHIAS ALTWICKER

While it is hard to imagine any contemporary city functioning without petroleum, it is harder to imagine Nueva Loja existing without petroleum. Nueva Loja grew up where no road or permanent human settlement previously existed, its creation is the result of the plentiful below ground oil resources. Every other quality of its geographic location has been wholly irrelevant to its development.

A post-petroleum city is like any post-industrial city – it can only survive by adopting a new economic and social identity; but with one significant difference: the petroleum city has no place-specific identity on which to base this reinvention. Having never been conceived of as a place in which infrastructure and growth are seen as long-term considerations, the petroleum city is simply a way station in an extractive economy. This attitude is not limited to petroleum. The inhabitants, themselves transient, often displaced, cannot rise above subsistence living. The growth of agriculture that followed the development of the city – the product of misguided public subsidies and settlement plans – is similarly extractive and destructive.

For all the extraction taking place – above and below ground – the products are insufficiently valuable to attract serious investment from any of the bodies involved. The oil corporations see ever diminishing returns, the government sees the successive failure of settlement plans and the inhabitants see a bleak future. Once existing at the periphery of the global economy, Nueva Loja now sits clearly in its rear-view mirror.

INTENTIONS

Given this background, it is hard to imagine the enormous population growth projected for the city. Unlike many post-industrial cities, the inhabitants of Nueva Loja have a variety of skills, can perform a multiplicity of jobs and, most importantly, are already doing many of those jobs simply to survive. The opportunity for future inhabitants of this city exists in its current inhabitants: the most important resource of Nueva Loja is resourcefulness. The single most crucial requirement for the realization of our plan for a new Nueva Loja is an educated, fixed population. Its resourcefulness combined with education (to broaden their passions and possibilities) would generate a dynamic relationship between the two and create the power of community. Constituent power, the first step to self-realization, precedes the realization of place.

Self-organization is not the intention of this plan. The romanticizing of self-realization through ad-hoc construction without parameters is rejected. Instead, we propose a loose municipal planning framework with multiple controls, but without strong limits to development – beyond the required, basic public infrastructure. Efficient, local management is possible in neighborhoods with a population ranging from 500 to 3000 people. Neighborhoods at this scale will develop their own identity, both social and physical, around a combination of public infrastructure and location-specific economic possibilities. This is consistent with strategies for the social legibility and inclusion of all – most notably the disurbanist planning movement of the 1920s and 30s – and the existing political structures of the city today.

Post-petroleum should not be misinterpreted as no-petroleum, though carbon-neutral development is essential along with buildings and spaces that are sensitive to the environment. Nueva Loja's reinvention will need to address the relative merits of forest regeneration and eco-tourism. Most importantly, building a post-petroleum Nueva Loja will not simply be about reducing the city's use of petroleum, but about healing the physical and social problems caused by it.

The rainforest and the waterways will set the vertical and horizontal limits to the new development. The survival and regeneration of the natural periphery are critical to the long-term, healthy reinvention of Nueva Loja.

URBAN FORM

The larger goals of a planning framework aim for maximum flexibility in both urban form and the distribution of public services. Many aspects of polycentric planning are here, but with a very specific difference – the vast dispersion of linked variety of a distributed polycentric city is collapsed into a concentrated, dense packing of urban experiences.

A ten minute walk from anywhere within the city limits, will take the walker to radically different – identifiable and essentially self-sufficient – spatial and social environments. This eliminates the need for ever more costly connected systems of movement – which themselves promote more distributed development.

The new city, Nueva Loja Nueva, will be made up of equivalent neighborhood entities: *micro barrios*. They will maintain their autonomy through specific design and their connectivity through localized, yet equally distributed, movement infrastructures, that link them together into *gran-barrios*.

Zoning in a conventional sense will be unnecessary and conventional definitions of blocks, streets and squares would be altogether unrealistic. Each neighborhood will be autonomous in form and content, yet related to one another for survival. While quantity and distribution are important, location and function are variable. In effect, it is a city without a center at all.

IDENTITY

This center-less city is a direct result of a precise understanding of the place. The proposals presented here show the variety of possible morphologies within the framework described above, each of them attempting to uncover or establish an identity for the city. In this sense they are about the location and specific (if not holistic) responses to it. The exuberance of the proposals is at once exciting and disconcerting; the articulation of the ideas is at once an indication of great potential for the area and one of possible misunderstanding. After a fourteen hour bus ride through the Andes and the rainforest, it was impossible to be sure when we had arrived. The pipeline appeared, disappeared, and reappeared throughout the city. Areas of rainforest were interspersed throughout the piecemeal density of the unfinished city blocks. There was no clear boundary from one urban condition to another, often roads would end without warning while buildings with steel reinforcement stood anxiously awaiting the next floor. An identity for the city did not exist.

This perception did not change over time, and in retrospect this was significant in the development of the ideas presented here. The city, and the movement from neighborhood to neighborhood, would not be defined by superficial contrast or difference but rather by subtleties learned over time by inhabiting the place – or perhaps never learned if one chose to remain in one's *micro-barrio*. The fact that these differences could become the result of choice, rather than circumstance, is the most important parameter of Nueva Loja Nueva.

BIBLIOGRAPHY

Abalos, Iñaki y Herreros, Juan. *Areas de impunidad*, Barcelona: ACTAR, 1997

Asner, Gregory P., et. al. "Selective Logging in the Brazilian Amazon", www.sciencemag.org

Asner, Gregory P., et. al. "Sustainability science from space: Quantifying forest disturbance and land-use dynamics in the Amazon", www.pnas.org

Asociación Americana de Geógrafos (AAG) y Grupo de Especialidad Latinoamericana. *"El Estado Actual de la Geografía en los Países Hispanoamericanos"*, Chicago: AAG, 2006

Bethell, Leslie (Ed.) *Colonial Brazil*, Cambridge: Cambridge University Press, 1984

Borges, Jorge Luis. *El hacedor*, Buenos Aires: Alianza Editorial, 2007

Borja Cevallos, Rodrigo. *Enciclopedia de la política*, México D.F.: Fce, 1998

Bravo, Elizabeth & Martínez, Esperanza (Acción Ecológica). *Campaña "Amazonía por la vida: Debate ecológico sobre el problema petrolero en el Ecuador*, Quito, 1993

Browder, John O. and Godfrey, Brian J. *Rainforest Cities*, New York: Columbia University press, 1997

Browder, John O. and Godfrey, Brian J. "Disarticulated Urbanization in the Brazilian Amazon" *Geographical Review*, Jul. 96, Vol. 86, Issue 3, p.441, 5p., 1 chart

Bunker, Stephen G. *Underdeveloping the Amazon*, Chicago: University of Chicago Press, 1985

Coorg, Satyan R. "Pose Imagery and Automated Three-Dimensional Modeling of Urban Environments," http://biblioteca.universia.net/html_bura/ficha/params/id/1488592.html <http://biblioteca.universia.net/html_bura/ficha/params/id/1488592.html>

Corboz, André. *"El territorio como palimpsesto", Lo urbano en 20 autores contemporáneos*, coord. por Angel Martín Ramos, Barcelona: ETSAB, 2006

Cuesta Zapata, Salomón & Trujillo Montalvo, Patricio. *La frontera de fronteras PUTUMAYO: violencia, narcotráfico y guerrilla*, Quito: Ediciones Abya Yala, 1999

De Freitas, Marcílio. *Amazônia e Desenvolvimento Sustentável: Um diálogo que todos os brasileiros deveriam conhecer Petrópolis*, Editora Vozes, 2004.

Descola, Philippe. *La Selva Culta: simbolismo y praxis en la ecología de los Achuar*, Quito: ABYA AYALA, 1987

Ferreira Lins, Eurípides. *O Amazonas e seus problemas*, Manaus: Imprensa Oficial do Estado do Amazonas, 2006.

García, Lorenzo. *Historia de las misiones en la Amazonía ecuatoriana*, Quito: Ediciones Abya Yala, 1985

Gerlach, Allen. *Indians, Oil, and Politics: A Recent History of Ecuador*, Scholarly Resources, 2002

Harris, Roger & Hutchison, Peter. *The Amazon*, England, Bradt Travel Guides Ltd., 2007

Hecht, Susanna and Cockburn, Alexander. *The Fate of Forests*, Chicago: University of Chicago Press, 1990/2010

Hough, Michael. *Cities and Natural Process*. London and New York: Routledge - Taylor and Francis Group, 1995

IIRSA. "Plan Estratégico 2004 – 2012", www.iirsa.org

IIRSA. "Comunicado de Brasilia", www.iirsa.org

IIRSA. "Taller Regional sobre la Visión Estratégica de la Integración Física Suramericana (VESA)", www.iirsa.com

IIRSA. "Taller sobre la Gestión Intensiva de Proyectos Estratégicos Orientada a Resultados", www.iirsa.com

IIRSA. "Agenda de Implementación consensuada 2005-2010", www.iirsa.org

IIRSA. "Proceso de revisión de la cartera de proyectos IIRSA: Metodología de planificación territorial indicativa", www.iirsa.org

IIRSA. "ANNEX: IIRSA PROJECT PORTFOLIO – 2007" Disponible en www.iirsa.org

IIRSA. "Annex 10: Indicative Territorial Planning. TECHNICAL EXECUTIVE GROUPS – GTEs in Spanish 2007: Results and Project Portfolio – 2007 (Annex)" www.iirsa.org

IIRSA. "IIRSA: Building a New Continent, Project Information Sheets, Priority Investment Portfolio in South America, Initiative for the Integration of Regional Infrastructure in South America" www.iirsa.org

Izquierdo Peñafiel, Juan. *La ecoarquitectura: asentamientos humanos huaorani*, Quito: Ediciones Abya-Yala, 2000

Jorgenson, J. P. and Coello Rodríguez, M. (Eds.). *Conservación y desarrollo sostenible del Parque Nacional Yasuní y su área de influencia. Memorias del Seminario-Taller 2001*. Ministerio del Ambiente/UNESCO/Wildlife Conservation Society. Quito: Editorial Simbioe, 2001

Keefe, Patrick Radden, *"Reversal of Fortune,"* The New Yorker, January 9, 2012, 38-49

Killeen, Timothy J. "A Perfect Storm in the Amazon Wilderness: Development and Conservation in the Context of the Initiative for the Integration of the Regional Infrastructure of South America" (IIRSA), Arlington: *AABS* (Advances in Applied Biodiversity Science), number 7, 2007

Koester, Friedemann. El Hombre y la Biosfera en Yasuní. Coca: *Nuestra ciencia* - Reportajes, 2001

Lévi-Strauss, Claude. *The Raw and the Cooked: Mythologiques*, Chicago: University of Chicago Press edition, 1983

Lévi-Strauss, Claude. *Tristes Trópicos*, Barcelona: Ediciones Paidos, 1988

Meggers, Betty J. *"Amazonia in the Modern World" in Amazonia: Man and Culture in a Counterfeit Paradise*, Washington D.C.: Smithsonian Institution Scholarly Press, 1996

Montoya Bonilla, Sol. *Mitología del encuentro y del desencuentro*, Bogotá: Editorial Universidad Nacional, 1994

Moraes, Péricles. *Os Intérpretes da Amazônia*, Manaus: Valer Editora, 2001

Mulholland, Catherine. *William Mulholland and the Rise of Los Angeles*, Berkeley: University of California Press, 2000.

Nepstad, D.C. "Large-scale impoverishment of Amazonian forests by logging and fire" www.nature.com

New Internationalist Magazine. Viva Yasuni! Life vs. Big Oil, July 2008, Issue 413

Nixon, Robert. "Crude awakening in Ecuador;" In *E Magazine*; August 1994; Earth Action Network, Inc.; v5; issue n. 4; p 12

Omestad, Thomas. "The New Food Superpower: As commodity prices soar, Brazil steps up to feed a hungry world" in *U.S. News & World Report*, July 7-14, 2008

OTCA. "Integrando la Amazonia Continental: Informe de Gestión" Brasilia: OTCA, 2005

Page, Joseph A. *Brasil: el gigante vecino*, Buenos Aires: Emecé Editores, 1996

Perkins, John. *Confessions of an Economic Hit Man*, San Francisco: Barret-Koehler, 2004.

Petroecuador. *El petróleo en Ecuador: su historia y su importancia en la economía nacional*, Quito: Petroecuador, 2002

Rentería Rodrígues, Carolina. *Guidelines for the Work Plan 2008*, Montevideo: IIRSA, 2008

Ricardo, Fany. *Terras Indígenas & Unidades de Conservação da natureza: o desafio das sobreposições*, São Paulo: Instituto Socioambiental, 2004

Sawyer, Suzana. *Crude Chronicles: Indigenous Politics, Multinational Oil, and Neoliberalism in Ecuador* Durham: Duke University Press, 2004

Silveira, Soares-Filho, Britaldo, et. al. "Modelling conservation in the Amazon basin," www.nature.com/nature/journal/v440/n7083/abs/nature04389.html

Sassen, Saskia. *Una sociología de la globalización*, Buenos Aires: Katz Editores, 2007

Sassen, Saskia. *Cities in a World Economy*, London: Sage Publications Ltd., 2006

Sassen, Saskia. *The Global City: New York, London, Tokyo*, Princeton: Princeton University Press, 2001

Sassen, Saskia. *Global Networks, Linked Cities*, New York: Routledge, 2002

STCP. O Apagão e o Brasil Forestal. Curitiba: Informativo STCP, N. 8, 2004/2005

STCP. Gestão Fundiária: Principal Problema de Setor Florestal Brasileiro. Curitiba: Informativo STCP, N. 9, 2005/2006

Theroux, Paul. Blinding Light, http://www.halliburtonwatch.org/news/theroux.html

The World Bank. Brazil Rain Forest Unit: Business Plan 2005-2008 Washington D.C.: The World Bank, August 2004

Tocantins, Leandro. *O rio comanda a vida: Uma interpretação da Amazônia*, Manaus: Editora Valer, 2000

Ugarte Pinheiro, Maria Luiza. *A Cidade Sobre os Ombros: Trabalho e Conflito no Porto de Manaus 1899-1925*, Manaus: EUDA, Edições Governo do Estado, UEA, 2003.

Villarejo, Avencio. Así es la Selva. Iquitos: Centro de Estudios Teológicos de la Amazonía, 2005. "Hackenberger, Michael and Góes Neves, Eduardo". "Amazonian Archaeology" in *Annual Review of Anthropology*, Vol. 28, p. 251-266, Oct. 2009. "Geopolitical Diary: The Obstacles to Latin America's UNASUR." www.stratfor.com/geopolitical_diary_obstacles_latin_americas_unasur "Free Trade Zones," www.kishtpc.com/Free-En/free?colombia.htm

WEB LINKS

www.iirsa.com
www.bicusa.org
www.ecoamericas.com
www.edelca.com.ve
www.amazonia.org.br
www.socioambiental.org
www.ft.com
www.caf.com
www.mercosur.int
www.comunidadandina.org
www.otca.org.br
www.amazonguide.com.br/mapas/mapmanaus.htm
www.kishtpc.com
www.mct.gov.br
www.petroperu.co.pe
www.cipam.gov.br
www.perspectiva.inf.br geo@perspective.inf.br
www.potlatch.com.ar/beta/index.php?option=com_content
&task=view&id=67&Itemid=2
www.senado.gov.br-web/Senador/Mestrinho/mapaum.htm
www.justice.gov/dea/index.htm
www.plosone.org/article/info:doi/10.1371/journal.pone.0002932
www.halliburtonwatch.org/news/theroux.html

BIOGRAPHIES

MICHAEL SORKIN received his architectural training at Harvard and MIT and holds degrees from the University of Chicago and Columbia. He is the principal of the Michael Sorkin Studio in New York City. He is founding President of Terreform, a non-profit organization dedicated to research and urban intervention. He is President of the Institute for Urban Design; Distinguished Professor of Architecture and the Director of the Graduate Urban Design Program at the City College of New York where he has taught since 2000; Professor of Urbanism and Director of the Institute of Urbanism at the Academy of Fine Arts in Vienna (1993 to 2000), and he has been professor at numerous schools of architecture. He lectures around the world, he is the author of several hundred articles, and he is currently contributing editor at the *Architectural Record*.

ANA MARÍA DURÁN CALISTO graduated from the Liberal Arts School of Universidad San Francisco de Quito, with a Major in Anthropology and Minors in Comparative Literature and Art History. She received a scholarship to pursue graduate studies in Architecture and Historic Preservation at the University of Pennsylvania. She established the design firm Estudio A0 with her partner Jaskran Singh Kalirai, 2002. She teaches architecture studios at the School of Architecture, Design and Arts of Universidad Católica del Ecuador and she has been invited as a guest professor at the GSD of the University of Harvard and the GSAPP of the University of Columbia. She directed the XV Quito Pan-American Architecture Biennale: Visible Cities (2005-2006) and, as Dean, the School for the City, Landscape and Architecture of Universidad Internacional (2008-2009). She is currently a Loeb Fellow at the GSD

MATTHIAS ALTWICKER is a principal in AB Architekten in New York City and an associate professor and Chair at the School of Architecture and Design at the New York Institute of Technology. His teaching and practice focus on affordable and environmentally conscious housing and neighborhood development. He has designed sustainable housing for the Long Island Housing Partnership, collaborated with the Long Island Power Authority to investigate photovoltaic integration with existing suburban homes, and developed self-sufficient, expandable school prototypes for Kenya. The firm acts as an urban design consultant to the Regional Plan Association (NYC), the Nassau County Planning Federation (Long Island), and the Potsdam Housing Collective (Germany).

DAVID LEVEN is a partner at LEVENBETTS, a New York City based architecture practice begun in 1997 with Stella Betts. The firm has won several NYC AIA awards (2008, 2005, 2004, 2003), the Architectural League's Young Architects Forum and Emerging Voices Awards (2009), Architectural Record's Design Vanguard Award (2007), I.D. Annual Design Review Award (2004). The work of LEVENBETTS has been published in various design magazines and books and in a monograph (Princeton Architectural Press, 2008). David has lectured widely at a variety of institutions and he is currently an Associate Professor and Director of the Graduate Architecture program at Parsons the New School for Design. He holds a Bachelor of Arts from Colgate University, a Master of Architecture degree from Yale University and attended the Institute for Architecture and Urban Studies.

ACHVA BENZINBERG STEIN is a professor and practicing professional who has taught and worked in the US, Europe, Israel, India, and China. Her projects with neighborhood groups, public agencies, and non-profit organizations concentrate on meeting social needs while seeking to heal the damage of poorly managed urban development. Her landscape designs, which have won numerous awards from the American Society of Landscape Architects, include school grounds, large-scale housing projects, parks, playgrounds, hotels, community gardens and private residences. She has won numerous awards, including the 1994 Chrysler Award for Innovation in Design, and has twice been the recipient of Fulbright grants.

OSVALDO PALADINES ZURITA graduated as an architect from the School of Architecture of the Pontificia Universidad Católica de Chile in 1989. He currently teaches courses on the history and theory of architecture, as well as design studios, at the School of Architecture, Design and Arts of Universidad Católica del Ecuador. Over the past five years, Osvaldo has directed the 3rd year Urban Design Studio, which is geared towards developing new ways of approaching urban problems in Quito. He has participated in several collaborative international studios with architecture schools located in New York (City College of New York and Parson's New School of Design), Bogotá and Medellín. He collaborated in the design for Quito´s Factoría del Conocimiento and recently won an architectural design competition to build one of the venues for the School of the Millenium project in Quito. Together with a team from FADA-PUCE, he is developing the book "Quito Muévete", which will feature an academic proposal for the future mobility of Quito, and its urban growth.

CREDITS

CCNY URBAN DESIGN STUDENTS

Pilyun Ahn
Matthias Altwicker
Mariana Castillo
Alan Fox
John Hill
Holly Kallman
Paul King
Roberta Korcz
Gareth Mahon

CCNY ARCHITECTURE STUDENTS

Edith Altamiranda
Iman Ansari
Javier Caracamo
Camille Dunn
Onur Ekmekci
Rommel Gordillo
Yulya Ilizarov
Patrick Isaac
Lawrence Jacquette
Sujin Jeong
Yuriy Tkachenkov
Erik Scanlon

CCNY LANDSCAPE ARCHITECTURE STUDENTS

Chris Syrett
Patrick Weisel
Heather Fuhrman

FADA-PUCE STUDENTS

Tatiana Armijos
Marialuisa Borja
Verónica Guerra
Catalina Moreno
Andrés Nivelo
Esteban Sáenz
José Luis Gallegos
Nicolás Gallegos
María José León
Andrés Peralvo

FACULTY

Michael Sorkin, Distinguished Professor and Director, Graduate Program in Urban Design, CCNY
Ana María Durán Calisto, Professor, FADA-PUCE
Osvaldo Paladines, Professor, FADA-PUCE
David Leven, Professor, CCNY
Achva Benzinberg Stein, Professor and Director, Graduate Program in Landscape Architecture, CCNY

ACKNOWLEDGEMENTS

SPECIAL THANKS

George Ranalli, Dean, School of Architecture, CCNY

Hernán Orbea, Dean of FADA-PUCE, 2002-2008

Alexis Mosquera, Chair of the Architecture Program, FADA-PUCE, 2002-2008 (current Dean)

Friedemann Koester, Director of the Yasuni Research Station, PUCE, 1998-2008

Lucy Baldeón, Assistant to the Director of the Yasuní Research Station, PUCE, 1998-2008

The Huaorani community, with special thanks to Mr. Wuampi Ahua and Ms. Omene Ima; her sons Ramón, Pablo, Germán and Eduardo; Mr. Huintoque Boya and Ms. Nambai Ahua

Carlos Flores, Field Administrator at the Yasuni Research Station

Marco Haro, architect in Lago Agrio

Fabián Torres, architect in Lago Agrio

Martha Medina, architect in Lago Agrio

Lenin Recalde, architect in Lago Agrio

Felipe Domínguez, architect in Lago Agrio

Máximo Abad, former Mayor of Lago Agrio

EDITORIAL TEAM

Matthias Altwicker

Zoe Blackler

Lynne Desilva-Johnson

Trudy Giordano

Yuliya Ilizarov

Rodolfo Leyton

BOOK Credits
Creative Direction by Belén Matos
Preface by Michael Sorkin
Edited by Oscar Riera Ojeda, Michael Sorkin, Ana María Durán Calisto, Matthias Altwicker
Essays by Patrick Radden Keefe
Production by Oscar Riera Ojeda
Copy Editing by Kit Maude

OSCAR RIERA OJEDA
PUBLISHERS

ISBN 978-988-16194-2-6
Published by Oscar Riera Ojeda Publishers Limited
Printed in China by Artron Art Center

Oscar Riera Ojeda Publishers Limited
Unit 6, 22/F.,
Far East Consortium Building,
121 Des Voeux Road Central, Hong Kong
T: +852-5311-1625

Production Offices | China
Suit 19, Shenyun Road,
Nanshan District, Shenzhen 518055
T:+86-182-0098-3774

www.oropublishers.com | www.oscarrieraojeda.com
oscar@oscarrieraojeda.com

MÁS ALLÁ DE
PETRÓPOLIS

EL DISEÑO DE
UNA UTOPÍA PRAGMÁTICA
EN NUEVA LOJA

GRADUATE PROGRAM IN URBAN DESIGN - CITY COLLEGE OF NEW YORK
GRADUATE PROGRAM IN LANDSCAPE ARCHITECTURE
UNDERGRADUATE PROGRAM IN ARCHITECTURE

FACULTAD DE ARQUITECTURA, DISEÑO Y ARTES -
PONTIFICIA UNIVERSIDAD CATÓLICA DEL ECUADOR

PREFACIO Michael Sorkin.
EDICIÓN Michael Sorkin, Ana María Durán Calisto, Matthias Altwicker and Oscar Riera Ojeda.
ENSAYOS Patrick Radden Keefe

ÍNDICE

PREFACIO 292

INTRODUCCIÓN

Bienvenidos a Petrópolis **294** Infraestructura, futuro y memoria: el Bicentenario de la integración territorial en Sudamérica **296** El diseño de un nuevo paisaje para Lago Agrio **301**
El fin de la era petrolera ya está aquí **303** El viaje **304** La ciudad **304** La selva **305** Urbanismo predatorio: sobre el nacimiento y crecimiento de Nueva Loja **306**

CONTEXTO

SOCIAL Demografía **308** Economía **308** Política **312**
MEDIO AMBIENTE Clima **313** Vegetación **314** Hidrología **314** El río Aguarico **314** Ecosistema **315**

INFRAESTRUCTURA URBANA

Petróleo **316** Energía **316** Agua **319** Recomendaciones: agricultura y alimentos **319** Residuos **319** Instalaciones Públicas **321** Infraestructura Pública **321** Educación **321**

PROPUESTAS

DISEÑO URBANO Organización regional **324** Límites de la ciudad **325** Organización de la ciudad **326** Barrio Vía Quito **326** Napo - Julio Marín **327** Barrio San Francisco **327** Universidad del Orienco **328**
El Barrio Chacra **328** Barrio La Florida **329** De-Central Park **329** Barrio La Esquina **329** Barrio Isegorida **330** Barrio Puerto Aguarico **331** El carbón encendido **331**
ARQUITECTURA Infraestructura arquitectónica para la ciudad post-petróleo **332** El techo-máquina **335** Cubrir, unir, colgar **335** El sistema **335** El prototipo **336** Prototipo de vivienda para un clima húmedo y caluroso **336** Prototipo 750 **336** Vivienda unifamiliar con paredes apersianadas **336** Viviendas en la naturaleza **337** Viviendas apilables **337** Viviendas multifamiliares: la partida de la ciudad **337** Viviendas multifamiliares: vivir en el Amazonas **337** Viviendas de Lago Agrio **337** Aula móvil: escuela pop-up **338** Aula móvil: prototipo de 0 basura **338** Aula móvil: escuela desplegable **338**
Escuela secundaria de Puerto Aguarico **338** Escuela primaria verdiazul **339** La escuela urbana **339** La escuela como herramienta de aprendizaje: la escuela de construcción de Nueva Loja **339**
Asentamientos humanos sustentables para la era post-petrolera en la Amazonía ecuatoriana: una introducción al Taller de Lago Agrio (FADA-PUCE) **340** Paisaje productivo - Vivienda productiva **341**
Sistemas sostenibles **341** Conector multicapas **341** Metabolismos autosuficientes **342** Bandas de crecimiento **342** Fusión material **342** Vivienda unifamiliar auto-sostenible **342** Capa protectora **343**

Inversión de la fortuna **344**

CONCLUSIONES

Postfacio: Una Nueva Loja post-petróleo **354** Créditos y Agradecimientos **356** Biografías **357** Bibliografía **358**

PREFACIO

Por **MICHAEL SORKIN**

Todos los años, el Programa de Posgrado en Diseño Urbano del City College de Nueva York viaja a una ciudad que esté sufriendo algún problema que resulte particularmente revelador. Con la colaboración de estudiantes y profesores de una institución local, los alumnos observan y analizan una situación urbana, se familiarizan con los contextos físicos, sociales, económicos y ambientales, diseñan un programa, y formulan una serie de respuestas físicas. A lo largo de la última década, hemos realizado proyectos en Nicosia, La Habana, Johannesburgo, Wuhan, Biloxi, Nueva Orleans, Tijuana, Hanoi y Bogotá.

En enero de 2007, junto con estudiantes y profesores de la Pontificia Universidad Católica del Ecuador y de los programas de arquitectura, urbanismo y paisajismo del CCNY, nos trasladamos a la pequeña ciudad de Nueva Loja, en el corazón de la Amazonía ecuatoriana. Elegimos este destino luego de consultar con nuestros colegas Ana María Durán y Osvaldo Paladines, porque esta pequeña ciudad experimenta de manera emblemática muchos de los difíciles procesos de desarrollo en América del Sur, en particular en lo tocante a la interacción entre la ecología social y la ambiental. Cuando visitamos la ciudad, Nueva Loja, que en ese entonces contaba con 100.000 habitantes, tenía el índice de crecimiento municipal más alto de Ecuador.

Había un motivo para explicar un crecimiento tan explosivo: el petróleo. Desde los primeros grandes descubrimientos de yacimientos en 1967, el Oriente ecuatoriano, con Nueva Loja como epicentro, ha sido testigo de un patrón de explotación desenfrenado. Ubicada en un paisaje extremadamente sensible, y habitada por pueblos originarios cuyo modo de vida no se había visto sustancialmente interrumpido por siglos, la ciudad que se fue desarrollando y sus territorios aledaños fueron particularmente susceptibles a los estragos de la exploración y la extracción petrolífera, las presiones del desarrollo y la violencia proveniente de la cercana frontera colombiana.

El influjo poblacional que acompañó la aparición del dinero del petróleo se mezcló con los sistemas sociales y naturales existentes, produciendo una metástasis de violencia y destrucción. Algunos patrones de vida se han visto severamente perturbados por la "modernización". Miles de kilómetros cuadrados de selva tropical, incluyendo algunos de los ecosistemas más complejos y menos estudiados del planeta, han sido desbrozados y divididos en lotes que sólo sirven para el pastoreo y la especulación. La connivencia de factores tales como el dinero, las drogas, el tráfico de personas, la guerrilla y la inestabilidad política ha creado una cultura de violencia, corrupción, dependencia y pobreza. También ha fomentado la organización y la resistencia. Y ha creado una masa crítica de personas y de necesidades que exige ser atendida con mayor eficacia.

De mantenerse las actuales tendencias demográficas, la población de Nueva Loja alcanzará los 150.000 habitantes en 2021. Se trata de una fecha significativa: es el año en que se acabará el petróleo. Ése era el problema que nos proponíamos investigar: imaginar una Nueva Loja post-petróleo. Por supuesto, no se trataba de un proyecto puramente arquitectónico. Si bien nuestra tarea tuvo que ver con el diseño en términos materiales, tengo la esperanza de que este libro dé cuenta de una serie de problemáticas más amplia. Hemos intentado imaginar qué tipo de producción podría sostener a la ciudad en el futuro, y hemos orientado nuestra intervención para que reflejara este objetivo. Hemos incluido la utilización de fuentes de energía renovables de origen indígena como alternativa energética. Hemos estudiado la gama de actividades económicas que podría llevar a cabo de manera sustentable una selva tropical regenerada. Hemos incluido instalaciones de educación superior porque no hay ninguna en la región, a fin de evitar la tan mentada "fuga de cerebros" hacia Quito. Hemos pensado en la recuperación de la producción de base artesanal y en formas de agricultura sustentable, incluyendo el cultivo de plantas medicinales. Hemos incluido instalaciones para el turismo ecológico. Hemos estudiado los ríos de la región como medios de transporte. Y hemos especulado acerca de una industria de la construcción que se adapte al bioclima y a los recursos de la zona.

También hemos estudiado minuciosamente la ciudad existente. A pesar de ser caótica, precariamente provista y mantenida, un páramo arquitectónico que carece de la mayor parte de la infraestructura básica, de todos modos Lago presenta características comunales y urbanas que es necesario alimentar a fin de que se conviertan en la base de su desarrollo. Lo más importante de todo es el capital humano de la ciudad, sus activistas y sus luchadores, sus vigorosos inmigrantes y emprendedores, sus cuadros profesionales. Si bien es víctima de un régimen fiscal que establece que los fondos municipales vengan del gobierno central, la administración local, con todo y las abrumadoras exigencias de la política ecuatoriana, parece estar auténticamente abocada al progreso de la ciudad. Hemos visto pruebas de mejoras en los servicios, en el espacio público, en la educación y en otros aspectos fundamentales que son la base de una buena ciudad.

La vida de Lago también dio pruebas de una vigorosa urbanidad, y nos dio a pensar numerosas alternativas para elaborar en el futuro. Curiosamente, la ciudad ha crecido dándole la espalda a su mayor recurso natural, el río Aguarico. Como podría esperarse, antes del petróleo las comunidades ocupaban sus orillas, pero la necesidad de acceso a rutas, grandes terrenos y territorio desocupado provocó el surgimiento de la ciudad lejos del río. El hecho de que este hermoso y delicado corredor de agua haya sido ajeno al caos y a un desarrollo insensible en materia ambiental se trata de algo positivo, que deja el futuro del río en manos de actores más sensibles y cuidadosos.

El nuevo centro de la ciudad es bullicioso y urbano, y las veredas de la calle principal están llenas de vendedores ambulantes. Hay un incipiente sistema de arcadas que ofrece a los peatones refugio del intenso sol y los frecuentes chaparrones, y una actividad comercial que justifica que se lo llame "el centro". Hay un mercado público precioso. Hay una gran plaza nueva, de diseño ambicioso. La enloquecida trama de construcciones informales, tanto en los intersticios como en la periferia, si bien a menudo es improvisada e insalubre, muestra a la vez un vigor y una autonomía que, con la ayuda y las limitaciones apropiadas, debe convertirse en un componente fundamental de cualquier nuevo proyecto que se piense para el lugar.

Este libro contiene propuestas en numerosos ámbitos. La primera pertenece al orden territorial: se trata de un intento por promover la recuperación a mayor escala de un paisaje devastado y por integrar en él, de manera simbiótica, el cantón de Lago Agrio. A continuación, hemos estudiado el patrón general de organización de la ciudad, basándonos en una estructura barrial. Los barrios pretenden ser distritos parcialmente autónomos que ofrecen tanto viviendas como una serie de instalaciones comerciales, educativas, recreativas; en ellos tiene lugar la actividad política a nivel local. También hemos investigado los sistemas naturales de la ciudad, la apropiación de sus vías fluviales, el tratamiento biológico de sus desechos, la restauración de su flora y su fauna desplazadas. Finalmente, muchos estudiantes han trabajado en propuestas arquitectónicas que tienen que ver en particular con viviendas e instalaciones compartidas. Todas estas investigaciones se han realizado con ánimo de privilegiar las habilidades, los materiales y las tradiciones locales por sobre sus equivalentes foráneos y por sobre la utilización de prácticas no sustentables.

El trabajo de un semestre apenas alcanza para hacerse una idea superficial del carácter y el diseño de una ciudad, y sólo permite una módica participación en las instancias cruciales de colaboración que son propias de un proceso de planificación democrática, que debe siempre conservar su carácter dinámico. Ofrecemos estas propuestas como una contribución al diálogo que actualmente tiene lugar entre las organizaciones comunitarias, los intereses comerciales, el gobierno y los individuos. En nuestra visita nos conmovieron especialmente el optimismo y el activismo de nuestros hermanos y hermanas arquitectos de Lago Agrio. Su compromiso con su ciudad y con la causa de la justicia ambiental nos inspiró a todos, y estamos ansiosos por continuar nuestra relación con ellos y con su fascinante ciudad.

INTRODUCCIÓN

- BIENVENIDOS A PETRÓPOLIS
- INFRAESTRUCTURA, FUTURO Y MEMORIA: el Bicentenario de la integración territorial en Sudamérica
- EL DISEÑO DE UN NUEVO PAISAJE PARA LAGO AGRIO
- EL FIN DE LA ERA PETROLERA YA ESTÁ AQUÍ
- CRONOGRAMA
- GEOGRAFÍA
- EL VIAJE
- LA CIUDAD
- LA SELVA
- URBANISMO PREDATORIO: sobre el nacimiento y crecimiento de Nueva Loja.

BIENVENIDOS A PETRÓPOLIS

Por **MICHAEL SORKIN**

Pink Floyd sonaba por los altoparlantes del ferry que transportó nuestro ómnibus sobre el río Napo hacia del Parque Nacional Yasuní, que se extiende a lo largo de 4.350 kilómetros cuadrados de la cuenca amazónica, en el Oriente ecuatoriano. Luego de un lento avance por rutas agrietadas, atravesando un paisaje en gran medida desolado, habíamos perdido el ferry anterior, y habíamos pasado una hora dando vueltas por la orilla del río, en donde se extendía un panorama de extrema informalidad: un sol abrumador, senderos cubiertos de barro y basura a lo largo de la orilla, perros vagabundos, casas diseminadas aquí y allá, un pequeño negocio y un estacionamiento de tierra para los vehículos que aguardaban la llegada del ferry. El panorama del otro lado del río, sin embargo, se parecía más a Guantánamo. Una vez desembarcados en el muelle, tuvimos que recorrer estrechos pasadizos entre cercas rematadas por alambres de púa, atravesar un magnetómetro, pasar el equipaje de mano por un detector de rayos equis, entregar nuestros pasaportes para que con expresión severa los confrontaran con una lista que les habíamos enviado previamente, y echarle un último vistazo a nuestro ómnibus mientras lo metían en un galpón de chapa pintado con camuflaje. Nada de carteles de Coca-Cola ni de cortesías de ningún tipo. Por el contrario, había torres de vigilancia, reflectores, signos que prohibían el alcohol y las drogas, y hombres de uniforme armados con M-16, tanto del ejército ecuatoriano como de empresas privadas de seguridad ecuatorianas con nombres orwellianos como Servisafe y Servipro. Era una inesperada entrada al paraíso.

El Parque Nacional Yasuní, que forma parte de la "reserva mundial de biósfera" de la UNESCO, es una de las zonas más biodiversas del planeta, una selva tropical llena de vida, que es el hogar de los indígenas huaoranis. Y del petróleo. Al cruzar el río, entramos en el "Bloque 16", una de las gigantescas concesiones que se reparten el Oriente desde que en 1967 un consorcio de Texaco y Gulf descubrió enormes reservas petrolíferas en la zona. Para mediados de 1972, la explotación estaba funcionando a todo vapor y se había construido un oleoducto de 500 kilómetros para transportar crudo del por entonces pujante pueblo de Nueva Loja (universalmente conocido como Lago Agrio, llamado así porque en aquella época las oficinas centrales de Texaco se encontraban en Sour Lake, Texas) hasta la costa, desde donde se lo envía al exterior, principalmente a los Estados Unidos. El propósito de tanta seguridad era proteger este recurso, proteger la selva de incursiones por parte de terroristas, contrabandistas, narcotraficantes, cazadores furtivos, leñadores y colonos. Por supuesto, no ayudó en nada a proteger la zona del impacto traumático del propio petróleo. Los efectos del petróleo en el paisaje ecuatoriano han sido profundos. Por un lado, ha alimentado una economía de alza que, especialmente en los dinámicos años setenta y ochenta, trajo aparejadas una gran prosperidad para las clases medias y altas e inversiones del gobierno en materia de obra pública. Por el otro, el petróleo ha sido un desastre ambiental. Miles de kilómetros cuadrados de selva tropical han desaparecido. Las vidas de numerosos pueblos indígenas se han visto alteradas para siempre. Y grandes extensiones se han vuelto tóxicas. Según una demanda colectiva iniciada en 2003 por 30.000 habitantes de la zona (que aun se encuentra atrapada en los infinitos meandros del Poder Jaúñdicial ecuatoriano), Texaco, y su sucesora, Chevron, no sólo han derramado 30 veces más petróleo en la selva que el que derramó el Exxon Valdez, sino que además vertieron casi setenta y cinco mil millones de litros de agua residual tóxica. La mayor parte del petróleo se extrae por inyección de agua a alta presión, y en vez de seguir el procedimiento acostumbrado de reinyección de los desechos, la empresa simplemente los arrojó en hoyos a ras del suelo, ahorrándose 3 dólares por barril. Según Judith Kimerling, en su libro *Amazon Crude* (1990), esta catástrofe, que a menudo es llamada "el Chernobyl de la selva", ha contaminado grandes extensiones de tierra y acuíferos, aumentado en gran medida la incidencia del cáncer, de los abortos espontáneos y otras enfermedades, propagando estos nocivos efectos incluso hasta territorio peruano. La demanda, que pretende cubrir los costos del saneamiento, estimados en 6.000 millones de dólares, avanza a paso de tortuga por los tribunales, así como una demanda del gobierno ecuatoriano que acusa a Chevron de fraude. Las concesiones petroleras, que se extienden por miles de kilómetros cuadrados, tienen una espacialidad muy específica, un formato que, por etapas, está convirtiendo la selva no sólo en un ambiente tóxico y degradado sino en un urbanismo, una ciudad que ostenta un nuevo carácter "desarticulado", que combina redes y nodos, formalidad e informalidad, densidad y dispersión. Los componentes de esta ciudad selvática incluyen el trazado de líneas sísmicas (senderos de tres metros de ancho en los que se abren pozos de 2 a 5 metros de profundidad cada cien metros, a fin de colocar de 10 a 20 kilos de dinamita para exploración acústica), redes de pozos y desechos tóxicos, estaciones de bombeo, refinerías, patios de tanques, oleoductos, pistas de aterrizajes de helicópteros, aeropuertos, rutas, controles de seguridad, instalaciones militares, y profusión de campamentos, depósitos y pueblos, negocios y edificaciones a la vera de la ruta y pueblitos. En una demanda ambiental presentada contra la petrolera estadounidense Atlantic Richfield en 1993, los demandantes inventariaron, para una única concesión, 339 pozos, 29.000 kilómetros de líneas sísmicas, 500 kilómetros de rutas, 600 fosas de desechos tóxicos y 1.368 pistas de aterrizajes de helicópteros. Bienvenidos a Petrópolis.

Las rutas que cortan la selva son focos tanto de extracción como de atracción, y se vuelven el medio para la reorganización territorial a una escala aun mayor. Con la construcción de los caminos, se tala la selva para hacerle espacio a parcelas agrícolas de 250 por 2.000 metros, creándose áreas de doce kilómetros de ancho y, en total, cientos de kilómetros de largo, un enorme asentamiento lineal ocupado por colonos que migran desde otras partes del país. Más de un cuarto de millón de migrantes se han trasladado al Oriente desde el descubrimiento del petróleo. Gran parte son tierras de pastoreo: los suelos de la selva tropical no son idóneos para la agricultura convencional, y el talado de la selva destruye la biodiversidad, fuertemente simbiótica, que ésta permite. Este patrón trae aparejada una nueva organización económica, así como nuevas formas de actividad agrícola, nuevas haciendas, nuevas aldeas y nuevos pueblos. En gran medida como el trazado jeffersoniano del Oeste de los Estados Unidos, la despiadada geometría de la subdivisión lleva a cabo un dramático cambio literal y conceptual: lo que antes era "jungla" deviene urbe, parte de un sistema mundial. Los largos kilómetros de granjas y aldeas en la selva desforestada y el puesto de control del Bloque 16 son parte del mismo urbanismo petropolitano que produce la morfología de las autopistas de Los Ángeles y Houston y el resplandeciente panorama urbano de Dubai o Kuwai City.

Por supuesto, un ambiente urbano necesita de ciudadanos urbanos, y este boom ha atraído a cientos de miles. ¿Pero qué pasa con los que ya estaban ahí, y con sus estilos de vida fuertemente no urbanos? Dos años después de que Texaco descubriera las enormes reservas de petróleo en el Oriente, el gobierno ecuatoriano creó una "reserva" protegida para los huaoranis. Desesperado por las regalías petroleras, pero preocupado por los potenciales conflictos que podrían generarse entre los pueblos originarios, los trabajadores del petróleo, y el flujo cada vez más grande de colonos y turistas, José María Velasco Ibarra, el presidente en ese entonces, le confió la administración del protectorado al Summer Institute of Linguistics (SIL), un grupo evangélico protestante en actividad en Ecuador desde principios de la década de 1950, que se especializaba en la traducción de la Sagrada Escritura a lenguas indígenas.

Como sus predecesores, los misioneros de siglos pasados, la trágica empresa del SIL supuso forzar a los "nativos" a vivir en aldeas, fundar escuelas en las que la Biblia estaba en el centro del programa de estudios, e introducir el capitalismo. Los resultados también comprendieron talar selvas para la creación de mayores extensiones de cultivo, la especialización agrícola y una economía monetizada, así como la rápida introducción de formas culturales extrañas, desde pantalones y radios hasta cerveza y techos de zinc. Los nativos estaban siendo urbanizados, convertidos en ciudadanos modelo de un nuevo orden. La resistencia no tardó en surgir, y hubo muchos casos de sacerdotes y trabajadores del petróleo asesinados. Lo que es más importante, los pueblos nativos empezaron a organizarse políticamente y a crear conciencia, lo cual dio como resultado un hecho crucial: la creación en 1986 de la Confederación de Nacionalidades Indígenas del Ecuador, CONAIE, que actualmente constituye una importante fuerza política que trabaja en pos de los derechos humanos y ambientales. En 1989, el gobierno ecuatoriano, ante la baja del precio del petróleo, y ansioso por mantener su flujo de ingresos, preparó (con financiamiento de Conoco Oil) un nuevo plan de "gerenciamiento" del Parque Nacional Yasuní, aún sin explotar. El parque fue dividido en dos: una mitad para la explotación petrolera, la otra para los huaoranis. En 1993, se implementó un plan modificado, por medio del cual se incorporaba nominalmente a los huaoranis a la administración de la entidad combinada. Para ellos, esto significaba un empleo como trabajadores del petróleo y como guardias de seguridad en su propio, y otrora pacífico, terruño. También significaba nuevas (y tremendamente inadecuadas) viviendas para algunos, generalmente agrupadas en lo que sólo puede describirse como campos de concentración. Todo esto para un pueblo que a lo largo de miles de años había vivido de manera nomádica. Asimismo, el plan trajo aparejados el desastre de las enfermedades importadas y una rápida educación en la modernidad.

No es éste el lugar adecuado para ocuparse de la cuestión de los derechos de los pueblos originarios ni para debatir los respectivos argumentos a favor de la alfabetización, la tecnología y la participación en la vida nacional frente a la lógica de proteger la capacidad de los pueblos "primitivos" de defender y continuar patrones históricos de vida y asentamiento. Se trata simplemente de que la vida de esta gente se ha visto destrozada y su cultura va en camino de extinguirse, todo esto en nombre de un bien mayor, que sería el de la economía ecuatoriana, que sigue dependiendo casi exclusivamente del petróleo (como en el pasado lo hizo de monocultivos como el cacao y las bananas). Las ventas de petróleo equivalen a casi el 50% de los ingresos del gobierno (del cual aproximadamente la mitad se destina a gastos militares) y la nacionalización del petróleo en 1989 ha colocado al gobierno en la admirable posición de ejercer la potestad de su propia fuente de ingresos.

Las maquinaciones en Yasuní, con la constante modificación de los límites del parque, las concesiones y las reservas étnicas (para un pueblo en cuya imaginación no entraba la idea de aquellos límites) son parte de un sistema más amplio de territorios superpuestos, definidos por relaciones de propiedad, que inscribe en la selva los modernos patrones del espacio y del intercambio. El norte del Oriente ecuatoriano muestra todo esto elevado a la más alta potencia de locura tóxica. Las tropas que vimos en Yasuní no estaban allí simplemente para proteger el petróleo sino para mantener a raya a la industria de la cocaína (cada vez más empujada contra la frontera con Ecuador, y más allá de ella, por el "Plan Colombia", patrocinado por los Estados Unidos) que tiene su propio sistema reticular de extracción y un laberinto paralelo de rutas, pistas de aterrizaje, laboratorios, pueblos y flujos de capital.

Como cualquier ciudad, Nueva Loja superpone infraestructuras, territorios, intereses, tecnologías, densidades, comunidades, historias y morfologías. Sus diferencias con las ciudades-margen "post-urbanas" que se han convertido en la modalidad característica del crecimiento urbano en tantas partes del mundo no son de tipo, sino simplemente de grado. Ambos patrones son perjudiciales para el medio ambiente, y ambos están basados conceptualmente en la supremacía de sistemas distribuidos antes que concentrados. Asimismo, ambos están basados en un modelo de desarrollo urbano que privilegia la extracción (de petróleo, de cocaína o del valor de la tierra) sobre la sociabilidad, la permanencia o la cultura. Si bien sólo la mitad de la población mundial, si se la mide de acuerdo a los métodos tradicionales, vive en ciudades, el planeta se encuentra inmensamente más urbanizado. Yasuní, y la cuenca amazónica, ponen en relieve este urbanismo acelerado de manera tan aguda, porque la selva tropical sigue siendo para nosotros el paradigma del "estado natural" por excelencia, la antítesis de la civilización urbana. A medida que va en aumento nuestra sensibilidad ecológica (y que la selva desaparece), vamos entendiendo hasta qué punto nuestra propia supervivencia depende del destino de la selva. De manera análoga, el respeto por los pueblos indígenas y sus tradiciones es fundamental para comprender los riesgos de la globalización, que amenaza con aplastar todas las diferencias y con coartar la libertad de acción económica. Los huoaranis parecen condenados, pero urge que en su ruina nos veamos a nosotros mismos.

VER IMAGEN, PÁGINAS13 a 15.

INFRAESTRUCTURA, FUTURO Y MEMORIA:

el bicentenario de la integración territorial

Por **ANA MARÍA DURÁN CALISTO**

"...En aquel imperio, el Arte de la Cartografía logró tal Perfección que el mapa de una sola Provincia ocupaba toda una Ciudad y el mapa del Imperio toda una Provincia. Con el tiempo esos Mapas Desmesurados no satisficieron y los Colegios de Cartógrafos levantaron un Mapa del Imperio, que tenía el tamaño del Imperio y coincidía puntualmente con él. Menos Adictas al estudio de la Cartografía, las Generaciones Siguientes entendieron que ese dilatado Mapa era Inútil y no sin Impiedad lo entregaron a las Inclemencias del Sol y de los Inviernos. En los desiertos del Oeste perduran despedazadas Ruinas del Mapa, habitadas por Animales y por Mendigos; en todo el País no hay otra reliquia de las Disciplinas Geográficas".

Del rigor en la ciencia, en *El hacedor*, por Jorge Luis Borges

El territorio es un documento en continua transformación: maleable, elástico, pródigo e indomable. No sorprende que la ciencia que lo estudia, la geo-grafía, se remita etimológicamente al acto de escribir: en sus diversos estratos permanecen registradas las acciones y presiones ejercidas por diversas fuerzas naturales y sociales a través del tiempo. Ya André Corboz, en 1983, lo equiparó con un palimpsesto, en cuyos trazos la memoria y el olvido se renuevan y reconstruyen. América del Sur esculpe ahora mismo un nuevo territorio y observarlo bajo la lente de la mirada satelital es decodificar la estructura económica y política que rige los nuevos principios de la integración continental y bi-centenaria, pues si bien la independencia sentó las bases para la unificación ideológica, y la celebración centenaria inauguró varias de las grandes obras de infraestructura industrial (las vías ferroviarias, por ejemplo), el bicentenario se encuadra dentro de un proceso sin precedentes de integración infraestructural, política, cultural, financiera y militar. Son varias las instituciones (UNASUR, Banco del Sur, IIRSA, CAF, MERCOSUR, OTCA, etc.) y varios los discursos de la integración. Sin embargo, el tablero donde se juega su realidad y donde se encarnan sus principios es el territorio, por eso me propongo reflexionar sobre el papel político y mercantil que juegan las infraestructuras de la unificación.

EL IIRSA: PRAGMATISMO INTEGRACIONISTA, GEO-ECONOMÍA Y MERCADO GLOBAL

A raíz de que se desencadenaron los procesos de expansión irrefrenable del mercado global en la década de los 90, gracias al surgimiento de las tecnologías digitales que los facilitaron, las ciudades en América Latina, Asia y África han explotado. El comportamiento anárquico y la relativa autonomía del mercado transnacional se han desplegado en un sinnúmero de patrones globales, entre los que cabe destacar el surgimiento de los gobiernos locales (versus nacionales) como principales nodos de gestión política y económica; el del sector privado como el portador de las principales "economías", cuyo ranking ignora cualquier forma de afiliación nacional; la apertura directa e indirecta de las fronteras políticas como la nueva modalidad de acceso e intercambio de recursos, capitales y personas; y el surgimiento de China, India, Brasil, Rusia y Medio Oriente como los principales mercados emergentes a escala global.

Es un evento sin precedentes en la historia moderna del hemisferio sur que un país sudamericano se haya consolidado como uno de los principales vórtices de desarrollo del mercado internacional. No sorprende, por tanto, que Brasil lidere el proceso pragmático – comercial e infraestructural – de integración regional. En el año 2000, Fernando Henrique Cardoso, entonces Presidente de Brasil, presentó a sus homólogos sudamericanos la Iniciativa para la Integración de la Infraestructura Regional Suramericana (IIRSA) junto con un equipo técnico del BID (Banco Interamericano de Desarrollo): una ambiciosa propuesta de planificación territorial que incluía en la cartera del periodo 2003-2006, 351 proyectos de infraestructura de transporte, energía y telecomunicaciones, con una inversión total de aproximadamente 37 billones de dólares estadounidenses. La cartera de proyectos se amplió hasta llegar a incluir 524 proyectos en el año 2010, cuyo costo estimado asciende a los 96.119 millones de dólares estadounidenses.[1] El plan divide al continente sudamericano en diez ejes de desarrollo, cinco transversales y cinco longitudinales. Y si bien se propone desarrollar infraestructuras de transporte multimodal, energía y telecomunicaciones, el 80% de su cartera actual está compuesto por plantas hidroeléctricas y carreteras .

Son dos las fuerzas principales que han despertado el interés del gigante sudamericano por sus vecinos hispanoamericanos: por una parte, la necesidad de abrir rutas hacia los puertos del Pacífico para poder comerciar con Asia, particularmente con China; y por otra, la necesidad de manejar la cuenca amazónica y la red hidroeléctrica que se espera alimente en el futuro. Si bien alrededor del 70% de su sistema hídrico ocupa territorio brasileño, la mayor parte de sus fuentes se ubican en los glaciares andinos fuera de su territorio.[2] Adicionalmente, es en las estribaciones de la cordillera andina donde existen pendientes idóneas para la construcción de grandes proyectos de generación de energía hidroeléctrica, mientras que la Amazonia brasileña es relativamente plana. Brasil se ha asociado con sus vecinos andinos para desarrollar represas hidroeléctricas en las estribaciones orientales de los Andes. El anterior Presidente de Brasil, Luiz Inácio Lula da Silva, y el ex-Presidente de Perú, Alan García, firmaron un acuerdo para construir seis represas hidroeléctricas en la selva peruana. "La mayor parte de la energía [generada por estas represas] será exportada, inicialmente, a Brasil, pero la proporción se revertirá gradualmente hasta que Perú, luego de 30 años, sea el único propietario de este proyecto de 4 billones de dólares estadounidenses".[3] La primera central hidroeléctrica ha sido proyectada para el río Inambari, en la intersección de los departamentos de Cuzco, Madre de Dios y Puno. Conforme aumenta la necesidad de la economía brasileña por suplir a su creciente industria y sus ciudades con la energía necesaria para mantenerlas, no sorprende que en el año 2003 se haya constituido otro instrumento de integración, la OTCA (Organización del Tratado de Cooperación Amazónica). El tratado responde a un reconocimiento de que grandes ecosistemas como el que compone la Amazonia, no pueden ser tratados aisladamente, dentro de las barreras que imponen las fronteras nacionales, menos aún cuando está en juego un quinto del agua fresca del planeta – un recurso que se prevé será en pocas décadas el más codiciado de la economía mundial. La organización aglutina a los ocho países que comparten la totalidad de la cuenca amazónica en un intento por coordinar su conservación y desarrollo.

LAS CARTOGRAFÍAS DEL PODER: TERRITORIOS Y VISUALIZACIÓN

Los documentos de la planificación territorial no son papeles inocuos, al contrario, las cartografías, más allá de ilustrar los territorios a los cuales se remiten, tienen la capacidad de transformarlos. Por eso, no debe subestimarse el papel que han jugado los Sistemas de Información Geográfica, Google Earth, las imágenes satelitales, el *remote sensing* y otras tecnologías de macro, tele, subte y supervisión en la reformulación del continente sudamericano: paradójicamente, la percepción de lo local ha sido renovada por una capacidad masiva de visión a la distancia. De hecho, un programa de planificación territorial a escala continental, que se propone alcanzar la mayoría de sus objetivos en el transcurso de dos o tres décadas, hubiera sido impensable sin estas herramientas. Y cada uno de sus trazos infraestructurales, desde que ocurre en el papel, constituye un gesto que altera para siempre el ecosistema sobre el cual se inscribe. Las infraestructuras del IIRSA atravesarán varios eco-sistemas frágiles en el continente sudamericano. Preocupa de manera fundamental el futuro que se avizora para la Amazonia, portadora de cuatro de los diez ejes de la Iniciativa.

En la coyuntura bicentenaria es de fundamental importancia reforzar los principios de una integración continental, necesaria de cara a los retos impuestos por la economía global, sin dejar de preguntarse cuáles serán las consecuencias de que áreas tradicionalmente remotas, que han permanecido relativamente invisibles durante siglos, hayan sido cartografiadas, cuantificadas, avaluadas y reconfiguradas como mega-inventarios geográficos y depósitos de materias primas (incluida el agua), prontos a la extracción y comercialización. Los flujos de personas, mercancías, capitales e información dependen de la construcción y consolidación de redes infraestructurales genéricas de transporte, energía y telecomunicaciones. Por su naturaleza industrial y estándar, las carreteras o los oleoductos permanecen inmutables ya sea que crucen pantanales, desiertos o forestas. La ingeniería de las infraestructuras no ha sido pensada para responder a las condiciones variables del medio geográfico y social que remontan. ¿Qué ocurre en los puntos de encuentro entre dichas infraestructuras genéricas y las condiciones medioambientales y culturales específicas de un asentamiento, una comunidad o un ecosistema? Habría que preguntarse, ¿está poniéndose en venta, una vez más y a una escala monumental, la geografía sudamericana?

El territorio no puede cartografiarse más allá de la economía, ni la economía planificarse fuera del territorio. Por otro lado, es deseable que el diseño de la infraestructura –su recuperación, construcción, articulación y expansión – responda a una lógica coordinadora, de modo que facilite el intercambio y permita complementar la oferta y demanda de las economías de los doce países que conforman el bloque sudamericano. Y si bien el Comunicado de Brasilia expedido el 1 de septiembre del año 2000, alude a dicha visión y aboga por una integración complementaria de los países de América del Sur basada, incluso, en la expansión de la educación y los sistemas de información y telecomunicaciones, las imágenes publicadas por el IIRSA no hacen eco de las palabras inscritas en el Comunicado. Es vital cuestionar si dicha Iniciativa es el proyecto visionario que responde a la incuestionable –valga la redundancia– necesidad de afianzar América del Sur como un bloque con un mercado, una economía y un territorio comunes, y que para alcanzar este fin propone equiparla con un sistema infraestructural capaz de articular nuestras rutas terrestres, fluviales, aéreas, marítimas y digitales, así como sintonizar nuestro sistema de producción energética, agrícola e industrial dentro de un nuevo campo regional de libre comercio ("regionalismo abierto"); o si su propuesta reproduce patrones típicos de las economías de extracción.

América del Sur, desde que la descubrió Europa, ha acumulado una larga historia que ilustra con claridad la lógica subyacente en la mentalidad extractiva que rige gran parte de su economía hasta el día de hoy. Ni la Independencia ilustrada ni el centenario con aspiraciones industriales lograron revertir los círculos viciosos de las economías de boom y depresión que se basan en la mera extracción de recursos naturales y exportación de materias primas o productos de monocultivos. A riesgo de caer en un reduccionismo que seguramente escandalizaría a economistas e historiadores por igual, me atrevería a decir que en el territorio se acumulan las marcas de un patrón perturbador. Puntean, estrían o rasuran la geografía sudamericana los paisajes de la extracción y las infraestructuras que facilitan los flujos de materia y energía a escala regional y global. En las décadas de la Modernidad fueron los Estados nacionales, dirigidos por dictaduras en la mayoría de los casos, los que promovieron la construcción de grandes obras de infraestructura encaminadas a usufructuar los recursos primordialmente minerales de diversos países. Con la geografía como hipoteca para obtener onerosos préstamos que incrementaron las deudas internacionales de América del Sur a niveles sofocantes, se financiaron las monumentales obras de la industria de la extracción. El problema que surge cuando una infraestructura se construye con fines meramente extractivos, es que sus beneficios no se distribuyen en la sociedad. Al contrario, suelen centralizarse en grupos de poder que difícilmente los redistribuyen: se convierten en capitales de fuga que se re-inyectan en el mercado financiero internacional, en un ciclo perverso que devuelve un hilillo al caudal que le dio vida. Basta ver las condiciones en las que viven las comunidades y asentamientos de la extracción para comprobar la asimetría que generan sus sistemas productivos. Por otra parte, la inversión tecnológica eventualmente cae en desuso. ¿Qué queda? Queda la colonización informal y desoladora de la infraestructura, queda la deuda externa, quedan la deforestación y el avance de la frontera agrícola, quedan los inmensos costos medioambientales.

El patrón no es menos vicioso cuando lo gobierna el sector privado, o una alianza entre el sector público y el privado. En la década de los 90 experimentamos un acelerado índice de privatización de la infraestructura en América del Sur. De hecho, los conductos son, per se, uno de los principales negocios en la era de los ramajes globales: la infraestructura no es únicamente medio, también es mercancía. Las corporaciones transnacionales acumularon un poder y una fuerza sin precedentes, y se convirtieron en las principales benefactoras de nuevas olas de extracción de materia prima que pudiesen alimentar el crecimiento inverosímil de las urbes a escala planetaria, sobretodo en mercados emergentes como el asiático, y apoyar la expansión de la industrial digital, que como lo ha demostrado Saskia Sassen, no es una industria "virtual" e intangible, pues su mundo evanescente se apoya en un sistema tangible, a veces macizo, de infraestructura [4]. Al finalizar la década de los 90, sin embargo, varias de las economías de América Latina comenzaron a descalabrarse (fueron diversos los nombres con los cuales se bautizaron las crisis: corralito, efecto tequila, congelamiento de fondos, etc.) bajo la presión de políticas neoliberales que reforzaron al sector privado, incrementaron la porosidad de las fronteras e instauraron a las corporaciones transnacionales en el pináculo de la economía global, a detrimento de los espacios y agencias públicos a toda escala. La reacción de péndulo en América del Sur fue que surgieron gobiernos de corte neo-socialista liberal a lo largo y ancho del continente. Las políticas económicas se revirtieron parcialmente y emergieron mecanismos de alianza gracias a los cuales los Estados, que se asumían encogidos bajo las presiones de las previas políticas neo-liberales, recuperaron su poder, jugando un papel estratégico que otorga concesiones a las empresas multinacionales (o no) y garantiza (o no) un nivel de seguridad mínimo a las inversiones extranjeras. Si bien dentro del nuevo orden global los estados nacionales parecen haber perdido jurisdicción y autonomía, reduciéndose a jugar el papel de substrato institucional, de anacronismo erosionado por los flujos de las economías transnacionales que los soslayan; sus poderes ejecutivos han adquirido una agencia sin precedentes al afiliarse con los intereses corporativos, cuya carrera en la lucha por los recursos naturales adquiere velocidades vertiginosas.[5] En este punto, conviene devolvernos a la cartografía. Tomemos el caso del mapa de Petroperú que muestra los bloques que han sido concedidos a más de veinte compañías con fines de prospección y potencial extracción de petróleo en la Amazonía peruana. [6] Basta una mirada para comprender que la noción misma de territorio nacional se pulveriza en un sistema de parches concedidos, relativamente autónomos, relativamente privatizados por un período de tiempo. ¿Cómo puede hablarse de integración en una etapa de pulverización territorial? Lo único que parece zurcir los fragmentos de una nueva forma de hacer extracción es, justamente, la infraestructura. Por eso la colosal importancia de la IIRSA, una propuesta que a pesar de su magnitud y el impacto que está destinada a tener en América del Sur, ha permanecido, como lo anotó el ex-Presidente de la República del Ecuador y primer Secretario Ejecutivo de UNASUR, Dr. Rodrigo Borja, en la penumbra.[7] Lo que no hay que olvidar es que las infraestructuras ligan e integran a la vez que rasgan y separan. El IIRSA es un arma de doble filo desde el punto de vista geográfico. Podría hilvanar a América del Sur, o terminar de fracturarla.

DE LOS TRATADOS DE LIBRE COMERCIO (TLC) A LAS ZONAS ESPECIALES DE LIBRE COMERCIO (ZELC)

Vale la pena, por ejemplo, detenerse a observar los patrones de proliferación de las Zonas (Especiales) de Libre Comercio que puntean cada vez con mayor ahínco el continente sudamericano y aparecen afiliadas con los aeropuertos que se edifican o reconstruyen en las costas, selvas, montañas, desiertos y pampas de Sudamérica. Las ZELC, al abrir portones de intercambio en países cuyas políticas neo-socialistas han impedido a menudo la ejecución de Tratados de Libre Comercio (y la apertura de sus cordones fronterizos) logran el mismo objetivo económico con una estrategia infraestructural que soslaya los engorrosos trámites políticos de la negociación. La estrategia alternativa desplegada por el sistema orgánico y aparentemente anárquico del mercado global (perforar compuertas versus abrir las bandas fronterizas) genera áreas de impunidad económica donde se permite el flujo ininterrumpido de productos de exportación e importación. Estas zonas pueden tener componentes industriales, tecnológicos y de servicios –el outsourcing es un caso en punto. Es decir, son verdaderas ciudades (una versión industrial del *gated community*) que se construyen ya sea para acomodar la manufactura (maquilas) de empresas transnacionales que aprovechan la diferencia en los costos de la mano de obra, mal llamada "ventaja comparativa", o que buscan implantarse de manera estratégica para facilitar el comercio de materias primas o la provisión de servicios. Es una táctica brillante, sin duda, porque como ya se ha anotado, soslaya los engorros, la corrupción e ineficiencia de la burocracia local. Las ZELC constituyen burbujas legales, en ellas no se aplican tarifas ni cuotas, todo es posible. Fronteras dentro de fronteras, fronteras de un sistema global de mercado que se insertan en un sistema nacional de Estado para inocular componentes o productos terminados o semi-procesados del exterior y aspirar recursos manuales, intelectuales o naturales del interior. Inevitablemente van acompañadas de un urbanismo infraestructural: la afiliación con el umbral, con la compuerta, con la infraestructura, las define.

Muchas de estas Zonas Especiales de Libre Comercio se están implantando en regiones remotas, como ocurre en la costa peruana, al occidente de Arequipa, donde una ZELC está siendo propuesta y financiada por un grupo de inversionistas chino, o en la isla de Santa Rosa en la Amazonia peruana, en las Tres Fronteras, donde la ciudad conformaría un triángulo estratégico con otras dos: Leticia, en Colombia, y Tabatinga, en Brasil. No sorprende que la ZELC más desarrollada y extensa de Brasil esté en Manaos: un centro industrial, comercial y agrícola en el corazón de la Amazonia. Su inserción en zonas remotas contribuye a descentralizar la economía, pero también altera el entorno en ecosistemas de fragilidad extrema. Si esto está ocurriendo conforme escribo, y los puntos portuarios se articulan con todo un sistema de intercomunicación global, todavía estamos a tiempo para rediseñar el futuro de zonas que de otro modo decantarán como entropía, como los desechos del "desarrollo". La coyuntura es crucial, pues en lugar de repetir los modelos de industrialización de Norteamérica, Europa y Asia, América del Sur podría convertirse en el terreno ideal donde poner a prueba modelos de desarrollo sostenible, post-industriales. Si los minerales fueron la sangre de la era industrial, es la materia orgánica el futuro de la era post-industrial. Si la biotecnología es el futuro, el Amazonas es el centro y América del Sur está llamada a jugar un papel pivote en la formulación de modos de producción, estilos de vida y urbes más sostenibles. Desde el punto de vista tecnológico e ideológico, ¿constituye el IIRSA un avance? ¿Promueve la construcción de infraestructuras verdes, poblaciones sanas y una industria con valor agregado? ¿Estimula el desarrollo de nuevas tecnologías que nos permitan elevar nuestros productos y servicios por sobre la línea base de la extracción? Un organismo crea el nicho que ocupa conforme ubica la existencia de un territorio inexplorado en el ecosistema. América Latina, a través de una diversificación, no de una reproducción, podrá abrirse un nicho en el competitivo mercado global.

URBANISMOS INFRAESTRUCTURALES

El IIRSA estipula claramente que uno de sus objetivos primordiales es "facilitar acceso a áreas con un gran potencial productivo que permanecen aisladas o sub-utilizadas".[8] Sabemos de sobra lo que abrirse paso a las fuentes de materia prima o las áreas con potencial energético involucra: se trazan ferrovías; rutas aéreas, marítimas y fluviales; pero por sobre todo, se construyen carreteras. Lo que diferencia a éstas últimas de todos los anteriores medios de transporte, es que el patrón de desarrollo que generan no responde a una secuencia, o columna vertebral, con intervenciones puntuales, sino más bien desencadena una entropía transversal y continua que se comporta como un fractal: las líneas de las carreteras se multiplican en caminos secundarios, que a su vez generan otros caminos. Abrirse paso a las fuentes de materia prima es abrir las compuertas de la colonización y desencadenar procesos de migración hiperactiva y multi-direccional. El fenómeno que ocurre en la intersección de las necesidades globales y los hechos de la materia local podría denominarse "urbanismo infraestructural" o "urbanismo infraestructural entrópico". Si América del Sur, para "desarrollarse" (y es éste un término peligrosamente malentendido), necesita desplegar una red infraestructural, es vital analizar cuáles son las consecuencias espaciales y geográficas –eventualmente sociales, culturales y medioambientales– de su construcción y renovación. Tradicionalmente, los imanes de la ocupación y la eventual urbanización del suelo han sido la proximidad a una fuente de agua, suelos ricos en nutrientes o rutas comerciales. Los urbanismos infraestructurales en las zonas remotas derivan de una lógica distinta: ocurren a lo largo de rutas de acceso en geografías a menudo hostiles, y suelen depender de la provisión de productos externos para sobrevivir. Por otra parte, se sabe que el crecimiento urbano no puede ocurrir sin una concomitante expansión de las zonas agrícolas. Cuando se estudian las contrapartes de una explosión urbana sin precedentes en la historia, se descubren los inmensos pastizales y mono-cultivos que la sostienen, por un lado; las úlceras de la minería, por otro.

INFRAESTRUCTURAS VERDES

Según el *Financial Times*,[9] para añadir cuatro puntos al crecimiento anual del Producto Interno Bruto se necesita invertir entre 5 y 9 por ciento de su presupuesto en infraestructura. Sin duda, la economía crece propulsada por un impulso infraestructural. Habría que preguntarse, sin embargo, si el retorno varía para elementos que sirven primordialmente a la extracción, así como delinear curvas de retorno e inversión a largo plazo, e incluir los costos medioambientales y sociales en estos cálculos. De lo contrario, una economía territorialmente ciega traza oleoductos, canales, diques, carreteras, puentes, puertos, redes de cables, y un sinfín de medios de movilización sin cuestionar su naturaleza, que podría ser distinta, si se presupuestaran de manera que incluyan los costos del impacto que provocan. Acaso entonces los gobiernos y la empresa privada invertirían mayores fondos en el desarrollo de infraestructuras verdes. Por ejemplo, si se toman en cuenta los costos medioambientales de la construcción de un sistema de generación hidroeléctrica, u otro proyecto cuya sola escala basta para detonar un impacto de elevadísimos costos sociales, se desarrollarían con mayor celeridad sistemas de micro-infraestructuras, que por su menor escala, tienen un menor impacto y cuestan menos a largo plazo. Una serie de micro-represas hidroeléctricas alcanza un mayor costo inicial si se quiere que produzca tanto como una sola mega-represa, pero a largo plazo, su impacto en el medio ambiente es mucho menor, y el ahorro que genera termina por beneficiar más a la sociedad que un mega sistema centralizado. Lo mismo podría decirse, por ejemplo, de micro-sistemas de captación, reciclaje y tratamiento de agua, que en vez de conectarse a una matriz central, actúen como una opción *wireless* o *un-plugged*, otorgando autonomía y capacidad de ahorro a los usuarios, y efectuando, por efecto multiplicador, una reducción de la degradación medioambiental. Sabemos por la matemática y el análisis de los sistemas dinámicos, que un cambio infinitesimal en las condiciones iniciales produce una transformación sustancial a gran escala en las condiciones finales. Los futuros desarrollos infraestructurales pueden beneficiarse del efecto detonador de lo minúsculo y ser capaces de mediar el encuentro entre la escala continental y aquélla local. Incluso desde el punto de vista de la seguridad, las micro-infraestructuras constituirían una mejor opción que las grandes obras de ingeniería, en la medida en que son estas últimas las que sirven de target al terrorismo, pues si se derrumban, se derrumba con ellas el sistema. En lugar de ser objetos de centralización de recursos, las infraestructuras pueden ser medios de democratización, y contribuir a distribuir servicios públicos, por ejemplo, o ampliar el acceso a la educación y salud a grandes sectores de la población.

América Latina, si se lo propone como parte de su plan de integración y desarrollo económico diseñado en el bicentenario para el siglo XXI, puede desencadenar un proceso de renovación global desde su marginalidad. El relativo aislamiento en el cual hemos permanecido nos provee una ventaja nos provee una ventaja: la ventaja de no habernos desarrollado bajo los lineamientos de un paradigma industrial insostenible.

NUEVAS CENTRALIDADES: LAS PERIFERIAS DE LA PERIFERIA - EL CASO AMAZÓNICO

La Amazonia es el laboratorio ideal para estudiar, en las dendritas de la inteligencia capitalista, las relaciones entre lo global y lo local, sus efectos en el límite mismo, en la periferia de periferias, donde están latentes, como en pocos otros lugares remotos, las restricciones mismas del sistema. En estos puntos críticos, se espera, puede encontrarse el terreno idóneo para formular un nuevo paradigma de desarrollo. Allí puede ponerse a prueba todo lo "verde": las infraestructuras verdes, la industria verde, los urbanismos ecológicos, las energías limpias, los sistemas agrícolas mixtos o agroforestales, los urbanismos agrícolas, las potencialidades de la biotecnología, las posibilidades de los paisajes y los suelos antropogénicos. Ya los arqueólogos demostraron que la actividad humana puede ser positiva en la Amazonia. Sus culturas prehispánicas supieron no sólo cuidar, sino además engrosar suelos pobres para incrementar su productividad agrícola. Con esto no quiero decir que favorezco una colonización masiva de la selva, o su conquista agrícola. Simplemente que miro con optimismo la relación entre el ser humano y la naturaleza, y que esta última puede cultivarse en un ecosistema de fragilidad y riqueza extremas. Por otra parte, permanezco optimista con respecto a la tecnología. Además de brindarnos soluciones de diseño medioambiental, puede proveernos con las herramientas necesarias para aliviar malestares sociales. Un caso puntual es un sistema de comunicación basado en la captación de energía solar que se ha implantado en varias comunidades indígenas de la foresta brasileña, para otorgarles el beneficio de la interconexión inmediata en un medio donde predominan patrones de dispersión poblacional.

EL VIAJE COMO RESPUESTA A LA CEGUERA TERRITORIAL DE LAS GEO-ECONOMÍAS

La lógica de la economía a menudo ha adolecido de una ceguera territorial. Se afilia con la ingeniería y resuelve el cómo extraer qué de dónde. Es decir, sus estrategias se han desplegado sin la debida planificación del espacio físico. Su herramienta primordial son las cartografías digitales: enormes bases de datos que correlacionan diversos parámetros útiles a la planificación econométrica. Los mapas que al trabajar con el territorio a la distancia lo pulverizan, desvelando patrones, estructuras y sub-estructuras, e incluso causas, gracias a la eliminación del detalle, deben ser complementados con otros que se dibujen caminando, navegando, recorriendo las minucias del espacio, tomando en cuenta que los observadores –¿lejanos o cercanos– son un componente inextricable de todo sistema.

Si miramos, por una parte, desde la lejanía, a la cuenca amazónica, veremos que infraestructuras como la carretera transamazónica o la BR 163 que liga a Santarém con la frontera boliviana, inevitablemente generan patrones de desbroce. Paradójicamente, los mismos sistemas cartográficos que permiten el diseño y la inserción territorial, se han convertido en medios para defender de diversas formas de invasión al territorio mismo. Los sistemas de información geo-referenciada como GEOSUR, las redes descentralizadas de servidores de mapas, el mecanismo geo-integrador (open source), los datos geo-espaciales, la visualización regional de datos nacionales y el programa CONDOR 2.0 (el primer intento por brindar una herramienta de mapeo interactiva sudamericana por parte de la CAF en coordinación con Conservación Internacional) proveen otra forma de integración y permiten analizar y evaluar de forma preliminar el posible impacto ambiental y social de grandes proyectos de infraestructura vial, así como establecer diversos mecanismos de control.

¿Por qué el control es una preocupación preponderante en la Amazonia? Porque está plagada de ilegalidades: se ha convertido en uno de los principales centros de plantaciones de coca y amapola; el río es una arteria vital en el tráfico de cocaína y opio; la explotación sexual de niños ocurre a lo largo de todo el trayecto fluvial; la deforestación selectiva provoca un encogimiento del dosel de la selva; la deforestación total se abre paso hasta en las zonas más recónditas; la apropiación intelectual de los conocimientos de las comunidades de la selva sigue a la orden del día; el tráfico ilegal de animales no cesa; y la esclavitud (en el sentido literal de la palabra) sigue constituyendo una forma de explotación laboral.[10] Incluso existen infraestructuras ilegales. No solamente aquéllas que se afilian con la industria del narcotráfico: muchas más. Según el Imazon (Instituto del Hombre y el Medioambiente de la Amazonia),[11] "la selva brasileña tiene al menos 95.355 kilómetros de carreteras ilegales, diez veces más que las vías oficiales" y muchos nuevos municipios o localidades fantasma son ilegales –acaso la razón por la cual el GPS no identifica varias de las localidades amazónicas, a pesar de su tamaño.

Es interesante observar que las ilegalidades que parecen encontrar en el dosel de la selva el encubrimiento ideal, han pulverizado las huellas que dejan justamente como respuesta a los sistemas de control satelital, cuya capacidad de supervisión y mapeo incrementa conforme se agudizan las estrategias de la fracturación territorial: la deforestación selectiva, la agricultura en archipiélagos, el uso de vertientes secundarias e incontrolables para la transportación de drogas, animales u otros productos vedados por la ley.

EL MUNDO CONSTRUIDO COMO RECURSO NATURAL Y LA IMPORTANCIA DEL DISEÑO

La arquitectura, la ciudad y la infraestructura necesitan ser re-conceptualizadas como recurso natural, y no pueden seguirse elaborando planes de desarrollo sin la participación de diseñadores (arquitectos, planificadores urbanos, diseñadores urbanos, arquitectos paisajistas, etc.) que puedan elaborar propuestas al unísono con ingenieros, economistas, ecólogos, matemáticos y expertos de diversos campos. La integración de las disciplinas es otra forma de unificación vital de cara a los retos que plantea el futuro. Al fin y al cabo, la industria de la construcción absorbe el 50% de la obtención y extracción de materiales, produce 217 tipos de impactos ambientales, consume el 26.15% de la energía final gastada y produce el 50% de la contaminación que sufrimos.[12] Tanto los diseñadores que trabajan del lado de la extracción, como aquéllos que diseñan en las zonas de acreción material, están llamados a proveer respuestas efectivas a la problemática medioambiental. Sin embargo, la participación del diseño ha sido mínima, acaso nula, en los programas de planificación territorial. Las consecuencias nefastas de la ausencia de diseño se vuelven aparentes en el mundo desarrollado, en contracción, donde un sinnúmero de proyectos de recuperación de grandes zonas industriales acuden ahora a las disciplinas del diseño para buscar formas de rehabilitar espacios que fueron diseñados con una lógica económica e ingenieril. Grandes infraestructuras de la era industrial están siendo remediadas como parques y espacios públicos. Si aprendemos las lecciones del norte, podríamos diseñar las infraestructuras del futuro tomando en cuenta su ciclo de vida en el sur.

Incluso queda por cuestionarse si desde el flanco del diseño, estamos equipados para responder a las condiciones únicas de un ecosistema con las herramientas de los estándares y la normativa medioambiental. Mecanismos que se asumen verdes, como la certificación LEEDS, colapsan cuando se aplican a ecosistemas como el amazónico. ¿Es posible responder a ecologías de características únicas con estándares "verdes", normas y certificaciones genéricas? ¿O constituye este sistema una mera variación de las generalizaciones de la mentalidad industrial? Acaso los urbanismos paramétricos y los modelos dinámicos de las ecologías urbanas provean mejores alternativas para el diseño de futuras intervenciones en diversos ecosistemas. Para el caso específico de la Amazonia, y tomando en cuenta que muchas las respuestas se encuentran en el territorio (ya sea en versiones formales o informales), la cuenca podría constituirse como un paisaje productivo donde los principales componentes de la infraestructura y el urbanismo son flotantes: podemos aprender de flotantes como Iquitos; e incluso, los hospitales o las escuelas que navegan el río en un intento por proponer alternativas educacionales y de salud acordes con el entorno al cual sirven.

Por otra parte, el sistema de parques y reservas naturales podría reforzarse. Sabemos gracias a la cartografía, que nos permite develar patrones, y por tanto, causas, que su presencia reduce los procesos de urbanización: la densidad poblacional se diluye en los alrededores de las zonas protegidas. Y además de las públicas, las reservas privadas, por ejemplo, también pueden jugar un papel cada vez más importante en términos de la conservación medioambiental. De hecho, lo hacen ya, generalmente afiliadas con la industria del turismo.

EL BICENTENARIO COMO DIMENSIÓN SIMBÓLICA DE LA INFRAESTRUCTURA

Las infraestructuras no son sistemas silenciosos, a-semánticos, objetos funcionales vacíos de contenido o ideología. Todo lo contrario: significan progreso y desarrollo; simbolizan fuerza y unificación. Muchos de los proyectos de infraestructura que los Ministerios de Obras Públicas de diversos gobiernos sudamericanos tenían planificado ejecutar, han sido incluidos en la cartera del IIRSA, y otros tantos, están siendo o serán inaugurados en conmemoración de los diversos Bicentenarios de la Independencia que la mayoría de países en América del Sur celebran, celebraron o se preparan para celebrar. La alianza es perfecta: cumplimos dos siglos de independencia y, para sobrevivir en la inclemente competencia del mercado global, nos unificamos infraestructuralmente. Además de una triple significación: autonomía, integración y progreso, el Bicentenario infraestructural provee una plataforma para la rememoración, la auto-evaluación y la evaluación del discurso ideológico, y el fin mercantil, de las infraestructuras del IIRSA. Y si puedo cerrar este ensayo con un optimismo atípico en el mundo contemporáneo, con el optimismo que me dejó un viaje a lo largo del río Amazonas, me atrevería a decir que si el Nilo es el padre de la civilización egipcia; el Volga, de la rusa; y el Yangtsé, de la China; la civilización que ha engendrado y está por engendrar el Amazonas, está destinada a ser grandiosa, y en consonancia con la fuerza selvática, el caudal de vida, la generosidad y magnificencia del río mar. América del Sur no se puede dar el lujo de ignorar el papel fundamental que está llamada a jugar conforme se escriben los paradigmas del futuro post-industrial, y Brasil deberá continuar liderando el proceso, como le corresponde al único país en América del Sur que comparte fronteras con todos los demás, salvo dos: Chile y Ecuador. Cada paisaje es una forma de pensar. El Amazonas es símbolo supremo de la juventud ancestral, del sistema que se renueva, perenne, y está hecho de pequeñas muertes continuas… del río y su selva sabremos derivar las nuevas estrategias del desarrollo.

VER IMÁGENES, PÁGINAS 17, 18, 21, 22, 24, 25, 30, 32, 33.

[1] Ver www.iirsa.org
[2] "Es importante anotar que los glaciares andinos están retrocediendo bajo las fuerzas del calentamiento global. La Amazonía sufre ya de inundaciones y sequías extremas debido a este fenómeno".
[3] Tomado de "Messing around with dams: First build a road, then flood it;" *The Economist*, Nov. 19, 2009.
[4] Sassen Saskia. *Cities in a World Economy*. Thousand Oaks, London, New Delhi: Pine Forge Press, 2006.
[5] Sassen, Saskia. *Una sociología de la globalización*. Buenos Aires: Katz Editores, 2007.
[6] http://www.petroperu.com.pe/
[7] Entrevista personal
[8] http://www.iirsa.org/
[9] www.ft.com/home/us
[10] www.csmonitor.com/2004/0907/P01s04-woam.html
[11] http://www.imazon.org.br/
[12] http://vlex.com/vid/materiales-construccion-medio-ambiente-41651434

EL DISEÑO DE UN NUEVO PAISAJE PARA LAGO AGRIO

Por **ACHVA BENZINGER STEIN**

El sistema del río Amazonas es una red compleja e interconectada de miles de ríos que se unen los unos con los otros. Cerca de Lago Agrio, el río Cuyabeno une sus aguas con las del Aguarico, que a su vez desagua en el río Napo, que finalmente desemboca en el Amazonas (también conocido como Solimões). Este ecosistema sigue alojando al mayor número de especies del planeta: más de 2.000 tipos de árboles y arbustos, casi 600 especies de pájaros, 100 anfibios, más de 80 reptiles y casi 80 murciélagos distintos. Hay 60 especies de abejas sociales y más de 100.000 especies de insectos por hectárea. Esto arroja un total de más de seis billones de seres vivientes.

Pero la presencia humana ha tenido un profundo impacto en esta región. Tradicionalmente, los pueblos indígenas de la provincia de Sucumbíos, donde se encuentra Lago Agrio, han mantenido un delicado equilibrio con el medio ambiente, que los alimentaba y protegía. Sin embargo, desde mediados del siglo pasado, con la construcción de caminos y la extracción petrolera, la llegada de nuevos colonos ha tenido efectos devastadores para la región y sus habitantes. La contaminación resultante en el curso superior ha creado el caos río arriba: las implicancias globales, políticas, sociales y económicas de esto aún no han sido comprendidas en su totalidad.

En su libro The Sixth Extinction: Patterns of Life and the Future of Humankind, Richard E. Leakey y Roger Lewin sugieren que los seres humanos están provocando una "sexta extinción" similar a las cinco que tuvieron lugar con anterioridad a la aparición de nuestra especie. A juzgar por lo que ocurre en la actualidad en Lago Agrio, y el accionar humano que ha ocasionado tanta destrucción, su tesis no sólo parece plausible sino también convincente.

Hoy en día el paisaje urbano de Lago Agrio –ambiental, físico, infraestructural– es en gran parte producto de asentamientos azarosos, facilitados por la exploración petrolera y la subsiguiente migración interna de mano de obra. Algunas de las estructuras que se erigen en la ciudad o alrededor de ella están bastante bien construidas, pero tantas otras son improvisadas o están venidas a menos, o ambas cosas. La tierra cultivada ha sido dividida en pequeñas haciendas, mientras que las colonias donde viven los migrantes tienden a estar ubicadas cerca de caminos y de pozos petroleros antes que junto a tierras cultivables, lo cual refleja el estado de pobreza rural al que se fuerza a los recién llegados.

La contaminación producto del petróleo está en todas partes: impregna el suelo, se filtra en los ríos y arroyos y se acumula en grandes depresiones del terreno; forma charcos tantos en la ciudad como en la periferia. En consecuencia, el ciclo hidrológico de Lago Agrio ha sido dañado, y sus ciclos del carbono y de nitrógeno se han visto perturbados. Donde han surgido asentamientos humanos, la vegetación natural ha sido afectada, en el mejor de los casos; en el peor, ésta ha sido destruida totalmente. Las poblaciones nativas, humanas y no humanas, así como los recursos necesarios para su supervivencia, han sido marginalizadas, y a veces desatendidas por completo.

La extraordinaria riqueza biológica que hay alrededor de Lago Agrio, y el daño constante que está sufriendo la tierra, desafían a los científicos a pensar cómo proteger la selva de la invasión humana. Sin embargo, aún no han surgido ideas claras acerca de cómo restaurar el equilibrio de esta red de fuerzas físicas, económicas, sociales e institucionales. La conservación, restauración y creación de nuevos paisajes constituye la tarea fundamental del diseñador ambiental. Les encargamos a nuestros alumnos la tarea de preparar diseños que sirvan para paliar, detener e incluso revertir la situación que encontraron en Lago Agrio. Los resultados aquí reunidos no intentan ser un conjunto de recetas sino un ejercicio crítico. En todos los casos, se trata de soluciones prácticas para un futuro humano sustentable, no sólo para el futuro de Lago Agrio.

Los estudiantes de diseño urbano y paisajismo que prepararon el master plan urbano para Lago Agrio hicieron suyo el desafío de reparar y sanear la tierra. Buscaron ofrecer una respuesta al inevitable incremento en desechos y aguas residuales que acompañarán el crecimiento futuro de la ciudad. Propusieron que se incorporaran sistemas químicos y biológicos de reciclaje al plan de desarrollo, en particular sistemas de almacenamiento y recuperación de agua. Estudiaron en profundidad los ciclos del agua y sus métodos de filtración. Entre sus propuestas, a la vez críticas y ecológicas, se cuentan la creación de estructuras flotantes en los pantanos para incrementar la vegetación fluvial y eliminar óxidos nítricos tóxicos, y la construcción de un sistema de pantanos artificiales para filtrar hidrocarburos volátiles y no volátiles y materiales orgánicos e inorgánicos en refinerías de petróleo y vertederos. También propusieron plantar vegetación ribereña (aquella que naturalmente se adapta al tipo de suelo adyacente a arroyos, lagos y otras fuentes de agua) para reciclar y filtrar las aguas contaminadas antes de que lleguen a los acuíferos y otros cuerpos de agua.
Dado que éstos son sistemas de tratamiento pasivos, sólo exigen un mantenimiento esporádico y una inversión pequeña en comparación con otras tecnologías, lo cual constituye un requisito obligatorio en un ambiente tan sujeto a las restricciones económicas. En todos los casos, se buscó lograr que todas las propuestas fueran no sólo sólidas sino también practicables.

Las soluciones que aquí se ofrecen no son meramente temporales. Estas medidas podrían suministrar un tratamiento a largo plazo; quizás a perpetuidad. Son soluciones que requieren grandes extensiones de tierra, lo cual es una ventaja en esta región dado que hay zonas muy extensas que se han vuelto inhabitables. La combinación propuesta de lagunas, pantanos y balsas de infiltración sería un aporte muy atractivo a estas áreas dañadas. Con el tiempo, surgiría un nuevo ecosistema, habitado por una flora y una fauna adaptadas a las nuevas condiciones.

Lago Agrio, de crecimiento irregular y carente de planificación, sufre la presencia de depresiones y surcos de erosión. Los alumnos proponen la creación de zanjas y jardines de lluvia que no dejen que el agua se acumule sobre superficies impermeables, senderos, caminos y bajantes, permitiendo a la vez que la lluvia sature el suelo. En los jardines de lluvia se plantarían especies nativas de bajo mantenimiento con sistemas de raíces apropiados, que filtren el agua antes de que ésta llegue al acuífero. Estos jardines reducirían en una tercera parte la cantidad de contaminación que llegaría a los arroyos y riachuelos. Se consideró a las granjas de energía solar y los techos con paneles solares elementos cruciales para la producción de energía alternativa, así como la utilización de turbinas sumergidas en el río. Este hincapié en el río dirigiría la atención de la ciudad hacia este importante recurso natural no sólo como fuente de energía, sino también como sistema de transporte que necesita de grandes mejorías y como área de recreación para los residentes.

El plan maestro urbano crea un sistema extensivo de agricultura urbana. Reintroduce las técnicas agrícolas indígenas y la cría de animales en las granjas en los márgenes de la ciudad; y usa árboles y arbustos nativos para reemplazar las plantas exóticas en las calles, plazas y otros espacios públicos abiertos. El plan también propone el cultivo de bambú con fines comerciales. El bambú es un material útil, sustentable y de rápida regeneración, que puede emplearse tanto en la construcción como en revestimientos para suelos.

Los alumnos plantearon la necesidad de mejorar los recursos educativos en todos los niveles; propusieron programas de educación primaria y secundaria, y la expansión de la oferta educativa a niveles superiores. Su plan ubica una universidad sobre el curso del río, a fin de que actúe como parque lineal que sea a la vez un lugar para el esparcimiento, el tratamiento de aguas y el estudio de los recursos naturales. De hecho, el plan para esta institución incluye un centro de capacitación multidisciplinario, orientado al manejo de los recursos comerciales y naturales, que sirva como centro de educación y formación de proyectos locales, comunitarios o regionales a mayor escala.

Si bien estas soluciones fueron diseñadas específicamente para poner freno a la explotación de los recursos y para reparar las áreas deterioradas, están llamadas a tener un profundo impacto visual, ecológico y socioeconómico en la fisonomía de Lago Agrio. La reparación de sistemas ecológicos dañados es una idea fácil de entender. Sin embargo, la conservación es un concepto más complejo, para estudiantes y profesionales por igual, puesto que no sólo tiene que ver con reparar los daños causados en el pasado, sino también con imponer restricciones en el presente y en el futuro. En aquellos lugares en que las principales necesidades de conservación son de naturaleza organizativa y educativa, las implicancias y el valor de estas medidas son particularmente difíciles de comprender.

Una estrategia de conservación común es hacer de la selva una "reserva" para uso recreativo. Pero este enfoque no puede evitar la contaminación del aire, el agua y el suelo, ni aquella que es producto del polvo y de los ruidos, y que destruye el hábitat y las vidas de plantas y animales. El espacio al aire libre con fines recreativos está pensado para uso humano y para lograr impacto visual, no para la conservación de los recursos. Incluso el turismo ecológico daña severamente la selva, desde la caza furtiva y la tala hasta la erosión provocada por las lanchas a motor que además perjudican a las aves que nidifican a baja altura. La apertura de nuevos senderos, para satisfacer la sed de novedades de los ecoturistas, llevan a graves pérdidas de hábitats. Además, es necesario desarrollar las zonas aledanas a la reserva para albergar a la gran cantidad de visitantes que llegan en temporada alta, convirtiendo la selva en un ecosistema aislado, minando la integridad de la reserva y gradualmente destruyendo por completo el área. El turismo ecológico, incluso cuando se lo lleva a cabo de manera cuidadosa, perturba a las culturas nativas, al crear falsas expectativas de ocio y evasión. Para que la conservación sea efectiva, debe ponerse en práctica un programa integrador que incluya todas las categorías del espacio abierto, desde la infraestructura urbana y la agricultura hasta los jardines, parques y reservas naturales, y no simplemente áreas verdes divididas en porciones.

No diseñamos paisajes. Un paisaje es el producto de un sinfín de acciones, grandes y pequeñas, que se llevan a cabo individual y colectivamente –refleja todos los procesos que a nivel global tienen lugar en él. Todo paisaje es un flujo constante de fuerzas ecológicas, sociales y económicas. Cuando las especies humanas y no humanas conviven en relativa armonía, un paisaje resulta "natural". Cuando reúne las distintas condiciones necesarias para la vida de todos, puede funcionar sin violencia, coerción, altos niveles de mortalidad o desorganización. Lograr semejante coexistencia en Nueva Loja exigirá cambiar de paradigma, de la explotación y la extracción a la reconciliación. Sólo cuando los profesionales que trabajan con el territorio dejen de tratar de separar cultura de naturaleza y busquen la integración, el diseño del territorio va a cambiar. Cuando eso ocurra, el territorio mismo reflejará esos cambios. Sin embargo, no basta con que el arquitecto, el urbanista o el paisajista diseñen un programa coherente. Hay gigantescos problemas que resolver. Antes de que se implemente ningún plan en concreto, será necesario atender y conciliar los numerosísimos problemas, a veces en conflicto unos con otros, que plantea la tierra. Un objetivo difícil.

VER IMÁGENES, PÁGINA 37.

EL FIN DE LA ERA PETROLERA YA ESTÁ AQUÍ

Por **OSVALDO PALADINES ZURITA**

Hace unos pocos meses, en una histórica decisión, Rafael Correa, el presidente electo de Ecuador, decidió que ni una sola gota de petróleo saldrá del subsuelo ecuatoriano si se encuentra en una zona protegida, reserva natural o parque nacional de la cuenca amazónica ecuatoriana. Como si esto no fuera suficiente, el gobierno también ha dictado una serie de nuevas normas para controlar la extracción de minerales preciosos, cuyo proceso durante décadas ha causado inmensa contaminación de ríos y tierra con mercurio y otros metales pesados. Con estas primeras reglas de control, se ha puesto por primera vez a la minería bajo escrutinio en este país.

Este giro, aparte de dar cuenta de una nueva conciencia medioambiental mucho más severa y estricta (algo no muy popular entre los defensores de la política de libre mercado imperante en casi todo el continente sudamericano), nos coloca en una disyuntiva que afecta tanto a arquitectos como planificadores urbanos. Aparentemente, el temido fin de la Era del Petróleo ha comenzado en Ecuador. Al menos en lo que se refiere a su explotación indiscriminada, que ha sido la característica de las ultimas tres décadas.

Cuando comenzamos a planificar el Taller de diseño e investigación conjunta con nuestros amigos del City College de Nueva York, optimistamente estimamos un plazo de 25 años para que los recursos petroleros del Ecuador se agotaran. Al parecer nos equivocamos por un amplio margen. Aducimos que las ciudades petroleras de la Amazonía tendrían tiempo suficiente para proyectar su futuro, y ajustar sus políticas de planificación antes de que la riqueza del oro negro terminara. El dilema de qué hacer con estos campamentos convertidos en ciudades parecía lejano. Pero los acontecimientos han precipitado tal cambio y nuestra experiencia ha adquirido resonancia primordial.

Desde un principio, el reto académico era fascinante. Visitar y conocer de primera mano la realidad de una ciudad particular: Lago Agrio o Nueva Loja, que por su cualidad fronteriza además poseía una serie de condicionantes únicas, como centro de distribución comercial, añadido a ésto sus relaciones innegables con la guerrilla colombiana y su estatus de asentamiento urbano de crecimiento rápido, sostenido y muy poco planificado. Analizar las políticas de crecimiento urbanas, la constante aniquilación del suelo selvático y el potencial de Nueva Loja como ejemplo tipológico de ciudad post-petrolera eran aspectos dignos no de uno, sino de varios talleres de colaboración.
Nos pareció que el aporte de una mirada externa de un grupo de interesados y curiosos colegas de diversos orígenes, en conjunto con ciertas autoridades civiles y un grupo de decididos arquitectos de Nueva Loja, nos permitiría estudiar, analizar y finalmente proponer unas primeras ideas sobre como debería ser el crecimiento de estas ciudades, históricamente aleatorias en su "planificación"; improvisadas en sus políticas de desarrollo humano; y reductos de violencia y olvido por parte del gobierno de turno. Ahora el problema es inminente. Está a las puertas de nuestras inquietudes y posiblemente no tendremos mucho tiempo para reconvertir costumbres, ideologías y prejuicios de planificación urbana.

Ecuador navega en una modernidad que se niega a desaparecer; y esto sucede en todos los ámbitos del diseño. Está tan arraigada la modernidad del siglo XX que pocos se dieron cuenta de que la posmodernidad con su carácter de llave de acceso, llegó y pasó. Este es un país anquilosado en las prácticas socializantes del urbanismo de los años 60-70, y todos sufrimos sin una ligera esperanza de cambio estas condiciones ciudadanas.

La tarea de presentar nuevas visiones de planificación a las autoridades fue un reto que nos impusimos desde el principio, y luego de un par de jornadas pudimos interpretar y retroalimentar el Taller con los anhelos y propuestas del grupo de arquitectos a cargo de la renovación urbana del centro de la ciudad.

Pero quizás la experiencia más gratificante fue la visita a la estación experimental que posee la Universidad Católica, muy adentro en la selva ecuatoriana, en los límites del Parque Nacional Yasuní. Y justo ahí, donde la selva aún persiste en una aparente virginidad solapada, pudimos encontrar campamentos de extracción petrolera, que definitivamente no deberían estar ahí.

El contraste entre ese escenario de explotación humana y la dignidad de la naturaleza es tan escalofriante que a la mayoría de nosotros, profesores y alumnos, nos despertó a una realidad desde la que no hay forma de volver atrás. Se arraigaron en nuestros cerebros con fuerza aquellas premisas que nos dictaminan entrar en una constante práctica de conservación ambiental, en todos los niveles del diseño y de la vida diaria.

Entre las experiencias más impactantes y vívidas de estas jornadas, recuerdo aquella en que compartimos una visita a una comunidad Huaorani. Alterados y un tanto abrumados por el choque cultural, observamos sus decadentes rituales ancestrales ya casi evaporados por la mezcla con costumbres occidentales, fuimos regalados con unos cánticos ancestrales y tratando de darles algo recíprocamente, se entonó Noche de paz, que resonó extraña, pero sincera dentro de la gran choza de paja para turistas.

La experiencia académica se completó con animadas jornadas de evaluación conjunta en las que expusimos nuestras propuestas y conocimos las que tan amablemente y con mucha dedicación habían elaborado los alumnos del City College. El intercambio fue enriquecedor y nos permitió reconocer muchas de las directrices esenciales que podrían alimentar la futura planificación de las ciudades post-petroleras. Despertamos y develamos algunas certezas, que es más de lo que un taller puede pedir, descubrimos el verdadero sentido de sinchi sacha (poder de la selva) y la capacidad que tiene el macizo amazónico de permear todas las actividades de la vida y de la ciudad. Nos alejamos de prejuicios y sentimos como cierto aquello que dice Van der Laan, en su famosa comparación de la casa con una sandalia: "En el caso de la casa, no es sólo una cuestión del encuentro entre nuestros pies y el suelo, sino el encuentro entre todo nuestro ser y el total del entorno natural. Los términos en los cuales se da esta armonía entre los dos, no son ya el de un trozo de suelo blando que llevamos bajo nuestros pies, sino el de un pedazo de espacio habitable que separamos del entorno natural por medio de muros... Mientras la sandalia está sujeta a nuestro pie para completar el cuerpo y permite tolerar el duro suelo, la casa debería ser vista como una adición a la naturaleza, por medio de la cual el espacio natural es completado y hecho habitable para nosotros"... (1)

Y así los alumnos del taller diseñaron sus propuestas de vivienda sustentable para la Amazonía. Los proyectos aquí presentados son el resultado de éstas y otras consideraciones alrededor del papel que juega el ser humano en entornos naturales fuertemente amenazados. Las conclusiones y resultados no se verán al corto plazo, lamentablemente. Habrá que esperar a que la próxima generación de arquitectos ecuatorianos, decididamente se atreva a dar el gran paso hacia la verdadera planificación sustentable, y con vehemencia salve del exterminio abusivo y descontrolado a todo ese gran recurso amazónico, que eventualmente, salvará al resto de la tierra.

[1] Dom Van der Laan (SJ), Naturaleza y Arquitectura, tomado del *El lugar de la arquitectura*, Ediciones ARQ, Editor y traductor: Alejandro Aravena Mori.

CRONOGRAMA VER GRÁFICO, PÁGINA 40

GEOGRAFÍA VER IMÁGENES Y GRÁFICOS, PÁGINAS 41 a 43.

EL VIAJE

Por **HOLLY KALLMAN Y ROBERTA KORCZ**

Comenzamos nuestro viaje con el aire cristalino de Quito y de los Andes. Urbana y Colonial, Quito tiene una historia maravillosa, con facciones católicas enfrentadas, autobuses de tránsito rápido y magníficas vistas y monumentos. Nos resulta difícil creer que es una ciudad "insegura". Somos de Nueva York y somos chicas duras. ¡Ja!

Un paisaje increíble se abre debajo de nosotros. Esta ruta es sumamente precaria: aquí no hay armadura urbana. Por la ventanilla se nos ofrece un corte seccional del paisaje. Las alturas volcánicas van bajando hasta encontrarse con la arcilla roja de los rápidos ríos. Los autos pasan a centímetros de nuestro autobús, que avanza a toda velocidad. Oímos las ruedas del autobús golpear algo metálico mientras cruzamos un puente que se eleva sobre las aguas procelosas de un río. A nuestro lado se divisa siempre la burda estructura metálica del oleoducto, que viborea silenciosamente entre la densa y colorida vegetación. La existencia de esta ruta se debe al oleoducto. Texaco construyó las dos cosas juntas en 1972, abriendo el Amazonas para nosotros, para cualquiera.

Llegamos al río Napo y lo cruzamos en un bote, sintiendo finalmente la furiosa corriente. El autobús cruza en otra embarcación. Nos auxilian manos hábiles y capaces; ésta es una tierra hábil y capaz.

Nueva Loja es una ciudad en toda regla. Comercial y competitiva, los mercados son bulliciosos y están bien surtidos. Pero lo urbano a lo que estoy acostumbrada, acumulado capa sobre capa a lo largo del tiempo, no es lo que encuentro aquí. Hay apenas una única capa, delgada y frágil como la capa vegetal de la selva tropical, e igualmente difícil de hacer crecer y echar raíces. Inundado de vívidos colores, el Amazonas es una explosión de áspera y salvaje belleza.

VER IMAGENES, PÁGINA 44.

LA CIUDAD

Por **HOLLY KALLMAN Y ROBERTA KORCZ**

Con el descubrimiento del petróleo en 1967, Nueva Loja se convirtió en una entidad municipal. La infraestructura petrolera determinó el trazado de la nueva ciudad. Fijó el trazado de las calles y la distribución de la gente. también provocó la destrucción de la selva tropical. Hoy en día, que la población humana está llamada a crecer exponencialmente a lo largo del próximo cuarto de siglo, este patrón de organización de origen petrolero se arraigará aún más en la estructura de la ciudad.

En ese mismo periodo de 25 años, el petróleo se agotará y la infraestructura de la ciudad se volverá innecesaria. Si bien es posible imaginar un futuro post-petróleo a largo plazo para Nueva Loja, en el cual la huella de la industria petrolera desaparezca del paisaje; el suelo y las aguas estén libres de toxinas; la vida vegetal y animal regrese y la economía se diversifique; el pasado de la ciudad determinará ese futuro.

Nueva Loja, una ciudad de frontera formada predominantemente por migrantes y asentamientos informales, es bastante diferente de una ciudad latinoamericana típica. Su forma urbana lineal se concentra a lo largo de la calle principal, la Avenida Quito. Dinámica y urbana, la Avenida Quito se interrumpe abruptamente en el margen oriental de la ciudad, en una zona llamada "el petromuro" por su concentración de infraestructura petrolera.

En contraste con el patrón de desarrollo urbano tradicional de grilla colonial alrededor de un centro común, Nueva Loja se organiza en torno de una red fragmentada de edificios, parques, granjas y calles principales. Irónicamente, este trazado recuerda el propio tejido amazónico, que comprende selvas, sabanas, montes y planicies inundables.

Nueva Loja es el punto de encuentro de dos paisajes en apariencia contradictorios: el tejido urbano que se extiende hacia fuera y la selva tropical que es empujada más allá de la periferia. Este patrón tiene algunas excepciones, y se pliega y superpone allí donde los límites entre los dos sistemas son más fluidos.

VER IMAGENES, PÁGINA 45.

LA SELVA

Por **GARETH MAHON**

Los ecoturistas que tengan pensado partir desde Quito, la capital de Ecuador, con destino al Oriente ecuatoriano y a la cuenca amazónica, sin duda alguna leerán en los folletos que Nueva Loja es la puerta de entrada de la selva y el punto de partida de su travesía amazónica. Es verdad que Nueva Loja, en virtud de su ubicación e infraestructura, es un punto de partida natural para una expedición por la reserva del Cuyabeno o el Parque Nacional Yasuní, pero a la hora de comenzar a pensar una propuesta de diseño para el futuro de esta ciudad selvática es preciso examinar en mayor profundidad nuestra idea de la selva, y cómo podemos relacionarla con un entorno urbano contemporáneo.

La "selva" ocupa casi el seis por ciento de la superficie total de la Tierra. En términos climáticos y geográficos suele definírsela como un bioma, la selva tropical, que puede encontrarse en las regiones ecuatoriales de África, Asia, América del Sur y América Central. Las selvas son zonas de extrema biodiversidad, y albergan más de la mitad de las especies vegetales y animales del planeta. El Parque Nacional Yasuní, en Ecuador, ha sido designado el lugar más biodiverso de la Tierra, y la selva amazónica produce el veinte por ciento del oxígeno mundial. Estos hechos, junto con el dato de que se tala 0,6 hectáreas de selva por segundo, nos ayudan a comprender mejor su significación actual. Pero la idea de la selva se ha venido formando desde mucho antes de que las estadísticas modernas estuvieran disponibles, y a menudo se ha visto determinada por la yuxtaposición de dos creencias o experiencias opuestas, que juntas dan origen a la idea de lugar que hoy reconocemos. Para los más de 200.000 pueblos indígenas de la selva tropical amazónica, ésta ha sido siempre un lugar que merecía respeto y reverencia no sólo porque les brindaba alimento y protección sino por los peligros a los cuales los exponía. Ante los visitantes, ya sean los conquistadores, los científicos, los empresarios, los misioneros o los turistas, la selva se ha presentado bajo numerosas apariencias: un reservorio de oro y recursos naturales que había que explotar, un lugar pagano que era necesario redimir, o una maravilla de la naturaleza que había que explorar y fotografiar antes de que desapareciera.

En los primeros años del siglo XIX, el naturalista y explorador alemán Alexander von Humboldt recorrió gran parte de América Central, y viajó por Ecuador y Perú. Sus vívidas descripciones de los paisajes, plantas y animales fueron recibidas calurosamente en Europa y Norteamérica por los seguidores del por entonces novedoso movimiento romántico. A lo largo de las décadas que siguieron, los estadounidenses en especial comenzarían a obsesionarse con el paisaje como un medio para conectarse con un ser superior. Mientras los Estados Unidos dirigían la mirada hacia el paisaje árido y salvaje del Oeste, muchísimos artistas de aquella época, incluyendo al pintor de la Escuela del río Hudson Frederic Edwin Church, viajaron a Sudamérica para plasmar en sus telas las escenas selváticas descriptas en tan vivo detalle por von Humboldt. Estas descripciones, cargadas de referencias a lo sublime, comenzaron a formar una de las ideas de la selva que aún conservan mayor vigencia. Esta visión romántica, a la que se sumaban ideas trascendentalistas, colocaba al hombre y a Dios firmemente en el paisaje. Con la desaparición de tantas de aquellas primitivas tierras salvajes en los Estados Unidos, la antorcha parecía haber pasado a la selva, en tanto paisaje espiritual por excelencia.

En contraste, los acontecimientos que comenzaron a desarrollarse más de trescientos años antes de la expedición de von Humboldt, con la llegada de los conquistadores españoles a Sudamérica, pusieron en juego una dinámica muy diferente. Los conquistadores venían en busca de oro y tesoros, a fin de consolidar la posición de España como la superpotencia del siglo XVI. También venían a traer el cristianismo a tierras paganas. Sus métodos eran brutales, y trajeron el genocidio y la destrucción de las sociedades incaica y azteca. Para justificar sus acciones, describían la selva y sus habitantes como salvajes alineados con el demonio. Cuando esas historias llegaron a Europa, se formó una mala imagen de la selva, que comenzó a ser vista como un lugar temible. Los exploradores europeos que estuvieron en África y en Asia ayudaron a perpetuar una visión peyorativa de los nativos y su entorno, contando historias de canibalismo. Este mito ha sido recogido y estetizado por la cultura popular, la literatura y el cine a lo largo de todo el siglo pasado, haciendo de la selva un escenario para la lucha entre el Bien y el Mal, y un santuario para el lado oscuro de la mente humana.

Reconciliar las representaciones enfrentadas de la selva, que hacen de ella un lugar ora paradisíaco ora infernal, ha generado una polémica que se extiende a lo largo de gran parte de los últimos dos siglos, y que aún continúa. En cualquier caso, debe quedar claro que una y otra no se excluyen entre sí, y que la jungla salvaje y la selva virgen son una misma cosa. La película más popular de todos los tiempos, Avatar, se ocupa directamente de este tema. En un escenario exuberante, se plantea una batalla entre los indígenas y los visitantes, los inocentes y los corruptos. En algún momento, los espectadores deberán tomar partido, pero ¿cómo evitar querer a los na'vi? El artista contemporáneo Walton Ford estudia esta dialéctica con gran éxito en sus cuadros de grandes dimensiones. Ford pinta animales salvajes en ambientes naturales. Si se los mira con atención, se intuye el sufrimiento y el dolor que emanan animales y hábitat. La verdad es que la selva es un paisaje complejo formado por sistemas superpuestos. Y para bien o para mal, muchos de estos sistemas son controlados o influenciados por hombres modernos o indígenas, a fin de que se adapten a nuestras necesidades siempre cambiantes. William Cronon, el historiador del medio ambiente, afirma en *Uncommon Ground* que cuando pensamos en la naturaleza y en la jungla "nos miramos en el espejo que [la selva] nos sostiene [y] nos es muy fácil imaginar que lo que estamos contemplando es la Naturaleza cuando en realidad lo que vemos es la imagen de nuestros propios anhelos y deseos no atendidos". La selva debe cargar con esto. Para algunos sigue siendo una abundante reserva de recursos naturales a explotar. Para otros será siempre el emblema del movimiento ambientalista y una metáfora de todo lo verde. O quizá seguirá siendo el último territorio salvaje, y nuestro punto de contacto más cercano con lo sublime. Para muchos es su hogar y su medio de vida. Una ciudad moderna en medio de la selva debe satisfacer todas estas necesidades y compartir la carga de la selva.

VER IMÁGENES, PÁGINA 47.

URBANISMO PREDATORIO: SOBRE EL NACIMIENTO Y CRECIMIENTO DE NUEVA LOJA

Por **ANA MARÍA DURÁN CALISTO**

"Quirino, dios de la producción, o Hermes, que preside los intercambios, pueden contener la violencia más eficazmente a veces que Júpiter [dios de las leyes y de lo sagrado] o Marte [dios de la guerra] y, para conseguirlo, utilizan los mismos procedimientos que éste último".

Michel Serres, El Contrato Natural

Aquéllos de ustedes que hayan visto la película "Los dioses deben estar locos" (Jamie Uys, 1980) probablemente recuerden la escena en la cual una botella de vidrio de Coca-Cola aterriza en medio del desierto de Kalahari. La historia de Nueva Loja sigue una trama análoga, pero lo que aterrizó no fue una botella de Coca-Cola, sino un avión ligero de Texaco; y el territorio no fue el desierto de Kalahari en África meridional, sino las márgenes noroccidentales de la selva amazónica, en América del Sur. ¿Y los personajes? No los Ju/hoansi del desierto, sino los Kichwas y Cofanes de la selva tropical. El factor común en ambas historias – si bien la primera es ficticia y la segunda es real –es la súbita presencia de un elemento foráneo que aterriza en un territorio indígena para alterar por siempre la vida de sus comunidades. Conforme escribo, otro grupo, el de los Huaorani, los famosos hacedores de tsantas (cabezas encogidas), que entraron en contacto con el mundo occidental en la década de los 50, encaran un dilema similar conforme el subsuelo de su territorio en el Parque Nacional Yasuní – reserva de la biósfera y una de las mayores reservas de petróleo de Ecuador– se negocia para intercambiar en el mercado internacional la conservación de la selva por créditos de carbono y otros "servicios medioambientales", bajo una política que propone mantener el petróleo bajo tierra: la Iniciativa ITT (Ishpingo-Tiputini-Tambococha). La meta final de este proyecto es evitar que esta tierra y sus pueblos reproduzcan el patrón de subdesarrollo que inició con Nueva Loja y continuó con otros asentamientos petroleros en la foresta tropical.

Nueva Loja es un pueblo innatural, y utilizo el término "innatural" desde un punto de vista urbano, no medioambiental. No nació de un asentamiento indígena que crece y prospera (los habitantes autóctonos de la Amazonía son –o fueron–, en su mayoría, nómadas o semi-nómadas). Tampoco fue un implante colonial con su estructura ósea en forma de cuadrícula, cuyas adiposidades crecen conforme se llenan las cuadras que rodean a la plaza central, con su Iglesia Católica y su gobierno municipal, en consonancia con las Leyes de Indias que dictaminaron el primero y más impresionante proceso de urbanización sistemática de las Américas. No nació del orden de las Misiones ni se desarrolló a partir de su patrón rural de hacienda agrícola. Tampoco fue el crecimiento espontáneo de las fuerzas comerciales que colisionan en las intersecciones principales de un urbanismo vehicular o fluvial. No es un puerto fluvial terciario de la época del boom del caucho que fue reactivado en la era moderna, ni fue jamás una company town. El corazón de Nueva Loja es un pozo petrolero; este pueblo es el hijo bastardo de las ciudades automovilísticas y nació en uno de los muchos ecosistemas que las sostienen –simplemente surgió. Un punto y una línea fueron su cuna, el mecanismo de su origen. Primero llegó el avión (a finales de los 50), luego llegaron las líneas de prospección, luego los puntos de los pozos petroleros que fueron interconectándose y ramificándose conforme se multiplicaban. Esta estructura lineal, una flecha abriéndose paso en la frondosidad de la selva, se vinculó por medio de un camino al asentamiento que originalmente fue campamento petrolero para convertirse luego en boom town. Una versión más "natural" de asentamiento se consolidó en las márgenes del río Aguarico, en una suerte de brazo que se abre paso hasta el agua para respirar. Como anunció la llegada pionera del avión, los pozos petroleros traerían consigo una pista de aterrizaje, carreteras y oleoductos: el Sistema Oleoducto TransEcuatoriano (SOTE) se construyó en 1972. Su capacidad de carga fue incrementada en el año 2003, cuando se inauguró el Oleoducto de Crudos Pesados (OCP). Ambos vinculan a Nueva Loja con Esmeraldas, un puerto en el Océano Pacífico, luego de remontar la Cordillera Andina. Podría argumentarse que un asentamiento secundario se instaló en la fuente de agua, otro principal en la fuente petrolera, y que la infraestructura de extracción proveyó el soporte para que se desencadene una colonización entrópica.

Si tratamos de forzar a Nueva Loja dentro una tipología urbana existente, no encaja, provoca un impulso taxonómico, deseosa de un nombre propio, una genealogía, conforme sus descendientes proliferan a lo largo y ancho de la Amazonía ecuatoriana y más allá de sus fronteras: ¿zona informal de extracción? ¿Asentamiento entrópico? Hernán Orbea Travez, ex Decano de la Facultad de Arquitectura, Diseño y Artes de la Pontificia Universidad Católica del Ecuador, la llama "urbanismo predatorio". Escogí este nombre preciso y decidor para el título de este corto ensayo, porque captura la esencia de habitantes y asentamiento. La mayoría de ciudadanos de Nueva Loja llegaron allí para irse: el pueblo es, o era, un pasaje hacia una vida mejor y más próspera, en alguna otra parte. Los ingenieros de minas y petróleo (generalmente hombres) se mudan temporalmente a Nueva Loja, desde Quito o el extranjero, con miras a regresar a sus lugares de origen; los trabajadores de las petroleras migran en bandadas desde diversas provincias atraídos por los jugosos salarios de las compañías petroleras; prostitutas migran al pueblo con la esperanza de llevarse una tajada de la recién descubierta riqueza; los desplazados por la violencia de Colombia construyen refugios temporales en sus periferias, esperando poder –un día– regresar a casa; comerciantes llegan a la zona para abrir tiendas de licores, supermercados, restaurantes y todo tipo de local de entretenimiento; narcotraficantes, paramilitares y guerrilleros cruzan la frontera para descansar, divertirse o quedarse; madereros vienen y van con sus sierras eléctricas y sus camiones rebosantes o vacíos; y los pocos que llegaron para quedarse se dedican a la siembra de cultivos comerciales o a la ganadería (muchos de ellos motivados por la Ley de Reforma Agraria y colonización de 1964), desplazándose cuando la tierra deja de ser productiva. El sector informal de Nueva Loja también constituye una fuerza comercial vibrante que sub-emplea a pobladores atraídos por la misma promesa de fortuna.

VER GRÁFICOS, PÁGINAS 50, 51.

Aquéllos que han decidido quedarse en Nueva Loja quizás hayan apostado por un lugar que vale la pena, puesto que a pesar de sus evidentes problemas (o gracias a ellos), se ubica en el corazón de un juicio que está destinado a transformar las leyes medioambientales y las relaciones del comercio internacional para siempre. Un grupo de aproximadamente 30.000 indígenas de la Amazonía ecuatoriana tuvo el coraje de enfrentar al gigante corporativo Texaco/Chevron, y demandar que limpie el desastre medioambiental que dejó cuando abandonó el país a inicios de los 90. Es en el asentamiento sujeto de este ensayo –la perdida e invisible Nueva Loja– donde "se está fraguando un precedente que forzará a las compañías que operan en el mundo en vías de desarrollo a cumplir con los mismos estándares anti-polución que se exigen en el mundo industrializado". Tanto la Iniciativa ITT de dejar el petróleo bajo el suelo, como el juicio en contra de Texaco/Chevron, constituyen un intento por desarrollar lo que Michel Serres ha denominado "contrato natural". La negligencia nacional y transnacional, lo que podría resumirse, en palabras de Serres, como "violencia objetiva" (la violencia causada por la crudeza de un razonamiento exclusivamente financiero) puede tener efectos sociales y medioambientales devastadores, equivalentes, en muchos casos, a los de una guerra no declarada. Hoy por hoy, no existe una ley internacional que regule estos encuentros. Gracias a Nueva Loja, quizás esta condición cambie en el futuro.

DEMOGRAFÍA

VER GRÁFICOS, PÁGINAS 56, 57.

ECONOMÍA

Por **GARETH MAHON**

UNA ECONOMÍA CAMBIANTE

Para 2025, Nueva Loja dejará de ser un centro de producción petrolera en Ecuador. Los pozos de la región se habrán agotado, la industria se habrá trasladado a otra parte y Nueva Loja deberá arreglárselas en una nueva era post-petróleo.

Una ciudad que nunca ha conocido una vida sin petróleo deberá enfrentarse a una nueva serie de desafíos. Las clases acomodadas, ligadas al petróleo, desaparecerán. Los emprendimientos locales creados para satisfacer la demanda de las empresas petroleras y sus empleados deberán buscar nuevos mercados. Algunos seguirán al dinero del petróleo. Por otra parte, mientras que la vieja economía favorecía el consumo de productos básicos importados por sobre los de producción local, aquellos se volverán prohibitivamente caros.

EL CAMINO HACIA DELANTE

La ciudad del futuro deberá interesarse tanto por el diseño de su economía como por el de sus calles, parques y viviendas. Debemos pensar cómo los actuales sectores económicos impactarán en la economía del mañana. La nueva economía necesitará de un marco que le permita desarrollarse de manera sustentable, con un crecimiento que venga desde el interior. Debe respetar el medio ambiente y fomentar el bienestar de todos los ciudadanos de Nueva Loja. Los nuevos sectores económicos deberán cumplir los requisitos de una sociedad en proceso de cambio y todos los nuevos sectores, ya sean microemprendimientos caseros o industrias ya existentes modificadas, deberán crecer de manera simbiótica a nivel de la región, de la ciudad y del barrio, así como a través del tiempo.

Debido a su ubicación en la selva, su clima, su suelo, su hidrología, sus recursos renovables y su siempre creciente población, Nueva Loja es un lugar extraordinario. Con un conjunto de principios básicos y un marco de apoyo sólido, la ciudad podría florecer y convertirse en un ejemplo para otras comunidades que enfrenten dificultares similares.

PRINCIPIOS PARA UNA ECONOMÍA SUSTENTABLE

Autosustentable: El crecimiento económico debe provenir del interior de la región. La industria y los consumidores deben comprar y vender artículos producidos en la región, sin necesidad de métodos proteccionistas ni una merma en la calidad de los productos.

Ambientalmente sustentable: Toda nueva actividad económica deberá respetar el medio ambiente. Será necesario evaluar toda actividad existente, y modificarla a fin de que cumpla con las nuevas normas, minimizando así el impacto ecológico.

Sustentable en términos de calidad de vida: Toda nueva actividad económica deberá respetar el comercio justo, los derechos de los trabajadores y un salario familiar justo.

ESTRUCTURA DE APOYO

Para alimentar los sectores económicos emergentes, es necesario establecer una estructura de sistemas y prácticas de apoyo. Una serie de servicios debe ponerse a disposición de las empresas, nuevas o existentes, a fin de ofrecerles asesoramiento acerca de las "mejores prácticas", tanto en lo financiero como en lo ambiental. Este apoyo debe asumir varias formas, incluyendo educación y capacitación, créditos y programas de microcrédito, infraestructura mejorada y programas de mercadeo regional. A su vez, todo esto debe ser instrumentado por medio de iniciativas gubernamentales, programas de asistencia internacional y una red de organizaciones no gubernamentales (ONGs).

LA MEDIDA DEL ÉXITO

La nueva economía debe incluir un sistema para medir los éxitos y fracasos. Se impone la necesidad de nuevos indicadores económicos integrales que den cuenta del bienestar de los ciudadanos y del medio ambientes además de informar acerca del estado de la economía. Se necesita de un indicador genuino del progreso para informar a las empresas ya existentes y para fomentar nuevos emprendimientos sustentables. En el futuro, cualquier lectura económica deberá prestar atención no sólo al capital financiero sino al capital natural y al humano.

ECONOMÍA: PETRÓLEO

La economía ecuatoriana se transformó en 1964 cuando el país abrió sus reservas petroleras a la exploración por parte de empresas multinacionales. Se desencadenó una serie de eventos que convirtió a Ecuador en el quinto mayor productor de petróleo de Sudamérica. Actualmente, la producción supera los 500.000 barriles por día. Sin embargo, con la inversión extranjera llegó la deuda externa, que hizo de Ecuador, per cápita, el país más endeudado de Sudamérica. En 2000, la baja en el precio del petróleo, a la que se sumó una rápida inflación, llevó al gobierno a reemplazar la moneda nacional por el dólar estadounidense.

Más del 40% de los ingresos por exportación del país provienen del petróleo, que a su vez financian más del treinta por ciento del presupuesto del gobierno central. Sin embargo, Nueva Loja, a pesar de ser el motor de la industria petrolera nacional, sigue siendo una de las zonas más pobres de Ecuador. Si bien en lo que respecta al empleo las cifras de la región son poco claras, hay indicios que permiten inferir que los trabajadores del petróleo no son nativos de la zona sino que son traídos en un régimen rotativo. Gran parte del petróleo que proviene de esta región se encuentra actualmente bajo control de la compañía estatal Petroecuador.

ECONOMÍA: AGRICULTURA

Ecuador es un país eminentemente agrícola; la región litoral y la andina son las más productivas. El sector aporta aproximadamente un 15% del producto interno bruto, y las exportaciones equivalen casi a siete veces la importaciones. Ecuador es el mayor exportador mundial de bananas, que aportan casi la mitad de las exportaciones. Camarones, café, cacao y flores aportan el resto.

Se estima que un 30% de la población trabaja en el sector agrícola; esta cifra trepa hasta el 50% en el Oriente ecuatoriano. La expansión urbana y el aumento de las prácticas agrícolas corporativas ponen en una situación particularmente difícil a los pequeños productores, mientras que los problemas relacionados con la posesión de la tierra y los títulos de propiedad son tan urgentes en Ecuador como en el resto de Sudamérica.

15% PIB
30% Población nacional
50% Población agrícola

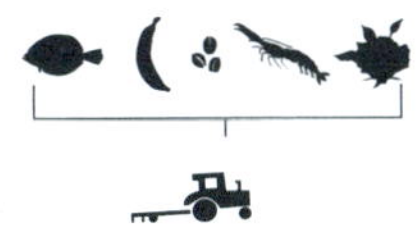

ECONOMÍA: ECONOMÍA INFORMAL

En Ecuador en general, y en Nueva Loja en particular, el trabajo informal equivale a un sector considerable de la economía. Las estadísticas nacionales ubican el desempleo en un 10% y el subempleo en un 50%; en Nueva Loja, la tasa oficial de desempleo es del 50%. Esta cifra quizá dé cuenta del nutrido y diverso sector informal que abarca comercio, servicios domésticos, jornaleros y microemprendimientos.

A pesar de su tamaño, el sector informal sigue estando desorganizado, por lo cual es vulnerable a la explotación; por otra parte, los bajos salarios y el trabajo infantil están a la orden del día. En 2006 el salario mínimo se estableció en US$ 166 por mes (el precio de la canasta familiar mensual se ubica en aproximadamente los US$ 440), y la mayoría de los empleados de los sectores formales ganaban más que eso. Sin embargo, existen informes que hablan de trabajadores informales del sector agrícola que ganaban sólo US$ 50 al mes.

Las prácticas informales son igualmente evidentes en lo que respecta a la propiedad de la tierra y a los métodos de construcción residencial. El dinero que envían al país los migrantes ecuatorianos residentes en España y los Estados Unidos constituye otro factor de la economía informal, que suele pasarse por alto.

ECONOMÍA: ECONOMÍA ILEGAL

Lago Agrio parece una ciudad de frontera y funciona como tal. A menos de veinticinco kilómetros de la frontera colombiana, lejos del ojo vigilante del gobierno central, posee una próspera economía ilegal. Conocido tradicionalmente como un lugar de descanso y entretenimiento para los rebeldes colombianos, también se ha convertido en la puerta de entrada de casi el 20% de las exportaciones colombianas de cocaína, así como de los productos químicos necesarios para preparar la droga una vez que ésta cruza la frontera. La dolarización de la moneda ha facilitado el lavado de dinero. El flujo y reflujo de acciones delictivas, como el robo de petróleo y los secuestros extorsivos, ha tenido como efecto secundario un incremento del empleo en las empresas privadas de seguridad. (La prostitución es legal en Ecuador, y por lo tanto no constituye un factor de la economía ilegal).

VER IMÁGENES Y GRÁFICOS, PÁGINAS 58, 59..

ES TIEMPO DE CAMBIAR

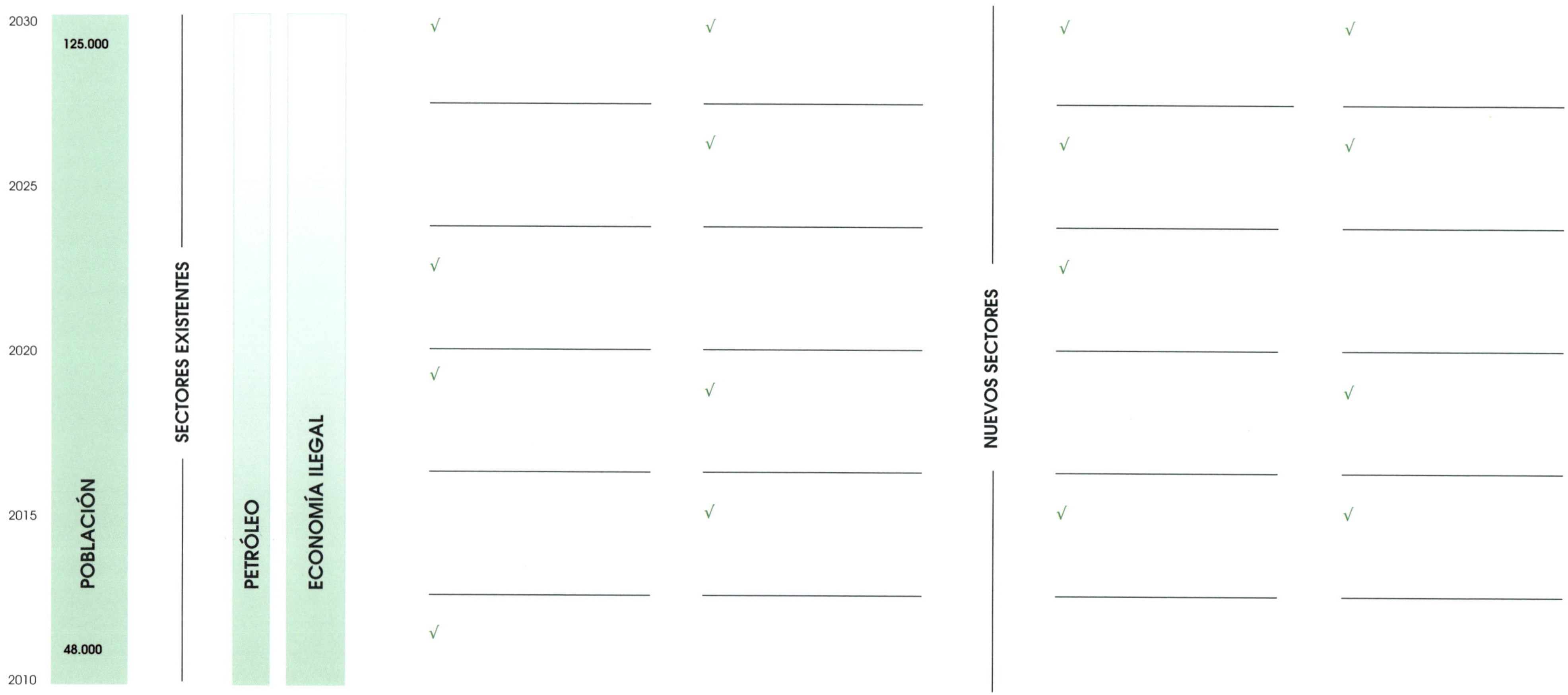

AGRICULTURA

La agricultura de exportación a gran escala continuará, pero deberán introducirse nuevas prácticas.

INFORMAL

La economía informal se fortalecerá y será reconocida.

CONSTRUCCIÓN

Se utilizarán nuevos materiales de producción local para la infraestructura municipal y residencial.

AGRICULTURA DOMÉSTICA

Impulsarán este sector nuevos métodos, cultivos y mercados.

SISTEMA DE APOYO	COMBUSTIBLES ALTERNATIVOS	BAMBÚ	EDUCACIÓN	TURISMO ECOLÓGICO
EDUCACIÓN Y CAPACITACIÓN	√	√	√	√
PATROCINIO DE ONGs	√	√		
INFRAESTRUCTURA			√	√
PROMOCIÓN				√
PROGRAMAS DE CRÉDITO			√	√
AYUDA AL DESARROLLO	√		√	
	El petróleo será reemplazado por tecnologías desarrolladas en la región.	El clima y los suelos resultan ideales para el cultivo de bambú y para la creación de una nueva industria en base a los productos manufacturados con ese material.	Nueva Loja se transformará en un centro de desarrollo sostenible a partir de la construcción de una universidad ecológica.	Ya constituye un sector emergente en Lago Agrio y continuará desarrollándose en base a principios sostenibles.

POLÍTICA

Por **JOHN HILL**

La política del Oriente ecuatoriano gira en torno a tres cuestiones fundamentales: el petróleo, la agricultura y la población indígena. Desde 1964, año en que Texaco llegó al país a buscar depósitos petrolíferos por invitación del gobierno ecuatoriano, se introdujeron reformas agrarias y se formaron las primeras federaciones indígenas; estas tres cuestiones han sido determinantes para la región, relacionándose entre sí con dificultad y a veces con violencia.

POLÍTICA: PETRÓLEO

Se ha extraído petróleo en Ecuador desde 1917. Sin embargo, recién después de 1964, cuando Texaco comenzó su exploración en el Oriente ecuatoriano,el petróleo se convirtió en un factor principal de la economía y la política del país. Anteriormente, la cuenca del Amazonas era un área inaccesible, transitable sólo por vía fluvial o a pie. Pero en los cinco años que siguieron al descubrimiento de petróleo en 1967, se construyó una red de caminos y oleoductos. El gobierno ecuatoriano se hizo cargo de los costos de la infraestructura que construyó Texaco empleando trabajadores locales escasamente remunerados.

En 1992, la petrolea nacional Petroecuador se hizo cargo de todas las operaciones. Si bien Texaco (actualmente Chevron) ha abandonado la región, una demanda colectiva presentada por los residentes de Lago Agrio contra la empresa por daños medioambientales sigue esperando resolución. Por su parte,

Chevron afirma que la responsabilidad es del gobierno ecuatoriano, por permitir el uso de prácticas deficientes en sus operaciones de perforación. Pase lo que pase con esta demanda, el gobierno ecuatoriano, determinado a construir una economía basada en la renta petrolera, sin duda alguna ha tenido que ver con el daño

infligido al medio ambiente.

POLÍTICA: AGRICULTURA

La Reforma Agraria implementada por Ecuador en 1964 definía la tierra como un recurso productivo. La agricultura y la ganadería fueron oficialmente consideradas los dos usos principales de la tierra en el Oriente ecuatoriano (por lo general, se la destinaba a monocultivos y luego se la empleaba como terreno de pastoreo). Las prácticas indígenas que cuidan la selva no se definen como agricultura porque no se las considera "productivas". Luego del descubrimiento del petróleo, llegaron agricultores migrantes, y comenzó el severo proceso de deforestación que continúa en la actualidad. La deforestación sigue siendo uno de los métodos para reclamar propiedad sobre la tierra, según la legislación en vigor.

POLÍTICA: PUEBLOS INDÍGENAS

La posición del gobierno en materia de tierra, petróleo y agricultura entra en conflicto con la de los pueblos indígenas. Mientras que el gobierno prioriza la explotación de la tierra, la población indígena insiste en su cuidado, a fin de asegurar la supervivencia de la tierra y la suya propia.

Desde que apareció la primera federación indígena en 1964, estas organizaciones se han multiplicado. En 1997, con el derrocamiento del presidente Abdalá Bucaram bajo presión de la CONAIE (Confederación de Nacionalidades Indígenas del Ecuador), la población indígena se convirtió en un actor fundamental en la toma de decisiones en materia política. Actualmente, los grupos indígenas suelen organizar protestas para expresar su descontento con las políticas gubernamentales en lo relativo al petróleo, la deforestación agrícola y la propiedad de la tierra. Ocasionalmente, se han producido disturbios, y los manifestantes han llegado a cortar rutas, dinamitar oleoductos e incluso asesinar.

El gobierno ecuatoriano ahora se encuentra en la incómoda posición de tener que balancear los intereses petroleros (internos y externos) con los de los agricultores y los pueblos indígenas, una tarea nada envidiable, pero necesaria para la supervivencia de la selva tropical, así como de todos los que dependen de ella.

POLÍTICA: LA FRONTERA

La ubicación de Nueva Loja, a sólo 18 kilómetros al sur de la frontera con Colombia, crea un contexto complicado y a veces violento para la ciudad y sus habitantes. Las características naturales de la zona: lo tupido de la selva, los numerosos ríos (incluyendo los ríos San Miguel y Putumayo, que circulan por los dos países) y la gran distancia respecto de zonas urbanas como Quito y Bogotá han facilitado el flujo de bienes, personas e incluso contaminantes aéreos de un lado de la frontera al otro. Desde 2003, Colombia, con la intención de reducir las actividades ilegales en su capital relacionadas con el tráfico de drogas, ha logrado empujarlas hacia la periferia, contra la frontera con Venezuela al noreste y con Ecuador al sur.

La insurgencia colombiana

Los actores principales de las actividades vinculadas con el narcotráfico en Colombia (fundamentalmente, de coca y amapola) son los movimientos insurgentes de izquierda, las FARC (Fuerzas Armadas Revolucionarias de Colombia) y el más pequeño ELN (Ejército de Liberación Nacional) y, del otro lado del espectro político, los grupos paramilitares de la AUC (Autodefensas Unidas de Colombia). Estas organizaciones necesitan de tierra, gente y armas para funcionar; las últimas dos son responsables de gran parte del tráfico ilegal a lo largo de la frontera entre Colombia y Ecuador. Los migrantes colombianos llegan a Ecuador buscando un refugio libre de insurgencia, mientras que los miembros de las organizaciones paramilitares cruzan la frontera para esconderse de las operaciones militares contra el narcoterrorismo. (A principios de la primavera de 2008, Colombia atacó un campamento en Ecuador, matando no sólo a uno de los principales comandantes de las FARC y a otros 20, sino también a un ecuatoriano). Al proteger a los insurgentes con el escudo de la neutralidad, ofreciendo un mercado dolarizado para el lavado de dinero y suministrando una fuente regular de armas que atraviesan la frontera, Ecuador contribuye de manera significativa a la actual inestabilidad colombiana.

La presencia de los Estados Unidos

Los Estados Unidos canalizan la asistencia a la región a través de dos estrategias diseñadas para combatir el narcotráfico y la insurgencia: el Plan Patriota y el Plan Colombia. Ambos intentan mantener a raya las actividades ilegales en el país y en sus zonas fronterizas, y ambos han sido ineficaces: ni el flujo de drogas ni la presencia de las FARC y del ELN han disminuido. Dado que ambos planes se centraban en el entrenamiento militar y policial y en el suministro de armas, su impacto social y económico ha sido insignificante. Los Estados Unidos han fracasado en encontrar una respuesta al flujo de personas, bienes y conflictos sociales a través de la frontera. Incluso ignora por completo la frontera, cuando rocía desde el aire cultivos ilegales, con lo cual peligrosos contaminantes aéreos llegan al norte de Ecuador.

La respuesta de Ecuador

El impacto de la insurgencia colombiana, el narcotráfico y otras actividades ilícitas en Ecuador se extiende mucho más allá de las zonas fronterizas. En varias ocasiones, el personal y la infraestructura de las empresas nacionales e internacionales ubicadas en las provincias del Oriente ecuatoriano, han sido víctimas de secuestro y vandalismo. Actualmente, las empresas petroleras gastan millones de dólares en seguridad. Y si bien Ecuador emplea a más de 10.000 soldados para vigilar los 600km de su frontera con Colombia, ésta sigue siendo permeable. En los campos de coca del norte trabajan ecuatorianos, el material en bruto se transporta al oeste dentro de Ecuador, luego vuelve a ingresar a Colombia para su proceso, y luego viaja al sur para ser distribuido a través de los puertos ecuatorianos de Esmeraldas o Guayaquil.

VER IMAGENES Y GRÁFICOS, PÁGINAS 62, 63.

MEDIO AMBIENTE

- Clima
- Vegetación
- Hidrología
- El río Aguarico
- Ecosistema

CLIMA

Por **MATTHIAS ALTWICKER**

La Región Amazónica del Ecuador yace sobre la ladera oriental de la Cordillera de los Andes y se encuentra en el extremo occidental de la cuenca amazónica, que se extiende hacia el este hasta la costa atlántica. Su posición geográfica produce un clima caluroso y húmedo. Las temperaturas suelen oscilar entre los 25 y los 36 grados, y el calor se ve exacerbado por la humedad y la falta de viento. La nubosidad se ubica en un promedio del 25% anual y las precipitaciones son elevadas; en invierno y en primavera llueve el doble que en verano y en otoño. Sin embargo, si se la aprovecha adecuadamente, la lluvia puede ser beneficiosa: puede reducir sustancialmente la sensación térmica y hacerla más llevadera.

RECOMENDACIÓN:
RESPUESTA ARQUITECTÓNICA AL CLIMA

De manera sorprendente, la arquitectura de Nueva Loja no ofrece una respuesta responsable a sus condiciones climáticas. Esta falla no se debe a la escasez de materiales o de espacio sino a la falta de conocimiento básico de la zona y de la forma más apropiada para construir allí, entre migrantes provenientes de otros climas de Ecuador. La utilización de sombras en las viviendas y en el espacio público es escasa.

La serie de transformaciones morfológicia que proponemos constituye una respuesta al clima en términos tanto de protección como de proacción. Despegar las edificaciones del suelo (o separar el techo de la pared) promueve la ventilación cruzada y ayuda a proteger la vivienda contra las inundaciones, además de crear un área sombreada que puede usarse para recolectar agua de lluvia y remediar las pérdidas por agua de escorrentía. Estos principios pueden aplicarse también al espacio público.

VER IMÁGENES Y GRÁFICOS, PÁGINAS 66, 67.

VEGETACIÓN

Por **CHRIS SYRETT**

La Región Amazónica del Ecuador es la región más biodiversa del mundo. Contiene entre 9.000 y 12.000 especies de plantas vasculares, muchas de las cuales sólo pueden hallarse en las selvas aledañas a Lago Agrio. Un informe reciente del Global Environment Fund encontró 1.200 especies de plantas en una extensión de apenas dos kilómetros cuadrados de la reserva Cuyabeno. Sin embargo, el número total de especies sigue siendo desconocido. Se estima que un 30% del total de organismos vivos de la región aún no ha sido identificado.

La bóveda de la selva supera los 40 metros; debajo de ella se ubica en numerosos estratos gran variedad de árboles: lianas, bromeliáceas, árboles y arbustos del monte bajo. Existen tres tipos principales de selva tropical en la Región Amazónica del Ecuador: tierra firme, várzea e igapó. La selva de tierra firme se encuentra en terrenos más elevados, no sujetos a inundaciones; la de várzea se ubica en las márgenes de los ríos de aguas blancas que producen inundaciones estacionales; y la de igapó crece en suelos inundados de manera estacional o permanente por aguas negras o ríos de baja sedimentación. En cada tipo de selva se encuentran tipos diferentes de vegetación.

Las plantas amazónicas son asimismo una rica fuente de alimento, medicamentos y materiales. Si logran sobrevivir a la deforestación del Ecuador, podrían convertirse en la fundamental fuente de riqueza sustentable para la región.

VER GRÁFICO, PÁGINA 68.

HIDROLOGÍA

Por **PATRICK WEISEL**

HIDROLOGÍA SUPERFICIAL

Como gran parte de la cuenca amazónica, el área en que se encuentra Nueva Loja es hidrológicamente compleja. En tiempos antiguos, la cuenca desaguaba en el océano Pacífico antes de que la deriva continental formara los Andes, obligando a los ríos que quedaron al este de la cordillera emergente a revertir su curso para a desembocar en el Atlántico. La selva inundada o igapó, que se halla al este de Nueva Loja en la reserva Cuyabeno, es un excelente ejemplo de los cambiantes sistemas de drenaje del continente, que aún no encuentran solución.

HIDROLOGÍA REGIONAL

En la peculiar hidrología de la cuenca amazónica, Nueva Loja es aún más particular. Ubicada en una elevación extremadamente baja y ambigua que divide la cuenca del Putumayo de la del Napo, Nueva Loja contiene los tributarios activos de ambos ríos, en algunas ocasiones separados por menos de un kilómetro de tierra firme. En consecuencia, la lluvia que cae en los barrios del norte de la ciudad no converge con la que se precipita sobre el resto de la ciudad hasta que ambas pasan a formar parte del río Amazonas, casi 1.000 kilómetros río abajo, en Brasil. La ciudad se encuentra en una encrucijada hidrológica, capaz de ejercer una poderosa influencia en dos cuencas de importancia.

HIDROLOGÍA LOCAL

El centro de Nueva Loja se ubica sobre otra elevación que divide los ríos Teteyé y Aguarico. Por lo general, las cuencas fluyen con dirección norte desde la Avenida Quito (que se encuentra en lo más alto de la elevación) y desembocan en el Teteyé y su afluente principal, el Oriencо. El agua que cae desde el sur de la Avenida Quito suele desembocar hacia el sur en varios afluentes más pequeños del Aguarico. Dentro las tres cuencas principales de la ciudad, la del Putumayo, la del Teteyé y la del Aguarico, existen ocho subcuencas. La cuenca del Putumayo se acumula en gran medida en Nueva Loja, mientras que otras tres, incluyendo la del Oriencо y la del Teteyé, serpentean lentamente a través de las tierras bajas saturadas al norte y al este de la ciudad, uniéndose eventualmente con el Aguarico 15 kilómetros río abajo. Estas cuatro cuencas del norte pueden contener enormes cantidades de agua de movimiento lento, de modo que el potencial de contaminación es considerable. Las restantes cuatro cuencas, dos al norte del río Aguarico y dos en Puerto Aguarico, al sur del río, se unen con el Aguarico luego de recorrer un tramo más breve atravesando pendientes más pronunciadas.

VER GRÁFICOS, PÁGINAS 69, 70.

EL RÍO AGUARICO

Por **MARIANNA CASTILLO**

El río Aguarico ocupa la parte central y noroccidental de la provincia de Sucumbíos. Uno de los principales afluentes del río Napo, a lo largo de generaciones, les ha proporcionado a las comunidades indígenas de Sucumbíos y de Nueva Loja gran parte de su sustento. En sus orillas, las mujeres lavan la ropa, las familias se bañan, los niños juegan y las comunidad cultiva sus alimentos.

Desde el comienzo de la explotación petrolera en Sucumbíos, las toxinas, producto del derrame de petróleo, han contaminado el río Aguarico. Si bien el daño no es visible de manera inmediata, ha afectado profundamente la vida de todos aquellos que dependían del río. Su fuente tradicional de agua ahora es tóxica, ya no hay peces y han aparecido nuevas enfermedades. Los pueblos indígenas ahora deben recurrir al agua de lluvia, incluso cuando la lluvia se ha vuelto negra a causa de las nubes de humo tóxico de los pozos humeantes de petróleo. Deben hallar la manera de proveerse de dinero para comprar comida que antes les suministraba el mismo río, para construirse pozos para obtener agua limpia y para pagarse tratamientos médicos para curar nuevas enfermedades.

El río Aguarico sigue siendo un recurso fundamental para los habitantes de Nueva Loja, como arteria de transporte para la comunidad indígena y para los turistas que viajan a través de la Región Amazónica Ecuatoriana. Durante la semana, las mujeres siguen lavando ropa y los niños continúan bañándose y jugando en sus orillas. Los fines de semana, la ribera es un importante centro de recreación.

RECOMENDACIONES: UN NUEVO RÍO AGUARICO

El río Aguarico es uno de los mayores capitales de Nueva Loja: un espectacular paisaje natural y una ruta de transporte muy conveniente. Con la restauración de la ecología fluvial, podría convertirse en el centro de nuevas actividades recreativas y económicas.

El río y su costa deben ser tratados como una parte fundamental de Nueva Loja. Debe incrementar la vitalidad de la ciudad; ofrecer una amplia gama de usos culturales, comerciales y recreativos; y debe ser física y visualmente accesible para residentes y turistas por igual. El plan de renovación del río Aguarico debe restablecer las partes del entorno natural que se perdieron con el tiempo, y su herencia indígena y su papel como arteria regional deben aportarle carácter y sentido al futuro desarrollo costero. La preservación de su pasado es fundamental para que el río vuelva a desarrollarse de manera sustentable.

VER IMÁGENES Y GRÁFICOS, PÁGINAS 71, 73.

DATOS

Origen: Cordillera de Pimampiro, 77°35'W; 0°25'N
Largo total: 390 km
Principales afluentes: Cofanes, Tetetes, Eno, Shushufindi, Zabalo, Pacayucu
Desembocadura: Río Napo
Área: 10,290 km2

	Abril - Junio	Noviembre - Febrero
PROFUNDIDAD mts.	4,58	2,37
ANCHO mts.	216	194
VELOCIDAD mts/sg	1,34	0,99
CORRIENTE m3/sg	1258	440

ABRIL - JUNIO

NOVIEMBRE - FEBRERO

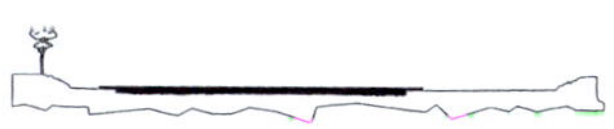

ECOSISTEMA

Por **CHRIS SYRETT**

La selva tropical amazónica es un ecosistema altamente complejo. En un solo árbol de la selva viven más especies de hormigas que en toda Inglaterra. Hay más especies de árboles en unas pocas hectáreas que en la totalidad de América del Norte. Pero si bien la biodiversidad de la selva es verdaderamente impresionante, la verdadera complejidad de este ecosistema se deriva no de la impresionante cantidad de especies sino de las numerosas relaciones e interdependencias que se establecen entre ellas.

La nuez de Brasil, por ejemplo, depende de una serie específica de criaturas para completar su ciclo vital. Sus flores, que se encuentran cerca de la bóveda de la selva, son polinizadas por una única especie de abeja, la abeja de la orquídea. Una vez que las nueces maduran, caen al suelo de la selva y son desparramadas por la zona por una única especie de roedor, el agutí.

La deforestación del oriente ecuatoriano ha perturbado profundamente este complejo tejido vital. Cualquier pérdida en la bóveda significa la destrucción del hábitat de numerosas especies y la perturbación de complejos sistemas ecológicos de evolución milenaria.

Se debe desarrollar un plan integral de utilización de la tierra para preservar la selva tropical y proteger estos ecosistemas. Históricamente, los territorios designados como "reservas" eventualmente sucumben a la deforestación a causa de las presiones originadas por la necesidad de tierras de siembra y pastoreo. Por consiguiente, cualquier nuevo plan que se elabore deberá incorporar programas multifacéticos y flexibles que resalten el valor de la selva. Esto podría llevarse a cabo mediante la extracción sustentable de recursos forestales, la agricultura forestal o las chacras.

DIAGRAMA

- El Oriente ecuatoriano es parte de la enorme cuenca de la Selva Tropical Amazónica.

- La deforestación de la Región Amazónica Ecuatoriana está llevándose a cabo a un ritmo acelerado.

- Si bien las perturbaciones son un aspecto importante de la sucesión y la diversidad de la selva, la perturbación causada por los seres humanos produce profundos, y a menudo perjudiciales, cambios en el ambiente.

VER IMÁGENES Y GRÁFICOS, PÁGINAS 74, 75.

INFRAESTRUCTURA URBANA

- PETRÓLEO
- ENERGÍA
- AGUA
- RECOMENDACIONES: AGRICULTURA Y ALIMENTOS
- RESIDUOS
- INSTALACIONES PÚBLICAS
- INFRAESTRUCTURA PÚBLICA
- EDUCACIÓN

PETRÓLEO

Por **ALAN FOX**

Desde que se instalaron los primeros pozos petrolíferos en 1967, Nueva Loja se ha convertido en el centro de la creciente producción petrolera de la región. Los oleoductos y los caminos construidos para alcanzar las reservas de petróleo se extienden por gran parte de la región.

Cuando Texaco abandonó la selva ecuatoriana en 1993, había derramado 30 veces más petróleo que el vertido en el desastre de Exxon Valdez, y había creado más de 600 fosas de desechos y otras instalaciones que continúan filtrando desperdicios altamente tóxicos. Esta catástrofe ambiental ha afectado a más de 30.000 personas de la zona. Con la multimillonaria demanda contra Texaco aún pendiente de resolución, Petroecuador y otras compañías privadas continúan con la degradación de la selva tropical. Hasta la fecha, la industria petrolera ha causado la deforestación de aproximadamente dos millones de hectáreas (20.000 kilómetros cuadrados) de selva tropical en el norte de la Amazonía ecuatoriana.

Sin embargo, el Ecuador sigue atado al petróleo, al igual que los países a los cuales se lo vende. El crudo equivale a casi el 50% de las exportaciones ecuatorianas. Los beneficios petroleros suministran el 50% de los ingresos del gobierno, que éste utiliza para pagar su considerable deuda con el Fondo Monetario Internacional. La economía petrolera ecuatoriana está condenada a correr la misma suerte del pozo petrolífero LA-01 de Lago Agrio. En 1967, la producción de LA-01 era de 1.500 barriles por día. Actualmente, produce apenas el 10% de eso. Mientras que la producción actual de petróleo de Ecuador asciende a 550.000 barriles por día, para 2037 se espera que ésta se reduzca al 10% del nivel de 2006. Se estima que los campos petrolíferos del país contienen 4.500 millones de barriles. Al ritmo actual de extracción, Ecuador se quedará sin petróleo en 2029.

DIAGRAMA

EL PRIMER POZO PETROLERO DE NUEVA LOJA, LA -01 ESTACIÓN DE SEPARACIÓN

Esta estación de separación contiene una piscina de petróleo, una de las muchas que se encuentran desparramadas por el noreste de Ecuador, y una estructura que quema el gas natural. Ecuador carece de la infraestructura necesaria para almacenar gas natural, de modo que gran parte acaba por quemarse.

VER IMÁGENES Y GRÁFICOS, PÁGINAS 78, 79.

ENERGÍA

Por **ALAN FOX Y HOLLY KALLMAN**

CONSUMO ELÉCTRICO: 2007

Ecuador cubre cerca del 60% de su demanda eléctrica a través de la energía hidroeléctrica generada por plantas hidroeléctricas sobre el río Paute, al sur de Ecuador, que satisfacen más de la mitad de las necesidades del país. El resto se genera por producción térmica convencional utilizando plantas alimentadas por gasoil y gas natural.

Satisfacer la creciente demanda eléctrica del país es un desafío constante. La economía de Ecuador se encuentra en expansión, y su apetito eléctrico crece aún más rápido. En agosto de 2007, el presidente de Ecuador declaró: "un estado de emergencia energética". El año pasado la demanda se incrementó en un 8%. A la vez, la oferta ha caído, a causa de una reducción en el volumen de agua que pasa por las plantas hidroeléctricas y a la escasez de inversiones. Nueva Loja sufre la misma escasez de electricidad que el resto del país. El gasoil es la forma de generar electricidad más económica y accesible con que cuenta la ciudad, pero los generadores diésel no alcanzan a producir lo suficiente, sobre todo en horas pico, como las últimas horas de la tarde y las primeras de la noche. Los cortes de electricidad en barrios enteros son comunes. Muchos de los residentes más ricos poseen sus propios generadores diésel de emergencia, por si falla la red eléctrica de la ciudad.

La Empresa Eléctrica Sucumbíos S.A. suministra la energía eléctrica en Nueva Loja. Su tendido eléctrico es el único que no se encuentra conectado a la red nacional. Cada vez más, se espera que los proveedores privados sean capaces de satisfacer la creciente demanda eléctrica.

PROYECCIONES ELÉCTRICAS: 2037

Para 2037, la población de Nueva Loja se habrá incrementado de 45.000 en 2007 a 150.000. El ingreso per cápita habrá crecido significativamente y sus habitantes gastarán el triple en electricidad que en 2007. Pero también tendrán más aparatos eléctricos, por lo que sus necesidades eléctricas habrán crecido más que sus ingresos. El costo del gasoil también habrá aumentado y las restricciones a las emisiones de dióxido de carbono restringirán aún más su uso, si bien los generadores diésel se seguirán utilizando para compensar la escasez en los horarios pico.

La energía hidroeléctrica será la principal fuente energética de Nueva Loja. La mitad de la demanda energética de la ciudad será cubierta por plantas hidroeléctricas ubicadas en la Cordillera de los Andes, que estarán en manos de la ciudad, de empresas privadas e individuos. La electricidad llegará a la ciudad por las mismas rutas empleadas para despachar la oferta cada vez menor de petróleo. Asimismo, la ciudad, el estado y los ciudadanos habrán invertido en paneles fotovoltaicos y en pequeñas y grandes turbinas de energía eólica. Estas importantes inversiones serán inicialmente considerables, pero en el largo plazo la adopción de combustibles gratuitos pagará sus dividendos. Para entonces, se habrán formado asociaciones energéticas que ayudarán a afrontar los costos.

La electricidad que sobre se venderá en el mercado abierto. La ciudad será dueña del sistema de distribución y estará encargada de mantenerlo, cobrándoles a sus usuarios una tarifa. Algunos individuos habrán construido pequeñas instalaciones hidroeléctricas en sus propiedades, y destinarán la energía generada para su consumo personal o la venderán a la ciudad.

VER GRÁFICOS, PÁGINAS 81 a 83.

CUADRO COMPARATIVO DE LA GENERACIÓN DE ELECTRICIDAD EN NUEVA LOJA POR kWh

	DIÉSEL	HIDROELÉCTRICA	FOTOVOLTAICA	EÓLICA
EMISIÓN DE C02	X X X X	X X		
IMPACTO EN LA SUPERFICIE		X X X X	X X	X
COSTO DE INSTALACIÓN	X X	X	X X X X	X X X X
COSTO OPERATIVO	X X X	X	X	X
COSTO DE COMBUSTIBLE	X X X X			
DISTANCIA DE TRANSMISIÓN	X	X X X X	X	X X
PRECIO EN 2007 EN DÓLARES DE 2007	.11	.05 - .15	.24 - .48	.10 - .20
PRECIO EN 2037 EN DÓLARES DE 2007	.30	.03 - .08	.12 - .25	.07 - .15
FUTURO	De rápida instalación, se trata de un método probado para la generación de energía. Requiere la utilización de combustible diésel A medida que se haga cada vez más caro y que se vayan limitando las emisiones de CO2, se lo irá reemplazando con la energía hidroeléctrica.	Bajo costo de construcción y mantenimiento. El combustible es gratuito. Sin embargo, implica un considerable impacto a nivel local, especialmente porque algunos sectores de la selva tropical y algunos asentamientos quedan sumergidos. El impacto global incluye la posibilidad de que las plantas que quedan sumergidas y se pudren en la represa hidroeléctrica produzcan emisiones significativas de CO2 y otros gases de efecto invernadero. Sin embargo, el impacto puede minimizarse actuando con previsión y escuchando las opiniones de los habitantes de la zona. Además, las represas no son un requisito ineludible para la generación de energía hidroeléctrica. La topografía y las lluvias hacen del Oriente ecuatoriano, que se encuentra especialmente cerca de la Cordillera de los Andes, una región ideal para la producción de energía hidroeléctrica.	El costo de los paneles es elevado, el combustible es gratuito y el mantenimiento es mínimo. La intensidad del sol en la región es óptima para la producción de electricidad. Sin embargo, el brillo del sol es variable debido a la alta frecuencia de nubes. Los costos seguirán bajando.	El costo de la maquinaria es alto. El combustible es gratuito y el mantenimiento es mínimo. Los vientos intermitentes y de baja velocidad no hacen de ésta una región óptima para la generación de energía eólica. Sin embargo, quizá haya un promedio de viento diario suficiente para que pueda competir con la energía fotovoltaica. Las turbinas de gran tamaño pueden comenzar a generar energía con vientos de apenas 14 km/h. Las pequeñas, con vientos de 5 km/h. Los costos seguirán bajando.

AGUA

Por **PATRICK WEISEL**

Nueva Loja recibe un promedio de 340 milímetros de precipitaciones diarias en temporada de lluvias y 190 milímetros durante la estación seca, lo cual arroja un promedio de 3.500 milímetros anuales. Administrar tal cantidad de agua es fundamental para la calidad de vida en un área urbanizada, pero las capacidades de infiltración y absorción eficaz de la selva originaria de la región se han perdido.

EL TERCIO PERDIDO

El dosel de la selva tropical, que anteriormente cubría el área en su totalidad, absorbe apenas un tercio del agua de lluvia antes de que ésta llegue al suelo. Incluso en ausencia de superficies pavimentadas impermeables, la absorción natural no puede compensar la pérdida de la bóveda de la selva. Las inundaciones, el incremento de la velocidad de los cursos de agua y la erosión destruyen el hábitat, desestabilizan la estructura del suelo y alteran la capa freática, todo lo cual tiene consecuencias potencialmente graves. La solución a un exceso de agua superficial parece evidente: recolectar la mayor cantidad de agua de lluvia posible y almacenarla para consumo hogareño y comercial.

TRATAMIENTO DE AGUAS RESIDUALES

Además de los problemas relativos al agua de lluvia y al agua potable, Nueva Loja carece de un sistema eficaz de tratamiento de aguas residuales. La creación de un sistema descentralizado de tratamiento de aguas residuales vinculado a la recolección, almacenamiento y administración del agua de lluvia podría reemplazar la función de la parte perdida del dosel de la selva.

HIDROLOGÍA ESTRUCTURAL

La recolección, almacenamiento y tratamiento del agua de lluvia son instancias que dependen unas de otras y no pueden ser consideradas por separado. Una asignación equilibrada al nivel del barrio y del lote determinará el emplazamiento de los edificios y las densidades habitacionales, lo cual dará como resultado una Nueva Loja hidrológicamente sana y sustentable.

VER GRÁFICOS, PÁGINAS 84, 85.

RECOMENDACIONES: AGRICULTURA Y ALIMENTOS

Por **CHRIS SYRETT**

La provincia de Sucumbíos actualmente está bien ubicada en la mayoría de los índices mundiales de hambre, pero en las próximas décadas alimentar a la población de Nueva Loja se convertirá en un desafío más difícil. El crecimiento poblacional, la degradación de los suelos, los cambios y la confusión en la propiedad de la tierra, las prácticas agrícolas deficientes y los efectos del calentamiento global podrían amenazar la producción de alimentos y la seguridad alimentaria de la región.

Sin embargo, si se adoptan las estrategias adecuadas, muchos de estos problemas podrían solucionarse, y podría desarrollarse una agricultura sustentable y dinámica en Nueva Loja. Por ejemplo, el sistema indígena de chacras con cultivos alternados podría utilizarse para preservar y recuperar los frágiles suelos de la selva tropical, así como para alimentar a la ciudad de manera efectiva. El cultivo de productos no forestales nativos podría proporcionar una alternativa lucrativa a la actual dependencia de cultivos industriales poco exitosos. Estos productos no forestales, como el aguacate, podrían complementar el acceso de Nueva Loja a frutas frescas, vegetales y frutos secos.

La agricultura urbana podría ser otra fuente de alimentos para los residentes, que podrían plantar huertas en sus jardines para producir alimentos, ya sea para complementar sus dietas o como fuente suplementaria de ingresos. La agricultura urbana tiene otros beneficios: elimina el costo ambiental y financiero que conlleva transportar alimentos, y reduce los desechos propios del empaque.

VER GRÁFICOS, PÁGINAS 86, 87.

RESIDUOS

Por **GARETH MAHON**

PROBLEMAS

COSTO

En los países en vías de desarrollo, se gasta entre el 30 y el 50% del presupuesto operativo municipal en el manejo de residuos sólidos. Los sistemas suelen ser centralizados, verticalistas y privatizados, por lo cual requieren grandes inversiones en bienes de capital. La financiación para estos proyectos generalmente viene de préstamos internacionales de organismos como el Banco Mundial.

EFICIENCIA

En la mayoría de las ciudades, sólo se recolecta sólo se recolecta entre el 50 y 80% de de los desperdicios hogareños.

EXCLUSIVIDAD

La comunidad informal recolectora de basura, particularmente activa en todo el Ecuador, es marginalizada cuando se implementan sistemas centralizados de administración de desperdicios.

SALUD

Los vertederos mal administrados suelen ubicarse cerca de asentamientos informales, creando problemas sanitarios y de contaminación.

OBJETIVOS DE LOS INVOLUCRADOS

LOS CIUDADANOS DE NUEVA LOJA
Vivir en barrios más seguros e higiénicos.

LA MUNICIPALIDAD
Crear puestos de trabajo.

Reducir los problemas sanitarios.
Reducir los costos de las materias primas.
Encontrar soluciones económica y socialmente viables.

RECOLECTORES INFORMALES DE RESIDUOS

Obtener empleos seguros.
Huir de la pobreza.
Mejorar su salud.
Disfrutar de seguridad.

EL MEDIO AMBIENTE

Eliminar la contaminación tóxica.
Reducir los vertederos.
Conservar recursos.

OBJETIVOS

MINIMIZAR La producción de desechos.
MAXIMIZAR La reutilización y el reciclado de desperdicios.
ABONO Exclusivamente material orgánico.

DESPERDICIOS: ¿QUITO, UN MODELO PARA NUEVA LOJA?

Lago Agrio no recicla sus desperdicios. La basura se recoge de las distintas partes de la ciudad y se traslada a un vertedero a 8 kilómetros al este de la ciudad. (La recolección de residuos en Lago Agrio parece ser bastante eficiente, si bien según el Banco Mundial los gobiernos locales en Sudamérica gastan del 20 al 50% de sus ingresos en servicios de recolección de residuos sólidos, pero de hecho sólo se recoge del 50 al 80 por ciento de los residuos).

Las primeras iniciativas de reciclaje en Quito, la capital de Ecuador, le ofrecen algunas enseñanzas a Nueva Loja. Quito comenzó sus primeros programas piloto de reciclaje en 1993 en barrios de clase baja y media baja. Los estudios publicados en 2002 muestran cómo han evolucionado en los años subsiguientes y algunos de los problemas con los que se encontraron por el camino.

Los programas de Quito aprovechaban los sistemas informales existentes de manejo de residuos. La separación inicial de los productos la realizaban familias; equipos o "microemprendimientos" barriales recogían por las calles los desperdicios reciclables (acambio de un salario fijo pagado por el gobierno); y la ciudad recogía los desperdicios de depósitos designados y los llevaba a reciclar. Los grupos barriales trabajaban con los microemprendimientos para asegurar los mejores precios y para redistribuir parte de las ganancias a la comunidad. El objetivo primordial era reducir los gastos municipales a la vez que se creaban puestos de trabajo a nivel local. Entre los efectos secundarios inesperados se registró una mejora en las condiciones de salubridad y un incremento en el orgullo barrial.

Sin embargo, con el paso del tiempo comenzaron a surgir problemas. Los residuos no se estaban separando correctamente y el volumen general de reciclaje comenzó a disminuir, como resultado de la insatisfacción local con el programa. Un posterior estudio, financiado por USAID y llevado a cabo en parte por la ONG local Corporación OIKOS 17, identificó los principales factores que causaron el fracaso del programa.

El estudio culpaba a la falta de educación y capacitación posterior; a la insatisfacción con la tarea realizada por los microemprendimientos; a las creencias culturales y a la imagen que tenían de sí mismos los residentes (muchos pensaban que dedicarse a la separación de residuos era denigrante, una tarea propia de mendigos); y a una resistencia generalizada a entregarles residuos valiosos a los microemprendimientos.

El estudio también descubrió que el programa de Quito le otorgaba una importancia insuficiente al sistema formal que venía a reemplazar. En un intento por reducir la práctica informal de los "minadores", que buscan sobras en los vertederos, también puso fin a la tradición de los "cacharreros", que iban de puerta en puerta a comprar sobras directamente. El género también tenía una incidencia. Por lo general, muchos de los microemprendimientos habían sido creados por mujeres, quienes también solían encargarse de la tarea de separar los residuos, pero a menudo los hombres, que no entendían el sistema o el esfuerzo que demandaba, se oponían a él por cuestiones de imagen personal o motivos financieros.

Los resultados de este estudio sugieren que si se pretende instaurar un sistema de reciclaje que funcione en Lago Agrio, se debe comenzar por obtener el apoyo de la comunidad, y luego continuar implementando iniciativas claras vinculadas a un programa de educación pública. Algún beneficio económico por la reventa de material reciclado debería llegar a los hogares, y cualquier sistema de reciclaje informal debería incorporarse.

DESPERDICIOS: RECOMENDACIONES

REDUCIR LA GENERACIÓN DE DESPERDICIOS

- Establecer programas de educación en escuelas y centros comunitarios.
- Fomentar la eficiencia en las industrias locales.
- Instar a las industrias locales a reducir el empaque.
- Introducir Códigos Municipales que promuevan el uso de productos reutilizables de larga vida.

DESCENTRALIZAR EL MANEJO DE LOS DESPERDICIOS A LOS GRANDES BARRIOS

ESTABLECER OBJETIVOS PARA EL SISTEMA INFORMAL

- Apuntar a reciclar el 90% de todos los desechos.

APOYAR UN SISTEMA DESCENTRALIZADO

- Reconocer los desperdicios como un recurso.
- Involucrar a todos los actores implicados en el manejo de este recurso.
- Permitirles a los recolectores informales formar cooperativas con ayuda de organizaciones de base (OBCs) y organizaciones no gubernamentales (ONGs).
- Identificar mercados locales, regionales y nacionalespara colocar los residuos reutilizables y reciclables.
- Suministrar espacio en cada comunidad para la separación y el almacenamiento de residuos.
- Suministrar espacio para el compostaje.
- Suministrar espacio para generadores de bio-gas.

Desarrollar un sistema de compensación

- Otorgar a los recolectores de residuos derechos sobre todos los desechos recogidos y/o crear un servicio remunerado.

Generar servicios secundarios

- Limpieza de las calles.
- Poda de árboles.

Identificar los problemas y trabajar para resolverlos

- Superar la mentalidad mezquina.
- Involucrar a los residentes que no participan del sistema.
- Implicar a los residentes que no llevan a cabo la separación inicial.

VER IMÁGENES Y GRÁFICOS, PÁGINAS 88 a 90.

INSTALACIONES PÚBLICAS

Por **MATTHIAS ALTWICKER**

La infraestructura de Nueva Loja, deficientemente distribuida, resulta tremendamente escasa incluso para su población actual, la cual, si las predicciones son correctas, está llamada a explotar.
Una nueva infraestructura pública para la ciudad debe centrarse en la cantidad, la distribución y la secuenciación. Los espacios públicos exteriores y las instalaciones educativas son fundamentales para el desarrollo de cualquier barrio.
Éstos deberían conectarse con un sistema de transporte público que llegue a toda la ciudad y convertirse en la base de la comunidad.
Durante una segunda fase de desarrollo, una serie de mercados deben enlazarse a la estrategia económica de la región.
En ambas fases, los vínculos entre los niveles local, urbano y regional serán fundamentales: determinarán la ubicación de la nueva infraestructura.
Cada barrio de 3.000 a 5.000 habitantes tendrá dos centros, uno económico y otro educativo, y el barrio se desarrollará entre ambos.
La infraestructura primaria que no se encuentre en estos barrios –el mercado central, la estación de autobuses y el estadio– se distribuirá de manera pareja a lo largo de la ciudad para promover el movimiento y la interacción entre los distintos barrios.

VER IMÁGENES Y GRÁFICOS, PÁGINAS 91, 92.

INFRAESTRUCTURA PÚBLICA

Por **MATTHIAS ALTWICKER**

COMPONENTES

I El primer elemento será una escuela primaria o una secundaria.
II Se ubicará junto a un espacio verde, cerca de las rutas de transporte público.
III Junto a la escuela se diseñará un espacio público con sombra.

MERCADOS

I **Pequeñas tiendas**
Pequeñas tiendas informales ubicadas a 150 metros de distancia en las zonas residenciales.
II **Mercados callejeros**
a 500 metros de distancia –una estructura independiente con productos importados y horarios fijos.
III **Mercados barriales**
Ubicados a 1.500 metros de distancia; próximos a rutas de circulación y a zonas de producción; contienen tanto espacios abiertos como cerrados.

ADYACENCIAS

I En el edificio de la escuela pueden funcionar programas públicos adicionales, o puede ubicárselos en otra parte.
II A medida que la escuela adquiera nuevos usos como resultado de estos programas, se agregará un espacio exterior adyacente que permita alojar 1.500 personas.
III No se permitirá la ubicación de servicios municipales y mercados en las cercanías de la escuela.

PARÁMETROS

I La municipalidad se ocupará de mantener el espacio público abierto.
II La comunidad será responsable de la ubicación de la infraestructura comercial y pública.
III Cada edificio y espacio debe ser accesible a todos.
IV La construcción deberá utilizar sistemas pasivos de sombra, iluminación y ventilación.

VER GRÁFICOS, PÁGINAS 93, 94.

EDUCACIÓN

Por **HOLLY KALMANN**

RECOMENDACIONES: LA ECONOMÍA DE UNA UNIVERSIDAD AMAZÓNICA

"La verdad es que el planeta no necesita de más gente 'exitosa'. Pero necesita desesperadamente de más conciliadores, sanadores, restauradores, narradores de historias y amantes de todas las formas y colores. Necesita gente que viva bien en su lugar. Necesita gente con coraje moral, deseosa de participar en la lucha por hacer el mundo habitable y humano".

David Orr, ambientalista.

La UNESCO sigue de cerca las estadísticas educativas mundiales. A través de su programa UNI TWIN dirige, apoya y supervisa la educación en los países en vías de desarrollo. La expectativa de educación de un niño constituye una de las brechas más significativas entre los países más ricos y los más pobres. Y la causa más significativa de esta diferencia es el suministro de educación terciaria.
El apoyo para una universidad amazónica podría provenir de una serie de universidades públicas y privadas que han expresado su interés por financiar y suplir con profesores a centros de investigación satelitales. Entre éstas podrían contarse a MIT, CityTech, CUNY, Penn State y Duke University. A la OPEP le interesa financiar las investigaciones destinadas a mitigar el impacto de la extracción petrolera. La Unión Europea, el Banco Mundial y empresas privadas como Intel también son patrocinadores potenciales.
La creación de una universidad en Nueva Loja reforzará el sentido de identidad amazónica, haciendo de Nueva Loja un emblema de la región y trayendo prosperidad sustentable a la ciudad. Los estudiantes aprenderán directamente del territorio que los rodea y se establecerá un nuevo modelo educativo, vinculado estrechamente con la "cultura de taller".

VER IMAGEN, PÁGINA 95.

INVERSIONES	2013	2018	2023	2028
CUERPO DOCENTE A TIEMPO COMPLETO	20	45	75	100
INSTRUCTORES	25	50	125	200
POBLACIÓN ESTUDIANTIL	500	1,000	2,000	3,000
MANTENIMIENTO INTERNO				
MANTENIMIENTO CONTRATISTAS CONSTRUCCIÓN INDUSTRIA	150 personas empleadas 20 nuevas empresas			1.500 empleados 150 nuevas empresas
SERVICIOS				
SUMINISTROS				
PRESUPUESTO ANUAL				

PROCESOS	2013	2018	2023	2028
CURRÍCULA				
PATROCINIO UNESCO EMBAJADOR	Investigación y desarrollo en fitorremediación	Se descubrirán curas para el cáncer	Nueva tecnología en la recuperación de agua potable	La generación de energía solar e hidroeléctrica se volverá confiable

RESULTADOS	2013	2018	2023	2028
CARRERAS DE GRADO				
BIOLOGÍA Y CIENCIAS DE LA VIDA		Se interrumpen las perforaciones petroleras, excepto para uso doméstico, que de todos modos se encuentra bajo un control estricto		
EDUCACIÓN	10% más profesores	Sube un 20%		Modelo de turismo ecológico
AGRICULTURA	Sostenible	Libre de pesticidas	Comercio en los mercados	
ENFERMERÍA	Las estadísticas mejoran a partir de la colaboración entre el sistema de salud, basado en la alopatía, y la aplicación del saber tradicional sobre hierbas autóctonas	El sistema de salud es coordinado por especialistas en enfermería	Modelo de medicina alopática, dado que los costos son apenas 1/20 de los costos médicos promedio en el primer mundo	Modelo mundial de construcción de riqueza
ARTES Y HUMANIDADES	Educación secundaria en la Amazonía	Se ofrece educación tanto de grado como de posgrado	Estudiantes y profesores comienzan a recibir premios de literatura importantes	Enfermeros/as capacitan a los médicos
TECNOLOGÍAS	Solar/Energía	Construcción-Reciclado	Reforestación	Destino educativo
ODONTOLOGÍA				
NEGOCIOS	Se crea el Departamento de Microemprendimientos	Se implementan mercados	Financiación de hipotecas y créditos para la adquisición de viviendas	Administración = gestión

BENEFICIOS

EDUCACIÓN SUPERIOR EN LA AMAZONIA

REVOLUCIÓN EN LAS TECNOLOGÍAS DE REMEDIACIÓN

MOTOR ECONÓMICO PARA LA CIUDAD Y LA REGIÓN

UNIVERSIDAD: DESTINO Y EDUCACIÓN

EGRESADOS DISTINGUIDOS

PRODUCCIÓN DE LÍDERES MUNDIALES EN MATERIA DE SOSTENIBILIDAD

ORGANIZACIÓN REGIONAL

Por **MATTHIAS ALTWICKER**

CIUDADES HERMANAS: NUEVA LOJA Y COCA

OBJETIVO

Nueva Loja es el centro regional de la provincia de Sucumbíos, y Coca su centro administrativo. Considerar a Nueva Loja y Coca ciudades hermanas ayudaría a fortalecer ambos centros urbanos y a equilibrar su dilatada periferia compartida. Cada ciudad mantendría su propia identidad local, si bien se vincularía simbióticamente con la otra a través de recursos y funciones compartidos.

POBLACIÓN

	Nueva Loja	Coca
Urbana - proyectada	150.000	60.000
Periferia - proyectada	40.000	20.000
Total	165.000	80.000

RECURSOS DISPONIBLES: GENERALES

Las ciudades hermanas compartirían las culturas indígenas, las reservas ecológicas y un vigo de educación primaria.

RECURSOS DISPONIBLES: ESPECÍFICOS

Conexiones internacionales	Colombia	Brasil
Conexiones nacionales	Andes	Oriente
Transporte	Aeropuerto	Río Napo

PRINCIPALES INVERSIONES NECESARIAS

Fuentes energéticas: Auspiciantes técnicos privados, subsidios de investigación.

Iniciativas educativas: Subsidios al desarrollo de la ONU, colaboradores de universidades privadas.

ZONAS FRONTERIZAS

OBJETIVO

Promover relaciones productivas entre las fronteras existentes. Cambiar la percepción que se tiene de la frontera entre Colombia y Ecuador, y que en vez de considerársela un lugar peligroso y hostil se la vea como un lugar seguro. Esto dará origen a un área "controlada" con incentivos para el asentamiento y oportunidades para la colaboración a través de la frontera.

UBICACIÓN / RECURSOS DISPONIBLES

Internacional: Frontera colombo-ecuatoriana.

Las ciudades fluviales dispersas se organizarán en colectivos. Los productos de la construcción formarán una base industrial que aprovechará la reforestación y los nuevos desarrollos a lo largo de la frontera.

REGIONAL: FRONTERA SUCUMBÍOS- NAPO

Se desarrolla una estrategia de conservación con las empresas petroleras que operan en el sur, de manera que limite el desarrollo de la zona fronteriza entre Sucumbíos, Napo y los centros urbanos.

PRINCIPALES INVERSIONES

Asentamientos: Las localidades municipales escriturarán títulos de propiedad y asistirán con la infraestructura básica.

Desarrollo: El dinero del Plan Colombia de los EE.UU. y el presupuesto militar ecuatoriano serán destinados a la inversión privada en el sector industrial.

ZONAS AGRÍCOLAS

OBJETIVO

La agricultura, si bien es la fuente principal de comercio de la región, es administrada de manera ineficiente. A través de la educación, la capacitación y la revisión de las prácticas del uso de la tierra, con el tiempo podría volverse más productiva y sustentable.

COMUNAS

Las cooperativas se han ganado la reputación de incurrir en administración fraudulenta y de aprovecharse de los nuevos colonos. Éstas serán lentamente reestructuradas en comunas vinculadas por su proximidad. Los cultivos se equilibrarán para asegurar colaboración dentro de la comuna en vez de competencia.

ACTIVIDAD AGROFORESTAL

Los nuevos colonos aprenderán técnicas de reforestación productiva y a manejar huertas para mejorar la eficiencia en la utilización de la tierra. El 80% de la tierra se utilizará para cubrir necesidades locales y nacionales.

CHACRAS: AGRICULTURA EFICIENTE

La adopción de este método de cultivo indígena constituirá una mejora con respecto a los actuales métodos de agricultura de subsistencia y permitirá la regeneración del medio ambiente así como la reintegración de la cultura indígena.

INVERSIONES PRINCIPALES NECESARIAS

El Banco Mundial y los Fondos de Desarrollo de la ONU para la reeducación; inversiones privadas en agroindustria.

ZONAS DE RESTAURACIÓN

OBJETIVOS

Restaurar y manejar la ecología de la zona por medio de prácticas de administración de la tierra y de la reducción de los asentamientos y del acceso. Esta zona remota, aislada del mercado mundial, se convertirá en un lugar de oportunidades locales.

REFORESTACIÓN: BORDES Y CORREDORES

Se creará un margen continuo de reserva forestal por medio del "llenado de huecos". Los colonos, contratados como guardias forestales, obtendrán su sustento de la tala selectiva y de la agricultura de subsistencia, así como por medio de subsidios del gobierno local y nacional. Se trata de un plan de restauración a largo plazo: pasarán diez años antes de que los resultados comiencen a apreciarse.

DESINTOXICACIÓN

Se recurrirá a la microrremediación (por medio de hongos) y a la fitorremediación (por medio de plantas) para limpiar las zonas contaminadas con petróleo. El proceso inicial demanda varios meses, pero en el transcurso de un año estas áreas producirán hongos y patatas. Este proyecto será administrado y estrechamente vigilado por el gobierno ecuatoriano, el sistema educativo y supervisores que garanticen la confianza para asegurar la confianza y la cooperación.

INVERSIONES FUNDAMENTALES

Reforestación: Gobiernos locales, turismo ecológico, ONU y Banco Mundial.
Desintoxicación: Gobierno ecuatoriano, empresas petroleras.

VER GRÁFICOS, PÁGINAS: 102 a 107.

LÍMITES DE LA CIUDAD

Por **ROBERTA KORCZ**

DISCREPANCIAS EN EL CRECIMIENTO

Tanto los datos municipales como los informales muestran que Nueva Loja se está expandiendo a un ritmo acelerado. Sin embargo, las dos fuentes revelan distintos patrones de crecimiento. Los mapas de la ciudad registran un patrón de crecimiento radial bastante parejo, mientras que las imágenes satelitales revelan que la expansión urbana y agrícola es más esporádica y fragmentaria, extendiéndose al costado de las líneas de infraestructura petrolera y de las principales carreteras.
Este patrón se debe en gran medida a la naturaleza informal de los asentamientos en el Oriente. Como resultado, la tierra forestada y aquella urbanizada están quedando cada vez más desconectadas, a medida que la tierra de cultivo se extiende formando corredores rurales. Simultáneamente, las distancias entre las zonas de asentamiento y los centros urbanos son cada vez mayores, creando dependencia de los automóviles.

OBJETIVOS DE LIMITACIÓN DEL CRECIMIENTO URBANO:

- Limitar la expansión descontrolada, a nivel urbano y agrícola.
- Evitar la fragmentación del hábitat ecológico.
- Delinear un patrón en red de utilización de las tierras urbanas, agrícolas y naturales.
- Evitar las interacciones negativas de la ciudad con los ecosistemas que la rodean.

CONDICIÓN FINAL

Las redes urbanas conectan las áreas pobladas periféricas directamente con el centro de la ciudad, creando zonas de posible crecimiento futuro. Las conexiones verdes crean corredores ecológicos para evitar la fragmentación del hábitat. Entre las zonas agrícolas, se crea una barrera protectora contra especies potencialmente invasivas.

ESTRATEGIAS DE IMPLEMENTACIÓN

Las estrategias de implementación combinarán diseño, políticas públicas e iniciativas comunitarias:

- Crearán conexiones directas entre las áreas urbanas periféricas y el centro de la ciudad.
- Crearán corredores ecológicos: todos los espacios verdes designados estarán conectados con otros espacios verdes designados.
- Incorporarán elementos ambientales como pantanos artificiales, nuevos bosques y reservas ecológicas en el sistema urbano, como condiciones semiporosas del borde urbano.
- Harán hincapié en prácticas de agricultura independiente para limitar la expansión de la frontera rural y para ayudar a contener el avance de especies invasivas como el bambú.
- Formarán zonas de fortalecimiento urbano que contendrán todas las instalaciones, servicios y economías municipales que necesita la comunidad local para funcionar de manera relativamente autónoma.
- Establecerán redes de infraestructura que incluirán (pero no se limitarán a) escuelas, consultorios públicos, parques y transportes, todos fácilmente accesibles accesibles dentro de los centros comunitarios.
- Implementarán incentivos relativos al valor de la tierra y a los títulos de propiedad, de modo que la tierra edificable se ofrezcaa un precio más asequible y la posesión de la tierra se asocie con el desarrollo personal.

VER IMÁGENES Y GRÁFICOS, PÁGINAS: 108 a 111.

ORGANIZACIÓN DE LA CIUDAD

MICRO-BARRIOS EXISTENTES

Un elemento fundamental en la constitución actual de la ciudad es el micro-barrio, una entidad política creada especialmente por los residentes para obtener representación política en la municipalidad. Los micro-barrios deben tener una población mínima de 500 personas. Sin embargo, esa representación política es limitada: no permite oponer resistencia a la municipalidad, ni influir sobre la fisonomía urbana.

PROPUESTA DE GRANDES BARRIOS

Proponemos que los micro-barrios se agrupen en organizaciones más amplias, los Grandes Barrios. Los Grandes Barrios superarían las barreras físicas que normalmente se utilizan para dividir electorados (calles y catastros). Y por el contrario, su fisonomía estaría determinada por problemas de infraestructura compartidos.

CORREDORES ECOLÓGICOS

Actualmente hay escasez de espacio abierto en Nueva Loja, por lo cual algunos espacios deberían dejarse sin construir a fin de establecer corredores ecológicos través de la ciudad –los ecosistemas que fueron empujados más allá de la periferia volverían a ser parte del desarrollo.

SISTEMAS DE TRANSPORTE

Las principales rutas de transporte de las industrias petrolera y forestal serán trasladadas al sur de la ciudad. Dentro de los límites urbanos, una serie de rutas de autobuses hilvanará la infraestructura pública.

ESPACIO PÚBLICO E INFRAESTRUCTURA

La infraestructura pública se utilizará para desarrollar los barrios. El espacio público urbano se distribuirá de manera pareja a lo largo de la ciudad, y se ubicará tanto hacia la periferia como en elnúcleo actual.

EDUCACIÓN Y ECONOMÍA

La educación y la economía deben conectarse y coexistir de manera productiva. La agroeconomía y la agroeducación son fundamentales para la supervivencia de la región. Estos espacios serán deliberadamente diferenciados y separados del espacio público municipal.

VER GRÁFICOS, PÁGINAS: 112, 113.

BARRIO VÍA QUITO

Por **PAUL KING**

El Barrio Vía Quito, ubicado en el margen sudoeste de Nueva Loja, será la entrada de los visitantes que lleguen desde Quito.

ECONOMÍA

El Barrio Vía Quito será un barrio de uso mixto (residencial, comercial e industrial) que desarrollará y promocionará una economía basada en derivados del bambú.

El bambú se cultivará en el sur, donde las condiciones del suelo lo permiten. Se cultivarán numerosas especies no invasivas de bambú en una zona forestal sustentable certificada por el Consejo de Administración Forestal (FSC, por sus siglas en inglés). (Esta certificación asegura el empleo de métodos sustentables de cultivo y producción. Adherirse al programa incrementa el atractivo comercial de los productos, que pueden ostentar el logo del FSC).

Luego de su cosecha, el bambú será traído al barrio para ser procesado. El ciclo de crecimiento y cosecha del bambú varía según su uso. El bambú para artesanías y tejidos puede ser cosechado luego de dos o tres años; los muebles y los materiales compuestos requieren de tres a cuatro años; y los productos estructurales, entre cinco y seis.

Los productos de bambú pueden dividirse en tres grandes categorías: artesanías y tejidos; muebles y productos compuestos; productos para la construcción y componentes modulares para viviendas prefabricadas.

Las artesanías y tejidos incluyen canastas, esterillas y otros productos trenzados, así como hilo de bambú y tejidos. El bambú produce un hilo naturalmente antibacteriano que puede utilizarse para fabricar ropa. La producción de muebles y productos compuestos requerirá de capacitación en carpintería. Los productos de mobiliario y cercas incluyen a los pisos de bambú y al "plyboo," un panel de plywood fabricado con bambú. Los productos de la construcción incluyen a los andamios estructurales y los módulos para las viviendas prefabricadas.

PROGRAMAS SOCIALES

El Barrio Vía Quito seguirá el modelo establecido por los proyectos de vivienda social de la Fundación Hogar de Cristo, en Guayaquil. Las viviendas serán prefabricadas, ensambladas y desarmadas en el lugar de producción, para luego ser nuevamente ensambladas in situ. Las personas que sean aceptadas para participar en el programa podrán comprar una casa, con la condición de que contribuyan con un programa de educación para mujeres emprendedoras.

EDUCACIÓN

Las escuelas de oficios del barrio Vía Quito se especializarán en capacitar a los alumnos para que se conviertan en miembros productivos de la economía del bambú. Una de ellas se centrará en los "productos blandos": artesanías y productos tejidos o trenzados (esterillas, textiles, indumentaria, etc.). Otra se especializará en los "productos duros", enseñando los rudimentos de carpintería necesarios para la producción de muebles, productos compuestos y componentes modulares para la construcción de viviendas prefabricadas. Ambas se encontrarán ubicadas a escasa distancia de la Plaza del Mercado.

Un sistema de aprendizaje de oficios se montará para mejorar las oportunidades laborales de los estudiantes y ofrecerles capacitación en los lugares de trabajo. Los fines de semana, podrán realizar exposiciones de ensamblaje de componentes de viviendas prefabricadas en la Plaza del Mercado.

El mercado se convertirá en un un nuevo centro para las actividades del barrio y en un escaparate para los distintos usos del bambú. En la entrada del mercado, una escultura en forma de tótem les dará la bienvenida a la ciudad a los visitantes. Al traspasar la entrada, y visible desde el camino, un gran pabellón de bambú al aire libre exhibirá las capacidades estructurales del material. Grandes grupos podrán darse cita en el pabellón, protegidos del sol y la lluvia. Los fines de semana, habrá demostraciones de productos manufacturados con bambú y se venderán viviendas prefabricadas.

PLAZA DEL MERCADO DE BAMBÚ

Además, habrá puestos de bambú que venderán productos terminados. Los edificios en el centro de la Plaza del Mercado alojarán grupos solidarios y harán las veces de aulas para la educación de adultos, que ofrecerá capacitación en la fabricación de productos a hechos con bambú, así como tutorías y apoyo.

PLAZA DEL TÓTEM

Ubicada a lo largo de la Vía Quito, esta plaza albergará el tótem de Nueva Loja, que marcará la entrada a la ciudad

GRAN PABELLÓN CENTRAL DE BAMBÚ

Un gran espacio al aire libre, flexible, que se utilizará para albergar reuniones comunitarias y para exhibir sistemas de viviendas prefabricadas de bambú y otros productos de gran tamaño.

PUESTOS DEL MERCADO AL AIRE LIBRE

Puestos más pequeños serán provistos en el mercado para facilitar la venta de productos fabricados con bambú, como canastas, esterillas, muebles, tejidos e indumentaria.

EDIFICIOS DEL MERCADO CENTRAL

Contendrán aulas donde funcionará una escuela para adultos que además brindará capacitación en el trabajo con bambú, e instalaciones que albergarán la iniciativa de viviendas fabricadas con bambú y otros programas sociales. Habrá asimismo un segundo pabellón de bambú al aire libre, más pequeño que el otro.

VER IMÁGENES Y GRÁFICOS, PÁGINAS: 114 a 116.

NAPO – JULIO MARÍN

Por **MATTHIAS ALTWICKER**

El desarrollo informal o auto-construido, que equivale al 40% de la construcción en Nueva Loja, tiene lugar en el barrio Napo-Julio Marín. El desarrollo informal acarrea una gran variedad de problemas.

Los colonos suelen ocupar tierras de propiedad pública o privada que tienen potencial como zonas de desarrollo urbano. Esta condición genera conflictos entre los colonos, la Municipalidad –el organismo a cargo de controlar el uso de la tierra– y los propietarios de las tierras.

Los colonos por lo general forman "comunidades" semi-legales para obtener títulos de propiedad o servicios de la ciudad. En muchos casos, el propietario oficial de las tierras le permite a la ciudad resolver el problema suministrando los servicios necesarios. Las regulaciones municipales en materia de construcción, medio ambiente, salud y seguridad no se ponen en práctica de manera igualitaria.

El sentido de comunidad que establecen los primeros colonos se desintegra una vez que la ciudad comienza a proveer servicios y los colonos pronto vuelven a una existencia competitiva, de subsistencia. La ciudad, que no está preparada para asumir los nuevos costos de estos desarrollos inesperados, es incapaz de continuar proveyendo servicios.

CONTRAPROPUESTA

Para solucionar estos problemas, la municipalidad debe adoptar una actitud más proactiva ante los desarrollos informales, monitoreando las tendencias e identificando los nuevos desarrollos cuando éstos son aún incipientes. Debe construir micro-infraestructura para los nuevos asentamientos que ponga en práctica tres controles esenciales para las construcciones informales, sin declararlas ilegales ni hacerse el de la vista gorda.

En primer lugar, la ciudad debe definir los límites de los desarrollos ilegales y establecer derechos de propiedad en las tierras adyacentes al asentamiento.

En segundo lugar, debe introducir un sistema que permita y do sopor le al crecimiento progresivo y contigente.

La municipalidad recuperará parte de su inversión en el corto plazo, al controlar el suministro de agua y de energía.

La ciudad también verá su inversión recompensada en el largo plazo, puesto que tendrá infraestructura para futuros desarrollos.

La ciudad comenzará a proveer servicios antes de que comience el desarrollo. El suministro de estos servicios tendrá lugar con métodos respetuosos del medio ambiente que asegurarán su mantenimiento a través del tiempo.

VER IMÁGENES Y GRÁFICOS, PÁGINAS: 117 a 120.

BARRIO SAN FRANCISCO

Por **JOHN HILL**

La estrategia de desarrollo para este área urbanizada al norte del centro del barrio Los Ángeles consiste en la construcción de viviendas en lotes vacíos y de infraestructura pública distribuida de manera equitativa.

Las propuestas incluyen la rehabilitación ecológica de terrenos deteriorados con acceso a la red de agua corriente; la creación de frentes de uso mixto con franjas comerciales; una red verde de bulevares, parques, vías fluviales y selva recuperada; y una red de transporte público que les otorgue prioridad a los peatones y a los ciclistas.

COMPLEJO EN TRES CAPAS

Este complejo de seis cuadras será una adición fundamental al barrio de San Francisco, tanto en lo económico como en lo ambiental y en lo social. El proyecto consiste en tres capas agregadas desde dentro hacia fuera (de allí su nombre): un parque central unido al límite norte por medio de un parque lineal ininterrumpido; nuevos edificios de la Universidad del Oriento, destinados al estudio agroforestal, a la investigación médica y a otros estudios en materia de conservación forestal; y una combinación de distintos usos con comercios y viviendas en la planta baja. Además, una plaza pública se ubica en la esquina sudeste, hay oficinas gubernamentales locales y nacionales en el límite este, y una torre con mirador entre medio de ambas.

Todas las partes del complejo dependen del centro: un parque público que a la vez será un centro de educación especializado en la recuperación ecológica de la selva que simultáneamente colaborará con su conservación y la integrará a la ciudad. Todas ellas, por consiguiente, tienen un interés fundamentado en su conservación: las instalaciones educativas, investigar la selva; los comercios, (proveer de servicios a la universidad); y el público, (disfrutar del parque, la plaza y el mirador).

COMPONENTES

Alrededor del perímetro del complejo se ubican pequeños lotes, estrechos y profundos, que serán construidos con el tiempo. Además de este acceso a la calle, hay entradas a callejones de servicio entre los edificios educativos y de uso mixto; pasajes de la calle al nivel principal –elevado– de la escuela, y "senderos selváticos", donde la selva se abre a la calle, invitando a los transeúntes a internarse en el parque. Los edificios de la escuela poseen ventilación natural, reciclado de agua de lluvia, tratamiento de aguas residuales y circulación exterior que alterna de un lado al otro, interactuando con los pasajes.

VER IMÁGENES Y GRÁFICOS, PÁGINAS: 121 a 124.

UNIVERSIDAD DEL ORIENCO

Por **HOLLY KALLMAN**

El río Orienco corre por el barrio más importante de Lago Agrio. Desde la entrada occidental hasta la ciudad, el río corre hacia el noreste a lo largo de la Avenida Quito, pasando por el ayuntamiento y la alcaldía.
En la mayoría de las ciudades en crecimiento, un río como el Orienco sería considerado un estorbo. Los residentes arrojan sus desperdicios en él, y es necesario construir puentes para cruzarlo. Con el tiempo, quizá la ciudad decida entubarlo, hasta que las inundaciones, con pérdidas materiales y quizás humanas, le recuerden a la ciudad su olvidada existencia.
El Orienco podría correr otro futuro. Podría convertirse en un "lugar", con mejoras y construcciones, quizá denso, para una serie de distintos usos. Podría convertirse en la sede de una universidad para la Región Amazónica.
Una universidad ubicada aquí también albergaría una escuela primaria y una secundaria, suministrando viviendas y aulas para la educación comunitaria y de adultos. Capacitaría a los adultos para trabajar como maestros, inicialmente a través de un sistema por medio del cual los padres y tutores recibirían una remuneración por acompañar a grupos de alumnos a sus escuelas.
La Universidad del Orienco trabajaría conjuntamente con la ciudad para establecer las bases de una sociedad próspera y humana, creando nuevos centros de conocimiento y atrayendo a los residentes involucrados con la salud, el bienestar de la comunidad y el desarrollo de los recursos de la región.
Los cursos que impartiría la universidad comprenderían las siguientes asignaturas: salud pública; agricultura sustentable; regeneración de la selva y de la vida silvestre; energía renovable; tecnologías de transporte y construcción renovables, locales e inteligentes.
La ubicación del río Orienco en el centro de Nueva Loja, y su importancia como intersección de distintas cuencas, lo convierten en el emplazamiento ideal para una nueva universidad. Se mantendría el actual nivel de las aguas, y el río funcionaría como un sistema de desagüe y reciclado de agua, y como lugar de recreación.
Para que la universidad tenga éxito, es necesario desarrollar el Orienco; podría convertirse en un sistema vivo para el procesamiento de las aguas servidas de la ciudad. Sin embargo, esto debe planearse cuidadosamente, dado que la construcción de una universidad incrementaría la densidad del área. El campus debe convertirse en un modelo, de carácter innovador, de esos sistemas.
La construcción de la universidad es un proyecto que se ejecutaría en 20 años, divididos en distintas fases.
El programa de fomento de UNESCO-UNITWIN podría establecer un plan para la universidad con una serie de objetivos determinados.
La universidad podría ser financiada por la OPEP y por empresas petroleras multinacionales, dado que a éstas les interesa investigar tecnologías de remediación. El tipo de investigación a largo plazo que se necesitaría para obtener verdaderos resultados tendría un costo prohibitivo si se llevara a cabo en los Estados Unidos. Este tipo de investigación atraería a a varios equipos líderes en diversos temas a la zona, donde también podrían enseñar.
La financiación para las facultades de Educación, Biología y Ciencias de la Vida, Agricultura y Estudios Forestales podría proceder de compañías multinacionales del sector energético, el Banco Mundial y ONGs.
La universidad atraería a educadores de nivel internacional a la región para cubrir la falta de especialistas locales.

VER IMÁGENES Y GRÁFICOS, PÁGINAS: 125 a 129.

EL BARRIO CHACRA

Por **CHRIS SYRETT**

El rediseño del Barrio Chacra se basa en una economía dinámica y sustentable, centrada en la agricultura y la explotación forestal.
El barrio se dividirá en 11 barrios más pequeños. Cada uno de estos "micro-barrios" incluye una parcela de selva en las afueras de Nueva Loja. Los productos forestales no maderables, los empleos y otros beneficios que se derivarán de estas pequeñas selvas individuales incrementarán el valor colectivo e individual de cada micro-barrio.
El barrio cuenta actualmente con 1.500 habitantes. Con la introducción de este esquema de chacras la población se duplicará.
Cada hogar de la comunidad recibirá dos parcelas agrícolas para suplementar su provisión de alimentos y sus ingresos. Utilizando el sistema indígena de chacras con rotación de cultivos, los hogares deberán mantener una porción considerable de sus tierras en barbecho. Esto permitirá la recuperación del suelo y de la bóveda de la selva. Se podrá acceder a las parcelas a través de pasarelas móviles de madera ubicadas sobre campos en barbecho.
Cada micro barrera tendrá un espacio central de encuentro y recreación, además de viviendas ubicadas en los lotes vacíos. Habrá asimismo al menos una tienda compartida por comunidad. El centro será un lugar para practicar deportes, celebrar reuniones comunitarias, llevar a cabo acciones políticas o simplemente pasar el tiempo y relajarse.

VER IMÁGENES Y GRÁFICOS, PÁGINAS: 130 a 133.

BARRIO LA FLORIDA

Por **ROBERTA KORCZ**

La Florida es la sección noreste de Nueva Loja. Limita con el aeropuerto al norte, con un importante campo de petróleo al oeste, con tierras bajas al sur y con una pequeña comunidad residencial al oeste. Se ubica sobre el "petromuro", una zona de la ciudad con enorme presencia de infraestructura petrolera. Son también características de la fisonomía de La Florida las irrupciones intermitentes de la selva tropical en la ciudad, que crean una yuxtaposición surrealista de acero y vegetación.

DISEÑO FINAL

El diseño de La Florida se basa en un sistema de corredores verdes que conectan los principales núcleos del barrio, según el esquema determinado por la infraestructura petrolera preexistente.
Cuando dentro de 25 años el petróleo se acabe, estos núcleos evolucionarán acompañando el crecimiento de las nuevas economías basadas en el bambú, el turismo, la horticultura y otras iniciativas ecológicas. A medida que éstas se desarrollen, la antigua infraestructura petrolera continuará siendo parte de la identidad de la ciudad.
Los corredores verdes permitirán recorrer a pie el barrio, reduciendo la utilización de automóviles. Un sistema de transporte público que rodeará el barrio hará posible acceder fácilmente al resto de la ciudad. Estos corredores verdes también aportarán fitorremediación, que ayudará a eliminar toxinas del suelo. Los corredores verdes crearán una red de tupidas franjas de selva en todo el barrio.
En el extremo sur de La Florida se encuentra un pantano semi-artificial. Esta zona se encuentra en un terreno más bajo, lo que la convierte en un sitio ideal para el drenaje de aguas de escorrentía. Este pantano será desarrollado como una reserva destinada el uso recreativo de residentes, turistas e investigadores, ofreciendo una alternativa que dará descanso a las reservas de selva tropical ubicadas en zonas aledañas.

VER IMÁGENES Y GRÁFICOS, PÁGINAS: 134 a 139.

DE-CENTRAL PARK

Por **PATRICK WEISEL**

CONSIDERACIONES INICIALES DE DISEÑO

El patrón de desarrollo de este barrio ha sido determinado por las redes de infraestructura petrolera; entre sus líneas de conexión se ubicaron comercios y viviendas. De-Central Park se encuentra sobre uno de los bordes más importantes de la ciudad, con grandes parques nacionales y reservas ecológicas al este y al sur. Su condición de límite produce la unión entre un entorno edificado y la selva.
Debido a la presencia del aeropuerto, al norte, las ordenanzas establecen limitaciones en la altura de las construcciones en ciertas zonas. Este barrio ubicado al noreste de la ciudad cumpliŕacuatro funciones principales: servirá de entrada a Nueva Loja desde el aeropuerto y los parques nacionales aledaños; conformará el límite noreste de la ciudad; sentará un precedente para la conversión de infraestructura petrolera en lugares funcionales y atractivos cuando se acabe el petróleo dentro de 25 años; y fomentará la industria turística de la región. Geográficamente, este barrio se dividirá en tres áreas principales de desarrollo. Al noreste, se conservarán los pozos petroleros agotados, que serán integrados en un nuevo paisaje. Estas áreas serán transformadas en parques, corredores verdes y áreas turísticas, sin perder de vista la rica historia petrolera de la ciudad. El aeropuerto, de importancia fundamental para este barrio atravesado horizontalmente por el petromuro, seguirá siendo una de las principales puertas de entrada a Lago Agrio. La zona se convertirá a la vez en símbolo de la historia petrolera de la ciudad y de su futuro sustentable.
El extremo oriental de la Avenida Quito alberga grandes campos petroleros aún en funcionamiento. Ésta es la primera sección de la ciudad que podrán ver los visitantes al llegar al aeropuerto y la última que verán al dejar la ciudad rumbo a los parques nacionales de las inmediaciones. La yuxtaposición de infraestructura petrolera y escenarios naturales podría crear un límite dinámico que sería a la vez atractivo y ecológicamente responsable.

VER GRÁFICOS, PÁGINAS: 140, 141.

BARRIO LA ESQUINA

Por **GARETH MAHON**

Todos los caminos conducen a la esquina: La Esquina se encuentra en la convergencia de varias arterias importantes de la ciudad, incluyendo la "Diagonal", el bulevar entre el río Aguarico y la Avenida Quito. Ubicada sobre la entrada sur del parque central, La Esquina se convertirá en un destino turístico así como en un barrio residencial. nUna plaza central multifuncional servirá de lugar de encuentro, entrada al parque y centro cultural, identificable en toda la ciudad. El barrio contará con una sólida red educativa que incluirá numerosas escuelas de enseñanza técnica. El sistema de espacios verdes del barrio comprenderá un sistema visible y descentralizado de manejo de desperdicios.

CONDICIONES EXISTENTES

Área	80 hectáreas
Viviendas	440
Población	1.600
Densidad	20 personas por hectárea
Distritos municipales	9

CONDICIONES PROPUESTAS

Población	8.000
Densidad	100 personas por hectárea

INFRAESTRUCTURA REQUERIDA

Centro médico	1
Consultorios públicos	6
Guarderías	6
Escuelas primarias	3
Escuela secundaria	1
Comisaría	1

SISTEMAS Y REDES

PARQUES, CANCHAS, HUERTAS COMUNITARIAS Y ENTROS DE RECICLADO

Centros de reciclaje descentralizados
Red peatonal
Espacios verdes protegidos al aire libre

CIRCULACIÓN

Bulevar "La Diagonal"
30-35m de ancho
Cuatro carriles para automóviles y bicicletas.
Edificios comerciales con mesas para comer en la acera
Calles secundarias
15m de ancho
Dos carriles para automóviles y uno para bicicletas
Actividad comercial a nivel de la calle
Corredores verdes
3-4m de ancho
Bicisendas de doble mano y sendero peatonal

EDUCACIÓN

Campo de deportes compartido
Escuelas: técnicas, primaria y secundaria.
Recursos
Consultorios públicos a 250 metros
Centro barrial a 500 metros
Campo de deportes
Parque o huertas comunitarias a 250 metros
Conexiones
Corredor verde a la escuela | Ruta de autobús a la escuela

CENTROS COMUNITARIOS

Uso comercial y servicios sociales
Identidad barrial
Vínculo con el resto de la ciudad
Vínculo entre la ciudad y el barrio
Autobús directo, corredor verde y calle/bulevar principal
Centro del barrio
Servicios de emergencia – cuartel de bomberos, comisaría y centro médico | Factor de atracción local principal | Parque o plaza que le dénidentidad al barrio
Conexión con otros barrios
Combinación de autobuses, corredor verde, calles de uso mixto.
Conectado a través de otros barrios.
Centro barrial
Servicios básicos, centro comunitario y consultorios públicos | Identidad local | Espacio al aire libre
Beneficia a 1.500 personas
Conexión interbarrial
Conexión a través del corredor verde y las calles de uso mixto
Recursos compartidos
Distancia mínima 500 metros

LÍMITES Y TERRENOS PRESERVADOS

Los límites del actual perímetro edificado se extienden hasta alcanzar una distancia de 15 metros de todas las vías fluviales.
El borde se mantiene ocupado con tierras destinadas a la explotación agrícola y agroforestal.
Se eliminan los lotes desocupados que indica el plano de la ciudad.

CONDICIONES Y TOPOGRAFÍA ACTUALES

Expansión formal e informal sobre las mayores elevaciones.
El cambio de elevación en todo el predio oscila entre los 10 y 15 mts.
La línea de barrancos sobre el límite norte del barrio aporta el cambio de elevación necesario para la plaza.
Arroyos y áreas más bajas de drenaje.

VER IMÁGENES Y GRÁFICOS, PÁGINAS: 142 a 147.

BARRIO ISEGORIDA

Por **ALAN FOX**

Isegorida será un nuevo barrio de artesanos para 10.000 personas, cuya fisonomía recordará la acogedora proporción y escala de una ciudad medieval europea. Las plazas, callejones, pasajes, parques y calles darán la sensación de ser una extensión de las salas de estar de los residentes. Esto fomentará un sentido de comunidad e inclusión. Los servicios públicos se encontrarán a 20 minutos de caminata los unos de los otros, reduciendo las necesidades de transporte.

CONDICIONES EXISTENTES. INFRAESTRUCTURA PÚBLICA.

EDUCACIÓN	
GUARDERÍAS	7
ESCUELAS PRIMARIAS	4
SECUNDARIA	1
ESCUELA COMERCIAL	1
SALUD	
CONSULTORIOS PÚBLICOS	7
CENTRO DE SALUD	2
HOSPITAL	1
MERCADO	
PEQUEÑAS TIENDAS	3
MERCADOS CALLEJEROS	30
CENTRO COMERCIAL	4
MUNICIPAL	
SALAS DE REUNIÓN	10
POLICÍAS	10
BOMBEROS	3
CALABOZOS	1

El Puente de la Noria, al igual que la ahora mejorada Avenida Quito, será no sólo una ruta de transporte sino también un destino turístico. Se ensanchará la acera en un tramo equivalente a la mitad del largo del puente para permitir que la gente pasee tranquilamente. Esta acera también tendrá bancos, árboles y pequeños puestos. La noria rodeará el centro del puente, y se convertirá en un punto de interés así como en una puerta de entrada al barrio. El río será su fuente de energía, conectando además a la gente con el agua.

VER IMÁGENES Y GRÁFICOS, PÁGINAS: 148 a 151.

BARRIO PUERTO AGUARICO

Por **MARIANA CASTILLO**

VER IMÁGENES Y GRÁFICOS, PÁGINAS: 152 a 157.

EL CARBÓN ENCENDIDO

Por **PILYUN AHN**

El nuevo pavimento permeable para las aceras se inspira en la trama de las alfombras.
El pavimento de las carreteras utiliza residuos de petróleo.

SISTEMAS NATURALES DE DRENAJE

Se construirá una red de zanjas, jardines y cascadas a ambos lados de las calles para que el agua de lluvia pueda ser absorbida directamente por el suelo o a través de canales de drenaje.
El sistema de drenaje está inspirado en el proyecto *Street Edge Alternative*, de Seattle, que comenzó como un experimento en un barrio residencial de casas unifamiliares, con una baja densidad poblacional. A raíz del éxito del programa, la secretaría de obras públicas de Seattle extendió el experimento a áreas urbanas cada vez más grandes y más densamente pobladas, demostrando que estas técnicas innovadoras podían aplicarse no sólo en zonas de bajo desarrollo urbano, sino también en tejidos consolidados de alta densidad poblacional.

EL MOTOR DE LA CREACIÓN

Este diseño se basa en una espiral que representa la creación.
Mide 18 metros de diámetro.
Crea un lugar de encuentro y esparcimiento.
Ayudará a incrementar el valor de la propiedad.
Las tres columnas representan recursos naturales, gente y ciencia.
Se ubica en el centro de una rotonda.

INFINITO

Una rotonda.
Una plaza de 30 metros de diámetro.
Su función: superficie para andar en bicicleta, patinar y trotar.
El árbol proporciona sombra.
El diseño es una espiral que representa el infinito.

A TRAVÉS DEL ESPEJO

El concepto es geométrico.
Una horizontal, una vertical y un rectángulo profundo.
A través del espejo.
Es lógico y orgánico.
Una pared de árboles da sombra.

UNA LUNA LLENA

Una escuela ateniense > un diseño lógico y clásico en la entrada
Un diseño en forma de ola interior> la educación produce nuevas olas de pensamiento

KARMA

Una plaza con sol – un reloj de sol y un reloj transparente
Una plaza soleada – cuatro en el barrio

PLAZA BAÑADA POR LA LUZ DE LA LUNA

Concepto: la yuxtaposición de la pasión y la fría abstracción geométrica
Fuego > yuxtaposición > frío
Un espacio bucólico: los agricultores necesitan un lugar de descanso

PLAZA DEL TRIUNFO

Una flor florecida, rectángulos infinitos, fases de la luna, un águila en vuelo.
La llegada de la marea > una plaza
Todos estos elementos se incorporan a una plaza activa

OLA

Giros, remolino, ilusión óptica
La tercera ola (científica) > una sensación activa

ORIGEN

CAPULLO

Función: circulación de automóviles, peatones y sombra

VER IMÁGENES Y GRÁFICOS, PÁGINAS: 158 a 171.

- Infraestructura arquitectónica para la ciudad post-petróleo
- El techo-máquina
- Cubrir, unir, colgar
- El sistema
- El prototipo
- Prototipo de vivienda para un clima húmedo y caluroso
- Prototipo 750
- Vivienda unifamiliar con paredes apersianadas
- Viviendas en la naturaleza
- Viviendas apilables
- Viviendas multifamiliares: la partida de la ciudad
- Viviendas multifamiliares: vivir en el Amazonas
- Viviendas de Lago Agrio
- Aula móvil: escuela pop-up
- Aula móvil: prototipo de 0 basura
- Aula móvil: escuela desplegable
- Escuela secundaria de Puerto Aguarico
- Escuela primaria verdiazul
- La Escuela Urbana
- La Escuela como herramienta de aprendizaje: la Escuela de Construcción de Nueva Loja
- Asentamientos humanos sustentables para la era post-petrolera en la Amazonía ecuatoriana: una introducción al Taller de Lago Agrio (FADA-PUCE)
- Paisaje productivo - Vivienda productiva
- Sistemas sostenibles
- Conector multicapas
- Metabolismos autosuficientes
- Bandas de crecimiento
- Fusión Material
- Vivienda unifamiliar auto-sostenible
- Capa protectora

INFRAESTRUCTURA ARQUITECTÓNICA PARA LA CIUDAD POST-PETRÓLEO

Por **DAVID LEVEN**

Lago Agrio, o Nueva Loja, como suele llamársela, es una pequeña y polvorienta ciudad petrolera ubicada en la Región Amazónica, en el Oriente ecuatoriano. A juzgar por las presiones a las que está sometida la ciudad, bien podría explotar o desaparecer en medio de la selva luego de sus cuarenta años de existencia. La explosión urbana podría tener lugar de varias maneras y en diferentes escalas: por el crecimiento económico debido a la migración interna; efecto de la agitación social debido a las bajo las presiones neoliberales del primer mundo y a las desigualdades de la economía petrolera; presiones del narcotráfico en la zona de frontera; producto de la degradación ambiental producida por las empresas petroleras y forestales; o por la explosión literal de un pozo de petróleo. Por otra parte, la disolución podría tener lugar si tras el agotamiento del petróleo en la región, no lo reemplaza otra base económica.

Sin embargo, al visitar la ciudad nos encontramos con un asentamiento efervescente, a menudo contradictorio y mayoritariamente informal, rebosante de actividad humana. La vida continúa, y abundan los patrones de habitación, interacción social, comunidad y coexistencia con el clima. Al estudiar estos patrones, es posible encontrar soluciones arquitectónicas integradas que hagan de esta ciudad un lugar saludable, sustentable, equitativo y hermoso; que albergue un sinfín de actividades, economías y pueblos. Los estudiantes de arquitectura, cuyo trabajo se muestra aquí, tuvieron que lidiar con las implicancias arquitectónicas de la interacción entre sociedades tradicionales y modernas. Sus propuestas, que prestan atención tanto a la tradición como al clima, se valen de materiales, métodos y procesos de construcción apropiados, tanto modernos como tradicionales.

PROPUESTA: INFRAESTRUCTURA ARQUITECTÓNICA

Dado que el ámbito del arquitecto es la construcción y la geografía social de los lugares, nos hemos centrado en dos tipos de construcción (con subtipos derivados): viviendas y escuelas. A estas últimas, las consideramos parte de una tradición del siglo XX (particularmente, de principios del siglo XX, cuando existía un gran interés por los ideales sociales) y de una metodología de diseño centrada en la comunidad.

Los estudiantes diseñaron viviendas en distintas escalas, desde el refugio unifamiliar hasta la aglomeración de viviendas en las que los servicios son compartidos y la organización de los edificios facilita las agrupaciones comunitarias. Cuando pasaron del estudio de la vivienda como entidad individual, separada del resto, a la disposición urbana de múltiples unidades, la vivienda comenzó a ser considerada "infraestructura", conectada al esquema urbano, diseñada para aportar eficiencia y continuidad urbana. También consideraron el acceso a una vivienda humana y sustentable como un derecho.

La idea de que la infraestructura determina la configuración de un lugar puede verificarse en la infraestructura petrolera del Oriente. El oleoducto ecuatoriano, una infraestructura mundial neoliberal, que atraviesa todo el país desde la costa pacífica, a través de la cordillera de los Andes, hasta la cuenca del Amazonas, se extiende paralelamente a la única carretera principal que une Quito con Lago Agrio, Shushufindi y otras ciudades petroleras amazónicas. Esta impasible tubería, muchas veces negra y lisa, otras pintada con eslóganes políticos, circunvala física y económicamente a la gente que vive a lo largo de ella, a pesar de que muchos se ven obligados a servirla. En contraste, las "infraestructuras" aquí propuestas por los estudiantes desafían las políticas neoliberales que colonizan el espacio en base a un conjunto muy estrecho de reglas económicas. Por el contrario, sus soluciones abren el debate acerca de la integración de distintas economías (incluyendo la petrolera, mientras dure), formaciones sociales y prácticas sustentables, capaces de reconfigurar la ciudad post-petróleo en torno a ideales urbanos y arquitectónicos positivos.

La idea, que podría parecer una herejía para el capitalismo occidental, de que la vivienda puede ser considerada una infraestructura que determina la fisonomía de una ciudad, presupone que, al igual que el agua potable, la vivienda es un derecho. Sin embargo, los estudiantes no concibieron la infraestructura como algo monótono, impersonal y verticalista, como gran parte de las viviendas construidas por los go-

biomos, sino más bien como algo táctil, tectónico, que fuera un reflejo de la comunidad y estuviera en armonía con la naturaleza.
Los principales modelos arquitectónicos que consideran a las escuelas un producto de la comunidad que a la vez la determina proceden de los arquitectos de mediados del siglo XX, Aldo Van Eyck y Herman Hertberger. Su trabajo constituyó la base para pensar una escuela selvática urbana centrada en la comunidad. También fomentó la comparación entre la construcción de escuelas luego de las Guerras Mundiales y en esta región post-petrolera, que también sufre las consecuencias del narcotráfico colombiano y la respuesta militar al mismo, así como del reclutamiento por parte de los grupos insurgentes y la prostitución (de hecho, hay un prostíbulo junto a una de las escuelas secundarias de Lago Agrio).

LAS VIVIENDAS POST-PETRÓLEO DESDE LA PERSPECTIVA DE LAS VIVIENDAS DE POSGUERRA

Es común que las ciudades que sufren las secuelas de una catástrofe experimenten un auge de la construcción.
Es menos típico, pero a veces ocurre, que se produzca una reevaluación del rol social de la arquitectura. En 1928, en la Europa de posguerra, un grupo de arquitectos modernos liderado por Le Corbusier y Sigfried Gideon fundó el Congress International d'Architecture Moderne (CIAM). El CIAM buscaba definir los principios de la arquitectura moderna, declarándola un arte social. La segunda conferencia del CIAM, que tuvo lugar en 1933, se centró en la vivienda mínima; allí se introdujo el concepto de Existenzminimum, que se presentó como un nuevo modelo teórico para la provisión de viviendas sociales y humanas. La sexta conferencia, en 1947, dos años después de que la Segunda Guerra Mundial hubiera dejado en ruinas numerosas ciudades europeas, se centró en la reconstrucción de las ciudades. Las conferencias del CIAM también formalizaron ciertos métodos materiales y tecnológicos que determinaron la fisonomía de los ámbitos edificados del mundo moderno. Estos tres temas, la vivienda social, la reconstrucción de las ciudades y los profundos efectos de la industria mundial dela extracción de materias primas tienen fuertes implicancias en esta lejana ciudad selvática.
Si bien no es en modo alguno equiparable a las consecuencias de una guerra mundial, el impacto de Texaco y otras compañías petroleras sobre la selva ecuatoriana puede considerarse catastrófico, dada la severidad de la degradación del medio ambiente y de la calidad de vida de sus habitantes, así como los efectos colaterales de la extracción petrolera en la cuenca amazónica. Cuando Texaco se estableció en la región, las formas de vivienda eran únicamente indígenas y primitivas, pero ambiental y climáticamente adecuadas y sofisticadas. Un buen ejemplo es la típica vivienda huaorani, de carácter intrínsecamente temporario, fabricada con largas y delgadas piezas de madera recubiertas de hojas, para formar una cubierta autoventilante. Asimismo, la simple innovación tecnológica de hileras de hojas estrechamente superpuestas hacía a esta cubierta altamente resistente a la filtración de agua proveniente de las copiosas y persistentes lluvias de la selva tropical.
Tiene una abertura cubierta en la parte superior, que permite que escape el humo de la cocina y que además fumiga la vivienda contra insectos de la selva, conforme se dispersa.Cuando los pueblos indígenas fueron recluidos en reservas, sus viviendas fueron transformadas en algo muy inferior: en los permanentes, modernos y ubicuos bloques de cemento o en barracas de madera, con un techo de hierro galvanizado que produce un calor asfixiante cuando brilla el sol y un ruido ensordecedor los días de tormenta. Estos bloques de cemento y los edificios del mismo material de mayores dimensiones son la resaca de la adopción por parte del movimiento moderno internacional del cemento como material con el cual construir la totalidad del mundo moderno, independientemente del clima, la estructura social o la cultura material.
Cuarenta años más tarde en Lago Agrio, ha surgido una ciudad informal con una estructura, en gran medida aleatoria, de manzanas y lotes, cuya fisonomía es producto de la adquisición y la contingencia individual. La ciudad forma una cuadrícula azarosa que rodea una pista de aterrizaje, unos campamentos donde se encuentran los depósitos de petróleo, una serie de arroyos convertidos en estanques de aguas servidas y un gran espacio verde protegido de la adquisición por parte de las compañías petroleras o el ejército por un propietario particular; todo esto antes de desaparecer hacia el sur, donde se encuentra con el río Aguarico. Las dimensiones de estas manzanas van de los 60x60 metros a los 60x90 e incluso 60x140 metros, con lotes y construcciones azarosamente distribuidos. Las construcciones residenciales en estos lotes a menudo toman la apariencia de un conjunto de casas, talleres y galpones agrupados muy cerca el uno del otro, que comparten medianeros con estructuras vecinas. Como siempre, la selva intenta volver a surgir allí donde no se la tala o se la cubre con pavimento. Los materiales con que está construida la ciudad son el cemento y el bloque de cemento, el hierro galvanizado y la madera. Establecidas de manera informal, algunas áreas muy densas de la ciudad contienen lotes y estructuras con usos residenciales, comerciales e industriales superpuestos en forma de delgadas franjas que se topan con los campamentos petroleros. Estas franjas miden aproximadamente 5 metros de ancho por 30-40 metros de largo, medidos desde la calle. Otras formas de vivienda son chozas informales sin acceso a servicios, o edificios de varios pisos sin terminar, en cuyos pisos más bajos generalmente funcionan viviendas, destinándose los más altos a depósitos o a secar la ropa.
El desafío para los estudiantes era, en primer lugar, comprender los patrones de vivienda anteriormente descriptos. En segundo lugar, determinar qué saberes, métodos, tecnologías y materiales locales podían resultar útiles. Tercero, proponer planes arquitectónicos integrales a nivel del lote y de la vivienda unifamiliar, y luego a nivel del conjunto de múltiples viviendas. Y finalmente, considerar tecnologías, morfologías y prácticas sustentables externas que puedan resultar apropiadas. A la hora de construir viviendas y escuelas, los estudiantes debieron trabajar desde un primer momento con un master plan urbano, para asegurarse de que sus propuestas se integraran a las comunidades aledañas. Asimismo, estos proyectos debían tener en cuenta qué infraestructura se encontraba ya presente, cuál había que reforzar y cuál era necesario construir antes de que sus ideas pudieran ponerse en práctica.

TRADICIONES CONTEMPORÁNEAS

Varios arquitectos contemporáneos y proyectos arquitectónicos sirvieron como precedentes para marcar el enfoque seguido por los estudiantes. Las viviendas sociales de Álvaro Siva en el Barrio de la Malagueira, en Évora, Portugal (1977-1999) configuran la totalidad del plan urbano alrededor de un sistema de acueductos infraestructurales que transportan agua y otros servicios a las viviendas. Los acueductos se construyeron primero, los planos y los edificios modelo se realizaron según los principios modernistas de existencia mínima, y la comunidad hoy en día sigue cumpliendo con el master plan. En el proyecto de Siza, el genio arquitectónico se evidencia en la dependencia de una infraestructura física visible que proporciona lo necesario para el crecimiento pero además crea una sensación de comunidad en el marco de una situación económica muy modesta. De manera análoga, la Quinta Monroy, realizada por Alejandro Aravena en la ciudad chilena de Iquique, en 2004, presenta una serie de módulos mínimos de vivienda con huecos entre unidades, que pueden ser completados por los residentes a medida que sus finanzas se lo permitan. El propietario de una unidad adquiere el espacio mínimo que puede pagar y la estructura general del complejo se va llenando con el tiempo. Como resultado, se plantean condiciones de comunidad dinámicas y en constante evolución.

El proyecto del Estudio Teddy Cruz realizado en la frontera entre San Diego y Tijuana constituye otro ejemplo de las posibilidades de lo informal y lo comunal. En la Casa Familiar, las configuraciones informales de viviendas y los edificios sociales se entrelazan entre sí para crear una comunidad que no se adapta a los códigos locales aceptados sino que responde a las necesidades y a las características de sus habitantes.

PROYECTOS DE VIVIENDA

Los proyectos de vivienda aquí presentados estudian una serie de problemas específicos de este entorno selvático. Inicialmente, los estudiantes redujeron los parámetros de diseño para las viviendas en la selva a tres operaciones: cubrir, unir, colgar. Como resultado, fue posible aislar las cuestiones climáticas, tectónicas y ergonómicas como problemas autónomos de diseño, y como condiciones que luego serían integradas en esquemas arquitectónicos completos.

Uno de los proyectos, un sistema de techado en forma de hoja, utiliza el bambú tradicional como sistema estructural y lo combina con ensambles/juntas de aluminio o acero. Otro, la Máquina del Techo, va un paso más adelante, proponiendo una configuración flexible que permite la modulación del flujo de aire en la estructura. El Sistema, un método de componentes estructurales, estudia los procesos naturales de las telarañas y las chinches de agua para lograr eficiencia formal y estructural. La genialidad del Sistema estriba en su sistema de uniones y en su separación de la tierra, producto del reconocimiento de la polución del suelo provocada por la explotación petrolera. El Módulo de Vivienda Prototipo se ocupa de cuestiones similares –la unión, la separación del suelo y la tecnología del bambú– y las aplica a través de sistemas de diseño no lineales y no jerárquicos adecuados al caos ordenado de la selva. Este proyecto sintetizaba el ejercicio inicial de "colgar, unir y cubrir" con el estudio prototípico de la vivienda unitaria. En el diseño del componente residencial de unidades únicas, los estudiantes determinaron inicialmente el tamaño, los materiales, los métodos de construcción, los requerimientos energéticos y los métodos de remediación adecuados para las viviendas de Nueva Loja. Se consideraron además otras cuestiones, como la cercanía a otras viviendas, la circulación de la comunidad y la reproducibilidad. En el proyecto de vivienda prototipo, se estudió en profundidad hasta qué punto y en qué convenía modernizar las viviendas indígenas. Los tres prototipos aquí presentados responden a la cuestión climática separando las estructuras del suelo y creando sistemas de paredes apersianadas o permeables para permitir el flujo de aire. Los sistemas estructurales también tuvieron una importancia fundamental en este ejercicio, como lo muestra el Prototipo 750, que usa tubo de acero –omnipresente desecho de la industria petrolera– para estructurar una flexible unidad de vivienda desmontable, que puede transportarse fácilmente en un camión e instalarse en cualquier zona de la ciudad o de la región. Otros proyectos empleaban sistemas desmontables fabricados con cañas de bambú de distinto diámetro, obtenidos de plantaciones existentes o propuestas.

Los proyectos de vivienda colectiva presentaban un conjunto de requisitos y condiciones diferentes, de mayor escala, complejidad y presencia urbana. En estos proyectos fue necesario realizar un plan maestro de todo el barrio para comprender el tejido urbano de cada escenario, tanto a gran como a pequeña escala. El plan maestro incluía cuestiones relativas al acceso; al carácter urbano; a la volumetría y la zonificación; a los bordes y el contexto; así como propuestas para mejorar los sistemas de transporte existentes y las mallas urbanas, y estimular el fomento de las actividades comunitarias y la provisión de servicios públicos. Una vez establecido, el master plan se desarrolló en configuraciones programáticas que tenían en cuenta las características del barrio, e incluían distintas unidades de vivienda, áreas comunales, acceso al transporte público y privado, estacionamientos para bicicletas y vehículos de uso comercial, instalaciones comerciales, estrategias de generación de sombra tanto a nivel de la unidad como de la comunidad, y programas y formaciones verdes.

PROYECTOS PARA LA CONSTRUCCIÓN DE ESCUELAS

El sistema escolar de Nueva Loja es seriamente inadecuado para la población existente: en el número de escuelas, en la calidad de los edificios e instalaciones para los alumnos, los docentes y la comunidad en general, y en sus métodos para lograr la sustentabilidad. El sistema escolar, que incluye guarderías, escuelas primarias y secundarias (Ecuador sólo divide sus escuelas en estos dos grupos principales) corre el riesgo de quedarse atrás en materia de instalaciones, con lo cual se vería sobrecargado por el aumento de la población, que según proyecciones trepará a los 125.000-150.000 en la próxima década. Además, en Ecuador es común que los alumnos asistan a la escuela en distintos turnos (mañana, tarde o noche) que permiten acoger el doble de alumnos en un mismo edificio. En Nueva loja, los edificios permanentes de las escuelas eran prioritarios. Pero también encontramos la necesidad de hallar soluciones temporarias, que permitan acomodar de manera flexible y rápida a una población en crecimiento.

Para ese fin, el primer ejercicio que desarrollaron los alumnos fue diseñar edificios temporarios, potencialmente móviles, de dimensiones flexibles, para satisfacer la necesidad cambiante de aulas, consultorios médicos y lugares de reunión. Como precedente, se estudió el modelo de la Clínica Móvil de Salud para la Atención del VIH/SIDA, creado por Architecture for Humanity en 2002 en el África subsahariana. Las ideas inherentes a este concurso de diseño –flexibilidad, asequibilidad, sustentabilidad, justicia social, diseño inteligente y eficiente– fueron el punto de partida para los proyectos.

El siguiente ejercicio, (el proyecto principal de los alumnos), fue el diseño de escuelas modelo de ambos niveles, primario y secundario. Como en los proyectos de vivienda colectiva, se realizó un exhaustivo análisis del programa y de la zona, se determinaron los conceptos del enfoque educativo que surgieron de estudios precedentes conducidos por gente como van Eyck y Hertzberger, se enfatizó la conexión con las comunidades, y se emplearon los métodos constructivos apropiados para la región y para garantizar la sustentabilidad de la construcción, todo a fin de crear diseños viables para estas escuelas.

VER IMÁGENES, PÁGINAS: 177.

EL TECHO-MÁQUINA

Por **IMAN ANSARI Y ONUR EKMEKCI**

Las condiciones tropicales de Nueva Loja –las abundantes lluvias y el potente sol– presentan desafíos específicos para el diseño de un nuevo sistema constructivo. Los elementos fundamentales que se necesitan son los techos y cubiertas. Debido a las problemáticas que plantean la sustentabilidad y el calentamiento global es necesario pensar en distintas formas de ventilación y generación de sombra, así como en el consumo y producción de energía del edificio.

El edificio contiene dos o más espacios, cada uno cubierto con un sistema de techado. Estos espacios están conectados entre sí por el costado, y el frente y la parte de atrás se abren para recibir ventilación y luz. Estos espacios podrían construirse en diferentes tamaños, según el uso que se les quiera dar. Cada sistema de techado, junto con el espacio que recubre, funciona de manera independiente con el fin, una vez más, de permitir diferentes usos.

Los sistemas de techos corredizos suministran sombra y cubierta, así como ventilación y recolección de agua. Además, los techos serían flexibles, permitiendo una cobertura máxima en caso de lluvias torrenciales o sol abrasador, o una cobertura mínima en otras ocasiones.

Un aspecto fundamental de este proyecto es el consumo reducido de energía. Además de la posibilidad de controlar el ingreso de luz del sol por medio de la utilización de techos deslizantes, el aire se comprime y se dirige al interior de la vivienda. Así, el sistema actúa como un sistema de refrigeración, sobre todo cuando la estructura del techo se llena de agua de lluvia. El agua que se recolecta es canalizada y almacenada para otros usos.

El diseño de la Máquina del Techo también surgió de un análisis del bambú como potencial material estructural. La Máquina del Techo consiste en una serie de cañas de bambú cortadas a la mitad y unidas por unas juntas que permiten el movimiento circular de las piezas. Una varilla larga de metal conecta las juntas a la pared. Unas guías instaladas dentro de la pared permiten que el techo se mueva en ambas direcciones. Aquí también hay un canal para recolectar y eliminar el agua del techo.

SISTEMAS DE BAMBÚ

El bambú es un material sustentable que tiene aplicaciones tanto formales como estructurales. La Máquina del Techo aprovecha la estructura interna del bambú, que es capaz de actuar como barrera contra el agua y de contenerla, así como su solidez y su largo: las piezas de bambú se conectan a través de un sistema de juntas, que permiten una variación y una flexibilidad infinitas. Cada junta puede conectar hasta seis piezas de bambú distintas. El sistema es capaz de soportar una cubierta estructural y de expandirse en varias direcciones. El sistema puede usarse también como malla espacial.

VER IMÁGENES Y GRÁFICOS, PÁGINAS: 178, 179.

CUBRIR, UNIR, COLGAR

Por **ROMMEL GORDILLO Y JAVIER CARACAMO**

EL DESAFÍO

Crear un sistema de cubierta / unión / colgado. ¿Cómo puede desarrollárselo como prototipo? ¿Cómo puede crecer?

EL CONCEPTO

La naturaleza es el sistema más complejo de crecimiento. Analizamos el crecimiento de las hojas y de los árboles para aprender sobre el crecimiento complejo.

LA ESTRUCTURA

Al principio, parece una simple forma geométrica. Está compuesta de dos sistemas sobre el mismo eje. El sistema adherente sigue el mismo patrón. Esto da lugar a un crecimiento vertical.

EL PROTOTIPO

Este sistema puede adoptar múltiples configuraciones, con sólo rotar la junta estructural. Algunas configuraciones crean espacios habitables. Varias configuraciones crean un sistema de unión, cubierta y colgado. El sistema surgió de un análisis de la estructura de las hojas. El concepto era aplicar la disposición y la unión de las hojas a una estructura que funcionara espacialmente.

El resultado es una forma estructural: un prototipo que incorpora esas tres ideas: unir, colgar y cubrir. Está construido en bambú, un material eficiente y sustentable, fácil de conseguir en climas calurosos.

VER IMÁGENES Y GRÁFICOS, PÁGINAS: 180, 181.

EL SISTEMA

Por **PATRICK ISAAC Y SUJIN JEONG**

El sistema es un híbrido entre la estructura de una telaraña y la técnica de suspensión de una chinche del agua. La idea era crear un refugio humano con una estructura separada del suelo para minimizar su impacto en el lugar.

El proyecto proporciona nuevas viviendas para la ciudad en expansión. Simultáneamente, fomenta una relación más directa entre los colonos humanos y el suelo, a medida que éste vaya descontaminándose. Además, ayudará a que se establezca un nuevo ecosistema en Lago Agrio.

La unión vertical tiene tres piezas: dos piezas horizontales paralelas y una diagonal, ubicadas en distintos ángulos.

Esta unión permite que una juntura interior, ajustable y rotativa, sostenga una pieza colocada con una inclinación.

Las piezas horizontales que conforman la telaraña serán fijadas con placas de metal a las que estarán atornilladas. Esto de todos modos permitirá que haya cierto juego entre las dos piezas conectadas, aunque en ningún caso les permitirá formar un ángulo de 90 grados.

VER IMÁGENES Y GRÁFICOS, PÁGINAS: 182, 183.

EL PROTOTIPO

Por **ERIK SCANLON Y YULYA LLIZAROV**

Este prototipo de vivienda amazónica está inspirado en los sistemas naturales de crecimiento. Los módulos están diseñados para integrarse de manera armónica en el medio ambiente. Serán colocados en un área de densa vegetación arbórea, que suministrará la estructura. Los módulos son variaciones sobre una forma triangular, puesto que esto requiere que haya el menor número de puntos de conexión con los árboles estructurales para crear un espacio cerrado. Los módulos se colocan en los árboles a varias alturas, dependiendo de si se encuentran sobre la tierra o sobre el agua.
La estructura de los módulos se basa en la construcción de andamios. En cada unión se colocan abrazaderas móviles que permiten varias opciones de conexión. Las paredes del módulo consistirán en una doble capa de soga penetrada por el follaje.

VER IMÁGENES Y GRÁFICOS, PÁGINAS: 184, 185.

PROTOTIPO DE VIVIENDA PARA UN CLIMA HÚMEDO Y CALUROSO

Por **YULYA LLIZAROV**

Este prototipo de vivienda para el clima húmedo y caluroso del Amazonas contiene zonas tanto públicas como privadas. La zona pública es el gran espacio central, con diferentes áreas separadas por leves cambios de elevación. Los nodos privados se disponen alrededor del espacio público principal. Hay variaciones tanto en las zonas públicas como privadas que permiten numerosas distribuciones.
La zona pública se divide en una cocina, una sala de estar y dos espacios exteriores. Su distribución puede variar para cambiar la relación entre los espacios interiores y exteriores. Los nodos privados permiten que numerosos grupos familiares distintos compartan la vivienda. Pueden agregarse según la necesidad, a medida que la familia extendida va creciendo. Los nodos se conectan con la zona pública central, que es el área donde se reúne la familia.
El prototipo tiene un armazón de bambú con cables tensores que se usan para colgar los nodos privados de la zona pública principal. Cada pared externa está cubierta de una doble capa de tiras finas de bambú, con follaje entre ambas capas para purificar el aire. Las tiras de bambú se entretejen en el armazón del prototipo. Es posible entretejerlas más sueltas o más apretadas, según el nivel de privacidad que se desee crear. El techo se recubre de un tejido fotovoltaico para producir energía. Debajo del baño hay un cubo de compostaje para recolección y uso por parte de la comunidad.

VER GRÁFICOS, PÁGINAS: 186, 187.

PROTOTIPO 750

Por **ERIK SCANLON**

El PROTOTIPO 750 es un modelo de vivienda urbana en Lago Agrio. Debido al aumento proyectado de la población, que se incrementará de 25.000 a 150.000 habitantes en 2021, el proyecto debía lograr la máxima eficiencia en términos de bajo costo, funcionalidad y construcción, y a la vez responder a las muy peculiares condiciones urbanas, climáticas, culturales y de desarrollo de Lago Agrio.

COMPONENTES DEL SISTEMA

El PROTOTIPO 750 es un sistema de viviendas prefabricadas de fácil ensamblaje construidas con materiales locales. El armazón estructural está hecho de segmentos de bambú conectados con inserciones de metal y luego atornillados. La superficie del suelo está hecha de soga que oculta un armazón mecánico ajustable de tres puntos que puede utilizarse, variando la posición, como cama, sofá, y superficie para sentarse o apoyar cosas. Este sistema de pisos se usa en las habitaciones y en la sala familiar. El sistema de pared exterior es una serie de paneles triangulares cubiertos por una trama de bambú y malla que puede abrirse a lo largo de la línea del techo para crear circulación de aire. Además, los paneles inferiores pueden desplegarse, ampliando el espacio de la vivienda de 70 a 150 metros cuadrados. Los mecanismos operativos del PROTOTIPO 750 ofrecen esas posibilidades.
Los materiales podrían reemplazarse por otros más accesibles o de más bajo costo, permitiéndole a cada familia expresar su identidad individual a través de su propio diseño. El principal objetivo del PROTOTIPO 750 es ofrecer una respuesta en lugar de ser la respuesta.

VER IMÁGENES Y GRÁFICOS, PÁGINAS: 188 a 191.

VIVIENDA UNIFAMILIAR CON PAREDES APERSIANADAS

Por **ROMMEL GORDILLO**

EL DESAFÍO

Diseñar un prototipo de vivienda unifamiliar para un clima caluroso. ¿Cómo puede este sistema convertirse en un prototipo? ¿Cómo puede crecer?

EL CONCEPTO

La naturaleza es el más complejo sistema de crecimiento. Analizamos el crecimiento de las hojas y de los árboles para comprender el crecimiento complejo.
La parte posterior de la vivienda se eleva para acomodar un sistema de reciclaje de agua. El espacio abierto en el centro de la casa sirve como filtro de agua.

ÁREAS PRIVADAS

Están en la parte posterior y los niveles elevados para ofrecer mayor privacidad.

ESPACIOS PÚBLICOS

Comienzan en la entrada y van circulando hacia arriba en forma de U. Las áreas públicas tienen persianas y vistas que abren al exterior.

TECHO

Se diseñó un techo en pendiente, que transporta el agua de lluvia hacia un pozo ubicado en el centro de la casa, donde se la almacena y usa. La estructura está compuesta principalmente de madera con persianas de aluminio que dejan pasar el aire, a la vez que evitan la entrada del aire cuando se las cierra. La estructura se coloca sobre las paredes principales que sostienen la casa.

VER IMÁGENES Y GRÁFICOS, PÁGINAS: 192 a 197.

VIVIENDAS EN LA NATURALEZA

Por **POR PATRICK ISAAC**

Nuestro punto de partida es la creación de una infraestructura que les permita a los recién llegados conectarse a la ciudad. En términos arquitectónicos, esto se traduce en "un periférico auto-construido en el cual [la gente construye] su propio hogar". Esto crea viviendas individuales y privadas, a la vez que las necesidades sociales de los residentes se convierten en la base del funcionamiento de la ciudad. Una solución es un edificio parecido a un garage: pura infraestructura que intenta reproducir la dinámica de las calles de la ciudad, pero en sentido vertical. Un individuo puede adquirir una parcela de espacio construido, similar a un lote de terreno, y edificarla a voluntad. La prolongación vertical de la calle en los edificios conectará a los individuos a los espacios y actividades sociales comunes.

VER IMÁGENES Y GRÁFICOS, PÁGINAS: 198 a 203.

VIVIENDAS APILABLES

Por **YULIYA ILIZAROV**

Este modelo de viviendas lineales está diseñado para un área escasamente poblada al sur del río Aguarico. El asentamiento lineal comienza en el límite artificial sudoeste de la ciudad. En el límite, las granjas públicas propuestas mantienen a esta comunidad en desarrollo con un mercado agrícola que abastece a toda la ciudad. Un trazado relativamente denso de viviendas, jardines urbanos comunales, mercados, caminos para la circulación de peatones, bicicletas y vehículos, y espacios públicos al aire libre acompaña las franjas de granjas lineales.

Las unidades de vivienda se disponen linealmente, con una serie de terrazas, aleros y patios que crean espacios al aire libre que van de lo privado a lo semiprivado y lo público. La mayor parte del espacio público al aire libre alberga los jardines urbanos comunales, que producen comida tanto para el consumo local como para su venta. Un entramado exterior de circulación, estructura e infraestructura sostiene la agrupación de unidades de vivienda.

VER GRÁFICOS, PÁGINAS: 204 a 207.

VIVIENDAS MULTIFAMILIARES: LA PARTIDA DE LA CIUDAD

Por **IMAN ANSARI**

El barrio se encuentra en el margen nororiental de la ciudad, y está alineado con la pista de aterrizaje del aeropuerto que existe actualmente. La estructura del lugar es una metáfora para la ciudad, conforme despega y desaparece. La densidad actual del barrio es bastante baja. Por consiguiente, el nuevo diseño busca resolver esta cuestión.

Un nuevo trazado crea oportunidades espaciales dentro del barrio. La densidad crece desde el centro y la circulación principal y el eje del trazado existente coinciden con el nuevo sistema.

VER IMÁGENES Y GRÁFICOS, PÁGINAS: 208, 209.

VIVIENDAS MULTIFAMILIARES: VIVIR EN EL AMAZONAS

Por **IMAN ANSARI**

Este proyecto es un nuevo sistema de viviendas a gran escala: se basa en la repetición de una única estructura plegada que contiene dos unidades de vivienda y dos jardines. La segunda estructura se ubica junto a la primera, pero mirando en dirección opuesta. El patrón se repite.

Cada unidad de vivienda está siempre rodeada de jardines por los cuatro costados. Asimismo, cada unidad tiene su propio jardín al frente para mejorar la eficiencia energética y la refrigeración. La planta baja se asigna a uso comercial y público. Esto crea un espacio público activo debajo del edificio. Hay un espacio comunal dentro del edificio para realizar actividades públicas.

VER IMÁGENES Y GRÁFICOS, PÁGINAS: 210, 211.

VIVIENDAS DE LAGO AGRIO

Por **LAWRENCE JACQUETTE**

Este proyecto depende de la finalización del puente, aún sin terminar, sobre el río Aguarico y de la construcción de un segundo puente para peatones y ciclistas al este.

Un proyecto de viviendas lineales multiformes se emplazará en la ribera sur del río, entre estos dos puentes, conectándolos.

El proyecto incluye varias soluciones sustentables de manejo de desechos, incluyendo tratamiento in situ de aguas grises. Los edificios son autoventilantes, sustentables, con guarderías para los niños de padres que trabajan en otras partes de la ciudad.
La combinación de viviendas y comercios en planta baja, y la creación de una plaza pública en la entrada del puente para peatones y ciclistas propuesto, creará una nueva infraestructura de gran importancia en la ribera sur del río.

VER IMÁGENES Y GRÁFICOS, PÁGINAS: 212 a 215.

AULA MÓVIL: ESCUELA POP-UP

Por **LAWRENCE JACQUETTE Y CAMILLE DUNN**

Esta escuela portátil y autosuficiente de dos habitaciones está diseñada para que la utilicen los pueblos indígenas de la selva tropical en las inmediaciones de Nueva Loja. De día, el interior flexible alberga la escuela, y fuera del horario escolar funciona como espacio comunitario donde tienen lugar reuniones y pequeñas asambleas. La estructura, la cubierta y el equipamiento de la escuela desplegable cabrían en un contenedor de madera, que a su vez se desplegaría para hacer las veces de piso de la escuela. Unas columnas de bambú aseguradas con soportes de metal sostienen el sistema de techado y crean un soporte para encastrar los paneles modulares. Estos módulos pueden disponerse según necesidades climáticas o programáticas.

VER IMÁGENES Y GRÁFICOS, PÁGINAS: 216, 217.

AULA MÓVIL: PROTOTIPO DE 0 BASURA

Por **ERIK SCANLON AND YULIYA ILIZAROV**

El Prototipo de Basura 0 de un aula portátil está fabricado con un contenedor metálico que se corta y se transforma en un contenedor plegable y portátil de dos niveles que alberga una oficina, un baño y un cuarto de servicio en el nivel inferior, y un aula/sala de reuniones en el superior.
El interior está revestido en contrachapado, mientras que el exterior es la brillante carcasa coloreada del contenedor metálico. Las paredes están hechas con un armazón metálico revestido de una malla que permite crear una sensación de espacio cerrado a la vez que deja pasar el aire y la luz. En las paredes del aula/sala de reuniones hay sillas y pupitres plegables en variedad de colores que pueden descolgarse y usarse según se necesite.

VER IMÁGENES Y GRÁFICOS, PÁGINAS: 218, 219.

AULA MÓVIL: ESCUELA DESPLEGABLE

Por **EDITH ALTAMIRANDA Y YURIY TKACHENKOV**

El éxito de una escuela móvil depende de cuán fácilmente pueda transformársela y ajustársela a las necesidades de diferentes usuarios y actividades.
Por tanto, el diseño del prototipo debía ser flexible y ajustable.
El proyecto emplea una combinación de particiones removibles y desplegables, que permiten configurar y reconfigurar los espacios; y combina materiales locales (bambú y madera) e industriales. También incorpora instalaciones sencillas basadas en tecnología simple pero fiable. Las particiones móviles y removibles minimizan el consumo de electricidad. Las particiones exteriores e interiores se diseñan utilizando tecnología similar para que sea más fácil empaquetarlas y guardarlas. Las particiones recubiertas de bambú producen sombra y permiten ventilar las aulas.

VER IMÁGENES Y GRÁFICOS, PÁGINAS: 220, 221.

ESCUELA SECUNDARIA DE PUERTO AGUARICO

Por **EDITH ALTAMIRANDA**

Puerto Aguarico, un municipio al sur de Nueva Loja, que se encuentra cruzando el río Aguarico, es una de las áreas más antiguas y atractivas de la ciudad. La falta de puentes limita su comunicación con el resto de la ciudad. Para acceder al puerto, se utilizan botes y canoas.
Los espacios del ala oriental de la escuela miran hacia la selva, dándole la espalda a las zonas urbanizadas de la ciudad. Los espacios sociales y de trabajo se ubican en el ala oeste de la escuela.
Un toldo de bambú que se extiende a lo largo de todo el edificio proporciona sombra y permite ventilación natural.

Texto tomado de diagrama:
Materiales locales: guadúa, cemento y madera.
"Manipular el ambiente dentro de los edificios trabajando con las fuerzas naturales que los rodean en vez de contra ellas".

AULA MULTIPROPÓSITO
Elementos para un ámbito de aprendizaje diverso.

AMBIENTAL
Espacios bien iluminados, vistas agradables y áreas funcionales.
PSICOLÓGICO
Diferentes métodos de aprendizaje adaptados a las asignaturas.
SOCIOLÓGICO
Grupos de aprendizaje individual formales e informales: talleres, conferencias y actividades individuales.

VER IMÁGENES Y GRÁFICOS, PÁGINAS: 222 a 225.

ESCUELA PRIMARIA VERDIAZUL

Por **YULIYA ILIZAROV**

La Escuela Primaria Verdiazul se organiza en torno a dos sistemas opuestos: el trazado urbano, artificialmente impuesto, y los ríos que naturalmente corren por la zona. Situada en un terreno sin construir en un barrio irregularmente trazado y dividido en dos por un río, la escuela rodea el río con un grupo de aulas, laboratorios y oficinas.
Los distintos elementos de la escuela se ubican como partículas diferenciadas pero conectadas debajo de una estructura contenedora que hace las veces de techo y de cubierta, y que incorpora en su diseño la estructura cuadricular del barrio. El patio interno es el centro de las actividades escolares: un espacio abierto, aunque privado y seguro, para el aprendizaje. La estructura contenedora se extiende más allá del haz de partículas que conforman la escuela para incluir un espacio protegido al aire libre abierto a toda la comunidad. Este espacio media entre el interior privado de la escuela y el exterior público de la calle peatonal.

VER IMÁGENES Y GRÁFICOS, PÁGINAS: 226 a 229.

LA ESCUELA URBANA

Por **IMAN ANSARI**

El barrio donde se ubicará esta escuela es probablemente el área más densamente poblada de Lago Agrio, y contiene los principales centros sociales, –sagrados y profanos– de la ciudad. Este, el súper barrio está rodeado de importantes avenidas como la Avenida Colombia al este y la Avenida Quito al sur, y se encuentra dividido en dos por el río que lo atraviesa. Esto interrumpe la cuadrícula urbana, creando manzanas de diferente morfología y extensión. La escuela se convertirá en parte de la nueva universidad, revitalizando las zonas abandonadas alrededor del río. Por consiguiente, deberá mantener su propia identidad en el campus de la universidad. Debido a la densidad poblacional del área, la escuela se construirá sobre lotes vacíos o desocupados a la vera del río, conectados por una serie de puentes.
La escuela recrea el trazado urbano a menor escala. Al elevar la escuela, la planta baja se abrirá al público permitiendo que fluyan los peatones, los vehículos y el comercio. Este sistema de llenado de espacios unidos con puentes a ambos lados del río, podría repetirse a lo largo de la orilla del río para ampliar la universidad o la escuela en el futuro.

VER IMÁGENES Y GRÁFICOS, PÁGINAS: 230 a 233.

LA ESCUELA COMO HERRAMIENTA DE APRENDIZAJE: LA ESCUELA DE CONSTRUCCIÓN DE NUEVA LOJA

Por **CAMILLE DUNN**

La Escuela de Construcción de Nueva Loja, o ECNL, es una escu la técnica para el desarrollo y la capacitación en materia de técnicas constructivas sustentables. Al impartir prácticas de construcción sustentables, la escuela difundirá ideas y estrategias para promover el crecimiento sustentable y fomentar la industria local en la provincia de Sucumbíos.
La Esquina se encuentra en la esquina de la Avenida Amazonas, la calle que se interna en la selva, y la Avenida Aguarico, la principal arteria que cruza la ciudad de noroeste a sudeste, desde el río hasta el corazón de la ciudad. Es un barrio que se prepara para recibir un incremento de tráfico, así como desarrollos sociales, infraestructurales y ecológicos (bajo la forma de un parque que se ha propuesto).
A partir del crecimiento de la ciudad, es necesario reflexionar acerca de los métodos constructivos que se utilizan aquí. Actualmente, gran parte del desarrollo es de carácter informal, construido sin permisos oficiales e insostenible a largo plazo. Los materiales son de baja calidad; los sistemas constructivos son improvisados y están mal ejecutados; y la infraestructura en materia de desechos, suministro de servicios y calles a menudo brilla por su ausencia. Como resultado, estos barrios residenciales informales corren el riesgo de desintegrarse y ser tragados por la selva en el corto plazo.
El proyecto de una escuela técnica consagrada a los medios, métodos y materiales de la construcción ocupa un predio a metros de la intersección entre las avenidas Aguarico y Amazonas. Ubicar la escuela allí, cerca de esta intersección, como remate de una zona de usos abierta, cerca de barrios residenciales, mirando al río (y al puente, que ojalá se reconstruya) y a la selva, reforzará la sensación de integración con el barrio y hará la escuela (y la tecnología y los saberes que producirá) accesible al resto de la ciudad. El diseño de la escuela busca reflejar la belleza del lugar, el carácter vibrante de la ciudad e ilustrar en sus materiales y sistemas constructivos la aplicación de métodos inteligentes y sustentables adaptados a la selva. La estructura de la escuela forma un armazón al que pueden agregarse o quitarse aulas. Los alumnos estudiarán en un lugar donde los materiales, las formas y los sistemas pasivos de diseño (ventilación transversal y proyección de sombra) enfatizarán la importancia de renovar la cultura constructiva en la región y mantener viva la misión de cultivar un entorno sostenible.

LABORATORIO VIVIENTE

La ENCL está pensada simultáneamente como un lugar donde aprender y sobre el cual aprender. Los estudiantes recibirán capacitación en materia de técnicas constructivas sustentables para aplicar a su práctica profesional.
Las aulas, centros de estudio y oficinas serán en su totalidad estructuras temporarias desarrolladas y construidas por grupos de alumnos, a fin de darles la oportunidad de poner a prueba nuevos métodos de construcción y materiales sustentables a escala real. La estructura de la escuela está diseñada para sostener y sujetar estas unidades experimentales por medio de un sistema de poleas que levanta los nuevos módulos y los coloca en su lugar.

ESTRATEGIA FORMAL:

Tropicalizar la Villa Académica de la Universidad de Virginia.
El célebre plan de Thomas Jefferson para la construcción de una "Villa Académica" en la Universidad de Virginia ofrece un precedente para el planeamiento del campus de la ENCL. Tanto la ENCL como la Universidad de Virginia tienen un plano en forma de herradura abierta con la biblioteca en el ápice. Esta forma da origen a un campus muy cohesionado, con un parque en el medio. Sin embargo, la ENCL se

diferencia formalmente de la Universidad de Virginia en varias cuestiones, ligadas a su respuesta a las condiciones climáticas y a la comunidad que lo rodea:

• Se rota el plano para minimizar la exposición a la luz directa y para que reciba todo el sol de la mañana.

• Mientras que la Universidad de Virginia tiene jardines privados, el ENCL tiene un paisaje urbano de calle y unos maceteros en la fachada para disfrute de todos.

• En vez de estar rodeada por una capa aislante de viviendas de profesores y autoridades, la ENCL se rodea de viviendas comunitarias.

• El volumen de la ENCL es más poroso, tanto para la libre circulación de aire como para hacer el interior más accesible a la comunidad, en vez de aislarla como la Universidad de Virginia.

ESTATEGIA FORMAL:

Refrigeración pasiva en áreas tropicales.

La ENCL utiliza estrategias de refrigeración pasiva en sus espacios internos. Para aprovechar las corrientes de aire fresco, la ENCL fomenta el movimiento de aire y la doble circulación en toda la escuela, manteniendo el edificio poroso y plano.

Para minimizar la exposición al sol de las superficies del edificio, la ENCL es alargada y angosta, orientada para minimizar la superficie de las fachadas oriental y occidental, expuestas al sol de la mañana y de la tarde. Al mediodía, cuando el sol pega más fuerte, los paneles de tracción, semejantes a sombrillas, semejantes a sombrillas, que conforman el sistema de techado, forman un toldo para arrojar sombra sobre las aulas y los espacios de circulación que hay debajo.

TECNOLOGÍAS PASIVAS:

La Máquina Viviente Integrada, un sistema de tratamiento de aguas residuales.

La ENCL tendrá un programa para educar a los estudiantes y a la comunidad en la construcción y mantenimiento de sistemas de tratamiento de aguas descentralizados, sustentables y de baja tecnología. Además, la escuela recolectará y tratará agua de lluvia para su utilización en el campus, proporcionándoles a los estudiantes experiencia de primera mano en la utilización de estos sistemas.

El agua de lluvia es se recoge en los paneles de tracción del techo. Estos la canalizan hacia columnas internas que a su vez la vierten en tuberías colectoras subterráneas que alimentan la Máquina Viviente, –el sistema de tratamiento de aguas. La Máquina Viviente es una serie de tanques y pantanos artificiales en los cuales un ecosistema de plantas, algas, bacterias, moluscos y peces actúa como biofiltro, procesando las aguas residuales y volviéndolas aptas para usos no potables como la irrigación y los retretes. Parte del agua tratada es luego canalizada a otros sistemas de filtración para potabilizarla. El agua potable y la no potable se almacenan separadamente en tanques para su uso en el campus.

LA TORRE BIBLIOTECA

La Torre Biblioteca es un hito dentro del campus que simboliza el compromiso de la escuela con las prácticas constructivas sustentables innovadoras e integradoras. En primer lugar, constituye una parte fundamental del sistema de refrigeración pasiva de la biblioteca. La fachada de la torre es una losa negra de hormigón plegada, inclinada para recibir el sol de la mañana. Al aplicarle una delgada lámina transparente de film de ETFE, los huecos en el hormigón se convierten en focos de aire caliente, producto de la masa térmica del hormigón. A medida que el aire caliente sube hacia lo más alto de la torre pasa por los conductos de ventilación de la biblioteca, produciendo succión (efectos del Principio de Bernouli). Esta succión alimenta el sistema de refrigeración pasiva, al tomar aire del exterior, a través del intercambio de calor producido por un circuito geotermal, y enfriar el interior de la biblioteca y del laboratorio de informática. En segundo lugar, la torre posee tanques llenos de agua gris y de agua potable, ambas tratadas por la Máquina Viviente. La altura de la torre genera presión que permite que el agua se distribuya en todo el campus, para ser utilizada en cocinas, baños e irrigación.

VER IMÁGENES Y GRÁFICOS, PÁGINAS: 235 a 239.

ASENTAMIENTOS HUMANOS SUSTENTABLES PARA LA ERA POST-PETROLERA EN LA AMAZONÍA ECUATORIANA:

una introducción al Taller de Lago Agrio (FADA-PUCE)

Por **OSVALDO PALADINES ZURRITA**

La ciudad de Nueva Loja, conocida como Lago Agrio, es un asentamiento urbano creado a partir de la aparición de la industria petrolera para satisfacer las necesidades de vivienda, recreación y comunicación de los trabajadores de las empresas extranjeras establecidas en esa zona del Oriente ecuatoriano. Por su ubicación estratégica, cerca de la frontera con Colombia, Lago Agrio se ha convertido además, en el centro de acopio y distribución de mercaderías y servicios ilegales introducidos hacia el país en forma clandestina. También es la puerta de entrada para la Reserva Natural Yasuní, una de las más ricas en biodiversidad del planeta.

El Taller de Lago Agrio que se llevó a cabo en la Facultad de Arquitectura, Diseño y Artes de la Pontificia Universidad Católica del Ecuador se dividió en dos etapas principales:

1. La visión a escala urbana del asentamiento humano en la Amazonía

El objetivo del Taller fue moverse oscilatoriamente entre la utopía y la realidad, con el fin de explorar en visiones creativas y novedosas los fenómenos urbanos, sus causas y los posibles caminos de solución. La meta final fue la de desentrañar el tejido urbano y proponer alternativas para una ciudad contemporánea sustentable, dentro de una visión general de crecimiento urbano.

Se estudiaron las distintas fuerzas de génesis y crecimiento de la ciudad de Lago Agrio y su impacto en la selva, reconociendo el tema del río, el árbol y los movimientos nativos nómadas como referentes, así como los posibles modelos de aplicación para un crecimiento proyectado de 100.000 habitantes. Para este propósito, se hizo hincapié en la experiencia directa del conocimiento del lugar, a partir de la visita programada.

El producto final de esta primera etapa fue una propuesta general de crecimiento para la ciudad de Lago Agrio, que se plasmó en un documento pedagógico para la población infanto-juvenil de la zona. Este documento expone clara y didácticamente las características principales que tendrá la futura ciudad de Lago Agrio y los compromisos individuales que cada miembro de la sociedad debe asumir para su correcto funcionamiento. La publicación estuvo apoyada por material audio-visual en formato digital que facilita su comprensión y puede ser presentada a los miembros de la comunidad.

2. La unidad auto-sustentable de vivienda para la futura ciudad de Lago Agrio

La realidad post-petrolera que se avecina en un lapso no mayor a 25 años, hace que el estudio de nuevas maneras de enfrentar las soluciones arquitectónicas en las ciudades del petróleo sea un tema de vital relevancia. Históricamente, aquellos asentamientos que florecen espectacularmente debido a la explotación de algún recurso natural, cuando éste se termina, se transforman en pueblos fantasmas y abandonados (véase el caso de las ciudades del salitre en Chile, los pueblos de la fiebre del oro, etc.).

Las ciudades del petróleo, por su ubicación estratégica y su potencial turístico, no deberían correr con la misma suerte puesto que podrían ser reestructurada de manera que se conviertan en ejemplos de uso sensible de los recursos y de conservación de la energía, en todos sus aspectos. Esto hace que el segundo tema de estudio se concentre en la unidad o sistema de unidades de vivienda, no como una caja/máquina enchufada que solo consume energía, sino como la unidad básica que garantiza la sobrevivencia de las ciudades y que son parte de un sistema que involucra las demás escalas urbanas.

En esta etapa del taller, se estudiaron los siguientes temas:

- Energía: Alternativas para la producción de energía: solar, eólica, etanol y su impacto en el diseño de las viviendas y la ciudad.
- Alimento: Capacidad del territorio para producir alimento, basado en la realidad del ciclo selvático.
- Agua: Análisis del ciclo completo del agua que garantice su uso eficiente, reciclaje, etc.
- Basura: Análisis de cada nivel del proceso de generación de desechos y como pueden ser reciclados de manera que el asentamiento no genere ningún tipo de huella contaminante.
- Tecnologías constructivas: Recuperar e implementar las técnicas constructivas acordes al lugar, la economía y la situación climática.
- Materiales: uso de materiales propios de la región, estructuras tensiles, fibras, maderas, caña guadúa.

Como meta final de esta parte del Taller, se diseñaron las viviendas y las agrupaciones que utilizando todas las posibilidades estudiadas, establecieron una aproximación contemporánea a una solución que, aunque se encuentre en los límites de la ficción, puedan establecer ideas para la ciudad post-petrolera de la Amazonía ecuatoriana.

PAISAJE PRODUCTIVO – VIVIENDA PRODUCTIVA

Por **TATIANA ARMIJOS**

En este proyecto se propone la generación de ejes viales que se desarrollan en torno a los corredores ambientales existentes (ríos y riachuelos) para producir una conexión permanente con lo natural y generar, a la vez, una serie de bordes dinámicos entre Nueva Loja y el agua, bajo la forma de una serie de espacios recreativos, agrícolas (espacios verdes productivos) y turísticos. Las funciones comerciales y agrícolas se introducen también en la propuesta de vivienda conforme se hibridan con sus fines habitacionales. Su perímetro se concibe como una piel que facilita el intercambio con el medio ambiente: respira, se alimenta y produce. La vivienda aprovecha las características del lugar en el cual se implanta: se nutre de la actividad comercial circundante; se desarrolla en varios niveles; optimiza el uso del agua (capturándola, reciclándola y reutilizándola en las zonas de riego agrícola) y los desechos (generando abono útil en las actividades agrícolas). La vivienda cuenta con áreas para la exhibición y venta de sus productos, así como con un lugar de almacenamiento. El hormigón y el ladrillo se seleccionaron para suplir expectativas culturales de solidez, mejora y capacidad de crecimiento. Su composición estructural se aprovecha para generar un sistema de llenos y vacíos que facilita la ventilación transversal sin obstruir la contemplación del exterior.

VER IMÁGENES Y GRÁFICOS, PÁGINAS: 242, 243.

SISTEMAS SOSTENIBLES

Por **JOSÉ LUIS GALLEGOS**

Planteamos que la futura ciudad sostenible y sustentable de Nueva Loja sea un gran sistema conformado por una serie de sub-sistemas o barrios situados en cuatro puntos estratégicos de manera que cumplan funciones específicas (turismo, comercio, piscicultura y agricultura) y trabajen independientemente de la ciudad actual a la vez que la sostienen y alimentan, en una era sin petróleo. Cada uno de estos barrios se encarga del manejo de la energía, el agua, los desechos y el transporte.

La vivienda constituye un tercer sub-sistema y refleja a escala arquitectónica las intenciones urbanas. Su estructura se construye con tuberías recicladas de la era petrolera; sus servicios están diseñados para que se abastezca de agua, la reutilice y recicle; sus desechos se aprovechan como combustible o se clasifican para conectar con el sistema de reciclaje del barrio y la ciudad. Debido a que la pluviosidad es alta en la Amazonia, a las fachadas de la vivienda se las trata como techos y el agua lluvia se recoge a través de un pozo de luz que atraviesa la vivienda. Además están diseñadas para facilitar la ventilación transversal. La forma del volumen arquitectónico es la de un cubo en torsión que busca reproducir las sensaciones de la selva.

La economía del barrio que se ubica a orillas del río Aguarico, así como de sus viviendas, se basa en piscicultura y cultivo de frutos amazónicos para las necesidades de consumo interno y de exportación.

VER IMÁGENES Y GRÁFICOS, PÁGINAS: 244 a 247.

CONECTOR MULTICAPAS

Por **ESTEBAN SÁENZ LAVERDY**

Nueva Loja ha crecido de una manera arbitraria y caótica. Es necesario revitalizar la ciudad y entregar soportes a su futuro crecimiento: generar nuevos nodos de desarrollo, nuevas oportunidades laborales y micro-empresas. Utilizando la metáfora de la selva y sus especies vegetales, que luchan entre sí por alcanzar la luz en las alturas, se pretende inyectar nueva vida al estero Orienco. Este atraviesa la ciudad y se espera que a lo largo de sus orillas compitan nuevos centros de comercio y recreación, beneficiados por un sistema de transporte público fluvial. En un segundo plano, se implementan espacios de exposición, comercio y transición de una orilla a otra. Con esta costura se busca incentivar el intercambio social, cultural y comercial en un ambiente colectivo, típico de una comunidad reunida. En un tercer plano, la vivienda se propone como un espacio doméstico sostenible. Es jerárquica en su diseño e implantación. Un sistema de persianas actúa como malla que facilita el crecimiento de la vegetación a lo largo de las fachadas. Esto, a su vez, permite evitar la concentración del calor y generar espacios cómodos y habitables. El agua lluvia se recolecta y filtra para consumo humano.

VER IMÁGENES Y GRÁFICOS, PÁGINAS: 248, 249.

METABOLISMOS AUTOSUFICIENTES

Por **MARÍA LUISA BORJA**

El proyecto es parte de una propuesta urbana para el crecimiento de la ciudad de Nueva Loja. Este modelo urbano propone la creación de varios núcleos que se generan a partir de un centro verde (parques) y se delimitan por grandes vías colectoras de transporte. Las densidades de las viviendas varían desde el centro verde hacia la periferia, de mayores a menores. El proyecto está localizado en una esquina frente a un parque, y de acuerdo con el plan urbano, debe tener una densidad alta de vivienda, comercio y espacio público. Además de la integración de estos elementos, el proyecto toma en cuenta varios parámetros de sostenibilidad con el objetivo primordial de lograr que la vivienda colectiva funcione, al igual que la naturaleza, como un sistema autosuficiente: produce su propia energía; renueva sus recursos y recicla sus desechos en un metabolismo circular cuyo fin es minimizar el impacto medioambiental en la selva. Asimismo, la propuesta urbana busca reproducir el modelo de sistema autosuficiente a gran escala. Se propone que, a futuro, las prácticas del quehacer humano se mimeticen (desde el punto de vista del impacto ecológico) con las de la naturaleza en un solo sistema simbiótico. El manejo de la energía propone disminuir el consumo de electricidad. Con dicho fin, la arquitectura satisface las necesidades de luminosidad, ventilación y temperatura cómoda a través de un diseño bioclimático que mantiene a la vivienda fresca, iluminada y ventilada. Los materiales utilizados se modulan para evitar al máximo el desperdicio y son certificados, en el caso de la madera.

VER IMÁGENES Y GRÁFICOS, PÁGINAS: 250 a 253.

BANDAS DE CRECIMIENTO

Por **ANDRÉS PERALVO**

La selva se encuentra en constante cambio; se adapta a su entorno para poder desenvolverse. La ciudad como organismo vivo no es diferente; ha sabido adaptarse a nuevas condiciones y necesidades. Cada parte de la ciudad ha encontrado su espacio. Lo que falta es un diseño que facilite el desarrollo de un crecimiento ecológico, en el cual cada organismo se pueda relacionar con el medioambiente, aprovechando los recursos propios del sitio.

Mi propuesta para Nueva Loja es densificar la ciudad y acercar diversos servicios a sus ciudadanos para disminuir al máximo su necesidad de trasladarse. El proyecto se implanta en una zona central de la ciudad y su desarrollo se basa en un sistema de bandas que se incrementan generando espacios diversos para diferentes tipos de vivienda. Las bandas de crecimiento se adaptan a distintas funciones y necesidades medioambientales; buscan replantear los bordes entre departamentos, entre exteriores e interiores, entre sociedad y naturaleza. En la vivienda misma, se ha privilegiado las zonas comunales que alojan actividades como agricultura urbana, lavanderías comunitarias (alimentadas por agua lluvia) y estacionamientos para bicicletas. Para lograr una mejor convivencia entre los entornos construido y natural, se han identificado los beneficios de los recursos y características locales, a la vez que se ha buscado disminuir al máximo el impacto ambiental de la intervención en una zona tan frágil como la selva.

VER IMÁGENES Y GRÁFICOS, PÁGINAS: 254 a 257.

FUSIÓN MATERIAL

Por **NICOLÁS GALLEGOS**

Desde el punto de vista programático, la vivienda propuesta cumple con los requerimientos básicos de cualquier morada, pero busca responder a las nuevas necesidades medioambientales a través del diseño bioclimático y una reformulación de las infraestructuras de servicios. Las fachadas se arman con un tratamiento de piel semipermeable que permite climatizar la vivienda o se abren completamente para facilitar la ventilación. La cubierta aprovecha las frecuentes lluvias amazónica para recolectar el agua lluvia que luego es reciclada y reutilizada en los servicios. Una serie de materiales se fusionan con el fin de optimizar al máximo sus propiedades. Las tuberías de acero de la era petrolera se reciclan en la estructura y la madera de árboles caídos de avanzada edad se absorbe en plataformas y pieles.

VER IMÁGENES Y GRÁFICOS, PÁGINAS: 258 a 261.

VIVIENDA UNIFAMILIAR AUTO-SOSTENIBLE

Por **VERÓNICA GUERRA**

Antes de empezar con el diseño del proyecto arquitectónico, se desarrolló una propuesta de crecimiento para Nueva Loja. Luego se analizaron los elementos que conducen a su desarrollo en una determinada dirección: están las tensiones naturales, como el río Aguarico o el lago; y las tensiones artificiales, como el aeropuerto. Se propuso el crecimiento hacia estos lugares, ya que poseen gran potencial turístico, comercial y natural. Se realizó un estudio de manchas urbanas, en base a la pixelación de los elementos que componen la geografía, para observar su comportamiento en el tiempo y poder aplicar lo aprendido en la morfología de crecimiento de Nueva Loja, los usos de su suelo y el diseño de sus viviendas.
Una vez llevado a cabo el análisis y la propuesta a escala urbana, se identificó un lugar relacionado con la agricultura y el comercio (actividades complementarias a la vivienda). Conceptos como capas, conexiones y pixeles fueron la base del diseño. Las fachadas se fragmentan en un mosaico de porosidades que permiten respirar a la vivienda. En la implantación se propone un sistema de agricultura rotacional que evite el desgaste de la tierra y se introduce un lugar para los paneles fotovoltaicos. El programa arquitectónico de la vivienda se amplía para incluir componentes productivos.

VER IMÁGENES Y GRÁFICOS, PÁGINAS: 262 a 265.

CAPA PROTECTORA

Por **MARÍA JOSÉ LEÓN**

El objetivo del presente proyecto fue crear un tipo de vivienda que se adaptara al clima de la región de Nueva Loja. Al analizar la Amazonia, y más concretamente, sus bosques, pude observar que a pesar de que su clima se define como tropical –húmedo y caliente– en el interior del bosque, bajo el efecto de los árboles y la vegetación, se engendra un micro-clima fresco y sombreado. El bosque provee una capa protectora que suaviza los efectos del clima tropical. En el proceso de diseño, se analizó esta
capa para desarrollar una vivienda que aprovechara el principio de protección de los árboles. La cubierta simula el dosel al independizarse del resto de las habitaciones. Las pieles se desdoblan para crear ambientes cerrados, abiertos o semi abiertos. La escala es pequeña y el programa arquitectónico mínimo. La estructura se construye con un recurso renovable, la madera, y en base a los mecanismos de renovación del bosque.

VER IMÁGENES Y GRÁFICOS, PÁGINAS: 266, 267.

INVERSIÓN DE LA FORTUNA

Por **Patrick Radden Keefe**
Publicado en *The New Yorker*, 09 de enero 2012

El puesto de avanzada selvático de Lago Agrio se encuentra en el noreste de Ecuador, donde las elevaciones caen a pico desde la cresta dentada de los Andes hasta las hondonadas pantanosas de la cuenca del Amazonas. Los ecuatorianos llaman a la región el Oriente. Durante siglos la selva estuvo poblada solo por tribus autóctonas. Pero, en 1967, perforadores estadounidenses de Texaco descubrieron abundantes reservas de crudo a tres kilómetros bajo el suelo de la selva. Durante veintitrés años un consorcio de empresas, liderado por Texaco, perforó pozos en todo el amazonas ecuatoriano. En un principio, la selva era tan impenetrable que el consorcio tenía que transportar los equipos necesarios con helicópteros. Pero los trabajadores abrieron sendas con machetes y, a la larga, Texaco pavimentó caminos y construyó un aeropuerto.

Hoy en día, Lago Agrio da una sensación de miseria. Los edificios parecen encimados unos sobre otros, como si nadie hubiese creído que la bonanza fuese a durar. Perros sueltos rondan las calles polvorientas, y una delgada tubería de petróleo bordea cada uno de los caminos principales, elevada sobre postes, a la altura de la cintura, como una barandilla interminable. La frontera colombiana queda a quince kilómetros al norte, y los traficantes de drogas y los paramilitares han infestado el Oriente, así como los sicarios –asesinos a sueldo— que ponen anuncios en Internet y a veces no cobran más de veinte dólares. En solo un mes de 2010, fueron hallados los cuerpos de treinta víctimas de asesinato en un trecho de camino cerca de la frontera.

Un día del pasado febrero, un juez de Lago Agrio, que presidía una despojada sala de audiencias de concreto, ubicada en un centro comercial en las afueras del pueblo, emitió un dictamen que reverberó mucho más allá del Amazonas. Desde 1993, un grupo de ecuatorianos venía entablando una lucha legal, en apariencia infructuosa, que buscaba hacer a Texaco responsable de la destrucción del Oriente. De acuerdo con la demanda, durante las décadas que operó allí Texaco habría derramado sesenta y ocho mil litros de desperdicios tóxicos. Según se dice, cuando la empresa cesó sus operaciones en Ecuador, en 1992, dejó cientos de fosas abiertas llenas de malignos sedimentos negros. El daño causado por Texaco —reclamaban los demandantes— podía medirse en muertes por cáncer, abortos no buscados, defectos de nacimientos, ganado muerto, peces enfermos y la casi extinción de varias tribus; el legado de Texaco en la región se presentaba como un "Chernobyl de la selva".

Cuando el juez, Nicolás Zambrano, hizo pública su decisión, la causa llevaba dieciocho años abierta. Había durado más que juristas en función en dos continentes. Zambrano era el sexto juez que presidía en Ecuador; un juez federal de Nueva York había muerto antes de fallar en la causa. El litigio duró incluso más que Texaco: en 2001, la empresa fue subsumida por Chevron, que heredó la demanda. Actualmente la disputa se considera una de las contiendas legales más acérrimas de las que se tenga memoria, un espectáculo casi tan desagradable como la contaminación que le dio origen.

Chevron, que opera en más de cien países, es la tercera corporación más grande de los Estados Unidos. Sus ingresos, que con frecuencia superan los doscientos millardos de dólares, son casi cuatro veces mayores que la producción económica de Ecuador. Los demandantes, que se autodenominan los afectados, incluyen a pueblos autóctonos y a pobladores incultos del Oriente; algunos de ellos firmaron documentos de la causa con una huella digital. Los representaba una coalición díscola de abogados estadounidenses y ecuatorianos, que en su mayoría trabajan a resultado. Una demanda medioambiental contra una enorme corporación se parece a una guerra de desgaste, y en 1993 pocos observadores habrían predicho que los demandantes soportarían tanto como lo hicieron. Pero el 14 de febrero de 2011 se recompensó su perseverancia. El juez Zambrano falló que Chevron era responsable de contaminación a gran escala y ordenó que pagara dieciocho millardos de dólares por daños y perjuicios: el fallo más grande nunca dictado en una demanda medioambiental.

Fue un triunfo extraordinario, en especial para uno de los abogados líderes de los demandantes, un tenaz estadounidense llamado Steven Donziger, que había sido una de las figuras clave desde el comienzo del caso. Donziger habla español y, desde hace años, viaja con regularidad entre Ecuador y Nueva York. "El juicio es histórico", ha dicho. "Es la primera vez que un pequeño país en vías de desarrollo ha prevalecido sobre una multinacional estadounidense".

Chevron niega de manera categórica las acusaciones de la demanda, e insiste en que no es responsable de la contaminación del Amazonas y en que las operaciones de Texaco se hicieron "completamente en regla con los estándares del momento". Un portavoz de Chevron me dijo que "no hay pruebas que corroboren" el vínculo entre la explotación petrolera en el Oriente y efectos nocivos para la salud, y culpó a los "abogados de la causa" de "perpetuar información falsa".

En los últimos años, Chevron ha invertido millones de dólares en reparar su imagen pública. Elegantes anuncios publicitarios televisivos, narrados por el actor Campbell Scott, hacen hincapié en que la compañía se propone "practicar y adherir a la conservación". Un anuncio gráfico trae la fotografía de dos mujeres africanas sonrientes y al pie se lee: "Las compañías petroleras deben brindar apoyo a las comunidades de las que forman parte". El otoño pasado, en un debate matutino sobre "Negocios y derechos humanos" hecho en Nueva York, la gerente de temas globales de Chevron, Silvia Garrigo, dijo que la compañía realiza "inversiones sociales" dondequiera que opere, puntualizando: "Nos instalamos en países a largo plazo".

En los tribunales, sin embargo, Chevron se ha mostrado mucho menos conciliador. No hace mucho, después de que la compañía rechazó exitosamente una demanda que buscaba hacerla responsable de las muertes por arma de fuego de unos manifestantes en una plataforma marina de petróleo costa afuera de Nigeria, trató de obligar a los empobrecidos demandantes nigerianos, algunos de los cuales eran viudas e hijos, a reembolsarle los honorarios de sus abogados. (La sentencia no incluyó honorarios, y el juez reprendió a Chevron por intentar obtenerlos.) "Así es como litigan", me dijo Bert Voorhees, uno de los abogados nigerianos. "El objetivo es amedrentar a cualquier otra comunidad que tal vez intente hacer valer sus derechos humanos".

Chevron se ha mostrado especialmente desafiante al enfrentar las acusaciones de Lago Agrio, que los abogados de la compañía han denominado "una sacudida". Además de defenderse en Ecuador, ha combatido la causa en más de una docena de tribunales federales de los Estados Unidos, contratando a cientos de letrados y produciendo lo que sus propios abogados defensores han llamado "una avalancha de papel". Donziger ha sostenido que Chevron está motivado no solo por el temor a una sentencia adversa sino por el deseo de "destruir la idea misma de que un pueblo autóctono pueda efectuar una demanda contra una compañía petrolera". En 2008, el miembro de un grupo de presión de Chevron que opera en Washington dijo a Newsweek: "No podemos permitir que países pequeños jodan a las grandes compañías". Uno de los portavoces de Chevron dijo: "Vamos a pelear esta causa hasta que se congele el infierno; y después vamos a seguir peleando en el hielo".

Cuando se pronunció el veredicto en Lago Agrio, Chevron declaró el juicio "ilegítimo e imposible de aplicar", y dijo que la compañía, que no tiene activos en Ecuador, no pagaría. En vez de hacerlo, contraatacó con una movida audaz: demandó a Steven Donziger, el arquitecto de la demanda que pesaba en su contra. En el preciso momento en que Donziger habría podido celebrar una victoria histórica en los tribunales de Ecuador, descubrió que enfrentaba acusaciones de extorsión y fraude en uno de Nueva York.

Cuando Donziger no está en Ecuador, trabaja en la cocina llena de papeles del departamento de tres ambientes que comparte con su esposa y su hijo, en el Upper West Side de Manhattan. Pero también se mantiene muy ocupado en restaurantes. Se instala a la hora del almuerzo en el Ocean Grill, enfrente del Museum of Natural History, y usa su teléfono hasta que todos los demás clientes se han ido. Dondequiera que vaya, lleva un MacBook Air bajo el brazo. Si la discreción es un imperativo característico del derecho, Donziger es un abogado poco ortodoxo. Es un hablador compulsivo; su torrente incesante de palabras sigue el curso de sus emociones volátiles. Animado por su propia oratoria, a menudo levanta la voz hasta que, de pronto, grita. Con más de un metro noventa de estatura, grandes rasgos faciales, pelo negro grisáceo cortado al ras y manos enormes, Donziger tiene una presencia física imponente. Los amigos de la facultad de derecho de Harvard lo llamaba "Steve el grandote". En Harvard jugó al básquet con Barack Obama, otro de los miembros de la promoción de 1991. Desde entonces, Donziger ha dedicado su carrera a un solo caso.

Pocos después de que Donziger se graduara, un abogado de Massachusetts llamado Cristóbal Bonifaz empezó a considerar una demanda contra Texaco. Bonifaz era un emigrado amable de una prominente familia ecuatoriana. (Su abuelo había sido, brevemente, Presidente.) En abril de 1993, tras enterarse de los daños medioambientales en Oriente por un informe de Oxfam, reunió un equipo de abogados, doctores y especialista de la Harvard School of Public Health, para hacer un viaje de reconocimiento al Amazonas. Bonifaz invitó a Donziger, un amigo de la familia, a unirse a la expedición.

Cuando Texaco halló petróleo en Ecuador, el país era inestable y muy pobre; su principal artículo de exportación eran las bananas. Como escribió Judith Kimerling, la autora del libro Amazon Crude, se hizo desfilar el "primer barril" de petróleo ecuatoriano por las calles de Quito. En 1972, cuando Texaco finalizó la construcción de un oleoducto para transportar petróleo hasta la costa del Pacífico, Ecuador se convirtió de inmediato en el segundo exportador de petróleo más grande de Latinoamérica, a la zaga de Venezuela. En una década, el PIB per-capita casi se duplicó.

Uno de los retos de perforar pozos de petróleo es qué hacer con el "agua producida": un líquido maloliente, enriquecido con metales pesados, que emerge con el petróleo al bombeárselo hasta la superficie del suelo. En los Estados Unidos, una vez que el petróleo se separa de la mezcla, el procedimiento estándar es "reinyectar" el agua producida, bombeándola hacia el fondo de pozos designados, para así evitar daños en el hábitat local. Pero la reinyección es costosa, y, en Ecuador, Texaco simplemente vertió el líquido en pozos del tamaño de una piscina. El agua producida no es biodegradable, y, cuando Donziger y sus colegas visitaron el Oriente, descubrieron que la superficie de la selva estaba marcada por cientos de lagunas grasientas.

Desde un principio, el gobierno de Ecuador había estado al tanto de la técnicas, y durante muchos años Texaco formó parte de un consorcio que incluía a la compañía petrolera nacional. Las prácticas de Texaco no violaban de forma directa las leyes de Ecuador; de hecho, por esa época el país no tenía normas medioambientales de sentido coherente. La mayoría de los ecuatorianos sabía poco sobre la ciencia de extraer petróleo, y la mayor parte de lo que aprendieron se lo enseñó Texaco. Lago Agrio recibió su nombre de Sour lake, el pueblo de East Texas donde se había establecido Texaco, y, cuando el campamento petrolero creció hasta formar un pueblo que se benefició del auge, los derrames de los oleoductos se volvieron corrientes. Los camiones de Texaco rociaban los caminos de petróleo para aplastar el polvo. En Quito conocí a una mujer llamada Margarita Yépez, que trabajó dieciocho años como asistente social para Texaco. En los primeros tiempos, me contó, los petroleros gringos le decían a los residentes locales, en chiste, que el petróleo era bueno para la salud; un jarro de café lleno de crudo podía curar la artritis o la calvicie en los hombres, con solo frotar un poco en la zona afectada. "Eran la autoridad, así que confiamos en ellos", dijo la mujer. "Fuimos unos tontos."

Al principio, las tribus autóctonas fueron los únicos ecuatorianos afectados por las perforaciones. Y aunque el petróleo estaba bajo su tierra natal, no gozaban de ganancia alguna, porque el gobierno retuvo todos los derechos "por debajo de la superficie". ("Los mansos recibirán la tierra por heredad", observó una vez el petrolero J. Paul Getty. "Pero no los derechos de explotación minera.") Las tribus derribaron árboles para cortar el paso de los camiones de Texaco, y lanzaron ataques contra los trabajadores. En 1987, un obispo de una misión capuchina local se ofreció a entrar en contacto con una tribu especialmente solitaria, los Tagaeri, asentada en tierras que otra compañía petrolera deseaba explorar. Un helicóptero depositó al obispo, junto con una monja, en el territorio tagaeri. Cuando el piloto regresó al día siguiente, descubrió sus cadáveres, clavados al suelo por veinte pesadas lanzas de madera.

De nada sirvieron esos gestos de rebeldía. En la década siguiente a la pavimentación de caminos, cien mil ecuatorianos se asentaron en el Oriente, atraídos por las tierras gratuitas y la promesa de trabajo. Arrasaron la selva para instalar sembradíos, y las tribus locales se vieron reducidas a vender baratijas en los campamentos petroleros o a internarse más adentro en la jungla. "Fue la destrucción absoluta de sus vidas", me dijo Miguel Cabodevilla, un monje español que lleva décadas trabajando con las tribus.

En noviembre de 1993, Cristóbal Bonifaz inició una querella colectiva contra Texaco en una corte federal de Manhattan, en nombre de treinta mil afectados. Texaco negó las acusaciones, manteniendo que había "operado de acuerdo con las prácticas seguras de la industria y acatado la ley ecuatoriana".

Al principio, Donziger participó menos de la estrategia legal que de una campaña de relaciones públicas contra Texaco. Antes de estudiar derecho, había trabajado en América Central como periodista y no tenía escrúpulos en emplear algo de teatro para dramatizar la historia de sus clientes. En importantes audiencias que tuvieron lugar en Manhattan, Donziger los presentó ante la prensa con collares de cuentas aborígenes y pintura de guerra. El desarrollo había expuesto a la mayoría de los demandantes a las costumbres modernas, y, tras aparecer vestidos de plumas en la conferencia de prensa, a menudo se ponían jeans en su hotel, para ir de compras en Times Square. Pero los periodistas quedaron prendados de los miembros transplantados de aquella tribu. Un artículo en la revista Times llevaba el titular: "SIMPLES TURISTAS EN BROADWAY, PERO DESCALZOS Y CON GANAS DE COMER MONO ASADO".

Durante ocho años, Texaco trató de que se desestimara la demanda, alegando que no debía juzgarse en los Estados Unidos sino en Ecuador. Donziger y sus colegas temían esa vuelta: el sistema judicial de Ecuador era notoriamente corrupto, y un tercio del presupuesto anual del gobierno dependía de las rentas petroleras. "Texaco controló el país por veinte años", me dijo Chris Jochnick, un amigo de universidad de Donziger que entonces vivía en Ecuador y ahora trabaja para Oxfam America. "Tenían a la embajada estadounidense metida en el bolsillo. Contaban con el ejército. En un sentido político, no había forma de que hicieran responsable a Texaco en Ecuador". Texaco negó que Ecuador fuese incapaz de ofrecer un juicio justo, insistiendo en que las normas legales del país eran "similares a las de muchas naciones europeas".

En 2001, Texaco prevaleció. Un juez federal de Nueva York sobreseyó la causa, dictaminando que "tenía todo que ver con Ecuador y muy poco con los Estados Unidos". Para entonces ya estaba en marcha la adquisición de Texaco por parte de Chevron. En un anuncio de prensa gráfica, Donziger y sus colegas advirtieron a los accionistas de Chevron que "Texaco viene con un haber abultado, y con un enorme pasivo". Pero debe de haber parecido que la demanda había llegado a su fin. Justo antes de la adquisición, un portavoz de Chevron dijo que la compañía no sentía la necesidad de "hacer especial hincapié" en las demandas ecuatorianas ante sus accionistas.

En 2003, Donziger y sus colegas reiniciaron la causa, ahora en Lago Agrio, pese a sus dudas en cuanto el sistema legal ecuatoriano. Contrataron a un equipo de abogados ecuatorianos, y Donziger empezó a viajar con frecuencia a la región. Al no tener permiso para ejercer el derecho en Ecuador, en apariencia cumplía un papel de asesor. Pero disfrutaba de los rigores del litigio en el Oriente sofocante, y, gracias a personalidad eléctrica y sus frecuentes visitas, poco a poco reemplazó a Bonifaz como motor del caso.

No todos aceptaron el liderazgo de Donziger. Esperanza Martínez, que está a cargo de Oilwatch Sudamérica, un grupo ambientalista de Quito, me dijo: "Confieso que la personalidad fuerte de Steve… me resulta una lucha". Sarah Lee Whitson, una vieja amiga de él que ahora trabaja en Human Rights Watch, reconoció que hay gente a la que chocan la terquedad y la teatralidad de Donziger. Pero fueron justamente esas cualidades, dijo ella, las que le permitieron enfrentarse a un gigante petrolero: "Es un líder, y lo cierto es que él lleva más de una década en el caso y lo ha mantenido vivo".

Mientras la demanda avanzaba en Ecuador, Donziger y su equipo se desalentaron ante lo que parecían ser graves desventajas. En su diario, Donziger se lamenta de que tratar de hacer responsables de las compañías petroleras "va contra la corriente de la economía entera". El país no tiene juicios con jurado, por lo que se enviste de un enorme poder discrecional a los jueces, quienes, en su mayoría, son funcionarios mal pagos; a Donziger le preocupaba que fuesen propensos a aceptar sobornos. En Estados Unidos, los abogados tienen prohibido reunirse con un juez "ex parte", sin la presencia de la parte opuesta. Pero, en esa época, en Ecuador no existía una ley así, lo que hacía difícil monitorear si un juez había estado sujeto a presiones indebidas.

Julio Prieto, un joven abogado ecuatoriano que trabaja para los demandantes, me dijo que, cuando estudiaba derecho en Quito, "siempre se decía que las cosas tiene que ser de cierta manera, pero en la práctica era pura cháchara". Le pregunté si era desalentador trabajar en un sistema así. "¿Alguna vez usted sobornó a un policía?" me preguntó. Negué con la cabeza. "En Ecuador, todo el mundo lo hace", dijo. "Pero eso no quiere decir que no necesitemos policías".

Chevron contrató a un flota de abogados locales, que en Lago Agrio a menudo iba acompañada de guardaespaldas. Donziger se obsesionó con el vasto poder de su adversario. "No importa lo que yo haga, me pueden superar con dinero", se quejaba. Cada vez que un nuevo juez o perito entraba en la causa, Donziger se preguntaba si esa persona estaba contagiada: corrupta. Algunos miembros del equipo legal de los demandantes llegaron a creer que se hallaban bajo la vigilancia de agentes de Chevron. En 2004, cuando el hermano de Pablo Fajardo, el principal abogado ecuatoriano defensor de los demandantes, fue asesinado cerca de la frontera colombiana, algunos miembros del equipo de Donziger insinuaron que Chevron estaba envuelto en ello. Donziger se preocupó por su seguridad, preguntándose si también se "convertiría en una víctima". (Chevron niega rotundamente estar envuelto en el asesinato, y los demandantes no han ofrecido pruebas que apoyen esa teoría.)

La mayor ventaja de los demandantes, en opinión de Donziger, eran las pruebas incontrovertibles de contaminación medioambiental: el bosque desfigurado, los pozos tóxicos. Cuando periodistas visitaban el Amazonas, los demandantes los llevaban en bote de un lugar a otro, en un rito que llegó a conocerse como la "visita tóxica". Al mismo tiempo, Donziger temía que el resultado legal acabara dependiendo, no de la verdad, sino de la manipulación del sistema.

Esas preocupaciones se acentuaron en 2006, cuando Donziger oyó acusaciones de que el nuevo juez que había sido asignado a la causa, Germán Yánez, era, en palabras de Donziger, "un mujeriego" y "un bebedor". (Por esa época, se acusó a Yánez de acosar sexualmente a una pasante, una acusación que él rechazó como motivada por cuestiones políticas.) El "perfil psicológico" de Yánez "cuadraba perfectamente con el chantaje y la corrupción", pensó Donziger. Algunas noches, alzaba la vista desde su laptop y, al ver su cara en el espejo, se asombraba de cuánto más viejo se veía con respecto a cuando la causa había empezado. Estaba inquieto por algo que había empezado a llamar para sus adentros "el problema de la misión inútil".

El estudio de Gibson, Dunn & Crutcher tiene más de cien años y cuenta con mil abogados. Un día del otoño pasado, visité las oficinas neoyorkinas del bufete, en el piso cuarenta y seis del MetLife Building, para reunirme con Randy Mastro, un socio de cincuenta años que, durante los últimos dos años, ha representado a Chevron en la causa de Ecuador. Mastro, que tiene cejas en punta y pelo blanco rebelde, habla con suavidad, pero, incluso para los estándares pugilísticos del derecho neoyorkino, tiene fama de ser un litigante despiadado. En los tribunales, vestido con un traje conservador, con los anteojos posados en la punta de la nariz, Mastro cobra vida. Rebota sobre las puntas de sus pies para acentuar lo evidente de su lógica y corta el aire con la mano al ritmo de sus deducciones, como un rapero. Su pavoneo es paralizante.

Como fiscal federal y, más tarde, teniente de alcalde bajo Rudolph Giuliani, Mastro luchó contra la mafia de Nueva York, limpiando el Fulton Fish Market y el San Gennaro Festival, pese a amenazas de muerte. En la Alcaldía, a veces blandía un bate de béisbol en las reuniones, para enfatizar un punto. El periódico Daily News observó en una oportunidad que Mastro era la única persona en el gobierno de Giuliani al lado del cual el alcalde parecía un buen tipo.

Cuando Mastro entró en la lujosa sala de espera donde yo lo aguardaba, llevaba un torre de carpetas que contenían miles de páginas con informes y declaraciones juradas de Chevron. Apenas se le veía la cara. Entonces las posó en una mesa con un golpe seco. "Los clientes vienen a nuestro bufete en busca del tipo de defensa entusiasta que puede ayudar a dar vuelta una causa", me dijo Mastro, y se ha alabado a Gibson, Dunn por los éxitos obtenidos al rescatar grandes corporaciones de amenazas legales. En 2010, Walmart, tras una defensa exitosa en un importante demanda laboral, elogió a los "abogados salvavidas" de Gibson, Dunn. Otros han sugerido que el bufete se extralimita. Hace varios años, en una causa sin relación con la anterior, la Corte Suprema de Montana reprendió a Gibson, Dunn por caer en actos de "matonería legal".

La demanda en el Amazonas no tiene méritos, me aseguró Mastro. Donziger solo quería "ganar plata". Pero el hecho de que Chevron solicitara la ayuda de Mastro sugiere que la compañía estaba nerviosa en cuanto al futuro de la causa. La estrategia de Donziger de cortejar a la prensa había resultado excepcionalmente efectiva. En 2005, Donziger abordó a Joe Berlinger, un respetado cineasta de Nueva York, para sugerirle que filmara un documental sobre el caso. La película, Crude, se estrenó en 2009. En ese mismo años, el programa de televisión 60 Minutes emitió un segmento sumamente crítico sobre Chevron. En el mismo, Silvia Garrigo daba la impresión de ser una caricatura de inhumanidad al restar importancia a los riesgos para la salud del petróleo. "Llevo maquillaje, y hay en mi cara aceites que se producen de manera natural", dijo. "Lo cual no quiere decir que vaya a enfermarme."

Además de sus roles de abogado y estratega de relaciones públicas, Donziger se ha vuelto, por necesidad, un experto recaudador de fondos. Fue incansable y creativo a la hora de sumar celebridades a la causa, incluyendo a Sting y a Darryl Hannah, y de conseguir el apoyo de patrocinadores adinerados como Russ DeLeon, un contemporáneo suyo de la facultad de derecho que ganó una fortuna en un emprendimiento de apuestas online. "Hay que encontrar maneras de sostener esfuerzos como este", explicó Donziger en un discurso reciente, porque cuando se lleva a juicio a una multinacional, la "estrategia principal de esta es dejarnos exhaustos". Durante años, el caso estaba respaldado por un bufete de abogados de Filadelfia, Kohn, Swift & Graft, que brindaba apoyo financiero y legal a cambio de un porcentaje de las ganancias eventuales. Pero, conforme la causa se prolongaba, las transferencias desde Filadelfia no llegaban con suficiente regularidad para cubrir los gastos.

Buscando otras fuentes de apoyo financiero, Donziger las halló en el sector emergente de las "finanzas de litigio". En los últimos años, ciertos fondos especulativos han empezado a invertir en querellas colectivas, proporcionando capital por adelantado para cubrir los gastos de un proceso a cambio de una parte de las ganancias si se el resultado es exitoso. Estos acuerdos no están regulados y son muy polémicos. Pero a Donziger le brindaron la oportunidad crucial de mantener vivo el litigio. Hizo a los inversores una propuesta de alto riesgo y grandes recompensas posibles. La sentencia podía alcanzar millardos de dólares, afirmó, de los que los abogados se llevarían más o menos un tercio en honorarios. Confidencialmente, notó que sus honorarios personales tal vez ascendieran a doscientos millones de dólares. Al final, un fondo llamado Burford Capital, que tiene su base en las Islas del Canal, hizo una inversión multimillonaria en el caso. Un poderoso bufete de Washington, D.C., Patton Boggs, también se unió al equipo de los demandantes.

Según Randy Mastro, los especuladores ricos que buscan sacar provecho financiando a Donziger revelan el cinismo subyacente a la causa de los demandantes. El proceso no está impulsado por ecuatorianos pobres, me dijo, sino por "abogados y consultores y financistas". La ambición de Donziger era por cierto grandiosa, pero parecía motivada tanto por un idealismo combativo como por el deseo de obtener riquezas. Quería recalibrar la dinámica de poder que, tradicionalmente, había hecho difícil que los extranjeros marginalizados demandaran a las compañías estadounidenses. Creía que estaba creando un "modelo de negocio viable para casos de derechos humanos".

En 2006, Ecuador eligió a un nuevo Presidente, el economista de izquierdas Rafael Correa. Donziger estaba eufórico. El día en que asumió Correa, Donziger les dijo a los camarógrafos de Berlinger: "No hay manera de que con un gobierno presidido por este hombre Chevron se salga con los procedimientos que suele emplear aquí, que son sobornos, reuniones secretas y manipulación del poder gubernamental". Al año siguiente, tras cabildeos hechos por los demandantes, Correa visitó el Oriente y contempló los pozos de desechos. "No nos engañemos", dijo en una conferencia de prensa en Lago Agrio. "Aquí ha habido un crimen contra la humanidad".

La señal más clara de que, en Ecuador, el viento había cambiado en contra de Chevron llegó el 26 noviembre de 2008, cuando un ingeniero geológico llamado Richard Cabrera, al que se había designado para que actuara como evaluador independiente de daños medioambientales, presentó un informe en el que recomendaba que el tribunal responsabilizara a Chevron y le impusiera un multa de veintisiete millardos de dólares por daños y perjuicios. Chevron denunció el informe, diciendo que contenía "pruebas falsificadas y erróneas" y sugiriendo que Cabrera tenía predisposición por los demandantes. Pero el equipo de Donziger encargó una evaluación de las conclusiones a Stratus, una consultora medioambiental de Boulder Colorado, que había realizado trabajo exhaustivo para el gobierno de Estados Unidos. Stratus respaldó el informe de cabrera caracterizándolo de "sólido, razonables y consistente con los enfoques utilizados en otras causas por daños al medioambiente".

En ese momento, quizá la dirección de Chevron lamentó los esfuerzos denodados que hizo Texaco en los años noventa por que se desestimara la causa en los tribunales de Estados Unidos. Los representantes de Chevron expresaron alarma ante el pésimo estado del sistema judicial ecuatoriano, comparando los juicios que ocurrían en el país con lo que cabía esperarse en Corea del Norte. El peligro, como explicó más tarde Mastro, era que el régimen de Correa pusiera "el pulgar en la balanza" de la justicia a favor de los demandantes.

En agosto de 2009, Chevron ofreció asombrosas pruebas en apoyo de su afirmación de que Ecuador era totalmente corrupto: dio a conocer material de video que, supuestamente, implicaba al entonces juez de la causa de Lago Agrio, Juan Nuñez, en una trama de sobornos. Un hombre de negocios ecuatoriano llamado Diego Borja había esperado obtener un contrato de limpieza en caso de que se fallara contra Chevron. Pero, según explicó la compañía, cuando Borja se reunió con el juez y con un funcionario del gobierno de Correa, se le informó que antes tenía que pagar un sendo millón de dólares a Nuñez, al gobierno y a los demandantes de Lago Agrio. Borja y un socio grabaron en secreto las discusiones, usando cámaras escondidas en un reloj y en una pluma fuente. Charles James, un ejecutivo de Chevron, declaró: "Esta información descalifica por completo al juez y anula todo lo que ha hecho en esta causa".

Jorge Nuñez se hizo a un lado. Pero siguió insistiendo en que era inocente. Los videos, que Chevron publicó en Internet, mostraban a Borja y al funcionario hablando elípticamente con Nuñez acerca de la posibilidad de un soborno, pero no ofrecían pruebas de que el juez hubiese solicitado o aceptado tal cosa. Nuñez me dijo que el escándalo fue una trampa, y Donziger ha llamado al incidente "una cama de las que hace Chevron". Más tarde salió a la luz que el supuesto funcionario del gobierno de Correa era, en realidad, un vendedor de automóviles y proveedor part-time de catering de Quito, cuyo nombre no aparece en la base de datos de los miembros registrados del partido. El hombre de negocios, Borja, era un ex contratista de Chevron.

Chevron insiste en que no incitó a Borja a iniciar discusiones sobre sobornos, y afirma que este no fue remunerado por sus esfuerzos. Pero, de acuerdo con documentos del juzgado, Borja y su esposa se mudaron a Estados Unidos a costa de Chevron y recibieron una casa, un auto, un generoso estipendio mensual y los servicios de un abogado criminalista de primer nivel. El abogado no le permitió a Borja hablar conmigo, pero un amigo de Borja, Santiago Escobar, me dijo que Jorge Nuñez era inocente y que Borja le tendió una trampa. "No es un buen Samaritano", dijo Escobar. "Quería dinero."

Hace unos meses, hice la visita tóxica. La mitad del día, mi guía fue un portavoz de Donziger y de los demandantes; la otra mitad, me acompañó un representante de Chevron. En la actualidad los dos bandos emplean especialistas en relaciones públicas a tiempo completo. De hecho, llevan tantos años contendiendo uno con otro que la controversia llega a parecer una injuriosa campaña política: un peloteo constante de argumentos y refutaciones. El bando opuesto disputa toda afirmación científica o histórica. (Miguel Ángel Cabodevilla, el monje, me dijo: "En la selva, hay más literatura que historia".) Chevron ha contratado a docenas de consultores ecológicos, que ponen en duda casi todas las reivindicaciones empíricas de los demandantes. La compañía niega que la contaminación y los riesgos sanitarios se encuentren siquiera cerca del nivel que alega Donziger. Cuando los demandantes presentaron un estudio que muestra porcentajes inusualmente altos de cáncer en el Oriente, Chevron respondió con un estudio propio, que mantiene que las tasas de cáncer son más bajas en esa zona que en otras partes de Ecuador. Silvia Garrigo, la ejecutiva encargada de los asuntos globales, se ha quejado de que los afectados culpan a Chrevron por cada uno de sus males: "Si su vaca se muere, es Texaco. Si su mujer tiene diabetes, es Texaco".

Durante la parte de la gira a cargo los demandantes, un lugareño llamado Donald Moncayo me mostró la zona. Con guantes blancos quirúrgicos puestos, levantó un puñado de lodo negro y lo sostuvo de manera de que la luz resaltara el tinte azul-anaranjado revelador de petróleo. En un pozo fétido que se hallaba en una claro de la selva, dio unos pasos con cuidado sobre la superficie, donde la materia sólida del agua producida se había endurecido hasta formar una costra como de alquitrán, que soportaba su peso. Sonriendo un poco, Moncayo se apoyó alternadamente en una pierna y después en la otra, hasta que toda la superficie empezó a ondular bajo sus pies. Parecía un niño en una cama de agua. De acuerdo con los demandantes, hay casi mil de esos pozos en Oriente, desperdigados en un área del tamaño de Rhode Island.

Al mirar a Moncayo, tuve una sensación de déjà vu. Él es el maestro de ceremonias habitual de la gira tóxica; yo había oído hablar de su número, y lo había visto en acción, de manera casi idéntica, en Crude, el documental de Berlinger. Pero, si el ritmo de Moyano era ensayado, su indignación no tenía nada de fingida. Me condujo por un barranco empinado hasta un arroyo. Bajo la luz vaporosa que se filtraba entre el follaje, el agua, de apenas treinta centímetros de profundidad, se veía cristalina. Moncayo hundió un palito en el lecho del arroyo y removió el légamo hasta que el agua se enturbió por los sedimentos. Cuando Moyano me animó a hacerlo, pasé la mano por la superficie del arroyo. Mi palma quedó recubierta de una película acre.

Moncayo me miró con satisfacción sombría. "Le decimos a Chevron: 'Si ustedes creen que esto es apto para el consumo humano, ¿por qué no beben ustedes de esta agua?", dijo.

Jim Craig, un portavoz de Chevron, me mostró Lago Agrio. Me contó que la compañía hizo sus propias mediciones en el agua del Oriente y jamás obtuvo una lectura positiva en cuanto a contaminación de hidrocarburos. Especuló que, en algunos casos, los demandantes deben de haber "adulterado" las fuentes de agua locales tras las pruebas de Chevron.

Craig me dijo que las infecciones cutáneas y los problemas gastrointestinales que los demandantes atribuyen a la contaminación de petróleo son causadas, más probablemente, por la red cloacal que corre en paralelo a los arroyos y ríos locales. "Cabe imaginarse que surgen problemas de todo tipo cuando se ingieren esas porquerías", dijo.

A unos kilómetros de Lago Agrio, nos detuvimos a la orilla de un de los pozos de desechos, y Craig me dijo que el residuo de aspecto inmundo que se hallaba en la superficie tenía solo unos pocos centímetros de espesor. Para demostrarlo, tomó una piedra y la arrojó al pozo. Esta aterrizó, con un débil golpe seco, en la superficie. "Si tuviera una roca más grande…", dijo, y arrojó una de mucho mayor tamaño. Tampoco esa se hundió.

Según entiende Chevron, de todas maneras, estas demandas y contrademandas medioambientales son algo irrelevantes, porque, en última instancia, la defensa de la compañía se apoya no en la ciencia sino en la ley. En 1995, Texaco reconoció que había dejado el Amazonas hecho un desastre y se comprometió, en cierta medida, a remediarlo. Pero la compañía subrayaba que había formado parte de un consorcio de Ecuador –el cual incluía la compañía estatal de petróleo— y que su participación en la sociedad era del treinta y siete por ciento. Por consiguiente, Texaco aceptó limpiar solo el treinta y siete por ciento de los pozos, pese a que, como el único "operador" del consorcio, había sido responsable tanto de hacer las perforaciones como de cavar los pozos.

Texaco gastó cuarenta millones de dólares en la limpieza, y en 1998 el gobierno de Ecuador le extendió a la compañía un documento que la liberaba de cualquier demanda futura que se hiciera en su contra. Chevron admite de buen grado que hay grandes pozos de residuos desperdigados en el Amazonas, pero niega que tenga la obligación legal de limpiar más de ellos. Sugiere, en cambio, que la responsabilidad debería recaer en la compañía petrolera estatal, Petroecuador, que se ha ocupado de la extracción en Lago Agrio desde la partida de Texaco y ha sido acusada de contaminar ampliamente la región. "El caso no es sobre la mugre que hay en Ecuador", señaló una vez un abogado de Chevron. "Es sobre un contrato y sobre cómo interpretarlo".

En enero de 2009, Donziger viajó a Park City, Utah, para asistir al estreno de Crude, en el Sundance Film Festival. La película lo retrata como una presencia dominante; en un momento, al pensar que los abogados de Chevron quizás han manipulado a un anciano juez de Quito, Donziger entra hecho un huracán en las habitaciones del juez, que es mucho más pequeño que él. "Tenga mucho cuidado con los abogados de Texaco", le advierte Donziger. "Juegan sucio." Hablando a cámara, concede que nunca haría nada semejante en Estados Unidos, pero explica que en Ecuador "se juega así".

En otra escena, Donziger instruye a uno de sus clientes locales, Emergildo Criollo, preparándolo para colarse en la reunión anual de accionista de Chevron, en Houston. Le dice que no se amedrente y le sugiere cierta retórica: "'Ustedes pasaron veintiocho años en mi país. Puedo quedarme tres minutos en el territorio de ustedes.'" Satisfecho con el resultado, dice: "Esa es buena, ¿no?" En la escena siguiente, Criollo pronuncia la frase ante los accionistas.

Cuando Randy Mastro y sus colegas examinaron la película, notaron una pequeña discrepancia entre la versión que se proyectó en Sundance y la que se comercializó más tarde en DVD. En la película hay una escena que muestra una consulta entre los abogados de los demandantes y la tribu a la que representan. En Sundance, se veía a un médico español llamado Carlos Beristain. En la versión en DVD, la edición lo eliminó. El hecho le pareció potencialmente significativo a Mastro, porque tras el encuentro en cuestión Beristain pasó a trabajar para el perito independiente en daños medioambientales. ¿El director lo había eliminado a pedido de los demandantes?

"Eso nos hizo parar las antenas", me dijo Mastro.

Se preguntó qué otras tomas de película descartadas podría haber de los tres años que Berlinger pasó filmando a Donziger, y en abril de 2004, solicitó a un juez federal de Nueva York que obligara a Berlinger a entregar todo el material en bruto. Mastro citó un estatuto poco utilizado que le da derecho a un estadounidense litigante que se enfrenta con una demanda en el extranjero a buscar "proposiciones de pruebas" extensamente dentro de los Estados Unidos. Chevron necesitaba las tomas descartadas, argumentó Mastro, para probar que se "había negado el proceso debido" en Ecuador.

Los abogados de Berlinger objetaron que Chevron estaba "de pesca", e invocaron el privilegio del periodista. Mastro respondió que Crude no era periodismo en absoluto sino "una descarada obra de propaganda". Dado que Donziger había propuesto a Berlinger rodar la película, argumentó Mastro, y dado que Berlinger había cortado la toma del médico español a pedido de los demandantes, no se trataba en realidad de un cineasta independiente.

Pese a la intervención de organizaciones periodísticas, incluido The Times, donde se argumentó que obligar a Berlinger a entregar el material crearía un peligroso precedente, tanto el juez, Lewis Kaplan, como un tribunal de apelaciones se pusieron de parte de Chevron. Poco después el equipo de Mastro tomo posesión de seiscientas horas de película.

Mastro no tardó en pedir otra audiencia con Kaplan, un cáustico pero respetado juez federal, que había trabajado como abogado de sociedades antes de su nombramiento en la magistratura, hecho por Bill Clinton en 1994. "Si estábamos de pesca, atrapamos un pez gordo", anunció Mastro en el tribunal. Al parecer Donziger se sentía tan cómodo con el equipo de Berlinger que pasaba por alto el hecho de que grababan cada cosa que decía. Cuando Mastro pasó ante el juez una serie de tomas descartadas, quedó por completo en evidencia que Donziger no tenía pelos en la lengua. Peroraba, indignado, sobre las deficiencias del sistema legal ecuatoriano. "Son todos corruptos", dice acerca de los ecuatorianos en un momento. "Tienen el derecho de nacimiento
a ser corruptos."

A juzgar por las tomas, el temor de Donziger a que la causa no se decidiera por sus méritos lo llevó a dudar de la importancia de las pruebas mismas. En una escena, un perito científico de los demandantes le anunciaba que una de las mediciones de contaminación en el agua subterránea no era tan fuerte como había supuesto. "Estamos en Ecuador, ¿sí?" dice Donziger. "Al fin y al cabo, si hay mil personas por los tribunales, uno conseguirá lo que busca." En cuanto a los datos científicos, agrega, no es más que "humo y espejos y tonterías".

Fue una presentación devastadora. En el mismo momento en que Chevron afirmaba que Ecuador era demasiado corrupto para garantizar un juicio justo, su adversario decía efectivamente lo mismo. El documental fue la "ruina" de los demandantes, me dijo Mastro.

En otra escena que Mastro mostró en el tribunal, se ve a Donziger conversando con sus asociados durante una cena en un restaurante. Alguien de la mesa, refiriéndose a la antipatía general que sienten en Ecuador por Chevron, sugiere que, si el juez de lago Agrio falla en contra de los demandantes, tal vez lo maten. "Tal vez no", responde Donziger, con una copa de vino tinto en la mano. "Pero cree que sí. Lo que es igual de bueno."

A lo largo de varias audiencias, el juez Kaplan dio muestras de sentir una palpable antipatía por Donziger. Lo describió como "el general de campo de una ofensiva política y mediática", y pareció ofenderse por lo que llamó las "frontales admisiones hechas por Donziger de que lo que ocurre en Ecuador es una lucha en el barro, no un litigio de buena fe".

Los abogados de Donziger trataron de minimizar sus palabras .Pero Mastro argumentó que las tomas revelaban una conspiración criminal, en la que Donziger explotaba la corrupción de sistema ecuatoriano para presionar a Chevron a llegar a un acuerdo de mucho dinero fuera del tribunal. De pronto, las mismas cualidades que le había permitido a Donziger mantenerse firme en medio de tremendas desventajas —su retórica desenfrenada, sus dotes para las relaciones públicas— lo había puesto, y había puesto a la causa entera, en peligro. "Los cuchillos sirven para cortar cosas", me dijo su amiga Sarah Leah Wilson. "Pero a veces uno puede rebnarse un dedo." Mastro, envalentonado por su triunfo con las tomas descartadas, decidió dar un paso más. El material de video revelaba una deshonestidad tan extraordinaria, le dijo al juez Kaplan, que Chevron debería tener derecho a ver los documentos personales de Donziger. Dado que gran parte de las tareas de Donziger consistían, sugirió Mastro, no en representación legal sino en hacer publicidad y recaudar fondos, no debería concedérsele el privilegio de confidencialidad de abogado y cliente; e incluso con derecho al privilegio, había renunciado a él al invitar las cámaras de Berlinger a que lo filmaran. "Le queda un solo privilegio", Mastro le dijo al juez Kaplan. "Puede acogerse a la quinta enmienda".

Normalmente, cuando un abogado recibe una citación crea un registro de documentos confidenciales que retendrá. Pero Chevron pedía el archivo entero de Donziger sobre la causa —documentos que abarcaban cerca de dos décadas— y Donziger no tenía personal de asociados que lo ayudasen a revisarlo. Cuando no consiguió presentar un registro confidencial que obtuviera el visto bueno de Kaplan, el juez concordó con Mastro en que "no se podía dar marcha atrás", y le otorgó a Chevron acceso a los documentos confidenciales de Donziger. Donziger se vio obligado a entregar doscientas mil páginas de material.

Veinte abogados de Gibson, Dunn empezaron a revisar pilas de memos y correos electrónicos marcados "Confidencial" y "Producto de trabajo legal". En promedio, leían cinco mil páginas por día. Gibson, Dunn también pidió, y recibió, las declaraciones de impuestos de Donziger, información sobre su cuenta bancaria y sus computadores personales. Personal técnico exploró sus discos rígidos, y Gibson, Dunn copió todo lo que encontraron. Un abogado de Donziger protestó que eso implicaba que los abogados de Chevron podían interrogar sus comunicaciones con su esposa, así como otros asuntos inconexos.

"No tiene otros asuntos", dijo Kaplan. "Este es su vida."

La decisión de Kaplan fue extrema; rara vez se le había otorgado a un adversario semejante cantidad de material sensible. Mientras los abogados de Gibson, Dunn se esparcían por todos el país, presentándose en diecisiete tribunales federales en busca de información, un juez de un tribunal de apelaciones notó que la magnitud de aquel tipo de proposición de prueba era "única en los anales de la historia judiciaria estadounidense". Kaplan incluso le dio permiso a Chevron de tomarle declaración a Donziger: una movida muy inusual.

"Ningún abogado quiere que le tomen declaración", me dijo Stephen Gillers, un legalista en ética de la New York University School of Law. "Nos pone nerviosos, en cuanto profesionales. Nos gusta creer que operamos en una zona privada que nada puede penetrar, a menos que así lo dejemos. En efecto, eso es lo que nos permite hacer nuestro trabajo."

Durante catorce días, en una sala de conferencias de un rascacielos en el midtown de Manhattan, Mastro y otros abogados de Chevron interrogaron a Donziger, bajo juramento, sobre la financiación de la causa y varias estrategias legales que había empleado. En poco tiempo Donziger se debilitó y quedó exhausto. Una de las tareas del interrogador es limitar al interrogado a dar simples respuestas por sí o por no. Pero Donziger insistía en defender su conducta locuazmente, hasta el punto de que Kaplan lo reprendió, comentando que "un hombre así haría carrera como senador filibustero."

En un momento, le preguntaron a Donziger si tenía un diario. Al principio dijo que no. Pero su diario, que había llevado por varios años, estaba guardado en una de sus computadoras portátiles, y Gibson, Dunn lo encontró en el disco rígido. Cuando Chevron presentó el texto, íntegro, en el tribunal, este se convirtió en parte de un los archivos públicos, una humillación más para Donziger. En su diario, detalla sus dudas y aspiraciones, y vuelve obsesivamente sobre el tema de su adversario, que abrevia simplemente como "Tex". Relata discusiones que tuvo con su esposa y hace duras observaciones sobre sus colegas.

Donziger también describe reuniones con el juez Yánez, el juez que, según temía, sería propenso a aceptar sobornos en vista de que supuestamente era un mujeriego y un bebedor. En una entrada, Donziger escribió: "Llamé al juez y pidió que le lleváramos whisky o vino. No lo hicimos." En otra ocasión, describió que Yánez le había pedido que lo ayudara a obtener una visa para que su novia pudiese visitar Estados Unidos. Dozinger no lo hizo, pero anotó en su diario que los demandantes habían redactado un denuncia acerca de la conducta de Yánez, y que le habían informado que "podemos presentarla si no se atiene a ley y a nuestras necesidades".

A Donziger le preocupaba que manipularan a Yánez para que forzarlo a dictar un fallo corrupto. Pero, al conminarlo a mantenerse recto, los demandantes explotaban la vulnerabilidad de Yánez en beneficio propio. "Así que en vez de tener juez fuerte que ve la viabilidad de nuestra causa", escribió Donziger, "puede que ahora tengamos un juez débil que quiere fallar correctamente por todo tipo de motivos inadecuados y personales".

Esperanza Martínez, la ambientalista de Quito, me dijo que, en el complejo paisaje moral de Ecuador, se pueden ejercer diferente tipos de "presión" sobre un funcionario público. Si se presiona a un oficial para que abrogue los derechos de alguien, se trata de un acto incuestionablemente corrupto. Pero si se presiona al funcionario para que haga valer los derechos de alguien", sostuvo Martínez, "se trata de lo más alejado que hay de la corrupción".

Conforme Mastro y sus asociados se abrieron paso por el tesoro hallado sobre Donziger, la información que más les interesó resultó estar relacionada con el perito independiente en daños medioambientales, Richard Cabrera. Originalmente, cuando se decidió nombrar a un solo perito en daños y perjuicios, Donziger se preocupó por el hecho de que cualquier individuo con semejante influencia en el resultado de un caso de varios millardos de dólares podía ser sobornado. Pero se alegró del nombramiento de Cabrera; de hecho, según descubrieron los abogados de Gibson, Donziger supo por adelantado que el tribunal elegiría a Cabrera. "Tenemos un perito", dice en un toma descartada. "El juez nombrará como perito a un tipo de Ecuador. Pero en realidad, ya sabes, le daremos nuestro apoyo con nuestro trabajo".

La decisión del nombramiento compitió al juez Yánez. Los demandantes nunca cursaron la denuncia en su contra, y Donziger tuvo la impresión de que Yánez había quedado debiéndole un favor. "Lo salvamos", escribió sobre el juez, en enero de 2007. "Y ahora cosechamos los beneficios." (Un portavoz de Donziger me dijo que "cosechar los beneficios" simplemente quería decir que el juez Yánez actuaba independientemente de Chevron.)

Otra toma captura la reunión de los demandantes el 3 de marzo de 2007, dos semanas antes del nombramiento oficial de Cabrera. Donziger estuvo presente, junto con el principal abogado ecuatoriano, Pablo Fajardo y Cabrera en persona. En el video, Fajardo explica al equipo que Cabrera les pedirá en poco tiempo que presenten una evaluación independiente acerca de la responsabilidad de Chevron. Este "dará su opinión, firmará el informe y lo revisará", dice Fajardo. "Pero todos tenemos que contribuir."

"Pero Chevron no", dice alguien: una broma, que causa risa.

Antes de que la reunión termine, la cámara captura a Donziger, que se vuelve hacia Cabrera. "Por supuesto, Richard, tienes que sentirte de verdad cómodo con todo eso", dice. Al cierre de la reunión, Donziger exclama: "Tal vez llevemos todo esto a treinta millardo en un día".

Mastro y sus colegas quedaron estupefactos. "Ese es el tipo de revelación que por lo general habría invalidado la causa de un demandante", me dijo. "Lo increíble de esta causa es que hay una prueba tangible tras otra."

Gibson, Dunn envió una citación a Stratus, la consultora de Colorado que había respaldado el informe de Cabrera recomendando una multa de treinta millardos de dólares para Chevron. Cuando Julio Prieto, el joven abogado de los demandantes, se enteró de que Chevron intentaba obtener información de Stratus, envió un correo electrónico desesperado a sus colegas. Que se revelaran los documentos de Stratus podía ser "potencialmente devastador", escribió, agregando que él y sus socios ecuatorianos "podían ir presos".

Lo que el equipo de Mastro obtuvo de Stratus fue un documento, redactado en inglés, que la compañía había enviado a Ecuador pocos días antes de que se publicara el informe de Cabrera. El primer renglón del documento de Stratus decía: "Este informe fue escrito por Richard Cabrera". Era un borrador de la valoración "independiente" de los daños. Como me dijo Mastro: "el equipo de los demandantes había escrito furtivamente el informe".

Desde entonces los demandantes insisten en que no había nada indebido en que Stratus enviara materiales a Cabrera para que los tuviera en consideración, y que Chevron habría podido hacer lo mismo. Pero Donziger, en su deposición, reconoció que el informe final de Cabrera fue redactado "más o menos textualmente" a partir del documento de Stratus.

Una peculiaridad de la proposición de prueba de Gibson, Dunn es que, casi en tiempo real, los abogados de Chevron obtuvieron correos electrónicos en los que Donziger y sus colegas debatían cuál era la mejor manera de tratar las revelaciones mismas. "Tal vez sería mejor explicar que somos los autores del informe", escribió uno de los asociados estadounidenses de Donziger, "en vez de dejar que Chevron cuente la historia como Nancy Drew". Posteriormente ese correo electrónico se le entregó a Gibson, Dunn.

Durante la deposición, le preguntaron a Donziger: "¿Habían acordado que Stratus redactaría el informe de manera tal de que Cabrera pudiese presentarlo al tribunal ecuatoriano?"

"Esa era la idea general", dijo él.

Puede que la lógica de la corrupción sistémica se empariente con la del doping en el deporte. Si uno tienen buenos motivos para sospechar que los demás sacan ventajas competitivas con transgresiones subrepticias, puede concluir que no hacerlo por una cuestión de principios uno socavará su propio caso. "Creo que es un milagro cuánto hemos logrado con tan poco", escribió Donziger en su diario. "Pero al fin y al cabo eso no significa nada si no ganamos."

La deposición de Donziger concluyó el 31 de enero de 2011. Al día siguiente, Chevron lo demandó en una corte federal, junto a otros miembros del equipo de los demandantes, alegando que eran parte de una conspiración de crimen organizado, que se habían confabulado con individuos corruptos de Ecuador para obtener millardos de dólares de manera ilícita.

Después de que surgieran cuestionamientos sobre la independencia del informe de Cabrera, Nicolás Zambrano, el juez de Lago Agrio, dijo que no se apoyaría en él para dar su veredicto. Pero eso no apaciguó a Chevron. El fallo de Zambrano sería fraudulento, argumentó Mastro, y le pidió al juez Kaplan que emitiera una orden restrictiva que impidiese a los demandantes intentar conseguir de Chevron compensación por daños y perjuicios. "Aquí nos enfrentamos a la máxima espada de Damocles", dijo.

Durante su proposición de prueba, Gibson, Dunn se había procurado un memo interno que describía el plan de los demandantes para hacer valer el fallo ecuatoriano apuntando a los activos de Chevron en países extranjeros. Mastro llamó a esa estrategia "vejatoria", y solicitó al juez Kaplan que prohibiera a Donziger y a sus colegas intentar cobrar la multa no solo en Nueva York sino además en cualquier parte del mundo. Mastro le aseguró a Kaplan: "Usted tiene el derecho de exigir un litigio aquí y también en el extranjero".

Kaplan comprendió la postura. Según dijo: "creo que no hay nadie en este tribunal que quiera entrar con su auto en una estación de servicio y descubrir que no hay gasolina porque estos tipos la han paralizado en Singapur o donde sea". Concedió el mandamiento judicial. Cuando, ese mismo mes, el juez Zambrano pronunció una sentencia de dieciocho millardos de dólares contra Chevron, no quedaba claro si los demandantes recibirían siquiera un centavo.

Una tarde de septiembre, en Nueva York, me reuní con un hombre llamado Humberto Piaguaje, que es miembro de la tribu Secoya. Nació en 1964 en el Amazonas ecuatoriano y lleva casi toda la vida involucrado en el caso. Nos encontramos en el Mandarin Oriental Hotel, en el piso treinta y cinco del Time Warner Center. Uno de los abogados de la causa se hospedaba allí, y Donziger y sus colegas habían colonizado el bar del lobby, convirtiéndolo en un espacio de reuniones. Piaguaje llevaba puestos un polo y vaqueros. Desde hacía años hablaba con periodistas estadounidenses, y recitó con calma las indignidades que habían sufrido él y su gente. "Somos pobres", dijo. "No hay animales que comer. No tenemos nuestras medicinas tradicionales de las plantas. No tenemos agua limpia. Chevron nos ha dejado en la miseria". En los últimos años, contó, siete de sus parientes han muerto de cáncer. Expresó indignación ante el hecho de que, después de negarles a los suyos la oportunidad de llevar la causa a los Estados Unidos, les dijeran que tampoco hallarían justicia en Ecuador. Tal vez, dijo, Chevron quiera hacer el juicio en el cielo. "Seguro que ni eso le parecería lo bastante bueno, y pediría transferirlo a otra parte", agregó.

Fuera de hotel, el ocaso se posaba sobre Central Park, y las luces parpadeaban en los edificios de Columbus Circle. Si a Piaguaje lo sorprendía lo incongruente de su entorno, no lo demostró. Le pregunté si alguna vez tenía la impresión de que la causa había cobrado vida propia, una vida disociada de lo que de verdad ocurría en el Oriente. Se encogió de hombros. "Buscamos justicia", dijo. "¿Cómo podríamos hacerlo sin abogados?"

Piaguaje había llegado en avión a Nueva York para asistir a una audiencia oral ante el Segundo Tribunal de Apelaciones, centrada en determinar si el juez Kaplan tenía autoridad para impedir a los demandantes cobrar la multa de Ecuador en cualquier parte del mundo. Si se confirmaba el mandamiento judicial de Kaplan, se sentaría un precedente muy importante, que en efecto permitiría a los tribunales estadounidenses emitir juicio sobre la transparencia de sus contrapartes extranjeras, y descartar veredictos contra compañías estadounidenses cuando se considerase problemático el sistema legal que los hubiese emitido. La posibilidad quitaba el aliento: Chevron parecía haberse posicionado no solo de manera tal no admitir su responsabilidad, sino además de adquirir mayor inmunidad en sus actos en el extranjero. Shell, Dole y Dow Chemical presentaron un informe al tribunal, alentándolos a ponerse de parte de Chevron.

El 16 de septiembre, tres jueces de apelaciones tomaron asiento en un tribunal ubicado en el downtown de Manhattan. Había en la sala un contingente de abogados de Chevron, y estaban Donziger, su equipo legal y Piaguaje. Randy Mastro argumentó que la malevolencia de los demandantes era tan severa que la única solución era invalidar el fallo del tribunal ecuatoriano. "En treinta años de práctica, y habiendo ejercido como fiscal, jamás he visto un registro tan escandaloso de conductas ilegales e indebidas", dijo. "No toleramos sentencias procuradas mediante fraude."

"¿En ningún lugar del mundo?" preguntó un juez, incrédulo. "¿No toleraremos una sentencia en Sudáfrica procurada mediante fraude que se hace valer en Rusia?"

Las exposiciones orales tuvieron lugar un viernes. Normalmente, tras oír las exposiciones los tribunales de apelaciones se toman varios meses para pronunciar un dictamen sobre un caso, pero los jueces estuvieron listos al lunes siguiente. En una decisión unánime y lacónica, revocaron al juez Kaplan, y disolvieron el mandamiento judicial.

El otoño pasado, tuve media docena de conversaciones con Steven Donziger sobre el tiempo que pasó en Ecuador y su batalla contra Gibson, Dunn. Por consejo de sus abogados, eligió, en última instancia, no responder ninguna pregunta de manera oficial. ("Sabe que cualquier cosa que diga puede usarse en su contra", me dijo un representante de Chevron.) En una declaración, Donziger argumentó: "La historia de este caso no es sobre los abogados. Es sobre la gente de Ecuador y sobre el sufrimiento que padecieron a manos de una empresa petrolera estadounidense que incumple la ley y que no se detendrá ante nada para proteger sus ganancias ilícitas".

De momento, la demanda de Chevron contra Donziger por crimen organizado ha sido suspendida, pero si se cursa es probable que Kaplan permanezca como juez de la causa. En un acto desesperado, Donziger solicitó formalmente que reemplazaran a Kaplan, argumentando que había mostrado consistentemente predispuesto a favor de Chevron. Pero el pedido fue denegado.

Las demandas civiles por crímenes organizados rara vez van a juicio, y algunos observadores han sugerido que Gibson, Dunn empleó la contrademanda como una táctica de acoso para calumniar e intimidar a los demandantes. "Desviar y difamar: he ahí la estrategia", me dijo un amigo de Donziger, que asistió con él a la facultad de derecho.

Cuando le transmití esa teoría a Randy Mastro, esbozó una sonrisa apretada y murmuró: "Espero ansioso el juicio".

Una persona cercana al caso me dijo: "Lo que es muy desafortunado en este caso es que nos enfrentamos a una corporación gigante que actuó de manera muy insensible. Ellos no quedaron expuestos por su actos, porque en cambio los reflectores apuntan a este abogado inconformista. Steve tendría que haberse dado cuenta. Si uno quiere emprender una lucha del tipo de la de David contra Goliat, tiene que concentrarse en su propia conducta. Porque, si no lo hace, le da a los otros exactamente las municiones que buscan".

Chevron ha apelado la multa ecuatoriana de dieciocho millardos de dólares. También intentó bloquear la demanda apelando a un tribunal de arbitraje internacional en La Haya. Pero puede que el caso termine en un acuerdo fuera de los tribunales. Dado el rencor que hay entre las dos partes, parece difícil imaginar algo así, pero casi ocurrió en una oportunidad. Cristóbal Bonifaz me contó que, en 2001, los demandantes indicaron por escrito que abandonarían la demanda a cambio de ciento cuarenta millones de dólares. Pero, en la víspera de la fusión de Chevron, Texaco le dio la espalda a la oferta. Chevron se niega a hacer comentarios, pero los demandantes estiman que la compañía gasta aproximadamente ese suma por año en la causa.

Un día de febrero de 2007, Donziger se sentó con un abogado de Chevron en Nueva York. El encuentro fue secreto. El abogado le indicó que Chevron estaba dispuesto a buscar una manera de concluir el asunto. "No queremos que nuestros hijo y nietos prosigan el litigio", dijo.

En su diario, Dozinger expresó su ambivalencia en cuanto a un acuerdo fuera de los tribunales, preguntándose cómo pondría fin a algo que había "definido tanto" su vida. Al final, las dos partes no se pusieron de acuerdo. "Nos hemos vuelto prisioneros de nuestras propia creación", escribió Donziger, en otra entrada. "Tenemos demasiado invertido para detenernos."

VER IMAGEN, PÁGINA: 268

Ecuador: Chevron no pide disculpas por la contaminación, ni siquiera para salvar $ 9.5 mil millones

Chevron dijo el viernes que no tenía intención de pedir disculpas por el daño ambiental a la selva amazónica para el cual una corte ecuatoriana gobernó responsable. Los abogados de ambas partes han dicho que si Chevron se disculpó, su responsabilidad legal de $ 18 mil millones que se han reducido a $ 9,5 mil millones. Poder Judicial del Ecuador había establecido el viernes como fecha límite para una disculpa. James Craig, portavoz de Chevron, dijo que una disculpa sería "una confesión falsa de la responsabilidad." Chevron no tiene activos en Ecuador, por lo que los demandantes deben tratar de recoger el premio en el extranjero.

Now York Times
Associated Press, 4 de febrero, 2012.

POSTFACIO: UNA NUEVA LOJA POST-PETRÓLEO

Por **Matthias Altwicker**

Si bien es difícil imaginar cualquier ciudad moderna que funcione sin petróleo, es aún más difícil imaginar que Nueva Loja exista sin petróleo. Nueva Loja surgió en un sitio donde anteriormente no habían existido ni caminos ni asentamientos humanos permanentes; su creación fue resultado de la abundancia de petróleo subterráneo. Todas las otras características de su ubicación geográfica han sido completamente irrelevantes para su desarrollo.

Una ciudad post-petróleo es como cualquier ciudad post-industrial: sólo puede sobrevivir si adopta una nueva identidad económica y social. Pero con una diferencia significativa: la ciudad petrolera carece de una identidad arraigada a un espacio en que basar esta reinvención. Dado que nunca se la concibió como un lugar en que la infraestructura y el crecimiento se pensaran a largo plazo, la ciudad petrolera no es más que una escala en el camino de una economía extractiva. Esta actitud no se limita al petróleo. Los habitantes, ellos mismos transitorios, a menudo desplazados, no pueden intentar más que una vida de subsistencia. El crecimiento de la agricultura que tuvo lugar con el desarrollo de la ciudad, producto de subsidios gubernamentales y planes de asentamiento equivocados, resulta igualmente extractivo y destructivo.

A pesar de todos los procesos de extracción que tienen lugar, sobre la tierra y por debajo de ella, los productos no son lo suficientemente valiosos para atraer inversiones de ninguno de los organismos involucrados. Las empresas petroleras obtienen cada vez menos beneficios, el gobierno es testigo de los sucesivos fracasos de los planes de asentamiento, y los habitantes ven un futuro calamitoso. Nueva Loja, que alguna vez se ubicó en la periferia de la economía mundial, ahora simplemente se refleja en su espejo retrovisor.

INTENCIONES

Dado este contexto, resulta difícil imaginar el enorme crecimiento poblacional que se proyecta para la ciudad. A diferencia de muchas ciudades post-industriales, los habitantes de Nueva Loja poseen gran variedad de habilidades, pueden realizar numerosos trabajos y, lo que es más importante, ya están realizándolos para sobrevivir. La esperanza de los futuros habitantes está en sus habitantes actuales: el recurso más importante de Nueva Loja será en su capacidad para inventarse recursos. El único y fundamental requisito para que pueda llevarse a cabo un plan como el que hemos propuesto para la renovación de Nueva Loja es una población fija y educada. Su ingenio para inventar nuevos recursos, sumado a la educación (para ampliar las pasiones y los intereses de los habitantes) crearía una relación dinámica entre ambos factores, dando origen a una comunidad y fortaleciéndola. El sentido de pertenencia a una comunidad, que es el primer paso hacia la realización personal, precede a la realización de un espacio.

La autoorganización no es la intención de este plan. Se rechaza la idealización de la realización personal a través de la construcción improvisada y carente de parámetros. En cambio, proponemos un esquema general de planificación municipal con controles múltiples, pero sin límites demasiado estrictos para el desarrollo, más allá de la infraestructura básica necesaria.

Es posible lograr una administración local eficiente en barrios con poblaciones que oscilen entre los 500 y los 3.000 habitantes. Los barrios de estas dimensiones desarrollan su propia identidad, tanto social como física, alrededor de una combinación de infraestructura pública y posibilidades económicas propias del lugar. Esto se condice con las estrategias para la legibilidad social e inclusión de todos, especialmente con las ideas del movimiento desurbanista de las décadas de 1920 y 1930, así como con las estructuras políticas que existen actualmente en la ciudad.

"Post-petróleo" no debería interpretarse como "sin petróleo", a pesar de que los desarrollos en materia de carbono neutral son fundamentales, junto con edificios y espacios que sean sensibles al medio ambiente. La reinvención de Nueva Loja deberá evaluar los méritos relativos de la regeneración forestal y el turismo ecológico. Lo que es más importante, construir una Nueva Loja post-petróleo no se tratará simplemente de reducir el buso de petróleo por parte de la ciudad, sino que tendrá que ver con remediar los problemas físicos y sociales causados por él.

La selva tropical y los ríos trazarán los límites verticales y horizontales del nuevo desarrollo. La supervivencia y la regeneración de la periferia natural son esenciales para reinventar, de manera saludable y a largo plazo, Nueva Loja.

FORMA URBANA

Los objetivos fundamentales de un marco de planificación apuntan a lograr la máxima flexibilidad, tanto en la forma urbana como en la distribución de los servicios públicos. Aquí aparecen muchos aspectos de la planificación policéntrica, pero con una diferencia fundamental: la vasta dispersión de la variedad conectada que representa una ciudad policéntrica y distribuida colapsa y se transforma en un paquete concentrado de experiencias urbanas.
Quien realice una caminata de diez minutos por cualquier lugar dentro de los límites de la ciudad pasará por ambientes sociales y espaciales radicalmente diferentes, es decir, identificables y autosuficientes. Esto elimina la necesidad de sistemas de movimiento más costosos, los cuales promueven un desarrollo más distribuido.

La nueva ciudad, Nueva Loja Nueva, estará compuesta de entidades barriales equivalentes: los micro-barrios. Éstos mantendrán su autonomía a través de su diseño específico y su conectividad a través de infraestructuras de movimiento localizadas, aunque equitativamente distribuidas, que los unirán en grandes barrios. La zonificación en el sentido convencional será innecesaria, y la definición convencional de manzanas, calles y plazas será directamente poco realista. Cada barrio será autónomo en forma y contenido, aunque deberán relacionarse entre sí para sobrevivir. Si bien la cantidad y la distribución son importantes, la ubicación y la función son variables. En efecto, se trata de una ciudad sin ningún centro.

IDENTIDAD

Esta ciudad sin centro es el resultado directo de una comprensión cabal del lugar. Las propuestas aquí presentadas muestran la variedad de morfologías posibles dentro del marco antes descripto, cada una de las cuales busca revelar o establecer una identidad para la ciudad. En este sentido, tienen que ver con el lugar y cómo responder de manera específica (si no holística) a él. La riqueza de las propuestas produce a la vez entusiasmo y desconcierto; la articulación de las ideas indica simultáneamente el gran potencial que podría tener la región así como la posibilidad de que exista un malentendido. Luego de un trayecto de catorce horas en autobús a través de la Cordillera de los Andes y de la selva tropical, no podíamos estar seguros de que habíamos llegado a nuestro destino. El oleoducto aparecía, desaparecía y volvía a aparecer a lo largo de la ciudad. Áreas selváticas se intercalaban entre las manzanas de la ciudad, a menudo sin terminar y dispuestas de manera poco sistemática. No había límites claros entre ambas condiciones urbanas, a menudo las calles se interrumpían sin advertencia previa, mientras que edificios con refuerzos de acero se erguían aguardando ansiosamente que les construyeran el piso siguiente. La ciudad carecía de identidad.

Esta percepción no cambió con el tiempo, y visto en retrospectiva, esto influyó en el desarrollo de las ideas aquí presentadas. La ciudad, y el movimiento de un barrio a otro, no podían definirse por contrastes o diferencias superficiales sino más bien por las sutilezas que uno aprende a reconocer cuando habita un lugar, o quizá que no aprende jamás, si uno opta por permanecer en su propio micro-barrio. El hecho de que estas diferencias puedan convertirse en el resultado de una elección, antes que en el producto de una circunstancia, es el parámetro más importante de Nueva Loja Nueva.

ESTUDIANTES DE DISEÑO URBANO DEL CCNY

Pilyun Ahn
Matthias Altwicker
Mariana Castillo
Alan Fox
John Hill
Holly Kallman
Paul King
Roberta Korcz
Gareth Mahon

ESTUDIANTES DE ARQUITECTURA DEL CCNY:

Edith Altamiranda
Iman Ansari
Javier Caracamo
Camille Dunn
Onur Ekmekci
Rommel Gordillo
Yulya Ilizarov
Patrick Isaac
Lawrence Jacquette
Sujin Jeong
Yuriy Tkachenkov
Erik Scanlon

ESTUDIANTES DE PAISAJISMO DEL CCNY

Chris Syrett
Patrick Weisel
Heather Fuhrman

ESTUDIANTES DE FADA-PUCE

Tatiana Armijos
Marialuisa Borja
Verónica Guerra
Catalina Moreno
Andrés Nivelo
Esteban Sáenz
José Luis Gallegos
Nicolás Gallegos
María José León
Andrés Peralvo

DOCENTES

Michael Sorkin, Catedrádico y Director del Programa
para Graduados en Diseño Urbano, CCNY
Ana María Durán Calisto, Profesora, FADA-PUCE
Osvaldo Paladines, Profesor, FADA-PUCE
David Leven, Profesor CCNY
Achva Benzinberg Stein, Profesora y Directora
Programa para Graduados en Paisajismo, CCNY

AGRADECIMIENTOS ESPECIALES

Hernán Orbea, Decano de FADA-PUCE, 2002-2008
Alexis Mosquera, Director del Programa de Arquitectura,
FADA-PUCE, 2002-2008 (actual Decano)
Friedemann Koester, Director de la Estación Científica Yasuní,
PUCE, 1998-2008
Lucy Baldeón, asistente del Director de la Estación Científica
Yasuní, PUCE, 1998-2008
La comunidad huaorani, especialmente al Sr. Wuampi Ahua and a la
Sra. Omene Ima, y a sus hijos Ramón, Pablo, Germán y Eduardo;
Sr. Huintoque Boya and Sra. Nambai Ahua.
Carlos Flores, Administrador de campo de la Estación Científica Yasuní
Marco Haro, arquitecto de Lago Agrio
Fabián Torres, arquitecto de Lago Agrio
Martha Medina, arquitecto de Lago Agrio
Lenin Recalde, arquitecto de Lago Agrio
Felipe Domínguez, arquitecto de Lago Agrio
Máximo Abad, ex alcalde de Lago Agrio
George Ranalli, Decano, Facultad de Arquitectura, CCNY

EQUIPO EDITORIAL

Matthias Altwicker
Zoë Blackler
Lynne Desilva-Johnson
Yuliya Ilizarov
Rodolfo Leyton

**Welcome to Petropolis fue publicado originalmente
en el *Architectural Record*, junio 2007**

BIOGRAFÍAS

MICHAEL SORKIN estudió arquitectura en Harvard y MIT, y también tiene títulos del University of Chicago y Colombia University. Es el principal del Michael Sorkin Studio en la ciudad de Nueva York y fundador y Presidente de Terreform, una organización sin fines de lucro que se dedica a la investigación e intervenciones urbanas. También es Presidente del Institute for Urban Design, Profesor Distinguido de Arquitectura, y Director del Graduate Urban Design Program en el City College of New York donde ha sido docente desde 2000. Ha sido Profesor de Urbanismo y Director del Instituto de Urbanismo en la Academia de Bellas artes en Vienna (1993 a 2000), y ha enseñado en varias escuelas de arquitectura. Ha sido conferencista en todo el mundo y ha publicado cientos de artículos. Actualmente es editor contribuyente en el *Architectural Record*.

ANA MARÍA DURÁN CALISTO se licenció en la Facultad de Artes Liberales en la Universidad San Francisco de Quito, especializándose en Antropología con asignaturas secundarias en Literatura Comparativa y en Historia de Arte. Consiguió una beca para estudios de posgrado en Arquitectura y Preservación Histórica en el University de Pennsylvania. En 2002, con su socio Jaskran Singh Kalirai, fundó la compañía de diseño Estudio A0. Dirige estudios de arquitectura en la Escuela de Arquitectura, Diseño y Artes en la Universidad Católica del Ecuador y ha sido profesora invitada en el GSD en la University of Harvard y el GSAPP en la University of Colombia. Fue directora del XV Quito Biennale de Arquitectura Panamericana. Ciudades Visibles (2005-2006) y, como Decana, la Escuela para la Ciudad, Paisaje y Arquitectura en la Universidad Internacional (2008-2009). Actualmente es Loeb Fellow en el GSD.

MATTHIAS ALTWICKER es principal en AB Architekten en la Ciudad de Nueva York y profesor asociado en la Escuela de Arquitectura y Diseño en el New York Institute of Technology. Su docencia y práctica están concentradas en construir viviendas económicamente accesibles con conciencia del medio ambiente y el desarrollo de barrios locales. Ha diseñado viviendas sostenibles por el Long Island Housing Partnership, colaborado con el Long Island Power Authority en la investigación de integración fotovoltaica en viviendas suburbanas existentes, y elaborado escuelas autosuficientes y expandibles en Kenya. Su compañía actúa como asesor para el Regional Plan Association (NYC), el Nassau County Planning Federation (Long Island) y el Colectiva de Viviendas en Potsdam (Alemania).

DAVID LEVEN es socio en LEVENBETTS, un estudio de arquitectura en Nueva York que fundó en 1997 junto a Stella Betts. La compañía ha ganado varios premios del NYC AIA (2008, 2005, 2004, 2003), el Architectural League's Young Architects Forum and Emerging Voices Award (2009), Architectural Record's Design Vanguard Award (2007), y el I.D. Annual Design Review Award (2004). El trabajo de LEVENBETTS ha sido publicado en varias revistas de diseño y libros y en una monografía (Princeton Architectural Press, 2008). David ha dado conferencias en muchas instituciones y es actualmente Profesor Asociado y Director del Programa de Posgrado en Arquitectura en Parsons the New School for Design. Se licenció en Colgate University, tiene un Master otorgado por Yale University y atendió The Institute for Architecture and Urban Studies.

ACHVA BENZINBERG STEIN es profesora y arquitecta profesional. Ha sido docente en EEUU, Europa, Israel, India y China. Sus proyectos con grupos barriales, agencias públicas, y organizaciones sin fines de lucro están enfocados en satisfacer las necesidades sociales y simultáneamente buscar sanear el daño causado por el desarrollo urbano que ha sido mal gestionado. Su paisajismo ha sido galardonado numerosas veces por el American Society of Landscape Architects, e incluye planos para terrenos de escuelas, proyectos de viviendas de gran escala, parques, patios de recreo, hoteles, jardines para comunidades, y residencias privadas. Ha ganado varios premios incluyendo el 1994 Chrysler Award para Innovación en Diseño y ha recibido una beca Fulbright dos veces.

OSVALDO PALADINES ZURITA se licenció en la Escuela de Arquitectura de la Pontificia Universidad Católica de Chile en 1989. Actualmente da cursos sobre historia y teoría de Arquitectura, así como de estudios de diseño, en la Escuela de Arquitectura, Diseño y Artes en la Universidad Católica del Ecuador. En los últimos cinco años, Osvaldo ha sido director del tercer año del Estudio de Diseño Urbano que está enfocado en nuevas maneras de abordar problemas urbanos en Quito. Ha participado en varios estudios colaborativos e internacionales con escuelas de arquitectura en Nueva York (City College of New York y Parson's New School of Design), Bogotá y Medellín. Ha colaborado en el diseño para la Factoría de Conocimiento en Quito y recientemente ganó un concurso para construir una de las sedes para el proyecto Escuela del Milenio en Quito. En asociación con un equipo de FADA-PUCE, está desarrollando el libro Quito Muévete, que presentará una propuesta académica para la movilidad de Quito y su crecimiento en el futuro.

ÁBALOS, Iñaki y HERREROS, Juan. *Áreas de impunidad.* Barcelona: ACTAR, 1997.

ASNER, Gregory P., et al. "*Selective Logging in the Brazilian Amazon*", www.sciencemag.org

ASNER, Gregory P. et al. "*Sustainability science from space: Quantifying forest disturbance and land-use dynamics in the Amazon*", www.pnas.org

ASOCIACIÓN AMERICANA DE GEÓGRAFOS (AAG) y GRUPO DE ESPECIALIDAD LATINOAMERICANA. "*El Estado Actual de la Geografía en los Países Hispanoamericanos.*", Chicago: AAG, 2006.

BETHELL, Leslie. (comp.) *Colonial Brazil.* Cambridge: Cambridge University Press, 1984.

BORGES, Jorge Luis. *El hacedor.* Buenos Aires: Alianza Editorial, 2007.

BORJA CEVALLOS, Rodrigo. *Enciclopedia de la política.* México D.F.: Fce, 1998.

BRAVO, Elizabeth & MARTÍNEZ, Esperanza. (Acción Ecológica). Campaña "*Amazonía por la vida: Debate ecológico sobre el problema petrolero en el Ecuador*". Quito, 1993.

BROWDER, John O y GODFREY, Brian J. *Rainforest Cities,* Nueva York: Columbia University Press, 1997.

BUNKER, Stephen G. *Underdeveloping the Amazon,* Chicago: University of Chicago Press, 1985.

COORG, Satyan R. "*Pose Imagery and Automated Three-Dimensional Modeling of Urban Environments*" http://biblioteca.universia.net/html_bura/ficha/params/id/1488592.html

CORBOZ, André. "*El territorio como palimpsesto*", Lo urbano en 20 autores contemporáneos, coord. por Angel Martín Ramos, Barcelona: ETSAB, 2006.

CUESTA ZAPATA, Salomón y TRUJILLO MONTALVO, Patricio. *La frontera de fronteras PUTUMAYO: violencia, narcotráfico y guerrilla.* Quito: Ediciones Abya Yala, 1999.

DE FREITAS, Marcílio. *Amazônia e Desenvolvimento Sustentável: Um diálogo que todos os brasileiros deveriam conhecer.* Petrópolis: Editora Vozes, 2004.

DESCOLA, Philippe. *La Selva Culta: simbolismo y praxis en la ecología de los Achuar.* Quito: ABYA AYALA, 1987.

FERREIRA LINS, Eurípides. *O Amazonas e seus problemas.* Manaus: Imprensa Oficial do Estado do Amazonas, 2006.

GARCÍA, Lorenzo. *Historia de las misiones en la Amazonía ecuatoriana.* Quito: Ediciones Abya Yala, 1985.

GERLACH, Allen. *Indians, Oil, and Politics: A Recent History of Ecuador.* Scholarly Resources, 2002.

GODFREY, Brian & BROWDER, John. "*Disarticulated Urbanization in the Brazilian Amazon.*" *Geographical Review*, Jul. 96, Vol. 86, Nro. 3, p.441, 5p., 1 gráfico.

HARRIS, Roger & HUTCHISON, Peter. *The Amazon.* Inglaterra: Bradt Travel Guides Ltd., 2007.

HECHT, Susanna and COCKBURN, Alexander. *The Fate of Forests.* Chicago: University of Chicago Press, 1990/2010.

HOUGH, Michael. *City Form and Natural Process.* London and New York: Routledge - Taylor and Francis Group, 1995.

IIRSA. "*Plano Estratégico 2004 – 2012*". Disponible en www.iirsa.org

IIRSA. "*Comunicado de Brasilia*". Disponible en www.iirsa.org

IIRSA. "*Taller Regional sobre la Visión Estratégica de la Integración Física Suramericana (VESA)*". Disponible en www.iirsa.com

IIRSA. "*Taller sobre la Gestión Intensiva de Proyectos Estratégicos Orientada a Resultados*". Disponible en www.iirsa.com

IIRSA. "*Agenda de Implementación consensuada 2005-2010*". Disponible en www.iirsa.org

IIRSA. "*Proceso de revisión de la cartera de proyectos IIRSA: Metodología de planificación territorial indicativa*". Disponible en www.iirsa.org

IIRSA. "*ANNEX: IIRSA PROJECT PORTFOLIO – 2007*" . Disponible en www.iirsa.org

IIRSA. "*Annex 10: Indicative Territorial Planning*". TECHNICAL EXECUTIVE GROUPS – GTEs, 2007: Results and Project Portfolio – 2007 (Annex)". Disponible en www.iirsa.org

IIRSA. "*IIRSA: Building a New Continent, Project Information Sheets, Priority Investment Portfolio in South America, Initiative for the Integration of Regional Infrastructure in South America*". Disponible en www.iirsa.org

IZQUIERDO PEÑAFIEL, Juan. *La ecoarquitectura:asentamientos humanos huaorani.* Quito: Ediciones Abya-Yala, 2000.

JORGENSON, J. P. y COELLO RODRÍGUEZ, M. (Eds.). 2001. *Conservación y desarrollo sostenible del Parque Nacional Yasuní y su área de influencia. Memorias del Seminario-Taller 2001.* Ministerio del Ambiente/UNESCO/Wildlife Conservation Society. Editorial Simbioe. Quito, Ecuador.

KEEFE, PATRICK RADDEN, "*Reversal of Fortune,*" The New Yorker, January 9, 2012, 38-49

KILLEEN, Timothy J. *A Perfect Storm in the Amazon Wilderness: Development and Conservation in the Context of the Initiative for the Integration of the Regional Infrastructure of South America* (IIRSA), Arlington: *AABS* (Advances in Applied Biodiversity Science), nro. 7, 2007.

KOESTER, Friedemann. *El Hombre y la Biosfera en Yasuní.* Coca: Nuestra ciencia - Reportajes, 2001.

LÉVI-STRAUSS, Claude. *The Raw and the Cooked: Mythologiques.* Chicago: University of Chicago Press edition, 1983.

LÉVI-STRAUSS, Claude. *Tristes Trópicos.* Barcelona: Ediciones Paidós, 1988.

MEGGERS, Betty J. *"Amazonia in the Modern World"* en *Amazonia: Man and Culture in a Counterfeit Paradise.* Washington D.C.: Smithsonian Institution Scholarly Press, 1996.

MONTOYA BONILLA, Sol. *Mitología del encuentro y del desencuentro.* Bogotá: Editorial Universidad Nacional, 1994.

MORAES, Péricles. Os Interpretes da Amazônia. Manaus: Valer Editora, 2001.

MULHOLLAND, Catherine. *William Muholland and the Rise of Los Angeles.* Berkeley: University of California Press, 2000.

NEPSTAD, D.C. *"Large-scale impoverishment of Amazonian forests by logging and fire".* Disponible en www.nature.com

NEW INTERNATIONALIST MAGAZINE. *Viva Yasuni! Life vs. Big Oil.* Julio de 2008, nro. 413.

NIXON, Robert. *"Crude awakening in Ecuador".* En *E Magazine*; August 1994; Earth Action Network, Inc.; v5; issue n. 4; p 12.

OMESTAD, Thomas. *"The New Food Superpower: As commodity prices soar, Brazil steps up to feed a hungry world"* in *U.S. News & World Report*, Julio 7-14, 2008.

OTCA. Organización del Tratado de Cooperación Amazónica, *"Integrando la Amazonia Continental: Informe de Gestión"*, Brasilia: OTCA, 2005.

OTCA. *Integrando la Amazonia Continental: Informe de gestión.* Brasilia: Gráfica y Editora Positiva, 2005/2006

PAGE, Joseph A. *Brasil: el gigante vecino.* Buenos Aires: Emecé Editores, 1996.

PERKINS, John. *Confessions of an Economic Hit Man.* San Francisco: Barret-Koehler, 2004.

PETROECUADOR. *El petróleo en Ecuador: su historia y su importancia en la economía nacional.* Quito: Petroecuador, 2002.

RENTERÍA RODRÍGUES, Carolina. *"Guidelines for the Work Plan 2008,"* Montevideo: IIRSA, 2008.

RICARDO, Fany. *Terras Indígenas & Unidades de Conservação da natureza: o desafio das sobreposições.* San Pablo: Instituto Socoambiental, 2004.

SAWYER, Suzana. *Crude Chronicles: Indigenous Politics, Multinational Oil, and Neoliberalism in Ecuador.* American Encounters/Global Interactions, Durham: Duke University Press, 2004.

SILVEIRA SOARES-FILHO, Britaldo, et. al. *"Modelling conservation in the Amazon basin."* Disponible en www.nature.com/nature/journal/v440/n7083/abs/nature04389.html <http://www.nature.com/nature/journal/v440/n7083/abs/nature04389.html>

SASSEN, Saskia. *Una sociología de la globalización*, Buenos Aires: Katz Editores, 2007.

SASSEN, Saskia. *Cities in a World Economy*, Londres: Sage Publications Ltd., 2006

SASSEN, Saskia. *The Global City: New York, London, Tokio, Princeton:* Princeton University Press, 2001.

SASSEN, Saskia. *Global Networks, Linked Cities*, Nueva York: Routledge, 2002.

STCP. *O Apagão e o Brasil Forestal.* Curitiba: Informativo.

STCP. N. 8, 2004/2005.

STCP. *Gestão Fundiária: Principal Problema de Setor Florestal Brasileiro.* Curitiba: Informativo STCP, N. 9, 2005/2006.

THEROUX, Paul. *Blinding Light* http://www.halliburtonwatch.org/news/theroux.html

THE WORLD BANK. *Brazil Rain Forest Unit: Business Plan 2005-2008.* Washington D.C.: The World Bank, August 2004.

TOCANTINS, Leandro. *O rio comanda a vida: Uma interpretação da Amazônia.* Manaus: Editora Valer, 2000.

UGARTE Pinheiro, Maria Luiza. *A Cidade Sobre os Ombros: Trabalho e Conflito no Porto de Manus* 1899-1925. Manaus EUDA, Edições Governo do Estado, UEA, 2003.

EUDA. Edições Governo do Estado, UEA, 2003.

VILLAREJO, Avencio. *Así es la Selva. Iquitos.* Centro de Estudios Teológicos de la Amazonía, 2005.

"Archaeology of the Amazon." Disponible en www.utexas.edu/courses/wilson/ant304/projects/projects97/jojinp/amarch.htmal <http://www.utexas.edu/courses/wilson/ant304/projects/projects97/jojinp/amarch.htmal>

"Geopolitical Diary: The Obstacles to Latin America's UNASUR." Disponible en www.stratfor.com/geopolitical_diary_obstacles_latin_americas_unasur <http://www.stratfor.com/geopolitical_diary_obstacles_latin_americas_unasur>

"Free Trade Zones." Disponible en www.kishtpc.com/Free-En/free?colombia.htm <http://www.kishtpc.com/Free-En/free?colombia.htm>

ENLACES DE INTERNET

www.iirsa.com
www.bicusa.org
www.ecoamericas.com
www.edelca.com.ve
www.amazonia.org.br
www.socioambiental.org
www.ft.com
www.caf.com
www.mercosur.int
www.comunidadandina.org
www.otca.org.br
www.amazonguide.com.br/mapas/mapmanaus.htm
www.kishtpc.com
www.mct.gov.br
www.petroperu.co.pe
www.cipam.gov.br
www.perspectiva.inf.br
geo@perspective.inf.br
www.potlatch.com.ar/beta/index.php?option=com_content&task=view&id=67&Itemid=2
www.senado.gov.br-web/Senador/Mestrinho/mapaam.htm
US Drug Enforcement Agency, http://www.justice.gov/dea/index.htm
http://www.plosone.org/article/info:doi/10.1371/journal.pone.0002932
http://www.halliburtonwatch.org/news/theroux.html

VIDEO:

Cineastas Indígenas Kuikuro

Créditos de la publicación
Dirección Creativa, Belén Matos
Prefacio, Michael Sorkin
Editado por Michael Sorkin, Ana María Durán Calisto, Matthias Altwicker and Oscar Riera Ojeda
Ensayos por Patrick Radden Keefe
Producción, Oscar Riera Ojeda
Corrección, Kit Maude

OSCAR RIERA OJEDA
PUBLISHERS

ISBN 978-988-16194-2-6
Published by Oscar Riera Ojeda Publishers Limited
Printed in China by Artron Art Center

Oscar Riera Ojeda Publishers Limited
Unit 6, 22/F.,
Far East Consortium Building,
121 Des Voeux Road Central, Hong Kong
T: +852-5311-1625

Production Offices | China
Suit 19, Shenyun Road
Nanshan District, Shenzhen 518055
T: +86-755-8336-6138

www.oropublishers.com | www.oscarrieraojeda.com
oscar@oscarrieraojeda.com